John Buridan

PUBLICATIONS IN MEDIEVAL STUDIES

John Buridan

Portrait of a
Fourteenth-Century
Arts Master

JACK ZUPKO

University of Notre Dame Press
Notre Dame, Indiana

Manufactured in the United States of America

Chapter 13 is a revised version of "What Is the Science of the Soul? A Case Study
in the Evolution of Late Medieval Natural Philosophy," first published in *Synthese* 110.2
(February 1997): 297–334. Copyright © 1997 Kluwer Academic Publishers, with kind
permission from Kluwer Academic Publishers.

Section 2 of Chapter 15 is a revised version of "Freedom of Choice in Buridan's
Moral Psychology," first published in *Mediaeval Studies* 57 (1995): 75–99,
by permission of the publisher. Copyright © 1995 by the Pontifical Institute
of Mediaeval Studies, Toronto.

Material from *John Buridan: 'Summulae de Dialectica'*, translated by Gyula Klima,
Yale Library of Medieval Philosophy (New Haven, Conn., and London:
Yale University Press, 2001), is used by permission of Yale University Press.
Copyright © 2001 by Yale University.

Library of Congress Cataloging-in-Publication Data
Zupko, Jack.
    John Buridan : portrait of a fourteenth-century arts master / Jack
Zupko.
        p.   cm. — (Publications in medieval studies)
    Includes bibliographical references and indexes.
    ISBN 0-268-03255-6 (cloth : alk. paper)
    ISBN 0-268-03256-4 (pbk. : alk. paper)
    1. Buridan, Jean, 1300–1358.   I. Title.   II. Series.

B765.B844 Z86   2003
189'.4—dc21

                                                        2002151564

∞ *This book is printed on acid-free paper.*

Now in regard to every matter it is most important to begin at the natural beginning.

—Plato, *Timaeus* 29B

· CONTENTS ·

·   ACKNOWLEDGMENTS   ·

·Reflecting on Aristotle's authority in psychology, Buridan writes, "nobody, however wise, can write or say everything that can be written or said about this science" (*Summulae* 6.5.10). This is also true for works in the history of philosophy, where it is not just that things get left unsaid but that so much of what is said (and a great deal of what is valuable in that) depends on the painstaking efforts of others. This book owes much to those primary source scholars who have brought Buridan's texts to light over the past few decades, as well as to discussions with many other historians of philosophy about their significance. Their influence is evidenced partly—but only partly—by the Works Cited bibliography below.

I would like in particular to thank my teachers Jenny Ashworth and the late Norman Kretzmann, who inspired me to pursue my love of philosophy and from whom I learned almost everything I know about philosophical scholarship. Mary Gregor, my late colleague at San Diego State University, offered valuable advice early in my career and showed me how it is possible to carry out a serious research program and be a conscientious teacher of large numbers of undergraduate students at the same time.

This book has benefited at every stage of its construction from the comments of wise and perceptive critics. Jenny Ashworth, Kent Emery, Jr., Jerry Etzkorn, Peter King, and Martin Tweedale all read the manuscript and offered helpful comments and suggestions. Jenny in particular drew my attention to some recently published articles in the history of logic, which led to many improvements in Part One. Gyula Klima's comments on chapter 1 alerted me to several errors, as did Henrik Lagerlund's on chapters 5 and 6. Some years ago, Terry Parsons helped me make sense of a difficult text on parts and wholes in Buridan's *Summulae*, and the results inform my discussion in the latter sections of chapter 10. I have learned a great deal from Calvin Normore's astute observations about Buridan over the years, and continue to marvel at the way he is able to knit medieval and modern concerns together so seamlessly. Gyula Klima, who embodies most every scholarly virtue I know, shared his expertise on Buridan with me from the beginning and served as a sounding board for many of my own ideas. I am also grateful to him for giving me access to his translation of Buridan's *Summulae* prior to its publication. Carole Roos, my editor at Notre Dame, read a long manuscript with patience and care, and saved me from numerous mistakes my author's eye prevented me from seeing. Many others, more than I could ever recall here, have assisted me in my travels with Buridan over the past decade. I have not always followed their advice, and where that is the case, I alone am responsible for the result.

Initial research for the book was completed in 1994–95 thanks to an NEH Fellowship for College Teachers and Independent Scholars (No. FB–31403–94), which enabled me to work at the Franciscan Institute, St. Bonaventure University. I am grateful for the hospitality shown to me by the members of the Institute during that year, especially Jerry Etzkorn, Rega Wood, and its then-director, Br. Ed Coughlin. My colleagues in the philosophy departments first at San Diego State and more recently at Emory University have always been supportive of the medievalist in their midst. I would also like to thank the Dean of Arts and Letters at SDSU, Paul Strand, and the former Dean of Arts and Sciences at Emory, Steven Sanderson, for support in the form of research leaves during which most of the book was written.

Several chapters are revisions of articles originally published elsewhere. Chapter 11 appeared as "How Are Souls Related to Bodies? A Study of John Buridan," in *The Review of Metaphysics* 46.3 (March 1993): 575–601; chapter 12 as "Buridan and Skepticism," in the *Journal of the History of Philosophy* 31.2 (April 1993): 191–221; chapter 13 as "What Is the Science of the Soul? A Case Study in the Evolution of Late Medieval Natural Philosophy," in *Synthese* 110.2 (February 1997): 297–334; and section 2 of chapter 15 as "Freedom of Choice in Buridan's Moral Psychology," in *Mediaeval Studies* 57 (1995 Annual): 75–99. I am grateful to these journals for permission to use this material here. I would also like to thank Yale University Press for permission to quote from Gyula Klima's translation of the *Summulae*.

This book is lovingly dedicated to my wife, Frances, and my son, Neil.

· John Buridan (c. 1300–c. 1361) was the most famous philosopher of his time, and probably the most influential, but we know very little about his life. From historical documents we are able to infer that he was born around 1300 in the Diocese of Arras in Picardy. He studied as a young man at the Collège Lemoine in Paris, where he was awarded a benefice or stipend for needy students, and later in the arts faculty at the University of Paris, where he received his master's degree and formal license to teach by the mid-1320s. There he remained until his death some forty years later. He received a number of stipends and benefices over the course of his long career. One of these, in 1348, was awarded by a committee consisting of a theologian, two members of the faculty of law, a proctor from each of the four nations at Paris, and the rector of the University—no mean feat in a period of uneasy relations among these competing educational constituencies. He twice served as rector of the University, in 1327/8 and 1340. He is last mentioned in a document of 1358 as helping to resolve a jurisdictional dispute between the English and Picard nations. He must have died shortly thereafter because in 1361, one of his benefices was awarded to another person.[1]

Buridan's academic career was unusual in two respects. First, he spent his entire career as a master of arts without ever moving on to seek a doctorate in theology, the more typical career path for academics in the later Middle Ages. Arts masters usually lectured for only a short time, leaving their teaching posts as soon as they were able to begin their studies in theology.[2] As a result, virtually all of Buridan's written work is based on the arts curriculum at Paris, and reflects his pedagogical concerns as a member of that faculty. His logical writings, for example, consist of textbooks and commentaries intended for use by actual students of logic. Likewise, most of his non-logical writings are in the form of literal commentaries (*expositiones*) and longer critical studies (*quaestiones*) derived from his lecture-courses on the works of Aristotle. In addition to the entire *Organon*, these include studies of the *Metaphysics, Physics, De Caelo, De Anima,* the books of the *Parva Naturalia,* and *Nicomachean Ethics.*[3] Buridan frequently lectured more than once on the same text, a fact which medieval scribes and editors were careful to note by marking their copies as containing Buridan's first, second, or "third or final teaching [*tertia sive ultima lectura*]" on, e.g., Aristotle's *De Anima*. But although these works make numerous references to each other, and can themselves be ordered according to their different versions, none can be dated precisely. What is certain is that Buridan's works were widely read. Handwritten copies and early printed versions were distributed by his students and followers throughout Europe, where they served as the primary texts for courses on logic and Aristotelian philosophy. This trend continued for nearly two hundred years after his death, with the *via Buridani* continuing to shape European thought well into the Renaissance.

The other way in which Buridan's career followed the road less traveled was that he remained a secular cleric rather than joining a religious order such as the Dominicans or the Franciscans. By the early fourteenth century, the distinct intellectual traditions created by these mendicant orders had transformed the study of theology at Paris, as the identity of each tradition began to coalesce around the thought of its major figures. These are the authors of many of the canonical texts of medieval philosophy: Albert the Great, Thomas Aquinas, Robert Holcot, and Meister Eckhardt on the side of the Dominicans, and Roger Bacon, Bonaventure, Duns Scotus, and William of Ockham on the side of the Franciscans. But the impact of Dominican and Franciscan thought was felt primarily in the more prestigious faculty of theology. By remaining among the "artists [*artistae*]," Buridan was able to develop his ideas independently of these traditions, freed from their authority as well as from doctrinal disputes that arose between them. We can see this in the occasionally eclectic character of his remarks, which borrow from both Dominican and Franciscan sources. Institutionally, his independence was reinforced by the fact that Dominican and Franciscan novices received their liberal arts training at custodial schools run by their own orders, rather than in the arts faculty at the university. This meant that most of Buridan's students were as secular as he was, and, like any good teacher, he tailored his message to the circumstances of his audience.

But even though we know very little about Buridan's life, his writings say a great deal about him as a philosopher. It is Buridan's vision of the philosophical enterprise that I aim to capture in this book. Rooted in the study of grammar, first among the liberal arts, this vision develops a distinctive philosophical method in the *Summulae de Dialectica,* the compendium of logical teachings that was Buridan's masterwork, and then puts it into practice through careful investigation of the Aristotelian speculative sciences. Accordingly, this book is divided into two parts. The first part, 'Method', deals with the picture of language and logical method presented in the *Summulae,* and is subdivided according to the particular treatises of that work. The second part, 'Practice', gives a reading of Buridan's philosophy by following the ap-

not physical science? time?

plication of this method through a threaded series of topics in Aristotelian metaphysics and natural philosophy. All readings of Buridan are threaded insofar as they must begin in logic, the "art of arts [*ars artium*]," and move out along one of several possible pathways in the speculative sciences. The path I have chosen to exemplify begins, like the others, in logic, but then proceeds through metaphysics to natural philosophy, as represented by the special, subaltern science of psychology, finishing up in moral psychology. This reading can be pushed farther, of course, into practical ethics, rhetoric, and poetry, though I do not do so here. It is in this sense that this book is an exercise in philosophical portraiture, an expression of what I take to be the most salient features of Buridan's thought in the different contexts in which it has come down to us. My judgments about what is important—about what belongs on this particular canvas—will be somewhat subjective and impressionistic, just like a 'real' portrait in oil or watercolor or pencil, but that just goes with the territory. There are other, equally valid, ways of exemplifying Buridanian practice. For example, instead of heading from metaphysics inwards to the natural science of psychology, we could have used Buridan's account of sublunary motion (which is related, interestingly enough, to his account of moral virtue, as we shall see in chapter 14 below) and journeyed outwards to the movement of heavenly bodies and disposition of the superlunary realm. The only claim I would make is that all of these readings must be based on a common method, which is to be found in the *Summulae*. This is what would make them all portraits *of* Buridan.

Anneliese Maier, one of the first modern scholars to study Buridan's writings, was absolutely right when she noted of later scholastic natural philosophy that "what changes is the method of knowing nature," so that "what is interesting is not the knowledge (*scientia*), but the method of knowing (*modus sciendi*)."[4] In much the same way, the nominalism most modern readers associate with Buridan is often misunderstood as a closely guarded set of doctrines when it would be closer to the truth to think of it as a parsimonious way of doing philosophy.[5] There is no nominalist manifesto in his writings, no treatise aimed at eradicating the creeping menace of real universals. That is because there was no creeping menace of real universals in mid-fourteenth century Paris.[6] Metaphysical nominalism, or more accurately, conceptualism, was assumed to be the default position of virtually everyone teaching at the University. Buridan does, to be sure, provide his students with an account of various solutions to the so-called 'problem' of universals, as well as rehearsing the standard arguments taken to refute the realist position, but he does so with the conviction of someone who knows that the real debate died out a long time ago. What interests him is the development of nominalism as a method for answering other kinds of philosophical questions, from specifying how souls and bodies are related to determining the nature of scientific knowledge. Parsimony—whether that involves denying the existence of real universals or economizing on the number of entities required to explain some natural phenomenon—is a feature of the nominalistic method, but the real work is done by extending the discipline of the *Summulae* into the speculative realm. For Buridan, the discourse of the *Summulae* is the discourse of philosophy.

A study such as the one undertaken in these pages is liable to be misconstrued along a number of lines. In some ways this cannot be helped, but let me try to clarify a few things at the outset. First, I make no claim to comprehensiveness. Buridan left an enormous number of writings, most of which have never been edited, let alone properly studied. Although interest in Buridan has increased at least tenfold since the 1970s, many of the finer points of his thought, his exact positions on a variety of particular topics and local debates, are still not well known. These are most properly addressed in particular studies and comprehensive, lengthwise treatments of particular works, such as the several versions of his commentaries on the *Physics* or *Nicomachean Ethics*. In contrast, my aim here is to provide some sense of what Buridan thought philosophy was about. My reconstruction of his method and reading of his practice through certain texts will, I hope, show what he thought he was doing when he addressed himself to philosophical questions, perhaps even providing a kind of 'starter-kit'—as my late teacher, Norman Kretzmann, used to call it—for the study of Buridan. But as an inventory of arguments and positions, my results are only partial because they are incidental to my main purpose. For the full particulars, there is no substitute for actually going to the texts, a task which has become much more straightforward now that the critical edition of the *Summulae* is nearly complete and has appeared in a reliable English translation by Gyula Klima.[7] There is also a large and growing body of secondary literature on Buridan, which has been immensely helpful to me in the preparation of this book, and to which the 'Works Cited' section below is but a partial guide.[8]

Second, because I emphasize local contexts and particular differences, I do not speak to the question of whether Buridan deserves a place in the pantheon of great philosophers. In my view, this is for the reader to judge, if it is to be judged at all. The problem with such judgments, of course, is that they fall all too easily into distortion and caricature. The same is true of approaches that seek to identify the "big theories" Buridan might have advanced or the "big questions" he was trying to answer. As far as I can tell, these terms have no referent in the texts. What we find instead is that Buridan's substantive views are developed within the specialized medieval genre of *quaestiones*. Part commentary and part treatise, *quaestiones* were not answers to philosophical questions in our sense of the term, but a stylized method of teaching authoritative texts.[9] Thus, Buridan is not investigating the problem of self-knowledge when he asks whether the human intellect can understand itself in Book III, Question 9, of the final version of his *Quaestiones* on Aristotle's *De Anima*.[10] Rather, the issue is what to make of Aristotle's aporetic remark at *De Anima*

429b10 about thought thinking itself. After reviewing the arguments on both sides, Buridan gives his own (affirmative) answer in an elegant, six-step proof of the mechanism of self-cognition in Aristotelian psychology. But the issue here is whether (and how) we can form a concept of the intellect based on its own, first-order cognitions. There is never any suggestion, in Buridan or in any of the other fourteenth-century arts masters who considered this question, that such an inquiry might tell us something about what we would now call the self, i.e., the personal or existential subject behind the thinking. It would never have occurred to a medieval thinker to infer from my inability to catch the elusive subject behind my thoughts that perhaps this is all I am, i.e., a bundle of perceptions. That is because Aristotelian empiricism, unlike Humean empiricism, is committed to the idea that there is something underlying our perceptions.[11]

Philosophical genres in the later Middle Ages also tend to deflate historicist assumptions about questions of influence. Buridan's *quaestiones* transmit the learning of authoritative texts to student audiences by means of passages that were seen as interesting or problematic or important to them, not necessarily to us. Views of other philosophers and other authoritative texts were invoked in the development and resolution of a question, but often anonymously— '*aliquis dicit* [someone says]'—or even silently, without explicit reference. The questions themselves were ordered not only by the text being commented upon, but also by the tradition of commentary on a given text, so that it is sometimes better to follow the treatment of a particular question through several authors rather than taking the views of a single author as definitive. Such complexities are familiar to medievalists. What they mean here is that it is very difficult to separate questions of influence and impact from the broader traditions shaping what Buridan says. In my view, the rush to determine Buridan's significance vis-à-vis what are assumed to be the main problems of philosophy has led to some of the most egregious misinterpretations of his thought, one of which is discussed in chapter 12 below. As things stand, it will take a generation or more of scholarly work on Buridan and other later medieval philosophers (and early modern philosophers too) before we will be in a position to entertain such questions meaningfully, i.e., in a way that is not simply speculative. Therefore, although I sometimes mention ideas that influenced Buridan and the impact his views had on others, I have studiously avoided making these into my main focus.

The first part of this book is organized around the two surviving parts of the *trivium* in fourteenth-century Paris, grammar and dialectic, or logic.[12] Buridan did not write grammars or grammatical commentaries,[13] but his teaching in the *Summulae* is clearly addressed to students who had completed their grammatical training and were familiar with Donatus and Priscian as well as classical authors such as Cicero, Virgil, and Horace. Accordingly, chapter 1 develops Buridan's conception of language from the perspective of an arts master, in which the successive discourses of grammar, logic, and speculative philosophy are linked by the practice of teaching. Chapter 2 is addressed to the theoretical and practical aspects of his conception of logic as a science (*scientia*), or body of knowledge. Chapters 3–9 follow the order of treatises in Buridan's *Summulae:* chapter 3 on propositions, predicables, and categories (*Summulae* Treatises I–III); chapter 4 on suppositions (IV); chapter 5 on syllogisms (V); chapter 6 on topics (VI); chapter 7 on fallacies (VII); chapter 8 on demonstrations (VIII); and chapter 9 on sophistic exercises (IX). Medieval philosophers convey meaning through order. By cleaving to Buridan's order, I hope to portray the pedagogical concerns that drive the text of the *Summulae.*

As mentioned above, the second part of the book concerns Buridan's application of his method to a threaded series of topics in metaphysics and natural philosophy. Chapter 10 begins by showing how Buridan sets the boundaries of metaphysics relative to theology (and vice versa), before moving on to consider the intersection of grammar, logic, and metaphysics in the traditional discourse of parts and wholes. Chapter 11 discusses the metaphysics of inherence as exemplified by the different modes of soul-body relation. Here we see Buridan's method under fire, confronting Averroistic arguments that threaten to undermine the unity of his account of human and non-human animal souls. In chapter 12, Buridan's remarks on the possibility of human knowledge are considered in the context of his commitment to naturalistic principles and patterns of inference. His conception of the natural science of psychology is the topic of chapter 13, its differences highlighted via the contrasting accounts of Thomas Aquinas and Nicole Oresme. Chapter 14 characterizes one of the best-known innovations of Buridanian physics, the theory of impetus, as a way of thinking about quantitative change that was also applied to model the internal push and pull of the virtues. Chapter 15 continues the narrative into Buridan's moral psychology with a discussion of human freedom as a perfection of the intellect. I offer some concluding remarks in chapter 16.

But even if we concede that logic is Buridan's method, his philosophical grammar, it seems rather tendentious to assume that his logic always matches pedagogical needs. I do not deny that Buridan had genuine systematic interests in logic, only that such interests are ever foremost in his mind. Buridan tends to be skeptical of systematizing pretensions in other fields, doubting whether anyone could show that the whole of physics is one, or even the whole of metaphysics (*QM* VI.2: 33vb).[14] Furthermore, logic and grammar are not speculative but "practical sciences, for they teach us how to construct good syllogisms and well-formed expressions [*orationes congruas*]" (*QM* VI.2: 34rb). When he is asked directly where the science of dialectic is taught, he does not reply 'in the *Summulae*'. Rather, the answer fragments along the lines of the division of sciences in the arts curriculum: "If it is asked where the science of dialectic is taught, we say that it is taught in the book of the *Metaphysics* as far as metaphysical conclusions are concerned, in the book of the *Posterior Analytics* as far as the conclusions of the posterior science [of demonstration] are concerned, in the book of the *Physics* as far as physical conclusions are concerned, and so on for the other [special] sciences" (*QM* IV.4: 15va).[15] If Buridan does have a *theory* of logic, it must be extracted piecemeal from these texts and the *Summulae,* and often with great difficulty, as historians of logic have found, for example, with account of modal syllogisms.[16] Even his most sophisticated logical work, the *Treatise on Consequences,* is clearly a kind of textbook for advanced logic students. The fact that we can usually identify practical ends for Buridan's logic but few evidently theoretical ends surely raises practice above theory as a hermeneutical strategy for dealing with these texts.

On the other hand, the fact that logic is Buridan's philosophical method does not mean that we should find the teachings of the *Summulae* everywhere apparent in Buridan's metaphysics and natural philosophy, any more than we find the teachings of the *Organon* throughout Aristotle's speculative philosophy. If we did, then Buridan's metaphysics and natural philosophy would read like another logic textbook, the reader's attention constantly being diverted to the role of some substantive logical principle in arguing for a certain view, or to the way in which an opponent's position has missed or misused the principle. Thankfully, logical considerations do not intrude so violently into his texts. Where he does question an opponent's reasoning, it is not to teach him the right rule, but to point out that he is not even speaking the same language, be it metaphysics, physics, or ethics. Thus, chapter 12 below discusses Buridan's attack on Nicholas of Autrecourt, who he sees as threatening "to destroy the natural and moral sciences" through his insistence that we cannot infer the existence of substance from the existence of accidents (so that 'An accident exists; therefore, a substance exists' is not a good consequence). Likewise, as we will see in chapter 4, Buridan criticizes Ockham's position in the debate over the modal status of scientific propositions with the rather tongue-in-cheek remark, "I believe that such great controversy has arisen among the disputants because of a lack of logic [*ex defectu logicae*]" (*QNE* VI.6: 122vb). He says this because he believes Ockham has failed to use logical resources plainly available to him—resources Buridan is only too happy to bring into play in his own solution. Like nearly everything else in his philosophy, this solution is developed through the same typology of term, proposition, and argument, whose proper use is taught in the *Summulae.* That is why logic and natural philosophy can be said to have the same subject matter, though differently conceived: "It seems to me that it must be said that the logician and the natural scientist speak of quiddity [*quidditas*] differently, for the logician stops at predicable intentions, whereas the natural scientist asks what things are signified by these intentions or by these predicable terms" (*QM* VII.12: 48rb).

What is my method in this book? If we think of philosophical archaeology as the task of recovering artifacts from historical texts that might interest us today, and philosophical anthropology—if I may separate that term from the way it is currently understood, as signifying the philosophy of human nature—as the attempt to reconstruct the philosophical life and practices of medieval thinkers, then my approach is anthropological rather than archaeological. I am not interested in what an artifact is so much as in what it says. The conceptual distance between medieval and modern philosophical discourse is bound to make reconstructing the context of Buridan's thought difficult. But actually, it will be both easy and difficult: easy to the extent that the institutional setting in which Buridan worked, the university, is still with us in a form remarkably unchanged since the Middle Ages; difficult because the temptation will always be there to wrench his ideas from their medieval context in order to compare them to those of modern philosophers. But Buridan is not a modern or even a proto-modern philosopher. Those who wish to mine Buridan for contemporary insights are welcome to read on, but they will not find what they read here very edifying because I regard the question of what Buridan means to us 'today' as unanswerable. On the other hand, those who take as much interest in philosophical questions as in our efforts to answer them will be closer to Buridan's own spirit of inquiry, and hence in a better position to appreciate his philosophical legacy.

CHLMP	Norman Kretzmann et al. (eds.), *Cambridge History of Later Medieval Philosophy*
CUP	H. Denifle and E. Chatelain (eds.), *Chartularium Universitatis Parisiensis*
DMA	*Expositio in librum De motibus animalium Aristotelis*
PL	J.-P. Migne (ed.), *Patrologiae Latinae*
QAnPo	*Quaestiones in duos libros Aristotelis Posteriorum Analyticorum*
QAnPr	*Quaestiones in duos libros Aristotelis Priorum Analyticorum*
QC	*Quaestiones in Praedicamenta*
QDA$_1$	*Quaestiones in libros Aristotelis De anima [prima lectura]*
QDA$_3$	*Quaestiones in libros Aristotelis De anima [tertia sive ultima lectura]*
QDC	*Quaestiones super libris quattuor De caelo et mundo*
QDI	*Questiones longe super librum Perihermeneias*
QDP	*Quaestiones de puncto*
→ *QE*	*Quaestiones Elencorum*
QGC	*Quaestiones in duos libros De Generatione et Corruptione Aristotelis*
QIP	*Quaestiones in Isagogen Porphyrii*
QM	*In Metaphysicen Aristotelis Questiones argutissimae*
QNE	*Quaestiones super decem libros Ethicorum Aristotelis ad Nicomachum*
QP	*Subtilissimae Quaestiones super octo Physicorum libros Aristotelis*
QPol	Ps.-Buridan, *Quaestiones super octo libros politicorum Aristotelis*
QR	*Quaestiones in Rhetoricam Aristotelis*
QT	*Quaestiones circa librum Topicorum Aristotelis*
S	*Summulae de Dialectica*
TC	*Tractatus de consequentiis*
TDI	*Tractatus de infinito*
TDUI	*Tractatus de differentia universalis ad individuum*

PART ONE

METHOD

CHAPTER ONE

Language

·John Buridan was a teacher. That is, he understood his own work as a ₨
philosopher primarily in terms of his role as a *magister artium,* an arts master, the position he held for his entire academic career at the University of
Paris. Traditionally, arts masters were charged with providing students with
their education in grammar, logic, and Aristotelian philosophy, subjects that
embodied the medieval conceptions of literacy and wisdom, as well as afford-
ing the intellectual tools for further study in the faculties of law, medicine,
and theology.[1] Arts was the cornerstone discipline in the medieval university
insofar as the language used in those other faculties was first taught by arts
masters and first spoken in the faculty of arts. Students became acquainted
with it through a highly structured curriculum in which they were required
to study, in ascending order, the exposition and interpretation of authoritative texts (grammar), the structure and modes of reasoning in conventional
discourse (logic), and finally, the analysis and systematic disclosure of the order
of nature (Aristotelian philosophy). More activity than concept, the language
of arts was a way of speaking whose mastery provided the key to all other
learning. No one could enter the intellectual community without it, and its
possession, in turn, betokened membership in that community.

The importance of language in Buridan's thought emerges on many levels, all of which are at some point driven by pedagogy. This latter fact would
for some historians of philosophy reduce his texts to a derivative status, as if
we must 'factor out' the audience or pupils in Buridan's lectures and textbooks in order to reconstruct what he *really* thought about an issue.[2] For reasons that will become clear below, I think this is quite mistaken. Buridan's

thought cannot be fully understood unless his role as a teacher is taken seriously. But taking pedagogy seriously means that we must avail ourselves of more appropriate, if unconventional, hermeneutical strategies. In this book, I use the notion of pedagogical order—the order of texts, teachings, and disciplines—to present Buridan's views on some of the main philosophical questions of his day. The advantage of this approach is that it will allow us to unify Buridan's teachings and make his texts accessible in a way that is more faithful to what he understood himself to be as a teacher and philosopher. The disadvantage is that the recursive and often repetitive style which comes so naturally to Buridan *qua* teacher obscures, rather than assists in, the task of revealing once and for all the edifice of his contribution to *philosophia perennis*. But if there is no such edifice, or if the aim of looking for one obscures Buridan's achievements *qua* philosopher—e.g., because he conceived of his roles as philosopher and teacher inseparably—then it would seem that the pedagogical approach is the next best thing. As we shall see, in Buridan's case, it is more than good enough.

1. Beginning at the Beginning

In the fourteenth-century arts curriculum, we begin with grammar.[3] Its origins in the curricula of ancient Roman schools are reflected in what came to be its standard medieval definition, from Isidore of Seville (c. 560–636), according to which grammar is "the art of speaking and writing correctly [*scientia recte loquendi et scribendi*]."[4] By the ninth century, this was already a serious understatement. Closer to the historical fact is Isidore's own elaboration of this definition (not always quoted with it): that grammar is also "the starting point and foundation of the liberal arts [*origo et fundamentum liberalium artium*]."[5] Medieval grammar was not only concerned with the study of vocabulary, word forms, syntactical rules, and other sorts of primary school lessons we now associate with the term, it was also the rubric under which one learned proper pronunciation,[6] etymology, semantics, and, at more advanced levels, literary skills such as textual analysis and composition. Indeed, in medieval universities, certain aspects of the study of grammar were functionally equivalent to what we now know as literary criticism.

Two further points distinguish medieval grammar from its modern counterpart, which, by comparison, begins to look a shadow of its former self. The first is that the subject matter of medieval grammar was essentially a foreign language, i.e., Latin, rather than one of the regional, vernacular languages people would have spoken at home, in the marketplace, or in other settings of secular life.[7] Yet Latin was also very much alive in other, more specialized, contexts: for almost everyone, it was the language of worship, i.e., of sacred texts and liturgy; for a smaller group, it was the language of administration and jurisprudence, a manifestation of the political order of medieval society; for a smaller group still, it was the language of scholarship and intellectual activity, the discourse of higher learning.[8] Buridan himself proposes being "very educated in the arts [*in artibus doctissimus*]" as one of the conditions for properly grasping the most difficult problem-sentences in logic, as if the philosophical issues raised by logic will simply escape the notice of those who lack sufficient training in grammar.[9] The second point is that medieval grammar had an investment in textuality unprecedented in the history of western literature. Students were taught the basics of Latin vocabulary and syntax via illustrations from sacred and literary texts, and were instructed in the arts of exposition and composition by imitating classical authors. 'Creative writing' was unheard of. The main grammar text in the universities, the *Institutiones Grammaticae* of the early sixth-century grammarian Priscian, was filled with examples from classical Latin authors such as Virgil, Cicero, Horace, Lucan, Ovid, and Juvenal.[10] And although controversies raged in the twelfth and thirteenth centuries over the relative prominence of grammar vis-à-vis the two other primary parts of the university arts curriculum (i.e., dialectic or logic, and rhetoric, which, together with grammar, formed the *trivium*), these disputes did not affect the way Latin was taught. Even the most minimally educated person learned the basics of Latin vocabulary and syntax, and had memorized a stock of exemplary modes of Latin discourse in the process of doing so.[11]

Textuality in the Middle Ages embraced both oral and written forms, with oral teaching being the predominant medium for the transmission of ideas in grammar schools and universities. The primary reason for this was economic. Books were rare and very expensive because they had to be copied by hand. Furthermore, such books as did exist were more often than not sequestered in private or college libraries to which only masters and advanced students had access.[12] The result of all this was an educational system organized from the ground up by the spoken word. Grammar school teachers "endeavored to impart and explain the text of [Donatus's] *Ars Minor,* word after word and sentence by sentence."[13] Arts masters used similar techniques to introduce university students to the texts of Aristotle, Porphyry, Boethius, Priscian, and Peter of Spain. As Jan Pinborg observed, these oral methods of teaching help to account for the different genres of written texts that have survived to the present day, because "most medieval philosophical literature reflects teaching practice and its form; even writings that were never delivered as lectures or held as disputations assume the traditional forms."[14] These include the *expositio,* or literal, line-by-line commentary on a given text; *quaestiones,* or question commentaries based on a series of problems or puzzles which are themselves informed by literal passages from the text; the *tractatus,* or independent treatise on a specific question or controversy, used both to introduce students to a particular field and to record the determination of the master on particularly vexing issues; and the *summa*, a detailed, systematic exposition of a whole field of inquiry, such as logic or theology. With few exceptions, these different forms of philosophical literature all began life as student lectures—living texts which were usually revived and delivered more than once before being committed to writing.[15] Buridan's works survive in all of these different forms, and bear the marks of the lecture hall at every turn. Thus, we find him at one point supplementing his logical masterwork, the *Summulae de Dialectica*, a commentary based on the *Summulae Logicales* of Peter of Spain, with a remark clearly aimed at his student audience (and later, readers): "we should note with respect to the entire chapter that the author of the *Summulae* [i.e., Peter of Spain] discusses modal propositions very briefly and incompletely. Therefore, to complete the treatise, I will not follow his text but provide a different text, to such an extent as will seem to me to be useful" (*S* 1.8.1: 67).[16] The criterion of utility here is student comprehension of the difficult subject of logic. In the same way, Buridan frequently preserves student queries in the written versions of his lectures on Aristotle—introduced by formulae such as, "if someone were to ask [*si ab aliquo quaeratur*]," or, "if you were to say [*si tu diceres*]"—even when these interrupt the expository flow and resolution of the question.[17] For Buridan, as for medieval arts masters more generally, the orality of their tradition was closely and naturally intertwined with pedagogy, and these two factors are what most influenced the shape of the texts which have come down to us today.

Grammar and pedagogy come together in a significant, but often overlooked, way in Buridan's philosophical work. His lectures and writings are based on the arts curriculum of mid-fourteenth-century Paris, and to the extent that he was a master of arts charged with teaching logic and natural philosophy, they reflect his efforts to make the canonical texts of Aristotle and his commentators both accessible and informative. To do this well he must, like any good teacher, have taken into consideration what students were bringing with them to the lecture hall, i.e., he must have had some idea of 'where their minds were at'. Where their minds were at was grammar. These students were coming to his lectures having absorbed the curriculum of the grammar schools. At one point, Buridan pauses to provide his audience with a kind of 'you are here' map of their location in the medieval arts curriculum, reminding them that shoemaking, grammar, and astronomy are all arts, ordered by virtue of their relative proximity to making (*facere*) and knowing (*scire*), opposite poles in the typology of human activity. He offers the standard gloss on these terms, appealing to their traditional etymology, an activity proper to the grammarian:

> We should note that some arts are mechanical or 'productive [*manuFAC-tivae*]', and there is practical knowledge of these. People [*laici* = laymen] 'produce [*FACiunt*]' [things by means of] them, as in the arts of shoe-

making and working in copper. Others are liberal arts, which are called 'liberal [*LIBERAles*]' because they 'liberate [*LIBERAnt*]' intellects that have been introduced to them from secular and worldly cares. And there are seven such arts, viz., grammar, logic, rhetoric, music, astronomy, geometry, and arithmetic. The first three of these are forms of practical knowledge. They are called 'practical' insofar as they instruct a man in how to converse, produce well-formed expressions, embellish his speech, construct syllogisms, and find [out about] the subject matter [in a dialectical inquiry]. For they teach how a Latin expression can be found, and the meanings [*significata*] of words, utterances, expressions, and propositions. But the other four are the 'speculative [*SPECULAtivae*]' arts, or arts in connection with which 'speculative knowledge [*scientia SPECULAtiva*]' is imparted, because they 'speculate [*SPECULAntur*]' about the highest causes: the orders of things, the essences of things, or almost everything else. (*QM* VI.2: 33vb; emphases mine)[18]

The *trivium* of grammar, logic, and rhetoric are thus bridge-disciplines between the practical and the speculative, joining one to the other through language, freeing us from the plough and enabling us to engage in a higher form of production by making our speculation about highest causes known to others.[19] Grammar is the first of these disciplines, and the foundation of the other two. Although Buridan did not lecture on grammar, nor contribute any independent works on the subject, he knew that his students had some training in the grammatical art of reading and interpreting texts, a skill crucial to the practice of dialectic in the Aristotelian tradition. As a result, one of the first things that becomes evident when we read the opening treatises of Buridan's *Summulae*—as well as his lectures on Porphyry's *Isagoge,* the traditional primer for Aristotle's *Categories*—is the attention paid to grammar and to "what the grammarians say," almost as if Buridan were consciously looking for intellectual hooks in his students on which to hang the new subject of logic.

It is in this context that the special character of Buridan's thought begins to emerge. Buridan understood his task as a logician as continuous with grammatical learning, so that logic becomes a natural outgrowth of grammar, another way of mapping the possibilities of human discourse. The primary unit in the study of logic is the assertion (*enuntiatio*), or proposition, whereas grammar is ordered towards the expression (*oratio*).[20] But logic uses many of the same categories and divisions as grammar, and indeed, the discourse of grammar is often appropriated wholesale in order to familiarize students with the discourse of logic. For example, for beginning students, the logical concept of supposition would have had antecedent significance in grammar.[21] Hence, it seems only natural to find Buridan the teacher recalling grammar as a contrast case in order to introduce the concept of supposition:

we do not deal here with supposition as it is understood by the grammarian, [namely,] as supplying the subject for a verb. For in this way the term 'chimera' could just as well supposit as the term 'man', since the expression [*oratio*] 'A chimera runs' is just as well-formed [*congrua*] as 'A man reads', and it is not in this way that, as logicians, we intend to take supposition. Again, if I say: 'A man is an animal', the term 'animal' supposits just as well as does the term 'man', which is not the case with supposition as the grammarian interprets it. (*S* 4.1.1: 221–22; cf. *S* 4.4.1: 281)[22]

In grammar, students would have understood supposition as the act of 'putting' or 'placing' something as the subject of a verb. In logic, however, supposition is the referential or denotative function of the subject and predicate terms in a proposition.

But besides providing a foil for the new vocabulary of logic, grammar also influenced the way logic was taught. In the very first section of the *Summulae*, Buridan gives precedence to grammar as that which makes all other learned discourse possible: "of course, positive grammar [*grammatica positiva*] has to be learned first, by means of which the master is able to communicate with the disciple, whether it be in Latin, French, Greek, or Hebrew, or whatever else" (*S* 1.1.1: 6). But the pedagogical debt to grammar was formal as well as material. Logic textbooks from the eleventh century through to Buridan's own day had certain structural similarities with grammar textbooks. For example, some of the earlier texts share a loose, question-and-answer format that bears witness to their origins in the oral context of the classroom. Consider the following (fairly representative) selection from the *Ars Minor*, the most widely used basic grammar text in the Middle Ages: "What is a pronoun? A part of speech [*pars orationis*] which is often used in place of a noun to convey the same meaning, and now and then refers to a person previously mentioned. How many attributes belong to the pronoun? Six. What? Quality, gender, number, form, person, case. In what is the quality of forms? It is twofold. . . ."[23] And so the student is taken through the rudiments of Latin grammar. Now if we look at the twelfth-century *Ars Montana*, an abridgement of an anonymous logic text from the influential school of Alberic at Mont Ste. Geneviève, we find the same format used to explain the rudiments of logic (in this case, the concept of conversion):[24] "What is it for a proposition to be converted simply? The predicate is turned into a subject, and the subject is turned into a predicate, while the signs remain the same. Universal negatives and particular affirmatives are converted with this sort of conversion. How? In this way: 'No man is an animal'; 'No animal is a man'; 'Some man is an animal'; 'Some animal is a man'."[25]

After the middle of the twelfth century, however, the pressure of increasing enrollments in the schools, which had since evolved into universities, made the old textbooks obsolete. Small classes were no longer the norm, and students needed something more than script-like reports or compilations of magisterial lectures to guide them through the thickets of grammatical and logical learning.[26] Thus, a new genre was born, the *summa,* and here again, grammar took the lead. The first *summa* was the *Summa super Priscianum* of Peter Helias, written around 1150, more than a century before Peter of Spain composed his logical *Summa,* and Thomas Aquinas his theological *Summa.* In the words of his modern editor, Leo Reilly, "Peter Helias is the inventor of the *summa* form, which became the standard genre of the Middle Ages. He sets the highest standard both for organization of material and eloquence of style. The *Summa* combines an organic treatment of each section [of the *Institutiones Grammaticae*] with a continuous commentary on the text. In about the same length as the original, it articulates the divisions and subdivisions of grammar and provides each with a prefatory summary in a style that is lapidary, formulaic and perfectly consistent with each context" (Reilly 1993, 16). Such a text gave students a "commentary complete in itself," which they "could struggle through by themselves," without having to cope with the text of Priscian on their own—a necessity given the large class sizes in the faculty of arts. The *summa* clearly had humble origins as a response to a specific pedagogical need, rather than arising from some critical re-conception or reconfiguration of the structure of human knowledge.

true?

Like the text on which it is based, Buridan's *Summulae de Dialectica* has clearly pedagogical aims. But why the need for a new *summa,* especially since Peter of Spain's *Summulae Logicales* was not even a hundred years old? These two texts stand in much the same relation as Peter Helias's *Summa super Priscianum* and Priscian's *Institutiones Grammaticae.* Buridan's *Summulae* begins as a kind of running commentary on Peter's *Summulae,* the text on which most logic courses of the period were based. But where Peter's text covers its topics in a brief, highly attenuated, format, Buridan's discussion systematically elaborates Peter's remarks, and, in the process, completely renovates the discipline using materials from the *logica moderna* or 'new logic'.

Here, for example, is Peter's presentation of the inference rule of simple conversion: "Simple conversion is making the subject into the predicate and vice versa, with the quality and quantity [of the propositions] remaining the same. And in this way, a universal negative and a particular affirmative are converted, e.g., 'No man is a stone'—'No stone is a man'; 'Some man is an animal'—'Some animal is a man'."[27] In his commentary, Buridan tries to get his students to look deeper for the reason why simple conversion applies to universal negative and particular affirmative propositions, but not to universal affirmatives or particular negatives. The form of his response does not attempt to mimic the quasi-dialogue of earlier texts, but it is just as if someone had asked him about it directly: "The reason is that in the conversion of a universal negative and a particular affirmative the terms supposit in the same way both in what is converted and in that into which it is converted, in that both [terms supposit] distributively in the universal negatives and both determinately in the particular affirmatives. . . . But the reason why a universal affirmative is not converted likewise by simple conversion is that its predicate is not distributed, as in 'Every man is an animal'. . . . And for a similar reason a particular negative is not converted simply either . . ." (*S* 1.6.2: 50).[28] It is not difficult, I believe, to hear the master's voice in this passage, echoing all the way back to the *Ars Minor* and *Ars Montana*. Buridan was as familiar as anyone in the arts faculty with these traditional primers in grammar and logic, and his anticipation of student queries reflects the straightforward, non-conversational tone of his object-text, the *Summulae Logicales*. His explanation of conversion also shows why it is necessary that "the signs remain the same" in the *Ars Montana* and that the propositions retain "the same quality and quantity" in the *Summulae Logicales:* if they didn't, the terms so signed or quantified would no longer *supposit* for the same things, and so the inference would fail. Conversion is thus explained in terms of supposition, the predominant logico-semantic doctrine of the fourteenth century.

2. FROM GRAMMAR TO LOGIC

In the later Middle Ages, the continuity between grammar and dialectic in the traditional arts curriculum is something that must be shown because it is hardly ever spoken of. Grammarians and philosophers from Peter Helias on were concerned with disentangling the two, so that if one focuses only on what medieval thinkers said, one would get the impression that the two disciplines were fully defined and compartmentalized by Buridan's time. But spoken differences sometimes mask unspoken continuities. How did the masters differentiate grammar and dialectic as arts teaching moved away from the *trivium* towards a curriculum based on the entire Aristotelian corpus?

This question is best answered, I think, by looking at two early, representative figures whose ideas profoundly influenced the subsequent debate. Peter Helias's efforts to separate grammar from dialectic, or logic, came after two generations of masters had witnessed a gradual blurring of boundaries between the two. Traditionally, grammar and logic were conceived of as sister sciences with a common, practical basis in natural language. "Every one of the logical arts is concerned with speech," Boethius said.[29] But as the teaching of grammar and logic evolved in the context of the *trivium*, doctrines from each began to infiltrate the other. As we saw above, logicians borrowed grammatical devices such as supposition in order to develop more sophisticated techniques of propositional analysis. Likewise, rather than primarily focusing on the origins of words, grammatical treatises began to show an increasing interest in their syntactical functions, as well as a tendency to systematize grammatical learning into a *scientia*, or proper body of knowledge, with reasons and arguments.[30]

Needless to say, controversy quickly ensued over the mandate of each discipline. On the side of the logicians, Peter Abelard (1079–1142), never one to avoid controversy, sought to elevate logic at the expense of grammar by drawing a sharp distinction between truth and mere congruence, or agreement: "But note that *syntactical* conjoining, which the grammarians are concerned with, is other than conjoining with respect to *predication*, which the dialecticians consider. For according to the force of the syntactical construction, 'man' and 'stone' (and any other noun in the nominative case) can be conjoined just as much as 'animal' and 'man' can with respect to making plain a certain understanding, but not with respect to showing the *status* of a thing." Abelard is insisting that the primary sense of predication, which was also a grammatical concept, must be determined by the logicians, whom he sees as concerned with the more properly philosophical task of connecting propositions with what makes them true. 'Grammatical' predication is the secondary or derivative sense of the concept. The passage continues:

> So a *syntactical* conjoining is a good one whenever it indicates a complete judgment, whether the judgment is so or not. But a conjoining with respect to *predication*, which we are concerned with here, pertains to the nature of things and to indicating the truth of their *status*. If someone says 'A man is a stone' he produces a well-formed syntactical construction of 'man' or 'stone' with respect to the sense he wanted to indicate. There was no grammatical mistake. With respect to the force of the statement, 'stone' is here predicated of 'man', with which it is grammatically construed as a predicate, insofar as false categorical propositions have a predicate term too. Nevertheless, 'stone' is *not* predicable of it in the nature of things. Here, when we are defining a 'universal,' we are concerned only with the latter kind of force of predication.[31]

On the Abelardian picture, the important difference between the grammarian and the logician is that the former is willing to accept all kinds of sentences, even nonsense sentences, just as long as "there was no grammatical mistake." This is because Abelard thinks that grammar and logic should both be concerned with discourse items that are context-free. As a result, poetry, liturgy, homiletics, and other, more literary forms of discourse get lumped together with the uttering of nonsense as all failing to pertain "to the nature of things." The benefit of such an approach is that it permits greater technical rigor in both disciplines. Logic is free to focus on the connotative and denotative functions of terms in propositional contexts, and, in doing so, to be ordered 'upwards', to the study of metaphysics: "when we are defining a 'universal', we are concerned only with the latter [i.e., logical] kind of force of predication."[32] Grammar, in turn, is depicted as the specialized study of syntax, the description and application of rules of agreement properly ordered to the production of "complete" sentences.[33] But the expense on both sides is a complete bracketing of the ambiguity and nuance of human discourse, because these phenomena require attention to the different contexts in which language is actually used, from literature to ordinary life. We have come a long way from Isidore's conception of grammar as the "art of speaking and writing correctly," in which the study and analysis of the Latin literary tradition played a significant role.

The story of Abelard's adversities, both political and personal, has tended to drown out the voices of those who rejected the sharply defined roles he set out for logic and grammar. Among these was Peter Helias. As Leo Reilly has pointed out, the latter Peter, unlike the former, understood the notions of truth and grammaticality in an inclusive rather than an exclusive sense.[34] In a passage probably directed against Abelard, Helias writes:

> 'Agreement [*congrua*]' must be understood [to apply to] speech as well as to meaning [*tam voce quam sensu*]. Then [we say that] there is a grammatical ordering [*ordinatio congrua*] of words in speech when utterances are joined to each other grammatically, in keeping with their accidental characteristics, e.g., masculine [gender] to masculine. . . . But [we say that] there is an agreement in meaning [*congrua sensu*] when, from words ordered in the aforementioned way, the hearer has an intelligible grasp of something [*habet auditor quid rationabiliter intelligat*], whether true or false, such as when it is said, 'A man runs,' or 'Socrates is a stone.' For although this [latter] proposition is false, the hearer understands something intelligibly through it.[35]

Peter Helias adopts a more holistic and humanistic approach to the study of language, redeeming semantics for the grammarian by clearing a middle path between syntax and truth. Whereas Abelard had sought to focus the study of logic on the actual meaning of terms, i.e., on the specific link to reality (*res*) forged by their propositional contexts, Helias insisted that words have natural meanings (*significationes*) that are open-ended, and hence capable of being shaped by a wide variety of discourse conditions. Thus, there is room on Helias's view to study the literary as well as the logical significance of a piece of discourse, a compromise achieved without denigrating the importance of either logic or grammar.

We can think of Buridan's conception of the relation of logic and grammar as striking a balance between the opposing perspectives of Abelard and Helias. On the Abelardian side, he adopts an exclusivist understanding of grammatical congruence and truth, so that at least on the surface, the grammarian and the logician seem to be involved in separate enterprises: "if I say 'Brownie is the king's donkey', everybody agrees that 'the king's donkey' is the predicate, and it does not appear that the predicate of this proposition could not become the subject and the subject the predicate by conversion, without any ungrammaticality offending the grammarian and without any falsity offending the logician" (*S* 4.2.6: 241). But things are not always as they appear. As we saw above, Buridan has pedagogical reasons for making the link between grammar and logic clear, introducing his students to the logical notion of supposition by differentiating it from the syntactical enterprise of supplying the appropriate subject for an incomplete expression.[36] Furthermore, grammar is brought into play in the *Summulae* as a practice whose rules make logic possible. This emerges in the fourth treatise, "On Supposition," where Buridan discusses a series of fourteen rules regarding the division of utterances into those which can and those which cannot be subjects and predicates, and from there, into those which can and those which cannot supposit. The fifth rule alludes to a "disagreement among the professors [*inter doctores*]" as to whether non-substantivated adjectives (e.g., 'white') can be subjects or predicates. Buridan writes:

> as regards non-substantivated adjectives I hold that they cannot be the subject of a proposition in themselves, i.e., without a substantive name, for the proposition would be ungrammatical, unless the substantive were implied. But I am doubtful whether they can be predicated in themselves by virtue of the implied substantive, since in a conversion the subject should become the predicate and the predicate should become the subject, and an adjective cannot become the subject in itself, unless it gets substantivated. And on this question we should have recourse to grammar, if the truth cannot be determined in logic. (*S* 4.2.6: 247)

Thus, the expression, 'White is (the) wall [*Albus est paries*]',[37] should be rejected as ungrammatical unless the adjective 'white' is adjoined to a proper subject, e.g., 'the white [thing]'—in which case the implied substantive 'thing' would be the proper subject, not the adjective 'white'. On the other hand, Buridan doubts whether non-substantivated adjectives can even be properly predicated, since the apparently innocuous proposition '(The) wall is white' would, by the logical rule of conversion, become 'White is (the) wall', which, again, would be ungrammatical without some implied substantive. In both cases, grammatical failures prevent an expression from entering the domain of logic.[38]

Buridan's explicit subsumption of grammatical rules as necessary conditions for the science (*scientia*) of logic indicates that although truth and congruence might be separable in theory, in practice the logician cannot determine the complete significance of a piece of discourse without appealing to both.[39] Hence, the context in which an expression occurs becomes crucial to its interpretation:

We should also note that some might ask whether it is the composite or the divided sense that is properly expressed by 'Every man or (a) donkey runs', that is to say, whether only the term 'man' or the whole subject is distributed. And I say that we have to respond differently, in accordance with the different manners of speaking and writing. For if immediately after 'man' there is a sign of division, namely, a pause or a period, then the proposition will be called divided, and only 'man' will be distributed, but if not, then it will be called 'composite', and the whole subject will be distributed. (*S* 4.2.6: 250)

Here we see a logical sign embedded not in the spoken or written proposition itself, but in the *way* it is spoken or written. Such are the linguistic raw materials with which both the logician and grammarian must work, and in contrast with which the Abelardian conception of logic as determining the truth conditions of context-free propositions vis-à-vis "the nature of things" begins to look like an activity proper to God, not to humans. Indeed, Buridan sums up his discussion here by bringing it full circle, back to the pedagogical concerns that motivated the whole inquiry. "And these are the major points," he says, "that, nevertheless, some people call into doubt owing to their poor education in grammar or in logic [*propter defectum instructionis in grammatica aut in logica*]" (*S* 4.2.6: 250).

3. Logic and Conventional Discourse

Although Buridan concedes that truth and congruence are separable in theory, he knows that the lines are not so easily drawn in practice. A more inclusivist conception of the relation between logic and grammar emerges when he discusses the office of the logician, which he sees as involving the practical art of interpreting human discourse—which is, of course, the activity Priscian counsels when he says that it is "for the exposition of authors" that the grammarian "must most diligently inquire" into the expression (*oratio*).[40] For his part, Buridan believes that the logician must likewise attend to the different modes of human discourse, an activity forced upon us by the conventionality of spoken and written languages:

an utterance [*vox*] does not have any proper import [*virtus propria*] in signifying and suppositing, except from ourselves. So by an agreement of the disputing parties, as in obligational disputes, we can impose on it a new signification and not use it according to its common signification. We can also speak figuratively [*transsumptive*] and ironically, according to a different signification. But we call a locution 'proper' when we use it according to the signification commonly and principally given to it, and we call a locution 'improper' when we use it otherwise, although we can legitimately use it otherwise. So it is absurd to say that a proposition of an author is false, absolutely speaking, if he puts it forth incorporating an improper locution, according to which it is true. Instead, we ought to say that it is true, since it is enunciated according to the sense in which it is true. . . . So it absolutely seems to me that wherever it is evident that an author puts forward a proposition in a true sense, although not as a proper locution, then to deny that proposition without qualification would be cantankerous and insolent [*dyscolum et protervum*]. But to avoid error, it should be properly pointed out that the proposition is not true in the proper sense, or by virtue of its proper meaning, and then it has to be shown in which sense it is true. (*S* 4.3.2: 256; cf. *QIP* 5: 144–45, ll. 800–829)

It is the business of the logician to expound the proper sense of a proposition. In Buridan's view, however, this cannot be done without determining the way in which a proposition is being used by its author, a procedure which involves carefully attending to both its internal features, i.e., the sense or meaning of the particular locutions incorporated in it, as well as its external features, i.e., the discourse conditions which surround it.

The notion that logic should, like grammar, focus on actual rather than ideal discourse is a key difference between the logic of Buridan and that of the other great nominalist thinker of the later Middle Ages, William of Ockham. It is important to notice, however, that this difference is methodological rather than substantive, although doctrinal differences, many of which are quite subtle, arise from it. What is especially interesting is that we know Buridan was acquainted with Ockham's *Summa logicae* from early in his career at Paris,[41] and so his decision not to follow the Venerable Inceptor's methods must have been deliberate, or at least as deliberate as his decision to use Peter of Spain's *Summulae Logicales* as the basis for his own *Summulae*. But whatever the reason, Buridan never mentions Ockham by name nor ever acknowledges his views as such, so it is impossible to know what he thought of Ockham's logic.

Both authors make the traditional assumption that propositions, be they spoken, written, or mental, are the proper bearers of truth and falsity. For Ockham, however, mental language is viewed as logically ideal or, in modern parlance, 'canonical'.[42] As Claude Panaccio points out, "mental language is prior to, and underlies, every reasonable speech utterance and provides it with meaning. Ockham's semantical theory, as presented in the [*Summa logicae*] and elsewhere, is primarily an explication of the various ways in which the natural conceptual signs that constitute the language of thought are linked with their external referents; and secondarily, of the ways in which conventional discourse is derived from this mental language."[43] By downplaying conventional discourse in this way, Ockham is able to conceive of a logic that abstracts from actual human reasoning and systematizes it in the direction of what we would now call theory. Spoken and written languages fail to be universal and logically perspicuous because they depend on the arbitrary naming conventions of fallible users. But these shortcomings can be filtered out metalinguistically once we realize that the meanings of their constituent terms depend on their corresponding mental concepts, which naturally signify the same for everyone.[44] By contrast, Buridan never privileges conceptual discourse, or suggests that the logician might use it to systematically reform spoken or written language. Buridan holds that spoken and written utterances—sometimes he uses the term 'utterance' (*vox*) where Ockham has 'term' (*terminus*)—signify concepts primarily: "the capability of speaking was given to us in order that we could signify our concepts to others and also the capacity of hearing was given to us in order that the concepts of speakers could be signified to us" (*S* 4.1.2: 222). Accordingly, "utterances are imposed to signify things only through the mediation of the concepts by which those things are conceived" (*QC* 1: 4, ll. 45–46).[45] Concepts serve as the medium of signification for Buridan, the cognitive aspect of the signification of a word. Ockham, on the other hand, holds that properly speaking, both concepts and spoken or written terms signify things outside the mind, although the latter do so in subordination to concepts,[46] which makes it easy to see why he thinks the logician should be interested in the semantics of concepts, or in the semantics of terms only insofar as they reveal the semantics of concepts.

Ockham and Buridan were also influenced by the different logical traditions at their respective universities. Ockham avoids making the *Summa logicae* dependent on any other text, whereas Buridan's *Summulae dialecticae* is structured as a commentary on Peter of Spain's *Summulae Logicales,* an authoritative text of the Parisian terminist tradition. Likewise, Ockham's logic has a more modern appearance in that he makes no effort to connect his ideas to his terminist predecessors, whereas Buridan consciously borrows concepts such as appellation and natural supposition from thirteenth-century logic and refits them for the *logica moderna.*[47] Again, Ockham's generalizing approach tries to reorganize the practice of logic around the basic notions of signification and supposition, whereas Buridan's remarks tend to be more localized,[48] where they are shaped by the particular text being commented upon and by identifiably Parisian debates such as the controversy over speculative grammar or the question of whether propositions signify.[49] When combined with their differing emphasis on spoken words or mental concepts as the subject of logic, these historical factors can make the differences between the two seem acute, even though their general doctrines are the same, or at least reducibly so.[50] Together, they explain why Buridan uses sophism sentences in the ninth treatise of the *Summulae* to test the functionality of the account presented in the first eight treatises—why Buridan thinks it important for logic to resolve paradoxes of self-reference whereas Ockham scarcely even mentions them.[51] It is significant, as Joël Biard has argued, that Buridan takes se-

Braid

riously the fact that self-referential propositions can at least be conceived. "In general," he continues, "there exists an opposition between logicians who, in one way or another, restrict the possibilities of our language—William of Sherwood, Walter Burley, William of Ockham—and those who, faced with the problem of insoluble propositions, accept that a proposition signifies something because it is grammatically well-formed and because a speaker used it with the intention of signifying—Thomas Bradwardine, John Buridan."[52] As a logician, Buridan is comfortable with the fact of human language.

With respect to the internal features of a proposition, Buridan says that "locutions [*sermones*] are to be understood in accordance with their subject matter," which he interprets in a broad sense, to include the speaker's intentions (*S* 3.1.5: 148).[53] Thus, if I predicate an abstract term denominatively—i.e., in the sense of 'being in a subject' rather than 'being said of a subject'—the resulting piece of discourse is called "denominative from the point of view of the [speaker's] intention," even though it is "not denominative properly speaking, for a requirement on the part of the utterance is not satisfied" (*S* 3.1.3: 146). Denominative terms are, after all, supposed to be concrete.[54] The distinction between proper and improper locutions is then used to conclude that "it is not a proper locution [*locutio*], although it is a true predication, when it is said that matter is privation, or that a magnitude is a shape, or that an action is a passion, or that time is motion, or that a blind [man] is a blindness" (*S* 3.1.3: 147). Buridan also appeals to the way in which words are commonly used to provide a context for the solution of logical puzzles that are puzzling precisely because they lack a proper context. For example, in expounding the sophism-sentence, 'At every time Socrates is running', he diagnoses the problem as involving an ambiguity in the proper signification of the term 'at every time', which he takes to be equivalent to the term 'always'. The solution is then rather straightforward: "it seems to me that according to common usage the word 'always' was imposed to distribute over every time, past, present, and future . . . and thus I reduce the whole [problem] to that of the conventional signification of the term 'always'" (*S* 9.7, 6th sophism: 948).

With respect to the external features of a proposition, Buridan is openly receptive to what we would now call non-truth functional modes of discourse.[55] This becomes clear in his *Questions on Porphyry's Isagoge*, where he addresses an objection that attempts to privilege literal meaning at the expense of metaphorical, ironic, and other "parabolic" meanings, so that the primary sense of a word is always determined by its personal sense in a proposition, i.e., when it is taken as standing for the thing(s) it signifies. Buridan's reply to this is direct and unambiguous:

> it seems to me that what they [i.e., the literalists] say is entirely mistaken, because a word does not have meaning in a proposition of itself, but from us, by convention [*ex nobis ad placitum*]. Therefore, if we use a word as

philosophers and others have customarily used it, we are not doing anything contrary to the meaning of the word. On the contrary, an utterance,
at least an articulate one, possesses the sort of meaning and capacity [for
signifying] that itself enables us to impose it to signify what we will, and
that, once it has been imposed for signifying, enables us to use it as we
will, viz., either significatively or materially. And in doing so, we are not
acting contrary to the meaning of the word. What is more, an utterance
 imposed to signify a certain meaning is imposed in such a way that it is
permissible for us to use it according to [1] the signification first and principally instituted for it, or [2] an analogous or metaphorical signification,
or indeed, even [3] a signification contrary to its primary signification,
such as when we want to speak ironically. Indeed, [these latter] uses agree
with the word by virtue of its primary signification, in keeping with
[their] attribution to it. And so such uses are in no way contrary to the
meaning of the word. (*QIP* 5: 143, ll. 739–53; cf. *S* 4.3.1: 252)[56]

Buridan proceeds to argue that the primary and proper sense of a word is not
necessarily the meaning philosophers ascribe to it, but rather, whatever the
corresponding utterance was first and foremost imposed to signify. Thus,
there is no a priori means of determining which senses of a word are primary
and which derivative, for "we can only know how, and to what, a word was
imposed to signify through the use of authors [*per usum auctorum*]," i.e., by
knowing the extra-propositional context of its imposition.[57] And where authorial intention is obscure or indeterminate, we must look to the way the
word is "commonly" used by the relevant class of experts, be they philosophers, poets, or 'simple old women'.[58] Buridan makes it abundantly clear that
the philosopher who practices his craft well must also be a good reader, trained
in the grammatical art of interpreting texts:

I immediately reply that the meaning of a word has never obliged us to
do this [i.e., to construe words only in their proper senses, and to concede or deny propositions only according to what is required by their
proper senses]. On the contrary, sometimes we must construe words in
their proper senses, and sometimes in improper senses, as in parabolic
or ironic [expressions], or in other ways even more removed from the
proper senses. For example, if we read the books of learned authors such
as Aristotle or Porphyry, we must construe their words according to the
senses those authors have imposed upon them, even if these are improper senses. And so we must concede that, strictly speaking, those
words are true because they are true as construed in those senses. But
even so, we must say that they have been imposed in such senses, and
that if they had been imposed in their proper senses, they would be false.
And if people reading the books of learned authors were to construe

their words differently than they believe them to have been imposed by these authors, they would be insolent and cantankerous, and unworthy to study or read the books of the philosophers. In the same way, we must say that every word of the Bible and the Gospels is strictly speaking true, and we must construe these words in the senses in which they have been imposed and according to which they are true. And those who do otherwise are mistaken, as well as being blasphemers, or perhaps even heretics. But even so, we can correctly state in connection with many of these words [of the Bible and the Gospels] that they are false, if imposed and construed in their proper senses. (*QIP* 5: 144–45, ll. 800–817)[59]

This is an attack not on what people read, but how they read. Buridan's target is a higher-level illiteracy—one that threatens to undermine students' understanding of the canonical texts of arts and theology.[60]

There is historical evidence that this threat was very real. According to William Courtenay, the University of Paris was troubled in the late 1330s by the growing popularity of "a narrow, somewhat sensationalist' method of propositional analysis according to which any proposition that did not meet the criteria of supposition theory (in its proper senses) was considered false."[61] Styles of teaching and debate based on this method were formally censured in an arts faculty statute of December 29, 1340. Among other things, the statute ordered that:

No master, bachelor, or scholar working in the faculty of arts at Paris should venture to assert that some famous proposition of an author whose book they are reading is strictly speaking or literally false, if they believe that in proposing it, the author understood it in a true sense. But they should either concede it or else divide the true sense from the false, because by parity of reasoning, one must deny propositions in the Bible [are true] in the strict sense—which is dangerous. . . . No one should say that every proposition which is false according to the personal supposition of [its] terms is literally or absolutely false, because this error leads to the previous error. For authors often use other [modes of] supposition . . . No one should say that a proposition must not be conceded unless it is true in its proper sense, because to say this leads to the aforementioned errors, since the Bible and [other] authorities do not always use words in their proper senses. Therefore, in affirming and denying [a proposition], one must attend more to words in relation to their subject matter than in relation to their properties. For a disputation attending to the properties of words, accepting no proposition except in its proper sense, is nothing but a sophistical disputation. Dialectical and doctrinal disputations that aim at true inquiry, [however,] exhibit a little concern about names [*modicam habent de nominibus sollicitudinem*]. (*CUP* II, n. 1042)[62]

The "concern" being recommended here is precisely the sort of sensitivity to discourse conditions Buridan wants to foster in his students. Logic does not primarily concern itself with names, but only insofar as names express intentions, which are its primary concern. Therefore, it is not for the logician to stipulate the meaning of a proposition from an authoritative text independently of the author's intention, although he can, of course, identify a range of possible meanings along with their truth conditions if the precise meaning is ambiguous. The practice of logic assumes that one has already acquired the maturity and good judgment to interpret a text properly, taking into account the circumstances of its composition—"we cannot know the [original] imposition except from the usage of authors" (*S* 4.3.2: 255)—and this is a descriptive task which takes the logician back to his grammatical training. Accordingly, truth and falsity are treated by Buridan as derivative notions, parasitic upon a broader understanding of authorial intention:

> Now then, with respect to our ordinary way of speaking, I say that although we are permitted to use words conventionally as long as we do not construe them in a false sense, by 'the meaning of a word' we usually understand its proper sense, conventionally and not strictly speaking. And so when we say that a proposition is literally true, we must understand by this that it would be true for someone construing it in its proper sense. And when we say that a proposition is literally false, we must understand by this that it would be false for someone construing it in its proper sense, although strictly speaking it is true, because we are construing it in another sense in which it is true. And if we understand our words of this sort differently, we are understanding them incorrectly.
>
> For this reason, it must be noted that the same spoken proposition can be true for me and false for you, since a spoken [proposition] is not true unless it designates a true mental [proposition]. That is why the same proposition, 'Man is a species', advanced by Porphyry, is true for me: because I construe it in material supposition, and thus it designates for me a mental [proposition] which is not false, but true in my mind. But perhaps it is false for you, because you intend to construe it only in its proper sense, according to which it designates for you a false mental [proposition]. (*QIP* 5: 145, ll. 818–36)[63]

There is relativism in Buridan's account of meaning, but only insofar as what is proper and improper must be defined relative to authorial intention, which is something any competent language-user can determine most of the time.[64] Going back to the arts faculty statute of December 29, 1340, it is easy to see why it would be a kind of beginner's mistake to think otherwise. The simple-minded insistence that propositions can have one and only one proper meaning—i.e., the one that connects them to what makes them true—places limits on what can be properly said. And Buridan, always respectful of the natural order, is unwilling to circumscribe the boundaries of language, and of philosophical inquiry, so radically.[65]

Convention is the principle to which Buridan returns again and again in his remarks on language. And conventions are, of course, determined by human need (S 9.7, 5th sophism: 946). By making language as it exists here and now the starting point of logic, Buridan forces his students to consider actual sentences from all kinds of different modes of discourse. Hence the necessity of determining speaker or authorial intention before one can determine the logical significance of a proposition. It is not possible, for example, to analyze contradictory propositions unless they "have the same subject and predicate in utterance and also in intention" (S 9.7, 2nd sophism: 943). Likewise, when testing a proposition for contradictoriness, we get the practical advice that "it is [sometimes] necessary to add other utterances when contradicting it. . . . For one should primarily attend to the intention, for we use words only to express the intention" (S 9.8, 11th sophism: 979). Again, where authorial intention is obscure or indeterminate, we must appeal to common usage: "a spoken proposition, outside of the context of such an [authorial] imposition or obligation, is to be taken to be true if it is true according to the signification that it commonly has for the listeners and speakers of the language, and false if false" (S 9.6, 6th conclusion: 933). Buridan tends to see human language as fluid and organic. Propositions do not exist unless they are spoken or written by an actual person. They are not timeless, nor do they 'say' anything without a human speaker or interpreter: "I deny that to affirm or to deny a proposition is something true or false, for to affirm or to deny is nothing else but the one affirming or denying, and this is a man, who is neither true nor false" (S 9.8, 6th sophism: 964). Under certain circumstances, a proposition does not even have to be expressed in language. Even a barrel hoop hanging in front of a tavern is a proposition, "for it is equivalent in its signification to the conventionally significative utterance that someone might yell at the entrance of the tavern: 'Wine is sold here!'" (S 9.6, 3rd sophism: 935–36).[66] Similarly, what a spoken or written proposition says is often determined by the conventions governing how it is said. This connects with the grammarians' traditional interest in pronunciation, recalled in Buridan's use of grammatical terminology (the 'form' and 'matter' of an expression) to comment on the logical fallacy of accent: "accent is a significant mode of uttering or writing an incomplex word. And that significant mode of uttering or writing belongs to the form of a word [pertinet ad formam dictionis]. Therefore a materially identical word is not absolutely identical in its utterance if it is uttered with different accents, as for example 'liber', uttered with its first syllable short ['book'] or long ['free']" (S 7.3.8: 533).[67] Not all such modes of uttering are significant and hence of interest to the logician, however, for Buridan hastens to add, "I said 'significant mode' so as to distinguish it from singing, in which the raising or lowering of the pitch of a voice does not make a difference in signification but only in the enjoyment of listening, and thus it does not give rise to a fallacy" (*S* 7.3.8: 533).

4. THE CONVENTIONAL AND THE NATURAL

Of course, Buridan's interest in linguistic convention is not without precedent in medieval philosophy. Other medieval thinkers acknowledged the conventionality of human language, a tradition going back to Boethius, Augustine, and Aristotle.[68] But as Jan Pinborg observed, Buridan "did something his predecessors did not: he took the arbitrariness of language seriously, sometimes to an almost shocking degree."[69] No one before Buridan placed so much emphasis on conventional meaning as a way of both shaping philosophical inquiry and indicating its limits.[70] First-time readers of Buridan are always struck by the frequency with which he reminds his audience that words are imposed to signify *ad placitum*—"conventionally," or, more literally, "at the pleasure of those who use them." When he has occasion to address this very question, i.e., of whether all words signify by convention, he replies as follows:

> We must briefly state that although there are propositions, expressions, and terms which are either mental, or spoken, or written, Aristotle only considered spoken ones in this book [i.e., *De interpretatione*] because disputations in logic must make use of them and also because determining the nature of concepts belongs to the *De Anima* or *Metaphysics*. And so it remains for logic to apply words corresponding to concepts in order to argue correctly and speak properly. Therefore, every noun considered here is vocal.
>
> But, you might ask, 'How do these vocal nouns and verbs signify at will [*ad placitum*]—according to my will, or yours?' I say that some nouns and verbs signify the same things and signify them in the same way for a single whole community, e.g., Latin words for every speaker of Latin, and French words for every speaker of French. And it is not in my power, or yours, to change or remove this sort of common signification, but it was in the power of the person or persons who first imposed those idioms, i.e., those who gave such-and-such meanings to such-and-such words according to their will. And even now, many people could by their mutual agreement create at will a single idiom that they might use among themselves, as in the case of those who speak slang [*garganicum*] to each other. Indeed, even I impose words to signify according to my will when disputing with you or teaching you, such as when I say, 'Let the major term be called *a*, and the minor *b*, and the conclusion *c*'. For I could speak differently if I wanted to. (*QDI* I.3: 16, ll. 4–23)[71]

There are two levels of convention at work here. Conventions originate from the ability of individual speakers of a language to impose words deliberately, so that they signify in a certain way. But this is not enough by itself. There must also be an agreement (*concordia*) with at least one other speaker of the language to use a word with the agreed-upon signification before actual communication can occur. Otherwise, the imposition would be pointless, since the various functions of language — teaching, disputing, speaking slang, and so on — could not occur. At a still higher level, such informal agreements are institutionalized into rule-governed systems of "common signification [*significatio communis*]," which individual speakers are no longer free to change "at will."[72] It is from these latter conventions that the proper use of a word is established. Yet the mutability of spoken and written languages means that it will always be possible for sufficiently dedicated speakers to attempt to impose a new signification upon others in their linguistic community, although this will be an uphill battle because of the sheer number of "wills" that need to be changed and the inertia of established discourse conventions. But he is shrewd about his strategy for reforming higher-order systems. As Gyula Klima remarks, "Buridan does not provide an explicit definition of any of the basic properties of terms that he covers in [the *Summulae*]. Instead, his aim seems to be to teach them in practice, by pointing out their differences through examples."[73] Buridan the teacher realizes that the right way to gain the assent of many wills is to show the implications of a particular imposition in practice. And we can easily imagine that where a large group of similarly trained students is concerned, a purely authoritative imposition would have surely fallen upon deaf ears.

Still, as a principle for understanding language, conventionality has some obvious shortcomings. For one thing, it threatens to break the link between truths and truth-makers, i.e., between the written, spoken, and mental propositions Buridan takes to be the bearers of truth on the one hand, and the states of affairs that make them true on the other.[74] The path to things appears blocked both externally, by institutionalized rules prescribing the form a significant utterance must take in different modes of discourse, and internally, by the need to discern the speaker's intentions based on the wider context of his or her utterance. The weakness of the link between truths and truth-makers has a temporal dimension as well. Like most medieval logicians, Buridan regards the propositions that are the bearers of truth and falsity as ephemeral, existing only when actually inscribed, or spoken, or thought.[75] On top of all this, the insistence on convention carries anti-realist connotations that do not fit well with Buridan's broadly Aristotelian worldview. Not once does he question the assumption that individual things really exist outside the soul, independently of our concepts of them.[76] Accordingly, it is not his view that philosophy is about conventional systems of rules governing contingent modes of discourse. There's more to it than talking.

Buridan never felt compelled to provide a general defense of conventionality for the simple reason that he did not think of it as a metaphysical position about the nature of reality. Conventionality is often understood this way in modern debates, where it is sometimes seen as an attempt to undermine our claim to objectivity by corralling philosophical problems and their solutions within certain forms of discourse, outside of which they have no significance. This is not Buridan's understanding of conventionality. For Buridan, philosophy is an activity conducted according to the patterns of speaking and reasoning outlined by Aristotle in the *Organon*.[77] The conventionality of philosophical discourse stems from the contingencies of human cognition, language, and social institutions. It is not that truth cannot exist outside of propositions. Rather, in acknowledging the Aristotelian commonplace that "as each thing is in respect of being, so it is in respect of truth," Buridan argues that the power to grasp the truth of a thing in its very being belongs to God, not to us.[78] For creatures possessed of empirical intellects such as ourselves, the comprehension of truth comes down to "nothing other than the comprehension of a true proposition."[79] But this means that our ability to comprehend truth is always conditioned by the fallibility of our intellects and the weakness of our wills, the former leading us to produce propositions which say the wrong things and/or say them about the wrong subjects, and the latter to assent too hastily or imprudently to whatever looks good.[80] Philosophical inquiry is supposed to guide us to the truth between these twin dangers. The development of appropriate conventions for evaluating the truth of propositions is thus central to the philosophical enterprise for Buridan, and must have struck his undergraduate students as an orderly expansion of grammatical propriety into the new fields of logic, metaphysics, and natural philosophy.

In grammar, the link between the material forms of words and what they signify was thought to be natural, and hence something we can discover via the more specialized discipline of etymology. According to Peter Helias.

> Etymology . . . is the exposition of any word by another word or words more known [to us], in keeping with the property of the thing [*proprietas rei*] and the similarity of the letters: e.g., 'stone [*LApis*]', as it were 'wounding the foot [*LAedere pedem*]'; 'window [*FENestra*]', as it were 'carrying us outside [*FErens nos extra*]'. For here, the property of the thing is closely attended to, and the similarity of the letters observed. Indeed, 'etymology [*ethimologia*]' is a noun made up of '*ethimo*', meaning 'true', and '*logos*', meaning 'speech', so we say that '*ethimologia*' is like 'speaking truly [*veriloquium*]', since the etymologist designates the 'true', that is, the primal origin of a word. But etymology differs from interpretation, which is the translation of one item of speech [*loquela*] into another.

Indeed, etymology is more often directed to the same item of speech. (Reilly 1993, 70, ll. 87–96; emphases mine)

What matters here is not whether the medieval practice of etymology is what we would call an empirical science. Many of the etymologies constructed by Isidore of Seville and others are based on merely accidental similarities between words. What matters is the grammarians' idea that conventions of orthography and pronunciation, the shapes and sounds of letters, are *naturally* guided by the properties or qualities of the thing signified. This same naturalism underlies Buridan's understanding of convention—the belief that the principles which guide our reasoning in logic, metaphysics, and natural philosophy are rooted, however circuitously, in the way things are.[81]

Buridanian conventions are not opposed to what is natural because they are natural.[82] He begins with the Aristotelian assumption that the conventional meaning of spoken and written languages is rooted in the discourse of thought, i.e., concepts which naturally signify the same for all: "mental terms are naturally significative, but other terms are conventionally significative, based on the voluntary imposition of those who first establish them" (*QE* 8, 3.1: 34, ll. 55–57; cf. Aristotle, *De Interpretatione* 1.16a3–8).[83] Writing and speaking are ordered upwards, towards thinking: written words signify spoken words, and spoken words "signify affections, i.e., concepts of the soul, and signify other things only by the mediation of the signification of the concepts" (*S* 9.1, 2nd conclusion: 832). What do concepts naturally signify? Concepts naturally signify things:

> by every concept something [*aliquid*] is conceived, though this need not be only one thing but can be several things together. For it would be absurd to say that someone understands, and yet he understands nothing; or that he sees, and yet he sees nothing. . . . For this reason we should hold that these are false: 'I read and I read nothing', 'I see and I see nothing', 'I understand and I understand nothing'; so I believe that all such [propositions] are false and not possible by nature [*non possibiles per naturam*]. (*S* 9.1, 3rd conclusion: 833)

Concepts or "mental terms" naturally signify the thing or things for which they stand in the context of a proposition, the basic unit of truth and falsity in Buridanian logical semantics.[84] But three other things are revealed in this brief passage.

First, the extramental objects of our cognitive acts are all individual or particular—"one thing" in the case of singular cognition, or "several things together" in the case of universal cognition. This looks ahead to the metaphysical side of Buridan's nominalism, which, as we shall see in chapters 10–11, recognizes the existence of only particular substances and certain qualities or "modes" of those substances.

Second, Buridan's criterion for rejecting the idea that a piece of conceptual discourse might have no real referent does not come from any a priori argument, but from lower down in the semantic hierarchy, viz., from conventional discourse—"it would be absurd to say that someone understands, and yet he understands nothing." Buridan understands the relationship between conventional languages and mental language dialectically or bi-directionally, as opposed to the more traditional, uni-directional picture, where concepts serve as the absolute and unchanging source of the meaning of all spoken and written words. Accordingly, Aristotle's "the same for all" in Buridan's mind refers to the natural capacity of concepts or "affections of the soul" to signify whatever thing(s) *first* generate them in the minds of human knowers, in the way that smoke means fire, rather than to what we would now call the 'content' of those concepts, since content is subtly shaped by the conditions in which actual thinking and speaking take place.[85] The difference is that in voluntary agents, concepts are produced naturally, though not ineluctably, through contingencies in the affective structures of individual agents.

Finally, this passage makes clear that nature also imposes limits on what concepts can signify, so that from the act whereby I understand something, if I really do understand—i.e., if "I understand [*intelligo*]" is true—there must be something that I understand; it cannot be that I understand when there is literally nothing (no thing) for me to understand. Non-referring significant concepts are "not possible by nature." Notice, however, that Buridan does not say "not possible absolutely [*simpliciter*]." This leaves open the possibility that God could, by virtue of his absolute power, operate outside the common course of nature to cause me to assent to the proposition that I understand something when there is nothing there for me to understand. As we shall see in chapter 12 below, Buridan does not regard such possibilities as philosophically relevant, since there is no way of confirming or disconfirming supernatural contingencies in terms that would make sense to us as empirical creatures.

It would be more in keeping with Buridan's way of doing philosophy to ask, '*How* do concepts (naturally) manage to signify what they do?' His answer is that concepts naturally resemble the extramental thing(s) they signify: "the passions, i.e., concepts, of the soul are natural likenesses of those things; and spoken words are only significative of those things in keeping with a voluntary, conventional imposition, and by the mediation of those concepts of the soul" (QDI II.11: 100, ll. 30–33).[86] Buridan accepts the idea that causes naturally resemble their effects, i.e., the uniformity of nature principle, as an explanatory primitive. When we signify something, the cause is the mental act of signifying and the effect is the thing made known to the intellect through that act of signifying.[87] It is important to note, however, that he does not run this naturalistic account of signification in the direction of essentialism, so that we might claim the ability to know the real definitions of things based on an intellectual grasp of their essences or forms. Buridan's Aristotelian assumption that all our knowledge is acquired through the senses is tempered by the recognition that this is a piecemeal and imperfect process in our wayfarer state.[88] This, together with his nominalism, is why he holds that concepts and what they are concepts of are related by similarity rather than by formal identity.[89] And if that were not enough of a move away from Aristotle, he also tells us that we should construe this similarity "broadly and figuratively [*large vel improprie*]," as referring "not to some quality, but only to a certain agreement appropriate to the agent as regards the effect" (*QM* VII.8: 46rb).[90]

As a result, we find throughout Buridan's philosophy an emphasis on function over form. In language, this emerges in his reliance on the actual use to which two words, or concepts, are put as the criterion for their sameness (or, more strictly, similarity), rather than on their definitions, or content. If two numerically distinct qualities, say, concept C in my mind and concept C' in your mind, both represent or make known to us the same extramental thing(s) in the same way, then they are the same concept. And, as we saw above, although Buridan would agree that concepts are "the same for all" in the sense that they are naturally produced by the same cognitive processes in such a way as to signify the same for all, their semantic values can be altered through their association with other concepts. Conceptual change is inevitable as a result of the dynamic relation between conventional discourse and individual understanding, between writing or speaking and thinking.[91] If Aristotle is right that children at first call all women 'mother' (*Physics* I.1.184b12), then what we see is a gradual refinement of the semantic value of that concept through the intervention of parents, teachers, and other purveyors of conventional meaning. What we do not see is the acquisition of a completely new concept, fixing the reference of 'mother' on its proper object, viz., the child's own mother. The philosopher uses the evidence of spoken and written discourse to reveal those diverse intentions of the soul on the basis of which all utterances and inscriptions have meaning. Buridan expresses this sentiment in a mixed prescription to his students, as if the best philosopher is one who is able to keep his eyes on two things at once: "in our expressions [*sermones*], where truth and falsity, consequences and oppositions are concerned, we should pay attention more to the intentions than to the utterances, although we should pay attention to both" (*S* 7.4.3: 566).

In the chapters which follow, we will see Buridan again and again appealing to our capacity to accurately describe and understand what we are saying in order to solve problems in logic, metaphysics, natural philosophy, and ethics. How this works in practice depends on the context, which itself must be determined through careful attention to actual discourse. But one moment in the *Summulae de Dialectica* stands out in particular. Buridan pauses in the midst of a technical discussion of the quantity of modal propositions to tell his readers: "in the present context I speak about necessity and impossibility broadly, for this is how we speak in the demonstrative sciences, although we speak differently in narrative stories [*historiae narrativae*]" (*S* 1.8.5: 76). Only Buridan would interrupt a logic text to remind us that what he is saying does not apply to narrative stories.

CHAPTER TWO

The Science of Logic

· Buridan's understanding of logic is based on two distinct, but complementary, conceptions of its purpose: theoretical (*logica docens*) and practical
(*logica utens*). The former, he says, is so-called because "it teaches us how, and
from what [materials], arguments should be constructed, whether those arguments be demonstrative, dialectical, or of some other kind." The latter derives its name from the fact that "it uses arguments in order to prove whether
some conclusion is evident, regardless of the subject matter of the conclusion" (*QIP* 1: 126–27, ll. 176–80).[1] What is striking about these remarks is that
both conceptions are, in essence, practical. Teaching how to construct arguments is no less a *praxis* than the use of arguments to construct proofs in
other disciplines. Buridan concludes that as a body of knowledge (*scientia*),
logic must be practical rather than speculative because a speculative science
"does not teach us how to do those things about which it thinks or speculates,
nor does it teach us to speculate in a certain way," whereas "a practical science
proposes that this must be done, or that it must be done by us in such and
such a way" (*QIP* 2: 132–33, ll. 372–78).[2]

This suggests a division of the study of logic into the practical-theoretical
and the practical-functional. The notion of the practical-theoretical is conditioned by the authoritative remarks of Aristotle in Book VI of the *Nicomachean Ethics*, who expresses it as the particular state or excellence of the
soul by which we deliberate.[3] Buridan follows suit, distinguishing those
intellectual states or "habits" which are practical from those which are
speculative:

I say, then, that *'praxis'* in Greek is the same as *'operatio* [activity]' in Latin—but not just any activity, only those produced freely by the intellect and will. That is why, if nourishment, growth, the movement of our hearts and lungs, and sleep or wakefulness are all produced in us via the nerves, activities of this sort are not called *'praxes'*, since they occur in us naturally and not voluntarily. Nor is there practical knowledge of how they are, but only speculative. But since activities which are capable of being performed by us are in the power of our free will, viz., such that we might perform them or not, and perform them in this way rather than that, then the habit teaching us when and where we should do this or forgo it, and how we should do it better, and so on in other circumstances— a habit of this sort is practical. (*QIP* 2: 130, ll. 292–302)[4]

What places logic squarely in the sphere of the practical is that it teaches us how to shape a particular form of discourse, the argument, to ends of our own choosing.[5] Logic is not itself directed to any end, and especially not to any natural end, since that would make it an activity like breathing or sleeping, beyond "the power of our free will." Thus, "so far as logic is concerned, the logician does not care for anything except whether the argument is good for proving the conclusion—regardless of whether it is in the service of justice, or used to perpetrate an injustice against and destroy a good man, or to separate his goods from him, in the way that advocates and advisors of rich men often argue against the good and the poor" (*QIP* 2: 132, ll. 345–50).[6] Buridan thinks it obvious that logic can be used for a "bad end," although the evaluation of ends he takes to be a matter of prudence, which is more properly treated in ethics.[7] This is what makes logic an art in the medieval sense in which it connotes a kind of professional or technical expertise.

Buridan's comments on the opening lines of Peter of Spain's *Summulae Logicales* show that Peter's text had already been corrupted by students or copyists confused over the place of logic in the hierarchy of learning: "we should note that a certain [other version of our] text has [the formulation]: 'dialectic is the art of arts, the science of sciences [*dialectica est ars artium et scientia scientiarum*] ... etc.,' but it is more correct to say only that it is the art of arts" (*S* 1.1.1: 6; cf. de Rijk 1972, 1). The latter formulation is more correct, he says, because the peculiar excellence of logic consists in "its utility and the generality of its application to all other arts and sciences." It is the task of the theoretical-practical side of logic, *logica docens,* to guide the practice of human reasoning by providing rules for the construction and analysis of arguments in any field of inquiry. Indeed, Buridan goes so far as to suggest that if logic were to have a proper subject, it would be argumentation, the "special product" of logical discourse.[8] The term 'argumentation [*argumentatio*]' is from Boethius, and Buridan is well aware of its practical import when he paraphrases the relevant passage from *De topicis differentiis*. An argument, he says, is the mental process of "inwardly coercing" the mind's assent, "but an argumentation is the vocal process expressing and significatively explicating this mental process" (*S* 6.1.2: 392).[9] Logic is therefore concerned with the perfection or completion of thought in conventional language.

These complementary conceptions of logic are further clarified through differentiation. Logic, unlike the speculative sciences, is about the way in which a body of knowledge is uncovered and expressed, so that "ultimately, speculative science is about knowing and practical science is about doing [*scientiam speculativam esse finaliter propter scire et practicam propter opus*]" (*QIP* 2: 132, ll. 359–61). But logic also resembles speculative inquiry on two fronts: internally, insofar as the logic student acquires certain "habits [*habitus*]" from the proofs which have been shown to him, "since in each book of [Aristotle's] logic, many conclusions are demonstrated by means of their proper and necessary principles" (*QIP* 1: 126, ll. 166–67); and externally, insofar as logic, like metaphysics, "has being in general as its subject" (*QM* IV.4: 15va).[10] Logic thus resembles metaphysics in terms of its reach, alternatively described as its "excellence," though they operate differently as ordering principles. Metaphysics is "the science of sciences" because of its access to the principles of all other speculative inquiries, but logic is the "art of arts," because no other art or science "can be satisfactorily acquired without a previous [training in] logic, since such a science needs to use syllogisms or other argumentations, the doctrine of which is taught by logic" (*S* 1.1.1: 6).[11] This permits us to see more clearly why logic must be practical rather than speculative. For even if it is specially concerned with argumentation, Buridan sees the subject matter of logic as embracing being more generally because of its role in structuring every other form of rational discourse. Thus, even though the proper subject matter of, e.g., psychology, is animate body, logic is also concerned with animate body to the extent that the primary objects of knowledge in psychology are conclusions whose truths are expressed in a process of demonstration governed by logic.[12]

The other side in this differential clarification of logic is also important, as it brings into play the mechanical arts, which are more obviously practical. If Buridan holds that logic is practical rather than speculative, what is there to distinguish logic from carpentry or shoemaking? As if to emphasize the utilitarian nature of logic, he says that the only difference is that the mechanical artist works with his hands on materials such as wood or leather to create houses and shoes, whereas logic does not involve manual work on things that exist outside the mind. The reader is left to draw the positive conclusion: logic involves intellectual work with "premises and principles [*praemissa et principia*]," using the raw material of concepts (internal) and expressions (external), to create products in the form of proofs, syllogisms, and other forms of argumentation (*QM* IV.4: 15va). We might think of the Buridanian conception of logic as 'carpentry for the mind', though this must be taken in the Aristotelian sense, where the primary products of carpentry—e.g., shelter "protecting us from wind and rain" (*QIP* 1: 131, ll. 324–25)—are external goods necessary for survival. The logician must never lose sight of the fact that even in its theoretical mode, logic is a practice ordered to the perfection of other, more properly speculative, forms of inquiry that are essential to our lives as rational creatures.

But what about the practical-functional side of logic? Here Buridan denies that logic has any determinate subject matter. Consequently, there can be only opinion, not knowledge, of what conclusions will be made evident prior to the actual application of the logical *processus* in other disciplines. But this indeterminacy of subject matter is what gives *logica utens* its versatility, for it is that by means of which "we can argue dialectically as regards all scientific conclusions [*ad omnes conclusiones scientificas possemus dialectice arguere*]" (*QM* IV.4: 15va). In response to what was probably a student query about where one might find this taught, Buridan replies: "in the book of the *Metaphysics* as far as metaphysical conclusions are concerned, in the book of the *Posterior Analytics* as far as the conclusions of the posterior science [of demonstration] are concerned, in the book of the *Physics* as far as physical conclusions are concerned, and so on for the other [special] sciences. That is why often in those books, probable arguments are usually posited and adduced by way of disputation, before the main thesis is demonstratively proved" (*QM* IV.4: 15va).[13] So logic as a practice is, appropriately enough, learned by watching others—in this case an exemplary other in the person of Aristotle. We become competent practitioners of dialectic by apprenticing ourselves to the metaphysics and natural philosophy of Aristotle, from which we learn the art of disputation.

But why does Buridan include the *Posterior Analytics* in this list, since that is one of the canonical texts of Aristotelian logic, and he has already denied that logic has a determinate subject matter? Is there some hidden science of logic after all?[14]

1. LOGIC AS *SCIENTIA*

It is when he considers the study of logic that Buridan first speaks about the divisions of the sciences and other fields of learning proper to the human intellect. The problem of how these various discourses are related to each other is as old as Plato, of course, and medieval thinkers inherited from philosophers of late antiquity a penchant for ordering them hierarchically. By Buridan's time, arts students were exposed to two methods of ordering, each with its own history and textual traditions. This situation created the new problem for arts masters of how to rationalize both systems within a single hierarchy of human learning.

The older and more traditional method found its expression in the seven liberal arts: the *trivium* of grammar, logic or dialectic, and rhetoric, and the *quadrivium* of astronomy, arithmetic, geometry, and music.[15] As we saw in chapter 1, the first two subjects of the *trivium* still determined the order of study in fourteenth-century Paris, a fact reflected in Buridan's frequent references to grammatical learning in his lectures on logic. But by the late twelfth century, another method had arrived on the scene, derived from the newly translated *Physics* and *Metaphysics* of Aristotle and reinforced for western thinkers by Islamic commentators such as Avicenna, whose works were also recently translated. Aristotle, as is well known, distinguishes between speculative and practical wisdom. Speculative knowledge, or *scientia,* is divided into three parts, which are ordered upwards in terms of the increasing intelligibility of their objects, beginning with physics or natural philosophy (which deals with what is sensible, imaginable, and intelligible), moving on to mathematics (which deals with what is imaginable and intelligible), and culminating with metaphysics or theology (which deals with what is purely intelligible).[16] Other sciences, such as psychology and astronomy, are teleologically ordered to physics or mathematics; as the universal science, metaphysics cannot be subdivided into fields.[17] But how can this newer, more systematic, Aristotelian picture of human wisdom be brought into communion with the older tradition of the seven liberal arts?

The answer is, 'by masterful compromise', an interpretive skill much in vogue in the later Middle Ages. Buridan himself was a master at harmonizing apparently contradictory authorities. His solution is to adopt the Aristotelian scheme wholesale and then adapt it where necessary to accommodate the liberal arts, not all of which emerge from the process unchanged. For example, on the side of the *quadrivium,* he eschews the traditional practice of subsuming the quadrivial arts under Aristotelian mathematics.[18] Arithmetic and geometry do seem to fit without remainder into Aristotle's conception of mathematics, but we should not assume the same for astronomy and music. Instead, Buridan classifies astronomy and music together with the Aristotelian science of optics as "middle sciences [*scientiae mediae*]," situated halfway between physics and mathematics (*QP* II.6: 34va; cf. *S* 8.9.2: 776). Here he notes a controversy concerning the classification of the middle sciences between Thomas Aquinas, whom he refers to as "Saint Thomas [*beatus Thomas*]" (Thomas had been canonized in 1324), and Averroes, "the Commentator" on Aristotle. Buridan, who must have been working from a copy of Thomas's *Commentary on Aristotle's Physics,*[19] ascribes to Thomas the view that the middle sciences are more "natural," i.e., proper to physics, because they proceed from mathematical principles to natural conclusions. On the other hand, he says, Averroes contends that they are proper to mathematics for the very same reason.[20] Realizing that the dilemma arises from differing conceptions about how subordinate sciences should be classified—i.e., whether a science derives its character from its starting point or its end—Buridan splits the difference between the two. Thus, astronomy is ordered to physics if we consider the heavenly bodies that are its objects under the concept (*ratio*) of movement, but it can just as well be ordered to mathematics insofar as those same bodies are considered as measurable objects.

The spoken arts of the *trivium* undergo a more radical transformation. First, Buridan rejects the idea of grammar as a science. Distinguishing between positive grammar (*grammatica positiva*), elementary instruction in the Latin language which makes communication between master and student possible, and normative grammar (*grammatica regulativa*), the systematic codification of rules of discourse found in authors such as Priscian or Peter Helias, Buridan does not consider either to be knowledge-producing. Because of its focus on the needs of the beginning student, positive grammar is too elementary, fragmented, and particular to generate anything like the propositions that might serve as the principles and conclusions of an Aristotelian science.[21] Likewise, normative grammar is prevented by the syntactical contingencies of spoken languages from reaching conclusions with the requisite universality—though, as we shall see below, Buridan does address himself to a late thirteenth-century effort to elevate grammar to the level of a science in just this way.

Rhetoric fares only slightly better than grammar. In his commentary on Aristotle's *Rhetoric*, Buridan states that although rhetoric is not usually considered a science in the sense that it has a theoretical aspect (*docens*), "nothing prevents it from being a science with respect to its many conclusions, like the science which is properly treated in *Posterior Analytics* I, because [rhetoric] is a habit of necessary conclusions demonstrated through its principles" (*QR* I.1).[22] But *rhetorica docens* turns out to be of minor importance as far as its classification in the hierarchy of human wisdom is concerned. Its proper place is secured by its practical or instrumental aspect, where it is subsumed not by any of the speculative sciences but by practical wisdom.[23] Thus, as Joël Biard points out, rhetoric for Buridan governs the discourse of moral teaching: "The principal part of the moral sciences includes the subdivisions of ethics, economics, and politics. But the 'supporting or instrumental [*adminicultiva seu instrumentalis*]' part, which plays the role that logic plays with respect to metaphysics, physics, and mathematics, is taught by [Aristotle's] *Rhetoric* and *Poetics*. These works accordingly constitute a kind of special dialectic, a 'moral logic.'"[24] The terms 'moral logic [*logica moralis*]' and 'special logic [*logica specialis*]' are coined by Buridan, and are intended to express the idea that, just as logic in the broad sense (*logica simpliciter*) is our means of expressing truth in the speculative sciences, so rhetoric is our means of enacting conclusions in the moral sciences. Rhetoric occupies this important position by virtue of its persuasive power, since "it is only with respect to morals that appetite is naturally suited to alienate the judgment of reason" (*QNE* Proemium: 2rb).[25]

The third trivial art, logic, or dialectic, is the one Buridan wishes to elevate to the level of a science.[26] Now this would seem to be a tall order, since Aristotle does not regard logic as a science and there is no obvious way of conceiving its objects as things without violating the principle of parsimony to which Buridan is generally committed in his thought. Buridan's solution is another masterful compromise: he elevates logic to the status of the science of discourse, rather than of things, thereby systematizing the teachings of two groups of authoritative texts along theoretical (*docens*) and practical (*utens*) lines. In the process, logic acquires a disciplinary autonomy it never really possessed before.

Buridan's reconception of the study of logic begins by noting that there is a difference between logic and the more properly speculative disciplines of metaphysics, mathematics, and physics. They are not sciences in the same sense. For, whereas the person doing, e.g., physics, is in the course of his investigations concerned with expressions, propositions, and demonstrations, logic is about the terms 'expression', 'proposition', and 'demonstration'. So there is a difference in the "concept [*ratio*]" by which the practitioners of these sciences approach a piece of argumentation. Speculative inquiry understands logic instrumentally, as our means of expressing truths about the structure and operations of the natural world. Furthermore, each of the speculative sub-disciplines is ordered in relation to all other forms of speculative inquiry. A valid proof in psychology will borrow its principles or starting points from physics, the higher science to which it is subordinated, and its conclusion will in turn supply principles for proofs in the more specialized studies of the senses and animal locomotion which are subordinated to it.[27] But logic, like the other practical sciences, is also an orphan discipline, governing only the mode of discourse it names. Buridan expresses this difference by holding that the subject terms proper to each of the speculative sciences are able to supposit personally, or stand for what they signify, such as when we consider the truth of the proposition, 'The human intellect is immaterial', in psychology. Here the question is whether the extramental things signified by the subject term, 'human intellect', are also signified by the predicate term, 'immaterial'. Discovering whether such a proposition is true means that we must find premises and principles sufficiently evident to demonstrate it, and this, of course, is the stuff of psychological inquiry.

The subject terms of logic, however—'expression', 'proposition', and 'demonstration'—are said to supposit materially. Buridan explains this idea when he introduces that part of the science of logic based on Aristotle's *On*

Interpretation: "the proper subject which must be ascribed to this science is the proposition, so that 'proposition' is not taken personally but materially, because what is principally determined here concerns the proposition and its parts, both subjective and integral, and its attributes, e.g., in constructions of opposition and equivalence. And in every respect, we give consideration in those cases to what is per se attributable to the proposition" (*QDI* I.1: 6, ll. 10–15; cf. *S* 4.3.2: 255–58).[28] Now according to Buridan, an utterance (*vox*) is said to supposit materially when it stands "for itself or for one similar to itself, or for its immediate significate, which is the concept according to which it was imposed to signify, as the term 'man' in the proposition 'Man is a species'" (*S* 4.3.2: 253). For example, "if I say, 'That a man is an animal is true', or 'That a man is a stone is false', the subjects of these propositions, the 'that-clauses', supposit materially for propositions," i.e., the propositions, 'A man is an animal' and 'A man is a stone' (*S* 4.3.2: 254). In understanding logic to be about words rather than things, Buridan takes himself to be following Aristotle: "although propositions, expressions, and terms are mental, spoken, and written, Aristotle only gave consideration in this book [i.e., *On Interpretation*] to spoken discourse, because that is the [form of discourse] which disputations in logic must use" (*QDI* I.3: 16, ll. 4–7).[29] But spoken words signify by convention, and "material supposition pertains to conventionally significative terms" (*S* 7.3.10: 538). So logic is a science of discourse, a conventional system of classifying the various modes and relations of human speech.[30]

The proper subject matter of logic becomes clearer if we ask not what logical terms stand for (answer: themselves) but what they signify, or make known. Here again it is helpful to contrast logic with speculative science. Although the details differ depending on the context of the discussion, Buridan's official position is that there are four objects of knowledge in any speculative science.[31] The primary object is the proposition, paradigmatically a proposition that is the conclusion of a formally valid demonstration employing premises whose truth is evident either immediately or from a superior science. But he also says that we can have knowledge "equivocally," or in a secondary sense, of the premises through which a demonstrated conclusion is known, of the significant terms in the premises and conclusion of a valid demonstration, and of the things signified by those terms (*QP* I.1: 2va). This last kind of knowledge is how our propositional knowledge extends outside the soul, i.e., how we can be said to have knowledge "of animals and stones, of God and the intelligences, and so forth" (*QAnPo* I.1).[32] Furthermore, the first three kinds of knowledge are for the sake of the fourth, so that whatever knowledge we acquire of propositions, premises, and terms is for the sake of knowing things.[33]

It is important to notice here that our knowledge of things is entirely derivative, occurring primarily through the medium of the proposition. This is a reflection of Buridan's Aristotelian conviction that the significant sounds of speech which are the building blocks of propositions are ordered via concepts or thoughts to the higher virtues of knowledge (*scientia*) and, ultimately, of wisdom (*sapientia*). It is not possible for human beings within the common course of nature to have knowledge of things *simpliciter*. The science of logic differs from speculative science, however, because its tier of secondary or derivative "knowable [*scibile*]" objects is much more circumscribed. That is, to put it in terms of the doctrine of supposition, the subject and predicate terms of propositions that are the primary objects of the science of logic supposit only materially, and as such do not stand for anything beyond the boundaries of human discourse. The contrast with the ultimate objects of speculative science is clear: metaphysics, mathematics, and physics are all modes of human knowing which ultimately reach out to the realm of nature, whereas logic never gets beyond the conventional.

Not surprisingly, when Buridan tries this as a means of classifying the objects of speculative science on logic, the garment does not always fit well. There is, he argues, no science of the *Prior Analytics* if by that we mean knowledge of terms or demonstrated conclusions, since the syllogisms that are its proper objects are not terms or demonstrated conclusions. Nevertheless, he allows that there is a science of the term 'syllogism' in the sense that the *Prior Analytics* contains many demonstrations in which 'syllogism' occurs in the subject or predicate position. There is even knowledge of things in the *Prior Analytics*. What things? Again, the answer is syllogisms, because it contains conclusions whose terms "signify syllogisms and supposit for syllogisms" (*QAnPr* I.1).[34]

We get a slightly different account in his *Questions on Aristotle's Posterior Analytics,* but the idea is still that the objects of knowledge in logic are to be understood materially. We do not know conclusions in the science of demonstration, since no demonstration—indeed, no syllogism—is the conclusion of a demonstration. Likewise, demonstrative science is not about terms because demonstrations are not terms but composites of propositions and terms (though again, Buridan concedes that sometimes a demonstration can occur in the subject or predicate position of another proposition as long as it is not taken significatively, or personally). Finally, we get the strange, but innocuous, argument that there is a demonstrative science of things because "the terms 'being', 'one', 'same', 'diverse', 'cause', 'effect', 'corruptible', 'incorruptible', and so on signify everything in the world, and from these terms many demonstrable conclusions can be constructed, in physics and metaphysics alike; so there is a science of all things through physics and metaphysics, and consequently, a science of demonstration" (*QAnPo* I.1). The operative phrase here is, of course, "through physics and metaphysics," since Buridan indicates that if we really want to "descend to the science of the

Posterior Analytics," we can go no further than the term 'demonstration'. "This is the science contained and taught in the *Posterior Analytics,*" he says, "for many conclusions are demonstrated in this book which contain the term 'demonstration' as the subject of a proposition, e.g., 'A demonstration is from what is true', 'A demonstration is from what is necessary'" (*QAnPo* I.1).[35]

Why does Buridan deny that logic is about things? The immediate cause was most likely a parsimonious reaction to the views of earlier contemporaries such as the *modistae* or speculative grammarians, whose interpretation of the modes of signifying reified the relations between intentions and extramental things. But if logic is no more than a *scientia sermocinalis,* a science of discourse, as opposed to a *scientia realis,* a science of things, or a *scientia rationalis,* a science of concepts, then logic must be about words and not things or concepts.[36] Since words already exist in the way Aristotle stated, as spoken sounds significant by convention, there is no need to find some new thing to be the proper subject matter of logic. But parsimony is more of a dividend of Buridan's position than its deeper motivation. For the latter, we must return to his initial characterization of logic as a practical science.

Logic, as we saw above, "teaches [*docet*]" us how to construct arguments, and also "uses [*utitur*]" those arguments as material for proofs in other disciplines (*QIP* 1: 126–27, ll. 176–80). To put it in terms of a modern distinction, we might say that logic is a 'know-how' rather than a 'know-that'. What it does is take the raw material of human speech and reshape it to create a higher and more specialized form of discourse capable of expressing human knowledge. But the higher discourse always presumes the lower. In keeping with his respect for convention, Buridan takes his raw material as given, refusing to apply the science of logic recursively to effect some kind of systematic reform of ordinary language.[37] The reason is fairly simple: the primary function of language is to communicate, not to communicate in a certain way. There is accordingly nothing illogical in the way "the untutored [*laici*]" speak, and it would be a category mistake—not to mention the height of presumption—for the logician to think otherwise.

There is also no solace to be found in the loftier realm of concepts. Logic cannot be about concepts or mental intentions for several reasons. First, although concepts play a crucial role as intermediaries in the process by which things are signified, or made known, through words—"significative utterances signify affections, i.e., concepts of the soul, and signify other things only by the mediation of the signification of the concepts" (*S* 9.1, 2nd conclusion: 832)—it is unclear what semantic value should be assigned to concepts themselves, or, if this could be specified, whether it would even be relevant to logic. It might seem obvious that extramental things are the significates of concepts, but then, as we saw in chapter 1, we run into the problem that concepts owe their existence to those same entities (which they are said to 'resemble') through sense perception. Second, concepts *per se* are causally inert, deriving at least part of their efficacy as signifiers from the act of understanding, which is proper to the intellect. And even if we weaken this to say that concepts are only naturally necessary conditions for the act of signifying, their causal powers remain highly circumscribed compared to other things in the natural order. Thus, certain terms are said to "appellate" their concepts "because we think of things by means of those concepts, but it is not in this way, i.e., not by means of a concept, that fire heats water or that a stone hits the ground" (*S* 4.3.8.4: 281). Buridan's general point here is nicely put by Paul Vincent Spade: "terms in mental language signify (make one think of) external objects only in the degenerate sense that they *are* the thoughts of those external objects."[38] To the extent that concepts are identified with the activity of thinking, it seems wrong to treat them as stable, discrete *termini* that can provide logic with its proper subject matter. Finally, Buridan unequivocally states that "investigating and determining the nature of concepts pertains to the *De Anima* or the *Metaphysics*" (*QDI* I.3, ll. 7–9: 16). Since they are natural and "the same for all," concepts would have to be the subject of a speculative science like psychology, not a practical science like logic—if, that is, there is a science of concepts at all. Although he offers no precise determination of the question, Buridan clearly does not regard the idea of a naturally significative mental language as a useful explanatory postulate in logic and semantics.[39]

So we are left with words.[40] But why, we might ask, must logic be the *scientia sermocinalis,* the science of discourse? Wasn't there an even more obvious candidate for the title in grammar, which, as we saw in chapter 1, had moved in an increasingly scientific direction since the twelfth century, partly through its engagement with logic? One reason Buridan *qua* arts master might have had for rejecting the elevation of grammar to the status of a science is that none of the traditional textbook authorities in grammar, including Peter Helias, refer to what they are doing as a science,[41] so that Buridan's students were not primed to think of their grammatical training along those lines. Thus, although Buridan concedes that "grammar is especially concerned with the similarities and dissimilarities of significative utterances" (*S* 7.5.5: 599–600), comparative studies of linguistic attributes will not yield any necessary and eternal conclusions, which is tantamount to saying that they do not amount to anything worthy of the name 'science'.

But historical considerations suggest that this can be only part of the explanation. Buridan's philosophical career at Paris was launched on the heels of the demise of the *modistae,* speculative grammarians whose aim was to turn grammar into the science of discourse, not by unifying the study of grammar per se, but by linking grammatical categories to Aristotelian ontology. The result was not so much a science of discourse, though *modistae* such as Siger of Courtrai were fond of describing it that way, as an effort to

treat syntactical forms or "modes" as the real effects of modes of understanding, and ultimately, of modes of being or real properties in the things understood.[42] Buridan was among the first masters explicitly to reject the teachings
of the *modistae,* who had dominated the Parisian logical scene for the previous half century, and restore the terminist approach to logic characteristic of
earlier authors such as Peter of Spain.[43] Although he hardly ever speaks of
the *modistae* (in what we may assume to be a rhetorical silence appropriate
for a discredited opponent), what he does say makes clear that he thinks the
whole movement rests on a mistake. There is nothing in the mere grammatical forms of spoken languages pertaining to truth-functional discourse,
and hence, nothing in grammar pertaining to the systematic acquisition of
knowledge in other disciplines. Consider the following passage from Buridan's *Summulae* discussion of the third mode of the fallacy of figure of words,
which, he says:

> comes about if we believe that to similar grammatical modes of signi-
> fication, although they involve words that do not sound similar, there
> correspond similar significations. Examples occur when we believe that
> all active verbs signify actions, and all passive verbs signify passion [being
> affected, being acted upon], or that since the genitive case in the expres-
> sion 'a man's donkey' signifies the relation of a possessor to a thing pos-
> sessed, we might believe that it signifies thus also in the expressions: 'the
> money's recipient', 'Robert's father', 'the city's sovereign', etc. (*S* 7.3.10: 536;
> cf. *QC* 17: 126–43)

The *modistae* are identified through a definite description in Buridan's explanation of the fallacy:

> The illusion involved in the third mode is promoted by the opinion of
> grammarians who hold that the modes of signification are derived from
> the modes of being, whence they believe that to similar modes of sig-
> nification attributed to utterances there correspond similar modes of
> being in the things signified. They believe, therefore, that the active voice
> of verbs and the masculine gender of names was taken from action,
> whereas the passive voice [*genus passivum*] in verbs and the feminine
> gender in names was taken from passion [*pati*], for the male acts on the
> female, and the female is affected [*patitur*] by him. Now there are pa-
> ralogisms [in this mode] such as the following: " 'to love' and 'to see' are
> of the active voice; therefore, they signify action," or " 'to be loved' and
> 'to be seen' are of the passive voice; therefore, what is seen or what is
> loved is affected [*patitur*]." For this is how some people believed that the
> senses were acting on the sensible objects in the course of sensing them.
> (*S* 7.3.10: 541–42)

However, the thesis that grammatical similarity has any relation at all to ontology is vulnerable to the most elementary of counterexamples:

> But this mode of arguing is defective, for although many verbs in the active voice do signify action, nevertheless, this need not hold for all, indeed, it need not hold, even if the names *activum* [active] and *passivum* [passive] may derive their vocal formation from the verbs *agere* [to act] and *pati* [to suffer, to be affected, to undergo (some action, influence, or change)]; they need not for this reason retain their signification with respect to just anything they are attributed to, for names signify by convention [*ad placitum*]. . . . And propositions are said sometimes to change the significations of the words of which they are composed. For it is absurd to say that if matter receives form, then its receiving is acting, even though 'to receive' is an active verb. (*S* 7.3.10: 542)

If we were to follow the *modistae* in maintaining that "a similar mode of predication should signify a similar mode of being or being related," then, on the basis of the grammatical form of genitive constructions such as 'Robert's father' or 'the city's sovereign', we would have to conclude that "the son possesses the father and the city its ruler"—which is absurd. But there is no science of the false or absurd. Therefore, speculative grammar fails to constitute a science, and a fortiori fails to constitute a science of discourse.

2. DOCTRINE AND DISCIPLINE

Like other bodies of knowledge or *scientiae,* logic is said to be a "habit [*habitus*]," which is a quality or capacity possessed by the relevant subject. In this case, of course, the subject is the human intellect. Habits are natural to the subjects possessing them in the sense that they are the dispositional fulfillment of certain of that subject's natural capacities or potentialities. This is brought out if we contrast "habit" with its opposing term, "privation [*privatio*],"[44] which refers to the absence or lack in some subject of a capacity it is naturally suited to have. Thus, blindness would be a privation in a human being, but not in a stone, since a stone has not been ordained to exercise the power of sight. Likewise, the ability to fly is natural to most birds, so that its absence would constitute a privation, but not for human beings, who are not deprived of anything by their inability to fly.

Buridan uses this distinction to characterize the teaching of logic. The remark in question is disarmingly simple, but expressed in a way that shows his virtuosity as a teacher: making a point about logic, a practical science, using grammar, first among the liberal arts, and connecting the result to natural philosophy or physics, lowest of the three speculative sciences. Logic, he says, is a habit, and the same habit is called 'doctrine' insofar as it is acquired from a teacher [*doctus*], and 'discipline' insofar as it is received by a student [*discipulus*], just as Aristotle speaks in the *Physics* of calling the same motion "'action' insofar as it comes from an agent, and 'passion' insofar as it is in a patient" (cf. *Physics* III.3.202a31–33).[45] The passage continues: "So in the most general sense every cognition that is thus acquired from someone else is said to be a 'doctrine'. Now some of these are sensory and some are intellectual. The sensory applies when a jester [*ioculator*] trains his dog to sit or to dance, or when a mother talking often to a baby teaches it her language; but this is not what Aristotle intends [to talk about], and neither do we" (*S* 8.3.5: 675–76). Teaching logic is not like training one's dog. It has a theoretical side in *logica docens*. Yet this seems to require something concrete on which to base the doctrine, which is, after all, properly grasped by the intellect.

Buridan is greatly assisted in his ordination of logic as a science of discourse by the fact that its two aspects, *logica docens* and *logica utens*, both have authoritative texts. The former, theoretical, side is based on Aristotle's *Organon:* "it is obvious, then, that *logica docens*, which Aristotle teaches in his logical books, is truly the science of argumentation—of dialectical, sophistical, and demonstrative forms of argumentation alike" (*QIP* 1: 127, ll. 195–97).[46] Furthermore, although the subject of logic in general is argumentation, or rather, the term 'argumentation', the particular sciences subordinate to it each have their own proper subjects, the inventory of which is once again provided by the *Organon*. After arguing that the proper subject of the science of interpretation is the term 'proposition [*enuntiatio*]', Buridan says:

> In the science of the *Categories*, we can designate [the term] 'term [*terminus*]' or 'expression [*oratio*]' as its proper subject. . . . Next, in the *Prior Analytics*, the term 'argument [*argumentatio*]' must be assumed as its proper subject, but only in the restricted sense in which it is said to concern entailment [*illatio*], and not in the broader sense as it applies to dialectical and demonstrative argumentation. (It is in the whole of logic that the subject is assumed to be the term 'argumentation', with various restrictions.) In the *Posterior Analytics*, it is 'demonstrative argumentation [*argumentatio demonstrativa*]' or 'demonstration [*demonstratio*]', which come to the same thing. In the *Topics*, it is 'dialectical argumentation [*argumentatio dyalectica*]'. In the *[Sophistical] Refutations*, it is 'sophistical argumentation [*argumentatio sophistica*]'. In the *Rhetoric*, it is 'rhetorical argumentation [*argumentatio rhetorica*]'. In the *Poetics*, it is 'poetic argumentation [*argumentatio poetica*]', which is called 'poetic' because it makes the soul, on the basis of certain attractive elements, [disposed] to hearing and believing, not from nature or from the circumstances of [our] deeds or of what we ought to

do or conclude, but from our admiration for words not commonly used, either from thoughts cloaked in metaphor, or by external imitation, and sometimes even by impossible images. For admiration is very enticing because it is pleasant, as is held in the first book of the *Rhetoric* [I.11.1371a22]. (*QDI* I.1: 6, l. 19−7, l. 3)[47]

Traditionally, the Aristotelian books in the *logica antiqua* (as opposed to the *logica moderna*, the distinctively medieval form of inquiry begun in the late twelfth century and represented by logicians such as Peter of Spain) numbered six: *Categories* and *On Interpretation* (which, together with Boethius's commentaries on these books and Porphyry's *Isagoge*, and later, the *Liber sex principiorum* associated with Gilbert of Poitiers, constituted the 'logica vetus' or 'ars vetus'); *Prior Analytics; Posterior Analytics; Topics;* and *Sophistical Refutations* (the recovered corpus of four books known as the 'logic nova').[48] But Buridan followed the later medieval convention, which was influenced by newly translated works of Islamic logicians,[49] in adding two books to the list, viz., Aristotle's *Rhetoric* and *Poetics*. This reflected the belief that logic must cover all forms of argumentative discourse, not merely its characteristic discourse of proof demonstration, but also its persuasiveness in moral contexts and beauty in aesthetic contexts.

Yet because logic is a practical science, Buridan does not use *logica docens* to order his own treatment of the subject. Although he writes literal and question commentaries on all of the texts included in the expanded *Organon* except the *Poetics*,[50] these works were produced on separate occasions, originally as lectures intended either to explicate a specific text or to elaborate and resolve particular interpretive problems raised by it.[51] There is no effort on his part to unify logic by producing a single, comprehensive treatment of *logica docens* as that is found in Aristotle. What he does instead is consult these texts, as well as his own commentaries on them, on an ad hoc basis in the course of working through the practical side of logic, *logica utens*, and the rest of Aristotelian metaphysics, natural philosophy, and ethics proper to his office as an arts master. Aristotle's logical writings are certainly authoritative as far as *logica docens* is concerned, but with respect to the practice of philosophy, they function for Buridan as an elementary corpus of logical learning— useful, but in the way that a library is useful.[52]

The role Buridan assigns to Aristotle's logic is not intended to demean it, of course. But it does reflect his own understanding of logic as first and foremost a practical science, concerned with the vagaries of human discourse and the very difficult business of how we can come into the possession of truth as empirical creatures who communicate with each other by speaking and writing. It also illustrates, at a disciplinary level, how far the *logica moderna* of the previous century had outgrown its roots in the *trivium*.

As Peter King observes, "Buridan was a brilliant logician in an age of brilliant logicians."[53] The brilliance of medieval logic consists in the way it reforged old doctrine with a new technique that could be directly applied to the speculative sciences. But the teaching of this new technique needed a new authoritative text, one that Buridan could use to initiate students into logic as a practice.

The authoritative text of the *logica utens* is, at least nominally, the *Summulae Logicales* of Peter of Spain, the text upon which Buridan bases his own massive compendium, the *Summulae de Dialectica*. In the prologue, he writes: "wishing to learn something in general about logic in its entirety without an excessively detailed investigation, I have chosen to deal in particular with that short treatise of logic which the venerable professor, master Peter of Spain composed a while ago, by commenting on and supplementing it; indeed, occasionally I am going to have to say and write things which differ from what he has said and written, whenever it appears to me suitable to do so" (*S* Preface: 4). However, Buridan makes so many changes and additions to Peter's brief text—aptly titled by the diminutive '*summulae* [i.e., little *summa*]'—even rejecting an entire treatise at one point and replacing it with his own,[54] that the result is a new text: a magisterial account of the *logica utens* that is both comprehensive and complete—except that now the '*summulae*' in its title is no longer apt. The real authoritative text of the *logica utens* is the *Summulae de Dialectica* itself. Now no text can serve as its own authority. But it became authoritative over logic within a generation of its composition, replacing the older, impoverished authority of Peter of Spain with a new text whose teachings were to dominate at European universities until well into the sixteenth century.[55] Buridan did not set out to replace Peter, of course. He chose to comment on Peter's text out of respect, intending only to reproduce its authority over the *logica moderna* for himself and his students. But if he did approach Peter's *Summulae* with the idea of writing a new authoritative text on the practice of logic, he succeeded beyond his wildest expectations.

Taking my cue from Buridan, the remainder of my remarks in the first part of this book will be ordered by the nine treatises that make up his *Summulae*.[56] References to his commentaries on Aristotle's logical works will be included only where necessary to clarify what he says in the *Summulae* or pursue his references to the authoritative texts of the *logica docens*. Needless to say, what follows does not pretend to offer a complete tour of the *Summulae*, an enormous work of approximately 360,000 words in English translation. Nor can it provide a detailed examination of the doctrines defended therein,[57] a task beyond the aim of the present book. Instead, I shall focus on a few of the salient features of each treatise, keeping my eye on the relation of logic to Buridan's understanding of his role as a philosopher, and connecting method to practice.

3. The Method of Logic

Medieval thinkers assigned a much greater importance than we do to the order of study or inquiry because they believed that the structure of knowledge reflects the providential order of creation, providing us with a guide for our intellectual journey in this life which ultimately points to its fulfillment in the next. Order becomes doubly important when one is authoring a textbook such as the *Summulae,* since the assumption is that the student will read or consult the work on his own, without necessarily having the master's authoritative voice to make that order transparent.[58]

So it comes as no surprise that order is everywhere in the *Summulae,* and everywhere made transparent.[59] Each treatise and section is prefaced by a paragraph indicating the material discussed in that particular subdivision of the text, and the subdivisions themselves are ordered by lemmata from the text of Peter of Spain, or by substitute and/or supplementary lemmata inserted by Buridan himself. The opening comment of the first treatise of the *Summulae* is a case in point. After quoting the first few lines of Peter's text, beginning "*Dialectica est ars artium* [Dialectic is the art of arts]," Buridan writes:

> We shall divide this book into nine treatises, the first of which is going to deal with propositions and their parts and attributes [*passionibus*]. The second will be about the predicables, the third about the categories, the fourth about suppositions, the fifth about syllogisms, the sixth about dialectical topics [*loci dialectici*],[60] and the seventh about fallacies. The eighth will be added to deal with divisions, definitions, and demonstrations, which our author did not treat of in this book; and the ninth will concern sophistic exercises [*practica sophistarum*] . . . (*S* 1.1.1: 4–5)

Peter's text, however, contains twelve treatises, not eight, and they are ordered differently. Although not all manuscripts of Peter's *Summulae Logicales* agree in their ordering, L. M. de Rijk has found that the best ones exhibit what he calls the "Avignon order," named after one of the exemplar manuscripts.

The following list gives the title and subject matter for each of the treatises in the Avignon order of Peter's text:[61]

I. *De introductionibus* [On Introductory Matters]: propositions; their grammatical parts (e.g., noun, verb, and expression); relationships between propositions (e.g., conversion, equipollence, opposition)

II. *De predicabilibus* [On Predicables]: the five predicables, i.e., genus, species, difference, property, and accident

III. *De praedicamentis* [On Categories]: the ten categories, e.g., substance, quantity, relation, quality, etc., and their interrelationships; the postpredicaments: 'prior', 'together', 'motion', and 'possession'

IV. *De syllogismis* [On Syllogisms]: moods and figures of the syllogism

V. *De locis* [On Topics]: rules for finding arguments in dialectical contexts

VI. *De suppositionibus* [On Suppositions]: referential function of terms

VII. *De fallaciis* [On Fallacies]: classification of modes of sophistical reasoning

VIII. *De relativis* [On Relatives]: properties of relative terms (e.g., 'who'; 'oneself')

IX. *De ampliationibus* [On Ampliations]: capacity of terms to extend their reference, e.g., to different times

X. *De appellationibus* [On Appellations]: capacity of terms to refer to existent things

XI. *De restrictionibus* [On Restrictions]: capacity of terms to restrict their reference, e.g., to a definite time

XII. *De distributionibus* [On Distributions]: capacity of distributive terms (e.g., 'every'; 'whole') to alter the referential function of common terms (e.g., 'man'; 'animal'); rules illustrated by means of sixteen sophisms

Buridan's first contribution to the terminist logical tradition is the complete overhaul of Peter's *Summulae*. This is so thorough that the resulting texts and treatises are only nominally the same. The most striking change is that the topics of four complete treatises, VIII–XI, have been folded into Buridan's own fourth treatise on suppositions, where they appear as chapters in a new text written not by Peter but by Buridan. This was a deliberate effort on his part to bring Peter's thirteenth-century text into line with the central place supposition had come to occupy among fourteenth-century practitioners of the *logica moderna*.[62] Other properties of terms, such as ampliation and restriction, which Peter treated separately, are viewed by Buridan as refinements of the doctrine of supposition covering the ways in which the reference of subject and predicate terms can be modified by other syntactical components of the proposition in which they occur—in this case, its extension or contraction by modal or tensed copula verbs.

A second major change is more explicit. "Since supposition belongs not to a proposition," Buridan says, "but to a term that can be the subject or the predicate of a proposition, the fourth treatise, dealing with supposition and some related matters, has to follow the treatise on predicamental terms" (*S* 4.1.1: 221). Buridan sees the *Summulae* as exemplifying an orderly progression of teachings based on the proposition, beginning with the consideration of propositions themselves (I), moving down to the categorial significance and referential function of their component terms (II–IV), then back up to propositions again, this time considered as parts in more complex patterns of reasoning: syllogisms (V), topics (VI), fallacies (VII), and finally, in demonstrations (VIII) and logical exercises (IX). In contrast, Peter places the treatise on suppositions sixth, after the treatises on syllogisms and topics. But this makes no sense to Buridan, since syllogisms and topics both assume an understanding of the categorical proposition as "an expression that affirms something of something or one that denies something of something," and the term as "that into which a proposition is resolved, as into a subject and a predicate" (*S* 5.1.1: 305).

Peter, however, does not seem to have intended his text to lead students through the rudiments of logic, at least not in any systematic way. The organization of his *Summulae* effects a much simpler division between the old and the new, with treatises I–V based on texts of the *logica vetus,* and VI–XII deriving from various twelfth-century treatises on the properties of terms.[63] By contrast, Buridan's text is not only systematically organized, it deliberately places the new over the old, devoting very little space, relatively speaking, to the first few treatises originating from the *logica vetus.*[64] The longest treatise by far is the eighth treatise on demonstrations, which begins with some remarks in which we can almost hear a disgruntled Buridan, chastising Peter for the omissions and indirection of his text: "Now it remains to discuss demonstrations. But these presuppose definitions; therefore, we should also treat of definitions. However, the investigation of definitions benefits [a great deal] from the art of division; hence, we also have to deal with divisions. But our author [i.e., Peter of Spain] did not discuss divisions, although [the art of divisions] is a very important and ultimate part of logic [*pars logicae magis notabilis et finalis*]" (*S* 8.1, Preface: 615). If this is a criticism of Peter, it is not exactly charitable, since Peter's *Summulae* was probably written not much later than the 1230s,[65] and Aristotle's *Posterior Analytics,* the theoretical source-text for much of the eighth treatise, had been commented upon for the first time in Latin only a decade earlier, by Robert Grosseteste. Regardless of what was available to Peter, Buridan wanted his *Summulae* to show that argumentation, understood as the practice of *logica utens,* is a well-ordered subject of study in its own right.

The third and final structural change was, as we have seen, the addition of a ninth treatise on "sophistic exercises [*practica sophismatum*]." The workbook format of the ninth treatise is in the spirit of Peter's twelfth treatise on distributions, which provides a series of rules and resolutions of sophism sentences containing distributive terms such as 'every [*omnis*]'. But the resemblance ends there, as Buridan's sophism sentences are designed to illustrate not just rules for distributive terms, but many other rule-governed topics in logic and semantics as well. There is a historical connection between Peter's and Buridan's uses of sophism sentences. We know that the medieval treatment of syncategorematic terms (of which 'every' was a standard example) evolved from being seen as presenting special problems of interpretation in introductory logic texts (which may have been Peter's aim in writing a separate treatise on distributions in his *Summulae*), to commanding separate and more sophisticated treatment in a new genre of texts on *syncategoremata,* or syncategorematic words (one of which was authored by Peter himself, more than a decade after he wrote his *Summulae*),[66] and finally, to being absorbed into the general literature on sophisms.[67] Buridan's treatment of syncategoremata reflects the final stage of this evolution. Although he mentions syncategorematic terms many times in the *Summulae,* and uses the distinction between the categorematic and syncategorematic senses of a word in order to solve philosophical problems (e.g., in *TDI* 18: 46–65; *QP* VI.4: 97rb),[68] he never discusses *syncategoremata* as such—this despite remarking at one point that syncategoremata "cause almost all the difficulties in logic" (*S* 1.2.2: 19). But these difficulties are not about syncategorematic words, which occur naturally in the languages from which the discourse of logic is taken. So we cannot treat the cause, or rather, we cannot treat the cause without possibly severing the connection between speaking and reasoning, between grammar and logic.[69] Buridan must have been thinking in this remark of the difficulties such words present in their effects, i.e., in the broader context of putatively knowledge-producing sentences or propositions. Thus, it is appropriate that they enter the world of the logic student through the problematizing discourse of sophismata.

CHAPTER THREE

Propositions, Predicables, and Categories

· The first three treatises of the *Summulae de Dialectica* consider propositions and their component parts, i.e., terms, whose power to signify makes discourse possible. After giving his audience an overview of the basic logical properties of propositions, Buridan tells us how we should understand terms with reference to two of the most widely consulted authorities in medieval logic, Aristotle's *Categories* and Porphyry's *Isagoge*.

1. PROPOSITIONS

Buridan prefaces his treatment of propositions with what amounts to an extended gloss on the first chapter of Aristotle's *De Interpretatione*, alluding first to the idea that logic is a practical science concerned with speech: "we should begin with sound," he says, "for in most cases the task of logic is exercised in a disputation, which cannot take place without speech, nor can speech occur without utterance" (*S* 1.1.2: 7). The genus of propositions is reached by carefully delineating the categories of speech. Thus, the broadest category of sound (*sonus*), which is "a quality sensible by hearing *per se* and properly," is divided into utterances and non-utterances, where 'utterance (*vox*)' refers to the natural production of vocal sound (*S* 1.1.3: 7). Utterances are either significative or non-significative, depending on whether they have the capacity to represent something in the mind of the hearer. If a significative utterance represents something conventionally rather than naturally, such as when "by the convention and agreement of disputants ... we say that A should stand for man, B for stone, C for animal, etc., as professors and disputants often do" (*S* 1.1.5: 10), then we have either (1) a name or a verb, in the case of non-complex, conventionally meaningful utterances, or (2) an expression (*oratio*) in the case of a complex, conventionally meaningful utterance. A proposition (*propositio* or *enuntiatio*) is then defined as "an expression that signifies something true or false" (*S* 1.3.1: 21).[1] Buridan closes the discussion by re-emphasizing its starting-point: "what is defined here is the spoken proposition, for 'expression' is given here as its genus" (*S* 1.3.1: 22).[2]

Buridan proceeds in the remainder of the first treatise to classify the various kinds of propositions in terms of their formal structure (categorical or hypothetical), their substance ('assertoric [*de inesse*]' or 'modal [*de modo*]'), their quantity (universal or particular), their quality (affirmative or negative), and their opposition and equivalence relations. These relations are briefly discussed using rules and examples. Of pedagogical interest is Buridan's graphical representation of Aristotelian logical space in terms of a "big figure [*magna figura*]" or cube of opposition, each of whose eight vertices contains nine equivalent propositional forms related to their equivalent propositions in the other vertices by one of the four Aristotelian relations of contradiction, contrariety, subcontrariety, and subalternation—to which Buridan adds disparity (*disparata*) for propositions which "obey no law [of opposition]" (*S* 1.8.6: 79).[3] There are two cubes of oppositions in the treatise on propositions, one for assertoric propositions and the other for modal propositions.[4] In both instances, they illustrate the basic inference relations between propositions having the same substance (i.e., assertoric or modal), but different qualitative or quantitative features introduced by what we would now call multiple quantification.[5]

But the cubes also show what is not properly said in a work such as the *Summulae.* The student who consults the *Summulae* needs to know the general idea behind these inference relations, as well as how to apply the more common inference rules to actual propositions. This is what the first treatise of the *Summulae* accomplishes. The typical student does not need to know the complete doctrine of assertoric and modal consequences, and certainly not its expansion into the doctrine of syllogisms with assertoric or modal propositions as premises. This is reserved for a specialist audience, for whom Buridan writes a separate treatise, the *Treatise on Consequences,* which aims to treat of the causes or reasons for consequences, reducing them "to the first causes through which they are said to hold" (*TC* I.1: 17, ll. 9–10).[6] The significance of this text in the history of logic is eloquently expressed by its editor, Hubert Hubien:

The four books [of the *Treatise on Consequences*] treat, respectively, of the general theory of consequences, corresponding to our propositional calculus, and of immediate inferences between non-modal categorical propositions; of immediate inferences between modal propositions; of non-modal categorical syllogisms; and finally, of modal syllogisms. If the title, '*Treatise on Consequences*,' is justified, it is because the entire subject has been reorganized around the fundamental notion of [logical] consequence. The method is quite modern: we have here what is without a doubt the first tentative, though certainly imperfect, axiomatic exposition of logic on the basis of a propositional calculus. . . . What is prefigured by the *Consequences* of Buridan, is not the Port-Royal logic, but the *Grundgesetze* of Frege and the first part of *Principia Mathematica*.[7]

Be that as it may,[8] the first treatise of the *Summulae* is devoted to the more mundane task of mapping the basic inference possibilities of discourse understood "by virtue of its proper meaning [*de virtute sermonis*]," which is what the two cubes of oppositions provide.

Buridan rarely misses an opportunity to make good on his claim that logic is a science of discourse. In his commentary on Aristotle's *De Interpretatione*, the theoretical text corresponding to the first treatise of the *Summulae*, we are told that the term 'proposition'—along with its species, 'affirmative' and 'negative'—is considered as such only in "the science of interpretation," although beyond their primary signification, these terms "connote a relation to argumentation [*connotant habitudinem ad argumentationem*]" (*QDI* I.1, l. 22: 7). This is, of course, how the subalternate logical sciences of interpretation, demonstration, and so on are connected to the science of argumentation, which is the concern of logic as a whole. But the common connotation of the subject-terms of these subalternate sciences is something Buridan *is* inclined to reveal in practice. For example, his teaching on "the division of propositions with respect to quality," i.e., into affirmative and negative, begins with a general rule: "since, therefore, the formal part of a proposition is the verbal copula, if the negation, i.e., the word 'not' affects the copula, then the proposition is called 'negative'; otherwise, it is called affirmative" (*S* 1.3.6: 34). But this is quickly supplemented by a more practical rule-of-thumb: "while we are on this point we should note that a negation does not affect anything that precedes it." The student learns that a negation immediately preceding the copula verb is sufficient to make the whole proposition negative, as in 'A man does not run [*Homo non currit*]', whereas if it precedes the whole proposition, as in '*Non homo currit*', the resulting proposition would be ambiguous between two senses: (1) read as affecting the subject-term only, the negation would infinitize it, rendering an affirmative proposition with an infinite subject-term, as in 'A non-man runs'; or (2) read as affecting the whole proposition, the negation would render the proposition negative and distribute the subject and predicate, as in 'No man runs'.

Anticipating the next question, Buridan says, "but then you ask: 'Which of the two senses described should the proposition *Non homo currit* have by virtue of its proper meaning? Should it be said to be an affirmative or a negative proposition?'" The answer forces the questioner to consider the discourse conditions of the original proposition. "If the utterance is continuous," Buridan replies, then "the negation affects everything that follows it" and the proposition is negative. The questioner must think back to *how* the proposition was said. Conversely, the proposition should be interpreted as an affirmative with an infinite subject-term "on the basis of the speaker's intention, or of the disputants' agreement, or on account of a sign of division, or a pause between [uttering] *non homo* and *currit*" (*S* 1.3.6: 35). The logician is obliged to gather the illocutionary evidence surrounding a proposition on the occasion of its use.

2. PREDICABLES

The second treatise on predicables is the shortest in the *Summulae*. But it is important because it enables Buridan to reinterpret a central text of the *logica vetus*, Porphyry's *Isagoge*, along the lines of the *logica moderna*, and thereby to introduce his audience to what might be called the 'technique' of nominalism. For Buridan, nominalism is first and foremost a semantic claim about how to interpret universal signs or words. It has metaphysical implications, of course, but none that Buridan cares to draw in this text.[9]

Buridan is quick to read along nominalist lines the resistance Porphyry offers Chrysaorius, the Roman senator to whom the *Isagoge* is addressed, to providing any answers to his "profound" metaphysical questions about the reality of genera and species.[10] "Porphyry," he writes in his question commentary on the *Isagoge*, "did not intend to teach us how to prove those predicables of their subjects, but only how to describe and distinguish them according to the different modes of predicating, and to point out their agreements and differences" (*QIP* 14: 187, ll. 2354–57).[11] What is it, then, that differentiates Porphyry's science from the other subalternate sciences of logic covered in the *Organon*—different, e.g., from the science of interpretation, which is concerned with the term 'proposition'? Buridan speaks for the nominalist majority opinion: "I say, together with other expositors of this text, that the genus 'universal' or the term 'universal' is the subject matter, or first and proper object, of the science [*scientia*] of Porphyry's *Isagoge*, because this term and its species, viz., of 'genus', 'species', etc., are principally determined in this book and in no others, except according to their attribution to the term 'universal' itself, and to its species, from whose unity the science as a whole is said to be one" (*QIP* 3: 135, ll. 459–65).[12] The species of the term 'universal' are the terms 'genus', 'species', 'difference', 'property', and 'accident', i.e., the names of the five predicables discussed in the *Isagoge*. But since the term 'universal', even construed materially (*QIP* 3: 136, l. 479; cf. *QDI* I.1: 6, ll. 10–15), is not exclusively logical in its application, Buridan shifts to another "equivalent" term as the main focus of the second treatise of the *Summulae*, i.e., the term 'predicable'. The two terms are related because being predicable of many is a "proper attribute [*passio propria*]" of the term 'universal' (*QIP* 3: 136, l. 501). "Therefore, a 'predicable', strictly speaking, in the sense intended here, is described as a term apt to be predicated of many things, i.e., apt to supposit for many things, and not for only one thing" (*S* 2.1.1: 105).

However, in saying that the terms 'universal' and 'predicable' are equivalent, Buridan is not saying that they are the same. How do they differ? Here he notes his disagreement with Peter of Spain, who takes the difference to consist in the fact that whereas a predicable is apt to be predicated of many things, "a universal is something that is apt to be in many things" (*S* 2.1.2: 105). For Buridan, however, 'predicate' and 'universal' are terms of terms, or terms of second intention, which are used to refer to the logical properties of terms rather than to the real properties of things (*S* 2.3.5: 120). The difference between the terms 'predicable' and 'universal' is merely that they are "diverse in their concepts, for they were imposed according to different concepts to signify the same things." 'Predicable' is used correlatively with 'subjectible' to refer to terms that can be predicated of a subject in a proposition. "But," he insists, "the same term is called a universal because it indifferently signifies many things, and is apt to supposit for many things . . . whether as a subject or as a predicate" (*S* 2.1.2: 105). Universality is thus assimilated by Buridan to the semantic properties of (1) signifying many things (in this case, other common terms) in the mind of a hearer, and (2) standing for many things (in this case, other common terms) in the context of a proposition. This is what 'universal' means.

The practical side of Porphyry's science of the term 'universal' is concerned with the term 'predicable'. But an individual, which Peter of Spain defines as "that which is predicated of only one thing, as 'Socrates' and 'Plato', and 'this man' and 'this donkey'" (*S* 2.3.5: 118), seems to present a challenge to the assimilation thesis, for a predicable individual would be equivalent to a universal, which is absurd. Buridan handles such objections by refusing to consider the possibility that what is at stake here is anything but the significance of the term 'individual', which, of course, is "not an individual" but "a name of second intention, suppositing for many terms, and . . . one species among the species and names of second intention." He then moves back to the difference in the "concept [*ratio*]" with which a name is imposed to explain how many distinct individuals could have the same proper name. Referring to himself and a nearby student, he notes that the name 'John' was not imposed "to signify me and you" with a single concept and in a single act of imposition; likewise, the actual reference of indexical expressions such as 'this man' is secured not by their grammatical form (since 'this man' is predicable of many things) but by the "different acts of pointing" which underlie the use of such expressions. In practice, we must attend not only to what is being predicated in a proposition, but to how it is being predicated. Buridan continues by arguing that, like the terms 'sun', 'moon', and 'world', the term 'god' is a species-term because "although on the part of the thing signified it is impossible that it should supposit for many, it is nevertheless not repugnant that it should supposit for many, either on account of its mode of signification, or because of the mode of its imposition" (S 2.3.5: 120).[13] The realists are mistaken if they think that language mirrors reality such that the term 'God' must be individual because there is only one thing to which it could refer. Human language is not that perfect. Indeed, Buridan seems to think that such a position could be arrived at only by totally ignoring the way people actually use words, perhaps by fixating on the "aptitude [*aptitudo*]" of a word as predicable, as opposed to its "actuality [*actum*]" as a predicate (S 2.6.2: 130–32). To avoid this error, we must attend not just to the 'what' but also the 'how' of predication.

3. CATEGORIES

The third treatise begins with the observation that although many *summulae* include a treatise on categories, many also do not. To this, Buridan adds that "since Aristotle quite amply discussed the categories in his book, *Categories*," he intends "to deal with them briefly, gathering Aristotle's most notable remarks and providing as brief a text" as he can (S 3.1.1: 143).

Why does Buridan exercise the option of including this treatise in the *Summulae*? The most obvious answer to this question is that he does so out of fidelity to his source-text. Peter of Spain includes a treatise on 'predicaments' or categories, although as L. M. de Rijk observes, this is "an innovation on Peter's part," since it is not found in other logical compendia of the period, such as those by William of Sherwood and Lambert of Auxerre.[14] This would explain Buridan's remark that many *summulae* omit this treatise.

But there is more going on here than meets the eye. As we have already seen, Buridan does not hesitate to abbreviate and/or replace Peter's text whenever it "suits" him, and he is certainly no slavish follower of either the ordering or topics of individual treatises. There is, I believe, a reason for its inclusion, but it is nowhere discussed explicitly. The reason is that a treatise on categories is needed in the *Summulae* as the *logica utens* accompaniment to the *logica docens* discussion of the subject in Buridan's question commentary on Aristotle's *Categories*. The third treatise of the *Summulae* functions just like the other treatises (with the exception of the fourth treatise on suppositions and the ninth on "the practice of sophisms"), as a guide to the application of the corresponding logical science presented by Aristotle in the *Organon*.[15] In his only sustained reflection on the ordering of the logical sciences, Buridan says that we can "designate [the term] 'term [*terminus*]' or 'expression [*oratio*]' as the proper subject of the science of the *Categories*" (*QDI* I.1: 6, ll. 19–20).[16]

For Buridan, there is a danger in applying the science of the *Categories* if we reify its classificatory scheme, making it into a science of things rather than of words. Thus, whereas Peter's discussion of the division of the categories alludes to some things being in a subject but said of no subject, "like genera and species and substantial differences, all of which are called substantial universals [*substantie universales*],"[17] Buridan abbreviates Peter's text into a paraphrase of the second paragraph of *Categories* 2: "Of those [things] that there are, some are said of a subject, but are in no subject, others are in a subject, but are said of no subject, still others are said of a subject and are in a subject, and yet others neither are in nor are said of a subject" (*S* 3.1.5: 148; cf. *Categories* 2.1a20–b9). He immediately comments that this text "is easy to expound if it is interpreted as being about significative terms. But it cannot be correctly expounded as being about other things, since a man is no more said of a subject than is Socrates, for a man is the same as Socrates, but the term 'man' is said of a subject, namely, of an inferior term, for example, of the term 'Socrates'. Further, it is reasonable that the whole [passage] be interpreted as concerning significative terms, for those are what Aristotle intends to discuss in the *Categories*, wherein he provides this classification" (*S* 3.1.5: 148). Buridan takes himself to be engaged in the exposition of Aristotle here, even though the *Categories* is notoriously ambiguous about whether the classification he refers to is merely linguistic, or both linguistic and ontological, i.e., about whether the distinction between being 'said of' and 'in' marks a twofold classification of names, or a distinction between names and things.[18] The remark has a transparently pedagogical aim in that it closes off for his students the possibility of understanding Aristotle's division to be about anything except significative terms.[19] Indeed, the ontological interpretation— and with it, the road to the inherence theory of predication—is dismissed as incorrect, without further comment. Buridan's commentary on the *Categories* offers little help, but enough for us to see that his linguistic interpretation of the categories is part of a broader program to recognize (via the doctrine of supposition) only particular substances, qualities, and quantities as possible referents of categorial terms, while at the same time preserving the significance of categorial discourse by recognizing (via the doctrine of connotation) that particular substances can be signified in different ways.[20] Moreover, although the semantic values of the latter terms are conventional, they are not arbitrary, for they are rooted in the speaker's intentions or concepts, which Buridan argues naturally resemble the particular "modes" or qualities of substances. Our conventional ways of speaking about particulars are the product of our manifold ways of understanding them:

> the distinction of the categories cannot be taken on the part of the things for which predicable terms supposit, because . . . the same heat is an action, a passion, a quantity, a quality, and a relation; and the same Socrates is a man, a white thing, three cubits tall, a father, and an agent, etc. Nor can their distinction be taken absolutely on the part of the spoken words, because one must not change the number [of something merely] on account of diverse idioms—which is what philosophers commonly assume. And spoken words are also imposed to signify conventionally; therefore, the categories would be multiplied according to our preference—which is absurd. But [these categories] are taken from the diverse intentions according to which terms are connotative and non-connotative in diverse modes. The diverse modes of predicating terms of primary substances come from these diverse connotations, and so a distinction is directly and immediately drawn between the wholly diverse modes of predicating [terms] of primary substances. For if they are predicated *in quid* or essentially of them, then such terms belong to the category of substance; but if they are predicated denominatively *in quale,* then they belong to the category of quality, and if denominatively *in quantum,* to the category of quantity [etc.]. . . . For when we ask, 'What is Socrates?' or 'What is Brunellus?' or 'What is this?', pointing to some stone or piece of wood, we are assuming that it is something, and we are asking for a specification in terms belonging to the category of substance. And if we also ask, 'How tall is Socrates?' or 'What does Socrates look like?', we are assuming that he has some height and some appearance, and we are asking for a specification through special terms subject to the terms 'how much [*quantum*]', 'in what way [*quale*]', and so on for the other [categories]. . . . And since we do not have common ways of inquiring about everything in an entire genus, we can distinguish the categories according to the diverse general modes of signifying in connection with primary substance. (*QC* 3: 17–18, ll. 89–121)[21]

The categories are also depicted in this passage as emerging from the primary elements of speculative inquiry, where they codify certain natural sequences of questions a student might ask of his master. For Buridan, however, the categories are ways of speaking and thinking about things in the world, which provide the basic definitions and descriptions that make speculative inquiry possible.

How many categories are there? The texts suggest that this question was always popular in the lecture halls at Paris. As for its origins, Buridan blames Aristotle: "And we should know that Aristotle never provided an argument to show that there are no other categories besides these ten, nor would it be un-acceptable to posit also others if other predicables were found that have different modes of predication, which are neither reducible to nor contained under the ones from which these ten categories are derived" (S 3.1.8: 151; cf. S 2.2.6: 114–15).[22] The question arises for medieval readers because Aristotle never argues that his ten categories are the only ones there could be. What would other predicables look like? One way of generating them would be to elevate specific divisions from one of the ten Aristotelian categories to categorial status, the most obvious candidate being Aristotle's four species of the category of quality, viz., habits and dispositions; capacities; affective qualities; and figure or shape.[23] But the question is evidently of little concern to Buridan, since he ignores the issue in the rest of the third treatise by simply assuming that "among all non-equivocally predicable terms there are ten that are the most common, and they are called 'most general genera' [genera generalissima], under which all others are contained" (S 3.1.8: 151).

His reticence is understandable if we turn to his question commentaries on the Categories and Porphyry's Isagoge. Because there is no common concept or intention, or univocal name, governing all of the categories, he says, those "who have wanted to assign a sufficient [reason] for the number of the categories, have labored in vain." Without such a concept, the possibility of finding a justification for some determinate number of categories is undercut:

> I say, therefore, that a sufficient [reason] for the number of the categories could be designated or proved only because we have found that so many diverse modes of predicating are not reducible to some more common mode of predicating, understood according to some single common concept, and therefore, that there must be that many. But also, we have not found common predicables that are not contained under those [ten] modes, or that are not reducible to them, and so we do not posit more categories. For this reason, if we find some common predicables exhibiting other modes of predicating besides the ten already mentioned, it is altogether apparent to me that it should not be denied that there are more [than ten] categories. (QC 3: 19, ll. 138–46)[24]

But although additional categories are possible, Buridan is careful about recognizing them:

> it is apparent to me for certain that even if there are others, [Aristotle's] ten categories are more manifest, and contain within themselves the greater majority of predicables. Therefore, it is more reasonable to list them. And one should not list others—assuming there are others—because from the consideration and determination of those ten, it would be easy to consider and determine others, whenever they occur, in keeping

with the similarity or proportion they exhibit in relation to those categories which have already been determined. (*QC* 3: 20, ll. 153–59)[25]

Without recognizing them as such, Buridan has provided a recipe for testing putative categorial terms: "Let inquirers diligently consider their circumstances and diverse connotations, and, as exigencies dictate, reduce them to the ten categories, or to one of them, or to the collection of many of them—if this is not possible, let other categories be permitted" (*QC* 3: 25, ll. 283–87).[26] For Buridan, the ten categories of Aristotle are an account of the modes of predicating.[27] They represent a range of discourse possibilities not *simpliciter*, but *secundum quid*, i.e., relative to our knowledge of the different, apparently irreducible, ways there are of signifying substance. It will always be possible for our language, or our language together with our concepts, to generate new ways of speaking and thinking. The absence of a common concept or univocal name covering all of the categories guarantees it.

Buridan ends his discussion of the number of the categories on a characteristic note, returning to the pedagogical aims which motivated the question. "I have said these things by way of example," he says, "so that through them, diligent inquirers might have occasion to speak more perfectly, both about the aforementioned [categorial] names, and about others" (*QC* 3: 29, ll. 374–76).[28] Like the grammarian teaching proper pronunciation, Buridan hopes to instill in his pupils the habit of proper predication.[29]

CHAPTER FOUR

Suppositions

· The fourth treatise abandons the brief discussion of supposition in the sixth treatise of Peter of Spain's *Summulae*. Instead, Buridan authors a new text designed to give practical expression to the notion of the supposition of terms, the definitive doctrine of the *logica moderna*.[1] But this means that, unlike every other treatise in Buridan's *Summulae* (except the quasi-independent ninth treatise), there is no theoretical text of Aristotle or Boethius, no *logica docens*, to which Buridan might refer those who wanted to consider the theory behind the doctrine. There was no shortage of such texts, of course,[2] but all were of fairly recent vintage, which would have made it difficult to treat them as authoritative. But it also suggests that the point of supposition would be missed by an abstract discussion of the semantics of terms. Supposition shows what different terms stand for (*supponere*) in the actual circumstances of their use, i.e., in the context of propositions.

As we saw in chapter 2, Buridan begins the treatise on supposition by explaining its position in relation to the *Summulae* as a whole: "since supposition belongs not to a proposition, but to a term that can be the subject or the predicate of a proposition, the fourth treatise, dealing with supposition and some related matters, has to follow the treatise on predicamental terms" (*S* 4.1.1: 221). This is a tacit criticism of the standard or Avignon order of Peter of Spain's *Summulae*, which ignores Aristotle's ordination of logic in terms of increasing complexity by placing the treatise on supposition sixth, after syllogisms and topical inferences. Buridan also wishes to remove any confusion that might arise from his use of the term 'supposition' by distinguishing logical supposition from the grammatical concept of the same name, which is concerned with words capable of "supplying the subject [*suppositum*] for a verb" in a "well-formed [*congrua*]" expression. He stresses to his audience, most of whom were fresh from their grammatical training, that the logician's use of the term differs from the grammarian's in two respects: (1) certain terms, such as 'chimera', can be the subjects of well-formed expressions in grammar, but not in logic;[3] and (2), for the grammarian, only the subject term of an expression can supposit, but the logician treats both the subject and predicate terms as having supposition (*S* 4.1.1: 222).[4]

What is supposition? Historians of logic divide the doctrine into two theories, a theory of supposition proper and a theory of the modes of personal supposition, assimilating the former to a theory of reference used to express, *inter alia*, the truth conditions of a proposition, and the latter to a theory (or technique, really) regarding the proper analysis of quantified propositions insofar as that pertains to the larger task of evaluating inferences.[5] Buridan's discussion of supposition assumes this division, although he does not acknowledge it explicitly.

As a logical property of terms, supposition is complementary to signification, which, like supposition, is based on a proto-linguistic act. But whereas signification stems from the way spoken sound "gives rise to some concept in the person hearing it," so that a term is apt to supposit if there is something pointed out [*demonstrato*] by the pronoun 'this' (or 'these' if there is more than one thing), and the term "can be truly affirmed of that pronoun" (*S* 4.1.2: 222; cf. *S* 9.3, 5th sophism: 866). This can be seen when we analyze the terms 'Socrates' and 'today' in the proposition, 'Socrates will die today': "the term 'today' is a discrete term suppositing only for this indicated day, just as 'this man' supposits only for this indicated man. Therefore, saying 'today' is equivalent to saying 'on this day'. Hence, pointing out Socrates, the term 'this man' supposits for Socrates and cannot supposit for something else where that act of pointing is concerned" (*S* 9.5, 10th sophism: 929). In signification, the causal vector is world-to-mind, so that a term is significant just in case the occasion of our hearing it effects some change in our understanding. But in supposition the causal vector is the other way around, i.e., mind-to-world, so that a term supposits just in case it picks out certain individual(s) outside the mind in the context of a proposition. Buridan's mention of the act of pointing here is doubly appropriate, for it is not only that we indicate to others the connection between our thoughts and the world through gestures, or conventional acts of demonstration, but also that the immediate objects of such gestures are particular individuals—which dovetails with his nominalist assumption that the world contains only particular substances and accidents. And although the techniques he presents in the fourth treatise quickly outstrip any literal meaning that might be attached to pointing or *demonstratio*,[6] pointing remains a helpful way of understanding Buridan's conception of the supposition of a term.

Thanks to its appearance over forty years ago in an edition by Maria Elena Reina, the treatise on suppositions has aroused more interest in the secondary literature than any other work in the Buridanian corpus.[7] It is not my aim here to engage this considerable body of scholarship, but rather to explicate Buridan's *De suppositionibus* 'from the inside', in terms of its position as the fourth treatise of the *Summulae,* taking its practical aims into account.

Supposition proper is connected to the logical concept of reference because it shows how a term occurring in the subject or predicate position of a proposition can stand for (*supponere*) another thing or things. Only terms occurring in a proposition can stand for things, the range of their supposition being a semantic function of the propositions in which they occur. It is important to distinguish here between a term's signification, or what we understand by means of it, and its supposition.[8] For example, the term 'white [*album*]' makes known to us a certain concept, and ultimately signifies every instance of the corresponding attribute outside our minds, i.e., the particular whitenesses of clouds, cathedrals, and horses.[9] But 'white' cannot supposit or stand for any of these when it is used significatively, since they are not things, but properties of things. Rather, 'white' stands only for the individuals that instantiate this property, each of which can be picked out by a proper name (Bucephalus), by the pronoun 'this' together with the common name of the object ('this cathedral'), or by a demonstrative gesture (the act of pointing to a certain cloud). Thus, signification is an account of meaning, linking concepts to those features of the world they are said to naturally resemble (*QDI* II.11: 100, ll. 30–33). Supposition, however, is an account of reference, indicating what things in the world our propositions are about, and how these things must be situated if a proposition is true.[10] Only propositions are true or false (*S* 4.3.2: 254–55). A proposition is true just in case its subject and predicate terms supposit for the same thing(s); otherwise—i.e., if they fail to supposit for the same thing(s), or if they supposit for nothing at all—it is false (*S* 9.2, 10th–14th conclusions: 855–59).

Buridan discusses several types or modes of supposition proper. The first division is into "proper" and "improper" supposition: "Supposition is called proper when the utterance supposits according to the nature or signification commonly instituted for it. It is called improper when the utterance supposits according to the signification of another utterance, figuratively [*ex transsumptione*], because of some similitude, or for the sake of irony [*propter similitudinem vel ironiam*], or for some other reason of this sort, as when we say that a meadow is smiling [*dicamus pratum ridere*]" (*S* 4.3.1: 251–52). As further examples of figurative or ironical discourse, Buridan cites the following propositions: (1) 'God is the lion of the tribe of Judah' (cf. Rev. 5:5); (2) 'He is ploughing the seashore [*litus maris aratur*]' (an old Roman proverb for someone embarked on a hopeless task);[11] and (3) 'Oh, you are a very good boy' (said sarcastically, by a father to his son). In each case, the proposition is not literally true

because: (1) God is not among the *supposita* of the term 'lion' (even if we assume that some large feline is now roaming the wilds of Judah); (2) the person
embarked on a hopeless task is not to be found among those actually ploughing the seashore (surely there are none); and (3) the individual referred to by
'you' is not presently a referent of 'good boy' (hence the sarcasm). Now only
a fool, or perhaps a beginner seduced by the power of truth-functional discourse, would insist that such propositions must be interpreted literally. But
the prudent logic teacher keeps them within the ambit of the doctrine of supposition as a preventative measure. We saw in chapter 1 that Buridan has a
realistic sense of what logic can and cannot achieve, and correspondingly, of
the importance of figurative, poetic, and other non-truth-functional modes
of discourse. The division of improper supposition provides an entry-point
for all of these other functions of language.[12]

Proper supposition is divided into personal and material supposition.
Supposition is personal when the subject or predicate term of a proposition
stands for what it signifies, or "for its ultimate significate, as the term 'man' supposits for men in the proposition 'A man runs'." On the other hand, supposition is material when a term either supposits for itself, or for a term similar to
itself (but which is, e.g., uttered rather than inscribed), or "for its immediate
significate, which is the concept according to which it was imposed to signify,
as the term 'man' in the proposition 'Man is a species'" (*S* 4.3.2: 252–53; cf.
S 9.1, 8th–9th conclusions: 836–38). The distinction between personal supposition and the first two modes of material supposition corresponds roughly to
our modern distinction between use and mention, where terms occurring in
material supposition are mentioned, rather than used—as in the propositions, '"Man" has three letters' or '"*Hominis*" is trisyllabic'. The third mode,
however, does not fit the use/mention analogy. That is because it has different
origins, in Buridan's effort to reduce the traditional divisions of proper supposition from three to two by eliminating the category of simple supposition.

A vestige of early terminist logic,[13] whose realist practitioners needed
some way of referring to common natures or universals, simple supposition
was still being used by nominalist logicians in Buridan's time to model reference to common concepts or intentions. Thus, William of Ockham, who is
about as far as anyone in the fourteenth century from conceding the existence of real universals, reformulates the doctrine so that a term exhibits
simple supposition when it supposits "for a concept in the mind [*pro conceptu mentis*],"[14] and is not being used significatively. What united Ockham
and the early terminists was their realization that if the proposition 'Man is
a species' is to be true, then the term 'man' cannot refer to the individual
men which are its ultimate significates, since it cannot be said of any man
that he is a species (Socrates is a man, not a species). Accordingly, the reference of 'man' must be to a common nature or to a concept.[15] But Buridan
will have none of this:

Of the first [section on the divisions of supposition], we should realize that some people have posited also a third member, which they call 'simple supposition'. For they [e.g., Peter of Spain] held that universal natures are distinct from the singulars outside of the soul. And so they said that a term supposits personally when it supposits for the singulars themselves, that it supposits simply when it supposits for that material nature, and materially when it supposits for itself. But I hold that Aristotle correctly refuted that opinion in the seventh book of the *Metaphysics* [VII.3.1038b1–1039a23] and so this kind of supposition has to be eliminated, at least according to this interpretation. In another manner, others [e.g., Ockham] call supposition 'simple' when an utterance supposits for the concept according to which it is imposed and material when it supposits for itself or another similar to itself. And this can be permitted, but I do not care [about this usage], for I call both 'material supposition'. (*S* 4.3.2: 253)

Buridan's rejection of simple supposition is of historical interest because it represents one of the two main respects in which his account diverges from Ockham's.[16] On the face of it, it seems an ironic effort to out-Ockham Ockham, using the razor against the very philosopher after whom it was eventually named.[17] Buridan sees that it is misleading to assign a special logical sense to terms being used to refer to themselves or to the concepts they express, as if this were any different from figurative or metaphorical uses, since only terms that refer to things existing per se are being used in their proper sense. Thus, terms can stand either for the things they ordinarily signify, in which case they supposit personally, or for something else, in which case they supposit materially. But what does he make of the 'Man is a species' argument that originally motivated the imposition of a separate category of simple supposition, and its preservation by the otherwise parsimonious Ockham?

Buridan's response is given with a teacher's concern for giving his students a succinct yet informative answer, and an arts master's awareness of the breadth of human discourse. He begins with the observation that "youngsters [*juvenes*] may have several questions concerning what has just been said." The remarks which follow indicate that he has in mind just the sort of beginner's worry about literal truth discussed in chapter 1: if the terms in propositions such as 'Man is a species' can supposit personally or materially, which supposition should they have if that proposition is interpreted literally, or "by virtue of its proper meaning [*de virtute sermonibus*]" (*S* 4.3.2: 255)? Three views on the question are distinguished. First, Buridan says, some people claim that 'Man is a species' is literally false because the principal kind of supposition is personal, and "we cannot carry the ultimate significata [of the terms in such propositions] to disputations." This is a joke, of course,[18] but it is an edifying joke because it brings in the rationale Peter of Spain and others used to defend a category of simple supposition, i.e., if 'man' supposited personally in 'Man is a species', that proposition could be true only if I carry all individual men with me to class and point them out—which is impossible. So the first view concludes that understood literally, the proposition is false.

With the laughter finally subsiding, Buridan introduces a second view:

> Another opinion states the contrary, namely that 'Man is a species' is true by virtue of its proper meaning. For speech [*sermo*], in signifying and suppositing significatively, only has any import [*virtus*] because of conventional imposition and usage, and we cannot know the [original] imposition except from the usage of authors. But authors and philosophers have used 'Man is a species' as a true proposition, and it is true only insofar as it incorporates material supposition; so in this proposition we have to consider this material supposition as based upon its proper meaning. (*S* 4.3.2: 255–56)

Buridan rejects this view for reasons he does not state, but which are evidently connected with the fact that it is often impossible to determine a term's original imposition, even if we carefully attend to its use. Medieval theologians were well aware of the difficulties this presented for the study of scripture, since the Bible is filled with ambiguous remarks whose literal sense is impossible to recover from the text, to say nothing of the many passages that are obviously not intended to be taken literally.[19]

This leads to the third view:

> The third opinion, with which I agree, is that an utterance does not have any proper import [*virtus propria*] in signifying and suppositing, except from ourselves. So by an agreement of the disputing parties, as in obligational disputes, we can impose on it a new signification, and not use it according to its common signification. We can also speak figuratively [*transsumptive*] and ironically, according to a different signification. But we call a locution 'proper' when we use it according to the signification properly and principally given to it, and we call a locution 'improper' when we use it otherwise, although we legitimately can use it otherwise. So it is absurd to say that a proposition of an author is false, absolutely speaking, if he puts it forth incorporating an improper locution, according to which it is true. Instead, we ought to say that it is true, since it is enunciated according to the sense in which it is true. (*S* 4.3.2: 256)

The view Buridan advocates here is motivated by the same sensitivity to nature and convention that informs his concept of language. Roughly, the idea is this: the default interpretation of any locution is its "proper sense," defined as "the signification properly and principally given to it." The proper signification of an utterance stems from the naturalistic consideration that "utterances were primarily and principally imposed to signify so as to stand for their ultimate significata, and not for themselves" (*S* 4.3.2: 256);[20] that is to say, just as concepts (at least in the first instance) naturally signify those extramental things which just as naturally gave rise to them, so utterances (at least in the first instance) are imposed to signify, via their corresponding concepts, the same ultimate significata.[21] For Buridan, this capacity is part of our nature as cognitive creatures. It is why he insists that determining the nature of concepts pertains not to logic but to psychology or metaphysics, speculative sciences whose conclusions cannot be otherwise (*QDI* I.3: 16, ll. 4–10).[22]

But there is another sense in which the *virtus propria* of an utterance can be said to "come from ourselves," for we can also use terms "by agreement," whether to refer to their ultimate significata, in which case we are said to use them properly, or to other things not primarily or principally associated with them, in which case we use them improperly. The latter category reflects the fact that we have established conventions of non-literal discourse; competent users of a language know when someone is speaking metaphorically or ironically, so that the secondary or "improper" association is not lost on them. The game of obligations in logic nicely illustrates this point, for its rules permit disputants to make *ad libitum* agreements regarding the signification of terms.[23] By endorsing the third view, Buridan wishes to evoke in his students the idea that no one who is honest about the variety and multiplicity of human discourse could fail to be judicious in using supposition to interpret propositions. In particular, such a person will recognize that literal truth is not the only kind of truth, and will take seriously the task of finding the sense in which a proposition is true. Thus, he says, "it absolutely seems to me that wherever it is evident that an author puts forward a proposition in a true sense, although not as a proper locution, then to deny that proposition without qualification would be cantankerous and insolent [*dyscolum et protervum*]. But to avoid error, it should be properly pointed out that the proposition is not true in its proper sense, or in virtue of its proper meaning, and then it has to be shown in which sense it is true" (*S* 4.3.2: 256).

Buridan's answer to the 'Man is a species' argument is that the proposition "is true insofar as it is put forth by authors"—by which he means the writings of authorities such as Boethius and Porphyry (so far he agrees with the second view)—but "not true according to its proper meaning, i.e., it would not be true if put forward as a proper locution." But as we saw above, in the third mode of material supposition, a term is said to supposit for the concept it was imposed to signify, or for its immediate significate, "as the term 'man' in the proposition 'Man is a species.'"[24] The appearance of impropriety is caused by the absence of an ultimate significate, as if the act of referring has been cut short at the conceptual level, without being carried through to its extramental completion. It is the functional proximity of words and concepts as types of signifiers that makes it appropriate to analyze such propositions using material supposition, since they present us with cases in which words of one kind (spoken) pick out words of another kind (conceptual or mental). Indeed, we might think of Buridanian material supposition as occupying the middle ground between a term's suppositing personally for its ultimate significate(s), and improperly, "according to the meaning of another utterance," such as when we say of a man performing a hopeless task, 'He is ploughing the seashore'. Referentially speaking, the middle ground is occupied by three kinds of immediate significate—inscriptions, utterances, and concepts—each of which is, in its own way, a mind-dependent linguistic artifact.[25]

The second main divergence between the supposition theories of Buridan and Ockham concerns Buridan's adaptation of the concept of natural supposition, a form of reference found in early terminist logic that had fallen into disuse by the fourteenth century.[26] Buridan divides personal supposition into common supposition, for terms such as 'man', and discrete, for terms such as 'Socrates' (S 4.3.3: 259). The former is further divided as follows:

> Common supposition is usually divided into natural and accidental sup-position. Supposition is called 'natural' when a term supposits indiffer-ently for everything for which it can supposit, present, past, and future; this is the sort of supposition we use in the demonstrative sciences. Sup-position is called 'accidental' when a term supposits only for present things, or only for present and past, or only for present and future things, as the verbs and predicates require, and will be explained later. Again, this is the supposition we use in telling stories, and this is also mostly used by sophists. (S 4.3.4: 259)

In reviving this dusty old terminology, Buridan must have surely raised eye-brows among his colleagues and more advanced students. In Peter of Spain, the terms 'natural supposition' and 'accidental supposition' are used to mark the distinction between the taking of a common term, such as 'man', "for every-thing for which it is naturally suited to be predicated [*aptus natus est praedi-cari*],"[27] and "for those things for which it needs something adjoined to it [*exigit adiunctum*]," i.e., where an adjacent term determines the thing(s) for which it stands. The 'accident' in 'accidental supposition' is accordingly the idea that the reference of such terms is determined by whatever other terms 'happen [*accidere*]' to surround them in the context of a proposition. The reference of naturally suppositing terms, however, is unaffected by accidents of context.

What is the meaning of this distinction? Buridan uses it to specify the range of a suppositing term's reference within certain temporal parameters. Now virtually all medieval thinkers understood 'proposition' to refer to what we would now call a declarative sentence, i.e., to a particular inscription or utterance (or thought) on the occasion of its use, rather than to what is ex-pressed therein.[28] Thus, terminist logicians assumed that all propositions

demonstrat science

contain some kind of temporal index, whether tacitly or explicitly.[29] In the most basic sort of case that index is to the present, so that if I utter the proposition 'Socrates is running', my proposition is true just in case there presently exists an individual named 'Socrates' who is among the things now running; otherwise (e.g., if he is not now running; or if nothing is running; or if he no longer exists), it is false. But obviously, not all propositions fit this paradigm. In particular, the verb in a proposition can also occur in the past or the future tense, and the presence of certain other terms (e.g., 'always'; 'dead'; 'know'; 'generable' and other verbal nouns ending in '-able') in a proposition can 'accidentally' alter the reference of its suppositing terms. To capture this feature of discourse, terminists devised rules of ampliation and restriction, where 'ampliation' refers to the capacity of certain words to extend the range of things for which a suppositing term stands to past and/or future things, and even to *possibilia,* and 'restriction' to the opposite capacity to contract its range of *supposita.*[30] So, for example, Buridan remarks, "it seems to me that according to common usage the word 'always' was imposed to distribute over every time, past, present, and future; and thus it would be an ampliative term, and 'Socrates is always running' would be equivalent to 'At every present, past, and future time Socrates is running, or will be running, or was running'" (*S* 9.7, 6th sophism: 948). It is important here not to lose sight of the qualification, "according to common usage [*secundum usum communem*]." Like other medieval logicians, Buridan took himself to be exploring and expressing the logical dimensions of ordinary discourse, an enterprise practiced in continuity with the other trivial arts of grammar and rhetoric. The common subject matter of all of these inquiries was language. This is not to say that medieval logicians did not occasionally devise more complex rules to cover more specialized forms of discourse—an example of which we will see in a moment. But it is to say that no one, including Buridan, thought that logic is about the study of inference relations within certain idealized and 'well-behaved' universes of discourse, or worse, that logic should be used to 'purify' common usage of its truth-functional infelicities. As far as the art of dialectic is concerned, most late medieval logicians would have been sympathetic to Wittgenstein's idea that philosophy "leaves everything as it is."[31]

In Buridan's logic, natural supposition develops the doctrine of ampliation, where it is presented as a kind of limiting case in which the range of a term's reference has been "ampliated to the fullest [*amplissima*]" (*QAnPr.* I.14). Yet "many modern authors [i.e., terminist logicians]," he says, "deny that there is natural supposition" (*S* 4.3.4: 259; cf. *QAnPo.* I.16). Instead of listing and then refuting their arguments, however, he believes it sufficient simply to "show that we often use it." By 'we', here, he does not mean his fellow practitioners of the science of logic, but his primary audience of grammatically trained students and other educated persons who look to the *Summulae* for help in dialectical matters. This becomes clear in the examples he gives of four kinds of discourse that exhibit natural supposition, only the last of which concerns the demonstrative sciences mentioned in the lemma heading this section of the fourth treatise. The examples are evidently designed to persuade his audience by moving from the easy cases, i.e., mundane and relatively uncontroversial uses of natural supposition, to its more abstract and controversial application in the demonstrative sciences, which happens to be the point at which Ockham's account will be rejected.

First, Buridan says, certain verbs such as 'understand', 'know', and 'signify' obviously "make the terms construed with them supposit or be taken for everything," as in 'A man is thought of', which is true just in case some past (e.g., Aristotle), present (e.g., Buridan), or future (e.g., the Antichrist) man is now being thought of. Second, natural supposition also occurs quite explicitly in propositions such as 'Everything that is or was or will be B runs,' for in such cases, "the subject supposits for present, past, and future things, whether it is true or false." Third, when a term such as 'perpetually', 'eternally', or 'always' occurs in a proposition, "it would appear from the usage of authors, to distribute [the suppositing term] for present, past, and future times." We find here yet another invitation to interpretation, for thus, he says, "it would not appear to be a correct usage of the term 'always' if we said that Socrates always runs, given that he ran only in this one hour, even if we only took that hour as the present" (S 4.3.4: 260). Fourth, and finally, he elaborates on his initial remark that natural supposition is the sort used in the demonstrative sciences.

According to Ockham, the necessity and universality of propositions in the demonstrative sciences can be preserved only if they are understood as disguised conditionals. The problem is that none of the particulars he is willing to accept as real seems an appropriate referent for the significant terms in those propositions he takes to be the proper objects of scientific knowledge. That is because none of them meets the Aristotelian criteria of necessity, eternality, and incorruptibility: "although it is incompatible with what Aristotle says, in truth no proposition made up of terms introducing corruptible things only, and that is merely affirmative, categorical, and present-tense, can be the principle or conclusion of a demonstration, because any proposition of this sort is contingent."[32] Yet since the propositional object of our knowledge must be categorical, he rejects the idea that any merely conditional proposition— the example he gives is, 'If a man exists, a man is a rational animal [*si homo est, homo est animal rationale*]'—could be the conclusion of a properly demonstrative syllogism. Nevertheless, he insists that we can still have scientific knowledge because "many conditional and non-assertoric propositions [*propositiones condicionales et de possibili*]" can be necessary in the required sense, for "this proposition is absolutely necessary, 'If a man exists, an animal exists [*si homo est, animal est*]'; and this, 'If a man laughs, an animal laughs [*si homo ridet, animal ridet*]'; and this, 'Every man can laugh [*omnis homo potest ridere*]', if the subject [term] stands for things which can be; and in this way [other] propositions equivalent to them are [also] necessary." This is a puzzling position. Has not Ockham just dismissed conditional propositions as objects of scientific knowledge? "Unfortunately," as Marilyn McCord Adams notes, "Ockham does not pursue any of these proposals systematically or in detail."[33] In essence—and this is certainly the way Buridan understands him (*QNE* VI.6: 122vb)—the solution looks to be an attempt to secure the necessity of demonstrative science by severing the connection between propositions and things. Thus, a scientific proposition such as 'Thunder is a sound in the clouds' needn't become false if uttered on a clear day, when there is no thunder (according to the doctrine of supposition, propositions whose subject terms *supposit* for nothing are false), because it is actually shorthand for another proposition, viz., 'If there is thunder, then it is a sound in the clouds', which is true regardless of whether it is thundering at the time of its utterance.

Buridan does not like this solution because, as he observes in a famous remark, "I believe that such great controversy has arisen among the disputants because of a lack of logic [*credo quod tanta fuit orta controversa inter opinantes ex defectu logicae*]" (*QNE* VI.6: 122vb).[34] By failing to make use of logical resources plainly available to him in the terminist tradition, Ockham has made it look as if we can have knowledge "of things which do not exist [*de non entibus*]," because his hypothetical propositions will be true even when their antecedents are false, i.e., even when their significant terms stand for nothing. But if that is so, how are we to distinguish true sciences from false ones, meteorology from chimerology?

Instead, Buridan moves the reader in a different direction by making a commonsense observation:

> it seems to me that names which signify things without consignifying any determinate time signify things indifferently [in the] present, past, and future. Nor is it surprising that I can understand a thing without understanding any determinate time along with it. That is why I can mentally combine the concept of a thing with the concept of a time in the past or the future, as well as in the present, such as when I say 'Caesar was' or 'Caesar will be'. And so it is not the least bit absurd that occasionally a term should *supposit* for past and future times, as well as for the present. (*QNE* VI.6: 122vb; cf. *S* 4.3.4: 260–62)[35]

This leads into a discussion of the way older terminist logicians (*antiqui logici*) handled the distinction by means of the division between natural and accidental supposition, so we can say that the propositional objects of demonstrative science contain terms which "supposit indifferently for all of their referents, whether past, present, or future."[36] Then, returning to the touchstone of ordinary discourse, Buridan reminds us that if we say in connection with Aristotle's *Meteorology* (for medieval thinkers, a paradigmatically demonstrative science) "that every thunder is a sound made in the clouds, or that every rainbow is a reflection or refraction of light, then we do not intend to say these things only concerning the present ones; indeed, even if there were no thunder or rainbow at the present time, we would nevertheless say the same things" (*S* 4.3.4: 260). Thus, the proposition, 'Thunder is a sound in the clouds' is true, referring to all singular instances of thunder, present, past, and future (*QNE* VI.6: 123ra). Ever the pedagogue, he also records a student's objection, together with his reply to it:

Ockham

> But someone might now say, 'Master, your opinion has coincided with the previous one [i.e., Ockham's], since you have assigned a hypothetical sense to the aforesaid knowable proposition [i.e., 'Thunder is a sound in the clouds'], and they conceded that in such cases that the hypothetical propositions are necessary and knowable'. I reply that perhaps my opinion and the other are the same in intent, but they differ in logic, in the way they are expressed. For those who hold the first opinion do not concede the categorical proposition in the aforesaid examples, understood in the categorical sense. But I concede that the categorical proposition is true according to natural supposition. (*QNE* VI.6: 123ra)[37]

In a flourish that accompanies only his *Summulae* discussion of natural supposition, Buridan speculates that even the souls of the blessed in paradise use natural supposition when they contemplate the propositions, 'God is good' and 'I am present to God'. For obviously, they would know "that there is no time, and so they would know that neither they themselves nor God did exist in the present time and that they did not coexist with the present time either" (*S* 4.3.4: 261). And equally obviously, the blessed do not take such propositions to be false, or senseless.

Having treated Buridan's innovations regarding the elimination of simple supposition and reintroduction of natural supposition, I shall not have much to say here about the other main branch of supposition theory, i.e., the modes of personal supposition or the theory of descent to singulars. Suffice it to say that the remainder of the fourth treatise suggests that descent functioned not so much as a theory as a technique embodied in a series of rules and illustrations. The technique shows how, from propositions containing what we would now call quantificational signs—e.g., distributive terms such as 'every' or 'no'; exceptive terms such as 'only'—we can 'descend to', or infer, other propositions which do not have such terms but which are nevertheless logically equivalent to them because they supposit for the same things.[38] Though there is some variation in the details, Buridan's presentation of the subject is generally in keeping with other fourteenth-century accounts, such as that found in Ockham's *Summa logicae* or William Heytesbury's *Regulae solvendae sophismata*.

CHAPTER FIVE

Syllogisms

·With the fifth treatise of the *Summulae,* Buridan returns to Peter of Spain as his source-text. But again, it is important to remember that Buridan's elaboration and practical presentation of syllogistic inference is approximately ten times as long as the corresponding chapter in Peter's *Summulae.* The result is, for all intents and purposes, a new account, one that reflects the centrality of supposition in later terminist logic. Because supposition is a semantic property of terms in propositional contexts, the fourth treatise serves as a thematic bridge in the organization of Buridan's *Summulae* between the first three treatises on terms and last four on arguments. The fifth treatise on syllogisms is the first and most general treatment of the rudiments of argumentation, leading naturally to its diversification in the sixth treatise on topics, the seventh on fallacies, and the eighth on demonstrations. Yet each of these treatises contains developments which indicate that Aristotelian syllogistic had been not so much modernized as utterly transformed by the terminists, even though the structure still looks the same from the outside.

Buridan regards it as the "principal intention" of logic to deal with syllogisms, an aim which he further subdivides, following Aristotle, into the goal of attaining knowledge (via the demonstrative syllogisms outlined in the *Posterior Analytics*) and the setting forth of opinions in the context of debate (via the dialectical syllogisms found in the *Topics*) (*S* 5.6.8: 347).[1] The treatise on syllogisms proper, which is traditionally connected to the model of inference presented in Aristotle's *Prior Analytics,*[2] will first direct the reader's attention to the classification of syllogisms by figure and mode, and then illustrate the concept of logical inference through a series of examples involving the various types of syllogism.

The conceptual apparatus of Buridan's syllogistic logic has all of the standard features. Quoting Peter of Spain, he notes that syllogisms occur in three figures, or arrangements of the syllogism's three terms in its two premises "according to their subjection and predication": the first figure, in which the middle term occurs in the subject position of the major premise and the predicate position of the minor premise (as in the inference, 'Every animal is a substance, every man is an animal; therefore, every man is a substance'); the second figure, in which the middle is predicated in both premises ('No stone is an animal, every man is an animal; therefore, no man is a stone'); and the third figure, in which the middle occurs in the subject position of both premises ('Every man is an animal, every man is a substance; therefore, some substance is an animal') (S 5.1.6: 310–11). Syllogisms are also classified according to mode, which is "an arrangement of premises in the quality and quantity required to necessarily infer the conclusion" (S 5.1.7: 311). Qualitatively, a premise can be affirmative or negative; quantitatively, it can be universal or singular or indefinite. The three figures of the syllogism have nineteen valid modes— nine in the first, four in the second, and six in the third—which Buridan expresses using the traditional mnemonic of nineteen names ('Barbara'; 'Celarent'; 'Darii'; etc.), each of which gives a typology of valid syllogism (S 5.2.1–2: 319–21). In this way, the student can "more easily formulate and better remember" the range of acceptable inference relations; 'Cesare', for instance, would be a valid syllogism of the second figure, of which the first premise is a universal negative ('e-form'), the second a universal affirmative ('a-form'), and the conclusion a universal negative ('e-form'), as in the syllogism above beginning 'No stone is an animal'. The mnemonic also encodes two sets of rules for the reduction of second and third figure syllogisms to the first four modes of the first figure, which are said to "conclude directly," or to hold via the class inclusion rules of *dici de omni* or *dici de nullo*:[3] (1) syllogisms with names beginning with the letters B, C, D, and F reduce to first figure syllogisms of the mode indicated by the same letter (i.e., 'Barbara'; 'Celarent'; 'Darii'; and 'Ferio'); (2) an 's' indicates that the proposition understood by the preceding vowel is to be converted simply (so that 'No stone is an animal' becomes 'No animal is a stone', reducing 'Cesare' to 'Celarent'), whereas a 'p' indicates that it is to be converted accidentally, an 'm' that the premises should be transposed, and a 'c' "anywhere but in the beginning" that the reduction should occur *per impossible* (S 5.2.3–4: 321–24). The result is an impressively compact model of the basic forms of logical inference, but there is nothing especially original or noteworthy in Buridan's presentation of it.

Nevertheless, it is in the context of his rendition of Aristotelian syllogistic that Buridan introduces some truly remarkable innovations, illustrating

Sten Ebbesen's observation that "Buridan proceeds like people who renovate old uninhabitable houses. He keeps the Aristotelian façade, but changes the interior so that it fits his purposes."[4] To continue the metaphor, two of the changes he makes in the field of syllogistic logic look more like additions than renovations, and the first of them threatens to dwarf the original structure.

Buridan's first change is to make the whole of syllogistic logic assimilable to the doctrine of consequences. I say 'make assimilable' rather than 'actually assimilate' because Buridan only gestures to this possibility in the fifth treatise of the *Summulae*. The gesture is made near the beginning of the treatise, where he replies to an objection to Peter of Spain's understanding of the inferential force of a syllogism as holding between two apparently quite separate entities: "a syllogism is an expression in which, after some things have been posited, it is necessary for something else to occur on account of what has been posited [*quibusdam positis necesse est aliud accidere per ea quae posita sunt*]" (*S* 5.1.3: 308).[5] The problem with this, the objection runs, is that a syllogism is composed of not one but several expressions which can differ in species as categorical or hypothetical—considerations which might block the otherwise unimpeded movement from premises to conclusion. Buridan's response makes it clear that the consequence expressed by a syllogism is to be understood seamlessly:

> I reply that although a syllogism is composed of several expressions, it is nevertheless a single hypothetical proposition, connecting the conclusion with the premises through the conjunction 'therefore'. Further, it can be relegated [*reducere*] to the species of conditional propositions, for just as a conditional is one consequence, so too is a syllogism, whence a syllogism could be formulated as a conditional, in the following manner: 'If every animal is a substance, and every man is an animal, then every man is a substance'. Strictly speaking [*proprie*], however, a syllogism has an additional feature in comparison to a conditional in that a syllogism posits the premises assertively, whereas a conditional does not assert them. Therefore it would not be inappropriate to place syllogisms in a species of hypotheticals different from those that the author [i.e., Peter of Spain] enumerated earlier; that species could then be described, as far as its nominal definition is concerned [*quantum ad quid nominis*], in terms of the following expression: 'a consequence that asserts the consequent and the antecedent'. (*S* 5.1.4: 308–309; cf. *S* 7.4.6: 581; *TC* I.3: 21)

The remark, "it would not be inappropriate [*non esset inconveniens*]," is something of an understatement, for what follows is a recipe for recasting the entire tradition of syllogistic logic handed down from Aristotle as "a species of hypotheticals," i.e., in terms of the theory of consequences.

This new approach to syllogistic, developed in Buridan's independent *Treatise on Consequences,* is governed by a set of comprehensive rules capable of dealing with categorical and hypothetical as well as modal syllogisms. Although he does not mention it in the fifth treatise of the *Summulae,* the third and fourth books of the *Treatise on Consequences* are addressed to syllogisms with assertoric and modal sentences, respectively, under the rubric of "syllogistic consequences [*de consequentiis syllogisticis*]" (*TC* III.1: 79, l. 8). It is the *Treatise on Consequences,* rather than Aristotle's *Prior Analytics,* or Buridan's own commentary thereon,[6] which serves as the companion-text for this new approach. Students who wished to explore the subsumption of Aristotelian syllogistic by consequences could go on to study the nineteen theorems (*conclusiones*) governing syllogisms with assertoric sentences in the third book of the *Treatise on Consequences;* likewise, they would also find a distillation of the *Summulae*'s lengthy discussion of arguments involving mixed and non-mixed modal syllogisms and reduplicative syllogisms (*S* 5.6–8: 335–71) in the twenty-eight theorems of modal syllogistic consequences presented in the fourth book of that work. The discussion of rules of inference does differ between the two works.[7] As befits a practical textbook—which almost certainly also found use as a reference work—the *Summulae*'s treatise on syllogisms gives inference rules in terms of the traditional figures and mnemonic names of syllogistic logic, and, in the case of modal syllogistic, in terms of the most readily apparent modal characteristics of the syllogism in question. This is clearly laid out in the table of contents at the head of each chapter. Thus, for example, a theologian puzzled by a syllogistic argument about the contingency of creation would have read that "the sixth [section of chapter 6 of the fifth treatise deals] with syllogisms consisting of propositions about contingency [*de contingenti*]" (*S* 5.6.1: 336), and found there a generous discussion with examples (and counterexamples) of valid syllogisms with contingent premises (*S* 5.6.6: 344–46). By contrast, the *Treatise on Consequences* is not organized around the modes and figures of Aristotelian syllogistic, and contains no such reader-friendly helps for discerning its contents. Instead, the discussion centers on the inference rules themselves.[8] These rules tend to be more complex than those found in the *Summulae,* and typically speak to a variety of syllogistic modes and figures, as in the Twenty-Second Theorem of Book IV, which reads, "For any premises from which a necessary, affirmative conclusion follows, from those same premises a contingent, negative conclusion also follows" (*TC* IV.3: 131, ll. 68–70).[9] The *Treatise on Consequences* was evidently written for a different kind of audience, one that had graduated from Aristotelian logic and was ready to use it to learn a newer and more powerful logic centered on the proposition.[10]

Buridan's approach to consequences is best seen as striking a compromise between the approaches of his older contemporaries, William of Ockham and Walter Burley. Ockham's *Summa logicae* preserves the traditional Aristotelian structure in its respective treatises on terms, propositions, and arguments, and, although he seems to have been aware that rules for consequences are independent of conversion rules for syllogisms, he deals only fleetingly with the former in the final chapter of the third section of the third treatise on topical syllogisms.[11] The reader is accordingly faced with the task of "sifting out" a theory of consequences from this section of the *Summa logicae*.[12] On the other hand, the presentation of general rules for consequences occurs first in Burley's *De puritate artis logicae* (both versions), with only a very brief outline of rules for syllogistic consequences appended to his remarks, almost as an afterthought.[13] It is for this reason that Ivan Boh has characterized Burley as "perhaps the earliest medieval logician who fully understood the logical priority of propositional logic and also developed it to a considerable degree."[14] Buridan's approach resembles Ockham's in the *Summulae,* but it is more like Burley's in the *Treatise on Consequences.* That is, inference rules are brought into play in the fifth treatise of the *Summulae* indirectly, by way of expounding particular kinds of syllogisms with assertoric and modal premises. But these same rules, expressed in a more general form, are brought into the foreground in the *Treatise on Consequences,* and the entire discussion is built around them. The main difference between Buridan's and Burley's work on the consequences consists, as Niels Green-Pedersen has shown,[15] in Buridan's very deliberate effort to systematize them. "I would like to treat of consequences," Buridan writes in the very first lines of the treatise, "by discussing—so far as I am able—their causes, concerning which many things have been previously demonstrated by others, but perhaps not reduced to the primary causes through which they are said to hold" (*TC* I.1: 17, ll. 7–10).[16] It would have been more in keeping with the pedagogical aim of the *Summulae,* however, to present these rules in a dialectical fashion, preserving in them as many references as possible to the traditional figures and modes of Aristotelian syllogistic.

But that said, Buridan still makes clear to his audience that consequences represent a definite break with Aristotle:

> It seems to me that Aristotle thought of a syllogism not as composed of premises and a conclusion, but of premises only, from which a conclusion may be inferred. Therefore, he took it to be a power of the syllogism that more than one conclusion can be drawn from the same syllogism [cf. *Prior Analytics* I.1.53a2–b2]. And so in the first figure, in addition to the four modes concluding directly and in the usual way of speaking, Aristotle posited only two other modes which, also in the usual way of speaking, conclude indirectly, viz., Fapesmo and Frisesomorum, setting aside those modes which conclude only in unfamiliar ways of speaking. And he did not list Baralipton, Celantes, and Dabitis in addition to Barbara, Celarent, and Darii, since they do not differ from them in what they say. (*TC* III.4: 92–93, ll. 263–73; cf. *S* 5.1.7: 311–12)[17]

As we saw above, Buridan rejects Aristotle's view, conceiving of a syllogism not as an inference between two propositions but as "a single hypothetical proposition, connecting the conclusion with the premises through the conjunction 'therefore'." The reason Aristotle did not list Baralipton (AAI) in addition to Barbara (AAA) as a mode of the first figure is that by his own account, "they have the same arrangement of premises in quantity and quality" (S 5.1.7: 311), differing only in their conclusions—which Aristotle considered to be separate from their premises. On Buridan's more holistic approach, however, the number of distinct syllogistic modes proliferates very rapidly. This is most evident in the case of modal syllogisms. G. E. Hughes calculated that there are only sixteen pairs of premises to consider in the case of non-modal syllogisms, since each must occur as an A, E, I, or O form. But things change when we are faced with a premise having:

> a necessity, possibility, contingency, or non-contingency copula in place of the non-modal one, and in each of these cases it may or may not have the 'which is' qualification [which blocks ampliation of the subject term—cf. QAnPr I.31]. This gives us not 4 but 28 possibilities for each premiss, and so 784 premiss-pairs; and if we subtract the 16 purely non-modal pairs, we are left with 768. Since the same holds for each figure, we have 3072 premiss-pairs in all. Of each of these we can ask whether it yields any of the 28 possible conclusions, and if so, which. So if we define a syllogistic mood in what is probably the most usual way, in terms of the forms of premises and conclusion, we shall have 3072 × 28 (86016) modal syllogistic moods, including of course all the invalid ones, as compared with the modest number of 256 for non-modal syllogisms.[18]

Buridan's way of handling this situation is to show how a certain range of examples can be tested for validity, leaving the rest as an exercise for the reader: "And whoever wishes to stretch the subtlety of his ingenuity with further rigor in pursuit of what has been said, will be able to find sufficient direction here" (S 5.7.7: 364). Beginning students are invited to explore on their own this rather monstrous 'modal' addition to the original house of Aristotelian syllogistic. But more advanced students can view the entire building from a different angle, using consequences, the simpler and more powerful way of modeling inferences between propositions.[19]

The second major change Buridan introduces to the treatment of syllogisms concerns, not surprisingly, his use of supposition to analyze the structure of certain complex terms that would remain unanalyzed on the traditional account. Of particular importance here is the doctrine of ampliation.[20] For example, although the syllogism, 'Nothing dead is an animal, some man is dead; therefore, some man is not an animal', is an acceptable fourth-mode syllogism of the first figure (Ferio), Buridan denies that the consequence is "formally valid." The reason is that in this syllogism, 'man' is an ampliative term, and "from an ampliated nondistributed term the same term does not follow nonampliated"; that is, "in the minor proposition the term 'man' was ampliated to past [things], whereas in the conclusion it was not ampliated," making the premises true but the conclusion false (*S* 5.3.2: 326; cf. *QAnPr* I.14). Similarly, terms referring to the divine persons will sometimes generate counterexamples to the traditionally accepted modes. Thus, "the following syllogism in *Barbara* is invalid: 'Every God is the Son, every divine Father is God; therefore every divine Father is the Son," for the transitivity of identity fails in cases "where the most simple unity is a trinity of really distinct persons" (*S* 5.3.2: 327). Buridan also cautions the reader to be wary of modal contexts introduced by verbs of knowing and believing, because "the verb 'know' ampliates the subject to supposit not only for present things, however, but also for future and past ones." This means that without suitable qualification, "although I know that every man is an animal, nevertheless, it does not follow that every man is known by me to be an animal; for then it would follow that every man, whether alive or dead or yet to be born, would be known by me to be an animal, which is false" (*S* 5.6.8: 348). What is noteworthy in these and other examples is the way Buridan uses doctrine of supposition to expand the range of 'truth-makers' for modal inferences, i.e., his assumption that "the presence of a modal copula—*any* modal copula—in a proposition ampliates the subject to stand for not only the actual things but also the possible things that fall under that term."[21] Because it makes merely possible objects relevant to the evaluation of modal inferences, ampliation functions here as the Buridanian equivalent of possible worlds semantics, though it would be a mistake to regard it as a remarkable anticipation of the twentieth-century theory of that name. Buridan's remarks on its larger significance are few.[22] Certainly he did not himself see it as a great innovation, but only as a further effort on his part to make existing schemes for checking inferences more practicable.

CHAPTER SIX

Topics

· The treatise on topics or *loci* is the first in a series of three treatises aimed at developing the concept of argumentation sketched in the fifth treatise on syllogisms. In this case, the practical goal is the generation of opinions or beliefs in others by means of persuasive arguments. What makes an argument persuasive is differentially defined, relative to sophistical arguments, which are the subject of the seventh treatise, and demonstrative arguments, which are the subject of the eighth. Buridan's sixth treatise gives an account of rules for syllogistic arguments that produce true opinion, rather than false opinion on the one hand, or knowledge on the other. Viewed synoptically, the treatises on topics, fallacies, and demonstrations are different applications of the notion of inference presented in the treatise on syllogisms.

In choosing to treat of the topics, Buridan is of course picking up on a very long tradition that began in Aristotle as an attempt to classify logical relationships among non-demonstrative arguments. This project was reconceived in a more rhetorical vein by Cicero, and eventually given a unified treatment by Boethius in *De topicis differentiis* and *In Ciceronis Topica*, two works which were the source-texts for all discussions of the subject in the Latin West until the recovery of Aristotle's *Topics* in the latter half of the twelfth century.[1] But even then, Boethius's work continued to inform the reading of Aristotle's *Topics* until interest in the subject began to die out in the early fourteenth century. Peter of Spain's own discussion of topics is, as L. M. de Rijk points out, "not a compilation from Aristotle's *Topica*, but from Boethius's *De topicis differentiis* I and II, with some additions from Aristotle's *Topics*."[2] Buridan is well aware of this fact, remarking in the very first sentence of the sixth treatise that "this treatise, which is about dialectical *loci,* has been excerpted by our author from Boethius's *Topics*" (*S* 6.1.1: 391).

Topical argumentation is an important chapter in the history of medieval logic, but it would be beyond the scope of the present study to rehearse it here. It has, in any case, been definitively treated by others.[3] But the attention Buridan gives to the doctrine raises an interesting question: why has he chosen to devote an entire treatise of the *Summulae* to a subject which had, for a variety of reasons, fallen into desuetude by the time it was composed in the second quarter of the fourteenth century? It cannot be for reasons of completeness, since hardly anyone after Abelard believed that topical rules were necessary or even desirable as warrants for syllogistic inferences.[4] Nor can it be for comprehensiveness, since Buridan does not extend the same special treatment to other subjects, such as the doctrine of syncategorematic words, which had played a much more central role in the evolution of terminist logic. Nor can it be for reasons of fidelity to his source-text, since, as we have seen, Buridan is not above reorganizing and rewriting Peter's *Summulae* to suit his own needs, transforming his own *Summulae* into an independent textbook rather than a commentary on Peter's work. So why the inordinate interest in topics?

The answer to this question can be found in the pedagogical aim of the *Summulae*. Buridan discusses the topics because topical disputation was still part of the Parisian intellectual milieu in the second quarter of the fourteenth century. Even if most of his students were unfamiliar with Boethius's *De topicis differentiis* because it was no longer taught, they would have encountered the doctrine via commentaries and lecture courses on Peter of Spain's *Summulae,* and, less frequently, on Aristotle's *Topics.* They would also have had some exposure to the topics as a method of discovering and presenting arguments through their observations of real life disputations among their teachers and peers.[5] But Buridan's own discussion of the topics serves not merely to cover a standard text and the increasingly archaic practices associated with it; rather, he seems intent upon redeeming the Aristotelian tradition of topics—and, in the treatises which follow, of fallacies and demonstrations as well—in the direction of epistemology, thereby linking logic to natural philosophy in a single, comprehensive vision of the *scientia* or body of knowledge constitutive of the liberal arts. Buridan's view is that the curriculum must not merely be taught but articulated.

As Buridan understands it, the doctrine of the topics consists of a collection of inference rules expressing relationships between the terms (*habitudines terminorum*) of an argument. The topic or *locus* just is this relationship, "on account of which the whole argument has its power and efficacy," i.e., to generate belief in its conclusion (*S* 6.2.2: 402). For practical purposes, the *locus* is exemplified by its maxim or maximal proposition (*propositio maxima*), a "self-evident proposition [*propositio per se nota*] ... which contains universally the whole power of the argument," thus giving the general form of the rule. It is by virtue of their 'containing' the force of the argument that the maximal proposition and its terms are called a 'place [*locus*]' metaphorically, just as a literal place "contains quantitatively that which is in the place" (*S* 6.2.2: 401–402). For example, in "arguing that 'A man is running; therefore, an animal is running', when it is asked 'Whence the locus?', I could reply: 'From the superior to the inferior', or, more specifically, 'From the universal whole to its subjective part', or even more specifically, 'From the genus to its species'. And the maxims are to be assigned analogously, both the more general and the more specific ones" (*S* 6.4.3: 425). The terms 'man' and 'animal' supply the difference (*differentia*) of the maxim, and hence the means of ordering *loci* or topics into "necessarily diverse" maxima—which is one of the principal tasks Boethius sets for himself in *De topicis differentiis*.[6]

The result was a system of rules whose truth and self-evidentness could be used to confirm arguments. As Niels Green-Pedersen describes it:

> In the argument to be confirmed an instance of this [topical] relation occurs between a term in the antecedent (or premiss) and a term in the consequent (conclusion). An argument may contain, e.g., the term 'man' in its antecedent and the term 'animal' in its consequent. The argument is confirmed or proved by means of the relation holding between the two terms. They relate to each other as a species to its genus, so we have here a particular instance of the relation of species to genus. Since a locus is a relation between two terms . . . Buridan stresses that we should not speak of a locus 'from the species', but of a locus 'from the species to the genus', for this is the only manner in which we can indicate the nature of the relation. The function of the maxim is to spell out and state the relation by which the argument is proved.[7]

The fact that topical relations are assumed to hold between terms and not things is a product of Buridan's nominalism. But lest the point be lost on his audience, he remarks, "in the argument, 'Every man runs; therefore every animal runs', we should not say that here we have a locus from man to animal, for neither a man nor an animal is put in the argument, but rather that this is really a locus from the term 'man' to the term 'animal', and it is on the basis of the relationship between these two terms that the consequence is valid" (*S* 6.3.1: 409). We are reminded of the fourth treatise joke about not being able to "carry the ultimate significata [of terms] to disputations" (*S* 4.3.2: 255). And the point is roughly the same: we should reject the claim of the literalists that 'Every man runs; therefore every animal runs' is invalid because it is not verified of actual men and actual animals.

For the same reason, Buridan later remarks that "a dialectical maxim more immediately confirms an argument formed with its terms taken materially than one formed with its terms taken personally, or significatively" (*S* 6.3.5: 418–19). But in the other direction, all this talk of the 'power' of an argument which is 'virtually contained' in the relation expressed by a topical maxim might lead one to ask, "What should we understand by the term 'relation' here, i.e., what does it signify, and for what thing does it supposit?" (*S* 6.3.1: 408). Could a topical relation stand for some kind of abstract entity? In a passage reminiscent of his fourth treatise rejection of simple supposition, Buridan argues that the things related are terms of second intention:

> If, therefore, descending [to the level of singulars], you were to ask what the relation [*habitudo*] of the term 'man' to the term 'animal' is on account of which the term 'man' is called a species, I would say that this is the same as asking what thing the relation of two to one is on account of which two are said to be the double [of one], or again what thing is the relation of Socrates to Plato on account of which Socrates is said to be Plato's father, or similar to Plato, or diverse from Plato. And this amounts to asking whether abstract terms from the category of relation supposit for the same things as their concrete [counterparts] or for some super-added dispositions, and this has to be and has been determined elsewhere. (*S* 6.3.1: 410–11)

Buridan is referring to Book V, question 6 of his commentary on Aristotle's *Metaphysics,* where he argues that the paternity of Socrates as regards Plato *just is* Socrates, and conversely, that the filiation of Plato as regards Socrates *just is* Plato. But although the term 'paternity [*paternitas*]' supposits for the same thing as its concrete counterpart, 'father [*pater*]', i.e., Socrates, Buridan says that it also "connotes or appellates Plato [*connotat sive appellat Platonem*]" (*QM* V.6: 30rb).[8] He makes the first claim explicitly about topical relationships: "I [accordingly] say that the relation of the term 'man' to the term 'animal' whereby the term 'man' is the species of the term 'animal' is the term 'man' itself" (*S* 6.3.1: 411). Presumably, he would also want to say that topical differentia connote their abstract counterparts. But the first claim is sufficient to banish any realist thoughts from the minds of his audience.[9]

Buridan's conception of the *locus* was the standard conception in the later Middle Ages.[10] But he adds a few twists of his own, most notably where the doctrines of topics and consequences overlap, creating a potential conflict between old and new on the question of how inferences should be validated.

For Buridan, a consequence is a relation holding between sentences as terms in a conditional proposition—as we saw in chapter 5 above, he argued that a syllogism, although it "is composed of several expressions, it is nevertheless a single hypothetical proposition, connecting the conclusion with the premises through the conjunction 'therefore'" (*S* 5.1.3: 308; cf. *TC* I.3: 21). Thus, in a consequence, "one proposition is antecedent to another, which is related to it in such a way that when both are proposed together, it is impossible for the former [i.e., the antecedent], howsoever it signifies, to be true, without the other [i.e., the consequent] howsoever it signifies, also being true" (*TC* I.3: 22, ll. 48–51).[11] This general notion of consequence is then divided into formal and material consequence. A formal or formally valid consequence is said to hold in virtue of the logical form or syntax of the proposition alone, regardless of the signification of its constituent terms; on the other hand, a material or materially valid consequence "does not hold for all like terms, even when the form remains constant [*non tenet in omnibus terminis forma consimili retenta*]," but is also a function of certain semantic considerations. Thus, 'A man runs; therefore an animal runs' is a material consequence, because it is unacceptable with these terms: 'A horse walks; therefore wood walks' (*TC* I.4: 23, ll. 10–14). Furthermore, a material consequence can be reduced to a formal consequence "by the addition of some necessary proposition or propositions, whose placement next to what has been assumed in the antecedent renders the consequence formal" (*TC* I.4: 23, ll. 16–19).[12] In the case of 'A man runs; therefore an animal runs,' it is easy to see that the addition of the proposition, 'Man is an animal', which Buridan says is "necessary according to Aristotle [*necessaria secundum Aristotelem*],"[13] yields a formal assertoric consequence whose conclusion is valid both directly ('An animals runs') and indirectly ('Something running is an animal'), and which is accordingly described as "useful [*utile*]" for making deductions (*TC* II.1: 56, ll. 13–22; cf. *TC* III.4: 93; *QAnPr* II.19). In Aristotelian syllogistic, this consequence corresponds to the valid third-figure mode with the mnemonic name *Disamis* ('Some M is P; all M is S; therefore, some S is P') (*S* 5.5.2: 333). In the alternative confirmatory scheme of the topics, 'A man runs; therefore, an animal runs' is likewise said to hold by means of the *locus* "from a species to its genus" (*S* 6.3.1: 409).

So Buridan has given us a recipe for reducing material to formal consequences, or consequences whose truth is "evident [*evidens*]" to us (*TC* I.4: 23, l. 15). The problem is that throughout the treatise on topics, he also seems to associate topical inferences with material consequences, an association which, in view of the reducibility of material to formal consequences, threatens to make dialectical *loci* superfluous as a means of validating inferences. Indeed, Buridan hints in the very last section of the sixth treatise that an argument cannot be both a formal consequence and based on a *locus*:[14]

> But some people say that the *locus* from division is not to be counted among the dialectical *loci*, given that the argument based on it is a formal[ly valid] consequence [*argumentum per ipsum est consequentia formalis*]. But to maintain [the opinions of] Boethius and Themistius and our author [i.e., Peter of Spain], and generally everybody else who has listed this *locus* among the dialectical *loci*, I say that the following is an

argument from division: 'A is an animal and is not rational; therefore, it is irrational'; and this consequence is not formal[ly valid], but it would indeed be rendered formal[ly valid] by adding the proposition 'Every animal is rational or irrational'.

But this does not matter, for this is so even where other *loci* are concerned. For if we argue by the *locus* from contraries in the following manner: 'A is white; therefore, A is not black', it is clear that a syllogism, or a formal[ly valid] consequence, would be effected by the addition of the proposition 'Nothing white is black'. And the same goes for the other dialectical *loci*: if they are not laid out in [a syllogistic] form, they do not conclude on account of their form; but they can be reduced to [a syllogistic] form by means of additions. (*S* 6.6.4: 491)

This is a remarkable suggestion. On the one hand, Buridan seems to be saying that his treatment of the topics is motivated by our need to respect tradition: we still teach and discuss dialectical *loci* to maintain ('*sustinendo*' is the Latin participle he uses here) the views of Boethius, Themistius, and Peter of Spain. But on the other, every topical inference is in principle reducible to a formally valid consequence if we add the right 'middle'—i.e., true or necessary proposition—to its antecedent. So the more propositional approach of consequences appears to trump the traditional method of confirming arguments by means of a maximal proposition and *differentia*.

What role is left for the topics to play? One might speculate that the reason why Buridan devoted an entire chapter of the *Summulae* to dialectical *loci* was to provide a kind of historical exercise for his students, exposing them to the traditions out of which the methods of the *moderni* had developed. But this cannot be the only reason, for we have already seen that he omits other material without much comment, including subjects that were standardly discussed by logicians only a century earlier. Buridan was too good a teacher, and too parsimonious a philosopher, to devote so much attention to a doctrine that had essentially become an idle wheel. But he was also a cautious thinker by temperament. A radical break with the past, which is what rejecting dialectical *loci* in favor of consequences would have amounted to, would have been considered only as a last resort. Buridan's strategy is usually to redeem the traditional in terms better suited to the philosophical concerns of his own day. So the question we need to ask here is not, 'What logical role does the tradition of the topics play in Buridan's thought?', for the answer to that will be 'Next to none', bringing us back to the idle wheel. Green-Pedersen is almost certainly correct when he says, "the topics seem hardly to be involved in the development which takes place within logic as a whole in the 14th century."[15] We should be asking instead how Buridan conceives of the topics so as to make it relevant to his own, systematic conception of the different *scientiae*, or bodies of knowledge, that are proper to the arts faculty.

faciens fidem

The first hint of the direction Buridan intends to take in recovering the topics occurs near the beginning of the sixth treatise, where he reflects on Boethius's definition of argument (*argumentum*) as "a reason producing belief [*ratio faciens fidem*] concerning some doubtful matter." This is contrasted with argumentation (*argumentatio*), which is "an explication of an argument by means of an expression [*argumenti per orationem explicatio*]" (*S* 6.1.2: 391).[16] Boethius explains his definitions along psycho-semantic lines,[17] which is also the interpretation advanced by Buridan:

> it does not seem to me that Boethius intended to call a single term an 'argument'; rather, Boethius's intention seems to be that an argument and an argumentation differ from one another as do a mental process and a vocal process. For an argument is a process in the mind [*argumentum enim est processus in mente*] whereby the mind, on account of the mental premises known to it, is compelled to concede a conclusion previously not known or doubted. And thus 'reason' is taken here for the whole mental process; whence it is called 'argument [*argumentum*]' as though it were '[something] arguing the mind [*arguens mentem*]', i.e., something inwardly coercing the mind to concede and to assent to what it has doubted, or what it would have doubted if it had been posed as a question. But an argumentation is a vocal process expressing and significatively explicating this mental process. (*S* 6.1.2: 392)

Despite giving a rather straightforward reading of Boethius's text, and despite the false etymology,[18] these remarks are the first indication that Buridan intends to redeem the topics in the direction of psychology, where it will link the practice of logic to natural philosophy by treating inference as a mental act productive of knowledge and belief. Traditionally, of course, both demonstrative and dialectical arguments were thought to be aimed at the production of beliefs in the minds of those who hear them.[19] In the sixth treatise of the *Summulae*, this translates into an interest in the internal or 'material' circumstances of particular inferences—which topical reasoning so effectively captures— rather than external considerations of formal validity. As we have seen, the topics had already been completely upstaged by consequences as a means of confirming inferences. There is, to be sure, enough of the original teaching left in the sixth treatise for those who are so inclined to try using topical maxims and *differentiae* to validate inferences, and it is true that Buridan nowhere forbids this activity. But it is also clear from his assimilation of topical inferences to material consequences, and his claim that material consequences are reducible to formal consequences, that he regards the traditional approach as a waste of time if one just wants to do logic. Inferences should be evaluated, wherever possible, using the new doctrine of consequences.

What distinguishes Buridan's approach in the broader history of topical argumentation is what is not present in it. There is no attempt to follow Boethius in trying to reconcile the lists of topical *differentiae* found in sources such as Cicero and Themistius. Such an effort would be pointless in Buridan's view, "for they were talking equivocally" (*S* 6.2.3: 404). Likewise, there is no attempt to develop the thirteenth-century terminist idea that Boethian topical arguments could be brought into line with the Aristotelian syllogistic moods.[20] Consequences had driven a permanent wedge between these two approaches to dialectic. Instead, Buridan's approach typifies what Green-Pedersen has identified as the final stage in the evolution of the medieval tradition of the topics, wherein topical arguments were assimilated to dialectical syllogisms and subsumed under a species of "proving" syllogism, in contrast to syllogisms as such, which were called "inferring" syllogisms.[21] The "proof" in dialectical syllogisms is not demonstrative, of course, but only persuasive, a fact which led authors such as Buridan to mine Aristotle's and Boethius's topics for material relevant to the evaluation of arguments as plausible, i.e., insofar as they have the appearance (*apparentia*), or 'ring', of truth. Buridan remarks, "an argument or argumentation requires not only the necessity of the consequence but also proof [*probatio*] of the conclusion, so that the consequent should be proved on the basis of the antecedent" (*S* 6.1.4: 394). What this means is that beyond formal validity, an argument or argumentation must satisfy a further criterion, which Buridan expresses in epistemic terms: "for such a proof to occur it is also required that the antecedent should be better known [*notius*] than the consequent" (*S* 6.1.4: 394).

But the term 'argumentation' turns out to be ambiguous. In his commentary on Aristotle's *Topics*, Buridan distinguishes between perfect argumentation, where the conclusion is inferred "of necessity [*de necessitate*]," and imperfect argumentation, where the conclusion is inferred only "evidently [*evidenter*]" (*QT* I.16: 370). Of the four species of argumentation commonly discussed—syllogism, induction, enthymeme, and example—only the syllogism as such is perfect because only in a syllogism is the conclusion inferred of necessity. But the syllogism as such drops out of the picture in the sixth treatise of the *Summulae*, as Buridan takes it to have been fully dealt with in "the preceding treatise" on syllogisms (*S* 6.1.4: 395). More interesting for his purposes is a particular kind of syllogism, viz., the demonstrative syllogism, which is said to be not just perfect but "absolutely perfect [*simpliciter perfecta*]," because only in a demonstration is the conclusion inferred of necessity from an antecedent that "is absolutely evident and known without any fear [that its contradictory might be true instead]" (*QT* I.16: 371).[22] The range of topical or dialectical argumentation is then expressed differentially, in terms of those syllogisms, inductions, enthymemes, and examples that suffice to make their conclusions evident, though not absolutely evident, because of some formal or epistemic defect in their premises. By means of the criterion of plausibility or evidentness (*evidentia*), then, Buridan enacts the traditional Aristotelian distinction between demonstrative and dialectical argumentation, making the boundary between them epistemic, rather than logical.

But if Buridan is right that every topical inference is reducible to a formal consequence by the addition of the appropriate true or necessary proposition to its antecedent, could not the same be said for dialectical arguments, i.e., could they not be reduced to demonstrations by adding some sufficiently evident clause(s) to their antecedents? The answer to this question is 'no', and it is within these newer, epistemic parameters that the older science of dialectic finds room to operate. With regard to inductive inference, Buridan is quick to resist those who would try to make it deductive, and hence demonstrative:

> we should note that an induction is not formally valid unless by the addition of another premise it becomes a syllogism, as will be explained in the following part [of the sixth treatise]. Some people, however, want to claim that by virtue of the clause 'and so on for the singulars' an induction concludes formally and of necessity. But I believe that that clause is not an integral part of an induction, and this is clear from the fact that that clause is neither a proposition nor part of a proposition. And if it is said that it is posited in place of a proposition, I would reply in saying 'Socrates runs and Plato runs . . . and so on for the singulars; therefore, every man runs', if the clause 'and so on for the singulars' is taken in place of a proposition, then that proposition should be more clearly explicated, and one would have to scrutinize what that would be, but this is not easy to state [*tunc oporteret quod perfectius illa propositio explicaretur, et oporteret videre quae esset illa, quod non est facile dicere*]. (S 6.1.4: 395)

In other words, there is no hope of legitimizing such "bastard reasoning," as Plato called it,[23] by any purely formal fix, since it would not be clear what the added proposition would mean. But then the inference would fail to be a demonstration, since if we don't know what it would mean to say 'and so on for the singulars', we certainly wouldn't be saying anything evident in asserting it. And if we specify the meaning of the added clause in terms of the requisite universal, we will have only begged the question (S 6.1.4: 395). For Buridan, there is no getting around the fact that inductive inferences work, i.e., generate beliefs, only through the contribution of the mind of the cognizer:

> we should say that it is not necessary in every valid induction to induce over all the singulars, for in many cases this would be impossible, as they are infinite from our perspective; rather it is sufficient to induce over many, and the intellect, on the basis of its natural inclination toward truth [*ex eius inclinatione naturali ad veritatem*], perceiving no coun-

terinstance in any of them, nor any reason why there should be a counter-instance in another, is compelled not only to concede that this is the case with them, but [it also has to concede] the universal proposition, which then becomes an indemonstrable principle, to be assumed in [the given] art or science without demonstration. For this is how we know the indemonstrable principle that every fire is hot, and that every magnet attracts iron, and that all rhubarb purges bile, and that everything that comes to be in nature comes to be from some preexisting subject, and so on for many other indemonstrable principles. (S 6.1.4: 396)

Buridan picks up the idea for this "natural inclination" from the opening chapter of Aristotle's *Rhetoric*, where it is used to explain the persuasive power of non-deductive arguments: "For the true and the approximately true are apprehended by the same faculty; it may also be noted that men have a sufficient natural instinct for what is true, and usually do arrive at the truth."[24] Buridan explicitly uses it to interpret Aristotle's remarks about how we come to be acquainted with the general principles of the arts and sciences,[25] and, as we shall see below, it becomes the centerpiece of his account of knowledge. It is the faculty of the intellect that registers the evidentness of a proposition. Together with the formal criterion of necessity, it serves to order the various species of dialectical argumentation along a continuum of rational acceptability, relative to their capacity to generate belief. Its effect is to give us epistemic access to a whole range of scientific principles whose truth is not as absolutely evident to us as the truth of a properly demonstrative syllogism.

More than any other logical art, dialectic reflects this harmonization of the knower and known:

And Averroes speaks about this beautifully [*pulcre*], in bk. 2 of [his commentary on] the *Physics*, when he says that a universal principle that was doubtful earlier is concluded by induction without surveying all the singulars, and that this is how induction comes within the scope of demonstrative science. And he adds that on account of such an induction a universal principle is sometimes accepted more quickly and sometimes more slowly, depending on the nature of the principle and the nature of the person considering [the case]. (S 6.1.4: 396)

But we should not for a moment suppose that the mind's natural inclination toward truth is sufficient to make dialectical syllogisms demonstrative, so that the proof of their conclusions would be evident from the form of the syllogisms alone:

But if an induction cannot be performed over all the singulars, as in the case of our concluding from the singulars that every fire is hot, then such an induction is not reduced to syllogism, nor does it prove its conclusion on account of its being a formally valid consequence, nor because it may be reduced to a formally valid consequence, but because of the intellect's natural inclination toward truth. For just as the vegetative soul is naturally inclined to generate something similar to itself but does not generate unless the appropriate dispositions preexist, so the intellect is naturally inclined to assent to the truth of indemonstrable principles but does not give its assent until it is disposed to do so by the consideration of many singulars, sometimes in more, sometimes in fewer cases, in accordance with the nature of the principle and the nature of the person doing the considering, as the Commentator said. (*S* 6.1.5: 399)

The importance of dialectical argumentation, whether it is in the form of an induction, enthymeme, or example,[26] is that it brings the perspective of the cognizer to bear on the evaluation of inferences. It is the bridge to natural philosophy, the diversification of consequences by means of human experience. In Buridan's view, the topics, or dialectical *loci,* can be redeemed as a series of evident rules and maxims which, when properly adduced, make empirical inferences more persuasive.

Buridan's presentation of the topics is driven by the same pragmatic considerations that govern the organization of the other treatises of the *Summulae.* His lists of *loci* "do not purport to be exhaustive," but "are propounded in this way because the loci that are listed are the principal ones, namely those which dialecticians tend more willingly and more often to use" (*S* 6.6.1: 485). His discussion of particular *loci* for the most part follows Aristotle and especially Boethius, emphasizing points that are in keeping with his view of the topics,[27] and occasionally rewriting traditional definitions in a way better suited to the logic of the *moderni.* Thus, when we look for the maxim, "we are looking for the self-evident proposition that confirms the argument, and that need not be composed of terms placed in the argument, but [may be composed] of terms of second imposition suppositing for terms whose relationship to one another is what accounts for the validity of the argument." For example, the inference 'A man runs; therefore, an animal runs' is confirmed by the maxim, 'Whatever is truly affirmed of the species is truly affirmed of the genus', where 'genus' and 'species' are terms used of other terms, standing here for the terms 'man' and 'animal' (*S* 6.3.1: 410). Buridan does not limit his discussion to dialectical *loci,* but includes demonstrative or knowledge-producing *loci,* such as the *locus* 'from the universal whole to its subjective part', whose consequences can also be confirmed by reduction to a syllogism (*S* 6.4.3: 423). But he stops short of adopting or even endorsing the topics as means of dialectical reasoning in natural philosophy. What he does instead is to bring inductive inferences "within the scope of demonstrative science" by elevating evident natural principles to the level of "indemonstrable principles" which then serve as the appropriate middles of demonstrations in the natural sciences. As a result, Buridan's natural philosophy develops what amounts to a parallel system of rules governing the conversion of its empirically conditioned material consequences into formal consequences. The reason the redemption of the old Aristotelian-Boethian account of dialectical *loci* is left incomplete, or rather, without practical import, must be that Buridan thought that his approach was simpler and more powerful. But again, the older tools are there for readers who wish to use them, as a first approximation to the general problem of how to model dialectical inquiry.

Buridan also foreshadows the approach he takes in the remaining treatises of the *Summulae*. In connection with the *loci* 'from the more' and 'from the less', he says, "when we are talking about more and less, however, it seems that we should not understand this to concern evident appearance, nor sophistic appearance, but plausible appearance. Therefore, such loci are neither demonstrative nor sophistic, but they should be regarded as dialectical, and as ones that generate opinion or persuasion by plausibility [*et secundum probabilitatem facientes opinionem vel persuasionem*]" (S 6.5.6: 474). If we look at arguments in terms of their capacity to produce belief, then we need to examine three alternatives, since arguments can appear to us to be either plausible, or sophistical, or evident. The sixth treatise dealt with the capacity of plausible appearances to persuade. The seventh and eighth treatises will be concerned, respectively, with the power of sophistical appearances to deceive, and the power of evident appearances to convince.

CHAPTER SEVEN

Fallacies

· The medieval tradition of the fallacies, or sophistical *loci*, evolved separately from the tradition of the topics, or dialectical *loci*, though it was widely understood to be its counterpart.[1] As *loci*, however, the dialectical context of the fallacies is much more palpable because the doctrine was developed to help the novice seeker of wisdom defend himself against a semi-fictional opponent seeking to deceive him. The doctrine of the fallacies began as a means of identifying and exposing his sophistical tricks, following Aristotle's divisions of arguments that "appear to be refutations [of the novice's reasoning] but are really fallacies instead."[2]

An indication of the importance of the fallacies within the terminist tradition is that they occupy by far the longest treatise of Peter of Spain's *Summulae.* Buridan also devotes considerable space to the subject in the seventh treatise. Like Peter, he would have understood the fallacies not as some optional appendix to the study of Aristotelian syllogistic, but as essential to the practice of logic. In his pioneering studies on the history of later medieval logic, L. M. de Rijk found that the doctrine of the fallacies formed the basis of terminist logic, inasmuch as it was from twelfth-century efforts to assimilate the newly recovered *Sophistical Refutations* of Aristotle that the most characteristic analytical techniques of the *moderni*—such as the doctrine of the properties of terms, and the illustration of such doctrines by means of sophism sentences—began to evolve.[3] In practical terms, the fallacies provided arts masters with a natural point of contact between the trivial arts of logic and grammar, both of which were concerned with interpretation. Everyone knew of Aristotle's declaration that sophistical arguments depend for their existence on ambiguity—an ambiguity which is unavoidable because "names are finite and so is the sum-total of their accounts, while things are infinite in number."[4] The doctrine of the fallacies provided a basic typology of errors of interpretation, as well as the means for resolving them through the systematic application of logical and grammatical learning. "If the solution [to a fallacy] is to be perfect," Buridan reminds us, "it is necessary not only to abolish what is false, but also to show the reason for that abolition" (S 7.6.1: 602). The latter task often brought to bear the whole range of subjects and texts taught by the arts faculty, as Buridan indicates in his remarks about the fallacy of figure of words: "Those, therefore, who have sufficient knowledge of the modes of signification in accordance with the rules of grammar, as well as sufficient knowledge about the distinction between the categories, the distributive signs properly pertaining to them, and the terms contained under them, can perfectly well solve the paralogisms of this fallacy and reveal their defects" (S 7.6.4: 607).[5]

Sophistical arguments arise in disputational contexts as *apparent* refutations by one party (the opponent) of the position defended by the other (the respondent) (S 7.1.3: 498). The instrument of disputation is the argument, but the kind of argument used in a disputation depends on "the diverse ends intended by the disputants." Reprising Aristotle in the second chapter of *Sophistical Refutations*,[6] Buridan divides these into doctrinal disputations, "the most powerful demonstrations," which argue demonstratively from the proper principles of each discipline; dialectical disputations, which "settle contradictions [by arguing from] probable principles"; examinatory disputations, which proceed from "things that appear true to the respondent," primarily to determine whether the respondent is able to demonstrate what he claims to know; and "litigious, or sophistic, disputations," which "syllogize from [principles] that appear to be, but are not, probable" (S 7.1.4: 499–501). It is the end or use to which it is put that makes a refutation sophistical. The only restriction is that "every elenchus properly so called be a syllogism, and not just any kind of syllogism, but one that proves the contradictory of the conclusion of the respondent." The sophistical refutation thus emerges as a misuse or misapplication of the basic forms of syllogistic argument introduced in the fifth treatise. As Buridan notes, the interest in syllogisms is "not because a sophist only uses syllogisms (for he uses whatever argumentation he deems advantageous for himself in order to appear to defeat the respondent), but because, aiming above all to appear to refute, he aims above all to appear to produce an elenchus [*quia maxime appetit videri redarguere, ideo maxime appetit videri facere elenchum*]" (S 7.1.1: 495–96).

There are two features of this account that need to be stressed because they tend to be overlooked by modern readers. The first is that for medieval thinkers, fallacies are uses to which arguments are put, rather than argument forms themselves. It is true, of course, that most of the fallacies inventoried in modern logic textbooks (usually on a list, inside the back cover) have medieval origins, some of which are still known by their medieval names: *petitio principii, secundum quid et simpliciter,* and so on. But for medieval arts masters and their students, these were names for techniques used in oral disputation that would have had only secondary or derivative significance as names of static patterns of reasoning encountered, say, in private study. Again, the appeal of a treatise on fallacies would have been practical because it offered a means of defending oneself against the dialectical onslaught of the sophist. Buridan's seventh treatise is accordingly laden with particular illustrations, commonsense examples, mnemonic formulae, and other bits of advice to assist the reader in identifying and exposing the fallacy in question.

The second feature is related to the first. It is that fallacies are techniques used by one person, traditionally known as the "sophist [*sophista*]," to deceive another person, the student—variously referred to as the "novice [*beanus*]" or "youngster [*junior*]"—who has not yet acquired the technique: "a fallacy, in the sense intended here, is the deception of someone unskilled in the art of sophistry by some sophistic argumentation" (*S* 7.1.7: 504). But the deception caused by a fallacious argument occurs for a reason—or for two reasons, actually. These were known as its "cause of appearance [*causa apparentiae*]" and its "cause of deficiency [*causa defectus*]" (*S* 7.1.7: 504).[7] According to Sten Ebbesen:

> The idea is this: for any fallacious argument it must be possible to explain why it is not a good argument. The reason may, for instance, be that its premises contain four terms, each occurring just once, which in medieval terminology could be called either 'the cause of not being' a good syllogism (*causa non existentiae*) or the 'cause of deficiency' (*causa defectus*). But while stating the *causa defectus* is a sufficient explanation why the argument is a bad one, it does not explain how anybody can be deceived by it, and so it is necessary to add, e.g., that as two of the terms are represented by one word, a semblance is created of there being only three terms, one of which is used twice. Indicating this fact would be stating the *causa apparentiae* or *principium motivum* of the paralogism. The meaning of the first term is clear; the original sense of the second term seems to be 'that which induces (*movet*) somebody to believe in the validity of the paralogism'.[8]

The concept of the *causa apparentiae* and *causa defectus* was a genuinely medieval addition to the Aristotelian doctrine of the fallacies, although as it began to take shape, it was easy for commentators to start reading it into the text of the *Sophistical Refutations.*[9] Buridan does not himself read it this way, but the idea is prominent in his analysis of sophistical arguments both in the seventh treatise of the *Summulae* and his commentary on the *Sophistical Refutations.* In both texts, it serves to bring out the psychological and epistemic dimensions of Buridan's understanding of the fallacies, i.e., their ability to produce deceptive appearances in the minds of human cognizers, causing them to make erroneous judgments: "Strictly speaking, every fallacy is in the soul [*proprie loquendo omnis fallacia est in anima*]" (*QE* 5, 5.3.1.1: 21). This is important because it links the fallacies to the tropes of deception discussed in his natural philosophy, such as the sick person tasting something sweet as bitter, the appearance to someone on a moving boat that the trees on shore are moving, and the reddish appearance of the sun at dawn (*QM* II.1: 8ra–b; cf. *QDC* II.22: 227; *QDA₃* II.11). It is no accident that the two are related. Buridan himself points out that his definition of 'fallacy' gives 'deception' as its genus (*S* 7.1.7: 504).[10] In both cases, the seeker of knowledge must learn how to defeat the deception, or mere appearance of truth, by exposing its defects and learning how it is produced.[11] Indeed, as we shall see in chapters 12–13, Buridan's account of empirical knowledge involves a kind of dialectical conversation between the intellect and nature, with the soul's sensory powers serving as the medium. For in sense perception as well, there are 'fallacies' which can fool us into thinking that what is false is true, the causes of which Buridan investigates just as carefully as the *causae* of sophistical arguments. What is different is that nature, unlike the sophist, does not intend to deceive. If left undetected, the sophist's arguments can even infiltrate the classroom, where students unwary of their nature repeat them. This is why Buridan argues that actual experience is almost always better than teachers and books when it comes to learning the principles of nature, for "teachers are capable of saying what is false, and even textbooks may contain falsehoods [*doctores possunt falsa dicere et in libris etiam falsa scribi possunt*]" (*QM* I.8: 7va).[12]

Like Aristotle, and virtually every other medieval author, Buridan recognizes thirteen species of fallacies divided into two general modes, six occurring "in words [*in dictione*]," and seven occurring "apart from words [*extra dictionem*]" (*S* 7.2.1: 506).[13] A fallacy is said to occur in words "if its cause of appearance [*causa apparentiae*] pertains to the conventionally signifying words," and to occur apart from words "if its cause of appearance pertains to the signified thing or intention."[14] For example, 'Every dog is an animal; a constellation is a dog; therefore, a constellation is an animal [*omnis canis est animal; sidus est canis; ergo, sidus est animal*]', is a paralogism of the *in dictione* fallacy of equivocation (*S* 7.2.1: 506–508). The *causa apparentiae,* or what makes it look good, is the "the unity of the utterance" which is its middle term, i.e. 'dog [*canis*]'. The *causa defectus,* or reason why the syllogism is bad, is that the spoken term 'dog [*canis*]' corresponds to "a diversity of intentions in the major and minor [premises], insofar as they are true." Specifically, the first premise is true only if the utterance 'dog [*canis*]' is understood to signify dogs that are members of the species *canis familiaris,* whereas the second premise is true only if the same utterance 'dog [*canis*]' is understood to signify the constellation *Canis Major,* whose brightest object is Sirius, the Dog

Star. But "a true argumentation not only requires identity of utterance, but also identity of intention" (*S* 7.2.2: 509). Therefore, the paralogism is resolved through the distinction of its middle term, revealing that its premises have different meanings, and thus different truth-makers.[15] An example of a fallacy *extra dictionem* would be the paralogism, 'Every man is an animal; a donkey is an animal; therefore, a donkey is a man [*omnis homo est animal; asinus est animal; ergo asinus est homo*]', which, according to Buridan, commits the fallacy of accident (*S* 7.2.1: 508). In this example, both the spoken middle term 'animal [*animal*]' and the concept it signifies are the same, so it looks like a good syllogism as far as the utterance and signified intention are concerned. But its *causa defectus* is that it supposits or stands for different extramental things on each occasion of its use, so that the first premise is true of some animals (viz., the rational ones), whereas the second is true of others (viz., the non-rational ones). The distinction in truth-makers produces the fallacy, thus making it *extra dictionem*.

The distinction between fallacies *in dictione* and *extra dictionem* is not so easily drawn in practice, however. One might think fallacies *in dictione* are primarily linguistic because they focus on ambiguities in conventional utterances and expressions, whereas fallacies *extra dictionem* are primarily mental because their *causa apparentiae* involves either the speaker's intention, or the things signified by that intention. Furthermore, Buridan tells us that no *in dictione* fallacy ever occurs in the mind, because "we do not use mental terms by convention [*ad placitum*] as we do with utterances and written marks" (*S* 7.3.4: 522). But here as well, appearances can be deceiving. All fallacies depend upon conventional spoken language in the sense that they are argumentations, and "significative utterances have to be used in all argumentations" (*S* 7.2.1: 507).[16] What the sophist does is present significative utterances as apparent syllogisms in order to deceive his opponent (*S* 7.1.1: 496). The difference between fallacies *in dictione* and *extra dictionem* is thus the difference between whether a syllogism presents an argumentation because of the particular expressions used (in which case it is a fallacy 'in words'), or regardless of the particular expressions used (in which case it is 'apart from words') (*S* 7.2.1: 507–508).[17] The same distinction is used in the fifth treatise between material and formal consequences. Recall that a material consequence "does not hold for all like terms, even when the form remains constant," but is partly a function of the signification of its constituent terms, whereas a formal consequence holds in virtue of the logical form or syntax of the proposition, regardless of the signification of its constituent terms. Similarly, *in dictione* fallacies turn on ambiguities in the meanings of the utterances used, whereas *extra dictionem* fallacies present formally defective syllogisms, or paralogisms (*S* 7.4.1: 549).[18] The *extra dictionem* fallacy of *petitio principii*, for example, is said to occur when an argumentation contains a conclusion validly inferred from its premises which contradicts the opponent's position, but which fails to refute him because the argumentation is not demonstrative in form, which is to say that it fails to prove anything because its premises are not better known than its conclusion (*S* 7.2.5: 513). In this case, of course, one of the premises is identical to the conclusion and hence equally well known, thus begging the question.

But it does not follow from this that there could be a concept of validity, or contradiction, or proof apart from words, if by that we mean a purely mental concept. Buridan does, to be sure, inherit the traditional specification of Aristotle's category of fallacies *extra dictionem* as those which occur on the part of the intention or things signified,[19] as well as the even more standard assumption, derived from Aristotle via Boethius, that such "affections of the soul [*passiones animae*] are the same for all" (*S* 7.3.4: 522; cf. *QE* 8, 3.1: 34).[20] But it would be a mistake to think of Buridan as defending the existence of mental language as a fully functional mode of discourse, parallel to that of spoken or written languages. It might come as a surprise to modern readers that Buridan never uses the term 'mental language [*lingua mentalis*]', nor anywhere suggests that the affections of the soul constitute what he would call a language. Part of the reason for this is etymological, since the most plausible Latin cognates corresponding to the English term 'language' are all derived from words associated with the physical production of speech.[21] But this is only part of the reason. The main reason Buridan does not regard mental language as a possibility worth thinking about is that it would have made no sense to him. If the purpose of language is to communicate one's ideas or intentions to others,[22] then it would be absurd for a 'speaker' of mental language to try to communicate with himself, since he already knows his own intentions. Buridan prefers to speak of concepts as 'conceiving' their objects, rather than as 'signifying' them—though he occasionally uses the 'signifying' terminology as well. He appears to reject the idea of a naturally significant mental language.[23] If concepts have a semantic value, that must be determined by psychology, not logic.[24] Buridan sometimes appears to confuse the issue by speaking of mental terms, mental propositions, and even mental argumentation (*S* 7.2.2: 509), and by attributing conventional semantic properties to them—"the principal intentions of the soul are diverse, as also are their distributions and suppositions and appellations" (*S* 7.3.10: 547). But we should not lose sight of the fact that every single one of these modes of characterizing mental discourse has been borrowed from the analysis of conventional discourse, which, as we saw in chapter 1, traces its origins to twelfth-century disputes between grammarians and logicians. We should therefore resist the temptation to interpret fallacies *extra dictionem* as the error theory of mental discourse. When Buridan glosses "apart from words [*extra dictionem*]" as "without the consideration of significative utterances, having their appearance in the mind [*praeter vocis significativae considerationem habentes in mente suam apparentiam*]" (*S* 7.2.1: 507), he is not saying that fallacies *extra dictionem* actually occur apart from words, only that one can conceive of them apart from words. No opponent, no matter how skilled in the art of sophistry, can beg the question against a respondent *solo in mente,* without presenting some argumentation embodying that fallacy in a well-ordered sequence of significative utterances.

The same point about existing "apart from words" is made several times in Buridan's question commentary on the *Sophistical Refutations,* but always counterfactually. Fallacies *extra dictionem* are said to be "deceptions arising from the reasoning process which could occur even if there were no conventionally instituted signs; but this fact notwithstanding, they can also occur in conventionally instituted signs" (*QE* 5, 5.3.1.3: 21–22).[25] In actual practice, both types of fallacy are expressed in conventional discourse, and differ only in their degree of dependence on it. Fallacies *in dictione* arise from the matter of the utterance, i.e., from what is said. Fallacies *extra dictionem* arise from the form of the utterance, i.e., from how it is said. In response to a student query, Buridan considers the possibility of self-deception with regard to fallacies *in dictione:*

> But in connection with this you will ask: 'So can someone be deceived by fallacies based on words, if he is merely thinking by himself, and without uttering anything?'. And I say that indeed, he can, but this is not without the consideration of significative utterances. For I can consider utterances and a spoken paralogism without uttering anything, and think that it has the same middle term, and on the basis of this identity I may believe that it is a valid syllogism, and that the one corresponding to it in the mind is also valid. (*S* 7.2.1: 508)

The only way that the mind can commit fallacies *in dictione* is by appropriating actual *dictiones* from a spoken paralogism, and then rehearsing them silently as if saying them out loud. The *persona* of the sophist would then, it seems, emerge as a split personality. But the same remarks apply to fallacies *extra dictionem,* since it is not possible to beg the question or otherwise err in one's reasoning without setting out the steps of that process in language. The conventionality of even fallacies *extra dictionem* is brought out by Duns Scotus, who finds it utterly absurd to suppose that a syllogism could be formally flawed and yet not be resolvable by natural reason, "because the intellect, as included among those natural things, has produced every art that deals with apparent syllogisms."[26] Since fallacies have been created by us, it must be possible for us to resolve them.

In his discussion of the modes of the *in dictione* fallacies of equivocation and amphiboly, Buridan touches on the issue of the distinction of propositions. Now this is an issue that would otherwise pass without comment, except that it happened to be the target of the infamous 1340 condemnation of teaching practices in the faculty of arts at Paris. As we saw in chapter 1, this statute attacked excessive literalness in the interpretation of biblical and other authoritative texts. Since "the Bible and [other] authors do not always use words in their proper senses," the statute contends, a good reading must pay close attention to the discourse conditions of a text, and try to discern the author's intentions wherever possible. For this reason, "a disputation attending [only] to the properties of words, accepting no proposition except in its proper sense, is nothing but a sophistical disputation." In the seventh treatise of the *Summulae*, Buridan takes a position in favor of the distinction of propositions that seems very much in the spirit of the 1340 condemnation. First, he cautions his students against becoming "someone who denies the authority of the wise and most reliable authors [*auctoritatem sapientium et probatissimorum*] or who speaks against them," since this invites the opponent's charge of implausibility, a dialectical fault relating to an argument's appearance. A broader strategy of interpretation is called for, because "it is well known that not only poets but even the Bible, and all theologians, preachers, and philosophers often use figurative and parabolical expressions, not only according to their proper signification but even by attribution" (*S* 7.3.4: 520). The respondent should therefore defend himself against sophistical arguments arising from premises with ambiguous terms by distinguishing the senses in which they are true, rather than by rejecting as false any premise—including those adduced from authorities—with terms whose primary sense is figurative or parabolical.

In this claim, the editors of Buridan's commentary on Aristotle's *Sophistical Refutations* have found what appears to be a rare change-of-mind by Buridan, for in the *QE*, he defends the thesis that "no proposition is to be distinguished in its literal sense [*nulla propositio est distinguenda de proprietate sermonis*]":

> I say, then, that except as regards the paralogisms of the fallacy of equivocation, one must reply by absolutely conceding or absolutely denying one of the premises [of the proposed syllogism]. And from this it is shown that the [opponent's] reasoning is invalid. Nevertheless, as an additional exercise for teaching others, and for the sake of those who are listening attentively [to the disputation, i.e.,], so that they don't come away with the impression that the respondent has contradicted himself and responded badly, the respondent can draw a distinction in one of the premises and show its diverse senses, of which one is true and the other false, to those who might be unfamiliar with them—although one must not do this as regards its literal sense. And in this way, we can speak to the authoritative passage of Aristotle [i.e., in *Sophistical Refutations* 18.176b35–36], where it is said that there is one resolution [of paralogisms of this fallacy] by abolition, i.e., by simple negation, and another by drawing distinctions. (*QE* 7, 3.3.4: 30–31)[27]

Besides the aforementioned remark from the seventh treatise of the *Summu-lae*, the editors cite other passages in which Buridan holds that the reader must be open to other interpretations besides the literal one if error is to be avoided and "human communication" is to be preserved. The basic idea underlying Buridan's arguments is that "words have meaning only by imposition, and imposition can be known only from use [*sermones non habent virtutem nisi ex impositione et impositio non potest sciri ex usu*]" (*QM* IX.5: 58va; cf. *S* 4.3.2: 256).[28] The editors conclude that the *QE* must have been composed before the 1340 statute, since "it is rather improbable that Buridan would have defended the thesis that no proposition is to be distinguished or would have used wordings in which he presents that thesis [in the text of the *QE*] *after* the promulgation of the statute."[29]

This conclusion is surely correct, but for different reasons, in my view, since Buridan does not in fact defend the thesis that no proposition is to be distinguished in the *QE*. What he says is that "no proposition is to be distinguished *in its literal sense* [*de virtute sermonis*]" (*QE* 7, 3.3.1: 30; emphasis mine). But this is not what is being attacked in the 1340 statute. What Buridan is defending is the eminently plausible view that there can be no distinction in the literal meaning of a proposition; instead, it must be either conceded or rejected or doubted (where its truth or falsity is not known) *simpliciter*. It would make no sense to say that the same proposition could be both literally true and literally false, or that it could be conceded and rejected in distinct but equally literal interpretations of its significance. The context of Buridan's '*nulla propositio est distinguenda*' is in response to the argument that there is no fallacy of equivocation properly speaking because the term 'equivocation' is itself equivocal between terms and propositions, so that even the principle of non-contradiction is equivocal by virtue of containing the equivocal term 'being [*ens*]' (*QE* 7, 1.3: 28).[30] Buridan notes that some unnamed thinkers have wanted to reply on behalf of the opponent that the premises of such arguments can still be distinguished, thereby preserving "the paralogisms of this fallacy [of equivocation]." But he will have none of this. Where *principia* such as the principle of non-contradiction are concerned, "no proposition is to be distinguished," which is to say that as a *principium*, a proposition has only one sense, i.e., the literal one. The consequence of denying this would be the destruction of knowledge, since there would no longer be any criteria for assessing beliefs, which would be propositions asserting 'truths' rather than truth.[31]

If a proposition has several senses [*plures sensus*], and is said to signify them equally, whether conjunctively or disjunctively, then these plural senses are easily reducible to a single sense by means of the rules for analyzing categorical propositions with conjunctive or disjunctive subjects, and so there is no need for distinction (*QE* 7, 3.3.3: 31; cf. *S* 4.2.6: 248–50).[32] The *Summulae* presentation of the rules closes with the remark that "these are the major points which, nevertheless, some people call into doubt owing to their poor education in grammar or logic" (S 4.2.6: 250), which dovetails with the QE remark that although there are no distinctions in the literal sense of a proposition, the respondent can still show the different senses of a proposition "to those who might be unfamiliar with them [*ignorantibus*]." To return to an earlier example, the respondent should not merely say to novices that the proposition, 'God is the lion of Judah', is literally false, but try to find its proper sense, in keeping with the author's intention (S 4.3.2: 256). Distinction is a pedagogical device aimed at remedying the higher-level illiteracy of those who don't know how to read texts. Its function is more grammatical than logical, insofar as it opens up other avenues of interpretation to the un-tutored besides the strictly literal one that is of interest to the logician.[33] It is therefore appropriate that Buridan should regard "sufficient knowledge of the modes of signification in accordance with the rules of grammar," in addition to knowledge of the rules of logic, as relevant to the solution of sophistical arguments (S 7.6.4: 607).[34]

CHAPTER EIGHT

Demonstrations

·The treatise on demonstrations is the last systematic treatise of the *Summulae*. It is also the longest. In relation to the text as a whole, it can be seen as applying the techniques for analyzing terms and propositions laid out in the first four treatises to the "ultimate [*finalis*]" manifestation of syllogistic inference first sketched in the fifth treatise, but more properly presented in its dialectical and sophistical forms in the sixth and seventh treatises, respectively. The eighth treatise is also the culmination of Buridan's account of the psychology of inference, based on the capacity of arguments to cause beliefs. As we saw above, the effect of dialectical or topical arguments is to persuade those who hear them with probable appearances, whereas sophistical arguments deceive them with sophistical appearances (hence, the analysis of such arguments focuses on their '*causa apparentiae*'). But demonstrative arguments produce conviction in the minds of their hearers by evident appearances, and conviction is for Buridan a necessary condition of *scientia,* or knowledge. Demonstration thus serves to link Buridan's logic to his natural philosophy, his other great pursuit as an arts master, by offering a paradigm of reasoning for acquainting ourselves—empirical creatures that we are—with what is true in the natural world. Without it, logic is an idle wheel, its practice a pointless diversion. Understood in this way, demonstration is nothing less than the key to all other branches of learning outside the *trivium.*

Because it is without precedent in Peter of Spain's *Summulae,* the object-text for the commentary in the treatise on demonstrations has been constructed wholesale by Buridan. It is interesting to speculate why Buridan felt he had to include the eighth treatise in his *Summulae,* even to the point of writing the text he was commenting upon, rather than simply authoring an independent treatise on demonstrations, like his treatises on consequences or relations. The answer is surely that without it, he understood logic to be incomplete and, more importantly, as lacking any practical connection with other forms of philosophical inquiry. If dialectic is truly the "art of arts, having access to the principles of all other inquiries" (*S* 1.1.1: 4), as Peter of Spain put it, then it must show how its practice actually leads to those principles. This is the purpose of the eighth treatise. The lemma-and-commentary format is preserved perhaps as an aid to readers, who would have found it easier to reference a subdivided primary text, with explanatory remarks below each of the divisions. The eighth treatise is divided into three different "subject matters [*materiae*]" on the basis of logical priority, with two brief sections on divisions and definitions followed by a much longer, ten-chapter section on demonstrations.

1. DIVISIONS

The art of division properly underlies the art of constructing definitions, the source of those evident "principles [*principia*]" which are the currency of the knowledge-producing syllogisms of demonstrative science. By beginning the eighth treatise with divisions, Buridan recovers the lost art of Boethius's *De divisione,* a text which had once formed part of the *logica vetus* but which was no longer being read, along with other works of Boethius whose relation to the logical writings of Aristotle was not evident. This was an unfortunate development from Buridan's perspective, because Boethius so clearly brings out the practical relevance of division in his preface to the work:

> The book *On Division* published by Andronicus, a most diligent scholar of old, treats of the considerable advantages the science of dividing brings to scholars [*quam magnos studiosis afferat fructus scientia dividendi*] and of the high esteem in which this branch of knowledge was always held within the Peripatetic discipline. Plotinus, a most profound philosopher, thought highly of Andronicus' book and Porphyry adapted it in his commentary on Plato's dialogue entitled *The Sophist.* It was also Porphyry who acknowledged the utility of his *Introduction to the Categories* with reference to this science [*Isagoge* 1, 3–6 B]. For he says that a knowledge [*peritia*] of genus, species, difference, property, and accident is a necessary prerequisite to, among several other things, partitioning, which is of the greatest utility [*propter utilitatem quae est maxima partiendi*].[1]

Boethius mentions four general types of division: genus into species; whole into parts; utterance into significations; and subject into accidents. Buridan groups things differently, recognizing only "two principal senses in which we talk about whole and parts," viz., the integral and the predicable (*S* 8.1.4: 617–19). The difference between them is expressed in terms of the second, indicating that Buridan considers it to be the primary sense: an integral whole is not predicable of each of its parts (no part of a house—e.g., the roof, the walls, the door—is the house), whereas a predicable whole is predicable of each of its parts (for every individual man 'n'—e.g., Socrates, Plato, Robert— it is true to say, 'N is a man'). The metaphor for integral part/whole relations suggests physical division, such as a loaf of bread cut into slices (of no slice would it be true to say, 'This is a loaf of bread'). But not all integral wholes are extended and hence physically divisible, for Buridan views "the separation of the form of a composite thing from its matter," e.g., when an immaterial form is separated from its matter "in the case of the death of a man," as the division of an integral whole (*S* 8.1.5: 619). The reason becomes clear when we use the predicability test: of neither the man's soul nor the man's body alone is it true to say, 'This is a man'. Boethius's third and fourth types of division, i.e., of utterances into significations and of subjects into accidents, are subsumed by Buridan's predicable whole/part division, since a whole can be predicated of its parts either (1) equivocally (which, according to Buridan, yields Boethius's division of utterances into their significations), or (2) univocally, or (3) denominatively (which, according to Buridan, yields the different kinds of Boethian subject/accident division) (*S* 8.1.6: 620–23).[2] In this way, (1) an equivocal term, such as 'dog', is predicable of other terms expressing its diverse significations, such as 'barking animal', 'celestial constellation', and 'marine fish'; (2) a univocal term, such as 'animal', is predicable of terms expressing the species into which it is "primarily" divided, i.e., 'man' and 'brute', by means of its differences, i.e., 'rational' and 'non-rational'; and finally, (3) a denominative term, such as 'white' or 'odd', expresses a mode or accidental determination of the thing which is its subject, such as when we say, " 'Of horses, some are white horses, others are black horses, and the rest are colored by intermediate colors [*equorum, alii albi, alii nigri, alii coloribus mediis colorati*]' " (*S* 8.1.6: 622).[3]

The kind of division that is most relevant to definition, and hence, to the construction of demonstrative syllogisms, is predicable whole/part division as that applies to univocal terms. But Buridan thinks it important to begin the eighth treatise by sketching the logical space in which the activity of defining takes place. Dialectical and sophistical forms of argumentation also use division, but neither in a way that is comprehensive and free of ambiguity. But demonstrative argumentation, if it is to produce knowledge, must have both. The logical form of a "good division" is given in the very last section of Buridan's discussion: "every good division [*bona divisio*] should be given in terms of opposites, and it should be twofold or reducible to a twofold division. It has to be given in opposites in this way, for of either member of a good division the opposite of the other member should be truly predicated. And I talk about 'opposites' in the sense of the opposition of finite and infinite terms" (*S* 8.1.8: 629). This is a gesture toward the essential role played by the principle of non-contradiction in demonstrative syllogisms. According to the Aristotelian account, the mechanism of human knowing works by bifurcating reality into mutually exclusive possibilities, one of which must be true and the other false. There is no third alternative.

2. DEFINITIONS

Buridan clearly has this model in mind when he moves on to discuss definitions, and "the eight common properties belonging to everything defined [*definitum*] and also to every definition": the definition and *definitum* are predicated (1) correlatively, and (2) convertibly of each other; (3) the definition "explicitly" makes the *definitum* known; (4) the definition is a complex expression, whereas the *definitum* is incomplex, or at least less complex than its definition; (5) there is no definition of singular terms; (6) no proposition is a definition or *definitum;* (7) "no definition should be expressed parabolically or figuratively [*parabolice vel transsumptive*]"; (8) definitions should be neither redundant nor deficient (*S* 8.2, Introduction: 631). In connection with the third property, Buridan reiterates that the purpose of giving a definition is so that "one can explicitly know what it is that the *definitum* supposits for, or what thing or things the defined term signifies and what thing or things it connotes" (*S* 8.2.1: 632). We can think of definitions in this way as bridges from unarticulated terms and concepts to propositions, the bearers of truth and falsity in his account of human knowledge—hence the sixth property that the proper parts of a definition, viz., the *definitum* and the expression making it known (also confusingly referred to as its "definition [*diffinitio*]"), cannot be propositions. Demonstrations use the power of definitions to make things known and, together with the rules of syllogistic inference, to lead us to the knowledge of other truths. That is why no distinctions can be drawn in the literal sense of a proposition, as was argued in the commentary on *Sophistical Refutations*. Again, "a definition is sought only for the sake of the explicit manifestation of the *definitum;* therefore, it should not be obscure, but it should be as clear as possible" (*S* 8.2.1: 635).[4] Figurative or metaphorical expressions can be used to great effect in rhetoric and poetry, but the obscurity that makes them so effective in those contexts excludes them from the discourse of knowledge.

Buridan proceeds to identify four modes of definition: nominal, quidditative, causal, and descriptive (*S* 8.2.2: 635; cf. *QAnPo* II.8). A nominal definition (*diffinitio explicans quid nominis*),[5] as the term suggests, gives the meaning of a name, though Buridan is quick to point that by 'name' he does not mean "the part of speech that Donatus distinguishes from pronoun, verb, etc., but broadly . . . any significative utterance [*vox significativa*], whether complex or incomplex, that needs explicit analysis [*expositio*]" (*S* 8.2.3: 636). The grammarian analyzes terms differentially in terms of their syntactical features, but the logician tries to get beneath the surface syntax to explain "what thing or things the *definitum* signifies or connotes," a task that is "properly speaking called an 'interpretation [*interpretatio*]'."[6] What the logician does is reveal what concept a word has been imposed to signify.

This gives us the two main kinds of definition: if "a word is imposed to signify a simple, or incomplex, concept, then such a word is not interpretable," and it has a real definition. On the other hand, if a word has been imposed to signify one or more complex concepts, then it is interpretable, and thus it has a nominal definition. The examples Buridan gives of each kind of definition are instructive. Even terms imposed to signify simple concepts can be "explained [*notificatur*]" to someone who does not know them, he says, by means of a synonymous word, "as when a [French] child is taught Latin by means of the French language; sometimes it is taught by pointing at the thing signified, as when a mother teaches an infant her language, and sometimes it is taught by means of a description of the word, or by a quidditative definition" (*S* 8.2.3: 636). The language-teaching example, whose Augustinian allusions would not have been missed by medieval readers of the *Summulae,* shows how real definitions sidestep the discursive act of interpretation to get at 'what the thing is'. Sometimes this can be accomplished simply and directly, by means of a gesture, but often we need help in the form of "an expression indicating precisely what a thing is [*quid est esse rei*] by means of essential predicates," i.e., a quidditative definition (*S* 8.2.4: 638). Nominal definitions, however, involve complexity, and complexity must be interpreted:

> But if a word has been imposed to signify a complex concept consisting of several simple concepts, then it needs an interpretation by means of several words that signify separately the simple concepts that make up the complex one. This is how 'philosopher' is interpreted as 'lover of wisdom' (for '*philosophos*' in Greek comes from '*philos*', which is love, and from '*sophos*', which is 'wisdom', thus yielding, as it were, 'lover of wisdom'), and so the word 'philosopher' should signify to us nothing more or other than the expression 'lover of wisdom', and conversely. (*S* 8.2.3: 636)

It is important not to see this as a reductionist strategy for analyzing linguistic complexes into simple concepts and their real significates, the first step on the road to a logically perfect or ideal language. For Buridan, human language is irreducibly conventional. If the function of language is to communicate our concepts or intentions to others, then the names we have imposed to signify these concepts, and the nominal definitions we use to expound them, will be at least as important to the enterprise of human knowledge as gestures, linguistic and otherwise, indicating what something is. Real or quidditative definitions serve to ground our discourse inasmuch as they pre-suppose "the existence of the thing" (*S* 8.2.4: 641).[7] But nominal definitions locate a term relative to other terms inside the web of language, and permit us, by means of propositions and proofs, to order the whole into a science, or body of knowledge.[8]

In Buridanian semantics, the distinction between terms having nominal definitions and quidditative, or real, definitions comes down to their corre-spondence to complex and incomplex concepts, respectively:

> the quidditative definition should signify much more, or something other, than the *definitum*. And this derives from the other difference be-tween them, namely, that to the *definitum* of a nominal definition there should correspond a complex concept, whereas the species defined quid-ditatively has an incomplex concept; for it is not the species but the de-finition of the species that is composed of genus and difference, whether with respect to utterance or concept [*sive secundum vocem sive secundum conceptum*]. (*S* 8.2.4: 646–47; cf. *S* 4.2.4: 234–35; *QM* VII.5: 44va)

This is explained at the level of terms using the doctrine of connotation. A simple, non-connotative term—e.g., 'animal', which signifies animals via its corresponding non-complex concept primarily and nothing else secondarily—must have a quidditative definition and cannot have a nominal definition. A connotative term—e.g., 'white', which signifies white things primarily via its corresponding complex concept, and whiteness secondarily—must have a nominal definition and cannot have a quidditative definition.[9] Quidditative definitions are not to be thought of as eternal or ideal. Rather, we construct them through the dialectical process of adding essential difference(s) to the genus of the *definitum* until we have "an expression indicating precisely what a thing is by means of essential predicates."[10] Hence, such definitions "most properly, and truly" answer the question, 'What is it?' (*S* 8.2.4: 638). A simi-lar process is involved in the construction of nominal definitions, except that here our aim is to get clear about the meaning of a complex concept, rather than to fix the reference of a simple or incomplex term.[11] This makes the study of quidditative definitions secondary, a point Buridan drives home on the authority of the Philosopher himself: "For this is how Aristotle puts it, in bk. 2 of the *Posterior Analytics*: 'Once we know whether the thing is, we ask what it is' [II.1.89b34–35], and later he adds: 'To ask what it is, not knowing whether it is, is to ask nothing' [II.8.93a26–27]" (*S* 8.2.4: 641).

Buridan's use of the term 'essential predicates' in connection with quid-ditative definitions can obscure the fact that for him, the difference between nominal and quidditative definitions is formal, corresponding to different ways or modes we have of conceiving things, rather than to the difference be-tween our names for things and their essences in any hypostatized, realist sense. If there are real essences, Buridan does not think we have any epistemic access to them as such—at least not in this life.[12] When questioned about the source of "the concept by which we originally conceive a thing to be," he replies, "things are perceived and judged to exist in the way they are perceived as [existing] in the prospect of the person cognizing them" (*QM* IV.9: 19vb).[13] What this means is that our quidditative knowledge of things derives from the empirical moment of our first contact with them. The verb 'to be [*esse*]' in this context connotes presence, he says—not temporal or successive presence, but presence "just as you are present to me [*sicut tu esses praesens mihi*]." It is only when "we intellectually free the concept of a thing from the concept of this presence, and also from the concept of the relation of the thing to this presence, that we impose the names 'essence', 'man', 'stone', [etc.] for signifying things" (*QM* IV.9: 20ra).[14] So Buridan appeals to no essence in his account of quidditative definitions, if by that we mean the innate or illuminated knowledge of a thing's nature.

But what is there to guarantee that the name 'essence' has been correctly imposed to signify the nature of a thing? There is no guarantee in the Cartesian sense of being certified by reason alone. Such an assumption would have struck most medieval thinkers as bizarre in view of the fallen condition of mankind and the impoverished epistemic circumstances we find ourselves in as wayfarers. The situation is by no means hopeless, however. When faced with such questions, Buridan always regains his naturalistic outlook, in this case focusing on the ways in which human cognition can reliably produce simple substance concepts "without the consequence of one proposition to another," i.e., without inferring them from other concepts. The worry here is that the alternative view would give rise either to infinite regress, or to the implausible notion that substance concepts are derived from concepts of accidents. The latter alternative, of course, really would undermine the distinction between essence and accident, and with it, the whole Aristotelian concept of "definitions arising out of divisions" on which Buridan bases his account of demonstrations:[15]

> Again, since there is no procession to infinity in definitions, but it is necessary to reach indefinable terms, and these are, strictly speaking, definitions only of substance terms, as is stated in *Metaphysics* VII [5.1031a1–14], and substance terms are not defined by accident terms, as is stated in the same place [VII.6.1031b18–22], it follows that we must arrive at indefinable substance terms. But to such indefinable substance terms there correspond simple substance concepts. For if complex concepts composed of simples corresponded to them, they would be definable, and definitively resolvable by terms and into terms corresponding to the simple concepts from which those complex concepts were composed.

Again, if the substance concept of man were complex—let us assume that it would be made up of three simples, viz., A, B, and C—and if no substance concept were simple, then A would be merely the concept of an accident, and likewise B and C. Therefore, the whole complex composed from them would be only a concept of an accident and not a substance concept, since the whole is nothing over and above its parts. But this is absurd, viz., that the concept of man is only the concept of an accident. (*QP* I.4: 5rb)[16]

Buridan then describes four ways in which our intellects can become non-inferentially acquainted with things in the form of simple substance concepts (*QP* I.4: 5rb–va; cf. *QDA*₃ I.6: 129va–vb). These are all identified adverbially, as if to suggest that they are modes of a single cognitive power, rather than separate faculties offering us independent—and possibly conflicting—views of the external world. First, simple substance concepts can be produced "objectively [*obiective*]": just as a concept or "notion (*notitia*)" in one of the proper senses is objectively related to common sense, so sensory concepts are related to intellective concepts. The generation of substance concepts from sensory concepts replicates at a higher level the natural process by which the sensory part of the soul judges the information presented to it by the various sensory modalities to have come from the same object.[17] Second, we acquire simple substance concepts "evocatively [*evocative*]," in the way Avicenna characterizes the elicitation of an unsensed intention from a sensed intention. The usual example here is a sheep's sensing hostility in the presence of a wolf. And since we find a similar power even among inanimate things—e.g., fire, in generating heat, can also generate lightness and thinness (*levitas et raritas*)—it should hardly surprise us that from one concept, the soul is able to "generate another naturally consequent upon the first [*generare aliam naturaliter consequentem ad priorem*]."[18] Third, we can acquire simple substance concepts "abstractively [*abstractive*]." Starting from "a concept representing substance and accident at the same time confusedly [*conceptum confuse et simul repraesentatem substantiam et accidens*]," e.g., the concept of something white, we realize that a thing differs from its whiteness when we see it gradually changing color. This could only happen, Buridan says, if "the intellect naturally has the power to divide that confusion and to understand substance in abstraction from accident and accident in abstraction from substance . . . forming a simple concept of both" (*QP* I.4: 5va).[19] It is by this same process of abstraction that we form universal from singular concepts. Thus, my concept of a horse is not inferred from anything, but distilled from confused concepts of particular horses that have at various times wandered into my presence (*prospectus*). Fourth, and finally, Buridan argues that we can form a simple concept from two other simple concepts "by forming a proposition [*formando propositionem*]." Now this seems more controversial, since it is not at all obvious how a proposition can be a simple concept if it is made up of simple concepts. The example he gives is the formation of the propositions 'A is B' and 'A is not B' from the concepts 'A' and 'B', where these are distinct propositions expressing distinct simple concepts, and his argument is a straightforward *reductio:* if 'A is B' and 'A is not B' were complex, they would be resolvable into the same simple parts, viz., 'A' and 'B', and we would have no grounds for distinguishing them. But obviously, these are distinct propositions. Therefore, there must be some third thing which figures into the formation of their corresponding concepts, "and it must be that this third thing concurring is a simple concept, since it is not 'A', or 'B', or 'A and B' together, but another distinct thing which is the formal element of the mental proposition by whose distinction the affirmative and negative mental propositions are distinguished as regards the same subject and the same predicate."[20] This amounts to the claim that assertion and denial are mental acts whose corresponding concepts do not add anything to the complexity of the propositions with which they are associated, but which do suffice to make them distinct—and fundamentally so. For Buridan, such acts are part of our endowment as intellectual creatures. Assertion and denial arise naturally for us from propositions, "either effectively or through some other kind of causation, without the consequence of one proposition to another proposition or propositions," i.e., without our having to infer them from anything.

It is important to notice that none of these modes of cognition establishes the existence of the things signified by our simple substance concepts, though they all presuppose it. This is what makes them relevant to the formation of quidditative or real definitions. 'Existence [*esse*]' itself has no quidditative definition because it corresponds to a complex concept, connoting the presence of the things signified to the person cognizing them. It must therefore be demonstrated. The function of quidditative definitions in Buridan's philosophy is to fix the reference of non-complex terms naturalistically. We might think of them as gestures to the semi-fictional moment of a term's imposition, where, in the presence of the thing signified, the term is connected to the simple concept mediating that signification: "names are imposed to signify through the medium of our conceptions of things [*nomina imponuntur ad significandum mediantibus intellectionibus rerum*]" (QM IV.8: 19ra). Analysis of the act of cognition that produced that simple concept is then used to guide the division of its corresponding term from other terms via certain baseline essential predicates, the collection of which gives its convertible *definitum.* For example, the reference of the term 'man' is fixed by means of the generic and differential predicates 'rational' and 'animal', abstracted by my intellect from confused concepts of particular men appearing in my presence. The resulting definition lends a kind of stasis to the semantic value of non-connotative terms, because although the signification of utterances is a matter of convention, the signification of their corresponding concepts is, as Aristotle pointed out, natural and the same for all. This is not to say that the signification of a non-connotative concept is acquired once and for all. Experience teaches that our ideas of things, even our ideas of substances, evolve over time in the direction of greater sophistication as we learn more and more about the world around us. But it is to say that the evolution of non-connotative concepts occurs within certain parameters determined by our natural cognitive abilities on the one hand, and the range of our experiences—i.e., of what actually does appear in our prospect—on the other. In psychological terms, non-connotative concepts are the intellectual equivalent of the deliverances of sense concerning proper sensibles such as white or black, sweet or bitter, and so on. Such judgments are not infallible, but Buridan claims that they are, under the appropriate circumstances, "certain and without any defect [*certe et sine aliquo defectu*]" (QDA$_3$ II.11: 171). Just as the ability to perceive proper sensibles is only part of what it means to have the power of sense perception, so the ability to form non-connotative or simple concepts is only one aspect of human intellectual cognition. Needless to say, Buridan nowhere attempts to reduce sense perception to the perception of proper sensibles, or intellectual cognition to the grasping of simple, non-connotative concepts.[21] To do so would have constituted an overly zealous application of the razor, rendering inexplicable all of the more complex acts of perception and understanding, i.e., those involving inference.

But beyond saying precisely 'what a thing is', Buridan does not think that a term's quidditative or real definition tells us much about its significate. It is therefore of limited interest as far as the acquisition of knowledge, or *scientia*, is concerned. The bridge between logic and the natural sciences is built by the other three kinds of definition—nominal, causal, and descriptive—for they deal with semantically thicker complex concepts. The terms corresponding to complex concepts all contain some connotative or relational element connecting the term in question to other terms and their concepts, and it is this added element, gesturing not to a term's absolute significate but to its surrounding causal circumstances, that enables us to order our piecemeal awareness of particulars into a body of knowledge. Buridan makes this point from a pragmatic perspective, looking not just at the kinds of definition, but at the use made of them by the different masters in the arts faculty. Thus, he says, when "the natural scientist conceives of man, or plant, or water, this is not according to an absolutely quidditative concept, but in relation to its movements and operations" (QP I.3: 4ra).[22] The proper subject of natural philosophy is intelligible, imaginable, or sensory being conceived in relation to motion and sensible matter. Quidditative concepts are what the metaphysician uses,[23] since "the first and most common substantial or non-connotative term is assumed to be the proper subject in metaphysics, e.g., the terms 'being [ens]', or 'thing [res]', or 'something [aliquid]'" (QP I.3: 4ra).[24] The science of metaphysics will accordingly be restricted in Buridan's view to the disclosure and ordination of substance concepts, either in themselves or as the proper subjects of other disciplines—lest the metaphysician illicitly cross into the domain of natural philosophy. The definitions used by the logician are different again. As might be expected of a practitioner of the science of language (scientia sermocinalis), "the logician [logicus] assumes that the question 'What is it?' concerns some definable term, and asks about its definition . . . just as Porphyry held that species is composed of genus and difference" (QM VII.21: 54vb).[25] The logician provides the dialectical starting-point for every inquiry by making its terms explicit (S 8.2.4: 642).[26]

But demonstration is not merely a form of dialectical argument:

> definition by genus and difference is usually called 'formal definition' by the logician because genus and difference are customarily referred to as 'forms'. And regarding formal definition, Aristotle states in the prologue to De Anima [I.1.403a2] that all such definitions are dialectical and useless [vane] for demonstrating, because they fail to manifest the causes of a thing and their accidents, but only state the nominal definition. Now the philosopher has no intention of stopping at this kind of statement of the nominal definition, but assumes it either from the grammarian or the logician, and then aims to discover what the thing is that is signified by such a term. (QM VII.21: 54vb)[27]

The problem with purely dialectical demonstrations is that they are limited to the realm of spoken discourse, generating no conclusions that could be applied to intelligible, imaginable, or sensible being. Thus, says Buridan, if we immediately cognize a man and believe that man is a simple thing because of the way we cognize him, and we have a name signifying him from the grammarian, and also a nominal definition, "we would no longer ask what thing is a man [non amplius quaereremus quae res sit homo]." But a moment's reflection should indicate that our cognitions are almost never that simple:

> That is why the philosopher, who seeks not the nominal but the real definition, does not ask only about the absolutely quidditative definition which is by genus and difference, because that is only to give the meaning of the name. For this reason, if I know what is mortal, rational, and animal, I do not thereby have distinct knowledge of what thing that mortal rational animal is, viz., of whether it is one simple thing or a composite, and, if it is composite, from what and how many parts it is composed. Therefore, the philosopher goes beyond this to seek the causal

definition, primarily with respect to its intrinsic causes, because the thing we are asking about is [the same as] its intrinsic causes in the way that a whole is [the same as] its parts. (*QM* VII.21: 54vb–55ra)[28]

It is noteworthy that Buridan's charge here is addressed not to the grammarian or the logician or the metaphysician or the natural scientist, but to the philosopher. The philosopher is someone who seeks speculative knowledge of metaphysics, mathematics, and natural philosophy by means of the liberal arts, but especially by means of the trivial arts of grammar and logic. As far as the philosopher is concerned, nominal and absolutely quidditative definitions are both deficient because they give only "the meaning of the name," the former in terms explicating its corresponding complex concept, and the latter in terms of the reference-fixing predicates of its *definitum*. Knowledge of this sort is still merely verbal, or conceptual, containing no indications of how we might descend to the qualities that make a thing what it is. What is needed is a definition capable of situating a term not merely externally—vis-à-vis other terms which give its "interpretation" or "exposition" (*S* 8.2.3: 636), or, if it cannot be interpreted, essential predicates which "signify many more things than the *definitum* does" (*S* 8.2.4: 639)—but internally, in relation to its constitution as a determinate mode of being. This knowledge is provided in the first instance by the causal definition, and secondarily by the description.

Causal definitions are built upon quidditative definitions in the sense that they indicate "what the thing is [*quid est esse rei*, the quiddity or essence of the thing]" (*S* 8.2.5: 655). But they also indicate "the reason why [*propter quid*] it is" via terms that would, were they taken in the nominative case, supposit for the cause or causes of the thing for which the defined term supposits. Such causes may occur in any of the four Aristotelian genera of causes: formal, material, efficient, and final. Thus, 'A man is an animal having a rational soul [*homo est animal habens animam rationalem*]' is a definition giving the formal cause or reason for man in terms of his possession of a rational soul, whereas 'Sleeping is the rest of the external senses for the sake of the well-being of the animal [*somnus est requies sensuum exteriorem propter salutem animalis*]' gives the final cause or reason for sleep in terms of the health of the animal—as opposed, say, to prayerful meditation, which also involves resting the senses. Buridan insists on placing the causal term in an oblique case as a formal marker of the fact that it does not supposit for the same thing as the term defined. The reason is fairly simple: "the same thing is not a cause of itself" (*S* 8.2.5: 657). He also emphasizes the epistemic role played by causal definitions as middle terms in *propter quid* or explanatory demonstrations, a role they fulfill because they demonstrate "that the description applies to what is described and that the attribute applies to the subject" (*S* 8.2.5: 658).[29] Their importance to the philosopher, or seeker of speculative knowledge, emerges when Buridan approvingly quotes Aristotle's remark that "accidents are very useful in the cognition of quiddity [*accidentia magnam partem conferunt ad cognoscendum quod quid est*]."[30] Of course, the words 'are very useful', or, more literally, 'play a large part', seriously understate the case. Accidents are in fact essential to the process by which we, as empirical creatures, come to cognize the quiddity of a thing. For Buridan, it is not at all surprising in view of the material constitution of our sensory and imaginative powers that "substantial terms in the category of substance are not altogether free from the connotation of accidents, [so that] at least in the act of imposing a term, we must consider accidents" (*QM* VII.17: 52vb).[31] So even if we are able to free a term from its accidents and provide it with a quidditative definition, it remains true that "we are led to the knowledge of substance through these accidents."

Buridan recognizes a fourth and final category of definition, which differs from the causal definition only insofar as the accidents or effects it concerns are not tightly enough bound to their subject to produce any explanatory or *propter quid* demonstration of it. They do suffice, however, for the weaker kind of factual or *quia* demonstration, i.e., of the fact that the subject exists, or exists in a certain way. Buridan expresses this in terms of epistemic priority. Generally speaking, descriptions operate by taking attributes that are better known to us and applying them to a subject whose precise nature is less known to us—though not absolutely, of course, since attributes are metaphysically posterior to their subjects, and would not be known first under ideal epistemic circumstances. In a memorable passage, Buridan reminds us that none of us is so situated. Thus, descriptions are like definitions in that "every definition is given for the sake of making the *definitum* known, and not for the sake of making it known to God, angels, or inanimate natures but to us, and it would not make it known unless it were itself better known to us" (*S* 8.2.6: 660). Definitions and descriptions would be pointless for God and angels because they have an immediate, non-discursive grasp of the essences of things and of every one of their related attributes. We, however, must 'bootstrap' our way to the knowledge of substances through naturally generated concepts of their accidents and effects. An example of description is, 'Fire is the lightest element'. According to Buridan, the descriptive predicate, 'lightest element', cannot be essential to fire, because it is possible for me to believe that some element is the lightest, but not fire, e.g., if I believe that a vacuum is lighter than fire. "But after I find out that there is no vacuum," and that "no other element is . . . lighter than fire, then I conclude that this is the description of fire, namely, that . . . 'Fire is the lightest element'" (*S* 8.2.6: 662). That fire is the lightest element is a contingent fact I discover upon learning another contingent fact, viz., there are no vacua in nature—though God could of course create one if God wished.[32] By contrast, in the causal definition of 'man', the attribute 'an animal having a rational soul' is essentially connected to the subject as its formal reason or cause, since it is not possible for there to be a man who does not have a rational soul.

3. DEMONSTRATIONS

In the final part of the eighth treatise, Buridan considers demonstrations themselves. The *Summulae* begins with a threefold division of the practice of logic: a dialectical part, which teaches the art of investigation, a doctrine of logical fallacies, which "eliminates false arguments," and a demonstrative part, which "regulates true reasonings" (*S* Preface: 3). It is by virtue of its regulative function that demonstration completes logic as a practical science. Instead of being directed to the discovery of arguments to support our opinions, or the development of a capacity to defend ourselves against fallacious and deceitful arguments, the formal machinery of inference is directed upwards, to the pursuit and proper ordination of truth. Demonstration quite literally becomes a guidebook, showing us the way from appearance to knowledge, given that "we want to find knowledge of a true proposition" (*S* 8.3.2: 666). And since, as we have just seen, the knowledge in question is our knowledge and not divine or angelic knowledge, a significant part of the story concerns the question of how it is generated, which for Buridan is to treat it as the natural effect of certain causal processes.

In the remainder of this section, however, I will focus on Buridan's remarks about the regulative function of demonstration, rather than on his account of how knowledge is produced. His eighth-treatise remarks about the latter are of a piece with certain discussions in his natural philosophy, which will be considered in chapters 12–13 below. Buridan himself practices this kind of scholarly division of labor. For example, in connection with four arguments on the question of whether we know the premises of an argument prior to its conclusion, he says, "we should only lightly touch on these arguments, for they do not belong to logic, except for the fourth" (*S* 8.3.7: 689). Although it is possible to reach every other art and science through dialectic, the wise arts master respects the boundaries between the disciplines and sub-disciplines of his faculty. To do otherwise would be to ignore the natural ordination of human knowledge, inviting a Babel-like confusion of its many discourses.

The difference between the dialectician and the demonstrator comes down to how they ask their questions: "the dialectician asks his questions in the form of a disjunction of both sides of a contradiction, giving the choice to the respondent. . . . But the demonstrator propounds assertively the proposition to be proved, and then it is a question, for it is a dubitable proposition, but the same [proposition] after the demonstration is the conclusion" (*S* 8.3.2: 666–67). Since demonstration is aimed at removing any doubts about a proposition from the minds of those considering it, there can be no options for the respondent, no alternative ways for the dialectic to unfold. The movement is always from a question or "dubitable proposition that is turned by a demonstration into a certain and known conclusion" (*S* 8.3.3: 670−71).[33] The demonstrator must therefore assert the proposition in question. The vehicle through which the movement takes place is the syllogism,[34] which is a "hypothetical proposition" (*S* 8.3.4: 674). Buridan reinforces this point by referring the reader back to the fifth treatise, where the syllogism was defined as 'a consequence that asserts the consequent and the antecedent' (*S* 5.1.3: 308). He also cites favorably Aristotle's view that the number of conclusions we can know is directly proportional to the number of demonstrable questions we can ask: "every demonstrable question can become a known conclusion and every known or knowable conclusion can be a demonstrable question to someone who does not yet know it" (*S* 8.3.2: 670). This is not a trivial truth, but an indication of how important it is to ask the right question if demonstration is to succeed in removing doubt.[35]

The account of demonstration given by Aristotle in the *Posterior Analytics* is riddled with obscurities that cannot be sorted out on any cursory reading of the text.[36] And medieval commentators were as perplexed as modern ones when it comes to stating just what Aristotle's concept is and what role it is supposed to play in his logic. Buridan warns readers of the corresponding sections of his *Summulae* that they are about to encounter a subject that is "obscure and very difficult" (*S* 8.3.3: 670), and elsewhere makes no secret of who he thinks is to blame for this: "Aristotle makes this great process [of scientific reasoning] more difficult [*Aristotiles faciat istum magnum processum multum difficile*]" (*QAnPo* II.4). Much of the trouble stems from Aristotle's belief that the basic definitions of substances in terms of genus and species, which are not themselves demonstrable, must somehow be related to demonstrations as the starting-points of scientific inquiry. The demonstrator's task, however, is not to analyze essential connections, but to synthesize the appropriate "middle [*medium*]," or minor premise, which will syllogistically connect what we already know with whatever question we want answered.[37] Demonstration is thus concerned with complexes.

To this end, the first chapter of *Posterior Analytics* II posits four kinds of question, corresponding to the four different kinds of things we can know about a subject, viz.: 'if it is', 'what it is', 'how it is', and 'why it is'. The discussion which follows has a strongly dialectical flavor, as Aristotle moves back and forth between basic definitions and explanations of more complex phenomena such as thunder, eclipses, and the Persian War, without ever producing a single perfect example of a demonstration.[38] In any case, for reasons barely discernible in the text, it emerges that only the third and fourth questions, i.e., the 'how it is' and the 'why it is', are strictly relevant to demonstration. Buridan devotes the majority of his discussion to these latter two, known in their medieval terminology as, respectively, '*demonstratio quia*', or 'demonstration of the fact [that something is the way it is]', and '*demonstratio propter quid*', or 'demonstration of the reason why [something is the way it is]', also known as 'explanatory demonstration'.

As far as Buridan is concerned, Aristotle's difficulties need not detain students who wish to learn the art of demonstration, for there is a simple reason why demonstrations can be only *quia* or *propter quid*. It is that the first two questions involve 'second adjacent [*secundo adiacens*]' or two-piece predications of the word 'is', and hence do not have enough logical parts for the construction of a demonstrative syllogism (*QAnPo* II.2). Syllogisms must have three terms: major, minor, and middle. But answers to the questions 'if it is' and 'what it is' will come in the form of terms corresponding to noncomplex concepts about either the subject's absolute being or the essential predicates of its quidditative definition: "By 'being absolutely [*esse simpliciter*]', I mean 'being as an absolute predicate [*esse secundo adiacens*]' "; on the other hand, the third and fourth questions, the 'how it is' and 'why it is', involve 'third adjacent [*tertio adiacens*]' or three-piece predications of the word 'is' together with some attribute, which can then serve as the middle term of a demonstration: "by 'being with qualification [*esse secundum quid*]' I mean 'being as a copula [*esse tertio adiacens*]' " (*S* 8.3.3: 672).[39] Thus, if we want to know whether it is true that all dogs have incisors, we can demonstrate this as the conclusion of an A-form syllogism by means of the attribute of being carnivorous, as follows: 'Having incisors belongs necessarily to all carnivores; being carnivorous belongs necessarily to all dogs; therefore, having incisors belongs necessarily to all dogs'.[40]

Demonstrations and definitions are both sources of knowledge for Buridan, though their objects are qualitatively distinct:

the conclusion of a demonstration is not known by its proper demonstration, nor is the term of a definition known by its definition, but rather, a thing is known demonstratively to be related to [its attribute] just as the conclusion signifies it to be, and it is known through a definition what thing it is that is signified by the term of the definition. And if we put the matter in this way, two conclusions should be proposed. The first is that the same thing is known definitively and demonstratively. The second is that the same thing is known definitively and demonstratively, but not in the same sense. For it is known demonstratively in the sense of its [corresponding] complex [concept or proposition], affirming or denying one term as regards another, and this is what we mean when we say that a conclusion is demonstratively known. But a thing is known definitively in the sense of its incomplex [concept], and this is what we are referring to when we say that something definable is known definitively. (*QAnPo* II.4)[41]

Complexity is what makes our knowledge of a thing amenable to syllogistic proof, a formal gesture that builds out from the subject either by demonstrating the fact that other things are naturally related to it, or by showing how these relationships account for its being the way it is. Simplicity, by contrast, is inward looking. As we saw above, it reveals its subject by means of a quidditative definition that serves not so much to expand our knowledge as to fix the reference of its corresponding subject term. It appeals to absolute being, but in an indemonstrable sense, derived from the absolute appearance of that thing in our prospect, "just as you are present to me [*sicut tu esses praesens mihi*]" (QM IV.9: 19vb). Definition is accordingly a necessary, but not a sufficient, condition for demonstration.

But lacking demonstrable parts, the quidditative definition is not designed for use in demonstrative syllogisms. In its place, Buridan recommends its close relative, the causal definition:

> in this broad manner of speaking, we call a 'definition saying what a thing is' not only a purely quidditative definition, but also a causal definition. And every cause that is sought in a demonstration *propter quid* can and should belong to the causal definition of the thing concerned in the question; and this causal definition is the appropriate middle in a demonstration *propter quid*. (S 8.3.3: 672–73)

Buridan's liberal attitude toward the use of causal definitions in scientific or knowledge-producing demonstrations represents a significant departure from the Aristotelian tradition.[42] What it does is open up the possibility of demonstrative discourse in natural sciences such as physics and psychology, which trade in nominal definitions and other kinds of descriptive phrases that suffice to identify their subjects, but fall short of being absolutely quidditative. "No science except metaphysics has to consider the quiddity of a thing absolutely," he tells us; "likewise, the natural scientist does not have to know absolutely what a man is or what a donkey is, although he can describe such things through some of their movements or operations" (QM I.3: 4vb).[43] The purpose of such descriptions and non-quidditative definitions is that they enable us to reach, via inferential rules, conclusions with terms whose significates are the proper and ultimate objects of knowledge in the natural sciences. By contrast, a strictly demonstrative proof gives knowledge only of the conclusion of the demonstration, which is to say that it gives knowledge only of a proposition (QM VI.3: 34va). This purely formal aspect of Aristotelian demonstrative science is assigned by Buridan to metaphysics, in which demonstration functions as a highly circumscribed mode of a priori reasoning about propositions taken to express the quiddities, or essential natures, of things.[44] But logic is not merely some self-contained, sterile activity in which we draw lines of symmetry between things we already know.

What Aristotle missed in the *Posterior Analytics* was that demonstration has
the practical application in natural philosophy of producing knowledge.
Buridan expands the scope of demonstrative science by weakening the formal criteria of demonstrative proof to include causal definitions, thereby
making possible the scientific investigation of how things change, beyond
what is true of their static essential natures.[45]

There is some evidence that Buridan discovered this practical side of
demonstration during the mid-point of his career at Paris. As Gyula Klima
has shown, Buridan's remarks about the definition of the soul in the first version of his question commentary on Aristotle's *De Anima* are inconsistent
with the concept of definition sketched in the eighth treatise of the *Summulae*.[46] In the former work, he claims, "there is one definition of the soul expressing its nominal essence [*exprimens quid nominis*], another expressing
its real essence [*quid rei*]" (*QDA₁* II.3: 242). The nominal definition of the
soul is provided by Aristotle in *De Anima* II.2, where he says that "the soul is
that by which we live, sense, are moved from place to place, and understand
[*anima est quo vivimus, sentimus, et secundum locum movemur et intelligimus*]" (414a12), whereas the real definition of the soul is found in *De Anima*
II.1: "the soul is the first, substantial, act of a physical, organic, body having
life potentially [*anima est actus primus substantialis corporis physici organici
vitam habentis in potentia*]" (412a20; 412a27). "Accordingly," Buridan adds,
this second definition "expresses not only the nominal essence, but also the
real essence, and not only the real essence, but also the explanatory cause
[*propter quid*]." Now in the *Summulae*, these definitions are said to be demonstratively related, for "the second is demonstrated by means of the first thus:
every principal intrinsic principle of living, sensing, and understanding is the
first substantial act of an organic, physical body potentially having life; and
every soul is such a principle; therefore, [every soul is the first substantial act
of an organic physical body potentially having life]" (*S* 8.2.7: 663). But the
Summulae stops short of characterizing the first as the nominal and the second as the real definition of the soul, classifying them instead as "complex."
This is a good thing, because the demonstration would fail if it did, because
the first, nominal, definition connotes the soul's operations, which are not mentioned in the second, whereas the nominal aspect of the second definition
connotes the subject of the soul, which is not mentioned in the first; but in a
proper demonstration, the term standing for the *definitum* must signify the
same concept each time it is used, and 'soul', by virtue of its different definitions, or, more precisely, by virtue of the different concepts (complex and
non-complex) signified by the predicate in each of its definitions,[47] does not;
therefore, there can be no demonstration of the real definition of the soul
from its nominal definition.[48] We can demonstrate a variety of things about
the soul, but its real definition, that essential predication expressing the "what
it is [*quod quid est*]" of the soul, is not one of them.

The third and final version of Buridan's commentary on Aristotle's *De Anima* brings the definition of the soul more into line with what is demonstrable according to the teaching of the *Summulae*. In this work, the two definitions of QDA_1 have become three, with the causal definition, now understood in distinction from the real definition, playing the leading role: "there is a certain definition of the soul stating its nominal essence, another purely quidditative definition, and another causal definition, explicating not only what the thing is but also that on account of which it is" (*QDA₃*, II.3: 35).[49] Note that the causal definition also "explicates [*explicans*]" its associated concept, rather than merely "stating [*dicens*]" it, or "expressing [*exprimens*]" it, which is what it did when it was bundled together with the real definition in *QDA₁*. The best explanation for this change, according to Gyula Klima, is that "in the problematic formulations of the *prima lectura* [i.e., *QDA₁*] Buridan simply followed an older line of interpretation, which he later abandoned upon realizing its conflict with his 'official theory' of definitions" in the eighth treatise of the *Summulae*.[50] The older interpretation is that of Thomas Aquinas, who is not committed to the view that the subject and predicate of a nominal definition must signify the same complex concept. "On the contrary," as Klima puts it, "in his conception we can obtain nominal definitions of terms subordinated to simple concepts by any sorts of indications somehow specifying what is meant by the corresponding term."[51] For Thomas, the different definitions of a subject become different ways of grasping the same simple nature, indirectly and by means of its effects in the case of its nominal definition(s), directly and by means of its categorial ordination in the case of its real definition. But Buridan's views on the primary and secondary signification of terms commit him to holding that the nominal definition of a term provides a description or analysis of its corresponding complex concept, whereas the real or quidditative definition of a term fixes the reference of its corresponding non-complex—and hence unanalyzable— concept by means of essential predicates.[52] This was to profoundly affect Buridan's conception of the proper method of inquiry in natural sciences such as psychology, as we shall see in chapter 13 below.

The other way in which Buridan opens up the possibility of demonstrative argumentation in disciplines other than metaphysics is to accept that there are many—indeed, infinitely many—principles capable of serving as the basis for demonstrations (*S* 8.5.2: 712).[53] He establishes this first in mathematics, where the infinity of "first principles" follows from the infinity of demonstrable conclusions. In geometry, for example, we need only reflect on "the infinity of figures":

> For just as a triangle has a proper attribute that can be demonstrated of it, namely 'having three angles equal to two right angles', so also does a quadrangle, namely 'having four angles equal to four right ones', and so

? not True

does a pentagon, namely 'having five angles equal to five right ones'; and so on to infinity. Therefore, there is an infinity of demonstrable conclusions in geometry. And I say, "there is an infinity," that is, there *can* be an infinity, so we need not be concerned about this [i.e., the possibility of actual infinities] in this context. And the same goes for the principles. And so it is as well in arithmetic, because of the infinity of the species of numbers.[54] (*S* 8.5.2: 716)

Likewise, it is possible to construct demonstrations in natural science by means of innumerable principles which are contingent in the sense that the intellect assents to them not immediately, through its simple apprehension of the nominal definitions of the terms involved, but mediately, through "its natural inclination to the truth [*ex naturali inclinatione eius ad veritatem*]" (*QAnPo* II.11; cf. *QAnPr* II.20).[55] Buridan therefore divides indemonstrable ✓ principles into two types. Principles of the first type arise from "concepts whose terms either manifestly include or manifestly exclude each other, once the nominal definition is known," as in the propositions, 'Man is an animal', 'Whiteness is a color', 'Nothing rational is irrational', all of which command the intellect's immediate assent. But principles of the second type, "although indemonstrable, first need the judgment of sense, memory, and experience." Thus, although the intellect is naturally inclined to assent to the principle, 'Every fire is hot [*Omnis ignis est calidus*]', it can do so only after it has been primed by the relevant experiences, and in the absence of any counterinstances.[56] That empirical cognition is a necessary condition for the generation of such principles is taken to be a simple fact of our wayfarer existence: "the intellect needs the assistance of the senses for forming the evident cognition of these principles, for all our intellectual cognition in this life depends on previous sensory cognition" (*S* 8.5.4: 721). The process by which this occurs will be discussed in more detail in chapter 12. As far as Buridan's logic is concerned, the important thing to notice is that his willingness to accept such propositions as principles of demonstrative proof opens up the whole of natural philosophy to the explanatory power of demonstration. This does not mean that we should read his commentaries on Aristotle's *Physics*, *De Anima*, and *Parva Naturalia*, for example, as part of a deliberate effort to reconceive Aristotelian natural philosophy along the lines of a strictly demonstrative science. We do not often find Buridan characterizing what he does in these commentaries as providing demonstrations.[57] The reason for this has to do with the different levels of discourse in his philosophy, an artifact of the traditional division of the sciences in the arts faculty. It would have struck a dissonant note to draw attention to the logical structure of an argument in the course of defending a thesis about the operations of the senses or the movement of the heavens, because the formal aspect of argumentation is the business of the logician, not the natural scientist. But it does mean that

not new ?

argumentation in the natural sciences will be assimilated wherever possible to the patterns of proof outlined in the eighth treatise of the *Summulae.*

This assimilation is expressed in terms appropriate to natural philosophy. What we find in Buridan is a sustained interest in the epistemic dimensions of argumentation, and specifically in the capacity of arguments to remove doubts in the minds of his readers or listeners. For example, on the question of whether the intellect must be free from any admixture that might hinder its capacity to be a perfect receptacle of forms, Buridan remarks that we cannot prove this by analogy to sense perception, as Aristotle and Averroes appear to do,[58] because these powers differ radically in terms of their dependence on material organs. For this reason, he observes, "although the argument or deduction [of such analogies] is apparent, it is not demonstrative [*quamvis haec ratio sive deductio sit apparens, tamen non est demonstrativa*]" (*QDA₃* III.2: 16). 'Apparent [*apparentia*]' is of course an epistemic term.[59] Arguments that are apparent 'look good' to the intellect, presenting 'the appearance of truth', or, to use a more familiar metaphor, 'the ring of truth'. Buridan concludes by noting that although the authoritative positions of Aristotle and Averroes on this question (with which he agrees) "have not been properly supported by demonstrative arguments, they could still be supported by probable arguments" (*QDA₃* III.2: 17)[60]—arguments which he proceeds to give in the subsequent questions. Now a probable argument is one that is readily believable, i.e., an argument whose premises, while falling short of certainty, are still such as to dispose most everyone who understands them to assent to its conclusion.[61] But, as we saw above, a probable argument is employed dialectically to persuade an audience to assent to its conclusion through its premises, which are the cause of the conclusion's 'looking good' (*causa apparentiae*), just as a sophistical argument is employed deceptively to the same end, although it suffers from a hidden defect (*causa defectus*), which the respondent aims to reveal. What, then, is the distinction between demonstrative and merely persuasive argumentation? Demonstrative proof is available in natural philosophy when the premises of an argument are such as to make their conclusion so apparent that we assent to it without any fear of the conclusion's being false. Buridan expresses this idea in terms of his concept of evidentness (*evidentia*), whose three modes are keyed to the two types of indemonstrable principles mentioned above, along with a third, weaker mode said to suffice "for acting morally well [*ad bene agendum moraliter*]" (*QM* II.1: 9ra). The extension of demonstration beyond metaphysics is achieved via his recognition of the second mode. This is the mode of relative evidentness (*evidentia secundum quid*), or evidentness on the assumption (*evidentia ex suppositione*), where a principle is said to command our assent indirectly, through the mediation of sense, memory, and experience, but—and here is the distinction between scientific proof and mere persuasion—without our needing to be further convinced of its truth by means of dialectical arguments.

The intermediate status of scientific proofs can be traced to how we know the indemonstrable principles from which they are derived. For example, in connection with the "common principle" that "every piece of red, burning, glowing coal is hot," Buridan remarks:

> one may doubt whether such an example or induction should be called a dialectical argument or a demonstrative argument. And I reply that it is not demonstrative, for it is not a syllogism, absolutely speaking. But neither should it strictly speaking be called dialectical, for dialectic does not produce certain and evident knowledge [*scientiam certam et evidentem*]. Rather, it is an argument producing the knowledge not of the conclusion of a demonstration but of a principle. Therefore, it exceeds the nature of dialectical argument, for it produces not opinion but evident and certain knowledge; and it falls short of a demonstrative argument, for it does not conclude necessarily and on account of its form, and thus it is not able of itself to direct the intellect to this knowledge [*non est potens ex se determinare intellectum ad illam scientiam*]. (*S* 8.5.4: 724; cf. *S* 8.12.2: 810)

What else is needed? Unlike the principle of non-contradiction, where we can say that the intellect's assent coincides with its act of understanding, a general principle in natural science must be made evident to us by the relevant particulars being placed in front of us, in the prospect of our senses.[62] This can occur directly, by experience, or indirectly, through the instruction of books and masters, whose *scientia* is based on singular concepts. Both options are left open in the following example:

> Many can doubt, although they know that the sun heats, that it generates fire by its light, for they did not see this, nor do they imagine how it would come about. And then this will be demonstrated and it will become known to them thus: 'Everything that burns and inflames something combustible and flammable can produce fire; but the sun burns and inflames something combustible; therefore, the sun can produce fire'. The premises are evident from [experience with] concave mirrors [*evidentes ad sensum ex speculo concavo*], and the consequence is evident. Therefore, this syllogism produces knowledge of the conclusion, and is a demonstration, even if the conclusion is necessary and the minor is contingent. (*S* 8.7.7: 748)

Of course, "if such examples or inductions were not sufficiently multiplied in several singulars, then the intellect would not rise up from this to assent [*consurgit ad assentiendum*] to the principle with certainty and evidentness, but rather with trepidation [*cum formidine*]" (*S* 8.5.4: 724). Again, the 'fear' in question is that the proposition to which we are assenting might be false.

Nature is the best teacher of principles, as it is with glowing coals and other things that are hot, because it is the best at dispelling fears that the contrary might be true.[63] But in the case of more complex principles, a good teacher is just as often someone who can assemble the relevant particulars quickly and easily, so that the student's mind is lifted from understanding to assent, without any residual doubt. It is the latter role that Buridan seeks to fulfill in his natural philosophy.[64]

CHAPTER NINE

Insoluble Propositions

· The ninth and final treatise of the *Summulae* is a workbook intended to accompany the preceding synoptic treatises, though, as we saw above, it was sometimes left out when the text was copied. Buridan himself indicates that he does not always "include the reading of this latter treatise along with the reading of the other eight treatises" (*S* 1.1.1: 5). Its relation to the rest of the text is that of the particular instantiation to the general rule. Thus, in the seventh treatise on fallacies, he remarks that the discussion will not descend "to the single defects of diverse arguments," because that "pertains to the treatise on sophistic exercises [*De Practica Sophismatum*]" (*S* 7.6.1: 602). The ninth treatise is organized around groups of individual propositions designed to appear puzzling or paradoxical either in themselves, or on the basis of some assumption that is part of the case [*casus*],[1] or hypothetical circumstances in which the proposition is to be entertained by the listener or reader.

Sophistical disputation had a long history at Paris. According to de Rijk, "as early as the eleventh century, ambiguous propositions or logical puzzles are interspersed in the compendia on logic in order to clarify the given expositions or to offer the reader practical exercises."[2] Buridan's opening remarks place his *Sophismata* squarely in this tradition. The ninth treatise, he says, is not only "about the practice of sophisms, namely, about their formulations and solutions," but also about the rules and principles introduced in the previous eight treatises: "I may recapitulate [*repetam*] in it some points discussed in the earlier treatises, and sometimes I will clarify them somewhat more, to the extent that I consider fitting for the solution of sophisms" (*S* 9.1, Prologue: 823). *Sophismata* were often orally disputed in the schools, and in a variety of formats. One of the most interesting of these genres was the *obligatio,* or obligational dispute,[3] so-called because it was based on the respondent's obligation to engage, according to certain rules, a sophistical proposition presented to him by an opponent. The whole exercise occurred under the watchful eye of the master, who also helped to set up the *casus:*

> it commonly happens in obligational disputations that the master stipulates that for the duration of the disputation the term 'donkey' should signify for the disputants precisely the same as that which the term 'animal' signifies for us when used in accordance with its common signification; and the respondent and the others agree. Then the proposition 'A man is a donkey' is true for them and is to be conceded by them, but a proposition similar in utterance would be totally false and impossible were it propounded outside the context of such an obligation in the church of Notre-Dame, to those there present. (*S* 9.6, 5th conclusion: 932)

The sort of linguistic artifice involved in the *obligatio* would be out of place in a church, of course, where we are bound by the higher obligation of speaking our heart, as in the sacrament of confession. Be that as it may, Buridan's *Sophismata* is not the record of the proceedings of a particular oral disputation — unlike the more formal *quaestiones disputatae* of the faculty of theology[4] — although parts of it were perhaps composed this way. Rather, the text seems to have been gradually refined through actual use in classroom lectures and discussions as well as in formal disputations. The result, in which the most important element is Buridan's careful analysis and resolution of each sophism, is a quasi-independent treatise capable of informing the reader quite apart from the circumstances that surrounded its composition.

The eight chapters into which the *Sophismata* is divided do not correspond to the eight main treatises of the *Summulae,* but instead represent sophisms grouped according to the semantic feature most relevant to their resolution, such as their signification, supposition, secondary signification or connotation (called 'appellation' in propositional contexts), and ampliation. The best-known chapter is the eighth, which deals with a special class of propositions known as 'insolubles [*insolubilia*]', or "propositions that are self-referential [*de propositionibus habentibus reflexionem supra seipsas*] on account of the signification of their terms" (*S* 9.8, Prologue: 952). Since it would not bring out what is distinctive in Buridan's thought merely to inventory the contents of the *Sophismata,* I shall focus on two questions given special attention in the ninth treatise: viz., (1) whether propositions signify anything beyond what is signified by their constituent terms; and (2) the conditions under which a proposition is said to be true (or false). The latter question will permit us to look at Buridan's treatment of self-referential paradoxes.

The question of whether propositions have their own significates is raised in the very first chapter of the ninth treatise in a sophism worthy of Lewis Carroll: "Complexly signifiables are chimeras [*Complexe significabilia sunt chimaerae*]" (*S* 9.1, 5th sophism: 829). What on earth could this mean? Nothing on earth—that is the whole point. A chimera is of course a mythical goat-stag, the commonplace example of a non-existent creature in medieval logic.[5] A '*complexe significabile*'—or 'complexly signifiable', in its awkward English translation[6]—is that which can be signified by a *complexum*, or proposition. Now the term '*complexe significabile*' would have raised a red flag for Buridan and his contemporaries because it happens to be the name of a controversial doctrine about the "immediate and adequate" object of demonstrative or scientific knowledge. The doctrine in this form appears to have originated with the English philosopher and theologian Adam Wodeham (c. 1298–1358),[7] who introduced it as a *via media* between what seemed to him the more problematic views of his Franciscan confrères William of Ockham (c. 1285–1347) and Walter Chatton (1285–1344).[8] Unlike Ockham, who held that the "total object" of assent in scientific knowledge is the *complexum*, or proposition, and Chatton, who argued that only "the extramental thing [*res extra*] is the object of the act of knowing, and of each and every act of assent,"[9] Wodeham believed that "the immediate object of the act of assent is the total object of the complex necessitating the assent—speaking of absolutely evident assent. [But] speaking more generally, the immediate total object of the act of assent is the total object or total significate of the proposition immediately conforming to it, concausing [the act of assent] and necessarily presupposed by it, or the total objects of many such propositions."[10] Wodeham's arguments indicate that this conclusion is, for him at least, a default position, so that "in positing the total object of assent as the total significate of the complex necessitating the assent, one avoids all of the inconsistencies mentioned in connection with the arguments [i.e., of Ockham and Chatton] advanced on both sides of the question."[11]

Wodeham's position is made possible by what I have elsewhere termed his 'epistemic holism', i.e., his belief that human knowledge is about irreducibly complex, mind-independent states of affairs.[12] Ockham and Chatton both confuse the parts with the whole (*totale*), proposing objects that are epistemically too derivative to serve as "the immediate total object" of scientific knowledge, which must be necessary and which must also say something about a world evidently in flux. In demonstrative terms, scientific knowledge results from the premises and the conclusion of a valid demonstration being taken together with the state of affairs they signify, which, in turn, "concauses" the intellect's act of assent. But as befits a former student and personal secretary of William of Ockham, Wodeham is concerned not to multiply entities beyond necessity. In response to a series of parsimonious objections to his approach, he is adamant that what is signified by the complex, 'man being an animal [*homo esse animal*]'—the formulaic noun-phrase he uses to represent the total significate of a proposition, in this case the proposition, 'Man is an animal [*Homo est animal*]'—is not a "what [*quid*]," but a "being-a-what [*esse quid*]," or, more loosely, that "something is in a certain way."[13] *Complexe significabilia* are not things, so that asking "What is man being an animal? [*Quid est: homo esse animal?*]" would be as absurd as asking "What is man is an animal? [*Quid est: homo est animal?*]." Wodeham dryly observes that "it should not be said that 'man is an animal' is a substance, or an accident, or something, or nothing, because none of these replies would be intelligible, or say anything [*nulla istarum responsionum esset intelligibilis aut aliquid dictu*]."[14] *Complexe significabilia* are modes of things rather than things, answers to questions about how things are rather than what they are. Wodeham accordingly understood them to be on a different logical level than things, and as such, to pose no threat to his ontology.

Unfortunately, the subtlety of Wodeham's idea was lost in its transmission a decade or so later to the philosophical community at Paris, where it made its most influential appearance in the *Sentences* commentary of the Augustinian theologian, Gregory of Rimini (c. 1300–1358).[15] Gregory does not adopt Wodeham's idea wholesale, but makes several changes to it in the course of developing his own account of the object of scientific knowledge. The result is a much less sophisticated account of *complexe significabilia*, which, in the words of the late Gedeon Gál, O. F. M., manages to give only "a mutilated presentation of the great debate between Ockham, Chatton, and Wodeham."[16] There is also no trace in it of Wodeham's epistemic holism, or of his careful insistence that the proper object of scientific knowledge must be regarded as a mode of being and not a thing. Instead, Rimini shows no compunction at all about referring to *complexe significabilia* or *enuntiabilia* as 'things' in two of the three senses he assigns to that term, an approach which was bound to rub those who valued parsimony the wrong way.[17]

That it rubbed Parisian theologians and arts masters the wrong way became evident almost immediately. The doctrine is mentioned among the "articles sent from Paris" in the 1346 condemnation of Nicholas of Autrecourt by the papal commission at Avignon charged with investigating his teachings: "That the complexly signifiable expressed by the proposition, 'God and creatures are distinct', is nothing.—[This is] false and scandalous [*Quod significabile complexe per istud complexum 'Deus et creatura distinguuntur' nichil est.—Falsum et scandalosum*]."[18] As Hans Thijssen observes, "the list of condemned articles does not furnish us with the grounds on which Autrecourt's theses were attacked,"[19] so we must exercise caution when interpreting them. But what is most striking about the above article, and significant as far as Buridan's views are concerned, is its very lack of context. Whether Autrecourt was friend or foe of the *complexe significabile* is irrelevant, and, given his few surviving works, probably undeterminable. As it stands, the article backs the reader into an *aliquid-nihil* dilemma on the status of *complexe significabilia*.[20] Either the *complexe significabile* expressed by 'God and creatures are distinct' is something (*aliquid*), or else it is nothing (*nihil*). If you say that it is nothing, beware that what you say may be deemed "false and scandalous." It is possible to speculate about why the "nothing" answer would have given rise to scandal, but the important point for Buridan and his contemporaries, i.e., students and teachers who actually read the articles of condemnation, is that the issue concerning *complexe significabilia* is one of ontology. There is no sensitivity here to the parsimony-saving arguments of Wodeham, who would have regarded it as unintelligible to characterize a *complexe significabile* as either something or nothing. Paris was primed for an ontological reading of the doctrine by Rimini, who omits these arguments in his exposition of Wodeham's ideas.[21]

The assumption that *complexe significabilia* present a problem, and that the problem is ontological, lies behind every occasion Buridan finds to discuss the doctrine. The sophism 'Complexly signifiables are chimeras' invites the student to consider the *complexe significabile* as being on a par with an exemplary non-existent, the chimera. The proof of the sophism begins by assuming that *complexe significabilia* "exist [*quia sunt*]," and proceeds to argue that, *qua* existing, they must be "substances or accidents, creator or creature, or chimeras"; but, since they cannot be any of the first four, they must be chimeras. The sophism is therefore true because its subject and predicate terms supposit for the same things, viz., chimeras (*S* 9.1, 5th sophism: 829). Conversely, the disproof of the sophism begins with the assumption that "chimeras do not exist [*quia chimerae non sunt*]," and argues that the same is true of *complexe significabilia* because they are neither God (being several, rather than one), nor creatures (they are purported to exist "before God created something"), nor accidents ("it would be impossible to determine what they were accidents of and in what they inhered"), nor substances (*S* 9.1, 5th sophism: 830–31).[22] The sophism is therefore false because its subject and predicate terms supposit for nothing, and sentences suppositing for nothing have no cause of their being true (*TC* I.2: 19).

In his resolution of the sophism, Buridan agrees with the opponent that the sentence is false, although he concedes that there is a sense in which a *complexe significabile* can be identified with the thing for which its subject terms supposit if the corresponding proposition is true. For example, since it is true that God is able to create B, 'God-being-able-to-create-B [*Deum posse creare B*]' simply "is God," just as 'Socrates-loving-God [*Socratem diligere deum*]' is Socrates, assuming it is true that Socrates loves God; otherwise it is nothing.[23] But it does not follow from this, of course, that *complexe significabilia* have any independent existence as things, which is what Buridan took defenders of the doctrine to have been arguing. And even if we identify a *complexe significabile* with some concrete individual, it does not make it into something capable of being true or false: "the one who declares a man to be an animal [*hominem esse animal*] is a man, who is neither true nor false, for he is neither a proposition nor a part of a contradiction" (*S* 9.8, 6th sophism: 963).

On the question of the role of *complexe significabilia* in the acquisition of scientific knowledge, Buridan has a twofold response, one which trivializes the doctrine, and another which argues that such knowledge can be explained more easily without it. The trivializing response interprets '*complexe*' as an adverb referring to whatever is signified by means of a complex term, phrase, or proposition.[24] "In this way, however," Buridan writes in his *Questions on the Metaphysics*, "everything in the world is a *complexe significabile*," because "even God, who is an absolutely simple being, is signifiable not only simply but also by means of a complex." Thus, "God is signified in a complex way by the propositions 'God is the first cause', 'God is the first act', and so on" (*QM* V.7: 31rb).[25] The second response begins with a passage showing just how suspicious Buridan is that defenders of the *complexe significabile* have engaged in some ontological slight-of-hand:

> Another conclusion that seems to me worth advancing against those who believe that God-being-the-cause-of-Socrates is a *complexe significabile* that is not identical with God, or Socrates, or both, nor even with any disposition inhering in God or Socrates, is this: given that it does not inhere in any thing, it would subsist per se even more than, or at least to the same degree as, a man or a stone. And so it would seem even more to be a substance. (*QM* V.7: 31ra)[26]

For the reasons mentioned above, it is difficult to imagine this argument cutting against Wodeham. But it is much less of a stretch to suppose that Buridan has Rimini's version of the doctrine in his sights, since Rimini's understanding of terms such as 'thing [*res*]', 'something [*aliquid*]', and 'being [*ens*]' is ambiguous enough to make any committed nominalist suspect that *complexe significabilia* are really just abstract entities.[27] Buridan accordingly disposes of them with the razor:

> if we can explain everything by positing fewer, we should not, in the natural order of things, posit many, because it is pointless to do with many what can be done with fewer. Now everything can be easily explained without positing such *complexe significabilia*, which are not substances, or accidents, or subsistent per se, or inherent in any other thing. Therefore, they should not be posited. (*QM* V.7: 31ra)[28]

It would be interesting to know what Buridan's reply to Wodeham might have been, since they could both be described as committed nominalists. But their differences on the proper object of scientific knowledge are fundamental enough to make speculating about it very difficult.[29]

Buridan's claim that the *complexe significabile* 'Socrates-loving-God [*Socratem diligere deum*]' is nothing if Socrates does not in fact love God is related to his account of truth conditions, and specifically to his account of what it is that makes a proposition false. In his view, what makes a proposition false is, quite literally, nothing. The idea that there is no special cause required for the falsity of a proposition, no "thing [*res*]" or "being [*ens*]" which makes it false, is something to which he returns often in his writings:[30]

> the falsity of an affirmative proposition has no cause because nothing is required in the thing or things signified, since it suffices that the proposition has been formulated and is not true. For if it has been formulated and is not true, it follows that it is false. Now, as for the fact that it is not true, there is no need for something to exist on the part of the thing signified, but it suffices that no cause exists on account of which it is true, if it is true.... [Thus] if there never was nor ever will be a horse or a donkey, this would still be false, 'A horse is a donkey', and this true, 'A horse is not a donkey'. And yet falsity of this kind is not in the things signified [by the terms of the proposition] by means of any cause. On the contrary, there is nothing in them because they are nothing. (*QM* VI.8: 39ra)[31]

Likewise, he says, no additional cause is required for the truth of a negative proposition because "whatever causes are required for the truth of any proposition, the same causes are required for the falsity of its contradictory" (*QM* VI.8: 39ra).[32] This conception of non-existence as present through its absence is not original with Buridan. Avicenna, for example, remarks, "the factor of existence comes by a cause which is a cause of existence, while the factor of non-existence comes by a cause which is the non-existence of the cause for the factor of existence."[33] But it plays a key role in Buridan's logic because he regards truth as a relational quality of propositions,[34] and specifically as a relation holding between (1) the subject and predicate terms of a complex or propositional subject, and (2) the thing or things (*res*) for which they stand:[35]

> Therefore, recapitulating, we put forth the 14th conclusion, namely, that every true particular affirmative [proposition] is true because the subject and predicate supposit for the same thing or things. And every true universal affirmative is true because for whatever thing or things the subject supposits for, the predicate supposits for that thing or for those same things.
>
> And every false particular affirmative is false because the subject and the predicate do not supposit for the same thing or things.
>
> And every false universal affirmative is false because not every thing or all things that the subject supposits for are also supposited for by the predicate.

And every true particular negative is true because the universal affirmative contradictory to it is false; and we have declared what the reason for this is.

And every true universal negative is true because the particular affirmative contradictory to it is false; and we have declared what the reason for this is. (*S* 9.2, 14th conclusion: 858)

The reason in question is simply the failure of the relation in the affirmative contradictory. What has changed is not anything on the part of the subject, but in the way things stand with respect to it.[36] The change in a proposition's truth-value is thereby assimilated to a particular species of relation Buridan elsewhere describes as that in which a subject "can be differently related at different times to something extrinsic to it, without any change on its part, through a change in that extrinsic thing, such as when a column is first on my right and then on my left [i.e., after I walk around to the other side of it]" (*QDA₃* III.11: 123).[37] The same sequence of steps is sufficient to make one proposition true, i.e., 'The column is on my left', and another false, i.e., 'The column is on my right'. I do not have to do anything else to make the second proposition false.[38] In the same way, absent causes are not really causes at all. Aristotle suggests that there is a sense in which we say that the absent pilot caused the shipwreck,[39] but Buridan glosses this by saying that "there is no causality [here] in the strict sense," for the absent pilot "does not strictly speaking move anything, and he does nothing more in this connection than he would if he were dead"; the same reasoning applies in natural philosophy should anyone wish to argue that the non-interposed earth is the cause of the absence of a lunar eclipse (*S* 8.10.3: 785–86). To think otherwise would be to reify what does not exist, when a simple change in what does exist is adequate to account for both eclipses and non-eclipses.

Buridan's account of truth works well as long as the things for which the terms in a proposition stand are extrinsic or non-identical to those terms. But what if a proposition is self-referential, such that the thing for which the terms must stand is the proposition itself? This is the question Buridan tries to answer in the eighth and final chapter of the *Sophismata*. The alethic paradoxes discussed there present a challenge to the correspondence truth conditions outlined in the second chapter because their truth-values appear to change depending on how they are assumed or considered, without any corresponding change in reality. Specifically, a proposition that appears true if false and false if true threatens to undermine the distinction between causes and non-causes of the truth of a proposition, for it presents a case in which a proposition's being false appears sufficient to make it true. Moreover, the same proposition, considered as a thing, possesses the same causal efficacy simultaneously as regards two contradictory states of affairs, viz., its being false and its being true. Yet self-reference is such an evident and obvious fact of everyday discourse that any formal system that cannot model it must be judged seriously deficient.

Now one might argue that a cursory examination of the different senses of 'true' and 'false' in ordinary discourse is all that we need to solve the problem, since a proposition could be false in its literal sense, but true in a metaphorical or analogical sense. But Buridan rejects such strategies as irrelevant to his task as a logician:

> I note that in our sophisms I intend to speak about the true or the false exclusively insofar as they are the appropriate properties of propositions [*nisi prout sunt appropriate differentiae propositionum*]. For I do not intend to investigate how God is true [*verus*] and how He is the First Truth [*prima veritas*], or how a man is false [*falsus*] [i.e., a liar], or how a denarius is false [*falsus*] [i.e., a counterfeit]. But I wish to speak about the true and the false insofar as they contradict each other, as is asserted in bk. 6 of the *Metaphysics* [VI.4.1027b17–25], for the logician does not intend to speak about truth and falsity in any other sense. (S 9.8, 6th sophism: 962)

The task Buridan sets for himself in the eighth chapter is that of dispelling the air of paradox surrounding certain self-referential propositions. His analyses of these sophisms pushed terminist logic to new heights, and remain impressive quite apart from their historical context, as is evidenced by the large secondary literature on the topic.[40] But rather than offering a meta-commentary on this literature (which would engage the literature, but not the text), or reviewing Buridan's solutions to the twenty sophisms discussed in the eighth chapter (which would engage the text, but not its significance for the method of the *Summulae*), I shall focus on his analysis of a single sophism which gets to the heart of his views on self-reference.

The seventh sophism Buridan considers is 'Every proposition is false'. The case posits "that all true propositions are annihilated while the false ones remain [in existence], and then Socrates propounds only this [proposition]: 'Every proposition is false'" (S 9.8, 7th sophism: 965). The question is then asked whether Socrates's proposition is true or false. The arguments on each side of the question illustrate the difficulties one faces if 'true' and 'false' are interpreted strictly. The argument that it is false assumes that "it is impossible for the same proposition to be true and false when propounded in the same language and understood in the same way by everyone hearing it," and proceeds to argue that the sophism is false because any proposition which entails its own contradictory is impossible, and therefore false. The opposite side begins by focusing on the logical form of the sophism as a universal affirmative that has no counterinstance in the case at hand, which stated that all true propositions have been annihilated with only the false ones remaining. Second, the sophism must be true because the subject and predicate terms supposit for the same things: if every proposition is false, then each and every propositional significate of the term 'every proposition' must be false, as it is, according to the case. Finally, the sophism must be true because "it signifies only that every proposition is false; and this is how things are [*ita est*]," according to the case (*S* 9.8, 7th sophism: 965).

Buridan writes as though this particular sophism enjoyed some notoriety among logic teachers at Paris, although all but one of the alternative solutions he mentions were discussed and criticized from the very beginning of the *insolubilia* literature. These involve various *ad hoc* proposals that either build new assumptions into the case or else make up new rules about how the terms of the sophism are to be interpreted.[41] Into the first category falls a solution known as the '*transcasus*', which involves the bizarre suggestion that the time Socrates utters his proposition and the time referred to by the verb of the proposition are not the same. This would allow us to say that if there are no true propositions during the first hour of a certain day, Socrates could utter his proposition at the end of this hour and it would be true, where he is understood as referring "not to the time at which he speaks but to the time of that first hour." But this is of no help if we stick to the case and assume that the times are the same. Alternatively, in a solution advocated by the '*restringentes* [restrictors]'—so-called because they avoided self-reference by restricting what a term can supposit for—we could make the proposition non-reflexive by stipulating that "terms that are apt to supposit for propositions are not put in propositions to supposit for the propositions in which they are put, but for others." But Buridan rightly rejects this second strategy as failing to take seriously our conventional understanding of terms, for when one uses the term 'proposition', he says, "one understands indifferently all propositions, indeed, present, past, and future ones, his own as well as those of another person." A moment's reflection should make it obvious that "this solution is worth nothing: for what one understands, of that he can speak [*quod aliquis intelligit, de hoc potest loqui*]" (*S* 9.8, 7th sophism: 966).[42]

Buridan's quick answer to the sophism is that Socrates's proposition is false in the case at hand. But before moving on to his final answer, he first discusses a solution described as being held by some people, including himself.[43] This is that there is another condition, in addition to the requirement that its terms stand for the same thing or things, which a proposition must meet if it is to be true. A proposition must also signify or assert itself to be true (*S* 9.8, 7th sophism: 967).[44] In her detailed analysis of this sophism, Fabienne Pironet has shown that the text in which Buridan defends this earlier view is his question commentary on Aristotle's *Posterior Analytics*, where it is expressed in terms of the traditional formula that "howsoever [a proposition] signifies, so it is [*qualitercumque significat, ita est*]" (*QAnPo* I.10).[45] Now Buridan holds that all propositions satisfy this condition trivially: "every proposition by its form signifies or asserts itself to be true" (*S* 9.8, 7th sophism: 967). The problem with self-referential paradoxes is that they also seem to signify that they are false. Thus, although the proposition 'I say what is false [*ego dico falsum*]' "signifies itself to be true in some fashion, nevertheless this is not so entirely, or howsoever it signifies [*licet aliqualiter sic significat, non tamen totaliter vel qualitercumque ita est*]. Therefore it is false" (*QAnPo* I.10).

Unfortunately, this looks no less *ad hoc* than the *transcasus* and restriction solutions he has just criticized. Why shouldn't other propositions, besides the paradoxical ones, be able to signify that they are false? Buridan does not say in his commentary on the *Posterior Analytics*, and in the *Summulae* he rejects his earlier view for the rather different reason that it is false "that every proposition signifies or asserts itself to be true" (*S* 9.8, 7th sophism: 968). His argument is not exactly clear, but the problem appears to be semantic: he cannot find an interpretation of the phrase 'itself to be true [*se esse veram*]' in the supplementary condition that will permit it to function as a general principle. Consider the proposition 'A man is an animal [*homo est animal*]'. If we understand it materially, i.e., as standing for a proposition, then it will signify 'The proposition "A man is an animal" is true', which is false because it refers to second intentions (concepts or signs by means of which we conceive of other concepts or signs as such), and the original proposition refers to things (human beings and animals), not concepts. But what if we say that a proposition signifies itself to be true if it is taken significatively for the things or first intentions, rather than materially? This will not work either, argues Buridan, because then the affirmative proposition 'A man is a donkey [*homo est asinus*]' would signify that a man is a donkey, which is false because the subject term 'man' does not supposit for anything (no human beings are donkeys).[46] Accordingly, we cannot base our solution to self-referential paradoxes on the idea that every proposition signifies or asserts itself to be true.[47]

The solution Buridan finally settles on receives the somewhat tepid endorsement of being "closer to the truth" than the previous solution—a reflection, perhaps, of his awareness of the imperfectability of any formal system that stays close to the fact of human language. Here, the idea that a proposition formally signifies itself to be true is replaced by the notion of implication from the doctrine of consequences. "Every proposition," he says, "virtually implies another proposition in which the predicate 'true' is affirmed of the subject that supposits for [the original proposition]" (*S* 9.8, 7th sophism: 969).[48] Unlike the old solution, in which the second proposition is signified by the first and hence part of its meaning, the new solution assumes only that the second proposition follows logically from the first, so that its meaning can be expounded separately. In this way, for the truth of any proposition P, it is required not only (1) that the subject and predicate terms of P stand for the same thing or things,[49] but also (2) that P implies another proposition, 'P is true', which must also be true. Otherwise, we would have a true antecedent and a false consequent, violating Buridan's fifth theorem regarding assertoric consequences, which states, "it is impossible for what is false to follow from what is true [*impossibile est ex veris sequi falsum*]" (*TC* I.8: 34, l. 97). Applying this to the seventh sophism, the constituent terms in the proposition uttered by Socrates—'Every proposition' and 'false'—stand for the same things, since in the posited case, "all true propositions are annihilated and the false ones remain, and then Socrates propounds only this: 'Every proposition is false'." So the first condition is satisfied. But the implied proposition, 'P is true' (where P is the name of 'Every proposition is false'), is false because its constituent terms, 'Every proposition is false' and 'true', do not stand for the same thing, since *ex hypothesi*, P stands for the antecedent proposition 'Every proposition is false', not for things that are true. But this gives us a true antecedent and a false consequent, and so the consequence does not hold. Therefore, the sophism is false.

Interestingly enough, Buridan gives very little consideration to self-referential paradoxes in the *Treatise on Consequences*, preferring to bracket them along with other *insolubilia* as minor annoyances more appropriate to logic workbooks such as *Sophismata*. He does, however, allude to the principles employed in his earlier and later solutions to the seventh sophism, though without indicating which is better: "I believe that every affirmative proposition is true whose terms *supposit* for the same, and in a way that is in keeping with its form; while at the same time not asserting itself to be false either formally or explicitly, or consecutively or implicitly" (*TC* I.5: 26, ll. 41–44).[50] The 'formally and explicitly' corresponds to Buridan's first solution, in which a proposition is said to signify or assert itself to be true, whereas the 'consecutively or implicitly' corresponds to the second, in which another proposition asserting the first to be true is said to be implied by, or taken to be a consequence of, the first.

Buridan's general attitude towards *insolubilia* confirms Paul Vincent Spade's assessment of the entire genre, which is worth quoting in full:[51]

> First, there was a tendency to multiply examples. Albert of Saxony, for instance, in *Perutilis logica,* 6, 1, discusses no fewer than nineteen insolubles [Buridan discusses twenty in his chapter on *insolubilia*]. Contrast the modern tendency to look for a paradigm case that shows the structure of the paradox with a minimum of inessentials. Second, the medievals do not seem to have had any 'crisis mentality' about these paradoxes. Although they wrote a great deal about them, there is no hint that they thought the paradoxes were crucial test cases against which their whole logic and semantics might fail. Again, contrast the modern attitude. Third, the medievals did not draw great theoretical lessons from

the insolubles. They did not seem to think the paradoxes showed any-thing very deep or important about the nature of language or its expres-sive capacity. Once again, contrast modern attitudes. One might do well to speculate on the reasons for these differences between medieval and modern semantic theory.

Taking up this invitation, then, if the main thesis of the first part of this book is correct, it should be apparent how Buridan's conception of logic as a way of doing philosophy, i.e., as a something that has meaning only when it is learned and applied in practice, is completely alien to the modern understanding of logic as a self-contained theory of inference. As we have seen, the *Summulae* is essentially a compendium of methods, a 'how-to' book for the philosopher. The student who masters its techniques will be equipped not only to read au-thoritative texts with confidence, but also to advance his knowledge through dialectical discussions with others. Likewise, the doctrines of the *Summulae* promise to guide the student as he reads another book, the book of nature, whose basic concepts and expressions are revealed in the metaphysics and natural philosophy of Aristotle. Logic as a freestanding discipline would have made little sense to someone accustomed to thinking of it as "the art of arts [*ars artium*]" because the value of logic is in terms of its relation to other dis-ciplines. That is why Buridan begins the *Summulae* with the quotation from the pseudo-Aristotelian *Rhetoric to Alexander:* "Just as the commander is the savior of the army, so is reasoning with erudition the commander of life [*ra-tiocinatio cum eruditione est dux vitae*]" (*S* Preface: 3).[52] What holds Buridan's logic together is not any common subject matter, but its relation to other sub-jects in the arts curriculum, over which it is said to rule.

PART TWO

PRACTICE

CHAPTER TEN

Ultimate Questions

· For the philosopher, ultimate questions are raised in the discourse of metaphysics. Yet Buridan's *Questions on Aristotle's Metaphysics* is among the shortest of his commentaries. The incunabular edition of this work runs to a mere 77 folios, as compared with 121 folios for his *Questions on Aristotle's Physics* and 214 for his massive commentary on the *Nicomachean Ethics*. Despite the position enjoyed by the *Metaphysics* at the height of the arts curriculum—it was typically studied only by candidates for the master's degree who had completed at least their bachelor's-level training in grammar and Aristotelian logic and natural philosophy—interest in the text was squeezed by jurisdictional concerns from above, and, in Buridan's case, by methodological considerations from below.

1. THEOLOGY AND METAPHYSICS

The impact from above can be seen in the sensitivity exhibited by Parisian arts masters to certain metaphysical questions, lest they be seen to violate their curricular authority by addressing issues proper to the 'higher' faculty of theology. Buridan, for example, bluntly qualifies his reply to an objection to his account of intellectual memory with the observation that "how we sense, understand, or remember after death and without a body is not considered a question this faculty [i.e., of arts] determines [*non spectat determinare ad istam facultatem*]" (*QDA₃* III.15: 173).[1] Remarks such as this can be found throughout Buridan's writings on metaphysics and natural philosophy.

They represent the institutional fallout from various attempts, some more successful than others, to accommodate Aristotle's teachings to revealed doctrine or "articles of the faith [*articuli fidei*]." The Parisian history of this conflict has been documented by others,[2] and I shall not attempt to retell it here. Suffice it to say that the significance of such remarks should not be overemphasized, as often happens with modern readers who, whether consciously or not, bring modern political sensibilities to the texts. As Hans Thijssen has observed:[3]

> At first sight the medieval academic condemnations seem to exemplify the facile generalization of older textbooks that the Middle Ages were "a millenium in which reason was enchained, thought was enslaved." Although probably no one any longer upholds this unbalanced view, the medieval academic condemnations do appear to the modern reader as striking manifestations of the limitations exerted by Christian faith on the thought and teaching of university scholars. Medieval scholars, however, perceived censure from a different point of view, namely, as the exercise of teaching authority, rather than as a restraint on academic freedom.

This is precisely how Buridan understood the question. Censure was a tool designed to check the tendency of teaching masters to make authoritative pronouncements in disciplines or fields over which they had no authority. Just as Buridan is loathe to pursue the consequences of intellectual memory for *post mortem* existence, since he would then be an arts master teaching theology, so a theologian would have no business making pronouncements about Aristotle's account of memory, since he would then be a theologian teaching arts.[4] As we shall see in chapter 12, Buridan reserves some of his harshest criticisms for Nicholas of Autrecourt, a theologian who dared to interpret Aristotle (and in a way that radically attenuated the scope of human knowledge),[5] as if the impropriety of his remarks made their error all the more acute, and dangerous.[6]

As far as Buridan is concerned, much of the confusion over the proper domains of metaphysics and theology stems from Aristotle himself, who in the *Metaphysics* identifies three kinds of speculative science: physics, mathematics, and theology.[7] Buridan provides the standard medieval interpretation of this passage in his commentary, reading 'theology' as 'metaphysics' and differentiating the three sciences in terms of the way they treat their respective subjects: whereas the natural philosopher considers things as qualified by motion, and the mathematician as quantified by number, the metaphysician considers them only insofar as they pertain to the "concept of being [*ad rationem essendi*]" (*QM* VI.2: 34ra).[8] For the difference between metaphysics and theology, however, we need to look at the very beginning of the commentary, where Buridan offers the following gloss of Aristotle's remarks:

It should also be noted that [when we ask whether metaphysics is the same as wisdom,] we are not comparing metaphysics to theology, which proceeds from beliefs that are not known, because although these beliefs are not known *per se* and most evident, we hold without doubt that theology is the more principal discipline and that it is wisdom most properly speaking. In this question, however, we are merely asking about intellectual habits based on human reason, [i.e.,] those discovered by the process of reasoning, which are deduced from what is evident to us. For it is in this sense that Aristotle calls metaphysics 'theology' and 'the divine science'. Accordingly, metaphysics differs from theology in the fact that although each considers God and those things that pertain to divinity, metaphysics only considers them as regards what can be proved and implied, or inductively inferred, by demonstrative reason. But theology has for its principles articles [of faith], which are believed quite apart from their evidentness, and further, considers whatever can be deduced from articles of this kind. (*QM* I.2: 4ra–rb)[9]

Might this passage suggest that Buridan was politically submissive, eager to 'toe the line' as regards the institutional primacy of theology over philosophy and the official prohibitions and condemnations that served to remind everyone of the proper domains of each faculty?[10]

It is difficult to answer such questions because medieval and modern conceptions of academic freedom are so different. But even by modern standards, it is clear that the threat of academic censure had anything but a chilling effect on Buridan's thought. This emerges in the discussion that immediately follows the above quotation, in which Buridan cites three traditional reasons why metaphysics is eminently qualified for the title of wisdom: (1) metaphysics is the universal science, as it considers "being in its entire universality"; (2) metaphysics is the most difficult of sciences, since it involves speculation about God, whose being is removed—in fact, "most removed [*remotissimus*]"—from the same senses without whose "assistance [*ministerio*]" we cannot cognize anything at all; and finally, (3) metaphysics is the most certain of the sciences because it considers the first and most evident principles of every field of inquiry. These arguments lead Buridan to reflect on the autonomy of metaphysics as the highest form of philosophical discourse:

Similarly, metaphysical inquiry is for the sake of itself, since it is speculative in the highest degree. Nor is it ordered in relation to the other speculative sciences. On the contrary, it is the other way around, since metaphysics is the most principal science and the ordering principle of all the other sciences. That it is the most principal is apparent from the fact that it considers the first and most universal principles of what we teach, through which all other principles of the other sciences are strengthened and formally stated, if they need stating. (*QM* I.2: 4rb; cf. *QAnPo* I.23; *S* 1.1.1: 6)[11]

As far as teaching in the faculty of arts is concerned, the roots of the other speculative sciences of mathematics and physics, as well as their various subordinate sciences, can all be retraced to metaphysics.[12] This is what it means for metaphysics to be the *ordinatrix,* or active ordering principle, as regards all other branches of learning.

I don't it

But because teaching naturally gravitates towards practice, moving out on the branches, and because metaphysics is so difficult, its imprint on the other sciences is evident only if we make it so. Buridan does not think it necessary to establish or justify the doctrinal hegemony of metaphysics by reductive proof; his view is rather that such proofs are available should it ever become necessary to strengthen or provide a formal statement of the principles of a subordinate science.[13] These latter sciences are sufficiently self-contained to be practiced by those who have mastered the relevant teachings without their ever having to produce a justification of the whole science, or even be in possession of such a justification.[14] This marks an important methodological distinction between later medieval and early modern philosophy. It would never have occurred to Buridan that philosophy begins in the search for some indubitable principle(s), our grasp of which provides the foundation for everything else we know. For one thing, it would have seemed the height of pretension to assume that an unaided intellect, a flawed instrument working with inferior materials, is capable of reaching the requisite degree of certainty. The notion that we must begin at the absolute beginning is incompatible with the flux of our wayfarer state. For another, since the proper object of belief is, like the proper subject of logic, an occurrent proposition, the degree of certainty attaching to any principle must fluctuate relative to how it appears "in our prospect" at any given time. But this, of course, is conditioned not only by its degree of evidentness, but also by whatever intellectual dispositions lead us to assent to it. As a result, even principles Buridan is prepared to describe as "absolutely evident," such as the principle of non-contradiction, can be presented to people in such a way that they withhold their assent from them.[15]

But what about theology, which "has for its principles articles [of faith], which are believed quite apart from their evidentness"? Can philosophers bask in the reflected certainty of their more prestigious neighbors, the theologians? The unequivocal answer here is 'no', and for good reason: the articles of faith studied by the theologians exhibit the wrong kind of certainty. As we shall see in chapter 12 below, articles of faith are said to be certain because they are deemed "maximally true" and held by the intellect with a firm and steadfast assent, though (and this is the crucial difference) not with an assent that is caused by their evidentness. In fact, Buridan notes, "it is compatible with this perfect certainty that because of the lack of evidentness we do not properly have knowledge of [the content of] these articles [of faith]" (*S* 8.4.4: 707). But philosophy is "about intellectual habits based on human reason, [i.e.,] those discovered by the process of reasoning, which are deduced from what is evident to us."

In a moment of political candor, Buridan comments on the status of philosophy as a subject in the faculty of arts vis-à-vis the other faculties at the University of Paris, viz., theology, law, and medicine:

> When it is argued that [metaphysics] is not the most principal [of the intellectual virtues], I say that this is true if we compare it to theology founded upon articles of faith. But leaving the faith aside, it is the most principal of all the other sciences. For the whole science of laws and decrees is subject to moral science or moral philosophy, and is subalternate to it—except insofar as those decrees and decretals take something from theology. Medicine, however, is entirely subalternate to natural philosophy. Therefore, neither [medicine nor law] merits being called a principal science. But why is our faculty [of arts] the lowest? It can be said that this is because of the wealth of those who profess in the other faculties, and because our faculty is also very common. For it includes grammar, logic, and rhetoric, and just because of them does not deserve to be called 'principal'. But along with those [trivial] arts it also contains natural philosophy, on account of which it is principal over medicine, moral philosophy, on account of which it is principal over law, and metaphysics, on account of which it is absolutely principal. (*QM* I.2: 4rb)[16]

Despite its pedestrian reputation, the dialectical inquiry taught and practiced by the arts masters produces a wisdom that "holds the key to the principles of every other method of inquiry"—to borrow the phrase of Peter of Spain.[17] It is almost as if Buridan thinks of his own faculty as the institutional embodiment of Luke 14:11, i.e., as worthy of exaltation precisely because of its lowliness. His remark that those who profess, or teach, in the higher faculties do so because of their wealth is also wonderfully ambiguous about whether the riches in question are intellectual or financial.[18] Without explicitly saying so— since that would almost certainly have landed him in hot water with the authorities—Buridan's identification of wisdom with the knowledge of metaphysics permits his audience to infer rather unambiguously what his own view is. Philosophical wisdom belongs to the faculty of arts. Whether there is another sort of wisdom proper to the faculty of theology is another question, which the theologians must answer for themselves.

Buridan does not attempt to argue that theology is subordinate to philosophy, however. Here, as elsewhere, his strategy is to grant *de jure* place of privilege to theology, while at the same time treating the two as *de facto* separate but equal. This is possible because the criterion that places theology ahead of philosophy is external to the practice of both disciplines. Both involve the rational articulation of beliefs, yet theology must come first because of the priority of faith over reason in the final ordination of human beings towards beatitude. Even so, Buridan, like Thomas Aquinas, does not think that the distinction between philosophy and theology comes down to a simple distinction in subject matter.[19] God can be studied by the arts master as well as by the theologian. In Buridan's writings, we find numerous discussions of God as omnipotent (*QM* IV.12: 21vb; *QP* VIII.2: 110va; *QNE* X.5: 213rb); as capable of freely creating other beings *ex nihilo* (*QM* VI.5: 36va; *QP* I.15: 19rb); as imparting inexhaustible motion to celestial orbs at the moment of their creation (*QP* VIII.13: 120vb–121ra); as completely independent in relation to creatures (*QC* 10: 72–74); as possessed of a perfect intellect whose activity makes human understanding possible (*QDA*$_3$ III.10: 326–29; *QM* XII.14: 75va–vb); as the cause of the miraculous transformation of eucharistic bread and wine into the body and blood of Christ (*QM* IV.6: 16va–17vb and V.8: 31rb–33ra);[20] as an eternal being knowable by us (*QNE* VI.3: 121vb–123vb); and as the source of the beatitude which is the perfection of human happiness (*QNE* X.4: 211rb–vb).[21] What all of these examples share is a creaturely orientation. God is in each case studied in relation to creatures, whose order and motion naturally draw our minds upwards to their principles, as well as providing us with evident appearances through which the divine author of these principles may be known. This much is proper to the arts faculty. In theology, however, God and creatures are considered through the divine light of revelation: "theology has for its principles articles [of faith], which are believed quite apart from their evidentness [*theologia vero habet pro principiis articulos creditos absque evidentia*]" (*QM* I.2: 4ra–rb). There is an important practical difference between the two approaches, which can be seen in the way Buridan argues for the existence of intellectual memory in humans without speculating about the role such a faculty might play in a disembodied intellect (*QDA*$_3$ III.15: 173; discussed in chapter 13 below), or in the way he treats of the relation between God and creatures without going on to consider the relation between the distinct persons of the Trinity (*QC* 10: 74).[22] Since the latter questions involve examining the consequences of particular doctrines or articles of faith rather than constructing demonstrations from evident principles, they are off-limits to the philosopher,[23] even if their subject matter is the same.[24]

What decides whether we should proceed philosophically or theologically in resolving a speculative question? We cannot say one way or the other a priori because our method of inquiry is determined by our starting-points, and Buridan holds that the intellect is free to choose the principle(s) it uses in rationally articulating a question (*S* 8.3.7: 691–92). This is how philosophy and theology can be *de facto* equivalent in the speculative realm. Metaphysics, or philosophical wisdom, cannot be ordained by theology because its methods, as rooted in its principles, are different. Philosophy is accordingly not inferior to theology, just different.[25]

2. METAPHYSICAL PRACTICE

Buridan ??

It was no mean feat for Buridan to establish a safe harbor for Aristotelian metaphysics in the faculty of arts. But this did not lead to the flowering of metaphysics as a secular discipline at the University of Paris. In practice, its sphere of operations was further attenuated because Buridan's method is critical, and tends to view traditional problems in metaphysics as based on confusions of logic or language. For example, when a cause is understood as being actual rather than merely potential, does our conception of it *qua* cause change in any way? Aristotle leaves this ambiguous in *Metaphysics* V.2, but some philosophers thought it necessary to posit an additional state of affairs to explain the dynamic aspect of causality, i.e., the fact that a contingent state of affairs needs to be brought about by some agent. Thus, if we think of God as the cause of Socrates, there must be something else, God's-being-the-cause-of-Socrates (*deum esse causam Sortis*), distinct from both God and Socrates, to account for his existence. This 'something else' then becomes not only what is signified by the proposition 'God is the cause of Socrates' (*complexe significabile*), but also the proper object of our knowledge that God is the cause of Socrates. Buridan replies by arguing that philosophers who think this way do not know how to interpret human language. They take everything too literally. But we should not be misled by what a proposition literally says, or seems to say, into thinking that there must be some new kind of entity corresponding to God's being the cause of Socrates, especially since such reifying moves do not help us to understand what is happening when a cause acts (*QM* V.7–8: 30va–33ra).[26] He concedes, of course, that there is an obvious and perfectly innocent sense in which propositions can signify, although again, what they signify is nothing over and above individual substances and accidents. Likewise, we might take Aristotle's *Metaphysics* II.1 remark about philosophy being knowledge of the truth as an occasion for asking how the comprehension of truth is possible for us. As we saw in chapter 8 (and will see again in chapter 12), Buridan uses this to explain the genesis of human knowledge, addressing skeptical concerns along the way and rebutting a rather virulent form of skeptical argument with the charge that by misconstruing terms such as 'certitude [*certitudo*]' and 'evidentness [*evidentia*]', it fails to see that 'An accident exists; therefore, a substance exists' is a perfectly good consequence.[27] Indeed, the error committed by these arguments is so outrageous and does such violence to ordinary scientific procedure that Buridan suspects those who advanced them to have done so deliberately.[28] But again, the problem is ultimately one of semantic or logical confusion, which he assumes any rational person can sort out, given the right dialectical tools.

With regard to the problem of universals,[29] Buridan does not so much create a new theory as show how our theoretical commitments can be expressed with a minimum of ambiguity and fuss. Like Ockham, he is a nominalist, although this term must be used with caution in later medieval philosophy because of the modern tendency to identify it simply with the denial of real universals. Most fourteenth-century philosophers were nominalists in this sense because they associated the contrary doctrine with Plato, with whom they were familiar only secondarily as one of the authors thoroughly discredited by Aristotle in Book I of the *Metaphysics*.[30] But medieval nominalism involved much more than rejecting Platonic universals. Its history can be traced to twelfth-century disputes over the reading of sacred texts, in which the techniques of logicians such as Abelard were pitted against those of grammarians such as Helias.[31] As these disputes matured, nominalism was gradually absorbed into the teaching of philosophers working in the faculty of arts, so that by Buridan's time, it is better to think of it as a practice or way of doing philosophy, rather than as a piece of doctrine.

When Buridan considers questions such as "whether universals actually exist outside the soul" (*TDUI:* 137), his remarks are almost always aimed at clarifying the meaning of the term 'universal' differentially with respect to terms such as 'individual', 'particular', and 'singular'. His rejection of realism is expressed in the claim that universal terms have no ultimate significate, i.e., nothing outside the soul they can 'make known' as such.[32] Hence, an account is needed of what such terms mean. Here, it is almost as if Buridan thinks there is something ill-formed about propositions where the term 'universal' occurs in the subject position, for when confronted with them his first move is always to tell us how the term 'universal' should be understood (*QIP* 3: 136, ll. 477–88).[33] He argues further that the primary signification of 'universal' is 'predicable of many', which makes it a term of second intention, or a term of terms, since only terms are predicable (*QIP* 3: 135–36; 4: 139; *TDUI:* 148).[34] The second-intentional status of the term 'universal' is also evident in propositions, where it does not signify a 'what' but a 'how', i.e., how we conceive of something— in this case how the term so designated is "indifferent to many supposits," or individuals (*TDUI:* 59).[35] As we saw above, logic is the study of terms such as 'proposition' taken materially, signifying actual tokens of the type (*QDI* I.1: 6). Moving from propositions to arguments, Buridan insists that terms in the premises and conclusions of demonstrative arguments must be taken as standing materially, i.e., for themselves in the particular discourse conditions which surround them, rather than personally, for their extramental significates (*QIP* 1: 128, ll. 223–37). Likewise, the proximate object of scientific knowledge is the actual demonstrated or demonstrable conclusion rather than the state of affairs it signifies, although he is willing to concede that "the terms of those demonstrable conclusions, or even the things signified by those conclusions" might be considered "remote," or secondary, objects of knowledge (*QIP* 1: 127, ll. 208–209).[36] Careful and systematic analysis is the best antidote for metaphysical perplexity because the trouble usually begins with untutored persons who don't know what a word or concept means.

It should be noted that Buridan's methods do not always produce parsimonious results. Like Ockham, he has only substances and qualities in his basic ontology, but he is much more willing than Ockham to expand this in the direction of modes or ways of being when confronted with recalcitrant phenomena. Thus, he argues that we must treat the question of *how* something is as distinct from *what* it is if we are to have a coherent understanding of motion, especially since the Ockhamist view posits an infinite succession of spatial qualities (*QM* V.9: 32va; *QP* II.3: 1ra–rb; *QP* IV.11: 77va–78rb).[37] Likewise, in a famous passage, Buridan is driven by his own experience to reject Ockham's explanation of condensation and rarefaction as kinds of locomotion. Why, he asks, does he find himself unable to compress further the air in a bellows which has been stopped up at one end? Not because of its matter, because more matter could exist in a much smaller space; nor because of the substantial form of the air, which would fill a much smaller space once it has cooled; nor even because of the heat it possesses, since more heat could exist in a much smaller space, such as at the end of a red-hot poker. No, the air must have a distinct quantitative form or magnitude preventing it from being moved. Against those who would do away with this distinction, Buridan argues that "a magnitude of this sort has not been posited in vain, for we have been compelled to posit it by arguments that make it seem as useful or even more useful to natural philosophy than [the qualities of] whiteness or blackness" (*QP* I.8: 11vb).[38]

Buridan's understanding of the problem of universals is also revealed in casual remarks. At one point he observes, almost as an aside, that "it would be easy verbally to persuade a person [who had never actually heard a horse] that horses do not utter any sound, if he had no training at all in philosophy [*facile enim esset tali persuadere verbis quod equi non vociferarent, si nihil esset edoctus in philosophia*]" (*QIP* 13: 181, ll. 2137–38). Now why should philosophical training matter here? Because it is philosophy, not empirical science, which teaches us the criteria for the application of a term or its corresponding concept. If we were to try to correct someone thus persuaded that horses are naturally silent by saying to him, 'Look, horses are capable of neighing,' we would be explaining to him what the term 'horse' means, not making an empirical observation. The evidence simply does not matter here.[39]

As L. M. de Rijk has shown, Buridan's predominantly semantic approach to the problem of universals is remarkably similar to that of his Parisian predecessor, Peter Abelard, some two centuries before.[40] Abelard enjoyed much celebrity in his own time as a master dialectician—he was known as 'the Socrates of Gaul'—and his reputation survived through his writings, including his ferocious attacks upon contemporaries who appear to have advocated various forms of metaphysical realism. But Abelard also made an important positive contribution to the medieval discussion of universals. This is his idea that to ask about universals is really to ask about the meaning of universal terms,[41] an idea in evidence in his *Glosses on Porphyry* when, after demolishing the views of several opponents, he remarks, "it remains to ascribe this kind of universality only to words."[42] For Abelard, the problem of universals is really the problem of how to characterize universal discourse, so that purely metaphysical questions—such as the question of whether any singular or collective "thing [*res*]" is a universal[43]—are at best incidental and at worst misleading as far as its solution is concerned. But if what is original in Abelard's solution is a matter of method rather than of doctrine,[44] then he and Buridan are fellow travelers on the problem of universals, and their approaches can be usefully compared—even if evidence of direct influence is lacking, and even if Buridan's own dialectical style was not confrontational enough to earn him the title, 'the Abelard of Arras'.

Abelard and Buridan share an interest in universals as a problem of what we now call mereology, or the theory of part/whole relations. Mereological questions arise here because medieval philosophers commonly understood universals as wholes that are divisible into subjective parts, i.e., the individuals of which they can be predicated. This understanding played an especially important role in the discussion of universals by philosophers trained in the schools of Paris.[45] The question for Abelard and Buridan, however, concerns not only what sense we should attach to the concept of a universal whole, but also how this construal of the term 'whole' should be articulated together with its other senses to produce a coherent language of parts and wholes. Nominalism enters the picture in the way each thinker tries to formulate these distinctions. Buridan's approach suggests a renovation of the Abelardian discourse, which is based on the *logica vetus,* using the techniques of the *logica nova,* such as the distinction between categorematic and syncategorematic uses of the term 'whole' in the fourth treatise of the *Summulae.*

Both Abelard and Buridan hold that universals are best understood in terms of the product or process of the cognitive act of signifying particulars. Abelard says that universal words such as 'man' "in a way 'signify' diverse things by naming them, not by establishing an understanding that *arises* from them but one that *pertains* to each of them."[46] He explains this rather cryptic remark with an account of how we grasp common natures:[47]

> For when I attend to this man only in terms of the nature *substance* or *body,* but not also in terms of the nature *animal* or *man* or *literate,* surely

I understand nothing but what is in the nature. But I do not pay attention to *all* the features it has. And when I say that I attend to the nature 'only' insofar as it has this or that feature, the term 'only' refers to the *attention,* not to the mode of subsisting. Otherwise, the understanding *would* be empty. For the thing does not *have* only this, it is only *attended to* as having this.

Abelard's strategy is to distinguish modes of understanding from modes of being, and then to deny ontological import to the former on the grounds that it would be a mistake to posit any kind of one-to-one correspondence between our ways of conceptualizing the world and the world itself.[48] Thus, the common term 'man' is not the name of any thing, although it does bring to mind a certain "confused" concept of "*animal, rational, mortal.*"[49] And when it does, Abelard says that he attends to the nature of man "simply in itself, not as regards any one man."[50]

Buridan takes a similar approach to the problem of universals, associating universality not with any kind of being, but with the cognitive act of signifying or representing particular things in a certain way:

> Some things are taken to be universal with respect to signifying or representing because they do not signify one thing or another determinately, but all things [that are] alike in genus or species indifferently, in the way that the term 'man' signifies all men, and the term 'color' all colors. And so universals are significative terms, whether vocal, mental, or written. And those mental or vocal terms exist as singularly as color does in a wall, although they are called universals with respect to signifying. And in this way, it must be conceded that universals are certainly as generable and corruptible in the mind or speech as the color is in a wall. (*QM* I.7: 6vb–7ra)[51]

Later in the same work, Buridan elaborates on this idea as follows: "something is said to be universal in predication or signification because it is predicable of many and indifferently signifies many and supposits for many. And then, by contrast, there is the signification of a singular or discrete term, which, by one imposition, is significative or representative of only one thing, such as Socrates [or] Plato. And so what is universal and singular are mental, spoken, or written terms" (*QM* VII.15: 50va).[52] Like Abelard, Buridan holds that universality should be ascribed to words alone, and that what makes a word universal is its capacity to signify or represent not just a plurality of particulars "alike in genus and species," but to do so in a certain way, viz., indifferently (for Buridan), or such that the resulting conception is confused (for Abelard). Buridan also follows Abelard in distinguishing between modes of understanding and modes of being, arguing that it would be a mistake to infer from our capacity to cognize universally that commonality is a feature of the world. "Everything which is in you exists as singularly as you do," he says, "but this does not prevent it from being able to signify many things indifferently; and so what is universal in signification certainly exists in you" (*QM* VII.15: 51ra).[53]

3. UNIVERSALS AS MEREOLOGICAL WHOLES

As is well known, Porphyry and Boethius set the stage for the medieval problem of universals. But Boethius also helped to define the parameters of the debate. His treatise *De divisione,* a systematic account of the different kinds of division,[54] crystallized for medieval thinkers the idea that substances and their attributes can be analyzed not only in terms of the predicables of genus, difference, and species, but also as part/whole relations.[55]

Boethius mentions three kinds of *per se* division in *De divisione:* of a genus into its species, of a whole into its parts, and of an utterance into its significations.[56] Part/whole division is differentiated from genus/species division using four criteria,[57] but the ensuing discussion indicates that he takes the notion of a whole to apply not just to things having integral parts, such as corporeal bodies, but also to species, and to what consists of "certain powers":

> We shall now discuss that class of division which is of a whole into parts, since that was the second one, following division of a genus. For we use the term 'whole' in more than one sense: The 'whole' is that which is continuous, e.g. body, line, or anything of that sort. We also speak of a 'whole' that is *not* continuous, e.g. a 'whole' flock, population, or army. We speak also of a 'whole' that is universal [*dicimus quoque totum quod universale est*], e.g. man or horse—for these are wholes pertaining to their respective parts, i.e. men or horses, which also explains why we call this or that man a *particular.* And then there is 'whole' in the sense of what consists of powers of some kind [*dicitur quoque totum quod ex quibusdam virtutibus constat*], e.g. in soul one potency is of understanding, another of sensing, another of imparting growth.[58]

Although the whole "that is universal" appears to be ambiguous between genera and species, Boethius regards only the *infima* (lowest) species in the tree of Porphyry as a mereological universal.[59] But there is little else said in *De divisione* about the division of such wholes, beyond the remark that "wholes that are not continuous and those that are universal are to be divided in one and the same way," i.e., into their discrete parts, so that "Of men some are in Europe, others in Asia, and others in Africa."[60] The questions of how we are to understand such wholes, and how their division should be effected, were therefore opened to posterity.

a. The Abelardian Analysis

Some six centuries later, Abelard was one of Boethius's most avid readers, composing a literal commentary on *De divisione* as well as devoting the fifth part of his independent logical treatise, the *Dialectica*, to the subject of division. Abelard makes clear from the outset that he sees the problem of division as semantic because it concerns the signification of the term 'whole [*totus*]' and the conditions under which terms standing for wholes and parts are predicated of each other. The introduction to his commentary on *De divisione* even echoes his famous remark about universality from the *Glosses on Porphyry:*

> It must be noted that all regular division is of terms only [*omnis regularis divisio tantum de terminis*] . . . the point of every division is that the things [produced by] the division receive the predication of that from which they have been divided only singly [*singillatim*], or only collectively [*collectim*], or in both ways [*utroque modo*], and that what undergoes division receives the predication of the things into which it has been divided particularly [*particulariter*]. . . . The goal [of this investigation] is so that we might know how to make divisions in a rule-governed way [*regulariter*], and how to discern composites. . . . This science is placed under the science of finding arguments, because we are teaching how to find arguments suitable for proving any questions that arise from division, without constructing syllogisms.[61]

Abelard's explicit connection of division to the doctrine of finding arguments, or topics (*loci*), is in keeping with his view that we cannot discern the truth of part/whole inferences from their formal structure alone.[62] Rather, such inferences are imperfect, which means that we must look beyond their logical form to what is signified by their terms in order to determine their truth.

What is signified by part/whole discourse? Abelard takes seriously Boethius's remark about the term 'whole' being used in different ways.[63] Beginning with 'the whole that is universal', he says: "a universal whole is one that is made up of parts which receive the predication of their whole singly [*singillatim*], in such a way that it is not a genus, nor like a genus."[64] Two things are worth noting in this definition. The first is that Abelard departs from Boethius in using the notion of predication to define universal wholes.[65] Boethius says only that wholes such as *man* or *horse* "pertain to their respective parts [*hi enim sunt toti suarum partium*]," without specifying their relation. The second is that Abelard does not explore universal wholeness beyond specifying the mode of predication possessed by the parts. What makes something a universal whole is the fact that it can be said of its parts in a certain way, i.e., such that the whole is predicated of each of its parts.[66] This is clear in his comment on another of Boethius's mereological metaphors. When Boethius speaks of individual human beings such as Cato, Virgil, and Cicero as elements of *man,* we are to think of them as "[individuals] who, because they are *particulars,* i.e., receiving the predication of their whole, nevertheless are joined together [*jungunt*] to make up the quantity of *man* as a whole, i.e., they confer upon *man* this quantity: such that it is said to be a whole [*conferunt homini hanc vim ut dicatur totum*] . . . , i.e., in such a way that with respect to those particulars, it is said to be a whole absolutely, and not a genus."[67] But a problem lurks in the Boethian account, for if the division of universal wholes is analogous to quantitative wholes, would not *man* cease to exist once Cato, Virgil, or Cicero perishes? How can a species-whole survive the loss of any of its parts?

Abelard's solution is to abandon Boethius's criteria for differentiating part/whole from genus/species division as far as universal wholes are concerned. Instead, he introduces the idea that universal wholes are distinguished by the distributive function of the term 'whole', which he contrasts with a primarily quantitative conception of integral wholes:

> 'whole [*totum*]' according to substance is said in one way insofar as it includes quantity [*secundum comprehensionem quantitatis*] (in which case it is called an 'integral whole'), and in another way according to the distribution of a common essence [*secundum diffusionem communis essentiae*] (in which case it is called a universal whole), e.g., when a species is distributed among its individuals in this way: 'This is one man, that is another'. . . . This latter whole makes its universality apparent by being predicated of its singular parts [*totum universale esse apparet quod de singulis praedicatur partibus*]. But this is by no means true of the integral whole, [for in that case the whole is predicated] of the entire collection taken together, in the way that the house is predicated of the walls, the roof, and the foundation, taken together. An integral whole cannot be a universal whole because universality does not have quantitative parts, but rather, consists in the distribution of its common nature over the many things of whose singulars it is predicated [*in suae communitatis diffusione permulta de quibus singulis praedicatur*]. The integral whole, however, has only singular predication in relation to itself, like Socrates, who is composed of these members. [68]

The difference between the species *man* conceived as a universal whole and the genus *animal* is that animal is divisible into what admits of further division: into the species man, horse, etc.[69]

This predicational account of universal wholes is in keeping with Abelard's teaching in the *Logica ingredientibus,* which is based on the idea that "a universal word is one that on the basis of its invention [*ex inventione*] is apt to be predicated of several things one by one [*singillatim*]."[70] A universal word is "imposed" on the things of which it is truly predicable in the way that the word 'man' "is imposed on all single men from the same cause—i.e., because they are rational, mortal animals."[71] Abelard treats wholes such as *man* and *horse* like universal words because for him, they *are* universal words.[72]

Integral wholes, however, call for a different treatment. Abelard defines integral wholes as those having quantitative parts: "the division of a whole, viz., an integral whole, does not involve the assumption of a quality, but comprehension of the quantity of a composite [*sed ad quantitatis compositi comprehensionem*] . . . only the comprehension of material parts is considered when the whole is divided into parts—something we can examine just as much with respect to those parts that are separable from it in reason alone, as with those that are actually separable."[73] But in addition to being marked by quantity, integral wholes are also distinguished by the fact that, unlike universal wholes, they are made up of parts "which do not receive the predication of their whole." This is true, Abelard says, whether we are talking about continuous integral wholes, which are destroyed upon any change in the spatial arrangement of their parts, such as a house or a person's body, or discontinuous integral wholes, which can survive such changes, such as a flock or an army.[74]

But here Abelard's predicational understanding of wholeness produces another divergence from Boethius's account. Boethius assimilates the division of discontinuous integral wholes to that of universal wholes, i.e., as both being divisible into their discrete parts, so that "of men some are in Europe, others in Asia, and others in Africa." Abelard cannot do this, however, since he holds that only universal wholes are predicable of their parts. At most, integral wholes are predicated "of all the collected [parts] taken together," so that '. . . is a house' is true only of the walls, roof, and foundation taken together. Abelard's view is that even if Boethius is right that universal wholes and discontinuous integral wholes both have discrete parts, they have them in an entirely different *sense,* which we can find represented in their different grammatical case endings:

> But the division of these [integral] wholes is not expressed in the same case, i.e., in the nominative, as the division of a universal whole. This fact prevents the integral whole from being predicated of its individual parts in the nominative case. The integral whole lacks this capacity, but it does accord with it to be expressed in the genitive, as in: 'Of this line, one part is this little line [*huius lineae alia pars est haec lineola*]' or 'Of this people, one part is this man, another is that man [*huius populi alia pars hic homo, alia ille*]'.[75]

Abelard connects this with the quantitative character of integral wholes, noting that "this populace is not one thing in nature, but naturally many, viz., as many as there are men in a place, for the plurality of things alone makes this a totality, not any composition of things in the same substance."[76] Conversely, universal wholes are said to have a "natural unity [*unitas naturae*]," since "a single substance can be constituted by natures altogether discrete in matter." This is what makes them predicable of their parts in the nominative case.

But integral wholeness involves more than simply "the plurality of things alone." There is also a difference between mere plurality and plurality that actually constitutes something. Abelard contends that the quantitative character of integral wholes can be found in three distinct modes: in "multiplicity [*pluralitas*]," in "aggregation [*congregatio*]," and in "structural unity [*unitas compositionis*]." Multiplicities are wholes whose integral parts need not be spatially (or temporally) proximate, but are more or less taken at random, in the way that "this unitary part of man [*unitas hominis*] living in Paris and that one living in Rome make a pair."[77] In contrast, "an assemblage of men [*conventus hominum*] makes a populace, and an aggregation of irrational [animals] [*irrationalium congregatio*] a crowd or a flock." Finally, there are integral wholes such as houses, ships, and individual human beings, which are said to consist "in a certain composition of things [*in certa rerum compositione*]."[78] The parts of these wholes are not merely multiple, or aggregate, but rather, must be arranged in a certain way: "for [even] if the walls and roof of a house lie above the foundation, and have been brought together in one place, they are not called a 'house' unless they have what pertains to the composition of a house." Abelard again finds a grammatical marker for this distinction in the fact that unlike plural or collective names, names whose invention is based on "a certain unity of composition" are not construed with plural verbs, so that we say 'Men run [*homines currunt*]', but not 'A house or a ship are [*domus vel navis sunt*]'.[79]

But just what is it that "pertains to the composition" of constitutive wholes? The problem here is that if their composition is formal, it is not formal in the way the composition of universal wholes is formal since constitutive wholes share with other integral wholes the feature of not being predicable of their parts. Abelard does realize that there is a difference between the names we apply to the parts of such wholes whether they do or do not actually constitute something: "although the [integral] parts are divided in keeping with [their] whole, nevertheless, they are not divided under the same name [*sub eodem nomine*], because when we say, 'the wall is one thing in the house, another outside the house [*paries alius in domo, alius extra domo*]', there is a division of genus into species, and so the wall does not remain under the same name."[80] D. P. Henry has shown that Abelard is very much aware that the notion of integral parthood is ambiguous between a constitutive and a non-constitutive sense, i.e., between actual 'parts-of-X' (which

Henry likes to call "genitively-moded parts") and mere 'X-parts'.[81] In the *Dialectica*, Abelard elaborates on the wall example as follows: "the wall is part of itself together with the other things with which it is conjoined, i.e., part of the whole house, but it is not part of itself *per se*. And it is said to be prior to itself and those other things with which it is conjoined, but not prior to itself *per se*. For the wall existed before the conjunction [of which it is a part] did, and it must be that each and every part is prior to the collection it makes [*efficiat*], and in which it is comprehended [*in qua comprehendatur*]."[82] He struggles valiantly with the question of what constitutes such a whole over and above the mere plurality of its parts, yet is unable to find any grammatical device for representing the distinction between parts-of-X and X-parts.[83] Notice that he cannot associate constituent wholeness in particular with the notion of being predicable of individual parts in the genitive, since that has already been used to define the broader notion of integral wholeness. We are left with the idea that the composition of constituent integral wholes representationally mimics that of universal wholes in that they have a unity worthy of a grammatically singular name, except that they fail to be predicable of their parts in the nominative.

With respect to wholes consisting of powers, Abelard follows Boethius in basing our conception of them on the two other kinds: "A whole consisting of powers [*virtuale totum*] has two definitions: one superior, according to which it is predicated of the singular parts, and has an affinity [*habet affinitatem*] with the universal whole; and another inferior, according to which it is not predicated of the singular parts, and according to which it has an affinity for the integral whole." Abelard's example here is the human soul, the "superior" definition of which is "The soul is the quality according to which the body is alive [*anima est qualitas secundum quam vivificatur corpus*]."[84] In this sense, the term 'soul' is predicable of each of its powers, since, e.g., the power of reasoning and the power of sensing are both "qualities according to which the [human] body is alive." The affinity with universal wholes consists in the fact that a soul distributes the quality of bodily animation over each of its constituent powers such that it is truly predicable of them. But the human soul also has an "inferior" definition, viz.: "The soul is a quality constituted by rationality, sensibility, and growth." Taken in this sense, the term 'soul' is not predicable of its powers,[85] since it is not true to say of any one of its powers, e.g., reason, that it is made up of rationality, sensibility, and growth.[86]

But Abelard is unable to extend his account so as to express the difference between inferior and superior qualitative divisions of wholes consisting of powers. Given their predicational affinity with integral wholes, quality would best preserve the contrast with the superior sense, which resembles universal wholes in being qualitatively divisible. Unfortunately, however, the inferior definition is also expressed in terms of quality. Abelard instead stresses the distinction between wholes consisting of powers in the inferior sense and integral wholes: "the fact that a soul is joined together from those powers [i.e., of growing, sensing, and reasoning] pertains to the nature of an integral whole, which is composed of its parts [*quod partibus suis constat*]. And there is an absolute likeness in the composition, [though] not in the mode of composition, for an integral whole is joined together from parts in one way, the soul from powers in another. For the former composition is material, in keeping with the quantity of essence; but the latter composition is in keeping with the reception and infusion of a difference."[87] Integral wholes and wholes consisting of powers are alike in that they both join non-discrete parts together into a single composite, although again, they do so in different ways.[88] On the other hand, the fact that wholes consisting of powers share with universal wholes a qualitative mode of division guarantees that they will be uniquely decomposable by means of sortal concepts, so that as wholes, human souls are divisible into vegetative, sensitive, and rational powers.[89] But again, as with the distinction between constitutive and non-constitutive integral wholes, Abelard has no formal means of representing this distinction.

b. The Buridanian Renovation

If Abelard gives the rudiments of a formal approach to part/whole discourse, Buridan can be seen as perfecting it through logical techniques capable of expressing the different senses of 'part' and 'whole'. As stated above, this is not to suggest that Buridan thought of himself as commenting on Abelard, or that he was directly influenced by Abelard's work, but it is to suggest that Abelard and Buridan are fellow travelers philosophically, and that in terms of reputation and influence, they are among the most important figures in the Parisian tradition of dialectic. The differences between them should not be minimized, of course, but many are attributable to extrinsic factors, such as differences in authorities or methodology. On the first count, we saw that Abelard's characterization of part/whole relations was developed in a commentary on Boethius's *De divisione*. Buridan, on the other hand, draws his inspiration from Aristotle's remarks about parts and wholes in the *Metaphysics, Physics,* and *De Anima,* works which had only became available near the end of Abelard's career and which do not appear to have influenced his thought, even if he was aware of them.[90] On the second, Buridan wrote at a time when medieval logic, long since transformed by the newly translated works of Aristotle, had reached its innovative zenith.[91] Abelard was, like Buridan, a brilliant logician,[92] but his ideas were expressed in the relatively impoverished genres of the 'Old Logic'.[93] The result is that although Abelard and Buridan approach the problem of characterizing whole/part relations in the same way, and with the same nominalistic temperament, Buridan is more successful at finding a solution to it.

Buridan recognizes only two kinds of whole: universal and integral. In this he consciously follows the classification of part/whole inferences in Boethius's *De topicis differentiis,* whose views he regards as consonant with Aristotle's. These authorities are connected in the *Summulae:*[94]

> And clearly Boethius is in agreement on this point with Aristotle in bk. 5 of the *Metaphysics.* . . . Boethius says: "Something is usually said to be 'whole' in two senses, either as a genus, or as something complete that consists of several parts" [*De divisionibus* 887D–888D; cf. *De topicis differentiis* 1188A13–14]. And Aristotle says: "A whole is that which contains those that are contained, so that they are some one thing [*unum aliquid*]; and this in two ways, for either so that each one of them is one, or so that that which is [constituted] from them is one"; and he meant to say that the whole has to be something one, as he says, "insofar as it is some totality" [*Metaphysics* V.26.1023b27ff.], and it is also necessary that the whole contain several things, which are its parts, and those several things also have to be or have to be said to be that one. And this can happen in two ways: either so that each one of those several things is said to be that one thing, i.e., so that the one whole is truly said, i.e., predicated, of each one of them, and this is the universal whole; for, as Aristotle says, the universal whole contains several things because of its being predicated of each one of them [*Metaphysics* V.26.1023b30–32]. In the other way the situation is such that the one whole is not predicated of any one of those several things but it is [rather made up] from and consists of them; and this is the integral whole, which is not only [made up] *from* its parts, but also *is* its parts [*non solum est ex suis partibus, sed est suae partes*]; whereas a universal whole *is not* its parts. (*S* 6.4.4: 427–28; cf. *S* 8.1.4: 617–19)

Aristotle does say in the *Metaphysics* that universal wholes are predicable of their parts, but neither he nor Boethius mentions the converse idea that integral wholes are those which are not predicable of their parts. For both Buridan and Abelard, however, predicability of parts is the *differentia* that separates universal from integral wholes.

About universal wholes, Buridan has little to say. This is a reflection of his view that the term 'universal whole' by itself does not stand for things, but only for other terms: "it is clear that the names 'universal whole' and 'subjective part', or even 'superior' or 'inferior in predication', are names of second intention, or imposition; for they appropriately supposit for predicable and subjectible significative terms" (*S* 6.4.4: 428; cf. *S* 6.4.3: 423; *QM* VII.11: 47vb). Buridan here invokes the important distinction—which the *logica nova* borrowed from Avicenna—between terms or concepts of first intention, which stand for things outside the mind, and those of second intention, which stand for other terms and concepts.[95] Buridanian universal wholes are thus twice removed from extramental things. But if the term 'universal whole' is just a term of terms, without its division producing anything having parts *per se,* the question of how universal wholes are divided as wholes points to this semantic hierarchy. Buridan remarks, "although the term 'universal' in your soul or mine does not have integral parts, it does have subjective parts, viz., the five predicables" (*QIP* 3: 136, ll. 505–507);[96] thus, he says, the term 'animal' is divided into 'rational' and 'irrational', "not in the way that an integral whole is divided into the parts from which it is made into something whole, but as a common term with respect to the terms subject to it" (*QIP* 4: 140, ll. 657–59; cf. *QM* VII.10: 47rb–va).[97] Conversely, he says, "the terms 'integral whole' and 'integral part' are terms of first intention or imposition, for they aptly [*bene*] supposit for external things, existing apart from the operations of the soul; for a house is an integral whole, as well as a man or a stone, for any of these consists of many parts and is those parts [*et sic illae partes*]" (*S* 6.4.4: 428).

Appropriately enough, it is in his natural philosophy, and specifically in his *Questions on Aristotle's Physics* and *De Anima,* that Buridan asks "whether a whole is its parts [*utrum totum est suae partes*]" in the sense in which this concerns integral wholes (*QP* I.9: 12va; cf. *S* 4.3.7.1: 167–68).[98] His answer involves a distinction between the term 'whole' understood properly or strictly, and according to what he calls "the extended and more customary use of the expression [*secundum locutionem impropriam et multum consuetam*]."

In the strict sense, 'whole' is a categorematic term,[99] signifying "the same as 'having integral parts' [*habens partes integrantes*]." But the proposition, 'The whole is its parts', turns out to be doubly ambiguous. If it means, 'The whole is some one of its parts', then it is false because "no part is the whole of which it is a part," just as the wall or the roof is not the entire house. Integral wholes, according to both Abelard and Buridan, are not predicable of their parts when those wholes are taken in their proper senses (*QIP* 7: 153). But if 'The whole is its parts' means, 'The whole is the sum of its parts', there is a further ambiguity between the compounded and divided senses of that proposition. It is false in the divided sense, i.e., with each addendum taken separately, because "it is not true to say that the whole is this part or that part." But in the compounded sense, i.e., with all of the addenda taken together, 'The whole is its parts' is true because "it is true to say that the whole is this part and that part." The reason for the distinction is that integral wholes have properties that are not distributed over their parts: "for example, we say in a divided sense that these foot-long stones are a foot long if each is a foot long, but we say in a compounded sense that those stones occupy two feet of space, as does what is joined together from them" (*QP* I.9: 12va).[100] Buridan is here expressing the Abelardian idea that integral wholes are not predicable of their parts taken one by one, but together, in terms of the distinction between the compounded and divided senses of the proposition,

'The whole is its parts'. This distinction had its beginnings in Abelard, but by the fourteenth century, it had become a standard tool of analysis for propositions in modal contexts.[101]

Buridan also introduces a less strict sense of the term 'whole' aimed at underwriting what he sees as its more common use in conventional discourse.[102] Here he employs the 'modern' distinction between categorematic and syncategorematic uses of a term. If we understand 'whole' less strictly as a syncategorematic term together with a categorematic term,[103] it makes the categorematic term with which it is construed signify each of its parts. For the term 'whole' "implies in itself [*implicat in se*] a universal sign distributing the name 'part' such that it means the same to say 'whole man [*totus homo*] and 'of a man, each part [*hominis quaelibet pars*]', or 'whole Socrates [*totus Sortes*]' and 'of Socrates, each part [*Sortes quaelibet pars*]'" (*QP* I.9: 12va).[104] The similarity between Buridan's exposition of 'whole'—with the categorematic name for the integral whole in the genitive, followed by the distributive adjective 'each' and the term 'part' in the nominative—and Abelard's notion that such wholes are predicable of their parts in the genitive is undeniable.

Returning to the ambiguous proposition, 'The whole is its parts', Buridan says that if we are referring to 'whole Socrates', then it is true in the sense of 'The whole is some one of its parts', because "of Socrates, each part is part of Socrates," i.e., each part of an integral whole is a part of it. But with respect to the other sense of this proposition, i.e., 'The whole is the sum of its parts', Buridan says that wholes can have parts in two ways: "there is one kind of which each part is divisible, e.g., a horse, a stone, and water, and another of which some part is indivisible but in which each part is divisible" (*QP* I.9: 12vb).[105] The truth of 'The whole is its parts' in the second sense then depends on how the whole in question is said to have parts: "I say that the whole is its parts, e.g., 'A whole horse is its parts', as is obvious in the following exposition: 'of a horse, each part is its parts', for each part has two halves, and the horse is those two halves, in keeping with what we have said above. But for those things in which some part is indivisible, it must be denied that the whole is its parts, e.g., it is not true that 'A whole man is his parts', for there is the counterexample of the intellective soul, which is not its parts, since it is indivisible" (*QP* I.9: 12vb).[106] Thus, each quantitatively divisible part of an integral whole simply is the parts into which it is further divisible—the whole horse is divisible into halves, quarters, and so on.

But then how are indivisible wholes such as the human intellective soul related to their powers, if not as wholes to parts? Buridan does not recognize wholes consisting of powers as such, but he does discuss them in Book II, Question 7 of his *Questions on Aristotle's De Anima*, which asks whether a whole soul is in each part of its body. Included there is a set of examples intended to instruct the reader on the proper analysis of propositions in which the term 'soul [*anima*]' occurs together with the term 'whole [*totus*]'.

Buridan begins by invoking his earlier distinction between the two senses of 'whole'. In the categorematic sense, 'whole' "signifies the same as 'having parts'," in which case it is true not only that 'In every horse is a whole soul of a horse [*in omni equo esset tota anima equi*]', but also that 'In each quantitative part of the body of a horse is a whole soul [*in qualibet parte quantitativa corporis equi esset tota anima*]' (*QDA₃* II.7: 104).[107] Since (as we shall see in chapter 11 below) Buridan conceives of brute animal and plant souls as homogenously extended throughout their bodies, they can have parts in the same quantitative sense in which bodies have parts. For the same reason, however, he denies, 'In a man is a whole soul [*in homine sit tota anima*]' because human souls are indivisible, and indivisibles do not have quantitative parts.

Buridan then distinguishes not one but two different syncategorematic senses of the term 'whole X'. In one sense, 'whole X' is expounded as 'of X, each part', so that 'of X' occurs first, in the genitive case, and 'each part' second, in the nominative, as in 'of a man, each part [*hominis quaelibet pars*]'. This is contrasted with another sense of 'whole', which reverses the order of the nominative and genitive words, as in 'each part of a man' or 'each human part [*quaelibet pars hominis*]'. Despite its trivial appearance, this change in word order represents Buridan's attempt to capture, in logical terms, the semantic distinction between constitutive and non-constitutive integral parthood. In the first sense, signifying a whole as constituted by integral parts, Buridan concedes, 'In the body of a horse is the whole soul of a horse [*in corpore equi est tota anima equi*]', because "in the body of a horse is of the soul of a horse each part, but not each equine soul-part [*quia in corpore equi est animae equi quaelibet pars, non tamen quaelibet pars animae equi*]" (*QDA₃* II.7: 102). The latter would not be true, he says, "unless every equine soul were in that horse [*nisi in isto equo esset omnis anima equi*]." In other words, each soul-part of a given horse inheres commensurably in its body, but not all soul-parts of horses existing anywhere. The placement of the genitive construction, 'of the soul [*animae*]' expresses the scope-distinction underlying these two ways of construing integral parthood. Buridan even suggests that the distinction ought to be reflected in the way his students refer to their corresponding wholes: "Some would ask how the phrase 'whole soul' should be expounded literally. And it seems to me that there is a difference between saying 'whole soul' and 'soul as a whole'. Therefore, let us say 'whole soul', that is, 'each part of soul', and 'soul as a whole', that is, 'of a soul, each part'" (*QDA₃* II.7: 103).[108]

Buridan's remarks here recall a passage from the *Summulae*'s fourth treatise, where he explains the difference in meaning between 'whole man [*totus homo*]', and 'man as a whole [*homo totus*]' in terms of the same scope-distinction: "It should also be known that, by virtue of its proper meaning [*de proprietate sermonis*], 'whole man [*totus homo*]' is expounded differently from 'man as a whole [*homo totus*]': 'whole man' is [expounded as] 'each part of a man [*quaelibet pars hominis*]' [i.e., 'each human part'], whereas 'a man as a whole' [is expounded as] 'of a man, each part [*hominis quaelibet pars*]'. These are quite different, for if Socrates is in this house and Plato outside, then 'Each part of a man [i.e., each human part] is in this house' is false, whereas 'Of a man, each part is in this house' is true" (*S* 4.3.7.1: 267–68).[109] Neither the categorematic nor either of the syncategorematic senses of 'whole soul' applies to human intellective souls, however, since they are indivisible.[110] To this end, Buridan says that 'whole' can also be understood "partly categorematically and partly syncategorematically." This exposition of 'whole' does not actually mention parts in either of those senses. Rather, 'the whole A is B' is to be expounded as 'A is B, and nothing belongs to A that is not B'. Buridan says that 'whole' in this sense is "rightly said of indivisibles [*bene dicitur de indivisibilibus*]" such as God and the human intellective soul, so that we can concede both 'The whole divine essence is God [*tota essentia divina est deus*]' and 'The whole intellective soul informs the human body [*tota anima intellectivae informat corpus humanum*]'. As an absolutely simple being, of course, God is identical with God's essence, so that the former proposition is expounded, 'The whole divine essence is God, and nothing belongs to the divine essence that is not God'. The same is true of the way in which the intellective soul animates the human body. The latter proposition is expounded, 'The whole intellective soul is informing the human body, and nothing belongs to the intellective soul that is not informing the human body'.

c. Nominalism as Praxis

In his 1966 translation of Buridan's *Sophismata*, T. K. Scott summarized the relation between the nominalism of Ockham and Buridan as follows:

> What Ockham had begun, Buridan continued, but with an even clearer realization of ends in view. While Buridan never acknowledges his debt to Ockham, it is obvious not only in his handling of specific issues, but also in his whole philosophic attitude. If Ockham initiated a new way of doing philosophy, Buridan is already a man of the new way. If Ockham was the evangel of a new creed, Buridan is inescapably its stolid practitioner. He cites Aristotle with approval, and at times with disapproval, but he seldom interprets him against the realists. He is a nominalist (a much more radical one than Ockham), but he is less concerned to defend nominalism than to use it.[111]

Scott's remarks remain a highly apt characterization of Buridan's philosophical outlook. We have since learned more about the details, and these tell us that Buridan's methods, as well as the actual uses to which he puts his nominalism, owe more to Parisian sources and traditions ranging from Abelard to Peter of Spain than to influences from outside the University. This is hardly surprising, of course, although it is easy to lose sight of it when the history of later medieval philosophy is told from the perspective of general trends and major figures. Buridan's contribution is more often than not in the details, and here, the particular character of his solutions has more in common with the nominalism of Abelard than of Ockham.

Abelard and Buridan share with twentieth-century philosophers such as Carnap and Wittgenstein the view that language is the source of pseudo-problems in philosophy. One such problem is the tendency of philosophers to reify terms and categories, insisting that there be some kind of isomorphism between the world and the language we use to describe it. In their view, the proper antidote for this is to be found in a semantics of terms—or, at a higher level, a system of rules governing the analysis of propositions and arguments—which does not have the same ontology-enriching consequences.

On the question of parts and wholes, Abelard insists that "all regular division is of terms only," and that the difference between a universal and an integral whole is only the difference between whether a term is predicable of its parts or not, i.e., whether we can say it of its parts or not. If someone were to ask him, 'Yes, but do universal wholes really exist?', Abelard's reply would be 'Wrong question: for when I think of Socrates or Plato as parts of *man*, I am only understanding Socrates or Plato in a certain way; nothing subsistent follows from my mode of conception'. It is by thinking that we can answer such questions that we find ourselves in perplexity. Abelard's main accomplishment was to establish a way of dealing with mereological questions semantically, by fixing upon syntactic differences between the uses of Latin words as a means of representing certain distinctions in meaning. This is evident in his observations that integral wholes are predicable of their parts only in the genitive case, and that constitutive integral wholes differ from aggregates and mere pluralities by being construed with singular rather than with plural verbs. But Abelard struggles with other distinctions, including the distinction between constitutive and non-constitutive integral parthood, never quite managing to move from the concept to its perspicuous representation in language.

Buridan employs several techniques unknown (at least in their developed forms) to Abelard in his analysis of parts and wholes, such as the theory of supposition and the distinctions between terms of first and second intention, the compounded and divided senses of an expression, and categorematic and syncategorematic uses of a term. His work can be seen as perfecting Abelard's strategy, first in the way it captures the distinction between constitutive and non-constitutive integral wholes in terms of the two different syncategorematic senses of 'whole [*totus*]', even going so far as to suggest that philosophers should conventionalize such differences by placing the term 'whole' either before or after the categorematic term with which it is construed. Second, Buridan shows that the standard categorematic reading of 'whole' as 'having parts' does not suffice to distinguish integral wholes from indivisible wholes, which do not have quantitative parts. To this end, he introduces a combined, categorematic/syncategorematic reading of 'whole', the exposition of which makes no reference at all to parts. This proves useful for interpreting propositions in which 'whole' is taken together with terms such as 'divine essence', or 'intellective soul', which are wholes in a quite different sense than animal souls and bodies, ships, houses, flocks, or armies. The result is a more nuanced presentation of mereological discourse, which will come in handy when he turns to the difficult question of how souls inhere in their bodies.

CHAPTER ELEVEN

Bodies and Souls

·How are souls related to the bodies they animate? Medieval answers to this question differed not only from each other but also internally, relative to the type of soul (and body) in question. Unlike modern philosophers of mind, medieval philosophers did not define their positions ontologically, in terms of whether one needs both mind and matter or just matter to explain psychological phenomena, but tended to infer differences within a broadly Aristotelian paradigm from capacities they saw actually being exercised by animate creatures.[1] Buridan is a case in point. He gives a different account of the soul/body relation, depending upon which of what he takes to be the two main varieties of animate, corporeal substance he is considering. Where human beings are concerned, he defends the thesis that the soul is an immaterial, everlasting, and created—as opposed to naturally generated—entity, actually inhering in each and every body it animates, and hence numerically many.[2] On the other hand, he argues that the sensitive and vegetative souls of non-human animals and plants are collections of material, extended powers exhaustively defined by their biological functions, and hence as corruptible as the particular arrangements of matter they happen to animate. This basic difference in souls yields a difference in what the natural philosopher can say about psychological inherence.

Buridan discusses what it means for the soul to inhere in the body at several junctures in the third and final version of his *Questions on Aristotle's De Anima* (QDA_3 II.4–7: 42–105; QDA_3 III.17: 20–56), though his remarks about non-human souls are of a piece with the more general picture of inherence presented elsewhere in his writings. Human souls call for special treatment.

In both cases, however, Buridan strives to explain body/soul relations in a way that is both naturalistic, i.e., in the sense that it acknowledges what our cognitive powers evidently tell us about the issue, and faithful to the patterns of reasoning he has so carefully modeled in the *Summulae*.

1. Non-Human Souls

The question of inherence is raised as such in the second book of Buridan's commentary. Like nearly all of the *quaestiones* in Buridan's commentaries, it is based on a lemma from the work being commented upon, in this case Aristotle's observation in the second chapter of *De Anima* II that it is possible for some plants and animals to survive physical division—a fact which leads Aristotle to conclude that before division, their souls are actually one but potentially many.[3] For Buridan, this invites us to ask how we are to understand the presence of the soul's nutritive and sensitive powers in animated, corporeal bodies: in what sense does the whole soul of an organism inhere in its body, if a single division of the quantitative parts of that body gives rise to two new whole souls? Since QDA_3 II is, like *De Anima* II, addressed to the nature and function of the sensitive soul, Buridan gives his answer from the perspective of the psychology of brute or non-human animals, creatures whose souls are paradigmatically sensitive. In addition, as we saw in chapter 10, since his answer must consider the soul of an animal as a 'whole [*tota*]', remarks are included on the proper interpretation of the term 'whole', thus instantiating the teaching of the *Summulae* (S 4.3.7.1: 267–68).

In the main section of QDA_3 II.7, Buridan introduces four metaphysical principles that he takes to govern the inherence of non-human animal souls, and hence to explain how the sensitive or vegetative souls of such creatures can be in each part of their bodies.

a. The Extensionality Principle

The first principle is attributed to Aristotle and defined as follows: "The vegetative soul, sensitive soul, etc., in a horse is not distinct in different parts of its body, but extended throughout the whole body of the animal as vegetative and sensitive and appetitive" (QDA_3 II.7: 89).[4] The vegetative and sensitive souls of plants and brute animals, together with their characteristic powers of nutrition, growth, and desire—which are sometimes called 'souls' in their own right, as in 'nutritive soul', 'appetitive soul', and so on—are said to be "extended throughout the whole body" because they are derived from its matter. According to the extensionality principle, when an animating principle has been derived from an extended subject, it must commensurably inhere in that subject.

Buridan elsewhere draws a distinction between two different modes of inherence that helps to clarify how one thing can be said to inhere commensurably in another. A power or capacity, he says, inheres in a subject (1) as a proximate potentiality (*potentia propinqua*), just in case it can act or be acted upon immediately, without the assistance of a mediating quality disposing it to act or be acted upon, or (2) as a remote potentiality (*potentia remota*), just in case it can only act or be acted upon with the assistance of a mediating quality so disposing it. In this way, some powers of the soul are said to be proximate, others remote:

> Although the human soul can exercise some of its operations immediately, it cannot so exercise all of them. For example, if we were to posit only one substantial form in a man, viz., the intellective soul by which some human body is informed, nevertheless, that soul has been abstracted in such a way that is not derived from a subjective potentiality nor extended by its extension—which is why it does not need to use a corporeal organ for its principal operations, i.e., willing and understanding. Yet even so, it needs a corporeal organ and certain qualitative dispositions of [such] an organ to exercise its other operations, for it needs an eye to see, an ear to hear, and so forth. (*QNE* VI.3: 118vb)[5]

What this means is that the intellective soul is proximately potential to its definitive or essential operations of willing and understanding, since it is possible for intellectual creatures to engage in those activities without needing any specific arrangement of matter in the form of an organ.[6] But the powers characteristic of the vegetative or sensitive souls—i.e., nutrition, growth, and sensation, which in human beings are subsumed under the single substantial form of the intellective soul—are only remote potentialities. They become proximate potentialities when they are considered along with their determining qualitative dispositions. Thus, we say that the sensitive power together with the eye, an arrangement of matter disposed to register light and color, is immediately capable of seeing; the sensitive power together with the ear, an arrangement of matter disposed to register vibrations in the air, is immediately capable of hearing; and so on.

The distinction between proximate and remote potentialities is crucial for understanding the precise sense in which Buridan understands powers of the vegetative or sensitive soul to be extended throughout the body. The extensionality principle is false if those powers are conceived as proximate potentialities, since the sensitive soul is proximately seeing or hearing not throughout the whole body but only locally, i.e., wherever it inheres in physical organs disposed to seeing or hearing. Thus, it is proximately seeing only in the eye, proximately hearing only in the ear, and so on. But the principle

is true of those powers conceived as remote potentialities, since each and
every part of the body of a plant or animal is potentially seeing or hearing,
but for the mediating qualitative disposition necessary for seeing or hearing.
Buridan explains his understanding of this distinction in response to a student query:

> But it is reasonable for you to ask whether the soul in the foot of a horse
> is capable of seeing. And I say that it is, speaking of a principal and re-
> mote potentiality, because in itself it is naturally suited to see and would
> see in a foot if God and nature were to form an eye in the foot for it. But
> it is not in the foot as a proximate potentiality for seeing because by
> 'proximate potentiality' we must understand either the necessary dispo-
> sitions together with the principal agent or the principal potentiality it-
> self in possession of the dispositions it needs to operate. And when it is
> without them, it is called a 'remote potentiality'. Nor is that [remote] po-
> tentiality posited pointlessly in the foot, since it exercises other opera-
> tions [besides seeing] there. (QDA_3 II.5: 66–67)[7]

So even if the sensitive soul's powers are manifested only locally, there remains a sense in which they are present throughout the whole body: "if there
were an eye in the foot in the same way as in the head as far as its qualitative
dispositions are concerned, we would undoubtedly see with the foot's eye just
as we do with the head's eyes. For the substance of the soul, which is naturally
suited to exercise its every operation wherever the organic dispositions necessary for it are present, exists everywhere throughout the whole body" (QNE
VI.3: 119ra).[8] Buridan's extensionality principle as applied to the soul, then, is
a claim about capacities of the soul conceived as remote potentialities.

b. The Subject Identity Principle

The second principle states that in non-human animals, "the sensitive soul
is not separate in subject from the vegetative soul [*non separata secundum
subiectum ab anima vegetative*]," but part of the same identical subject of
which the vegetative soul is also a part (QDA_3 II.7: 91). In defense of this principle, Buridan notes only that it raises the question of whether there is a plurality of souls in any living thing, which he says he has already answered in
the negative. This is a reference to an earlier question in the same commentary, where he presents five arguments against the view that the same animal
is possessed of vegetative and sensitive souls distinct not only in definition,
but also in reality (QDA_3 II.4: 49–54). The first three of these are aimed at reducing the pluralist position to absurdity. If the vegetative and sensitive souls
are really distinct, Buridan argues, then:

(N1) In a horse, God could separate one soul from the other, making the horse into either an animal or a plant. But then the horse would be composed of both animal and plant, which is absurd.

(N2) The vegetative soul of a horse would be nobler than its sensitive soul, since the former acts on substance through nutrition and generation, whereas the latter is merely the passive recipient of external sensible species. But this is absurd.[9]

(N3) Since the sensitive souls of a dog and a horse would have the same substantial nature, they must differ in some specific, substantial form added to them. Proof: this added form will be either a soul or else some other kind of form. If the latter, then it would be less noble than the sensitive soul, which is absurd since souls are the noblest natural forms, and specific form is related to general form as act to potentiality, from which it follows that a specific form must be nobler than the general form it perfects. If the former, then that added soul would be either capable or incapable of cognition. If incapable, it would be less noble than the sensitive soul, which is absurd. But if it is capable of cognition, it will cognize as either a sensitive or intellective power. Since a horse or dog cannot understand, however, it must be sensitive—but then it would not be distinct from the sensitive soul it supposedly differentiates, which is absurd.

Buridan's fourth argument proceeds to attack the pluralist claim that though really distinct, the vegetative or sensitive souls found in different creatures are specifically the same:

(N4) If the vegetative soul had the same nature in human beings, horses, and fish, then it would nourish in the same way, and produce similar flesh and similar limbs in those creatures possessing it, which is plainly false.

In his final argument, Buridan appeals to what he regards as the main problem with the pluralist position. We are possessed of empirical intellects. And although we can only argue to the specific diversity of substantial forms on the basis of diversity in operations, he says, "one does not argue to a diversity of substantial forms on the basis of any specific diversity in operations at all [*non quaecumque diversitas specifica operationum arguit diversitatem formarum substantialium*]" (QDA₃ II.4: 54). For this reason:

(N5) Not every operational diversity is attributable to specific difference. Thus, we do not argue from diverse operations in the intellect (e.g. understanding, willing, apprehending), the vegetative souls of plants (e.g. nourishment, growth, foliation, bearing fruit), or even from the natural dispositions of elements (e.g. the cooling and moistening capacities of water), to a diversity of substantial forms.

In Buridan's view, the pluralists' mistake lies in always inferring substantial from operational diversity. Buridan himself regards operational diversity as an indicator of substantial diversity, but his inferences are constrained by the more fundamental metaphysical principle that forms of a superior degree and greater actuality subsume, in their nobler operations, the operations of lesser forms, in the way that a mixture is said to retain the qualities and capacities of its predominant elements (QDA$_3$ II.4: 54–55; cf. QDA$_3$ III.3: 24). The soul/body inherence relation is thus not many/one but one/one, since one soul can have a variety of operations, some of which are nobler than others.

Although Buridan seems to be following Aristotle on the question of how many relata are on the soul side of the soul/body relation,[10] he is also motivated by considerations of parsimony. In the corresponding question on the intellective soul, Buridan reasserts the subject identity principle on the grounds that "it would be pointless to posit more than one soul if everything could be explained by just one [frustra ponerentur plures animae si omnes possent salvari per unicam]" (QDA$_3$ III.17: 192). One consequence of this is that language improperly implying the existence of a plurality of souls needs to be reformulated so that "the soul is said to be intellective to the extent that it is naturally suited to understand [anima dicitur intellectiva secundum quod innata est intelligere], sensitive to the extent that it is naturally suited to sense, vegetative to the extent that it is naturally suited to nourish, and locally motive to the extent that it is naturally suited to move a body locally" (QDA$_3$ III.17: 192–93; cf. QDA$_3$ II.4: 56–57). Likewise, Buridan finds that language used to refer to animate capacities must be carefully interpreted so as to avoid falling into the pluralist trap of assuming that distinct capacities must inhere in really distinct essences or natures:

> we say that Brunellus through his same essence and nature is Brunellus and a horse and an animal and a living thing and a body. And when we say that sensitive being is in Brunellus insofar as he is an animal and not insofar as he is a living thing, we understand by this that the proposition 'An animal is sensitive' is true per se and in the first instance, although not 'A living thing is sensitive'. Thus, by 'being in some respect' we understand an essential predication of terms either in first metaphysics or something of the sort . . . such that the expression was not about real inherence. (QDA$_3$ II.4: 56)[11]

Buridan holds that there is an order of predication between the various natural capacities of the soul and the soul itself conceived as sensitive, moving, living, and so on, but denies that such distinctions are ontologically significant in the sense that they entitle us to posit distinct entities. This is for the straightforwardly nominalistic reason that merely predicational distinctions do not real distinctions make. What is the basis, though, for this definitional or predicational sense in which the various powers of a single soul may be said to be distinct from each other? The final two principles are intended to answer this question, from the standpoints of logic and metaphysics, respectively.

c. The Definitional Distinction Principle

Founded upon Aristotle's assertion that the various parts of the soul, though incapable of existing separately, remain distinct in reason or definition,[12] Buridan's third principle is presented as a claim about how we should understand the terms 'vegetative', 'sensitive', and so on:

> Aristotle's second conclusion is that the names 'sensitive' and 'vegetative' attributed to a horse are not synonymous, but differ in reason because there is one concept according to which we understand the soul to be the principle of sensation and according to which it is called sensitive, and another according to which we understand the soul to be the principle of nutrition and according to which it is called nutritive, and so on for the others. (QDA_3 II.7: 91)[13]

Buridan argues that even though the powers of the soul are not really distinct,[14] we impose different names (e.g., 'sense', 'intellect', 'vegetative soul') to signify them as diverse operations, in keeping with the principle that active and passive potentialities take their proper denomination from their operations.[15] Such powers are said to be distinct in reason or definition, since their names signify the same thing according to different natures (QDA_3 II.5: 64; cf. QNE VI.3, ff. 188vb–119ra; QM IV.1, f. 13ra–rb).

"A definition," says Buridan, "must explicate the concept of the defined term [diffinitio debeat explicare conceptum termini diffiniti]" (QNE VI.3: 118vb). But understood in their proper or literal sense, the concepts of defined terms may differ while still suppositing for the same thing:

> I say that the same thing is conceived by very different concepts, either because of the diverse properties found in it or because of their extrinsic connotation, whether what is connoted is extrinsic to it or inhering in it. It is for this reason that the same thing is properly signified by the names of the ten categories. And so it seems concepts still possess an original distinction on the part of the things signified, although not always on the part of the things they signify or for which they supposit, but more often on the part of their connotation. (QM IV.1: 13ra–rb)[16]

The possibility of terms such as 'vegetative soul' and 'sensitive soul' standing or suppositing for different things is ruled out by the subject identity principle. As Buridan states, "I believe . . . that the soul in a horse is singular and that there is no vegetative soul in it [really] distinct from the sensitive soul, nor sensitive soul distinct from the vegetative soul [*credo quod . . . in equo unica sit anima et quod non sit in eo anima vegetativa distincta a sensitiva nec sensitiva distincta a vegetativa*]" (*QDA₃* II.4: 48). But the principle is applied here by means of a logico-semantic device whose rudiments are discussed in the *Summulae* (see *S* 2.5.2: 127–28; *S* 3.1.3: 145–48; and *S* 9.4, *in toto*). In their most literal sense, the expressions 'vegetative soul' and 'sensitive soul' are to be treated as connotative terms having the same referent, but making that referent known in different ways, i.e., signifying what they properly signify (souls) in relation to something else (capacities for nutrition/growth and sensation, respectively).[17] The doctrine of the connotation of terms, or 'appellation' as Buridan calls it in propositional contexts, thus becomes the vehicle for expressing a substantive view in the science of psychology. As L. M. de Rijk notes, it functions metaphysically "to make our different modes of thinking the same thing explicit," while avoiding the danger of Platonism which lies in "hypostasizing accidental features" of substances.[18] Where the single-substance soul is concerned, the features Buridan wishes to avoid hypostatizing are not accidental but essential, viz., the definitive operations of the soul variously conceived as sensitive, living, and so on. To this end, connotation grounds the language he uses to speak properly and scientifically about different psychological operations without committing him to the view that those operations must inhere in different things. Thus, we avoid the needless multiplication of entities.

d. The Homogeneity Principle

Buridan's fourth and final principle concerns the manner rather than the mode of inherence. The homogeneity principle states that the sensitive and vegetative souls of non-human animals are composed of quantitative parts "having the same nature [*ex partibus eiusdem rationis*]," like the form of air. This Buridan offers as the metaphysical basis for claiming that the parts of the soul "receive the predications of the whole to the extent that they are quidditative predicates [*partes recipiunt predicationes totius quantum ad praedicata quidditativa*]" (*QDA₃* II.7: 93; cf. *QDA₃* III.17: 192–93): it is because substantial predicates apply to each quantitative part of homogenous entities that we can say that each part of air is air; each part of water is water; each part of an animal is an animal; and each part of a horse is a horse.

But what is it, exactly, that is homogenous in sensitive and vegetative souls? The answer may be found in Buridan's discussion of the extensionality principle. The animate capacities of plants and non-human animals conceived as remote potentialities are homogenously extended throughout their entire bodies, since, as we saw above, even the foot of a horse would see but for the mediating qualitative dispositions necessary for seeing, the presence of which would make the foot into an eye. Notice, however, that the homogeneity thesis would be false if 'animal' or 'horse' were taken as signifying those dispositions or physical organs through which the soul happens to operate, since they are composed of heterogenous and dissimilar quantitative parts. Thus, Buridan argues that if we say that an animal "is substantially constituted by prime matter and a single substantial form not having substantially dissimilar parts belonging to diverse natures," then the term 'animal' is truly a substance term that does not signify or connote "arrangements [*organizationes*]" of organic matter such as we find in the eyes and ears of living things (*QDA₃* II.7: 94).[19]

Buridan offers two arguments on behalf of the view that the terms 'animal' and 'horse' are non-connotative substantial terms by means of which we conceive of an animal or a horse as a composite of matter together with a single soul having homogenous parts. First, if God were to separate, *per potentiam divinam,* a matter/soul composite from the organic dispositions through which it happens to operate and then preserve it separately, only on the substantial term view could 'animal' be truly predicated of the remaining composite—whereas if it were a term connotative of the qualitative dispositions through which the soul happens to operate, or of the soul conceived as an entirety, it would not be true to say of the remaining composite that it is an animal. Second, in an argument originating from Aristotle's remarks about animals that can survive physical division, it might look as if such animals are really two or more animals, since: (1) once divided, the names used to signify their parts will stand for something living, sensing, and subsisting *per se,* and everything of that sort is an animal; and (2) if the parts of an animal will be animals tomorrow, surely they are animals now.[20] But Buridan observes that construing 'animal' as a substantial term provides an innocuous way of conceding the truth of this consequence, for 'animal' may be truly predicated of both distinct substances and distinct quantitative parts of the same substance in the sense that each is a body/soul composite, although not in the secondary and connotative sense that each is a whole substance, having distinct quantitative parts (*QDA₃* II.7: 95–97).

By way of contrast, Buridan also discusses how terms such as 'animal' and 'horse' function when construed as connotative rather than substantial terms. Here the homogeneity principle does not apply. The reason is that if 'animal' is connotative of the animal taken as a whole, it cannot be predicated of each of its quantitative parts prior to their actual physical division, since by 'whole being [*ens totale*]', Buridan understands "that which is a being and not part of another being [*quod est ens et non est pars alterius entis*]," and by 'whole substance [*substantia totalis*]', "that which is a substance and not part of another substance [*quae est substantia et non est pars alterius substantiae*]." On this view, says Buridan, if we call the foot of a horse A and the rest B, "it is obvious that B is not a horse," although it immediately becomes a horse once A has been cut off. That is because being 'whole' or 'part' signifies not only some thing, but also that thing's being somehow related to something else. Thus, if the term 'animal' connotes a totality, Buridan concludes that one would be committing the fallacy of figure of speech by arguing, 'Whatever B is now, it was that before', or 'B is now an animal; therefore, it was an animal before'. The consequence fails because B has changed not in what it is, but in how it is related to another thing, in this case to (what was) another integral part of the whole animal (*QDA*$_3$ II.7: 97–99).[21]

But the change in truth-value of the proposition 'B is now an animal' is rooted in an important feature of Buridan's ontology. What kind of change would make that proposition false at one time but true at another? There is no change in the supposition or reference of its constituent terms, since on both occasions of its utterance, the subject 'B' refers to the horse minus a foot, the latter designated as 'A', and the predicate 'animal' to mobile, animate things. But there does appear to be a change in what is signified secondarily or connoted by the term 'animal'—recall Buridan's assumption that 'animal' is being used here as a connotative and non-substantial term—because 'animal' connotes a mobile, animate thing taken as a whole, and that connotation fails in the first instance, i.e., when A is still joined to B. But one must be careful here, since no thing either comes into or passes out of being as a result of this change. 'B is now an animal' is true in the second instance only because of a change in the way B is related to something external to it. The question this raises for nominalists such as Buridan is how to explain changes in truth-value that do not arise from the generation or corruption of anything, but merely from relational changes. If we assume that the world is austerely furnished to begin with, how should we describe subsequent rearrangements of that furniture?

As Calvin Normore has argued, Buridan resolves this problem by embracing realism about modes, which are qualities or accidents that define not what a thing is, but how it is.[22] Such relational changes are sufficient to ground changes in connotation. Buridan notes, e.g., that relational terms may connote "another thing" either inherent in, or extrinsic to, the things for which they supposit:

> sometimes it happens that a relative concrete term not only signifies or connotes the thing for which it supposits, and the thing to which the comparison is being made, but also connotes another thing either inhering in some one of them, or perhaps sometimes extrinsic to them. For example, if I say, 'Socrates is similar to Plato', the term 'similar' not only signifies and connotes Socrates and Plato, but also connotes the quality according to which he is similar to him. And so if I say, 'Socrates is equal to Plato', the term 'equal' connotes, beyond Socrates and Plato, their magnitudes. And if I say, 'Whiteness inheres in a stone' or 'Form inheres in matter', then the word 'inheres' connotes the disposition added apart

from the form and the matter, viz., the inseparability, as was stated in another question. Likewise, if I say, 'Socrates is at a distance from Plato', the term 'is at a distance' connotes another thing apart from Socrates and Plato and also extrinsic to Socrates and Plato, viz., the intermediate dimension by which Socrates is at a distance from Plato. (*QM* V.9: 32va; cf. *QM* V.8: 31rb–33ra)[23]

Although the proposition 'B is now an animal' does not contain any relational terms, Buridan's assumption that 'animal' functions in it connotatively suggests that the above distinction is the right model for understanding its change in truth-value. In this way, the term 'animal' may be said to signify an animate, mobile thing, but also to connote it in some way, viz., as a whole. What it connotes is the spatial continuity of its integral parts, something Buridan, oddly enough, takes to be extrinsic to the thing possessing it.

Buridan's unusual conception of spatial continuity begins to make sense if we look at another passage, where he says that there are three ways in which "something, while remaining the same, is able to be differently disposed, such that contradictory predicates are verified at different times of it, i.e., of the term suppositing for it, or such that the same predicate would be affirmed and denied at different times of that term."[24] Only one of these three ways could apply to 'B is now an animal', however, and that is the first, which Buridan describes as follows:

> The first way is, if the predicate is connotative of something extrinsic to it, for then it is possible for that to happen on account of the existence or non-existence, or on account of another change, of the extrinsic thing. For example, a man is a father if his son exists, and without him existing, he is not a father. And a man is rich if riches are joined to him, and poor if they are lost or joined to another. And body A is next to body B if there is no other body or space between them, and it is remote or more remote if there is a lesser or greater body between them. And to be differently disposed on account of another in this way does not require any change in it or in its parts. (*QP* II.3: 31ra–rb)[25]

The spatial continuity of the integral parts of an animal, i.e., the fact that there is no other body between them, is the extrinsic 'how' or mode connoted by the term 'animal'. That connotation fails for 'B is now an animal' as long as B remains spatially continuous with A, because the term 'animal' connotes the spatial continuity of the integral parts of its referent. However, once A has been physically separated from B, i.e., once there is some "body or space between them," then the connotation holds, since A is no longer one of the spatially continuous parts of the animal. The conclusion Buridan reaches is that although B "is not different than it was before, it is differently disposed . . . for being 'whole' or 'partial' not only signifies being something, but also being disposed or not disposed in some way towards another thing" (*QDA₃* II.7: 98).[26]

According to Buridan, then, the souls of non-human living things are homogenously extended throughout their bodies. In addition, we should understand the various animate powers we see being exercised by living things as different functions of the same identical subject.

2. HUMAN SOULS

Human souls call for a different strategy. Buridan begins by likening the metaphysical proximity of human souls to their bodies to the way in which God is said to be present to the world: "I imagine that just as God is present to the whole world and to each of its parts principally and immediately, so in a certain way is the human soul immediately present to the whole human body. And yet there would be a difference, since God is not a form inhering in the world, but the human soul informs the human body and inheres in it" (*QDA₃* III.17: 192).[27] At the risk of explaining the obscure by the more obscure, Buridan does make the point here that the human soul/body relation presents a special problem. But besides being "immediately present" to it, how is it that an immaterial and indivisible whole actually inheres in a material and divisible whole?

Buridan's first step is to appeal to the medieval distinction between being definitively and circumscriptively in a place.[28] According to this distinction, the intellective soul of a human being inheres definitively but not circumscriptively in its body, i.e., such that it is present to its body whole in whole and whole in part, rather than whole in whole and part in part (*QNE* VI.6: 143rb)—the latter being the mode of inherence exhibited by the sensitive souls of non-human animals and the vegetative souls of plants.

But Buridan also wishes to assert the subject identity and definitional distinction principles as regards the intellectual soul (*QDA₃* III.17: 191–96), so the more specific aim of his account is to explain how it is possible for a single immaterial substance possessing different powers to be definitively present in a single physical body. He outlines his position in response to Averroes's argument that it is impossible for indivisibles, such as the human intellect, to inhere in divisible subjects, such as the human body. This argument "can be set out deductively," he says, in three steps: (1) If an indivisible existing intellect inheres in a divisible body, then it must inhere either (a) in each part of that body, or (b) in some part of that body and not in another; (2) it cannot inhere in one part and not in another, because then "it could not be consistently attributed to each part and quantity" of that body (not 1b); (3) likewise, it cannot inhere in each part of that body, since as an indivisible, it will have to be taken as a whole (not 1a). Because it is inconsistent with the requirement that

? enai ?

the intellective soul be predicable of each part of its material subject, (1b) is rejected (*QDA₃* III.4: 30).[29] Buridan is more interested in (1a), however, since it was apparently the rejection of that premise that led Averroes to conclude that the immaterial part of the intellect does not inhere in the body.

Why does Averroes resist the idea that an immaterial soul could inhere as a whole in each part of its body? Buridan suggests that this notion gives rise to a number of seeming absurdities:

(A1) The same thing would as a whole be moved and at rest simultaneously. Proof: if your foot is at rest and your hand is moving, your soul would be moved as a whole with the motion of your hand, and at rest as a whole with your resting foot.

(A2) The same thing would be moved as an entirety by contrary motions simultaneously. Proof: if you move one hand to the left and the other to the right, your soul would be at a distance from itself, which is impossible.

(A3) Your foot would understand, because the intellect would be present in it as a whole. Proof: the principal operation of the intellect is to understand, and your intellect as a whole is present in your foot.

(A4) Your foot would be a human being, because the human substantial form would be present in it as a whole. Proof: the intellect is the substantial form of the whole human being, and your intellect as a whole is present in your foot.

(A5) Substantial forms would travel from subject to subject, as the parts of a body change. Proof: the intellect as substantial form is present in each part of the body, but some of these parts can come to be or pass away without the corruption of their original subject. (*QDA₃* III.4: 30–31)

Buridan, of course, rejects Averroes's conclusion that the human intellective soul must be a transcendent substance, firmly asserting the contrary thesis that "your intellect, by which you understand, inheres in your body or your matter [*intellectus tuus, quo tu intelligis, inhaeret corpori tuo sive materiâ tuâ*]." This obligates him to reply to each of the above objections.[30]

In response to (A1), Buridan points out that although the intellect is moved in the hand and at rest in the foot simultaneously, "this is not a contradiction" because "those motions do not inhere in it, nor are they commensurably related to it." As a model for the way in which human intellects inhere in their bodies, Buridan appeals to the theological doctrine of real presence in the Eucharist: "when it is said that the intellect is moved by contrary motions, we can speak of this just as we speak of the body of Christ in

religion
R

the consecrated host when one priest carries the body of Christ to the right
and another to the left. For the body of Christ is neither moved in itself, nor
by a motion inhering in it, just as the size of the host does not inhere in it"
(QDA_3 III.4: 35).[31] Buridan assumes here that there are two kinds of inherence relation: "real" inherence or inherence proper, the relata of which are
commensurably related to each other, and definitive inherence, the relata of
which are non-commensurably related. The commensurability of properly
inherent relata follows from their mutual, finite extension: one thing commensurably inheres in another just in case both are extended; otherwise,
their mode of inherence is non-commensurable. Immaterial substances such
as the intellectual soul would therefore be present in extended bodies according to the second, non-commensurable, mode of inherence.

The notion of non-commensurable or definitive inherence is made
clearer in Buridan's reply to (A2). Here the doctrine of real presence again
provides the model, this time for understanding how a non-commensurably   *model?*
inherent substance could be in two places at once:

> To the second objection it is said that the intellect is not at a distance from
> itself because it is not in the hand or the foot commensurably, since it is
> not extended by the extension of the hand or the foot. And it is not absurd
> for the same thing to be non-commensurably and wholly present in differ-   *supernatural*
> ent places at a distance from each other, although this would be by super-
> natural means, as the body of Christ is simultaneously in paradise and on
> the altar (for the body of Christ in the host on the altar is not commensu-
> rate with the magnitude of the host, but [exists as a whole] in each part of
> the host, even if the parts are at a distance from each other—and it is not
> on that account at a distance from itself). And so in the same way, the in-
> tellect is somehow in the hand and foot, and in neither commensurably,
> since it is not extended in any of those members. (QDA_3 III.4: 36)[32]

Following his reply to (A1), Buridan's reply to (A2) appeals to the fact that non-
commensurably inherent forms cannot be moved in conjunction with the
motions of any commensurable part(s) of their material subjects. Inherent
forms can be moved only if they are part in part present in their subjects.

Buridan replies to the worries about a foot (A3) becoming an understanding thing, or even (A4) becoming a human being, by returning to the   *semantics?*
semantics of the terms 'total [*totale*]' and 'partial [*partiale*]', a technique introduced in Book II of his commentary.[33] If the phrase, 'total understanding
[*totale intelligens*]', is properly expounded as "that which is not part of another understanding," he says, a foot cannot be called a 'total understanding'
because it is part of another whole understanding, viz., the human being.
Likewise, nothing is called a 'human being' "in public and ordinary speech
except the whole substance, i.e., that which is not part of another substance"

(QDA_3 III.4: 36).[34] The Averroists' mistake in (A3–4) was to multiply substances by the (infinite) number of divisible parts possessed by their material subjects, rather than by each of those subjects taken as a whole. But it does not follow from the assumption that the intellect is whole in each part of the human body that each part of the human body is a whole intellect. That would be to commit the fallacy of division.

The final Averroist argument, (A5), claims that substantial forms wholly present in each part of their material subjects would migrate from subject to subject as the extended parts of their bodies change (in modern terms, we might think of the souls of blood-donors coming to exist in the bodies of their recipients). Buridan replies by pursuing the suggestion in his reply to (A2) that non-commensurable inherence has a supernatural cause: "It will be said that the way in which the intellect inheres in the human body is not natural but supernatural. And it is certain that God could supernaturally not only form something not derived from a material potentiality, but also separate what has been so derived from its matter, conserve it separately, and place it in some other matter. Why, then, would this not be possible as regards the human intellect?" (QDA_3 III.4: 37).[35] In other words, because supernaturally inherent forms such as the human intellect are not subject to material change, they are not themselves divided when the extended parts of their bodies are divided. Rhetorical questions aside, it is puzzling to find Buridan, *qua* natural philosopher, pinning such a crucial metaphysical doctrine on divine omnipotence.[36] But the picture is more complicated than first appears.

Buridan's reply to (A5) contains two significant claims. First, non-commensurable inherence is not a natural state of affairs, meaning that it cannot be explained by appealing to the same principles that govern the inherence of material forms. Second, there is nothing contradictory in supposing that God could create an indivisible, unextended substance and put it in matter. Thus, Buridan is making the subtle but important point here that although no naturalistic model of explanation can explain how human souls inhere in their bodies, we have no a priori reason to suppose that only naturalistic models need apply. This is, in other words, a claim about where a theory of non-commensurable or definitive inherence should begin, rather than some *ad hoc* appeal to the miraculous. In the case of human souls and their bodies, Buridan is very clear about the *explanandum*. This is: "the truth of our faith, which we must firmly believe: viz., that the human intellect is the substantial form of a body inhering in the human body, but not derived from a material potentiality nor materially extended, and so not naturally produced or corrupted; and yet it is not absolutely everlasting, since it was created in time. Nevertheless, it is sempiternal hereafter [*sempiterna a parte post*] in such a way that it will never be corrupted or annihilated, although God could annihilate it by God's absolute power" (QDA_3 III.3: 22–23).[37] Again, since the human soul is not an extended or material thing, neither the extensionality principle nor the homogeneity principle will suffice to explain its mode of inherence in the human body. Some other principle or principles must be found to support the view that the various powers of the human soul are one in subject and yet distinct in definition.

But now that we know where to begin, what about the *explanans* of non-commensurable inherence? Here Buridan is less forthcoming, for two, not un-related reasons. First, as we saw in chapter 10, he is wary of encroaching on territory outside the traditional domain of an arts master, often mentioning his reluctance to treat a question which would be more properly addressed by theologians.[38] Given Buridan's belief that non-commensurable inherence should be understood on the model of real presence in the Eucharist, it is easy to see how any philosophical discussion of the former could become em-broiled in the theological controversy surrounding the latter.[39] Second, per-haps also because he was an arts master, Buridan sees himself as committed to philosophical explanation, which for him involves the construction of demon-strative or at least persuasive arguments based on *evident* premises. Where such arguments are lacking, he is inclined to indicate their absence and leave it at that, rather than to engage in theological speculation.

He takes a similar approach to the question of the human soul's status as an immaterial form:

> Although this thesis [viz., that the human intellect is not a material form] is absolutely true, and must be firmly maintained by faith, and even though the arguments adduced for it are readily believable, nevertheless, it is not apparent to me that they are demonstrative, [i.e., drawn] from principles having evidentness (leaving faith aside), unless God with a grace that is special and outside the usual course of nature could make it evident to us, just as he could make evident to anyone the article of the Trinity or Incarnation. (*QDA*₃ III.3: 25–26)[40]

Buridan's point here is that since the immateriality of the human intellect is not evident to us, or apparent to our senses, he is in no position to construct empirical arguments about it. God could, of course, make such truths evi-dent to us directly and non-empirically, but in that case our *scientia* would not be natural, but revealed.[41]

This leaves Buridan the philosopher with little to say when it comes to explaining how the various powers of the human soul are attributable to a single, unitary subject. Though he argues for this thesis, he does so, as we saw above, on the grounds that it would be pointless to imagine a plurality of souls inhering in a human being when operations such as nutrition, sensa-tion, and intellection can be attributed to just one. Thus, one and the same human soul may be called "sensitive to the extent that it has been naturally suited to sense [*sensitiva secundum quod innata est sentire*]," although unlike the sensitive souls of non-human animals, the human sensitive power is neither extended nor naturally generated. Rather, it is said to "inform" corporeal and extended matter by means of an act that "coexists" with the material dispositions of sense organs. The human sensitive soul can thus remain incorruptible, even if "the corporeal dispositions required for sensing naturally are corrupted" (*QDA₃* III.17: 193).

If the human sensitive soul cannot be both incorruptible and extended, however, it also follows from what Buridan says that, except for purely material similarities in the organs through which humans and non-human animals operate, sensation in human beings will differ specifically from sensation in non-human animals. This gives rise to a certain discontinuity between the two accounts, since our understanding of the internal causes of, e.g., equine vision will not apply to human vision. Buridan acknowledges this problem and reflects on it:

> It is certainly true that there is a great difficulty if we posit just one soul in a human being, for it must be intellective and indivisible, not extended in any way by the extension of matter or subject. And then that unextended soul is [also] a sensitive and vegetative soul. How, then—since sensation is supposed to be materially extended in organs—could it be inherent in an indivisible subject and, as it were, derived from its potentiality? This seems to be miraculous, since the only extension form has is extension in its subject. And how could a divisible and extended thing inhere in an indivisible and unextended thing? This seems to be miraculous. And I reply with certainty that it is miraculous, because the human soul inheres in the human body in a miraculous and supernatural way, neither extended nor derived from the potentiality of the subject in which it inheres, and yet also inhering in the whole body and in each part of it. This is truly miraculous and supernatural. (*QDA₃* II.9: 138)[42]

To modern ears, this passage has an unfortunate ring. It strikes us as a capitulation, a philosopher giving up the game because he believes that his subject matter is beyond rational comprehension. But seen in the context of his other remarks about psychological inherence, Buridan's claim here is actually much more limited. Recall his suggestion above that God could, if God wished, make the immateriality of the human intellect evident to us outside the common course of nature. Buridan is not suggesting here that the inherence of the human soul is utterly inexplicable, only that it cannot be explained naturalistically, i.e., with demonstrative or persuasive arguments based on premises whose truth is apparent to our senses.[43] He is only making a negative claim

about the failure of empirical knowledge in a certain field of inquiry. His remarks do not entail that some a priori mode of knowing might not reveal to
us the principle governing the human soul's inherence in its body, although
again, he does not speculate about this. Similarly, his conception of the miraculous is not absolute, but relative to the epistemic situation of human beings.
Thus, when he calls the inherence of the human soul in its body miraculous,
he has nothing in mind like the Humean conception of miracles as violations
or transgressions of the laws of nature, but something more in the spirit of
Augustine's remark that a miraculous event "does not occur contrary to nature, but contrary to what is known of nature."[44] Substituting 'outside the
common course of nature' for each occurrence of 'supernatural', and 'not empirically evident' for 'miraculous', would give us a reading of the above passage
that better reflects Buridan's thinking on this question.

For both human and non-human souls and bodies, Buridan holds that
the animate functions of a living thing belong to one and the same subject
(the subject identity principle), and that such functions are distinct from
each other not really but only in definition (the definitional distinction principle). The main difference between the two accounts consists in his assertion
that brute animal or plant souls are also extended throughout their bodies
(the extensionality principle) and have the same nature in each part (the homogeneity principle). The latter two principles do not apply to human intellective souls, which lack extension and hence also integral parts. The human
soul is, on the contrary, non-commensurably or definitively present in the
body in which it inheres.

Buridan sees psychology as a naturalistic endeavor, which for him means
that it is concerned with the construction of arguments based on empirically
evident principles. But his approach has its limitations when it comes to the
question of how human intellective souls inhere in their bodies. Buridan appeals to the notion of non-commensurable or definitive inherence to avoid
Averroes's conclusion that indivisible human souls cannot actually inhere in
divisible human bodies, but no naturalistic explanation seems possible for a
mode of inherence that is, by his own admission, brought about by a force
outside the common or usual course of nature. The result is that although
Buridan is able to block the Averroist *reductio* argument that an inherent soul
would be moved as an entirety by simultaneous contrary motions, he does so
at the cost of moving part of his practice beyond his own method. Understanding the precise relation between the human soul and its body turns
out to be a matter best left to the theologians, who use the notion of non-
commensurable inherence to explain the real presence of Christ in the consecrated bread and wine of the Eucharist.

Buridan openly acknowledges the evidential shortcomings of his account, but is quick to point out that the Alexandrian and Averroist positions

are no better off in that respect. What little evidence we do have is insufficient to establish philosophical truths about the nature of the human body/soul relationship. His own convictions are hardly agnostic, of course: "on the basis of <u>our faith</u> we posit some special forms to be separable from their subjects without their corruption, as in the case of the intellective human soul, which is not educed from the potentiality of its matter, or its subject" (*S* 6.4.12: 446). As we shall see in the next chapter, however, he is not about to let the strength of his convictions confuse him about what he *knows* to be true.

CHAPTER TWELVE

Knowledge

·Buridan's conception of human knowledge has received considerable schol-arly attention over the past five decades.[1] Much of this interest has been vicari-ous, aimed not at understanding Buridan's conception of knowledge but at sorting out the complex relationship between his remarks and a number of skeptical propositions associated with his Parisian contemporary, Nicholas of Autrecourt (c. 1300–after 1350). Since this relationship has often been misun-derstood, the present chapter will reconsider the question. It will serve as well to illustrate Buridan's general position on the question of human knowledge, since, as we shall see below, his reply to Nicholas makes no sense unless certain doctrines implicit in his remarks are brought into the foreground.

As far as Buridan and Nicholas are concerned, two facts stand in need of explanation: on the one hand, the fact that Buridan and Nicholas were con-temporaries at Paris, making it highly improbable that Buridan did not have at least some acquaintance with Nicholas's notorious skeptical theses, several of which were formally condemned in 1346; on the other, Buridan's apparent failure, despite his philosophical reputation and stature at the University, to attempt anywhere in his known corpus of writings a serious, sustained de-fense of the possibility of knowledge against Nicholas's skeptical challenges. Portions of questions in two different works are widely thought to contain replies to Nicholas's arguments, but neither discussion seems to do much more than merely gainsay Nicholas's position by rejecting his criterion of cer-tainty. Not surprisingly, commentators have been disconcerted by Buridan's silence on the matter. It has been suggested that he had not read enough of Nicholas's work to understand it, and that his reply might have been directed not against Nicholas but "some anonymous, or perhaps illusory, opponents." Buridan has even been diagnosed with a "schizophrenic attitude" towards articles of faith, accounting for his failure to take seriously the implications of divine omnipotence for our claim to know anything at all.[2]

But Buridan's failure to reply directly to Nicholas's arguments can be understood in terms of a broader and perfectly sensible anti-skeptical strategy rooted in his account of evidentness and certainty. It is true that Buridan does little to engage Nicholas's arguments, but not because he was unfamiliar with them. Rather, he thinks that some kinds of skeptical doubt are simply not worthy of philosophical consideration, a view supported by various remarks which, when properly interpreted, preclude any direct reply to the skeptic. One consequence of this is that the dispute between Buridan and Nicholas must be located at a different level than has hitherto been appreciated. Most commentators seem to have been expecting some kind of classical foundationalist reply from Buridan, and proceed to judge him harshly when they do not find it. But that assumption has no basis in the texts. It is possible to raise the issue of epistemic justification in Buridan, but if we want a contemporary analogue, then the position we should be looking to is not foundationalism but reliabilism, i.e., the externalist theory that the justifiability of a belief is a matter of the reliability of the cognitive process(es) which produced it, where reliability is a contingent (and only a posteriori determinable) matter of the way those processes operate under normal conditions, or as Buridan might say, "in the common course of nature."

This is not to suggest, however, that there is some hidden epistemological agenda lurking in Buridan's writings, or a remarkable anticipation of contemporary reliabilism. Far from it, even the most cursory examination of the texts reveals that he is more interested in explaining *how* we come to have knowledge than in exploring the grounds for knowledge claims, an orientation his work shares with most pre-Cartesian epistemology. The question here concerns what Buridan actually says about evidentness and certainty in response to Nicholas's arguments—remarks which, when seen from a reliabilist perspective, clearly refute the conclusion that his reply is "largely ineffectual," "uncritical," and "primitive."[3] But to understand this reply, we will have to look briefly at the views of his opponent, who is never actually named in Buridan's writings.

1. NICHOLAS OF AUTRECOURT

The skeptical conclusions drawn by Nicholas of Autrecourt are based on his theory of evidentness (*evidentia*).[4] In his Second Letter to Bernard of Arezzo, he contends that "the certitude of evidentness has no degrees," and that "except for the certitude of the faith, there is no other certitude except the certitude of the first principle, or that which can be resolved into the first principle."[5] The principle of non-contradiction is his criterion of certitude: on the one hand, we cannot have certain knowledge of any proposition unless it would be contradictory to believe its opposite; on the other, we cannot be certain of any inferential knowledge unless it would be contradictory for the premise(s) of that inference to be true and its conclusion false.[6]

The consequences of this view are far reaching, to say the least, and Nicholas is only too happy to enumerate them for Bernard. In the First Letter, Nicholas argues that "every appearance we have of objects existing outside our own minds can be false," since the awareness can exist whether or not the object does. For the same reason, "we cannot be certain by the natural light of reason [*in lumine naturali*] when our awareness of the existence of external objects is true or false." It follows that there can be "no evident certitude about the existence of external objects," including objects of the five senses. In response to Bernard's suggestion that inferences from appearances to the existence of external objects are valid when the former are naturally caused, Nicholas challenges Bernard to identify those instances in which this is not the case, i.e., when God intervenes in the natural order to impede the effects of natural causes.[7]

In his Second Letter to Bernard,[8] Nicholas uses this same criterion of certainty to place the conclusions of Aristotelian metaphysics in jeopardy. From "the fact that some thing is known to exist, it cannot be evidently inferred, by evidentness reduced to the first principle, or to the certitude of the first principle, that some other thing exists," Nicholas argues that "Aristotle never had evident knowledge of any substance other than his own mind, meaning by 'substance' a thing other than the objects of the five senses, and other than our formal experiences."[9] This is because substances neither appear to us intuitively (since if they did, Nicholas contends, even "rustics" would know that they exist), nor can their existence be inferred from antecedent perceptions (since "from one thing it cannot be inferred that another thing exists," as the above application of the principle states). Furthermore, Aristotle did not even have probable knowledge of any consequence of this kind, since for that one must be "evidently certain" that the antecedent and the consequent will both be true at some time. But no such certainty is possible. Thus, it is never probable to me that if I put my hand into a fire, I will be hot, since no inferential connection between distinct things, e.g., fire and feeling hot, is ever evidently certain.[10] Nicholas notes further that the assumption that an omnipotent God may at any time intervene in the natural order blocks any appeal to the evident reliability of natural processes in the formation of beliefs:

> And it is apparent that we do not possess certitude about any substance conjoined to matter, except for our own soul, because when one is pointing

to a piece of wood or a stone, this will be most clearly deduced from a single belief accepted at the same time. For by some power, e.g. divine, it can happen that, together with the appearances and prior to any reasoning of this sort, there is no substance there. Therefore, by the natural light of reason, it is not evidently inferred from those appearances that a substance is there.[11]

As for Bernard's apparent objection that such consequences can be made evident if we add the antecedent premise, 'God is not performing a miracle', Nicholas refers to his First Letter's challenge to show how we can be evidently certain when God is intervening in the natural order and when he is not. Nicholas concludes, "in the whole of his natural philosophy and metaphysics, Aristotle had such [evident] certainty of scarcely two conclusions, and perhaps not even of one."[12]

Nicholas draws other skeptical conclusions from his use of the principle of non-contradiction as the criterion of certainty,[13] but the main thrust of his attack is against the claim that we have certain and evident knowledge of causes and substances. Still, as Marilyn Adams has argued,[14] one must be cautious about seeing Nicholas as a medieval Descartes or Hume. For one thing, Nicholas does assume the reliability of human reason. He also states unequivocally that no power, including divine power, could make contradictories simultaneously true, or make the opposite of the consequent in a valid consequence compatible with its antecedent. For another, he represents his skeptical conclusions as a *reductio* of Bernard's position, rather than as part of some broader philosophical program to which he himself subscribes.[15] Clearly, Nicholas would not have viewed himself as a skeptic. But that still leaves the question of how Nicholas's arguments actually played in mid-fourteenth-century Paris, since his conclusions have obvious skeptical consequences once they have been lifted from their epistolary context. In Buridan's hands, they are fashioned into several *bona fide* skeptical arguments, including a rather virulent form of skepticism based on divine omnipotence.

2. Buridan's Presentation of Nicholas's Arguments

In Book II, question 1 of his *Questions on Aristotle's Metaphysics,* Buridan considers no fewer than eighteen arguments against the thesis that it is possible for us to comprehend the truth of things. Most of these arguments point to various ways in which cognitive mechanisms such as sense perception can and do fail naturally, causing conflicting or erroneous judgments in the course of their ordinary or non-miraculous operations. Buridan gives many traditional examples in this vein: the healthy person judging something to be sweet which the sick person judges to be bitter; the appearance, to a man on a moving ship, that the ship is standing still and the trees on the shore are moving; and the reddish appearance of the sun at dawn versus its whitish appearance at midday; and so on.[16] Nevertheless, he does not see any of these examples—which he calls '*instantia*', or 'counter-instances'—as raising doubts about the possibility of knowledge. Even though perceptual judgments are often in error, their reliability is restored once the intellect passes judgment on the matter: "I say that if the senses are naturally deluded, the intellect has the power to inquire when a man is and when he is not in error, and also the power to correct illusory judgments" (*QM* II.1: 9rb).[17] The intellect can appeal to other beliefs more reliably produced in order to correct the mistaken judgments of sense. It is known, e.g., that the presence of a certain humor in the sick man's tongue inhibits his gustatory powers; that judgments of vision are affected by the position of the eye relative to the object(s) seen; and that the refraction and diffusion of light in a mixed medium affects its propagation.[18] Buridan concludes that none of these natural *instantia* gives him any reason to doubt the possibility of knowledge based on sense perception.

But he also mentions three arguments that look to have been inspired by Nicholas of Autrecourt, two of which correspond directly to objections raised by Nicholas in the Bernard correspondence. First, observes Buridan (here presenting the skeptical argument):

> the senses can be deluded, as is commonly said, and it is certain that the species of sensible things can be preserved in the organs of sense in the absence of sensibles, as is held in *De somno et vigilia*. And then we judge about what does not exist as if it existed, and so we err through the senses. And the difficulty is made worse by the fact that we believe on faith that God can form sensible species in our senses without the sensible things themselves, and preserve them for a long time, and in that case, we judge as if there were sensible things present. Furthermore, since God can do this and greater things, you do not know whether God intends to do this, and so you have no certitude and evidentness whether there are men before you while you are asleep or awake, since God could make a sensible species in your sleep as clear as—indeed, a hundred times clearer than— what sensible objects could produce. And so you would then judge formally that there are sensible objects before you, just as you do now. Therefore, since you know nothing about the will of God, you cannot be certain of anything. (*QM* II.1: 8rb–va)[19]

The possibility of divine interference in the natural order is one of Nicholas's main points against Bernard in the Second Letter. It renders any appeal to the reliability of cognitive processes moot, for there can be no certainty if God can make me believe that I am perceiving something when I am not, and do so in ways undetectable to me.

A second argument, which reprises a skeptical argument also considered in Buridan's *Questions on Aristotle's Physics*, is based on the thesis that because only consequences reducible to the principle of non-contradiction are evident, the existence of one distinct thing cannot be demonstrated with evidentness and certainty from the existence of another. This thesis is readily applicable to our claim to know causes and effects, as Buridan's version of the argument recognizes:

> neither the conclusion nor the effect can be known through the cause, nor the cause through an effect, since the cause is neither essentially nor virtually contained in an effect; nor is an effect known through the cause, since causes are less known to us . . . it seems that we can never have an evident [cognition] about one thing through another, since the only evidentness is by reduction to the first principle, which is founded on contradiction. But we can never have a contradiction where two diverse things are concerned. (*QM* II.1: 8va)[20]

Finally, there is a third argument not found in the Bernard correspondence,[21] although it does closely resemble a skeptical conclusion drawn by Nicholas in his independent treatise, *Exigit ordo executionis*. There Nicholas argues that we can have no certainty about things known by experience, but only what he calls a "conjectural habit" (*habitus conjecturativus*), e.g., that rhubarb cures cholera or that magnets attract iron.[22] This is because we can never be certain that those effects will accompany those causes in the future:

> when it is proved that certainty [arises] through the proposition latent in the soul, i.e., 'What is produced in many cases by a non-free cause is its natural effect', I ask what you mean by 'natural cause'. Is it that which produced the effect in many cases in the past, and which will, if it continues to exist and be applied, still produce the effect in the future? Then the minor premise is not known. Even if [one assumes] that something has been produced in many cases [in the past], it is not certain that it must be likewise in the future.[23]

Buridan's version of this argument focuses on the question of whether universal conclusions can be justified by induction from particular experiences. Inductive inferences are fallacious, it is said, because "experiences only have the force of establishing a universal principle by way of induction from many, and a universal proposition never follows by induction unless every singular of that universal is included, which is impossible" (*QM* II.1: 8va).[24] Thus, the conclusion that every fire is hot is unwarranted if it is based solely on experiences of particular fires, each of which has been

skeptical

judged to be hot. It would be warranted only if that judgment has been made as regards each and every particular fire, and, as Buridan puts it, "it is known that those are all of them [*sit scitum quod illa sunt omnia*]" (*QAnPo* II.11). But no human intellect is ever in that position. Buridan notes further that the formal validity of inductive inference is not saved by the addition of the clause, 'and so on for the others', since that clause is itself neither known nor certain to the intellect.[25] Thus, our claim to have generalized a posteriori knowledge about the world is undercut, a prospect which threatens the possibility of natural *scientia*.

As we saw above, it is doubtful whether Nicholas actually subscribed to a position as radical as the one implied in these arguments. Although Nicholas's real views are difficult to discern, his arguments are compatible, e.g., with the straightforwardly rationalistic demand that all empirical knowledge be founded with deductive certainty on self-evident principles. But it is also clear that regardless of Nicholas's own views, or his reason(s) for challenging Bernard's position in the way he does, Buridan sees Nicholas's arguments as having dangerous skeptical consequences. I shall therefore call 'Ultricurian skepticism'—after the Latinized version of Nicholas's name—the position Buridan takes himself to be opposing. Buridan's versions of Nicholas's arguments in the *Questions on Aristotle's Metaphysics* reveal its main tenets, viz.:

(1) We cannot judge veridically about the existence of any object of the senses, since God could at any moment choose to deceive us in ways we could never detect. And we know nothing about the will of God;[26]

(2) Causes and effects cannot be known through each other with certainty, since causes are distinct from their effects;

(3) No conclusion reached by induction is certain unless the induction is based on every singular covered by that universal.

It is not difficult to see how each tenet could be generated if one insists, as Nicholas does, that we can be certain only of what is equivalent or reducible to the principle of non-contradiction. On that criterion alone, Buridan says, we could never with certainty infer the existence of one thing from another, for "if A and B are distinct, it would never be a contradiction for A to exist and B not to exist" (*QP* I.4: 4vb–5ra).[27] The result surely counts as a skeptical position, for although it does not imply that we have no knowledge at all, it does imply that we have a lot less knowledge than we think we have, which is why Buridan wants to reply to it. It is of course possible that Nicholas himself was not an Ultricurian skeptic, but again, since Buridan is replying to Nicholas under the guise of Ultricurian skepticism, Nicholas's own views, whatever they were,[28] are not relevant to the debate.

3. Buridan's Reply to Ultricurian Skepticism

After examining Buridan's replies to the second and third tenets of Ultricurian skepticism, I shall turn to its first and perhaps most important tenet, expressed in skeptical arguments based on God's omnipotence and absolute freedom.

a. Causal Knowledge

To the argument that causes cannot be known through their effects, or vice versa, since causes are neither contained in their effects "essentially or virtually" (ruling out demonstration from effect to cause), or at least as well known to us as their effects (ruling out demonstration from cause to effect), Buridan replies as follows:

> I say that effects are known through [their] cause *propter quid,* since the cause is more known, and also more known to us, than the reason why the effect exists. Likewise, a cause is known through [its] effect as to the fact that it exists, since the effect bears a certain likeness to the cause, and so can represent the cause together with the intellect's natural inclination to the truth. And when it is said that one thing cannot be conclusively known through another, I deny it and say that there are almost infinitely many principles known per se—whether through sense, experience, or the inclusion of terms—without needing to be demonstrated by [reduction to] the first principle. (*QM* II.1: 9rb–va)[29]

Buridan replies in similar fashion to this argument in his *Questions on Aristotle's Physics,* denying that every premise in a demonstration must be made evident by reduction to the principle of non-contradiction because knowledge is also justified by a posteriori principles acquired through sense, memory, and experience. Thus, he says, we can evidently conclude the existence of a heart from the existence of a man once we understand that it is physically impossible for a man to exist without a heart (*QP* I.4: 5vb–6ra).[30]

Likewise, although effects do not essentially or virtually contain their causes, Buridan argues that they do resemble them, so that we may acquire evident knowledge of causes on the basis of that resemblance together with the natural inclination of our intellect to the truth. What evidential status does Buridan assign to the uniformity of nature principle? It is easy to follow some recent commentators in assuming that Buridan takes it to express an a priori truth, needed to justify inductive reasoning in the natural sciences. From this it is a short step to claiming that he misses the point of Nicholas's argument entirely, which is to question such gratuitous assumptions about causality. But this interpretation is based on the mistaken assumption that

Buridan has the same view of causal knowledge as Duns Scotus, who does think it is self-evident that causes resemble their effects.[31] The passage quoted above, however, indicates that Buridan would disagree with Scotus. The uniformity of nature principle cannot be self-evident for Buridan because he contends that there is only one type or mode of universal principle to which the intellect can assent immediately, without experience or demonstration, i.e., principles expressed in propositions whose terms have nominal definitions manifestly either including or excluding each other.[32] The examples Buridan gives indicate that this category covers what have come to be known as analytic or definitional truths: e.g., 'Being is being'; 'Whiteness is a color'; 'Man is an animal'; 'Whiteness is not blackness'; 'No rational thing is irrational', and so on (*QNE* VI.11: 127ra).[33]

Universal principles belonging to the second mode have terms whose nominal definitions manifestly neither include nor exclude each other. Buridan describes these as follows:

> there are also some universal principles that the intellect concedes on the basis of experience with many similar singulars and its natural inclination to the truth: e.g., that every fire is hot, that the sun is a warming agent, that all rhubarb purges bile, that everything produced is produced from something already existing, that every mixture is corporeal, and so on as regards many natural principles. And these principles are not cognized immediately from the beginning, but we are able to have doubts about them for a long time. But even so, they are called principles because they are not demonstrative and cannot by any means be demonstrated nor even proved as the formal conclusion of an argument. Indeed, they are conceded only because we have seen many singulars like that, and have been unable to find a counter-instance in any of them. (*QM* II.2: 9vb)[34]

Second-mode universal principles are made evident to the intellect through experiential acquaintance "with many similar singulars," by the process of induction (*QM* I.8: 7va).[35]

Buridan clearly regards the uniformity of nature principle as second mode.[36] His reply to the skeptical argument about causal knowledge assumes that causes are neither essentially nor virtually contained in their effects. If he held the opposite view, we would surely find him refuting the skeptic by arguing that since causes and effects are not really distinct entities, there is no reason why the existence of the one could not be demonstrated from the existence of the other by means of an a priori definitional principle stating their essential connection.[37] It is worth noting that Buridan elsewhere shows no hesitation in appealing, when necessary, to the principle of non-contradiction. In his reply to this skeptical argument in the *Questions on Aristotle's Physics*, he points out that it is possible to demonstrate the existence of something by reduction to the first principle if the consequent of the demonstration contains an existential claim implied by the antecedent (*QP* I.4: 5vb; cf. *QM* IV.9: 19vb). But he employs no such strategy here to defend our claim to have causal knowledge.

But if beliefs about causal relations are justified only if the intellect is justified in assenting to inductive generalizations about them, then the skeptical problem about causal knowledge turns out to be a special case of another skeptical problem, i.e., concerning induction, to which Buridan offers a separate reply.

b. Induction

To the argument that inductive inferences are fallacious because "experience is not valid for concluding to a universal principle," Buridan replies as follows:

> I say that this is not an inference on the basis of the form, but that the intellect, predisposed by its natural inclination to the truth, assents to the universal principle by experience. And it can be conceded that experiences of this kind are not valid for absolute evidentness, but they are valid for the [kind of] evidentness which suffices for natural science. And along with this there are also other principles arrived at from the inclusion or opposition of terms or propositions, which do not require experiences, as is the case with the first principle. Indeed, it is evidently true that a chimera exists or does not exist; that a goat-stag exists or does not exist; and that man is an animal, if the signification of the terms is known. (*QM* II.1: 9rb)[38]

Here Buridan concedes that no inductive inference is absolutely evident. But he rejects reduction to the principle of non-contradiction as the sole criterion of certainty. Behind this lies his theory of evidentness.

Buridan indicates that all knowledge or *scientia* must satisfy three conditions: assent, evidentness, and truth. Assent and evidentness, however, come in degrees, some of which fail to yield knowledge:

> it must be noted that certitude and evidentness are required for knowledge. And there are yet two further requirements, namely, certitude of truth and certitude of assent. I say 'certitude of truth' first, because if we assent most firmly and without any hesitation to a false proposition, as heretics do, who sometimes would rather die than deny what they have assented to, there is still no knowledge on account of assent of this kind, since it lacks truth, and the certitude and firmness of truth. (*QAnPo* I.2)[39]

Buridan defines belief as the disposition to assent to an appearance or state of affairs apprehended by the intellect (QDA_3 III.16: 181) and knowledge as "the certain and evident assent supervening on [*superveniens*] the mental proposition, on account of which we assent to it with certainty and evidentness" (*S* 8.3.7: 688).[40] This cognitive act "through which we assent or adhere to a true proposition" is one of the means by which it is possible for us to comprehend truth.[41] Assent is a necessary condition for knowledge "because we can have doubts about a proposition of the most firm and certain truth, and on that account not assent to it firmly; in such a case, we would have no knowledge of it" (*QAnPo* I.2).[42]

But, in addition to assent and truth, knowledge must also meet the requirement of evidentness, for evidentness is what separates known propositions from those that are merely believed.[43] The latter category includes propositions expressing opinions, which can be true, and those expressing articles of faith, which must be true. We cannot know such propositions because in neither case is our assent "based on the evidentness [*per evidentiam*]." The assent we give to opinion is said to be "derived by human reason from the senses," whereas that which we give to articles of the faith arises from an act of the will, "on the authority of sacred scripture alone" (*QAnPo* I.2; cf. *QM* II.1: 8rb).

Buridan further states that there are three kinds of evidentness pertaining to acts of assent,[44] two of which figure in his reply to Ultricurian skepticism.[45] First, there is absolute evidentness, which commands our assent immediately, such that "a man is compelled without necessity, on the basis of sense and intellect, to assent to a proposition in such a way that he cannot dissent from it" (*QM* II.1: 8vb).[46] This is the sort of evidentness we have for the principle of non-contradiction, and indeed, for any first-mode principle. Our assent to such propositions does not require experience because they are evident as soon as they are put forward in the intellect and the signification of their terms is known.

Second, there is "relative evidentness [*evidentia secundum quid*]," or "evidentness on the assumption [*evidentia ex suppositione*]." We are told that this kind of evidentness "would be observed in entities in the common course of nature; and in this way, it would be evident to us that every fire is hot and that the heavens are moved, even though the contrary is possible through God's power" (*QM* II.1: 8vb–9ra).[47] To this Buridan adds the same qualification that accompanies his reply to the skeptical argument about induction, i.e., that relative evidentness, or evidentness on the assumption that the common course of nature holds, suffices for the principles and conclusions of natural science.

To absolute and relative evidentness there correspond different levels or degrees of certainty. Absolutely evident principles afford us the highest degree of certainty and the only degree accepted by Nicholas in the Bernard correspondence: certainty of the principle of non-contradiction. Absolutely evident principles meet this requirement because it would be contradictory to believe the opposite of propositions whose terms have nominal definitions manifestly including each other, such as 'Whiteness is a color', or conversely, to believe propositions whose terms have nominal definitions manifestly excluding each other, such as 'Whiteness is not blackness'.

The principles and conclusions of natural science also afford us certainty, but in a degree that is less than absolute. It is here that Buridan takes his stand against Nicholas's single criterion of evidentness and its consequences in the form of Ultricurian skepticism. Second-mode principles such as 'Every fire is hot' and 'The sun is a warming agent' are expressed in propositions not reducible to the principle of non-contradiction, and such principles, he says, are evident not absolutely, but relative to the assumption that they "would be observed in beings in the common course of nature."[48]

Returning to the problem of induction, how can our assent to such principles as 'Every fire is hot' be warranted unless it is based on "every singular of that universal"? Buridan denies that induction alone is sufficient to cause the intellect to assent to second-mode principles. The reason is that induction does not reach conclusions universally, or "on account of the form (*gratia formae*)."[49] It is in this connection that Buridan posits "a certain innate power in us, naturally inclined and determined to assent to the truth of principles, if they have been properly presented to it, just as fire is naturally inclined to burning when it has been placed next to something combustible. And that innate power in us is the human intellect" (*QAnPo* II.11).[50] Buridan's idea is that our knowledge of second-mode principles is produced by (1) an inductive inference based on the particular evidence of sense, memory, and experience; and (2) the act of assenting to the universal proposition arising from that inference. In practice, the process of knowing begins when induction presents empirical generalizations to the intellect. Then, if there are no counterinstances or other reasons for deferring judgment, the intellect naturally assents to those that are true. Under those conditions, Buridan speaks of the intellect as "rising up to assent" to universal propositions such as 'Every fire is hot', and even as being "compelled by its natural inclination to the truth to concede the universal proposition" (*QM* I.8: 7va; *QP* I.15: 19ra).[51]

Buridan would agree with the skeptical argument that no absolutely universal conclusion follows by induction unless the induction is from every singular covered by that conclusion, "and it is known that those are all of them." Thus, he concedes, "induction is not sufficient to determine the intellect unless the intellect is of its own nature so inclined and determined" (*QAnPo* II.11).[52] But even so, we are not naturally disposed to assent to principles unless our intellect has first been primed by particular experiences. Before they can be known, second-mode principles

first need the judgment of sense, and also memory and experience: e.g.,
the intellect does not immediately concede that every fire is hot and that
all rhubarb produces bile, and for this reason it would not be known by
your intellect whether every fire is hot if we suppose that you had never
seen a fire, or that if you had seen one, you did not touch it. Therefore,
it must be firmly conceded that as far as this sort of principle is concerned, the intellect needs sense, memory, and experience first, as follows: first you cognize by sense that this fire is hot, and then the intellect
immediately and consequently judges fire to be hot. (*QAnPo* II.11)[53]

In other words, there can be no knowledge that all fires are hot without at
least some acquaintance with particular fires, which is why Buridan claims
that "actual knowledge of principles is not innate in us, but acquired [*actualis
notitia principiorum non est nobis innata, sed acquisita*]" (*QAnPo* II.11).

But if induction alone "does not causally constitute an intellective cognition, or its certitude" (*QNE* VI.11: 126vb),[54] neither does the intellect's natural
inclination to assent to truth. It is tempting to read this 'natural inclination' as
an attempt to justify induction, if only because of its resonance with the conceptual innatist doctrine of the *lumen naturale*.[55] But Buridan clearly thinks of
it analogously to other animate powers of living creatures, rather than as some
supernatural ability to penetrate through to the essence of things: "For just as
the vegetative soul is naturally inclined to generate something similar to itself
but does not generate unless the appropriate dispositions preexist, so the intellect is naturally inclined to assent to the universal truth of the indemonstrable
principles but does not give its assent until it is disposed to do so by the consideration of many singulars" (*S* 6.1.4: 399). The *explanandum* here is simply
the observed fact that almost everyone immediately assents to first principles,
i.e., those that are equivalent or evidently reducible to the principle of non-
contradiction, and dissents from their opposites (*QM* I.5: 6ra).[56] We assent to
'Whiteness is a color' as soon as we see that the nominal definition of the predicate includes that of the subject. We are then said to know such propositions
because our assent to them is based on their evidentness, which is in this case
absolute or unqualified. But no evident assent follows our understanding of
second-mode principles because the nominal definitions of their constituent
terms neither include nor exclude each other. Rather, our evident assent to
such principles is caused from without, through judgments based on sense,
memory, and experience. Thus, although it is possible for the intellect to assent
to 'Every fire is hot' before being acquainted with particular hot fires, that
proposition would not be known by it, since its assent would be based solely on
an act of the will, and not on the evidentness of the proposition.[57]

The hypothesis that the intellect's natural inclination to the truth suffices
to make our beliefs certain also does not explain the fact that we can be in

error even about evident acts of assent. For even assuming the common course of nature, Buridan contends that assent based on the evidence of books and teachers is more prone to error than that based on direct acquaintance with the objects of our belief.[58] Furthermore, he agrees with Aristotle that the firmness of assent is no mark of knowledge, since some people "do not hesitate, but think they know exactly," based on reasons they only believe to be evident.[59] As he notes in the *Summulae,* we can fail to assent to a true proposition because "its arrangement into a necessary consequence is often lacking," which means that the evidentness of the consequence—which would otherwise compel our assent—is also lacking (*S* 8.3.7: 691). Finally, he notes that it is possible to draw mistaken inferences from the natural experiences that make our assent to scientific propositions evident. "Although poor and insufficiently examined experiences often lead to error," he says, "much experience properly examined in a wide variety of cases never leads to error [*licet experientia pauca et parum examinata saepe fallat, tamen experientia multa et bene in diversis casibus examinata numquam fallit*]" (*QAnPo* I.2).

But if neither inductive inference nor the intellect's natural inclination to assent to the truth suffices to make our assent to second-mode principles certain, the only candidate left would appear to be both capacities working in tandem. And herein lies Buridan's justification of our claim to know such principles. Our knowledge of 'Every fire is hot' or 'The heavens are moved' is justified because the intellect, together with the evidence of sense, memory, and experience, is a reliable detector of the truth of propositions expressing second-mode principles. Moreover, Buridan clearly regards the reliability of induction and assent as something that cannot be settled a priori, but that depends upon contingent facts about both human cognition and the nature of the external world.

Buridan's reliability claims fall into two general categories. First, he argues that although they are not infallible, intellectual judgments of assent do tend to produce beliefs that are free from doubt and error. Our disposition to assent to truth helps to secure the reliability of such judgments:

> As far as second-mode principles are concerned, there does not seem to be any doubt that in order to state the truth promptly, easily, and firmly, we need an acquired disposition, above and beyond the power of the intellect, because in relation to those things it is naturally suited to direct or lead astray, a power is not sufficiently determined in itself, without such an added disposition, to direct them firmly, promptly, and easily, and never lead them astray. (*QNE* VI.11: 127rb)[60]

Buridan then argues for the reliability of this added disposition on a posteriori grounds. In the case of scientific knowledge, we all know by experience that the intellect's inclination to assent to inductive generalizations is stalled as soon as it apprehends a counter-instance, or sees some other reason for deferring judgment.[61] For example, its inclination to assent to 'All swans are white' would be blocked by the appearance of a black swan, or it would at least defer judgment upon reading or hearing accounts of black swans. Buridan's view is that while sense and intellect have the power to apprehend similarities in sensible particulars and group them together by means of induction, no knowledge is produced unless the intellect itself judges which of those collections represent principles.

Second, Buridan argues that the particular sense perceptions upon which inductive generalizations are founded are reliably produced.[62] We are not deceived if our senses are at an appropriate distance from their objects, if the medium of sensation is clear, and if our sense organs are properly disposed (QDA_3 II.11: 169).[63] Furthermore, as we saw above, we can also know when each of these external conditions has been satisfied. We know that sense perception becomes less reliable the farther its objects are from the actual organs of sense; that because vision is ordinarily disposed to see any color at all, placing a colored glass between the eye and the object of vision will make color judgment unreliable; and that certain illnesses can affect the disposition of bodily humors and hence the judgmental capacity of physical organs.[64] In short, Buridan finds no reason within the natural order of things to suppose that inductive inference, together with the intellect's natural inclination to the truth, does not justify our claim to have empirical knowledge.

c. Perceptual Knowledge and Divine Omnipotence

Buridan replies to the skeptical arguments about sensory delusion and the possibility of divine interference in the natural order first by reminding his audience that the intellect has the power to correct illusory sensory judgments, provided the source of error is also part of the natural order. But he concedes that it is not possible to correct for errors that have a supernatural cause: "if God operates simply miraculously, it must be concluded that he can; and so there is only evidentness on the assumption [viz., that the common course of nature holds] which, as we have already said, is sufficient for natural science" (QM II.1: 9ra).[65] Of course, if God could produce in me a cognition of something that does not actually exist, causing me to mistakenly affirm that it does, our warrant to treat the ordinary operations of sensory and intellectual cognition as justifying knowledge claims would seem to be destroyed. Nevertheless, Buridan maintains that at least in the natural sciences, belief claims that are not absolutely evident are still justified. How is this a reply to Nicholas's argument?

There is one kind of response to skeptical doubt about perceptual knowledge available from an account of human knowledge that was circulating in fourteenth-century Paris, but to which Buridan did not himself subscribe.

This is the direct realist view that there are certain sensory and/or intellectual states through which we are directly and non-inferentially aware of the existence of external objects. Although neither employed it to refute skepticism, both Duns Scotus and Ockham maintained that there is an unmediated act of sensory or intellectual apprehension, the act of intuitive cognition, which produces an evident judgment of existence when its object exists, and of non-existence when it does not.[66] These judgments are evident because the cognitions from which they are formed are caused in the natural order only by objects that exist and are present to the cognizer.[67] It is therefore possible to have evident knowledge of contingent things whenever the intellect assents to propositions whose terms stand for intuitively apprehended objects.

Buridan, however, cannot take this route. Although his psychology posits an act of simple apprehension, the singular cognition of something as present to the senses, this will not work against the skeptic. The reason is that it fails to be veridical even within the natural order, for we can experience this most evident act of cognition even while dreaming. Buridan is well aware of the implications for veridicality: "often those concepts [of dream-objects] are fictitious, because they do not have a consistent correspondence to any external thing, for there is no absurdity in there being fictitious singular concepts, just as there are fictitious common concepts" (*QM* VII.20: 54va).[68] No criteria are offered, however, for distinguishing dreaming from waking states, nor does Buridan appear sensitive to the difference between fictitious dream-objects, such as chimeras, and dream-objects that could actually be present to my senses as objects of waking singular cognition, such as Socrates or Plato.

This points to an important difference between Buridan's singular cognition of something as present to the senses and intuitive cognition as defined by Scotus and Ockham. Intuitive cognition is the direct, unmediated awareness of an object as present to the senses or intellect, whereas Buridanian singular cognition is an indirect operation through which the intellect or sense apprehends an object by means of a species representing it. In Buridan's view, both sensory and intellectual singular cognition must occur through the medium of a species:

> Although exterior sense cognizes Socrates, or whiteness, or white, this is only in connection with a species representing it confusedly with the substance, the whiteness, the magnitude, and the location according to which it appears in the prospect of the person cognizing it. And sense cannot sort out this confusion, i.e., it cannot separate the species of the substance, the whiteness, the magnitude, and the location from each other, and so it can only perceive the whiteness or the substance in the manner of something existing in its presence. Therefore, it can only cognize the aforesaid things singularly. . . . I say that when the intellect re-

ceives the species or intellection of Socrates from the phantasm with this kind of confusion of size and location, making the thing appear in the manner of something existing in the prospect of the person cognizing it, the intellect understands him in a singular manner. (QDA_3 III.8: 76, 79)[69]

Unlike Scotus and Ockham, then, Buridan does not subscribe to a direct realist account of cognition, and so it is not open to him to appeal to our capacity to intuit certain objects directly in order to reply to skeptical doubts about the reliability of perceptual judgments.

true?

Still, the real problem Buridan faces in this Ultricurian argument is the *logical* possibility of our being deceived by an omnipotent being. The traditional reply to such arguments is to block the skeptical implications of one divine attribute with another, which is what Descartes does when he argues that a deceiving God would be doing something he cannot do, i.e., violating his own essential goodness.[70] Buridan cannot adopt this strategy, however, because he subscribes to both main assumptions of the Ultricurian argument, i.e., to the doctrine of divine omnipotence ("since God can do this and greater things"), and the belief that God's will is inscrutable ("since you know nothing about the will of God, you cannot be certain of anything").[71] From this it follows that "God would not be acting badly in [deceiving us], even if he annihilated all human beings and the entire world, because it all belongs to him absolutely. And so if he would not be acting badly in annihilating human beings, it also seems right that he would not be acting badly if he creates a false belief in someone, since that false belief would not in that case be bad" (*QM* IV.12: 21vb).[72] But this means that in Buridan's hands, the first tenet of Ultricurian skepticism has the same epistemological force as a Cartesian evil demon. Buridan's first reaction to it is predictably visceral. He calls those who improperly use the concept of divine omnipotence "wicked men" who, by means of their insistence that principles and conclusions "can be falsified through cases supernaturally possible [*possunt falsificari per casus supernaturaliter possibiles*]," are bent upon destroying the natural and moral sciences (*QM* II.1: 9ra). Even if this is not a reference to Nicholas, it applies to his argument that no evident inference from appearance to substance can be drawn by the natural light of reason if we take the notion of divine omnipotence seriously.

But Buridan has another, more considered response to this argument, which begins with his assertion that we can have knowledge, or as he puts it, that "the comprehension of truth with certitude is possible for us" (*QM* II.1: 9ra). This is possible only if relative evidentness, or evidentness on the assumption that the common course of nature holds, is accepted as adequate for empirical knowledge claims. Supernatural considerations are omitted from the discussion of human knowledge because they wreck the justificatory enterprise in two ways. First, as Buridan argues (departing here even from

Nicholas) not even absolutely evident judgments, i.e., those equivalent or reducible to the principle of non-contradiction, are secure in view of God's power, for there is no reason why God could not, if God wished, make us assent to a contradiction.[73] Second, by casting doubt upon the possibility of empirical knowledge, supernatural considerations nullify the primary task of the natural philosopher, which is to explain natural phenomena.[74]

Buridan thinks supernatural considerations are too easily misapplied in natural philosophy. In his *Questions on Aristotle's Meteorology*, for example, he suggests that appealing to the miraculous is not only unphilosophical, but also base and unlearned:

> There are several ways of understanding the word 'natural'. The first is when we oppose it to 'supernatural' (and the supernatural effect is what we call a 'miracle'). . . . And it is clear that meteorological effects are natural effects, as they are produced naturally, and not miraculously. . . . Consequently, philosophers explain them by the appropriate natural causes. But common folk, ignorant of these causes, believe that these phenomena are produced by a miracle of God, which is usually not true . . .'[75]

Likewise, although Buridan concedes that God could bring about directly any effect caused by a secondary agent, he does not see this as having any relevance to natural science. His discussion, e.g., of the operation of the agent intellect begins with the following proviso:

> It must be noted that although the universal agent who is God can bring about each and every thing determinately and without any other determinate agent, that action would not be called natural but miraculous. In natural actions, however, it must be the case that in addition to the universal agent, particular and determinate agents play a role in the fact that this happens rather than that, as when an agent fire determines the fact that a fire comes to be, or is produced, and not water, and the semen of a horse determines the fact that a horse is produced, and not a goat. (QDA_3 II.10: 154)[76]

Buridan recognizes that considerations based on divine omnipotence do nothing to *explain* natural phenomena.[77]

In keeping with this naturalistic tendency in his philosophy, Buridan defines epistemic error relative to the natural order. When asked whether one could be in error about first principles such as the principle of non-contradiction, he replies, "it is impossible to be in error about a first principle, at least naturally [*impossibile est sic circa primum principium errare, saltem naturaliter*]." The latter clause reflects his concession that God's power is such that he could "miraculously and supernaturally" produce and conserve contrary beliefs in the same intellect at the same time—a possibility which, Buridan says, "I dismiss because it is not natural [*dimitto quia hoc non est naturale*]" (*QM* IV.12: 21va–vb). Epistemological inquiry for Buridan is driven by the question of how error is possible given the way our powers of sensory and intellectual cognition happen to operate here and now, leaving aside the merely logical possibility of divine interference in the natural order. The result would not be such as to satisfy the Ultricurian skeptic, but that hardly worries Buridan, since he rejects the idea that only propositions equivalent or reducible to the principle of non-contradiction can be known with certainty.[78]

As far as Buridan is concerned, then, the proper philosophical response to skepticism based on God's power to deceive us is to acknowledge the possibility, and then to ignore it. He is committed to the former by his assumption that God's will is inscrutable, whereas the latter is a product of the view, implicit everywhere in his discussions of human knowledge, that it is unreasonable to accept the skeptic's demand that everything we know be equivalent or reducible to the principle of non-contradiction. That is why he argues that evidentness on the assumption of the common course of nature is sufficient for our assent to the principles of natural science. This is a perfectly valid anti-skeptical position, which has the additional virtue of explaining why Buridan is not much gripped by the skeptical arguments he confronts. He remains confident throughout that natural science can proceed using its own high standards of justification, regardless of what the skeptic says:

> For a good astronomer knows that today there is a lunar eclipse because [*propter hoc*] today the earth will be located diametrically between the moon and the sun; and he knows this also because he knows that today there is an opposition of the sun and the moon, and that the moon is in the head or the tail of Draco; and he also knows that there will be a lunar eclipse on such and such a day, because he knows that on that day the earth will be between the sun and the moon. And this knowledge of the astronomer and its demonstrations of this sort are with the certainty and evidentness that are required for natural science, although they can be falsified by supernatural power. (*S* 8.7.7: 747–48)

But it is easy to miss this if we try to read Buridan as a foundationalist. The contemporary theory of epistemic justification with which he has the most in common is reliabilism. This emerges if we look closely at his rejection of the direct realism of Scotus and Ockham, his treatment of the principle of the uniformity of nature as evident only a posteriori, and his justification of induction and sense perception on the a posteriori grounds that both tend to produce beliefs that are free from doubt and error (although not infallible beliefs), and with checkable results.[79] And although he is no precursor of Descartes,[80] Buridan is forced, unlike either Aristotle or Thomas Aquinas, to confront the Cartesian question of how knowledge can be justified given the existence of an all-powerful being capable of deceiving us in ways we could never detect. His answer is very un-Cartesian, but entirely consistent with the naturalism that underlies his conception of philosophical inquiry.

CHAPTER THIRTEEN

Natural Science

·Buridan's innovative conception of philosophical practice extended beyond dialectic to change the way speculative philosophy was done. In physics or natural philosophy, we see the gradual attenuation of what can be inferred about the nature of causes from their evident effects, together with a corresponding shift in attention from the formal to the productive aspects of knowledge. How do we come to know about the structure of the natural order, and how can such knowledge be reconciled with the fallibility of our cognitive powers and weakness of our wills? Much of Buridan's natural philosophy, from psychology (treated in this chapter) to ethics (treated in chapters 14–15), is driven by his attempts to answer these two questions. But again, methodological shifts are subtle. Buridan offers no definitive account of the possibility of knowledge in natural philosophy, nor could he, since the transcendental dimensions of the problem would not have been apparent until the modern period, when the separation of philosophy from theology was almost complete. Instead, questions about the generation of knowledge are raised in a variety of contexts in the special sciences, whose Aristotelian ordering Buridan still regards as authoritative. Thus, the Autrecourt controversy, which strikes us as epistemological and therefore paradigmatically modern, is discussed in at least three different contexts: in the *Summulae*'s eighth treatise on demonstrations and the *Questions on Aristotle's Metaphysics* (as we have seen), as well as in the *Questions on Aristotle's De Anima* (as we will see below). It is to these discussions, and their particular surroundings, that we must look for the crucial differences.

It was Autrecourt's strikingly modern focus on the limits of epistemic justification, among other things, that led Ernest A. Moody, one of the founders of American scholarship in medieval philosophy, to describe the fourteenth century as a period in which "empiricism was the prevailing philosophical position."[1] He attributed this on the one hand to "the powerful and drastic critique of knowledge which had been developed during the period between Thomas Aquinas and Ockham," and on the other to "theological reaction against the necessitarianism of Arab metaphysics and natural theology."[2] As an attempt to characterize the general spirit of a period, Moody's thesis has a good deal of surface plausibility. It is undeniable to anyone who has read Thomas and Ockham, for example, that these are profoundly different thinkers, and that their differences consist not only in what philosophical questions they regard as important, but also in how they think they should be resolved.

For a variety of reasons, however, Moody's thesis has never really caught on among historians of philosophy.[3] This is due in part, I think, to the suspicion with which such attempts at large-scale categorization are generally, and often quite rightly, regarded. But in this case, it also reflects the fact that we are all taught that empiricism is something that came along much later, well after Descartes, and medieval empiricism, if there be such, can easily look anemic and unsophisticated next to the modern or contemporary paradigms everybody associates with that doctrine. The difficulty with this, however, is that if fourteenth-century philosophers were empiricists, they were certainly not empiricists in anything like the way David Hume or Rudolf Carnap was an empiricist, to pick two rather different tokens of the type. We do not, for example, find fourteenth-century philosophers trying to reduce all ideas to sense impressions, or embracing an empiricist theory of meaning. Is there some more charitable way of understanding Moody's thesis?

I believe that there is, as long as we are willing to interpret 'empiricism' more broadly, as Moody himself surely did. For if we understand empiricism in terms of a cluster of broadly epistemic doctrines concerned with the methodology of knowing, and emphasizing in particular (1) the evidentness of sensory appearances and judgments (as opposed to their intrinsic, formal content) as the primary criterion for their veridicality, (2) the reliability of a posteriori modes of reasoning, such as induction (as opposed to modes based on the notion that empirical truths are deductively demonstrable),[4] and (3) the utility of naturalistic models of explanation, including their analogous application to non-physical phenomena (as opposed to their disuse, or limited application to specific natural phenomena), then much of what fourteenth-century philosophers did can count as empiricist, especially in contrast to the thirteenth century. The 'especially' is important here because it is the historically proximate differences that are most relevant as far as Moody's thesis is concerned, and the most interesting philosophically. It tells us nothing about fourteenth-century philosophy to note that it fails to match up to some historically remote paradigm of empiricism, be that British or logical.[5] Moody was surely attempting to characterize a subtler change of orientation, which means that if we want to properly evaluate what he said, we must turn to particular authors and texts, and look at the particular differences between them. If we look at particular differences, it emerges that a significant change occurred in the practice of physics, or natural philosophy, between the thirteenth and fourteenth centuries, and that Buridan was one of the agents of this change.

To illustrate this, I will look at differences between thirteenth- and fourteenth-century psychology, a division of Aristotelian natural philosophy where one might expect to find the changes of "method in the acquisition and evaluation of knowledge" Moody had in mind. In particular, I will compare the treatment of certain key issues in Buridan's *Questions on Aristotle's De Anima* with its most influential thirteenth-century predecessor, the *Sentencia De Anima* of Thomas Aquinas (1225–1274), as well as with one of its immediate successors, the *De Anima* commentary of Buridan's younger colleague, Nicole Oresme (c. 1320–1382).[6] I should add as a proviso that I do not believe that any of these figures should be seen as representative of philosophy in their centuries as a whole—as if 'typical fourteenth-century philosopher' is a referring term, any more than 'typical twentieth-century philosopher'—but I do think that their work exhibits trends typical of the periods and places in which they worked. And since these trends are what Moody was really concerned with, they will allow us to see if a more plausible interpretation can be attached to his thesis about empiricism.

First, I will compare Thomas, Buridan, and Oresme in terms of their differing conceptions of psychology as a science, or body of knowledge, focusing on their understanding of its subject matter and peculiar difficulty. Then, to show how their methods apply in practice, I will examine their differing explanations of intellectual memory, the phenomenon whereby the intellect is said to retain the capacity to cognize objects with which it has been previously acquainted.

1. THE PROPER SUBJECT OF PSYCHOLOGY

Thomas, Buridan, and Oresme all agree with Aristotle that psychology is part of the more general study of the "science of nature," or physics, and that it studies affections of the soul insofar as those involve matter, or body.[7] But other than to remark, "the soul is in some sense the principle of animal life," Aristotle does not attempt to characterize the subject of those affections at the beginning of *De Anima*,[8] and it is here that we find some interesting divergences among our authors.

The proper subject of psychology is the topic of the first two lectures of Thomas's *Commentary on De Anima*, a literal commentary based on a Latin version of Aristotle's text, which had been newly translated by his Dominican confrere, William of Moerbeke. The text is divided using lemmas from Aristotle's text. Paraphrasing Aristotle's query about whether soul can be defined by a single, unambiguous formula, Thomas remarks, "For this reason, then, there is a question whether we should seek one common account [*ratio*] of soul, as the Platonists said, or an account of this soul or that one, as the natural philosophers [*naturales*] said—as, for instance, the soul of a horse, or a human being, or a god. (He says 'of God' because these philosophers believed that the heavenly bodies are gods and said that they have souls)."[9] Although Aristotle leaves the question open at this juncture, Thomas is confident that Aristotle "holds that we should look for an account of both: both a common account of the soul and an account of each single species."[10]

But how can we discern the nature of something that cannot itself be sensed? Thomas calls this "the difficulty inherent in the knowledge [*scientia*] of the soul as regards the soul's substance and what it is [*quod quid est animae*]."[11] Aristotle hints at a solution with respect to human souls when he speculates that rather than belonging to the soul/body composite, some affections of the soul might be peculiar to the soul itself—to which he adds, almost as an afterthought, that if there were such affections, the soul "[would] be capable of separate existence." In his comment on this passage, Thomas mentions Book III of *De Anima*, where he says that Aristotle clears up this problem with a distinction between two senses in which the act of understanding depends on the body: understanding needs a body as its object—since, as he says, "the soul never thinks without an image"—but not as its instrument, since the act of understanding is not realized by corporeal organs.[12] Thomas's next comment moves even farther from the text of *De Anima*. Here he suggests that the psychologist can use this distinction to speculate about the nature of the human soul itself:

> Two results follow. One is that having intellective cognition [*intelligere*] is an operation that is special to soul and needs a body only as its object (as was said). Seeing, however, and other operations and states [*passiones*] belong not to the soul alone but to the compound [*coniunctum*]. The other result is that what has its operation on its own has its existence and subsistence on its own; what does not have its operation on its own does not have its existence on its own. Hence intellect is a subsistent form; the other powers are forms in matter. And here lay the difficulty of this question: for all the soul's states give the appearance of belonging to the compound.[13]

For Thomas, it is part of the science of the soul to offer a definitive account of its subject in virtue of the fact that we can reason to the essential nature of

the soul from its independent activities. Thus, from the evident per se operation of our intellects—e.g., when a mathematician actualizes certain dispositions to consider the transformations of a geometrical configuration in
topology, and does so apparently at will—we conclude that the human soul
must be something that exists per se.

But lest psychology be confused with metaphysics, Thomas emphasizes
that the 'raw data' of psychology always involves matter. Following Aristotle's
view of the psychologist as a natural scientist who studies attributes of the
soul not in terms of their purely formal natures or exclusively material conditions, but inseparably from their matter, Thomas argues that the psychologist's way of studying attributes differs from those used by craftsmen, meta-
physicians, or (here) mathematicians:

> [the] soul's states [*passiones animae*], like rage, fear, and this sort of thing,
> are not separable from the physical matter of animals insofar as they are
> such. They are not, that is, separable insofar as they are states that do not
> exist without a body [*quae non sunt sine corpore*] and are not like line
> and plane (i.e., surface), which can be separated from natural matter con-
> ceptually [*ratione*]. So if this is how things stand, then it is a matter for
> natural philosophy (as was stated above) to consider these things and soul
> as well.[14]

In the prologue to his commentary on Aristotle's *De sensu*, Thomas argues that
the criterion which separates metaphysical from psychological approaches to
the soul is the subject matter's degree of abstraction from (or, conversely,
contraction to) matter:

> the intellect is not the act of any part of the body, as is proved in *De
> Anima* III. That is why it cannot be studied by means of its contraction
> [*concretio*] or application to the body, or in relation to any corporeal
> organ. For its greatest contraction is in the [human] soul, whereas its high-
> est abstraction is in separated substances. Thus, other than *De Anima*,
> Aristotle did not write a book on the intellect and intelligibles—or, if he
> had, it would not have pertained to natural science, but more to meta-
> physics, whose province it is to study separated substances.[15]

But even so, the intellect's need for material objects in its mode of least abstraction, i.e., in particular acts of human understanding, is sufficient to secure a place for the human soul in the study of psychology. The psychologist
seeks to explain the workings of the human soul and, indeed, of every other
kind of living body, through its relations with matter.[16]

Like Thomas, Buridan begins his most comprehensive work on psy-
chology, the third and final version of his *Questions on Aristotle's De Anima*, *and earlier version?*

by delineating its proper subject matter. This is to distinguish psychology on the one hand from metaphysics, which, he says, considers the definition of the soul "in terms of its simple nature [*secundum simplicem rationem ipsius*]," and on the other from natural philosophy more narrowly conceived, which considers the soul's vital operations as such, or those operations which involve corporeal dispositions attributable to "the entire composite of soul and body [*ex parte totius compositi ex anima et corpore*]" (*QDA₃* I.1: 122va–123ra). Unlike Thomas, however, Buridan does not think that the science of psychology provides any special insight on the nature of the soul, nor does he see the difference between metaphysical and psychological investigations of the human soul in terms of their degree of abstraction from the body. For Buridan, the divisions are much sharper. He concedes that psychological inquiry presupposes a certain nominal definition of the soul, but its real definition belongs to metaphysics, not to psychology: "in this science [of the soul], the nominal definition of the soul is presupposed. Nor, as it happens, do we investigate the [real] definition of the soul here, except by means of a superior habit, viz., through metaphysics. For the definitions of each being in act and power, permitted [by Aristotle] in the second book of *De Anima* in order to investigate the definition of the soul, concern metaphysics, to which it belongs to establish the principles of the other sciences" (*QDA₃* I.1: 123ra–rb).[17] This is why Buridan does not think it proper for the psychologist to consider such 'metaphysical' questions as "whether the human soul understands after death, separated from the body [*si anima humana a post mortem intelligat separata a corpore*]."[18] For him, the science of the soul is limited to investigating the same corporeal dispositions that Aristotle treats in a more physicalistic vein in the *Parva Naturalia*. The difference is one of perspective: whereas the biologist studies them extensionally, as physical operations "common to all animate things [*communes animatis*]" and ultimately attributable "to the entire composite of soul and body [*ex parte totius compositi ex anima et corpore*]," the psychologist treats them as powers of the soul in particular, and hence as attributable to it as their proper subject (*QDA₃* I.1: 122ra–va).

But saying that psychology is neither metaphysics nor biology doesn't establish what psychology is. Buridan argues that it is a little of both:

> Aristotle thinks [i.e., in *De Anima* I.1.403b17–18] that although the soul is inseparable from the body, and although its operations could not exist apart from a body, it is possible to study the soul in itself by studying dispositions and attributes proper to the soul in itself and not to the entire body. For there are many dispositions and attributes of this sort: e.g., that the soul is the act of the body (for this is not proper to the body, nor to the composite of soul and body); and likewise, that the soul conceived as agent, form, and end is the principle of the body; that the soul is di-

de anima studie
only s ml us pat of
body

vided into several powers according to its diverse vital operations; and so
on. (*QDA₃* I.1: 122vb)[19]

But from these "dispositions and attributes proper to the soul in itself" we
can conclude only that the soul has certain functional characteristics: that it
is the act and principle of the body, as well as the subject of different powers
in keeping with its diverse vital operations.[20] This suggests that Buridanian
psychology conceives of the soul as no more than the bare, empirically indis-
cernible, subject of animate qualities. In contrast with Thomas, who wants to
attribute more robust qualities, such as per se subsistence, to the human soul, *true?*
Buridan does not think that psychology is in a position to reveal anything
about the inherent nature of the soul, and so he does not speculate about it.
The natural science of psychology is concerned with explaining the relation
between animate qualities and the soul itself as their proper subject, not with
some "simple concept" of the soul arrived at by abstraction from this relation. Buridan is keen to stress this later in the same work:

> Note that the natural scientist does not study substances according to
> their absolutely quidditative natures, but only the metaphysician. For the
> natural philosopher only studies substances in relation to their motion
> and operations. And since natural forms require for their operations a
> determinate matter made suitable for them by qualitative and quantitative
> dispositions, natural scientists must define forms through their proper
> matter. Therefore, in its natural definition, the soul must be defined by
> means of a physical, organic body. (*QDA₃* II.3: 34)[21]

To the objection that psychology cannot count as a natural science because
the soul itself is not a mobile being, Buridan replies rather bluntly, "I say that
it suffices for the fact that this science is natural that it considers some integral or essential part of mobile being in relation to its vital operations"
(*QDA₃* I.1: 123ra).[22] Since psychology is really about that relation, Buridan is
not inclined to question its legitimacy as a natural science, even if one of its
relata, viz., its proper subject, has an abstract mode of existence.   *no*

Nicole Oresme approaches the question of the proper subject of psychology in much the same way as Thomas and Buridan, although his conclusion indicates that he has an even more naturalistic conception of the science
of the soul. In his own question commentary on Aristotle's *De Anima,* he
observes that some regard soul as the proper subject of psychology, others
the animate body.[23] The first view is, of course, differently defended by both
Thomas and Buridan, but Oresme would have most likely associated it with   *R*
Buridan, whom he probably knew personally. Without actually refuting it,
however, Oresme adopts the second view, noting that the term 'body' in

'animate body' can be taken: "in one way for the matter and [material] dispositions, leaving aside the soul or form, just as we say that a man is composed of soul and body; in another way, 'body' is taken for the entire composite, and in this way it is a certain genus in the category of substance: in this way we say that a man is a body—though not from a body."[24] It is the first way of understanding 'body' which for Oresme characterizes the wholly physicalistic approach of the *Parva Naturalia*. As a positive reason for choosing 'animate body' understood in the second sense as the proper subject of psychology, he remarks that the various animate functions with which psychology is concerned "are not suited [*non competunt*]" to the soul itself, but only to the composite of soul and body, because (paraphrasing Aristotle) "the soul does not see or touch or nourish or generate, but the man or the animal."[25] How is such an inquiry into the functions of animate body worthy of the name 'natural science'? Oresme replies in a way that is reminiscent of Buridan: "it suffices that [animate body] is an integral part [of a natural science], that is, that it signifies an integral part of what is signified by the subject of an entire natural science [i.e., 'mobile being' or 'mobile body']."[26]

The difference between Thomas, Buridan, and Oresme on the subject matter of psychology would appear to be this: whereas the psychologist for Thomas seeks to understand the nature of the soul itself through its vital operations, and the Buridanian psychologist studies the soul as the logical subject of those same operations, Oresme takes the further, even more naturalistic, step of insisting that body (*corpus*) itself be mentioned as part of the subject matter of psychology. What we are seeing here is the migration of the concept of the soul in Aristotelian psychology from a substance whose essence can be revealed by studying its motions in Thomas, to the imperceptible and undisclosable subject of those movements in Buridan, and finally, to something of which corporeal matter must itself be mentioned as an essential part in Oresme. What accounts for this shift? To answer this question, we will need to look briefly at what Thomas, Buridan, and Oresme each have to say about the special difficulty of psychology.

2. The Difficulty of Psychology as a Natural Science

Aristotle begins his *De Anima* with the sobering remark, "to attain any assured knowledge about the soul is one of the most difficult things in the world."[27] In their comments on it, our authors provide different diagnoses of the problem.

Thomas sees Aristotle's difficulty in terms of the difficulty of knowing either "the soul's substance," or "its accidental or distinctive [*proprias*] states."[28] As far as psychology is concerned, however, he focuses on the second difficulty because it concerns the elements of a definition that will "make known the thing's essence [*notificat essentiam rei*]."[29] Thomas follows Aristotle in assuming that definition is "the starting-point [*principium*] for demonstrating things."[30] He assumes further that the science of the soul is, like other natural sciences, demonstrative to the extent that it proceeds by syllogistic inference from premises to conclusions productive of *scientia*, or knowledge, and that the premises are prior in the epistemic sense that they come from "sensible effects better known [*magis noti*] than their causes."[31] But the project of defining the soul involves us in a further difficulty "regarding the support that in definitions necessarily comes from the soul's accidents."[32] This contribution is necessary because

> in a definition one must reach a cognition not only of essential principles [*principia essentialia*] but also of accidental ones. For if the essential principles were rightly defined and could be cognized, then the definition would not need the accidents. But because the essential principles of things are concealed [*ignota*] from us, we must use accidental distinguishing characteristics in designating essential characteristics [*utamur differentiis accidentalibus in designatione essentialium*]. (For 'biped' is not essential but is introduced in designating what is essential.) It is through these accidental distinguishing characteristics, consequently, that we reach a cognition of essential characteristics. And that is why this is difficult. For we have to characterize what the soul is [*quid est animae*] in order to cognize readily the soul's accidents. . . . Conversely, also, if the accidents are grasped in advance, then this adds much to our cognition of what it is to be such a thing, as was said.[33]

Although the soul's essence cannot be directly revealed in this life, Thomas assumes that we can still have knowledge of it via its manifestations in the form of these "accidental distinguishing characteristics." We saw an example of this above, where he took the quasi-independent operations of the act of understanding to be indicative of the per se subsistence of the intellect to which it belongs. Resolving the special difficulty of psychology, then, becomes a matter of finding the right dialectical balance between inquiry into the nature of the soul, which is known through its accidents, and inquiry into the operations of the soul, which become easier to grasp once we have some understanding of the essence that is their organizing principle.

For Buridan, the difficulty of psychology stems from the epistemic consideration that human intellects are simply too weak to apprehend anything "without reasoning and deductive inference from the knowledge of sensible things [*sine processu et deductione ex notitia sensibilium*]" (QDA₃ I.4: 126ra). Despite this weakness, however, Buridan agrees with Aristotle that psychology is the "most certain" of the natural sciences.[34] On Buridan's view, the kind of certainty involved here is metaphysical rather than epistemological:

whereas the difficulty of psychology stems from our inability to apprehend its subject directly, its certainty is due to the nobility of its subject, since from a God's-eye point of view, the soul is "a great being, perfect and prior to [other natural things] in terms of its dignity [*anima esse magis ens, scilicet perfectus et prius via dignitatis*]" (*QDA₃* I.4: 126rb). With this in mind, he draws two conclusions:

> The first is that the science of the soul is exceedingly difficult for us and consequently uncertain with respect to the cognizing agent and compared to all other natural things (leaving aside God and the intelligences), because our intellect cannot be sensed. And yet it is on our part, arising from the weakness of our intellect, that we can comprehend only what can be sensed or by deduction from what can be sensed, as has been stated.
>
> The second conclusion is that, on the side of the things to be understood, the science of the soul is the most certain and the easiest, since among other natural things, the soul has the most being and is the highest object of cognition. (*QDA₃* I.4: 126ra)[35]

But if the same intellect is both cognizing and being cognized, why doesn't the difficulty of the former carry over into the latter, and conversely, why doesn't the ease of the latter somehow make the former less difficult? Buridan replies by claiming that we cognize the intellect itself under a different concept (*ratio*) than we do when cognizing it merely as something cognizing, an appeal to the distinction between cognizing the attribute of a subject (relatively easy) and cognizing the subject itself (relatively difficult).

Buridan also sees the particular difficulty of psychology on two levels. First, he says that psychology "is more difficult and uncertain absolutely, insofar as the intellective soul is concerned, in the way that the intellective soul is related to the body and to matter, because it is unextended and not derived from a material potentiality, but comes to inhere in the body in a supernatural way" (*QDA₃* I.4: 126rb–va).[36] On a metaphysical level, psychology is difficult because the exact relation between the human intellective soul and its body cannot be explained in a naturalistic fashion. As we saw in chapter 11, what Buridan means when he says that the human soul inheres in its body in "a supernatural way" is that the principles governing this relation are not instantiated anywhere else in the natural world. This is not to say that the inherence of the human soul in its body defies rational explanation, but only that its explanation cannot appeal to principles derived from reasoning about what is evident to our senses. But that is sufficient, Buridan argues, to push the question beyond the domain of psychology and into that of theology, which uses purely metaphysical and doctrinal considerations to address other, similar questions, such as how the body of Christ is present in the consecrated bread of the Eucharist.

Second, Buridan argues that, "based on the vast majority of doubtful questions, the science of the soul can be said to be more difficult than those of other natural forms because more than those other forms, the soul requires diverse [material] arrangements in a body, and in fact possesses exceedingly complex arrangements [of matter] and diverse powers and operations" (*QDA*₃ I.4: 126va).[37] From a purely investigative standpoint, psychology is more difficult than the other sciences because of the divergence and complexity of the material conditions needed for the soul's operations. Thus, we cannot understand the soul's power of vision without having at least some knowledge of the physiology and function of the eye, or the power of hearing without some knowledge of the physiology and function of the ear—neither of which is easily acquired.

In his own discussion of this issue, Oresme seconds Buridan's motion that the special difficulty of the science of the soul is attributable to the epistemic problem of explaining how evident knowledge is possible in psychology. But whereas Buridan points to the complexity of the various physical processes through which the soul operates, Oresme locates the problem more specifically in the sensory powers by means of which we are aware of them: "the difficulty [of psychology] occurs on the part of the bodily senses and organs. That is why, because of a certain indisposition [in them], there is a certain resistance and a certain difficulty in the operations of the interior senses—operations that are most of all required for understanding. And in this way, Plato said in the *Phaedo* [67d] that the intellect is impeded because of the shackles of the flesh."[38] In Oresme's view, the senses are not up to the task of producing images with an informational content rich enough to provide a basis for evident knowledge. He is careful to add that this difficulty does not occur on those occasions when we reason about general principles in psychology, but only when its conclusions are said to be removed or remote (*remotas*) from those principles. In the latter sphere, we find that the consequences are usually "non-formal," by which Oresme means a piece of reasoning whose truth is not deductively certain—at least not on the model of the A-form syllogism Aristotle regards as the paradigm producer of demonstrative knowledge.[39] For Oresme, what psychology features most of the time are informal inferences about the nature and functions of animate bodies, based on general principles and particular sensory evidence.

Although he is less confident than Buridan about the epistemic adequacy of our sensory powers, Oresme offers basically the same diagnosis of why psychology is so difficult: since the soul itself, or animate body qua animate, has no empirical manifestations, we can only infer what it is like from its vital effects. There is no such problem for Thomas, who, again, sees the difficulty in terms of balancing our efforts to define the essential nature of the soul and characterize its operations, given that our knowledge of one is conditioned by the other. Thus, Thomas does not query Aristotle's remark at the beginning of *De Anima* that knowing the accidents of a thing contributes to knowing its essence.[40] Both Buridan and Oresme worry about this, however, and it occurs to them that if psychology is to be a science, it must address the epistemic problem of how we can reliably draw inferences from natural phenomena to the nature of soul or animate body itself. Both authors turn to this next.

3. BURIDAN AND ORESME ON EMPIRICAL INFERENCE IN PSYCHOLOGY

If psychology is a natural science concerned with the relation between souls or animate bodies and their vital operations, then, like other natural sciences, it must start by reasoning from what is more evident to us—in this case, particular subject/attribute pairs such as (Socrates, Socrates's thinking)—to a general principle "more knowable by nature" which explains their connection.[41] But, unlike the subjects of other natural sciences found in the genus 'mobile being' (e.g., heavenly bodies), the subject of psychology is not evident to our senses. How, then, can we hope to discover its nature?

Buridan sees this problem in terms of the more general epistemological problem of whether substance can be cognized through accidents. He gives seven arguments on the negative side of the question, the fifth of which mentions a standard of certainty defended by Nicholas of Autrecourt, whose views, as we saw in chapter 12, were vigorously opposed by Buridan.[42] As Buridan describes it, Nicholas's position is that

> substance is not cognized through accident by a direct representation because accident and substance are exceedingly different. Nor is it obvious that this happens discursively, because there can be no evident consequence from the existence of one thing to the existence of another [distinct from it], since this cannot be reduced to the first principle, which is founded on contradiction. For there can never be a contradiction in the fact that one thing exists and another thing [distinct from it] does not, since a contradiction must involve the affirmation and negation of the same [predicate] as regards the same [subject]. (*QDA₃* I.6: 128va)[43]

The challenge to the defender of psychology as a natural science is to show that Autrecourt's criterion of certainty either (1) can be met, as the soul's accidents are not distinct from its substance; or (2) should be rejected, because although the soul's accidents are distinct from its substance, they are not so different that we cannot draw reliable inferences from one to the other, though the certainty of those inferences falls short of that guaranteed by the principle of non-contradiction.

Buridan opts for the second strategy. First he notes that a dog naturally attributes representations of its master under different sensory modalities to the same subject, so that even dogs seem able to apprehend substance per accidens.[44] He mentions several ways in which intellectual creatures seem to be indirectly acquainted with substance, whether consciously or not. First, he interprets Aristotle's remark that knowing the accidents of a thing contributes to knowing its essence much less literally than Thomas, suggesting that the intellect has the power to elicit a "concept [*intentio*]" of a substance—notice that he does not say 'essence of substance'—from "the concepts of accidents falling under the imagination," in the way that "a sheep sensibly elicits the intention of hostility from the color, figure, and motion of the wolf" (*QDA*₃ I.6: 128vb–129ra).[45] Second, he supposes that even if substance is at first apprehended confusedly, the intellect "naturally has the power to abstract from that confusion proper and distinct concepts"—notice that he does not say 'determinate and definitive concepts'—"of which it conceives substance without accidents in one way, and accidents without substance in another" (*QDA*₃ I.6: 129rb).[46] Third, he invokes the principle that effects seem to resemble their causes, arguing that since substance and accident are related to each other as cause and effect, it is possible to cognize a substance through its accidents. This leads him to assert further that, however else we might describe the psychological operation of cognition, we can be assured that "a thing is apprehended and cognized through its likeness [*res apprehenditur et cognoscitur per suam similitudinem*]."[47] Finally, he argues that although it is possible for the human intellect to have knowledge of substance, it cannot do so unless it has first been "predisposed by the knowledge of accidents."[48] Such knowledge is primary in the Aristotelian sense that the intellect cannot know anything without first being acquainted with particular images and sense perceptions.

On Buridan's view of the science of psychology, then, it is possible for us to acquire knowledge about the soul because the particular animate qualities with which we are more immediately acquainted happen naturally to resemble the subject(s) to which we attribute them. How do we know that these accidents of the soul resemble their subjects, given that the actual subject of the soul, its substance, cannot be sensed? Buridan says simply that "the agreement between accidents and substances is considerable, for heat is very agreeable, and natural, to fire. But when it is said that substance and accident differ from the first, this is conceded in relation to the modes of predicating according to which the categories are distinguished. And even if they are far apart in degree of being and perfection, different accidents properly generate likenesses and representations of different substances insofar as they are natural dispositions of them" (*QDA*₃ I.6: 129vb).[49] As we have already seen, Buridan's reply to skepticism about induction is to say that we have no reason to doubt the reliability of such reasoning. It is logically possible, of course, for

a given instance of heat to bear no real resemblance to the fire in which it inheres, but at least as far as our epistemic situation in this life is concerned,
there is simply no evidence to support such a belief.[50] As he remarks:

> it can be said that by means of a direct representation, a substance repre-
> sents itself to sense confusedly with accidents, and, by the assistance of
> sense, to the intellect, which can then abstract from it in the way stated, etc.
> I also say that we can know the one from the other discursively. And that
> argument [i.e., Autrecourt's] makes a false assumption, viz., that nothing is
> evident unless it is stated or proved by the first principle. On the contrary,
> there are as many indemonstrable principles as there are demonstrable
> conclusions, as must be seen in *Posterior Analytics* I [cf. I.32.88b4–10]. And
> what that argument says about the affirmative syllogism also makes a false
> assumption, viz., that one can proceed [in natural science] only by means
> of demonstrations from categorical premises. (*QDA*$_3$ I.6: 129va)[51]

Buridan's reply to Autrecourt's argument is in keeping with an anti-skeptical
strategy that ignores the skeptic on the grounds that no rational person
would accept logical certainty as a criterion for empirical knowledge. In psychology, as in other natural sciences, we are within our epistemic rights in
forming concepts about the nature of the soul by drawing inferences from
the accidents which represent it, that is, from the various qualities of the soul
with which we are empirically acquainted.

Oresme's position on whether the soul can be known via its sensory manifestations is similar to Buridan's, but with a slightly different focus. Like Buridan, Oresme develops his view in counterpoint to Autrecourt's argument,
which he sees as beginning from the assumption that "the concept or likeness
[*notitia vel similitudo*] of one thing is not the likeness or representative of another thing entirely different from it, it being immediately obvious that representation is based on likeness; but accident and substance are entirely different."[52] But Oresme sees more clearly than Buridan that there are really two
issues at stake here for the science of the psychology. For, in addition to the
skeptical worry about the lack of resemblance between the soul and its qualities, there is the more fundamental concern that our cognitive awareness of
accidents might not even entitle us to conclude that substances *exist*, for "from
the cognition or the proposition, 'A exists' [the cognition or proposition],
'therefore, B exists', never follows principally [*precipue*], or per se; hence, some
say that from one thing, no other follows—i.e., from the fact that one thing
exists, the existence of another does not follow."[53] Oresme directs his reply to
the more specific issue of whether we can conclude that substance in the form
of the soul, or animate body, exists as the subject of animate qualities.

Like Buridan, Oresme gives hardly a moment's thought to the possibility
that Autrecourt's criterion of certainty might be satisfied in psychology by

assuming that the soul's accidents are not distinct from its substance. The problem with those who subscribe to the principle of non-contradiction in this way, he says, is that "they state it too generally [*nimis generaliter enunciant*]," applying it to all modes of reasoning when it really only concerns consequences such as 'Something has been caused; therefore, a cause exists' or 'A father exists; therefore, a son exists'. The source of the misapplication Oresme finds in a misreading of Aristotle:

> [some] say that it is not absolutely evident that any substance exists, but only probable [*probabile*]. And they also manufacture difficulties which follow from this, such as that accident would then produce substance in its proper virtue, and others like this, which Aristotle never believed. And so their interpretation [*via*] is a long way from the opinion of Aristotle, which was that accident is inseparable from substance not only in existence, as they gloss him, but also in quiddity, because it does not have being strictly speaking. Thus, he supposed that just as it is impossible for there to be figure without something figured, so also as regards any other accident. And this is true, unless a miracle occurs [*Et hoc est verum nisi per miraculum*].[54]

It would be closer to Aristotle's intention, Oresme argues, to conclude that "the cognition of substance by necessity [*necessario*] accompanies the cognition of any kind of accident, since ... accident is not a being unless because of a being, i.e., unless because a substance exists." Experience shows that the cognition of accidents is always accompanied by the cognition of substance by means of "a confused and accidental concept"; therefore, "if someone is seen from far off, then it is conceived that this is white and that this is something, but not determinately that this is a man."[55]

But, in reply to Autrecourt, how does Oresme know that a soul-substance really underlies its animate attributes? It is important to see that the sort of necessity Oresme refers to in this passage is not logical but natural necessity. Claiming that there is a logically necessary connection between substance and accident would, of course, constitute a direct reply to Autrecourt by affirming that the science of psychology meets his criterion of certainty. But this is ruled out by the qualification Oresme adds here and in many other places: "unless a miracle occurs." Since miracles are conceived by Oresme—and by Buridan—in an Augustinian fashion as exceptional events that are contrary not to the rules of logic, but to the common or ordinary course of nature,[56] it must be due to a naturally necessary connection between the soul and its accidents that Oresme says we can, "from a cognition of those accidents, arrive a posteriori at a determinate and quidditative, i.e., definitive conception of its substance."[57] Of course, God could annihilate whatever substance underlies the accidents we perceive, but that is of no interest to the science of psychology, which concerns the construction of evident conclusions from premises whose truth is simply not a priori determinable.[58]

4. INTELLECTUAL MEMORY

The different conceptions of the science of the soul in Thomas, Buridan, and Oresme give rise to differing ways of explaining psychological phenomena. This emerges very quickly when we compare their accounts of the power of intellectual memory.

For Thomas, Buridan, and Oresme, the intellect evidently possesses the capacity to recall or reactivate its own prior cognitions. Furthermore, it must be some kind of internal difference that explains the relative ease with which the mathematician, as opposed to the student of mathematics, solves a complex deduction, since the perceptual data are the same for each. Aristotle acknowledges this when he remarks that the intellect of the knower is in potentiality to new knowledge, "although not in the same way as before it learned or discovered."[59] How are we to explain this difference between the intellects of learners and knowers, between the abilities of the calculus student and the mathematician? This is a question for the psychologist.

Thomas believes that the human intellect has the power to reactivate intelligible forms at will, once it possesses them "just as a knower [*sicut sciens*],"[60] but otherwise shows no interest at all in explaining the process by which this occurs, or in providing a model of the relation between the intellect and intelligible forms that will explain the differences between learners and knowers. Rather, his concern is to refute the competing theory of Avicenna, according to which intelligible species exist in the intellect only when it actually understands, so that the recollection of any form must be attributed to a transcendent, agent intellect. Thomas notes that contrary to Avicenna: "the Philosopher clearly says here that intellect brought to the actuality of species (in the way that knowledge is an actuality) is still intellect in potentiality. For when the intellect cognizes actually, the intelligible species are in it in respect of a completed act; but when it has the disposition of knowledge [*habitum scientiae*], there are species in intellect in a way that is between pure potentiality and pure actuality [*medio modo inter potentiam puram et actum purum*]."[61] But other than to suggest that once the intellect "in some way becomes actualized [*quodam modo in actu*]" with respect to an idea, it can entertain it at will, Thomas does not explore the question of how an intelligible species could exist in the intellect in either of the distinct modes he mentions— "pure" and "middle"—or how such modes are acquired and lost.[62]

Thomas's other writings offer little help here. His most comprehensive account of intellectual memory is in Book II, chapter 74 of the *Summa contra gentiles*, where he again wants to refute Avicenna. But besides reprising his argument that Avicenna's view runs against what Aristotle says in *De Anima* III.4, he offers only three a fortiori arguments in defense of his own view that such forms are preserved: (1) since the existence of the possible intellect is "more firm [*magis firmum*]" than that of corporeal matter, and since forms flowing into corporeal matter are conserved in it, this should be all the more true of the possible intellect; (2) since intellective cognition is more perfect than sensory cognition, and sensory cognition has the ability to conserve what it apprehends, the intellect should all the more have this power; and (3) since distinct things which belong to distinct powers in an inferior order belong in a higher order to one, the distinct powers of apprehension and preservation in the sensory part of the soul "must be united in the highest power, viz., in the intellect."[63] On this basis, he assigns a distinct operation to the intellect parallel to that of sensory memory, but concerned with different objects: "memory is certainly located in the sensory part of the soul because it concerns things subject to determinate times, for there is memory only of what is past. Therefore, since it does not abstract from singular conditions, it does not pertain to the intellective part of the soul, which is concerned with universals. But this fact does not prevent the possible intellect from preserving intelligibles, which abstract from all particular conditions."[64] But again, other than to remove conceptual obstacles to its existence, Thomas seems genuinely uninterested in telling us how intellectual memory actually works, or in trying to integrate the mechanism of species retention with the intellect's other activities.

Commenting on the same passage as Thomas, Buridan sees three possible ways of understanding Aristotle's remark. The difference could be explained (1) solely in terms of the nature of the intellect itself, without positing any distinct quality that the knower's intellect has but not the learner's; (2) by supposing that distinct thoughts are somehow retained in the knower's intellect, albeit in a diminished way; or (3) by positing an intellectual disposition, distinct from both the intellect and from actual thoughts, to serve as the medium by which cognitions are retained in the intellect. Despite his oft-stated desire to avoid multiplying entities, Buridan adopts the third proposal. As we shall see, this has everything to do with the inadequacy of the first two proposals, making it necessary for this nominalist to posit some entities.

Buridan's critique of the first proposal[65] is historically interesting because, as Anneliese Maier has shown, it represents a direct attack on a position associated with John of Mirecourt and eventually condemned at Paris.[66] A radical advocate of the principle of parsimony, Mirecourt had apparently argued that just as there is no reason to suppose that accidents are distinct from each other, so there is no reason even to distinguish accidents from substances. Buridan is sympathetic to at least part of this reductionist program, as he himself wants to argue that figure is not distinct from magnitude (*QP* II.3: 42vb–44va). But the difference between him and Mirecourt consists in the fact that he is unwilling to take the further step of reducing the accident of motion to a mere "mode [*modus*]" of moving substances.[67] What does the analysis of motion have to do with the relation between the intellect and its actual or dispositional qualities? The answer is that Buridan sees Mirecourt as having the same position on both:

> Now then, some have revived an opinion held by certain of those ancients [i.e., the atomists], which I believe has been sufficiently disproved in this day and age, so that no one would care to dispute about it any longer, viz., that in our understanding and knowing, intellect and intellection are the same and do not differ, and your knowledge and every one of your intellections are the same, and all of the intellectual dispositions by which you understand or think or are able to think are the same as your intellect. And the more formal arguments they adduce in support of this are those we have laid down at the beginning of the question. They base their position especially on the fact that we can explain everything by means of the same thing's being differently disposed, as was said about motion and figure. . . . And so for similar reasons, some of the most ancient authorities assumed that accidents are not beings distinct from their substances, but must be called 'modes of substances'. . . . And those who have held and now hold this opinion do so, I think, not because they believe it to be true, but because it is difficult to refute them demonstratively. (QDA₃ III.11: 118–19)[68]

Against Mirecourt's proposal that the intellect and its various "modes" suffice to explain all of its operations, Buridan offers four arguments, the first two of which actually mention two articles from the 1347 condemnation of Mirecourt's views.[69] But only the fourth argument is relevant to the question of intellectual memory,[70] and this is that modes of substances simply do not differ enough from substances themselves to explain how belief-changes can be attributed to the same intellect:

> 'being differently disposed' signifies the same as 'being disposed in different modes'. If, therefore, our intellect, being disposed in different modes, is now of one opinion, and tomorrow will be of the contrary opinion, this mode will not be that mode, because the modes are supposed to be different. So if there are several modes, and they differ from each other, and the intellect is not now and will not be something else, but is always the same, it is necessary that the intellect differ from those modes [taken together] and from each one of them—and then all of the difficulties that arose in connection with the difference or identity of those opinions return even more in connection with those modes. And so it is better to take a stand at once on the side of the difference of those opinions. It is true that, when it comes to have contrary opinions, the intellect is

disposed in different modes. But those modes are not those opinions. . . .
In general, being differently disposed requires some difference, and it
must be that it is given in the case we are considering, and that it can be
correctly given only of those dispositions in relation to each other or to
the intellect. (QDA_3 III.11: 122–23)[71]

What Buridan is saying is that in psychology, as in other natural sciences,
there is absolutely no explanatory advantage to be gained from positing substances and their modes, instead of plain old substances and accidents. The
problem with Mirecourt's view is that if these modes are identical to the intellect, they would, by transitivity of identity, also be identical to each other,
leaving it an open question what the difference is between an intellect first *sitting*
believing that Socrates is sitting, and later that he is standing up. How can the
evident difference between the content of such beliefs be spelled out in terms
of the internal structure of the soul?

Buridan's solution to this problem is to argue that dispositions inhere in
the intellect as qualities distinct from it. But this is no mere default position.
He sees the inherence of dispositions in the intellect as a special case of another inherence relation, proper to the more inclusive natural science of mobile being—of which he takes psychology to be a part. This becomes clear in
his reply to an objector who points out that one could "argue in the same way
about figure, that is distinct from magnitude," which is in fact the opposite of
what Buridan holds about those qualities (QDA_3 III.11: 123). Buridan replies *fn 72*
by appealing to a distinction in his *Questions on Aristotle's Physics*,[72] which is
then applied to explain the relation between the intellect and its dispositions
as follows:

if a thing is said to be differently disposed earlier and then later . . . then
the difference designated by 'being differently disposed' can only be explained by the generation or corruption of some disposition inhering in
it and distinct from it. For it is like this with water, if it is first hot and
later cold; with matter, if it is first in the form of water and then later in
the form of fire; and with the intellect, if it was first believing one thing
and then the contrary. For, when a man is asleep and without access to
any of his sensible representations, he would still be disposed differently
later than he was earlier—which can only be explained by the difference
of those beliefs from each other and from the intellect. Otherwise, it
could not be shown that not all things are one in the way Parmenides
and Melissus believed, as I said before. (QDA_3 III.11: 124)[73]

As Maier and others have shown, Buridan uses this same analysis in his explanation of projectile motion to underwrite the existence of *impetus,* or
impressed force, as a distinct quality of moving bodies.[74] It is almost as if

Buridan wants us to think of intellectual dispositions as *impetus* of the soul, i.e., as various inherent tendencies for the intellect to cognize in certain ways, provided no obstacles intervene.[75] Again, since physics and psychology are both natural sciences for Buridan, it should hardly be surprising to find him borrowing analytical principles from the one to apply to the other.

But what of the second possibility, according to which the intellect has the power to retain whatever it thinks, albeit in a certain diminished way? Buridan spells this out as follows:

> The second conclusion is that this [intellectual] disposition is not of the nature or species of the intellection, but differs from it only in intensification or diminution, as some say, so that when it has been intensified it is a thought, and when it has been diminished it is no longer called a thought but a disposition. This conclusion is proved because when an act of understanding no longer exists, there is a diminished disposition in someone who has studied too little, and so it is quickly annihilated unless he perseveres in study. In someone who has studied for a long time however, there is now an intense disposition, movable or annihilable with difficulty, although it is not an actual thought. (*QDA₃* III.15: 163)[76]

The "some" who have held this view are not identified.[77] But Buridan's criticism indicates that he thinks it suffers from the same defect as Mirecourt's view, viz., that the distinction in question cannot explain the evident difference between the master's and the student's knowledge:

> let us suppose, following an opponent, that a thought is a form intensified by ten degrees on the same scale [as the disposition], and the disposition left behind is a form diminished by five degrees, always on the same scale as those degrees which belonged to the intensified form. Thus, when the actual thought ceases, the five degrees belonging to that intensified form are corrupted. And it is agreed that a thought of this sort ceases quickly, easily, and almost instantaneously. Therefore, the [first] five degrees are corrupted quickly and easily. And yet the five remaining, which belong to the disposition, are not quickly corrupted but persist for a long time and are movable only with difficulty. But no one could give a reason relating to the difference between the five remaining and the five corrupted, why they are placed opposite each other on the same scale—something no intellect determines for itself. Therefore, the position of the opponent was fictitious and false. (*QDA₃* III.15: 163–64)[78]

Buridan is quick to point out that the strategy of treating thoughts and dispositions as intensive magnitudes does nothing to explain the easy fluidity of thoughts on the one hand, and the stubborn persistence of dispositions on the other. Saying that the mathematician is able to move so quickly from proof to proof because her actual thoughts diminish quickly whereas their corresponding dispositions do not, does not tell us what it is about her intellectual qualities themselves which causes this to happen. Again, some internal difference is needed.[79]

Buridan's answer is to argue that thoughts and dispositions must be different kinds of qualities. Only this assumption, he says, can explain how the intellect, "once actualized by first thoughts, is potentially actually thinking everything deducible from those first thoughts, or from others similar to them, whose dispositions have remained in it" (QDA_3 III.15: 165).[80] Furthermore, he argues that his opponent's view deprives thoughts of their usual causal powers with the arbitrary assumption that if these thoughts happen to exist in a diminished state, they could fail to make the intellect into an actually thinking substance. Positing distinct intellectual dispositions allows us to explain how thoughts can be recollected without compromising the very process by which thinking is understood.[81]

Oresme sides with Buridan on the first question of whether we need to posit accidents distinct from the substance of the soul, claiming the intellect's capacity to recall or reactivate its own prior cognitions cannot be explained simply by assuming that there is one thing, viz., the intellectual soul, which exists in different modes. First, he says, if "we could not say of any accident that it is distinct from its subject," then "there does not seem to be any reason or difference to distinguish these accidents [any more] than others." Second, we know by experience that the intellect is differently disposed "by an internal change [per sui mutationem]" when it understands and then does not understand one thing; but this always involves the acquisition or loss of some quality, since alteration "is motion towards a quality [est motus ad qualitatem]." Third, if the intellect is to be "naturally changed by an intelligible [naturaliter transmutatur ab intelligibili]," it must somehow acquire a new accident. Fourth, the will [voluntas] sometimes plays a role in the fact that we begin to understand something, but since the will is part of the intellect, volitions are really changes internal to the intellect. Finally, Oresme points out that the opposite view, i.e., that substance and accident are not distinct in the soul, "has been condemned by a certain Parisian article," which looks to be a reference to article 28 of the condemnation of John of Mirecourt.[82]

Unlike Buridan, however, Oresme devotes hardly any space to Mirecourt's views or to their proper refutation, almost as if he sees that task as having been accomplished by his senior colleague. The argument that "local motion is not a thing distinct from what is mobile; therefore, neither is the movement of the soul distinct from the soul" is mentioned briefly, but rejected even more briefly with the remark, "I say that local motion is an accident just like other accidents because it happens [accidit] to a man that he is moved."[83] Again, Oresme seems to take it for granted that intellectual accidents are natural qualities of the soul, just as motion is a natural quality of a moving thing. The interesting question for the psychologist concerns how the various internal states of the soul should be distinguished from one another.

Oresme differs from Buridan, however, on the need to posit dispositions qualitatively distinct from intellectual acts. Although he does not appeal to the doctrine of the intension and remission of forms as such, Oresme does seem to think that intensive magnitudes are the only way to go when trying to distinguish natural qualities of the soul. First, he reminds his audience that "an act of the soul ... is the same as the motion of the soul," and that "a disposition [*habitus*] is nothing but an inclination to an act, or that by which we are inclined to such an act, just as a stone is inclined to downwards motion by gravity."[84] Then, relating these dispositions to other intellectual qualities, he argues as follows:

> a disposition is that same likeness [*similitudo*] which is called a species, but connoting a greater firmness and also the fact that it inclines the intellect, because not any degree of intensity at all can incline the intellect. To sum up, then, it is obvious that it is the same as the quality which, while it is being acquired and while the intellect is cognizing it, is called an act; and when it is not being acquired or cognized, only then is it called a species. And when it is firm enough and inclining [the intellect], it is called a disposition. And since this is also an act, it can certainly be taken for the successive flow [*pro fluxu successivo*] [of the quality], as has been stated.[85]

Oresme does not seem to have been aware of Buridan's argument that such an analysis cannot explain how the same quality can be both fluid as a thought, and persistent as a disposition. Nevertheless, he concludes by pointing out that if psychology is to provide a rationally acceptable account of intellectual qualities, it must appeal to our understanding of the workings of other natural qualities with which we are better acquainted:

> It should also be known that if distinct qualities are assumed [to exist in the intellect] in some other way, this could not be demonstratively disproved. Still, it does not seem reasonable that such a multitude should be assumed without a corresponding reason, and, in a case where such a reason is lacking, this is not the more probable or truthful belief. And precedents [*exempla*] are found in other, better known, subjects: just as we see that it is the same gravity which, while it is being acquired, is called 'alteration' and 'movement'—when it is small, it cannot yet incline [something] perfectly to downwards motion; [but] when it is intense enough, then it can do so; and analogously in the subject at hand.[86]

Although Buridan and Oresme do not share Thomas's view that psychology is a strictly demonstrative science, its epistemic position is far from hopeless. For they see no reason to assume that qualities of the soul behave any differently than other, more familiar, natural qualities, viz., those we attribute to moving bodies. But since we already have a theory of moving bodies, why not use that as a model for understanding the thinking soul? That, I believe, is the guiding methodological assumption of both Buridan's and Oresme's theories of intellectual cognition.

5. Empiricism and Psychology

The changing conception of the natural philosophy of psychology in the *De Anima* commentaries of Thomas, Buridan, and Oresme suggests that Moody was at the very least on the right track when he described the fourteenth century as an age of rising empiricism.[87] Indeed, if the meaning of 'empiricism' can be separated from the eighteenth- and twentieth-century contexts in terms of which it is usually defined, and associated instead with the cluster of broadly epistemic doctrines described above, then Moody's thesis looks no longer (trivially) false, but both plausible and interesting.

Because he shares Aristotle's conceptual empiricism, Thomas acknowledges the role of sensory appearances and judgments in providing images that the soul needs in order to think. But he does not regard the epistemic import of appearances and judgments as exhausted by their evidentness. Rather, as we saw above, he sees the accidental differences we cognize as marks or indicators of their underlying substance. In the case of the human soul, the seeming independence of the act of understanding from corporeal organs entitles us to infer the per se existence of the intellect which is its subject. If we add to this the fact that Thomas does not see any problem with constructing inferences about the substance of the soul from its accidents, we can see why he does not bother defending the use of a posteriori modes of reasoning in psychology. The only difference between psychology and absolutely demonstrative disciplines such as geometry is, for Thomas, that psychological demonstrations must start from definitional premises based on "sensible effects better known [*magis noti*] [to us] than their causes." The result is a conception of psychology more akin to metaphysics—and indeed, differentiated from metaphysics only by its lesser degree of abstraction from matter—than to other disciplines concerned with natural phenomena, such as biology.[88]

Contrast this with the conception of psychology found in Buridan and Oresme. Though they differ in what they take to be its proper subject, Buridan and Oresme both see psychology as a natural science for which evident appearance is the only basis for explaining the relation between the soul and its activities. They agree with Thomas that the special difficulty of psychology stems from the fact that its subject is somehow hidden from view, but do not share his confidence that its real nature can be made intelligible by reasoning demonstratively from its operations, which are evident to us. Rather, faced with Autrecourt's skeptical argument that all psychological knowledge must be deductively demonstrable, Buridan and Oresme both reply that it is unreasonable to expect judgments in natural science to conform to the same epistemic standards we find in logic or geometry. Instead, they maintain that, in the absence of evidence to the contrary, our perceptual and judgmental capacities are reliable (though not infallible) detectors of what the world is really like—a dialectical move which shifts the burden of proof back onto the skeptic. Buridan and Oresme thus share the assumption that from an empirical and practical point of view, the science of psychology is a well-founded discipline.

The epistemic naturalism of Buridan and Oresme carries over into their treatments of psychological questions. In contrast to Thomas, they virtually assimilate psychology to physics, looking to their analyses of the motion of inanimate bodies for the right model to explain thinking. Indeed, if we were to formulate a slogan to capture their view of intellectual cognition, it would be 'thinking is like moving', though without the extended subject. If that sounds incoherent, we should remember that the primary analytical concept in their accounts of motion is *impetus*, which is an impressed incorporeal force. Since Buridan and Oresme both saw psychology as part of the science of mobile being, and since they already had a fairly sophisticated theory of motion at their disposal in physics, borrowing the concept of *impetus* to explain psychological phenomena would have seemed to them, well, only natural.

CHAPTER FOURTEEN

Virtue

·Buridan opens his extensive commentary on the *Nicomachean Ethics* with the observation that we must not take Aristotle literally when he says that ethics "is not for the sake of theoretical knowledge, for one does not inquire so that we might know what is [*quid est*] the excellence for which we are searching, but in order to become good, since otherwise our inquiry will have been of no use" (*QNE* Proemium: 2ra).[1] The reason we must not take Aristotle literally is that if true happiness is activity of the soul in accordance with excellence or virtue,[2] then speculation about the virtues—which, after all, belong to the soul—would be more noble and more likely to perfect the intellect than speculation about the objects of virtually any other science. Buridan includes here both physical sciences, whose objects are "minerals, plants, and animals," and even the more abstract objects of geometry and arithmetic. Therefore, he says, "in moral science it is necessary to treat thoroughly of the virtues of the soul, as well as of the habits, dispositions, and activities connected with their use, so that this science might be taught to others, and with the nobility of a speculative inquiry" (*QNE* Proemium: 2ra).[3] Unlike Aristotle, Buridan is determined to give the knowledge of virtue equal billing with its practice. Although he concedes that happiness is ultimately achieved through action—"For what can be better for a man than being brought to happiness through what he has chosen [*Quid enim homini melius esse potest quam quod ad felicitatem per optatam perducatur*]?" (*QNE* Proemium: 2ra)— both he and Aristotle define virtue as a habit of choice,[4] and that, in Buridan's mind, makes it more appropriate to study it first as a habit or principle of human action, rather than examining its effects in the form of temperate or courageous or just activities. The place of moral philosophy as a science is thus secured by pedagogical needs, so that students might grasp the order governing the affective side of our nature.

Buridan makes good on his commitment to examine virtue from a speculative or theoretical standpoint in a series of questions in the first two books of his commentary addressed to the nature of moral knowledge and the metaphysical status of virtue, understood in terms of its definition, cause, location, activity, and degree. What is most striking about Buridan's approach to the study of virtue is that it uses the same naturalistic methods we have seen exemplified in his writings on physics and psychology. In particular, moral *scientia* is conveyed to the students by assimilating the virtues to other natural tendencies and dispositions such as motion and magnetism, and using some of the same analytical procedures. The naturalistic approach is made possible from the outset when Buridan declares that "although human actions are contingent in relation to man taken absolutely, they are nevertheless determined in relation to their causes, for virtuous acts proceed from virtue and vicious acts from vice, always or for the most part [*semper vel in pluribus*]" (*QNE* I.1: 2vb).[5] But if virtue and vice proceed "always or for the most part," of course, then they can be proper objects of scientific knowledge. Buridan understands moral philosophy to be continuous with natural philosophy, so that his remarks not only about virtue but also about human freedom and the role of practical reason in moral judgment are always guided by the assumption that the internal order of the soul mirrors the external order of nature.[6]

1. Defining Virtue

Although Buridan follows Aristotle in defining virtue as a "habit of choice [*habitus electivus*]" (*QNE* I.1: 2va),[7] he is much more interested than Aristotle in clarifying the exact place of virtue in the taxonomy of human action. According to this definition, what is distinctive about virtue is the fact that its mode of generation as a habit must at some point involve choice. Thus, Buridan concedes, "virtue can exist without actual, present, choice, but not without any previous choice, since it is generated from chosen activities or from preceding choices" (*QNE* II.14: 33ra).[8] Now choice is that act of the will, or intellective appetite, by means of which "a voluntary agent can, with everything else disposed in the same way, freely determine himself to either of [two] opposites" (*QNE* III.1: 37va).[9] Virtue, then, is a kind of habit originating from choice.

Buridan also agrees with Aristotle that as a habit, virtue is neither a quantity nor a relation, but some quality of a thing (*QNE* II.8: 27vb).[10] But whereas Aristotle draws only a general distinction between habits and dispositions in the first species of quality—the former being "more lasting and more firmly established" than the latter[11]—Buridan wants something much more fine-grained where the virtues are concerned. He observes that since "every generable and corruptible form whose being does not consist in something divisible is capable of being increased and diminished," we need to consider whether or not virtue is such an indivisible quality (*QNE* II.8: 27vb).[12] Now the term 'virtue', he says, can be taken in one of two ways: first, for "the limit of excellence [*secundum excellentiae terminum*]" in a thing, in which case, it would be indivisible, and rarely or never found; or second, "for any praiseworthy moral disposition by which a person acts diligently, firmly, and agreeably [*pro omni habitu morali laudabili quo quis studiose, firmiter, et delectabiliter operatur*]," in which case "it would have a latitude [*habet latitudinem*]," and be commonly found (*QNE* II.8: 27vb–28ra). The analogy presented in the text at this point is Aristotelian in origin,[13] but, as we shall see below, Buridanian in its implementation: "For just as health is related to body, so moral virtue is related to soul. But a body is said to be healthy in relation to every disposition in which that body, both as a whole and in its parts, is naturally suited to exercise every activity ordained to it without difficulty and agreeably. However, the proportion of humors and qualities which makes this possible is not indivisible, but rather, differentiated by that very body every day, independently of the activities ordained to it. Therefore, moral virtue will be likewise" (*QNE* II.8: 28ra).[14] That moral virtue is a quality with a latitude Buridan takes to be evident from the fact that good people can be made better through the exercise of virtue. Conversely, the existence of people who are bad and worse suggests that evil can also be augmented. Buridan, then, wants us to think of moral virtue as a quality of the soul. But the way he wants us to think of it, at least as commonly found,[15] is as a divisible quality, i.e., as something which can be held "sometimes in a diminished way, and sometimes more perfectly [*aliquando diminutae et aliquando perfectius*]" (*QNE* II.8: 28rb), in the way that the health of a physical body is determined by the quantitative proportion of its qualities and humors. Not satisfied to differentiate such qualities by vaguely gesturing, as Aristotle does, at how long lasting or firmly established they are, Buridan seeks a greater degree of exactitude by assimilating moral virtue, a quality of the soul, to quantifiable physical qualities, such as health.

Turning to the classification of virtue as a psychological quality, Buridan acknowledges what everyone concedes, viz., "moral virtue is a certain principle of human actions pertaining to the appetitive part of the soul" (*QNE* II.14: 33va).[16] But what kind of principle is it: a passion, a power, or a habit? As we have seen, Buridan follows Aristotle in defining virtue as a habit of choice, but the way in which he differentiates it from the other two principles is instructive. First, he defines habits in relation to passions, viz., as "dispositions according to which we suffer passions well or badly [*habitus* esse secundum quos ad passiones habemus bene vel male]: e.g., in the case of anger, if we feel it strongly or weakly [vehementer vel remisse], then we suffer it badly; but if moderately [mediocriter], then we suffer it well" (QNE II.14: 33vb).[17] Second, he suggests that a similar relation obtains between virtuous habits and powers: "a power is strictly speaking the principle of an active or passive activity. Virtue, however, is not strictly speaking and in the primary sense a power, but a certain determination of an active or passive principle as regards acting or being acted upon in a certain way. For this reason, virtue is strictly speaking not the principle of an activity, but its quality" (QNE II.14: 33rb).[18] What this means is that in metaphysical terms, virtues are qualities of qualities in the sense that they help either to determine the strength of certain activities of the soul, or else to modify the effect of its passions. Buridan therefore conceives of the virtues not as 'whats' but 'hows', i.e., as qualities or modes of the soul that determine not what state the soul is in, but how it acts and is acted upon.[19] Thus, when a virtuous man acts for the sake of long-term happiness, he does so more forcefully and immediately; likewise, if he feels pangs of regret because he must forego sensual pleasures along the way, he feels them less acutely.

2. THE LOCATION OF VIRTUE

But if virtue is a quality or mode of the soul, in which part or parts of the soul should we expect to find it? Buridan answers this question in two ways, based on his earlier contention that "the use of virtue, i.e., the activity of virtue, must be distinguished from the virtues [themselves]" (QNE I.16: 14vb).[20] If we consider virtue to be a quality belonging to a subject, i.e., to a soul, then Buridan is quick to remind us that "doctors [of theology] have been radically opposed to one another on this question, for some try to prove that moral virtues are in the sensitive appetite, others that they are in the will" (QNE I.22: 20[xix]vb).[21] Ever the conciliator, Buridan argues that both sides prove "irrefutably [insolubiliter]" to him that there must be, on the one hand, "some habit generated in the sensitive appetite inclining it against the judgment of reason or against the will itself when it is supporting the judgment of reason, in connection with the fact that a man is made virtuous," and, on the other, "some habit generated in the will, inclining it against the judgment of reason itself, in connection with the fact that a man is made virtuous" (QNE I.22: 21ra–rb).[22] Moral virtue is then defined as the contrary habit that tilts the sensitive appetite and will, respectively, back in the other direction, i.e., "in keeping with the end which that power can achieve, that is to say, in keeping with the most perfect activity of which that power is capable" (QNE I.22: 21rb).[23] Buridan makes it especially clear that in the case of the will, "we need a certain habit inclining it to the judgment of reason to explain the fact that [virtuous persons] consent to the judgment of right reason promptly, agreeably, and without grumbling. And the faculty of reason would be influenced [by this habit] just as it was influenced by sensitive appetite. And this habit seems to be none other than moral virtue" (*QNE* I.22: 21ra).[24]

Conceived in relation to its subject, then, Buridan's first view is that moral virtue can be either (1) a quality in the will inclining it to follow the judgment of right reason; or (2) a quality in the sensitive appetite inclining it "to obey the will's completed act and the judgment of right reason." Nevertheless, he qualifies this by noting that it is "the virtue belonging to the will that is primarily and principally said to be the virtue of man *qua* man, and not the virtue of appetite, except insofar as the latter follows from and is ordered to the former" (*QNE* I.22: 21rb).[25] As we shall see below, Buridan takes this qualification even further in his remarks about the generation and activity of virtue, which are inconsistent with the idea that moral virtue could inhere in the sensitive appetite. So despite his initial conciliatory stance, Buridan's *de facto* position on the location of the moral virtues is at one with the broadly Franciscan view that all moral virtue is to be found in the will.

But because Buridan follows Aristotle in defining happiness as an activity in accordance with perfect virtue (*QNE* I.1: 1vb),[26] the question of where the use or activity of virtue is located is even more important for him. Primarily, virtue is found in the activity of choice consonant with right reason, exhibited by the rational appetite or will.[27] Buridan also believes, however, that any power of the soul contributing to human action can be affected by a virtuous quality.[28] This gives him occasion to invoke the traditional scholastic distinction between elicited and commanded acts of the will: "the activities of virtue must be distinguished. For some are from virtue itself, or are elicited from a power in which virtue exists and are immanent with respect to it: e.g., reasoning, judging, choosing, and, of course, willing or desiring. Other activities are commanded, and are transmitted to corporeal limbs and things outside the body: e.g., giving to the poor, waging war against enemies, giving to each his due; or further—and speaking privatively—abstaining from pleasures, giving injury to no one, etc." (*QNE* I.10: 10rb).[29] With respect to the moral virtues, this activity is transmitted and diversified in four distinct stages:

> Activities of the moral virtues can be ascribed in four ways: first, as immanent to the will itself; next, as immanent to sensitive appetite; third, as existing in our corporeal limbs, which we use physically to perform acts outside the soul; and fourth, as existing outside us, transmitted to the external world. For example, in the activity of liberality, once practical reason has

judged that such-and-such a gift should be given to so-and-so, the will first chooses to do this, and then commands the inferior powers to do it. Second, sensitive appetite, consenting to the will's command, desires to do the same thing, and so moves the corporeal limbs to do it. Then third, the corporeal limbs receive that motion from the appetite. And fourth, it is possible, in the performance of such an act, for motion to be received in external things from the movement of the limbs. (*QNE* II.4: 25rb)[30]

Now, since virtues are qualities of qualities, they are naturally related to the powers in which they inhere. The same is true of virtuous activities. When asked whether a moral virtue is actively or passively related to virtuous activities, Buridan replies that it is disposed "just like the power of which it is the virtue" (*QNE* II.3: 24vb),[31] so that the causal disposition of the virtue and power at any given moment matches that of the activity, whether one is giving to the poor or abstaining from sensual pleasure. Later, he adds that the virtues in themselves belong to "the same natural kind [*in genere naturae*]" and "moral kind [*in genere moralis*]" as the activities which give rise to them, and which they in turn modify (*QNE* II.5: 26ra).[32]

3. THE DISTINCTION OF VIRTUE

How, then, do we distinguish moral virtues from their interior and exterior activities? Here again we must look at the powers to which they belong. Because those powers are conceptually distinct,[33] Buridan remarks that "it should not be surprising what some find incredible, viz., that diverse moral virtues are posited in the will and sensitive appetite, i.e., from the acquired habit; indeed, it should be added that they must also be posited in the vegetative power, and in similar motive powers, or in any mode of operation possessed by all of the limbs" (*QNE* II.4: 25vb).[34] Thus, moral virtues in the will, sensitive appetite, and limbs, are as distinct as the natures [*rationes*] of those powers, which we see exhibited in their characteristic activities of choosing, desiring, and moving, respectively.[35] There is a causal connection between them in that virtuous activity in the will has a kind of 'trickle-down' effect on the activities of the other, lesser, powers. In order to distinguish between these levels of activity, Buridan insists that "virtue has a twofold activity: one interior, which is the true end of virtue (and that activity together with the virtue is what perfects a man and makes him truly good); but also another, external, activity, in connection with which it increases its goodness in other things" (*QNE* I.16: 16rb).[36] Buridan regards this distinction between the intrinsic and extrinsic activities of virtue as something we tacitly assume in the moral evaluation of others, for although the intrinsic activities of virtue are better than its extrinsic activities in that they "perfect the soul from within [*anima interius perficitur*]" rather than merely "adorning it from without [*exterius decoratur*]," only the extrinsic activities are evident to us (*QNE* I.10: 10va). He asks us to imagine "the king of the Franks and a lone pauper: let them both possess in themselves the virtue of bravery or liberality, in keeping with which they always have a good and perfect desire to act bravely and liberally, whenever the opportunity presents itself." Now, which man is better? Buridan favorably cites what he takes to be the opinion of Seneca, viz., that "those virtues and their activities do not make the king any better than the pauper *in himself*, but they do make him better as far as the entire country is concerned" (*QNE* I.16: 16rb).[37] This means that we must exercise restraint when passing moral judgment, for "although the external actions of a man are apparent to us, the interior activities of which we speak here, and which truly make a man good or bad, are hidden. For if someone is praying to God, I don't know whether he does so fraudulently or devotedly. Indeed, if we know that someone has often acted badly, even given that he has sometimes done the best thing and in the best way, we still think that he is a fraud and that he is not acting for the right reason" (*QNE* I.10: 10vb).[38] For this reason, Buridan says, "we do not judge a man to be good on the basis of a single and best action," but on his performance of many "good external actions which are evident to us," because the sum of these are for us, at least, "the sign of a good habit" (*QNE* I.10: 10vb).[39]

4. The Generation of Virtue

But asking about the causal relation between the virtues as qualities of powers of the soul naturally leads us to wonder about how they come to be there in the first place. Buridan seems to have something quite naturalistic in mind here, for, as we saw above, he suggests that the virtues might be assimilated to other "generable and corruptible forms" which are not indivisible, but "capable of being increased and diminished." What principles guide the process by which the virtues come into being?

In the first question of Book I of his commentary, Buridan remarks that virtue has three "determinate causes": viz., "reason, distinguishing between what is good and bad; will, choosing what is good and rejecting what is bad; and habituation to good actions, in keeping with the aforementioned choice of the will and judgment of reason" (*QNE* I.1: 2va).[40] He adds that these causes are connected to each other not per se, but accidentally, since it is possible for the will to reject what reason has determined to be good, and thus for the soul to fail to become habituated to it. A second, three-stage, description is offered of the process by which the virtues are generated. The virtues are produced in us, he says, "incipiently by nature [*per naturam inchoative*] . . . excitatively or provocatively by teaching [*per doctrinam excitative sive provocative*] . . . [and] perfectively by custom [*per consuetudinem perfective*]" (*QNE* II.1: 22ra).[41] Buridan's explanation of how the virtues are generated in us consists in his application of these latter three principles to the determinate causes of virtue: i.e., to reason, will, and habituation.

As we have seen, Buridan follows Aristotle in defining virtue as a species of habit concerned with choice. Now habit is the quality produced by habituation, which, in turn, "is produced by similar actions [*assuetudo fiat ex similis operibus*]" (*QNE* VI.1: 116va).[42] Where the virtues are concerned, the similarity in question is goodness or rightness. Buridan says that "virtue can only be generated from good and right acts [*virtus generari nisi ex bonis et rectis operibus*]" that are frequent and repeated, though, once established, it can also give rise to them on its own (*QNE* I.10: 10va).[43] Referring to the will, the primary faculty in which virtue is found, he remarks: "virtue is generated per se in the will from choices of the will itself that are consonant with right reason, and it is agreed that similar choices are elicited in keeping with the virtue generated. Therefore, since choices of the will are good or bad in the moral sphere because they are consonant or dissonant with right reason, it is apparent that choices of this sort, [i.e.,] those which precede virtue and from which virtue is generated per se, as well as choices which follow virtue, have the same nature in the moral sphere" (*QNE* II.5: 26ra).[44] Like other natural powers, the will tends to act in the direction to which it has been disposed, so that it will tend to make good choices in the future if it has done so in the past.

But why is 'commensurate with right reason' the *differentia* of virtuous habits of choice? The answer is that Buridan does not think it possible for the will to act, whether in pursuit of good or avoidance of evil, without the intellect first passing judgment on the goodness or badness of an object, thereby causing it to appear to the will as good (*sub ratione boni*), as bad (*sub ratione mali*), or under both aspects at the same time. This, in turn, causes the will's primary, receptive act, in which it feels a certain agreement (*complacentia*), or disagreement (*displicentia*), or both, depending upon which aspect(s) the willable object has. As we will see in chapter 15, since this primary act of agreement or disagreement is necessary, Buridan argues that freedom of the will must lie elsewhere, viz., in the will's second act of acceptance (*acceptatio*), rejection (*refutatio*), or deferment (*differre*), which is based on its first act, though not causally determined by it (*QNE* III.3: 42[lxii]va).[45] Moreover, Buridan thinks that the will cannot positively choose anything that the intellect has not judged to be good in some way or other (*QNE* III.5: 44vb; cf. *QNE* III.4: 44ra). In other words, virtuous habits cannot be formed unless the will is first primed by the judgment of practical reason about what is good and worthy of pursuit. However, since Buridan maintains that prudence, or the intellectual virtue of choosing rightly, admits of degrees depending upon how "articulately [*dearticulate*]" it is used to judge practical matters (*QNE* II.8: 29ra), the rightness of such judgments is always contingent, without any guarantee that the moral habits we acquire and cultivate will be virtuous ones.

5. VIRTUES AND POWERS

Still, Buridan does not believe that the will is meant to be utterly indifferent to the ends that motivate it. If virtue is produced when the will is habituated to choose in accordance with right reason, what does the will itself, as subject of this process, bring to it? There are two answers to this question, one given from the perspective of the relation between powers and their acts in general, and another addressed to the relation between the will and its choices in particular.

From the general perspective, Buridan places powers of the soul such as the intellect and will on a continuum with other natural powers and their dispositions to act. There are three ways, he says, in which a power can be related to its act: (1) as "determined in itself [*secundum se determinata*]"; (2) as indifferent but determinable by a single extrinsic action; and (3) as indifferent but determinable only by many extrinsic actions of the same kind. In the first case, a power is said to be "so determined to one act that it does not need to receive some impression from another in order to perform that act," in the way that an unsupported heavy body moves downwards (*QNE* II.2: 23ra).[46] Buridan denies that it is possible for such a power to be habituated to the opposite of its inclination because its operation is simply not vulnerable to that kind of external influence. As Aristotle points out, one cannot "train" a stone to move contrary to its natural motion, even if one throws it up ten thousand times.[47] Second, a power can be "indifferent to different acts, so that in order to pursue some action determinately, it needs to receive some prior impression determining it to that act, like a piece of iron that has the power to move towards a magnet" (*QNE* II.2: 23ra).[48] Buridan denies that such a power can be habituated to the opposite of its natural inclination, however, because it is "sufficiently determined to act by a single motion or action alone," whereas "habituation is, strictly speaking, produced by many similar acts" (*QNE* II.2: 23ra–rb).[49] Finally, a power can be indifferent to different acts in the sense that before it can be determined to one of them, "it needs many persistent acts of the same nature [*indiget multiplicatis perseveratis operationibus eiusdem rationis*]" (*QNE* II.2: 23rb). Now an indifferent power of this sort can be habituated contrary to its natural inclination, and Buridan remarks that this last power is found in many of the soul's powers, although not among corporeal powers such as taste and vision, which he regards as determinable by a single external action or motion. What this means is that only powers associated with the intellect and will are truly determinable by multiple actions, and hence, appropriate subjects for the process of habituation.

But even so, what is it that makes such incorporeal powers receptive to specific external actions? Why is it that the intellect and will can become differently inclined by virtuous actions, but not by the action of a magnet? Or why can a magnet incline a piece of iron contrary to its natural tendency to remain at rest, but not a rock (one that is relatively free of iron, let us suppose)? Buridan appeals to the metaphysical structure of natural subjects to explain why they are receptive to some external influences, but not to others. As we saw in chapter 11, his view is that a power or capacity inheres in a subject (1) as a proximate potentiality (*potentia propinqua*) just in case it can act or be acted upon immediately, without the assistance of a mediating quality or agent so disposing it; and (2) as a remote potentiality (*potentia remota*) just in case it can act or be acted upon only with the assistance of such a mediating quality or agent (*QNE* VI.3: 118vb; cf. *QDA₃* II.5: 66−67). The application of this distinction is clear in the case of powers or capacities belonging to inanimate subjects. A rock supported by a tabletop would possess only a remote potentiality to downwards motion, since it could not describe such a motion immediately; the table is in the way. But it would be proximately disposed to moving downwards if the table were removed, since unsupported heavy bodies are 'determined in themselves' to move in that way. Likewise, by virtue of its internal constitution, the piece of iron would have a proximate potentiality to move toward the magnet, meaning that it can do so immediately, without the assistance of some other agent. What is interesting about this distinction is that Buridan also uses it in his *Questions on Aristotle's De Anima* to explain how corporeal powers of the soul actually operate only in those parts of the body which are naturally suited to them. Thus, although the vegetative and sensitive powers of the soul are commensurately extended throughout the body as remote potentialities, their activities are manifested only locally, i.e., where mediating qualitative dispositions exist sufficient to make them proximate. Thus, the sensitive power of vision is found only in the eye, an arrangement of matter capable of registering changes in light. It is for this reason that we see with our eyes and not with our feet (*QDA₃* II.19: 326−27; *QNE* VI.3: 119ra).

But how does the distinction between proximate and remote potentialities apply to incorporeal powers of the soul, viz., to the intellect and will? Here, Buridan sees the same model as applying to both. In the case of the intellect and its proper act of understanding, Buridan argues that the intellect is naturally inclined to assent to truth, so that when presented with, e.g., the principle of non-contradiction, it cannot but assent: "the intellect has been so determined to assent to the truth of first principles, viz., to grasping the truth of those things that are absolutely first and known per se, that it cannot be habituated to deny them. But it can certainly be habituated to deny any principles that are not absolutely first and known per se, because it is not entirely determined in itself to their truths" (*QNE* II.2: 23rb).[50] In other words, the intellect is proximately disposed to assent to any truths it knows per se. Unfortunately, however, because we are empirical creatures, very few propositions appear to the intellect with their truths inscribed on their faces. Although the intellect will immediately assent to definitional truths as soon as it knows the meanings of their constituent terms, the vast majority of propositions are such that one first needs the judgment of sense, memory, and experience before one will feel confident in assenting to them without fear (*sine formidine*), i.e., without fear of being in error. This means that the intellect is only remotely disposed to assent to the truth of most empirical propositions, since this depends upon the mediating quality of evidentness (*evidentia*), which is provided by the testimony of sense, memory, and experience. Thus, I will not believe that there is a book on the table, or be disposed to assent to a proposition to that effect, unless it actually looks to me as if there is a book on the table.[51] Our intellect lacks the power to discern the truth of such propositions on its own.

Buridan clearly wants us to think of the relation between the will and moral virtue as analogous to that between the intellect and true belief, and indeed, between any natural power, corporeal or incorporeal, and its tendency to act:

> And so it seems that we should speak of the virtues in us just as we do of other natural forms perfecting their matter: from nature, they have in their matter only a kind of beginning, which is its proper receptivity and which is perfectible by them. Consequently, those things that have inclinations are naturally receptive towards them, just as matter is inclined to form. In addition, the perfectible pre-exists by nature in us in order to receive its perfection, for this receptivity is the appetitive or intellectual or sensory power of the soul. (*QNE* II.1: 22va)[52]

The intellect and will are both naturally receptive to the forms that perfect them: truth in the case of the intellect; rightness in the case of the will. Thus, although Buridan says that we are "naturally suited to be indifferent to virtues and vices," we do have, from birth, "a certain ability or inclination to receive such virtues [as temperance and fortitude] easily" (*QNE* II.1: 22va).[53] Now whether this ability becomes operational or not is a contingent matter, depending upon whether it is "firmed up [*firmatur*]" by teaching and practice. This means that as far as moral virtue is concerned, our will is only remotely disposed to choose rightly, meaning that it will act on that disposition only with the assistance of teaching and practice, external influences which habituate the will to choose in a certain way. What moral virtue does, in short, is turn the will's remote potentiality to choose in accordance with the dictates of right reason into a proximate potentiality, so that it can so choose whenever it wills.[54]

6. THE GRADATION OF VIRTUE

Buridan also thinks that virtue, like any other natural disposition, is a matter of degree. Just as the iron's proximity to the magnet determines the strength of its inclination to move toward it, and the evidentness of a proposition determines the degree to which the intellect assents to it without fear of being in error, so the effect of a virtue upon the will's choices varies proportionally with its strength. Virtuous habits are, like other natural dispositions, strengthened in the powers in which they inhere by their continual exercise. Buridan describes the effect of habit as "inclining and firming the will always to will in a certain way" (QNE II.6: 26vb).[55] Furthermore, the strength (firmitas) of a habit is what determines its permanence. In a helpful comparison, Buridan says that the virtues are more permanent than knowledge in subject and in act, but not in object, since the objects of the virtues, particular actions, are situation-relative (QNE I.19: 19ra). Although knowledge concerns universal truths, which are immutable, it is easily forgotten and difficult to apply. Virtues, on the other hand, are not so easily lost once acquired, and are easier to apply than knowledge, but the particular ends they aim to achieve in acting are determined by highly changeable external circumstances. As we saw above, one's success in acting depends upon how "articulately" the intellectual virtue of prudence is used to judge what ought to be done in a particular situation. For this reason, Buridan leaves the situational side of ethics open to debate, so that "it is possible that it would be good to give one denarius to this pauper, better still to give him two, and best for three to be given to him" (QNE II.8: 29ra).[56]

7. THE ACTIVITY OF VIRTUE

How do the virtues operate once they have been established? The answer to this question can be framed within this same general account of the relation between powers and their inclinations to act. The primary function of the virtues is to combat and counteract inclinations in the sensitive appetite contrary to what right reason dictates (QNE I.1: 2vb). Now what is interesting about sensitive appetite is that it is, like vision, a corporeal power of the soul, i.e., an animate power whose activity is located in corporeal organs. However, on Buridan's view, corporeal powers are not strictly speaking capable of being habituated because they can be inclined by a single action or motion. That sensitive appetite is a power of the latter sort is suggested by a passage in which, after discussing the magnet-and-iron example, he remarks, "we can also give an example of this distinction in moral philosophy, for the appetitive power is indifferent to virtue or vice, or even to acting diligently or perversely. Therefore, so that it is determined to virtue or vice with determining actions, it also needs a moral virtue impressed on it, determining it to act diligently, or a vice, determining it to act perversely" (*QNE* II.2: 23ra).[57] Sensitive appetite has whatever inclination it has on the basis of a single action, meaning that it cannot be affected any more profoundly by the repetition of single actions of the same kind.

With respect to the operation of the will, then, sensitive appetite can be either a helpful ally or a formidable opponent, simply because it is so easily 'tippable' for or against what the will has decided to do. Buridan tells us that sensitive appetite is naturally suited to pursue what is pleasurable and avoid what is painful (*QNE* II.9: 29va), and that although it is also naturally suited to obey reason, it is not compelled to do so, but rather, does so "freely [*libere*]" (*QNE* I.21: 19vb). What this metaphor suggests is that although we are naturally disposed to desire things that appear good to us (*sub ratione boni*), the volatile character of sensitive appetite simply does not allow it to stay fixed on such goods for very long. As a result, we often find it opposed to reason, obstructing both reason and will with sensory pleasures and other kinds of fleeting experiences contrary to what we have resolved to do (*QNE* I.21: 20[xix]ra). Buridan must have noticed, for example, that the mere sight of food is enough to make someone who has not eaten for a while desire it, regardless of his/her higher-order desires.

But how can sensitive appetite—which is, after all, merely a corporeal power—pose a threat to the autonomy of the will? Buridan says that sometimes the will can consent to the pleasure sought by sensitive appetite out of sympathy for it, even though reason has dictated the opposite (*QNE* I.21: 20[xix]rb; *QNE* I.22: 20[xix]vb–21ra). The metaphor he uses is that of the master who sympathizes with the plight of his servants by indulging their desires from time to time. One might wonder here why the will, a higher power, would deign to indulge a lower power, especially if doing so involves rejecting the counsel of reason. However, Buridan replies with an interesting hypothesis: perhaps this happens, he says, because before the use of reason, nature "made sensitive appetite tend in its object toward sensory apprehension without the rule of reason," because of the "necessities of life" (*QNE* I.21: 20[xix]va).[58] The picture we get here is of the will torn between two natural tendencies: reason and sensitive appetite. It will follow the dictates of right reason, but since those dictates are obscure to recognize and difficult to follow, it must be trained to do so—in contrast to sensitive appetite, which is inclined by single actions without any deliberation at all. The moral virtues are the result of that training.

Again, the danger sensitive appetite poses to someone who wants to act rightly rests in its volatility. Sensitive appetite might at any moment become "impassioned [*passionatus*]" against the will, even if the choice of the will is commensurate with right reason (*QNE* II.4: 25rb). Typically, the agent feels this either as regret in the amount of effort required to do what the will wants, or as sensual pleasure in some activity opposed to it. Thus, to borrow an example Buridan uses in another context, the sensitive appetite of a student might shrink from the effort required to listen to the precepts of his master, with the result that he chooses to play instead (*QNE* III.9: 47ra–rb). Indulging sensitive appetite in this way, however, can have a long-term effect on the will in the form of vice, i.e., a habit of choice in the will that conforms to sensitive appetite, not the judgment of right reason. The effect of vice is to obscure, pervert, and distort the judgment of reason to such an extent that it practically forces the will to conform its choices to the judgment of sense (*QNE* I.21: 20[xix]ra; cf. *QNE* II.7–10: 27vb–30rb). By over-indulging sensitive appetite, the will can freely acquire habits that will cripple its ability to act in a way commensurate with right reason. The effect of vice, once acquired, is rather simple. A vicious will is unable to control its sensitive appetites enough to permit its intellect to deliberate coolly and attentively about different possible courses of action. Instead, it leaps to the first goods presented to it as a kind of quick fix, without ordering them in any way with respect to some more ultimate good, since "sense cannot sufficiently compare the object presented to it with what accompanies or follows it, nor even the present with the future" (*QNE* II.9: 29rb).[59] Buridan thus arrives at the Socratic account of moral evil—viz., that the depraved person does not do evil knowingly—but he does so via the Augustinian idea that the ignorance in question is culpable because the vices that give rise to it were willingly acquired.

On the positive side, Buridan says that moral virtue is "for our ultimate benefit [*finaliter prodest nobis*]" because it harmonizes all of our actions with right reason (*QNE* I.10: 10vb). Its effect on sensitive appetite is threefold: moral virtue (1) "reins it in, so that it does not follow the judgment of sense too quickly, but waits for the judgment of reason;" (2) "determines it to obey the judgment of reason, even though the judgment of sense fights against it;" and (3) "tempers and orders sensory pleasures and pains so that their *impetus* can never draw the appetite away from, or contrary to, the judgment of reason" (*QNE* II.9: 29va).[60] Thus, even if the will can do nothing about the volatility of the inclinations of sensitive appetite—a volatility perfectly natural to it—it can still resist acting upon them by habituating itself in the other direction, e.g., by helping to "extinguish the regret [*tristitiam extinguit*]" that accompanies rejecting some short-term pleasure (*QNE* I.22: 21vb). For Buridan, the moral virtues act as an insurance policy against our own, undeniably natural, animal impulses.

8. Moral Psychology as Applied Physics

Walsh

James J. Walsh was the first to draw attention to Buridan's profession of "a full-fledged moral naturalism—naturalism in the sense that moral knowledge is held to stem from the nature of things."[61] This is a sound assessment. Buridan's working assumption is that the virtues can be assimilated to other psychological qualities, and indeed, to other natural forms both corporeal and incorporeal, so that if we are looking for the right model to explain the generation, location, and activities of virtue, we need look no further than his general analysis of physical change. The telling phrase here occurs in the first question of Book II of Buridan's commentary: "it seems that we should speak of the virtues in us just as we do of other natural forms perfecting their matter" (*QNE* II.1: 22va).[62] Buridan's explanation of moral virtue reflects the outlook of someone who sees moral psychology as applied physics. This emerges in his treatment of the virtues as "generable and corruptible forms" which are not indivisible, but "capable of being increased and diminished [*augmentabilis et diminutibilis*]" (*QNE* II.8: 27vb); his conception of inclinations in the will and sensitive appetite as being on a continuum with those of other natural powers, such as the tendency of heavy bodies to fall and magnets to attract (*QNE* II.2: 23ra); and his elaboration of these inclinations as involving not only the pursuit of good and avoidance of evil, but a "fixation on the good once it has been obtained, just as if we were to say that a heavy body not only has an inclination to move down when it is up, but also, when it is down, an inclination to be at rest there" (*QNE* II.14: 33va).[63]

More specifically, Buridan uses the propagation of light in the air as a model for understanding how the repetition of good acts both generates and intensifies virtue:

> Now as for the generation of virtue, let us say only that it can be understood by analogy to the generation of light in the air. For one candle produces something in the air and another [placed beside it] produces something, and the same light in the air is made greater, and likewise as regards a third candle, and a fourth. And so as well, one action produces something of virtue, and a second something further, and a third, and a fourth, and that form is produced which, when it has been perfected, is called 'virtue'. And just as one great luminous body produces a greater light in the air than ten smaller ones, so also one great and excellent act generates more virtue than ten acts which are remiss. (*QNE* II.7: 27va)[64]

Likewise, Buridan regularly describes moral virtue as an '*impetus*' (the Latin and English words are the same) to will in a way commensurate with right reason. The appeal to *impetus*, an intensional quality of a magnitude, is of course one of the things for which Buridan is famous, although his reputation has derived from his use of the concept in physics, to replace the flawed Aristotelian notion of antiperistasis in the account of projectile motion.[65] It might seem strange to suggest that a virtuous man is like a moving projectile, but the commonality, of course, is at the level of the explanatory principle. Buridan sees psychology, including moral psychology, as part of the more general science of mobile being, so that he would have found it perfectly natural to explain virtue in terms of impetus, the relatively sophisticated analysis of motion already at his disposal in physics. Indeed, if, as we saw in chapter 13, the right slogan to capture Buridan's account of intellectual cognition is 'thinking is like moving', then the virtues are like tendencies to move in a certain direction at a certain speed, like putting some weight or muscle behind our actions. The prescriptive idea is to habituate ourselves to virtue so that it becomes truly ponderous, determining our actions according to right reason without needing any special assistance from us.

CHAPTER FIFTEEN

Freedom

•Medieval discussions of free will are enormously complicated. Examined in terms of our modern conception of the problem, things get even worse, for the free will debate appears to break out on several fronts at once, in relatively straightforward questions about whether human volition is exempt from causal determination within the natural order, or the extent to which practical reasoning is moderated by virtue, as well as in other, more abstract questions about the redemptive effect of grace on wills marred by original sin and, of course, the compatibility of divine foreknowledge and human free will. There is no hope of trying to confine the inquiry to the natural order by reconstructing a particular author's interpretation of Aristotle since, almost without exception,[1] medieval accounts of the natural order are deeply informed by doctrinal and theological considerations rooted in the authority of scripture. In short, medieval discussions of free will potentially implicate the whole of creation, and God's relation to that whole.

Is it possible to fit all of these distinct concerns into a single, coherent picture? This may be the wrong question to ask, since no systematic account of the medieval conception of human freedom seems possible without flattening out, or unduly emphasizing, some elements at the expense of others. And it is not at all clear that medieval thinkers shared our taste for simplicity and explanatory power, although of course they may have believed that spiritual creatures above us are capable of synoptic cognition. Even Thomas Aquinas, who articulated an entire system of Christian wisdom, recognized that there are limits to human inquiry. Some of these limits are confronted when we seek the truth about the will. For example, Thomas says, "the Holy Spirit so inclines us to act that He *makes* us act voluntarily [*Spiritus autem Sanctus sic nos ad agendum inclinat ut nos voluntarie agere faciat*]."[2] But when speaking about the natural or created order earlier in the same text, he denies that another being can "directly insert a will-act into us or cause our act of choice to occur," because such an act is incompatible with what is voluntary. Accordingly, "it is impossible for the will to be moved by an extrinsic principle as by an agent; rather, every movement of the will must proceed from within [*oportet quod omnis motus voluntatis ab interiori procedat*]."[3] So why isn't the Holy Spirit's making us act voluntarily incompatible with what is voluntary? The paradox is resolved once it is realized that the gift of the Spirit, despite the fact that it actively transforms the will from without,[4] is not part of the natural order, and hence is neither involuntary nor violent in the medieval sense of being contrary to that order. Contrariety is a principle of difference that is proper to a given order; there is no contrariety between orders.

Now it might be argued, of course, that we should not be content with this *via negativa,* since the activity of the Holy Spirit and the freedom of the will must be, and are in fact, positively reconcilable in a higher order embracing both kinds of agency, natural and supernatural. But this is where we confront a limit, since our wayfarer intellects cannot discern providence except insofar as it is manifested in the natural order.[5] So, the pond remains murky at the bottom, even though we are able to see some distance below the surface.[6]

Buridan thought that important questions can be raised about the nature of human freedom, but the remarks he makes throughout his writings must be understood with a similar proviso. These are not expressions of a single, overarching theory, but responses to certain well-defined problems within the tradition, whose sources can be found in the mixture of authoritative teachings of Aristotle and the faith. These remarks fall into four general categories, which will be discussed in turn below: (i) the demonstrability of freedom; (ii) freedom of choice; (iii) freedom of final ordination; and (iv) intellectual freedom. It is not my intention to suggest that it is impossible to distill any unified account of human freedom from these discussions, but only to consider the matter in a way that reflects his context-dependent approach to the problem. And, in any case, there is another kind of unity discernible here: the reassuring sameness of method that runs throughout his speculative philosophy, a method characterized above as naturalistic and rooted in conventional discourse. His remarks on the metaphysics and psychology of human freedom are an extension of this approach.

1. How Do We Know That We Are Free?

By the time Buridan was writing, it was common for those who defended voluntarist positions on the will—i.e., those who viewed the will as an independent, self-determining power—to argue for the will's freedom as simply evident by experience. In discussions of this question by Duns Scotus and Ockham, for example, we find the concession that the will's freedom cannot be demonstrated from the nature of the will tempered by the argument that we can still know that the will is free simply because we have experienced it as such. Scotus writes, "Why postulate this indeterminacy in the will if it cannot be proved to follow from the nature of the will? . . . [Reply:] the proof is here *a posteriori*, for the person who wills experiences [*experitur*] that he could have nilled [*nolle*] or not willed [*non velle*], according to what has been explained more at length elsewhere about the will's liberty."[7] In a similar passage, Ockham comments:

> The first [difficulty] is whether it can be sufficiently proved that the will is free. . . . To the first difficulty I reply that the thesis in question cannot be proved by any argument, since every argument meant to prove it will assume something that is just as unknown as, or more unknown than, the conclusion. Nonetheless, this thesis can be evidently known through experience, since a human being experiences [*experitur*] that, no matter how much reason dictates a given thing, the will is still able to will that thing or not to will it or to will against it [*velle vel non velle vel nolle*].[8]

The assumption underlying both views is brought out by Duns Scotus, who argues that the causal action of the will is *sui generis*, meaning that it cannot be assimilated to any kind of natural agency:

> there is simply no appropriate [natural] example whatsoever that could be given, because the will is an active principle distinct from the whole class of active principles which are not will, by reason of the opposite way in which it acts. It seems stupid [*fatuum*], then, to apply general propositions about active principles to the will, since there are no instances of the way it behaves in anything other than the will. For the will alone is not this other sort of thing. Hence, one should not deny that it is the sort of thing it is, just because other things are not like it.[9]

Naturalistic proofs of the existence of free will miss the point because the will is not a kind of natural agency.

Scotus's and Ockham's arguments for the freedom of the will are reminiscent of Augustine's proof strategy in *On Free Choice of the Will*, where he gets Evodius to concede first, that the existence of the will follows simply from Evodius's desire to know whether it exists or not (for he cannot have this knowledge without first wanting to have it); and second, that this will can be either good or evil, depending upon the nature of its desires.[10] This leads Evodius to remark later: "There is nothing I feel so firmly and so intimately as that I have a will by which I am moved to enjoy something. If the will by which I choose or refuse things is not mine, then I don't know what I can call mine. So if I use my will to do something evil, whom can I hold responsible but myself?"[11] From the inside, then, the will's freedom is simply evident on the basis of our own experience as agents in the world. Augustine does not consider the matter further in this text.

The evidentness of the will's freedom re-emerges, however, in Book VII of the *Confessions*, where it is raised against the backdrop of Academic skepticism. Here Augustine struggles with the question of how he can know anything for certain, having recounted in the previous book his brief, post-Manichean, flirtation with the skeptical strategy of suspending judgment in the face of conflicting appearances.[12] That our will might not be free is not the issue here, although the moral significance of that freedom clearly is:

> I directed my mind to understand what I was being told, namely that the free choice of the will is the reason why we do wrong and suffer your just judgement; but I could not get a clear grasp of it. I made an effort to lift my mind's eye out of the abyss, but again plunged back. I tried several times, but again and again sank back. I was brought up into your light by the fact that I knew myself both to have a will and to be alive. Therefore, when I willed or did not will something, I was utterly certain that none other than myself was willing or not willing. That there lay the cause of my sin I was now coming to recognize.[13]

In an attempt to discern the nature of the second person of the Trinity later in the same book, Augustine suggests that the will's power to determine itself is not just internally, but also externally, evident: "To move the body's limbs at will at one moment, not another, to be affected by an emotion at one time, not another, to utter wise judgement by signs at one moment, at another to keep silence: these are characteristic marks of the soul and mind with their capacity to change."[14] Both passages are in keeping with Augustine's main anti-skeptical strategy, which is to reject the skeptical notion that nothing can be known for certain unless it is absolutely demonstrable.[15] What this means is that as far as the existence of free will is concerned, the awareness of our own freedom, even if it is only a posteriori evident, is sufficient to justify the belief that we are free. It does not constitute a demonstrative proof of free will, of course, but then Augustine surely knew that no proof meeting the skeptical criterion is possible.

Buridan likewise appeals to experience to establish the existence of human free will. But there is an important contextual difference between Buridan's experiential argument and those of Scotus and Ockham. Buridan's remarks have, like Augustine's, the implicit aim of rebutting skeptical objections against the possibility of knowledge, including the knowledge that we are free.[16] Unlike Augustine, however, Buridan's target is not Academic skepticism, but certain skeptical propositions associated with his Parisian contemporary, Nicholas of Autrecourt. As we saw in chapter 12, from his account of evidentness (*evidentia*), according to which the principle of non-contradiction is the sole criterion of certainty, Nicholas had argued that we can have no certainty about things known by experience, but only what he calls a "conjectural habit" to assent to them.[17] On the question of the will, Buridan is especially interested in replying to a skeptical objection from certain unnamed opponents who contend that the 'evidence' of the experiential argument equally supports the conclusion that our will is not free, but determined: "they say that experience seems to be such that the immutations of the will by its objects, by which [they say] it is necessitated to will or nill, are not manifest to us. But if they were manifest to us, we would experience that the will itself is determined by something else in every one of its acts" (*QNE* III.1: 37rb).[18] The upshot for the free will argument is that even if our impression of freedom is undeniable, it is not enough to make us free, because the experiences on which it is based do not entitle us to draw any such conclusion.[19]

Buridan's first reply to this objection is harsh, to say the least. "Without a doubt," he says, "this opinion is loaded, and exceedingly dangerous in both faith and morals [*procul dubio haec opinio est gravis et periculosa valde in fide et in moribus*]" (*QNE* III.1: 37rb). The resemblance between this and his thinly veiled attack on Autrecourt in his *Questions on the Metaphysics*—where, as we saw above, he speaks of "certain wicked men" who want "to destroy the natural and moral sciences" by insisting that the conclusions of natural philosophy can all "be falsified through supernaturally possible cases" (*QM* II.1: 9ra)—can hardly be accidental. Buridan does not stop there, however. He also offers a more considered reply, which must have struck his listeners and readers as echoing Augustine:

I want to believe absolutely and firmly with one faith, along with some experience and the sayings of the saints and the philosophers who agree with this belief and firmly adhere to it, that, with everything else disposed in the same way, the will can [choose between] opposites in acting, as was said before. And no one should shrink from common opinion because of arguments he finds irrefutable, especially in those matters that can touch upon faith or morals. For whoever believes that he knows everything and is deceived in none of his opinions is a fool. For regarding a piece of straw present to your senses, a hundred arguments or questions will be formed about which the most learned doctors [of theology] will form contrary opinions, because in each case one or both sides will be deceived. And so it does not surprise me if in this exalted matter [i.e., concerning the will's freedom], I cannot satisfy myself with [demonstrative] arguments and proofs. (*QNE* III.1: 37va)[20]

This is in keeping with Buridan's general reply to Nicholas's skeptical arguments, which is to reject his standard of certainty. Moreover, as we saw above, he offers in their place an account of knowledge based on the reliabilist assumption that belief-forming procedures such as induction are justified on the *a posteriori* grounds that they tend to produce beliefs that are free from doubt and error, even if the result is not infallible. Thus, Buridan's empirical defense of free will is even more Augustinian than either Duns Scotus's or Ockham's. First, his disinclination to prove the existence of free will does not stem from negative considerations, such as we see in Ockham's doubts about whether such a proof is possible, but, like Augustine, from his own positive rejection of the absurdly high criterion of certainty insisted upon by the skeptic. Both Buridan and Augustine have the same axe to grind in epistemology, and each has a definite target in mind: Autrecourt's skeptical arguments in the case of Buridan; Academic skepticism in the case of Augustine. Second, Buridan's and Augustine's arguments are similar in that both regard evident experience as sufficient to justify empirical beliefs. Their idea is that although our impression of freedom does not make us free, the very inescapability of that impression helps to justify the belief that we are free.[21] In the case of the will, that impression, together with the inconceivability of moral responsibility in the absence of free choice, is sufficient to make our belief in free will both rational and justified.

What sort of influence did Augustine exert on Buridan? On the question of the will, the texts show that he remained a gray eminence in Buridan's thought, hardly ever emerging in the course of argument as such, but always subtly shaping both the kinds of questions he asked and how he answered them. Thus, surface differences can be misleading. Buridan, for example, is more interested than Augustine in clarifying the exact place occupied by virtue in the taxonomy of human action—a tendency he inherits from Aristotle—whereas Augustine tends to see virtue almost transcendentally, in terms of its ultimate reference "to that end where our peace shall be so perfect and so great as to admit of neither improvement nor increase."[22] But Buridan still chooses to begin his *Questions on the Nicomachean Ethics* on an Augustinian note by distinguishing between speculative inquiry about ethics and everyday moral learning, referring to the importance of rhetoric, or what he sometimes calls 'moral logic', for teaching people how to act:

> we need a twofold logic or dialectic [in ethics]: one which teaches how to find doubt and truth *simpliciter* (and this we call logic or dialectic *simpliciter*), and another, abridged sort, which teaches how to find both doubt and truth at the same time, and how appetite is affected or disposed in such a way that it does not determine or impede the intellect in conceding what has been argued (and this is called moral dialectic, which is beneath dialectic *simpliciter* as something subalternate to it, for dialectic *simpliciter* concerns what is understood *simpliciter*). However,

rhetoric, or moral dialectic, concerns the intellect when reason has been restricted, viz., in connection with the fact that it can be carried away by appetite. Therefore, since it is only with respect to moral actions that appetite is naturally suited to alienate the judgment of reason, so it is that in morals, we need a special logic, whereas in other arts and sciences, logic *simpliciter* is sufficient for us. (*QNE* Proemium: 2rb)[23]

Buridan then divides moral logic into two parts: rhetoric, "which seeks a clear meaning and uses words retaining their proper signification"; and poetry, "which playfully seeks to obscure meaning through the metaphorical use of words or in other ways" (*QNE* Proemium: 2rb).[24] Evidently, he does not want philosophers to forget about the art of moral instruction, where teachers must take account of their audiences and be sensitive to the prejudices that cloud their judgment in real life. Augustine likewise sees rhetoric as motivated by paternalism towards one's students: "Yet, because in the pursuit of the things that are rightly commended as useful and upright, unwise men generally follow their own feelings and habits rather than the very marrow of truth—which indeed only a very exceptional mind beholds—it was necessary that they not only be taught to the extent of their ability, but also frequently and strongly aroused as to their emotions. To the portion of itself [i.e., the 'science of dialectic'] which would accomplish this . . . so that the crowd might deign to be influenced for its own good—to this portion, it gave the name of rhetoric."[25] Perhaps Buridan also acquired from Augustine a kind of pastoral concern with the practical side of ethics, i.e., with the dialectical efficacy of moral arguments, rather than with their straightforward rational acceptability. Confirmation of this hypothesis, however, must await a detailed study of Buridan's commentary on Aristotle's *Rhetoric*.

2. FREEDOM OF CHOICE

In his writings on human action, Buridan develops a complex account of choice that attempts to find a "middle ground [*media opinio*]" between a pair of more extreme views. The first of these maintains that the will can, with everything else remaining the same, choose the lesser of two incompossible goods presented to it by the intellect. The second counters that the will can never act directly against the intellect in choosing which goods it should pursue and/or evils it should avoid (*QNE* III.4: 43rb–44ra). The first view is a consequence of the 'voluntarist' position traditionally associated with Franciscans such as Duns Scotus and William of Ockham, for whom the will is an active power that is both superior to the intellect and free.[26] The second describes what is often referred to as the 'intellectualist' position of Thomas Aquinas and his followers.[27] According to this view, the intellect is the pre-eminent power in human beings, presenting the will with its ultimate object as well as the means for achieving it. Although the intellectualist will is said to exercise free choice in selecting the means, it can only choose less-than-optimally through ignorance or impediment, since it is not possible for it to contravene the dictates of reason.

The middle ground Buridan seeks to occupy contends that although the will can choose only what has been presented to it as good, it retains the ability to defer its choice whenever the goodness of its object is in some way doubtful or uncertain. And since the goodness of a thing is hardly ever judged with certainty, at least in this life, the Buridanian will seems to enjoy a considerable amount of freedom in practice.[28]

In addition to freedom of choice (*libertas oppositionis*), however, Buridan argues that human agents possess freedom of final ordination (*libertas finalis ordinationis*), which they exhibit whenever they act principally for their own sake, rather than for the sake of anything else.[29] This second kind of freedom is very much in the intellectualist tradition, for, like Thomas, Buridan maintains that (1) the ultimate end of a human being is not a matter of choice, but is naturally determined for him by God (*QNE* VI.5: 121va);[30] (2) freedom of choice is subordinate to freedom of final ordination in the sense that it has been ordained to assist the will in choosing the best means to its ultimate end (*QNE* X.2: 207[ccxv]vb);[31] and (3) the perfection of freedom of final ordination, or ultimate human happiness, consists in an intellectual act, viz., "in that perfect apprehension of God [*in illa perfecta dei apprehensione*]," rather than in an act of volition, viz., "that consequent act of willing and loving [*in actu volendi et amandi consequente*]" (*QNE* X.5: 213rb; 567).[32]

The primacy Buridan assigns to freedom of final ordination might suggest that his account of volition falls most easily and obviously into the intellectualist camp. However, things are not that easy or obvious. Because of his peculiar, hybrid account of free choice, the question of how his remarks ought to be understood in relation to other medieval writings on the question has proved to be a thorny one in Buridan scholarship. A whole spectrum of views has been defended in recent decades. It has been argued that, despite the presence of certain voluntarist influences in his account of free choice, Buridan remains essentially an intellectualist: "The necessity of the will to will the absolute good when presented with it as such, the will's inability to choose the lesser good as such, the will's final acceptance of the object in accordance with the judgment of the practical intellect, the subordination of the liberty of opposition to the liberty of final ordination, and the intellectual act in which beatitude consists: all these are clear marks of Buridan's intellectualism."[33]

Conversely, it has been argued that although Buridan has an intellectualist view of freedom of final ordination, his account of free choice clearly favors voluntarism, though in a more attenuated form than is defended by Scotus and Ockham: "in his commentary Buridan examines, in addition to the problem of the freedom of man, that of the freedom of choice. And if he takes the side of intellectualism in treating of the first of these problems, then conversely, he comes out in favor of a modified voluntarism when he speaks of the second. It seems . . . that Buridan, in searching for a dual formula to elucidate the problem of the freedom of man, and in speaking of *libertas oppositionis* and of *libertas finalis ordinationis,* was looking for a compromise between advocates of the two positions."[34]

Korola

Finally, Buridan's compromise between intellectualism and voluntarism has been located not in the abstract distinction between freedom of final ordination and freedom of choice, but in the latter doctrine itself: "for Buridan, uncertainty is the central concept which explains both free will and incontinence. If all judgments were firm, neither free will nor incontinence would exist. Buridan's psychology is thus based on the primacy of the intellect, but he sees human action as the result of an uncertain and ambiguous process in which the will is often free to choose its reason."[35] Buridan's account is thus said to differ from "Aristotelianism and Thomism as well as from Franciscan voluntarism."[36]

Saarinen

There is some truth in each of these views. In my view, however, Buridan is best understood as an intellectualist, though not merely on the relational grounds that he subordinates freedom of choice to freedom of final ordination. Rather he is an intellectualist in the much stronger sense that in the realm of free choice, the will is never free to act directly against the dictates of reason, not even when deferring its act of acceptance or rejection. Thus, contrary to what some commentators have supposed, Buridan's act of deferment does not represent a significant voluntarist departure from what would otherwise be a straightforwardly intellectualist account of volition. The reason is that, despite its novelty, the act of deferment does not make the will any more autonomous or free. This raises questions, of course, about the proper function of deferment in Buridan's moral psychology, to which we will turn next.

?? ?

I disagree

a. Willing, Nilling, and Deferring

Buridan begins by arguing that the will, like the intellect, is both an active and a passive power: "And so as far as the act of willing is concerned, I will say that when the soul has been informed by some prior act, e.g., either by a judgment about the goodness or badness of something willable, or by a certain agreement or disagreement, . . . it can move itself to an act of willing. So then, the same thing, viz., the soul, is called 'passive will' insofar as it can receive an act of willing, and 'active will' insofar as it can produce this act—but this is to the extent that it has been informed by the aforementioned prior act" (*QNE* III.2: 41rb).[37] He insists that the will, like the intellect, cannot act without being informed by some prior act because he believes that nothing is "sufficiently active and sufficiently passive in the substance of our soul [*in substantia animae nostrae non est sufficiens activum et sufficiens passivum]*" for volition, or intellection, to occur spontaneously. The soul must in both cases be primed by an object: something willable in the case of volition; something intelligible in the case of intellection (*QNE* III.2: 41va).[38]

The intellect supplies the will with something willable whenever it passes judgment on the goodness or badness of an object, thereby causing it to appear to the will as good (*sub ratione boni*), as bad (*sub ratione mali*), or under both aspects at the same time. This in turn causes the will's primary, receptive act, in which it feels a certain agreement (*complacentia*), or disagreement (*displicentia*), or both, depending upon which aspect(s) the willable object appears under:

> So judgment—or, ~~once~~ the soul ~~has been~~ informed by judgment about the goodness or badness of an object—first produces in the will a certain agreement or disagreement in relation to the object by the mediation of which the will can accept or reject the object. Indeed, the acceptance or rejection is now an actual inclination of the will upon which motion follows, if there has been no impediment. . . . Now ~~then~~, it ~~would~~ be said that if an object has been presented to the will as good, then immediately, the aforementioned act of agreement will be caused by necessity in the will. And if it has been presented to it as bad, an act of disagreement will be caused. And if it is presented as good and as bad simultaneously, both acts will be caused in it simultaneously, viz., an [act of] agreement and disagreement based on that object. (*QNE* III.3: 42[lxii]rb)[39]

Since the agreement or disagreement is produced by necessity, Buridan readily concedes that "the will is not free or master of its own first act," so that perhaps "one should say that the simple act of agreement or disagreement is not properly an act of willing or nilling" at all (*QNE* III.3: 43ra).[40] The proper activity of the will, and hence its freedom in choosing, must reside elsewhere.

Where freedom of choice properly resides is in the second act of the will, in which the will freely produces from its primary act a secondary act of acceptance (*acceptatio*), rejection (*refutatio*) or deferment (*differre*). Unlike its first act, the modes of the will's second act are incompossible: "But because acceptance and rejection are impulses towards an act of pursuit or avoidance, and those motions, viz., the pursuit or avoidance, are, due to [their] contrariety, incompossible in the same thing, so for the same reason, an acceptance and rejection of this sort cannot be produced in the will simultaneously. But the will can freely accept the act without rejection, or reject it without acceptation, or even neither reject nor accept it, but defer, as it seems to me any man can experience in himself" (*QNE* III.3: 42[lxii]va).[41] The relation between the will's first and second acts is that the primary act of agreement (or disagreement) is a causally necessary, but not sufficient, condition for its consequent

act of acceptance (or rejection). The will's first act cannot be causally sufficient for the second because then the will would not be free, but determined to
either accept or reject whatever seems agreeable or disagreeable to it.

For Buridan, freedom of choice stems from the epistemic consideration
that appearances often conflict.[42] Thus, the same object might seem both
agreeable and disagreeable to the will if the intellect presents it under both
aspects at once. Likewise, two or more distinct but incompossible objects
might produce two or more agreeable appearances in the will. Buridan contends that under such circumstances, the will is free to either (1) positively
will or accept one such object as good; or (2) positively nill or reject it as
bad;[43] or (3) defer its choice by not positively accepting or rejecting either
course of action. It is in this third and final mode of the will's second act that
Buridan appears to diverge from the intellectualist tradition. There is nothing like an act of deferment in Thomas Aquinas's account of volition.[44] Furthermore, it seems to indicate some structural similarity between Buridan's
remarks and the supposedly undiluted voluntarism of Ockham, who also ascribes to the will a threefold option when confronted with its final end, such
that "the will can absolutely either will it, or not will it, or nill it [potest absolute voluntas eum velle vel non velle vel nolle]."[45]

b. *Contra* Voluntarism

When considering limitations on willing and nilling, however, Buridan
comes down firmly on the side of intellectualism. Still, he says, it is not the
case that the will is determined to will what appears good, or nill what appears bad, "for otherwise, it would not be master of its own act" (*QNE* III.5:
44[lxiiii]vb).[46] One reason the will is not determined by such appearances is
that it has the power to defer willing/nilling an object that the intellect has
judged to be in some way good/bad: "the will can defer an act of willing to
make a preliminary inquiry if there was some bad consequence or condition
accompanying the apparent goodness. Moreover, it can not will it because of
the accompanying difficulty or effort. And in the same way, it must be said
that the will can not nill what the intellect judges to be bad" (*QNE* III.5:
44[lxiiii]vb).[47]

Buridan's second argument, however, leavens this with the standard intellectualist qualification that the will cannot will what the intellect has not
judged to be good in some way or other: "the will cannot will that with respect to which no aspect of goodness appears in the intellect because such a
thing would have in no way been presented to the intellect or will under a
willable aspect. And in the same way, it must be said that the will cannot nill,
although it could not will, that with respect to which no aspect of badness
appears in the intellect because such a thing has in no way been presented to
the intellect under an avoidable or rejectable aspect" (*QNE* III.5: 44[lxiiii]vb).[48]

Finally, Buridan's third argument explains how the first two fit together, i.e., how a will capable of willing only what appears good is not determined to will *whatever* appears good. The determinism fails here because the will can will against part, though not the whole, of an intellectual judgment: "the will can will that which has been judged to be bad in some way and nill that which has been judged to be good in some way: e.g., if an adultery has appeared [both] disrespectful and pleasurable, the will can, the disrespect notwithstanding, will the adultery by means of the pleasure, or it can not will it by means of the disrespect. It is likewise for the man who throws his goods into the sea during a storm [cf. Aristotle, *Nicomachean Ethics* III.1.1110a8–12]. . . . So then, it is obvious that the will can will against part of the judgment, but not against the whole, or in addition to the whole" (*QNE* III.5: 44[lxiiii]vb).[49]

on account of?

In these arguments and in the discussion which surrounds them, Buridan plainly subscribes to the intellectualist principles that (1) the will can never act against the counsel of reason as such, since it cannot will (or nill) what reason presents to it as bad (or good); and therefore that (2) if the will does choose a lesser good, it acts against reason only indirectly.[50]

true?

How is it possible for the will to act indirectly against the counsel of reason? Buridan mentions two ways. First, the will can act out of ignorance, which in turn can be either culpable or non-culpable. It is non-culpable "if the intellect's judgment was erroneous due to the invincible ignorance of some circumstance [*si iudicium intellectus fuerit erroneum propter circumstantiae alicuius invincibilem ignorantiam, non erit peccatum sequi iudicium rationis*]"(*QNE* III.3: 43ra). Ignorance is invincible "when someone, with every diligence of which he is capable or which is held to be appropriate, cannot know the thing" (*QNE* III.9: 47rb).[51] Thus, Buridan notes that it is possible for a judge to act well and meritoriously in hanging an innocent man, provided witnesses and other evidence make it sufficiently apparent to him that the man is a murderer (*QM* II.1: 9ra).[52] On the other hand, ignorance is said to be culpable if the will fails to keep its epistemic house in order, e.g., by deliberately blinding itself to some morally relevant aspect(s) of its object, or by engaging in activities that impede the use of reason. As an example of the former, Buridan mentions the ordinary phenomenon of asking someone not to tell you about something because you would rather not know (*QNE* III.9: 47ra).[53] The latter form of ignorance can arise in three ways:

> first, when an impediment to the use of reason follows upon some action we intend: e.g., from too much drinking, there follows a drunkenness which obliterates the use of reason. In a second way, when we intend to exercise some other operation, which, although it does not obliterate the use of reason, prevents it from taking into consideration what we ought to know: e.g., if someone wants to play when he ought to hear the master's precepts. In a third way, e.g., if it is our intention, while

in a state of inactivity, to be idle and to do no work, upon which there follows (due to negligence) a failure to take into consideration what we believe and can easily know. (*QNE* III.9: 47ra–rb)[54]

It is also possible for the will to act indirectly against reason through impediment, or operational deficiency. Like ignorance, impediment can be either culpable or non-culpable: non-culpable if naturally produced, in the way that defects in the material dispositions through which the soul operates might adversely affect its power to choose rightly (*QP* II.12: 38vb; cf. *QDA*₃ III.19: 212); culpable if the agent himself is responsible for skewing the operation of his will. Buridan concedes here that although the will has been "naturally suited to obey reason" and "to freely rule over sensitive appetite," it has also been "naturally suited to feel a certain agreement towards sensitive appetite, and to be sympathetic toward it," perhaps as the source of the objects required for its operation, viz., appearances with willable and nillable aspects (*QNE* I.21: 20[xix]rb; *QNE* I.22: 21ra).[55] But the overall effect of indiscriminately pursuing objects that look good to sensitive appetite is that "some habit must be generated in the will inclining it against the judgment of reason [*in voluntate oportet aliquem habitum generari inclinantem ipsam versus iudicium rationis*]" (*QNE* I.22: 21rb). If a sufficient number of such ill-considered choices are deliberately made, the will can become sinful, and "a sinful will is naturally suited to pervert the judgment of reason" (*QNE* VII.7: 144vb).[56] Buridan does allow that an incontinent man might know that he is choosing wrongly when pursuing pleasure, although not "with an actual, particular, and perfect knowledge [*scientia actuali particulari et perfecta*]," since that would mean that his will would be acting directly against reason—something it cannot do. Rather, when pursuing pleasure, the incontinent will either does not permit the intellect to judge that the pleasure should not be pursued, or else it somehow "obscures or suspends that decree [*obnubilet illud decretum vel suspendat*]" (*QNE* VII.7: 144rb–vb).

But even if the will's natural impulse in willing and nilling is to seek the good, and even if it cannot operate in either mode unless it receives objects under some willable or nillable aspect, there is still the act of deferment. Is the Buridanian will any more free because it has the power to defer its choice? The answer to this question is 'no', and for two reasons, the first of which appeals to the role played by deferment in the teleological structure of the will, and the second of which looks to the actual mechanism of deferment in acts of free choice.

According to Buridan, the end for which freedom of choice has been given to us is so that "in both intellect and will we may act freely with the freedom of final ordering, that is, laudably and well, to our salvation and perfection" (*QNE* X.2: 207[ccxv]vb; 531).[57] Deferment contributes to this end by better enabling rational yet fallible creatures to find the means to their ultimate good, the intellectual act of apprehending God perfectly (*QNE* X.5: 213rb).[58] What deferment does is to assist practical reason in making sound judgments about the normative status of what appears to it in the natural order of things:[59]

> As evidence of this, it should be known that the freedom according to which the will can not accept what has been presented to it as good or not reject what is presented to it as bad is of great benefit to us in the direction of our lives, so much so because in many things in which some *prima facie* aspects of goodness are apparent, thousands of evils often lie hidden, either as adjoined to them or as consequences of them. For this reason, accepting what appeared good would be inappropriate and detrimental to us. And so as well, what seems *prima facie* bad sometimes has hidden goodness, in relation to which it would be bad for us to have rejected it. (*QNE* III.3: 42[lxii]va)

As we have seen, the Buridanian will is constrained by appearances: it cannot act without being informed by some prior cognition of its object as good or bad. Buridan's idea is that if such a power is not to be driven, willy-nilly, by whatever our fallible intellect presents to it as good (or bad), it must be capable of suspending its act of acceptance or rejection in order to command the intellect to consider that *prima facie* good (or bad) object more fully.[60] The role of deferment within the natural order is to make morally responsible choice possible for rational creatures whose epistemic situation is poor, but improvable given enough time and effort.[61] Without it, the intellect would be unable to perfect the conclusions of its practical judgments beyond the level of *prima facie* appearances: "freedom was not given to us finally for evil but for direction. Let us ask, then, what if a judgment concerning the goodness of an object is not perfect? The freedom not to accept what has been judged, or to accept less, is beneficial to us, either immediately, for not accepting evil, or else as a precaution or safeguard against accepting what is perhaps evil" (*QNE* X.5: 212va–vb; 564).[62] In this way, deferment has been ordained not to oppose reason, but to help it make informed and reliable practical judgments:[63]

> the power of not accepting an apparent good, or of not rejecting an apparent evil, is for our ultimate benefit not so that we might stand firm in this mode of non-acceptance or non-rejection, but so that, before accepting or rejecting an object, we might inquire into every goodness or evil which follows upon that object, or is annexed to it, so that at last we would accept what is absolutely good and reject what is absolutely bad. Therefore, once a full inquiry has been made, so that the judgment is a judgment perfectly made with all fear [of error] removed, a power of not accepting would be of no further benefit, but would only be a hindrance,

since we could be frustrated by it in [attaining] our good, even when it is manifestly shown to us. (*QNE* VII.8: 145va)

The first point, then, is that the purpose of deferment is to permit the intellect to enhance its judgments in conditions of uncertainty. Buridan mentions no conative role for it to play beyond that.[64]

But although Buridan's concern with the purpose of deferment has all the marks of an intellectualist's interest in the teleological structure of volition, it does not follow from it that the power of deferment could not be exercised directly against an intellectual judgment. First, what is there to guarantee that a particular power will be used for the good purpose for which it was designed? If a genuinely free agent can, with everything else disposed in the same way, freely determine himself to either of two opposites,[65] then it should be possible for him to act non-optimally, e.g., by failing to defer even when that seems the best option. Second, global teleological considerations do not speak to the question of free choice, which is concerned with the range of the will's activity when confronted with particular conclusions of practical reason, not with the much broader question of what it was designed to do. And here, Buridan agrees with Aristotle that the will is not moved by speculative reason, nor even by practical reasoning about universals, but only by practical reason "descending to singulars [*descendens ad singularia*]" (*QDA₃* III.20: 220).[66]

Nevertheless (and this brings us to our second point), the teleological structure of deferment turns out to be local as well as global, since it is never possible for the Buridanian will to defer for no reason at all, i.e., without the judgment that to defer its choice with regard to a particular object would be a greater good than either willing it or nilling it.[67] In other words, deferment cannot occur unless the intellect has judged that the reason for the deferment is good, and has so presented it to the will. This is a conclusion, it should be pointed out, Buridan nowhere specifically endorses. Although he often asserts that we have the power of deferment, and that this power contributes to our freedom as rational agents, he is uncharacteristically vague about the actual mechanism of deferment in situations of free choice. But it clearly follows from what he says, for reasons to which we will now turn.

Like most scholastics, Buridan distinguishes in the will between elicited acts, which the will brings about in itself, and commanded acts, which follow upon the will's elicited acts and which it brings about externally. As we saw above, his account of free choice posits three elicited acts of the will—acceptance (or willing), rejection (or nilling), and deferment—each of which is said to be an impulse upon which certain motions, or commanded acts, follow, as long as there is no impediment. Corresponding to each elicited act, there are also three commanded acts of the will:[68] pursuit in the case of acceptance; avoidance in the case of rejection; and what is variously described as deliberation, consideration, and further inquiry in the case of deferment.[69]

We have already seen that Buridan does not think that the will can nill something good as such, "because such a thing has in no way been presented to the intellect under an avoidable or rejectable aspect"; likewise, he rejects the notion that it can will something bad as such, "because such a thing would have in no way been presented to the intellect or will under a willable aspect." For this reason, the will is said to be "able to pursue and avoid nothing unless it has been judged to be worthy of pursuing or avoiding" (*QNE* III.4: 43va).[70] But what about the elicited act of deferment and its commanded act of deliberation? Is that exempt from the general requirement in Buridan's model of volition that "we will nothing unless it has been judged to be good by the intellect," and that "if the will must choose, it chooses the greater good by necessity"?

It would appear not. Again, acts of deferment have a purpose, which is to make an inquiry in the intellect concerning the object of volition (*QNE* III.5: 44vb). Furthermore, provided the will does not "stand firm" in deferment, such inquiries always have the beneficial effect of informing subsequent choice by revealing good or bad aspects of a choice not initially evident to the will.[71] Thus, if the will is faced with conflicting appearances concerning its object (i.e., if it feels both agreement and disagreement in it), the act of deferring in order to consider the matter further will appear to it as good. This occurs, for example, when the will is confused about which means it should adopt in seeking some chosen end: "the will moves the intellect to consider in order to find an effective means of attaining the willed end. But this cannot be unless the fact that there is deliberation in order to find such a means has been presented to the will by the intellect under the aspect of goodness" (*QNE* III.5: 44[lxiiii]va).[72] So the prospect of deliberation, the commanded act of deferment, is no different from other volitional objects in being subject to evaluation in terms of its goodness or badness. And the judgment that it would be good (or bad) to deliberate is due to the intellect, not the will: "I say that the will never moves the intellect to deliberate unless the intellect has already made the judgment that to consider that object is good. Nor is it inconsistent that the act of the intellect should cognize some object under one aspect and have doubts about it under another, and that in that case, it would judge it to be good to consider the matter further" (*QNE* III.5: 44[lxiiii]vb).[73] Since there is no reason to believe that the good of further consideration is incommensurable with any other good motivating the will's act of acceptance or rejection, the activity of the will in deferring must conform to its activity in willing and nilling.[74] Typically, this will mean that if the will is to defer in a particular case, further consideration will appear to it as a greater good than either pursuit or avoidance, although the same considerations that govern the will's ability to choose the lesser good in acceptance or rejection apply as well to deferment. From this it follows that the deferment does not provide the will with some new kind of freedom, beyond what it already possesses as a result of exercising its more characteristic modes of choice.[75]

c. Buridan's "Middle Ground"

How 'Scotistic' is Buridan's account of free choice? Based on the above considerations, I believe that the answer to this question is 'not very'. Although voluntarist terminology regularly appears in his writings on human action, nothing in Buridan's remarks supports the idea that the will is free in the sense that its act is capable of transcending an agent's natural tendencies, including his/her intellectual tendencies. What we find instead is that when Buridan uses Scotistic vocabulary, he does so in a different sense—one that is in keeping with his own, more naturalistic, conception of the will as intellectual appetite.[76] His application of Scotus's celebrated distinction between the natural and the voluntary is a case in point.[77] Although he seems aware of how Scotus used the distinction,[78] Buridan understands free choice as an expression of our intellectual nature, not as something belonging to an order incommensurable with it. That is why his account places the will on a continuum with other appetitive powers, distinct from them not because it is free, but because it is cognitive:[79]

> the sensitive appetite and the intellective appetite (which is called 'will') are called cognitive appetites not because they cognize in keeping with the common nature of appetite, but because their acts follow upon prior cognition of their objects by necessity. For sensitive appetite and intellective appetite are distinct from natural appetite in this: natural appetite is brought to an object without prior cognition of that object. Therefore, those who suppose that sensitive appetite or will could be brought in uncognized are denying their proper nature, [viz.,] according to which they are distinct from natural appetite. (*QNE* III.5: 44[lxiiii]va)

Buridan sees the distinction between natural and non-natural appetite in terms of the distinction between animate and inanimate agency, so that the relevant difference between the tendency of an unsupported heavy body to fall and of a will (or even a sensitive appetite) to seek the good is that the latter, unlike the former, can operate only by means of a prior cognition of its object.[80] The fact that the will is free is not mentioned in this context.

Buridan's naturalistic approach to explaining human action is also evident in the way he characterizes the will's freedom. Even if a voluntary agent "can, with everything else disposed in the same way, freely determine itself to either of two opposites," Buridan insists that this "is the natural property of a voluntary agent, just as the ability to laugh belongs to man."[81] Likewise, he describes freedom as "a noble condition," which "has been naturally, indeed divinely, occasioned in the will [*libertas sit nobilis conditio et naturaliter, immo divinitus, indita voluntati*]" (*QNE* III.3: 42[lxii]va).[82] As for the alleged incompatibility of the natural and the voluntary, he distinguishes six different senses of the term 'natural', only the last of which is opposed to 'voluntary'.[83] Thus, it is possible for a property such as freedom of choice to be voluntary and yet natural in the fivefold sense that it does not owe its existence to (1) chance; (2) action(s) contrary to the common course of nature; (3) what is accidental or contingent; (4) supernatural influx; or (5) deficiency or superfluousness in the operations of nature (*QNE* II.2: 23ra).[84] Buridan concedes that there is in another sense (6), in which 'natural' is opposed to 'voluntary', but since voluntary action originates in the will, this opposition accords with his assumption that the will differs from other appetites and specifically from natural appetites in its inability to act without prior cognition of its object.[85] The Scotistic idea that the will must be capable of acting "nonmaximally upon natural inclinations, precisely in virtue of the possibility of transcending a purely natural appetite,"[86] plays no role in Buridan's account, and would probably have struck him as far-fetched.

All of which leaves us with a puzzle: why did Buridan feel it necessary to appropriate voluntarist terminology in his account of the will? One clue might be found in the moderation and restraint with which he expresses his own views—a reflection, perhaps, of his sense of propriety, knowing that similar ideas had been proscribed in the Condemnation of 1277. Another might be found in the respect he shows for the views of his predecessors in the intellectualist tradition, even when arguing that his own conclusions about the relation between the intellect and will do not have the same heterodox consequences. In discussing articles 166 and 169 of the Condemnation, for example, he says that "since many of the most devout doctors [of theology] held those conclusions, perhaps they should not be abandoned," especially when neither side has demonstrative, but only "readily believable" arguments in its favor (*QNE* VII.7: 144vb).[87] What this suggests is that Buridan's way of cleaving to the middle ground in this debate was to provide a doctrinally acceptable defense of intellectualist principles, rather than to invent some kind of compromise position between intellectualism and voluntarism.

3. FREEDOM OF FINAL ORDINATION

As we have seen, Buridan thinks freedom of choice has been given to us so that we can act freely with a freedom of final ordination, i.e., "laudably and well, to our salvation and perfection [*laudabiliter et bene ad nostram salutem et perfectionem*]" (*QNE* X.2: 207[ccxv]vb; 531). What is the final ordination to which freedom of choice is subordinated? Buridan's definition is expressed contextually, in terms of how an agent acts relative to other agents, rather than in terms of some absolute act: "an agent is said to act freely by freedom of final ordering if it acts by chief purpose for its own sake and is said to act like a slave [*serviliter*] if it acts for the sake of another" (*QNE* X.2: 205rb–va; 516). The need for a contextual definition becomes clear in what follows, in which Buridan maintains that it applies in different degrees to different agents:

> Hence God alone acts simply and entirely freely in this way, and in relation to God all other agents act like slaves, because all things that exist and act both exist and act for God's sake; and hence we too ought to be God's slaves—and every external thing God produces and conserves is produced and conserved in its primary and chief purpose for God's own sake, for all existing things are 'finally ordered' to God. Yet despite this, a particular agent is said to act freely if it acts for its own sake *more chiefly* than for the sake of any other particular end which does not 'finally contain' it according to the natural connection and order of ends. (*QNE* X.2: 205rb; 516)[88]

The examples Buridan gives suggest a hierarchical conception of agents and ends: just as God is said to contain us and all other things ultimately, so human beings contain all other things inferior to them, "for example, brute animals, plants, and inanimate things [*puta bruta, plantas et inanimata*]" (*QNE* X.2: 205rb–va; 517). Thus, we are capable of acting "more principally" on account of ourselves than on account of anything else except God. Glossing Aristotle's remark at the beginning of the *Metaphysics*,[89] Buridan also says that this kind of freedom comes only from the knowledge of metaphysics, for among all human sciences, "only metaphysics is the cause of itself." To this he adds: "by 'metaphysics', [Aristotle] means 'theology': from 'meta', which is 'beyond', and 'physis' which is 'nature', and 'icos', which is 'science', as if to say: 'the science of things that are beyond nature'" (*QNE* X.2: 205va; 517).[90] What is interesting about this remark is that where freedom of final ordination is concerned, Buridan glosses 'metaphysics' in the direction of theology rather than interpreting it as an autonomous subject, as he did in his *Questions on Aristotle's Metaphysics*. In the latter work, as we saw in chapter 10, he defines metaphysics as the science of being, the primary *ordinatrix* with respect to every other branch of learning in the faculty of arts. Unlike the account of freedom of choice, freedom of final ordination must have at least some of its starting-points in "articles of faith, which," as Buridan puts it, "are believed quite apart from their evidentness [*creditos absque evidentia*]" (*QM* I.2: 4rb). The account of freedom of final ordination begins with the belief that only God acts with a freedom that is absolute and complete, so that everything in the natural order is subservient to God. Because God's freedom transcends the natural order, it cannot be made evident to us as empirical creatures, and so must be accepted as an article of faith. The problem with empirical knowledge is that it is proper to our wayfarer state. It is also inherently imperfect, or at least always subject to further perfection. Buridan asserts, for example, that the concept of the Trinity we have in this life by faith is "much more perfect than the evident and demonstrative science that a triangle has three [angles]," but he also recognizes that this is an apples-and-oranges comparison, since the Trinity is not something "of which we can have evidence" (*QNE* X.5: 212vb; 565).[91] He flatly denies that human happiness consists in an act of faith based on evident judgment, whether in this life or in the next. The faith we have now in the Trinity carries over into the next life, but it is not thereby transformed into evident knowledge of the Trinity.

But given the distinction Buridan wants to draw between our natural and beatific conditions, could the introduction of freedom of final ordination signal a Scotistic trend in his thought? Duns Scotus, after all, distinguishes very clearly between the natural and voluntary orders, claiming that "the intellect falls under the heading of 'nature', for it is of itself determined to understanding and does not have it in its power to both understand and not understand."[92] Conversely, the Scotistic will has, in Allan Wolter's helpful terminology, a "superabundant sufficiency" or "positive indeterminacy" to actively determine itself in contrary ways, and thereby to exempt itself from the natural flow of cause and effect.[93] Can this be the inspiration for Buridan's remark that freedom of final ordination comes from knowledge that transcends the natural order?

Again, it would appear not. There is an important difference in scope between the views of Scotus and Buridan on the will's transcendence, which is in Buridan's case much more restricted. For although the 'natural' covers both sensual and intellectual goods, it is only the former which Buridan believes are transcended when we act freely according to final ordination: "It is therefore obvious that [vicious acts] are not finally ordered to the intellect and the will according to the natural ordering of ends. For it would be absurd to say that something unsuitable to me and wicked and harmful exists by the natural ordering of ends for my sake and is finally ordered to me. It is clear, then, that in such acts intellect and will do not act by chief purpose for their own sake but for the sake of sensual pleasures contrary to their natural perfections" (*QNE* X.2: 207[ccxv]rb–va; 529).[94] Transcendence is thus for Buridan a case of one natural appetite overcoming another natural appetite, so that moral virtue at least partly consists in our ability to subvert the senses' natural desire for pleasure and self-gratification in favor of the intellect's natural desire for wisdom and self-perfection. There is no suggestion here of the will participating in a different order than other animate powers, or of its operation being any less natural than that of the intellect or the senses.

Buridan's other remarks about freedom of final ordination confirm its distance from the Scotistic idea of transcendence. As we saw in section 2 above, he maintains that the perfection of freedom of final ordination consists in the intellectual act of perfectly apprehending God rather than in an act of volition. Indeed, the evidence suggests Buridan is deliberately opposing the Scotistic view, though he never mentions Scotus by name.

4. Intellectual Freedom

A further complication in medieval discussions of free will is the tendency Buridan shares with several other authors to extend the notion of freedom, ordinarily thought to be proper to acts of the will, to the operations of the intellect. But when Buridan speaks of 'intellectual freedom', of course, he does not mean the sort of freedom Bertrand Russell had in mind in "Why I Am Not a Christian," where we are told that "a good world . . . needs a fearless outlook and a free intelligence." No medieval author would have understood freedom in this way, to say nothing of the suspicions they would have had about freedom as a political concept. Rather, the idea seems to have been confined to psychology, where it was argued that just as the will is free in exercising its most characteristic act of choosing, so the intellect is free in exercising its own proper act of understanding.

Why would anyone want to characterize the operations of the intellect as 'free'? The motivation appears to have been twofold. First, virtually everyone subscribed to the Neoplatonic principle that the perfections of lower powers are in some way taken up by the higher power(s) to which they are subordinated. If we assume that we are essentially intellectual creatures possessed of wills rather than volitional creatures possessed of intellects, then the will must be a proper part or aspect of the intellect, dependent upon the intellect for its being. But then it would seem strange if such an obvious and unalloyed good as freedom were to be found in the will but not in the intellect. Therefore, there must be some way in which the intellect manifests the perfection of freedom in its own operations.

But to this it might be objected, 'Well, then why isn't the intellect also photosynthetic?' that is, 'Why doesn't the intellect subsume all of the perfections found in lower animate beings?' The reply is that perfections are providentially ordered to the natures of the beings that possess them. Not only is photosynthesis proper to material being, which the intellect is not, but it is also the perfection of a particular kind of body, i.e., a plant body, which, because it "forms a continuum with the earth," as Maimonides so vividly puts it,[95] is qualitatively inferior to animal bodies which are capable of being moved from place to place. So we have not been deprived of anything relevant to our proper perfection as creatures if we lack the ability to produce our own food, or see in the dark, or fly unaided. But the will is proper to our perfection as intellectual creatures, and so the principle does apply there.

Second, there is a special problem of authoritative texts. The source of the trouble appears to be Aristotle, who remarks in *De Anima* that "when thought has become each thing in the way in which a man who actually knows is said to do so (this happens when he is now able to exercise the power on his own initiative) . . . thought is then able to think of itself [*de auton*]."[96] In his gloss on this passage, Thomas Aquinas sees that Aristotle is attributing autonomous activity to the intellect: "For before [intellect] had the disposition of knowledge, which is its first actuality, it could not operate when it wanted to but had to be brought to actuality by something else. But when it already has the disposition of knowledge, which is its first actuality, it can go on, whenever it wants, to its second actuality, which is operating."[97] Thomas notices a similar passage in Aristotle's *Physics* which claims that in the case of a person who possesses the knowledge of a science without actually exercising it, "if something does not prevent him, he actively exercises his knowledge."[98] This last clause is understood as, "he is himself able to exercise his knowledge at will [*potest ipse exire in actum considerationis ut vult*],"[99] thereby describing the operation of the intellect using terminology appropriated from another faculty, viz., the will. But this presents us with a problem, and specifically an ordering problem concerned with the intersection of the two faculties most essential to us as agents. If the will as a faculty, or collection of powers, is ordered to the intellect, then intellectual freedom must be primary, ranked ahead of any freedom in the will, since the intellect is the faculty which commands the will. Yet our concept of freedom seems to have its source at some distance from the intellect, in experiences proper to the will. It is the control we seem to exert over such mundane activities as walking, talking, raising our arms, and so on that gives us the unavoidable impression that we are free. Our attribution of freedom to the intellect seems, at best, only a kind of metaphor. How could our intuitive notion of what it means to be free be so at odds with the metaphysical reality of freedom? Is our tendency to attribute freedom to the will rather than to the intellect a consequence of our inferior, empirical mode of understanding, attuned as it is to appearances rather than reality?

Buridan's solution to this ordering problem reveals him to be a sympathetic expositor of the intellectualism found in Thomas's moral psychology. But he also takes seriously the experiential side of human freedom, since any account that stays close to the facts must recognize the clarity and evidentness of the appearance that we are free. As an arts master, Buridan was in many ways uniquely situated to deal with the principles and authoritative texts surrounding the question of intellectual freedom. One point that is not often noticed is that some of the content of the medieval conception of freedom was supplied by the very etymology of the term 'liberal arts', which students would have encountered in their grammatical training. As we saw in chapter 1, Buridan glosses the term etymologically when he mentions it in his *Questions on Aristotle's Metaphysics:* the liberal arts "are called 'liberal [LIBERales]' because they 'liberate [LIBERant]' intellects that have been introduced to them from secular and worldly cares" (QM VI.2: 33vb; emphases added).[100] That is to say, by 'freeing' us from the plough, the liberal arts make possible the more self-sufficient, speculative activities associated with our natural desire to possess truth.

Buridan discusses the attribution of freedom to the intellect in a number of places, but his reasons for doing so are nowhere more clear than in the final version of his *Questions on Aristotle's De Anima*. Question 15 asks whether the intellect preserves intelligible species once actual thought has ceased. The issue here concerns the autonomous thinking we saw Aristotle alluding to in *De Anima* III.4 and Thomas in his commentary on this text. Buridan distinguishes between thoughts and dispositions, a kind of diminished species left behind by thinking, on the grounds that if thoughts were the only kind of currency in the intellect, the intellect would remain perpetually thinking whatever thoughts it happened to have. Some unnamed objectors reply that this distinction is superfluous, since the intellect is free, "and a free power need not produce its act, once it has everything needed to produce it ... but it can, with everything else in place, produce the opposite, or defer, and produce neither the act nor its opposite" (QDA_3 III.15: 167).[101] Buridan's reply is instructive: "on this point, I say that this freedom has a place only in voluntary acts and in other consequences of voluntary acts. . . . But no voluntary act can contribute to the formation of those first thoughts, since the will does not enter into intellectual cognition uncognized, and nothing was understood prior to the formation of the first thought. Therefore, the will has no place there, insofar as it is called 'will'" (QDA_3 III.15: 167–68).[102] What the objectors have unwittingly done is put the will in charge of the intellect. Buridan rejects this with the principle cited early and often in his psychological writings: 'the will never enters into the intellect uncognized'. In other words, every one of the will's movements is transparent to the intellect. There is no way for the will to climb over the fence and enter the intellect's compound without being immediately detected, a position entirely in keeping with the primacy of the intellect in Buridan's moral psychology. But notice that he also indicates that intellectual freedom is not like "this freedom," i.e., the freedom of the will, in that its operations do not consist in the acceptance, rejection, or deferral of its object.

One might wonder how the intellect manifests its freedom. Buridan fills out the picture in reply to what looks to be a student query:

And to clarify the matter, someone could then ask how the intellect is able to compound, divide, and reason discursively. I say that once it has been activated by several primary and simple apprehensions, the intellect can embrace other concepts either affirmatively or negatively as long as those phantasms remain. And once it has done this, it can again gather together several of those propositions, order them in a syllogism, and draw other conclusions following from them. And it can freely move itself from one consideration to another in matters to which it has been predisposed, dismissing this one and pursuing that, for the will freely exempts itself from such things. (QDA_3 III.15: 170–71)[103]

Intellectual freedom consists in the intellect's ability to range freely and without constraint among those objects which are proper to it, viz., the complex concepts or propositions which are the proximate objects of human knowledge. At one point, Buridan argues that the intellect must have the power to freely determine itself because without it, the will would have to initiate every act in the process of reasoning, something which would greatly hinder its operation (*QNE* X.2: 206rb). But there is more to it than that. Intellectual freedom can be likened to the play of ideas in the mind of an artisan creating a work of art. The difference is that, unlike the will, the intellect is not ordered to acts of acceptance or rejection or deferral, since all of these are defined in terms of the specific outcomes of practical reasoning.[104] The thought of the artisan trades in generalities, moving between concepts whose boundaries are more fluid than fixed. Ideas can be picked up, set aside, or combined with other ideas, without that process exhibiting any formal, syllogistic structure, and without any single idea encountered therein coalescing under the aspect of truth—an appearance which, if sufficiently strong, would command the intellect's assent just as surely as the will is reduced to act when presented with something unqualifiedly good. But the thought of the artisan is something we all experience, of course, whenever an apparently intractable problem compels us to change not what we think, but how we think. Buridan's concept of intellectual freedom embraces this fact of human experience, and would form at least part of his answer to what it means to be creative.

Creativity is very difficult to articulate within the Aristotelian worldview, however, because there is no obvious place for it. It connotes thinking outside the box, and Aristotelian psychology is full of boxes. Buridan's conception of intellectual freedom in terms of the intellect's autonomous activity within those boxes is probably the closest a medieval Aristotelian can come to the aforementioned Russellian notion of "free intelligence," as it represents a compromise between the formalized patterns of thinking held out in the *Posterior Analytics* as the model of truth-seeking discourse, and the fact that our intellects are not directed to the truth ineluctably, in the way that fire is ordained to burn. That is why Aristotle conceives of the man of science as possessing a kind of self-mastery through the pursuit of wisdom: "evidently then we do not seek [knowledge] for the sake of any other advantage; but as the man is free, we say, who exists for himself and not for another, so we pursue this as the only free science, for it alone exists for itself."[105]

The sense in which the intellect "exists for itself" is nicely characterized by the later fourteenth-century follower of Buridan, Nicholas of Vaudemont, first by means of a term appropriated from the will, and then using another term more in keeping with its proper activity: "With respect to many of its acts, the human intellect is free with qualified freedom of opposition [*libertate oppositionis secundum quid*] and with consecutive freedom [*libertate consecutiva*]. The conclusion is obvious, because with respect to mental propositions [*complexionum mentalium*], the human intellect freely forms different complex acts which are commanded and consequent upon first acts. And so it is obvious that the intellect is free" (Ps.-Buridan, *QPol* VII.5: 98va–vb). The "*secundum quid*" is attached to the first description because freedom of opposition, or freedom of choice, is proper to the will, not the intellect. As we saw above, the objects the intellect pursues and dismisses are more abstract than the clearly defined alternatives that activate the will. The second description, "consecutive freedom [*libertas consecutiva*]," suggests that the intellect is free to consider any of the possible consequences of a given concept. Presumably, it is impossible for it to consider concept B as a consequence of concept A if it knows that B is not a consequence of A, but beyond that, there is no restriction on the free range of the intellect.

On the ordering problem, Buridan is understandably circumspect. The problem with trying to determine which freedom is greater or more primary, intellectual or volitional, is that he regards the intellect and will as really identical, though they are differentiated in practice through their acts (*QNE* III.2: 41ra; cf. *QNE* X.1: 104va). That is, just as it is the same soul that nourishes, senses, and understands, so the same faculty of the soul houses (at least) two different operations, viz., understanding and willing. Therefore, we must say that the intellect and will are equally free (*QNE* X.1: 105ra). To hold otherwise would be to argue that the same thing is freer than itself, which is absurd. Nevertheless, when push comes to shove, Buridan is willing to take a position on which freedom is more primary, and when he does, it is the intellect which comes out on top, not the will. Freedom of opposition is proper to the will, he says, but it is ordered to freedom of final ordination, and, with respect to the latter, "the soul more principally, and consequently more freely, produces volition *qua* intellect than *qua* will" (*QNE* X.3: 209ra; 539).[106]

For Buridan, then, human freedom originates in the intellect. The fact that we ascribe freedom to the will is a consequence of our poor epistemic position in this life, where we are led to attribute primary perfections to whatever most evidently manifests them. But even if appearances are for the most part reliable, medieval thinkers knew that the way things appear is hardly an infallible guide to the way they are. If we remember the principle that the perfections of lower beings are subsumed by the higher, we can easily see that the will, which is completely dependent upon the intellect for its being, must owe the freedom that perfects its proper act to the intellect. So it should come as no surprise that the intellect is free, and that although they remain dialectically related, intellectual freedom is the source of freedom in the will.[107]

Thomas, on the other hand, is explicit about two things Buridan seems to take as given. First, he uses the metaphor of the intellect as artificer in order to characterize the intellect's autonomy in exercising its proper operation: "the form understood, through which the intellectual substance acts, proceeds from the intellect itself as a thing conceived, and in a way contrived by it; as we see in the case of the artistic form, which the artificer conceives and contrives, and through which he performs his works [*ut patet de forma artis, quam artifex concipit et excogitat et per eam operatur*]. Intellectual substances, then, move themselves to act, as having mastery of their own action."[108] The very next sentence reads, "it therefore follows that they [i.e., intellectual substances] are endowed with will." Incredibly, although Thomas argues for the existence of autonomy in the intellect, he concludes from this not that the intellect is free but that it must be possessed of another power, the will, which can serve as the agent or executor of its freedom. Now this might have struck Buridan as objectionable on grounds of parsimony. Why do we need to assign this freedom to some other power when it is the intellect's own ability to contrive and conceive of forms that is at issue?

But there is another problem here which might have given Buridan pause. According to Aristotle, the will is the rational appetite in the sense that it reduces the conclusions of practical reasoning to act: "that which is last in the process of thinking is the beginning of the action."[109] However, in order to move the will, the conclusions must be particular, not universal, as Buridan points out:[110]

> Then also, when a man is moved in accordance with reason and intellect, Aristotle shows which reason is the mover and which not when he says that speculative reason is not a mover, since it does not conclude that something should be done or not done, pursued or avoided [cf. Aristotle, *De Anima* III.10.433a13–25]. And so as well, universal practical reason is not a mover, e.g., if it is argued that one must always act well when an aptitude for acting well is present; but to act justly is to act well; therefore, one must act justly. I am not moved by this argument. But practical reason descending to singulars is a mover, e.g., if I argued that a feverish and thirsty person must drink herb tea; but I am feverish and thirsty, and this is herb tea: I will be moved to drink it at once, as long as there is no impediment [cf. Aristotle, *De Anima* III.11.434a16–21]. (QDA$_3$ III.20: 220)

Accordingly, the question for Thomas is: how does the existence of the will follow from the purely speculative and creative abilities of the intellect, given that the will is *ex hypothesi* concerned with particulars? If one wants to say that the intellect has mastery over its own operations, why not take the Buridanian line and simply assign freedom to the intellect, leaving the will to its assigned task of executing the conclusions of practical syllogisms?

The reason Thomas wants to expand the scope of the will is related to his efforts to refute the positions of Alexander of Aphrodisias, Averroes, and Avicenna on the nature of the intellect. All of these thinkers compromise the unity of the intellect as the substantial form of a human being: Alexander by assimilating it to material forms; Averroes and Avicenna by making different aspects of the intellect transcendent, or external to the individual cognizer. Against them, Thomas takes up a position which draws together all of the different facets of human consciousness into a single metaphysical entity, the intellectual soul. Along the way, more properly intellectual roles must be found for powers such as the will, which in Aristotle is concerned with particulars. Thomas does think that there is precedent in Aristotle for doing this, though the phenomenon he points to is attributed by Aristotle not to the will, but to emotion: "And the act of the will is clearly directed to the universal; as Aristotle says in the *Rhetoric*, 'we hate robbers in general, but are angry only with individual ones'. Therefore, the will cannot be the act of any part of the body, nor can it follow upon a power that is an act of the body. Now, every part of the soul is an act of the body, with the single exception of the intellect properly so called. Therefore, the will is in the intellective part . . ."[111] The problem with placing man's will outside of 'him', that is to say, outside of his intellect, is that then "a man would not be master of his own actions, since he would be acted upon by the will of a separate substance. But," Thomas adds, "this is impossible and would destroy all moral philosophy and sociality." This anti-Averroist point is repeated, almost verbatim, in a later attack on Avicenna where we are told that "if the agent intellect is a substance outside man, all man's operation depends on an extrinsic principle. Man, then, will not act autonomously, but will be activated by another. So, he will not be master of his own operations, nor will he merit either praise or blame."[112]

The stakes are obviously high in Thomas's elevation of the role of the will in human action. 'Deny it,' he seems to be saying, 'and the moral fabric of society will be rent, since the whole enterprise of praising and blaming people assumes not just that they are in control of their actions, but that this autonomy has a metaphysical basis in their very nature as persons'. The human moral agent thus acquires a kind of intrinsic dignity that is all the more compelling because it is rationally defensible.

Thomas's solution to the ordering problem, then, is to place the intellect in charge of the will: "For, primarily and directly [*primo et per se*], the intellect moves the will . . . the will would never desire the act of understanding unless, first of all, the intellect were to apprehend the act of understanding as a good. . . . Hence, it is evident that the intellect is, without qualification, higher than the will [*Unde apparet intellectum simpliciter esse altiorem voluntate*]."[113] Again, it is puzzling why Thomas wants to take back with one hand what he has given with the other. The Buridanian solution of ascribing freedom to the intellect on the grounds that the now elevated will and the intellect are only nominally distinct as powers of the human soul would seem the obvious route to take if one wants to preserve the dialectical balance between understanding and willing.

If the above picture is right, Thomas's contribution to the notion of intellectual freedom is to make the crucial first step of elevating the will from its position of Aristotelian servitude, in which it is merely the executor of practical syllogisms, to the level of an auxiliary power in the intellect, in which it appears as the engine that drives speculative inquiry. In his own words, "the act of the will is clearly directed to the universal." However, Thomas sees the ordering problem this would create and therefore stops short of assigning any dominance to the will, claiming that "the intellect is, without qualification, higher than the will." As a result, it is unclear whether this move in any way enhances the freedom traditionally ascribed to the will's proper act. That is, Thomas seems to have made little more than a house slave out of a field slave, increasing the will's range of responsibility without increasing its autonomy. This may be one reason why Thomas's moral psychology is so complicated, and often, confusing.[114]

It remains for Buridan to concentrate the highest perfections of the human person in the intellect. This is what gives rise to the concept of intellectual freedom. He encountered some awkwardness in doing so, since, together with his assumption that the intellect and will are not really distinct, this seems to entail that we must bracket our traditional way of speaking about the will as free. But Buridan has no intention of undermining traditional discourse, or of reforming it so as to bring it more into line with the metaphysical fact of freedom as primarily belonging to the intellect. Returning to the method of the *Summulae,* he diplomatically splits the difference between the voluntarists and intellectualists, arguing that the term 'happiness' primarily signifies an act of contemplation, but connotes the act of love which naturally follows from it (*QNE* X.4: 110ra). At most, he offers the gentle reminder to those who wish to speak of free will that all such freedom has its source in the intellect. This is not merely a friendly amendment to Thomas's philosophy of the human person, but a perfection of it.

True

CHAPTER SIXTEEN

Buridan's Legacy

·John Buridan stands as a kind of Boethian figure near the end of the Middle Ages. Just as Boethius is often described as an important transitional thinker, with one foot in antiquity and the other in the early Middle Ages, so Buridan bridges the gap between what are referred to as the 'medieval' and 'early modern' periods in standard histories of western philosophy. This makes his thought difficult to categorize, but also fascinating to study.

Like Boethius, Buridan modernized philosophical traditions that were on the wane, bringing about their transformation and redeeming them for posterity. In the field of logic, he overhauls Peter of Spain's *Summulae logicales,* apparently in an effort to bring this key thirteenth-century text into line with the central place the doctrine of supposition had come to occupy among fourteenth-century practitioners of the *logica moderna*. The result was a new *Summulae* with an orderly progression of teachings based on the proposition, which exemplified much more powerfully the idea that logic is the *ars artium,* the art of arts, whose method guides us to the principles of inquiry in all other disciplines. Buridan's logic is important not only because Buridan was a great logician whose insights are of interest to logicians today, but also because logic is how he makes sense of the world as a philosopher. The *Summulae* is a compendium of methods for the philosopher, not unlike the great doctrinal *summae* of the theologians in terms of its sheer range and comprehensiveness. It is easy to lose sight of this if one reads it only looking for doctrinal novelty. There is innovation in the text, but, as we saw above, logic is of purely instrumental value for Buridan. Its techniques can be studied as such, but they are really part of a larger whole whose meaning is expressed in relation to other disciplines. This is what it means to be the *ars artium*. There is no art of logic, and hence no subject of study at all, without other disciplines in the arts curriculum for it to belong to.

Buridan also did much to modernize the study of metaphysics and natural philosophy. Working within the bounds of authoritative texts and their traditional readings, he applied his method with the aim of perfecting Aristotelian philosophical practice. In his view, metaphysics and natural philosophy are in the first instance about language, since the significant terms of their respective discourses must be understood as suppositing materially, i.e., for other terms. Unlike logic, however, the terms of these higher discourses ultimately signify things in the natural order that are beyond the power of the human will to determine. To use Buridan's example, it is fire that heats the kettle, not the concept of fire, or the word 'fire' (*S* 4.3.8.4: 281). But the overlap between lower and higher discourses in the medium of conventional language had a profound effect on the way Buridan conceived of philosophical problems.

Buridan is confident both that the human intellect has been naturally ordained to assent to what is true (*QM* I.5: 6ra; *QP* I.15: 18vb–19ra), and that our cognitive capacities are reliable producers of evident appearances (*QDI* II.11: 100; *QM* VI.17: 52va). This means that more often than not, a problem exists because something has been conceived, or spoken about, in the wrong way. Buridan's famous remark in the debate over the nature of scientific knowledge—"I believe that such great controversy has arisen among the disputants because of a lack of logic [*ex defectu logicae*]" (*QNE* VI.6: 122vb)— is emblematic of his conception of the task of philosophy. The philosopher cannot answer all the questions we might have about nature and the place of human beings in it. Some of them such as 'Is the number of the stars even?' have answers which are simply not at all evident, or such as to produce in us a proposition which 'looks good', i.e., is good enough to command our assent. Others, such as 'How do we sense, understand, or remember after death and without a body?' (*QDA*₃ III.15: 173), have some evident propositions that can be marshaled on their behalf, but also appearances to the contrary, which, when taken together, prevent the conscientious philosopher from giving a decisive answer. Some of the questions generating mixed judgments can be resolved with the aid of another method of inquiry, e.g., by invoking articles of faith, but Buridan is very clear that when we do this we are no longer doing philosophy. Theology works from principles accepted because they are part of the doctrine of the faith and not because they are evident.

Of the remaining questions, many require only a perspicuous representation in our intellects. This is much harder than it appears, however, because our speaking and thinking are structured by language, and the expressive power of language naturally falls short of its object, created being, which is the language spoken by God. Medieval thinkers understood this as having a scriptural basis. Thus, the *Quodlibetal Questions* of Duns Scotus begins, "'All things are difficult,' says Solomon, and immediately adds the reason why he thinks they are difficult: 'Because man's language is inadequate to explain them' [Eccl. 1:8]."[1]

But the inadequacy of human language can be remedied, if not entirely cured. This is where the philosopher enters the picture, according to Buridan, using logic to clarify and resolve the sorts of questions raised in Part II of this book: the nature of universals (by determining the significance of terms such as 'universal', 'whole' and 'part'); the relation between bodies and souls (by establishing which names have been imposed on the soul to signify distinct natures and which signify merely diverse operations); the limits of human knowledge (by asking how the existence of a substance can be inferred from the existence of an accident); the proper subject matter of psychology (by distinguishing the various definitions of the soul); the nature of virtue (by representing it in terms of the analytical concept of impetus); and the basis of human freedom (by examining the epistemic character of those propositions the will is capable of accepting or rejecting). There are any number of topics in Buridan that can be studied and threaded together in this way. What they have in common is their basis in the dialectical method taught in the *Summulae.*

It is possible to read Buridan as a systematic logician, just as it is possible to read Buridan as an interpreter of Aristotle. But the result will not be an accurate portrait because he did not conceive of what he was doing in these terms. If he were driven by systematic concerns, we would expect to find his 'system' intruding regularly and explicitly in the texts. We do not. Logic intrudes, but always subtly, in the way we would expect of a method. Likewise, it makes no sense to ask whether Buridan was a faithful expositor of Aristotle because his Aristotle was a series of aporetic remarks and the commentary tradition that surrounded them. It would make more sense to try to locate Buridan within that tradition, relative to the other medieval authors and texts that defined it. But even this runs into the problem that commentaries were not constructed in order to respond to one's opponents, and that in those few places where the remains of a dispute does emerge onto the pages of a text, it is often far from clear who the disputants were, what the exact issue was, and what authorities were being used to resolve it. Even where we have enough information to narrate a dispute, as in the case of the debate over *complexe significabilia,* there is much that remains unknown and downright puzzling. But regardless of their role in intellectual controversies, we do know that commentaries on Aristotle were used to educate students about the order of nature and the practice of philosophical wisdom. Buridan's commentaries are almost perfect models of the genre in this regard.

In the same way, it would be possible, but not very enlightening, to compare Buridan with other later medieval philosophers as practitioners of Aristotelianism. Yet there are a number of ways of completing peripatetic doctrine on any given subject—Alexander, Averroes, Maimonides, and Aquinas all perfected Aristotle's teaching on the agent intellect, though they did so quite differently—and the effectiveness of a particular strategy must be judged relative to the larger system of which it is a part. But here the Buridanian readings appear to have been more influential than most, largely because of the fame of his first generation of students and the rapid dissemination of his works in the new universities of eastern Europe. When people read Aristotle, it was frequently with the assistance of Buridan's commentaries or abridged versions thereof, a practice that continued into the sixteenth century with early printed editions of his works. The same was true of his logic in the *Summulae*.

Let me conclude by suggesting that the real impact of Buridan on western thought has yet to be appreciated. That is because we have been looking for the wrong things. Questions of influence are almost always raised in terms of doctrine. We want to know what the new ideas were, who advanced them, and how they were passed on to posterity. On this criterion, Buridan looks less than impressive, although he does make original contributions in logic and natural philosophy. But even his best-known contribution, the *impetus* theory of projectile motion, is something for which he receives credit only as a popularizer, given that the doctrine itself derives from Philoponus via certain Islamic philosophers. But this in itself ought to give us a clue. Buridan's real philosophical legacy can be found not so much in new ideas as in new ways of thinking about old ideas. He made his most lasting contribution as a teacher, supplanting older techniques with the much more powerful method of the *Summulae*. Buridan never says why he remained a career arts master, but beneath the official posture of deference to the theologians was someone who felt very passionately about the independence and autonomy of his faculty, who believed that philosophy as properly practiced belonged to the faculty of arts, not to theology, or law, or medicine. It is not difficult to see how such an idea might lead to the secularization of philosophical practice, which of course is one of the features distinguishing later medieval philosophy from that of the early modern period. Whether or not Buridan's teachings played any discernible role in this development remains to be seen. But he would have approved of it, I think, since it was in this newer, secular space that he exercised his own philosophical genius.

Unfortunately, Buridan is like many other medieval authors in that few modern editions and translations exist of his works, though the situation has been improving in recent years. For a complete survey of the textual tradition up to 1978, see Michael 1985. At present, the most commonly used editions and translations of Buridan's commentaries and independent treatises are as follows:

COMMENTARIES

Expositio in libros Aristotelis 'De Anima' [*Literal Commentary on Aristotle's 'De Anima'*]. There are three versions of Buridan's literal commentary on *De Anima*, indicating that Buridan lectured more than once on this text during the course of his career at Paris. Moreover, each version has a corresponding question commentary (see below), since Buridan's lectures usually covered the literal text and the philosophical issues raised in it at the same time (see Flüeler 1999). The first version, or *prima lectura,* is critically edited in Patar 1991. The second and third versions are unedited.

Expositio in librum 'De motibus animalium' Aristotelis [*Literal Commentary on Aristotle's 'On the Motions of Animals'*]. Critical edition: Scott and Shapiro 1967.

Expositio in libros quattuor De caelo et mundo [*Literal Commentary on the Four Books of 'On the Heavens and the Earth'*]. Critical edition: Patar 1996.

Quaestiones circa librum Topicorum Aristotelis [*Questions on Aristotle's 'Topics'*]. Unedited. The text of Book I, question 16, from a single manuscript, is available in an appendix to Green-Pedersen 1984, 369–74.

Quaestiones Elencorum [*Questions on Aristotle's 'De Sophisticis Elenchis'*]. Critical edition: van der Lecq and Braakhuis 1994.

Quaestiones in duos libros Aristotelis Posteriorum Analyticorum [*Questions on the Two Books of Aristotle's 'Posterior Analytics'*]. Unpublished edition by Professor Hubert Hubien of the University of Liège.

Quaestiones in duos libros Aristotelis Priorum Analyticorum. [*Questions on the Two Books of Aristotle's 'Prior Analytics'*]. Unpublished edition by Professor Hubert Hubien of the University of Liège.

Quaestiones in duos libros De Generatione et Corruptione Aristotelis [*Questions on the Two Books of Aristotle's 'On Generation and Corruption'*]. Unedited. Manuscript copy consulted for this book: Wissenschaftliche Allgemeinbibliothek, cod. Amplon. F. 357, ff. 96ra–129va, Erfurt. The text of Book I, questions 1 and 3 appears in an appendix to Braakhuis 1999.

Quaestiones in Isagogen Porphyrii [*Questions on Porphyry's 'Isagoge'*]. Critical edition: Tatarzyński 1986.

Quaestiones in Praedicamenta [*Questions on Aristotle's 'Categories'*]. Critical edition: Schneider 1983.

Quaestiones in Rhetoricam Aristotelis [*Questions on Aristotle's 'Rhetoric'*]. Unedited. For this book, I was able to consult an unpublished working edition prepared by Bernadette Preben-Hansen.

Quaestiones in tres libros De Anima Aristotelis [*Questions on the Three Books of Aristotle's 'De Anima'*]. There are three versions of Buridan's question commentary on *De Anima*. The first version, or *prima lectura* (first course of lectures), has been critically edited in Patar 1991, the appendices of which contain excerpts from the second and third versions as well. Some scholars have expressed doubts about whether Buridan is in fact the author of this text (for a summary of the controversy, see Patar 1991, 67–98), but in absence of decisive evidence to the contrary, I have continued to treat it as authentic. The third version has been partially edited: Book II in Sobol 1984 and Book III in Zupko 1989. There is an early printed edition by George Lokert (1516; rpr. 1518) featuring commentaries on Aristotle's *De Anima* and *Parva Naturalia* which are ascribed to Buridan on the title page, though it is unclear whether these texts come directly from his lecture courses because they do not fit easily or obviously into any of the manuscript traditions, and we know that his commentaries were sometimes abridged by later copyists (see Markowski 1984). The complete text of the Lokert edition is reproduced in Patar 1991. There are translations of four questions from Book II of the third version (Sobol 1984 and 1996) and of the whole of Book III (Zupko 1989).

Quaestiones super libris quattuor De caelo et mundo [*Questions on the Four Books of 'On the Heavens and the Earth'*]. This work is widely available in a 1942 Medieval Academy edition by E. A. Moody, though it is based on only two of the (now) three known manuscripts. An updated critical edition can be found in Patar 1996.

Quaestiones longae super librum Perihermeneias [*Long Questions on 'De Interpretatione'*]. Critical edition: van der Lecq 1983.

Quaestiones super decem libros Ethicorum Aristotelis ad Nicomachum [*Questions on the Ten Books of Aristotle's 'Nicomachean Ethics'*]. There is an early printed edition (Paris 1513) available in a photomechanical reprint (Frankfurt a. M. 1968) under the title, *Super decem libros Ethicorum,* but no modern edition. John Kilcullen has emended the text of Book X of the 1513 edition on the basis of several manuscripts and kindly made the revised version available on his website (Kilcullen 1996), the translation of which can be found in McGrade, Kilcullen, and Kempshall 2001. There is also a translation of Book VI, question 6 in Hyman and Walsh 1987.

Quaestiones super duodecim libros Metaphysicorum Aristotelis [*Questions on the Twelve Books of Aristotle's 'Metaphysics'*]. There is no modern edition of this important work, though there is an early printed edition (Paris 1518) available in a photomechanical reprint (Frankfurt a. M. 1964) under the title, *Kommentar zur Aristotelischen Metaphysik* (the original publication date is mistakenly given as 1588 on the frontispiece to the reprinted edition). The 1518 edition describes Buridan's questions on its title page as '*argutissimae*' ('most eloquent'), so this text is often listed in library catalogues as the '*Quaestiones argutissimae Iohannis Buridani super duodecim libros Metaphysicorum Aristotelis*'. There are translations of the main sections of Book II, question 1 and Book IV, questions 8–9 in Hyman and Walsh 1987.

Quaestiones super octo Physicorum libros Aristotelis [*Questions on the Eight Books of Aristotle's 'Physics'*]. There is an early printed edition (Paris 1509) available in a photomechanical reprint (Frankfurt a. M. 1964) under the title, *Kommentar zur Aristotelischen Physik,* but as yet no modern edition of the complete work. The sub-treatise on infinity ('*Tractatus de Infinito*') contained in Book III, questions 14–19, has been edited by Hans Thijssen in a preliminary study for such an edition (Thijssen 1991a). A modern critical text is being prepared by a team of editors under Thijssen's direction at the Center for Medieval and Renaissance Natural Philosophy, University of Nijmegen. There are translations of the main sections of Book III, question 7 and Book VIII, question 12 in Hyman and Walsh 1987.

INDEPENDENT TREATISES

Quaestio de puncto [*Question on the Point*]. Critical edition: Zoubov 1961.

Summulae de Dialectica [*Compendium of Dialectic*]. Four of the nine treatises from the critical edition of this mammoth work have been published to date: Treatise 2 *De Praedicabilibus* [*On Predicables*] (de Rijk 1995), Treatise 3 *In Praedicamenta* [*On Categories*] (Bos 1994), Treatise 4 *De suppositionibus* [*On Suppositions*] (van der Lecq 1998, superseding the earlier edition of Reina 1957) and Treatise 8 *De demonstrationibus* [*On Demonstrations*] (de Rijk 1999). In addition, there is an edition of Treatise 9 *De practica sophismatum* [*On the Practice of Sophisms*] (Scott 1977, to be superseded by Pironet forthcoming), and an edition with translation of Chapter 8 of Treatise 9 on self-referential propositions (Hughes 1982). An early printed edition (Venice 1499) of the *Summulae* was published in a photo-mechanical reprint (Frankfurt a. M. 1965), though the text is seriously flawed (e.g., Treatise 4 is actually by Marsilius of Inghen, not Buridan). In any case, there is now a reliable English translation of the entire *Summulae* based on the critical edition (Klima 2001), which also replaces the earlier translations of Treatise 4 (King 1985) and Treatise 9 (Scott 1966).

Tractatus de consequentiis [*Treatise on Consequences*]. Critical edition: Hubien 1976. Translation: King 1985.

Tractatus de differentia universalis ad individuum [*Treatise on the Difference between the Universal and the Individual*]. Critical edition: Szyller 1987.

・ NOTES ・

Notes to the Introduction

1. The authoritative source for Buridan's life and works is Michael 1985, though the previous standard, Faral 1950, is still worth consulting. See also Flüeler 1999; Sobol 1984, x–xx; Zupko 1998, 131–32 (from which some of the material in this section is taken); and Klima, Introduction to S, i–iv. Like other famous and public persons, Buridan attracted his share of rumors, legends, and apocryphal stories. There is no truth, however, to the rumor mentioned by the fifteenth-century poet François Villon that the king of France ordered him to be thrown in a sack into the Seine River because of a scandalous affair with the queen, or that he went on to found the University of Vienna after being expelled from Paris for his nominalist teachings, or even that he hit the future Pope Clement VI over the head with a shoe while competing for the affections of the wife of a German shoemaker (the blow apparently causing the prodigious memory for which Clement became known). Nevertheless, they illustrate what Faral called the "*bruits de ville*" or 'buzz' surrounding his name in Parisian circles, which continued for some time after his death.

2. For this reason, arts masters tended to be "quite young, and they were often pursuing more advanced studies while carrying out their teaching" (Jan Pinborg, "Medieval Philosophical Literature," *CHLMP*, 15). See also Marenbon 1990, 265.

3. There is also a commentary on Aristotle's *Politics* attributed to Buridan, although Christoph Flüeler (1992, 1:132–68) has shown that it is actually the work of Nicholas of Vaudémont, a late fourteenth-century Parisian arts master. In an important study of the method of composition of Buridan's texts, Flüeler argues on the basis of the oldest copies of Buridan's commentaries on the *Metaphysics* that Buridan's question commentaries almost always correspond to an *expositio* or literal commentary, and that both commentaries were prepared at the same time, written down in alternating fashion during the same lecture-course. Moreover, like most arts masters of the period, Buridan revised these "reports [*reportationes*]" of his lectures into what he called "compiled [*compilata*]" commentaries (one scribe even notes that his copy of Buridan's commentary on the *Metaphysics* VI has been "compiled in the presence of the master [*compilata ante magistrum*]"). The latter, revised, copies seem to have formed the subsequent manuscript tradition, although it was usually only the question commentary that was preserved. For the details, see Flüeler 1999.

・ 279 ・

4. Maier 1964–67: "was sich ändert, ist die Methode der Naturerkenntnis" (1:434); "was interessiert, ist der *modus sciendi,* nicht die *scientia*" (1:439).

5. Actually, the caricature is almost as old as the doctrine of nominalism itself. As Damasus Trapp puts it, "From the 15th century down to our own days the research in 14th-century theology has suffered from the incubus of nominalism" (1956, 186).

6. Things were different in England during the same period, where it appears that only William of Ockham and Robert Holkot explicitly denied real universals, and nominalism had to compete with more sophisticated versions of realism developed by Duns Scotus and Walter Chatton.

7. Only Treatises II–IV of the critical edition of the *Summulae* have appeared to date: *In Praedicamenta,* ed. E. P. Bos (1994); *De Praedicabilibus,* ed. L. M. de Rijk (1995); and *De suppositionibus,* ed. R. van der Lecq (1998). Although I have used Klima's translation of the *Summulae* in this book, I have in every case consulted the Latin text, whether in the published versions of Treatises II–IV and VII or else in the unpublished working edition of the remaining treatises, to which I had access (gratefully acknowledged here) as a reader for Klima's translation. All other translations, unless otherwise noted, are my own.

8. For secondary literature on Buridan, see Fabienne Pironet's "Bibliographie Spéciale sur Jean Buridan," available online at www.brise.ere.umontreal.ca/~pironetf/download/JBBiblio.pdf.

9. For discussion, see Jan Pinborg, "Medieval Philosophical Literature" in *CHLMP,* 30–33. The genre of *quaestiones* involves further complexities. As Edmond Faral (1950, 38) notes:

> Les questions sont qualifiées de façons diverses selon le côté considéré de l'opération. Elles sont dites *institutae* en tant qu'elles sont formulées; *disputatae,* en tant elles ont été discutées. Cette discussion suppose que l'auteur a recueilli tous les éléments susceptibles d'y intervenir: les questions peuvent donc être dites *collectae,* ou *compilatae,* ou *congregatae* (sans que ses termes se réfèrent à la composition de recueil). Puis les arguments doivent être mis en ordre: les questions seront donc dites *compositae* ou *ordinatae.* Elles sont dites *pertractatae* ou *determinatae* en tant que l'auteur y soutient une thèse. Enfin, en tant que produits en public, sous forme orale ou écrite, elles sont dites *datae* ou *editae.*

See also Flüeler 1999.

10. For the text of this question, see Zupko forthcoming.

11. The role of empiricism in Buridanian psychology is discussed in chapter 13 below.

12. The third subject of the *trivium,* rhetoric, did not fare as well, though Buridan does find a place for it in the discourse of moral teaching. For discussion and references, see section 1 of chapter 2 below.

13. Buridan was not alone in not writing or lecturing on grammar. The last Parisian arts master to compose a treatise on grammar was Radulphus Brito (c. 1270–1320) (for discussion, see Ebbesen 2000). What appears to have happened is that during the thirteenth century, the teaching of grammar gradually migrated to colleges and other small schools at the periphery of the University. Buridan probably received his own grammatical training at the Collège Lemoine.

14. Buridan has a more contingent and organic conception of the unity of each speculative science. Thus, "the whole of metaphysics derives its unity from our attribution of everything in it to the term 'being', just as an army is unified by its commander" (*QM* VI.2: 34ra). The commander metaphor is used of logic in the preface to the *Summulae,* but in the sense of leading reason to its desired goal (demonstrated truth) and repelling the invader (fallacies), not in the sense of unifying the study of dialectic. See n. 52 of chapter 9 below.

15. *QM* IV.4: 15va. The Latin text is quoted at n. 13 of chapter 2 below.

16. See chapter 5 below. Of course, by treating Buridan's logic as *praxis* rather than *theoria,* I am not calling into question all of the good scholarship that has been done on its different aspects over the past few decades, and from which I—like every other student of Buridan—have learned a great deal. These books and articles give legitimate readings of the text, but in a different way, by showing Buridan's place within the broader thematic traditions of medieval logic, i.e., as regards doctrine of supposition, syllogisms, consequences, sophismata, etc. It would be possible to write a book that simply gathers these horizontal strands together along the axis of Buridan's particular contribution (perhaps distinctive, perhaps not) to them, but this would only incidentally be a book about Buridan. My approach is to insist upon a vertical perspective throughout, reading Buridan wherever possible in terms of his own philosophical vision.

Notes to Chapter 1

1. The mendicant orders, i.e., the Dominicans and Franciscans, were different in that they formed their own schools for training novices in the arts disciplines, and were by papal decree exempt from the requirement of a master's degree for matriculation into the other faculties of the university—much to the consternation of students and faculty who were not members of mendicant orders, it should be added.

2. To some extent, this view has been fueled by the growing division between teaching and research in present-day universities, where questions about the compatibility of conscientious teaching and *bona fide* scholarship are very much alive. I will not pursue this here, but suffice it to say that faculty members at medieval universities experienced no such tensions—though they did experience others, of course.

3. The following history is much abbreviated, as it seeks to cover only those points relevant to introducing Buridan's thought. For more comprehensive treatments of medieval grammar, see de Rijk 1962 and 1967; Hunt 1980; Ziolkowski 1985; Bursill-Hall, Ebbesen, and Koerner 1990; Reilly 1993; Kneepkens 1995; and Reynolds 1996.

4. Isidore of Seville, *Etymologiae* 1.5.1. Cf. Peter Helias (c. 1100–1166), who basically recapitulates Isidore's definition in the second sentence of his magisterial *Summa super Priscianum,* the most widely used grammar text in universities of the later Middle Ages: "Grammar, then, is the skillful [*gnara*] art of speaking and writing correctly" (Reilly 1993, 61).

5. Isidore, *Etymologiae* 1.5.1. Isidore's definition became a *leitmotif* in discussions of the place of grammar in the medieval curriculum. Cf. John of Salisbury (c. 1120–1180), who, in commenting on Isidore's definition, personifies grammar

maternally in its relation to philosophy: "Grammar is the cradle of all philosophy, and in a manner of speaking, the first nurse of the whole study of letters. It takes all of us as tender babes, newly born from nature's bosom. It nurses us in our infancy, and guides our every forward step in philosophy. With motherly care, it fosters and protects the philosopher from the start to the finish [of his pursuits]" (*Metalogicon* I.13, tr. McGarry 1955, 37; quoted in Ziolkowski 1985, 92). John makes the reason clear in an earlier passage: "Grammar prepares the mind to understand everything that can be taught in words" (*Metalogicon* I.12). More than two centuries later, we find William Wykeham writing that "grammar is the foundation, gate and source of all the other liberal arts, without which such arts cannot be known, nor can anyone arrive at practicing them. . . . Moreover . . . by the knowledge of grammar justice is cultivated and the prosperity of the estate of humanity is increased" (Foundation Deed of Winchester College, from Leach 1911, 321; quoted in Ziolkowski 1985, 89–90).

6. Suzanne Reynolds (1996, 9) cites an interesting *exemplum* from the sermon collection of Jacques de Vitry (d. 1240): "A cleric in the choir of the church sees a devil weighed down by a heavy sack; the devil reveals that his burden is made up of the syllables mispronounced by the choir. These mispronunciations are a kind of vocal sin and, so the devil explains, mean that the choir have in effect stolen the prayers from God."

7. This raises the question of how Latin was taught in the first place, if not by techniques familiar to us now, such as immersion. The answer, of course, is that it was taught in one of the vernacular languages. For example, historical records indicate that in 1349, the grammarian John of Cornwall was the first master in England to use English instead of French as the language of Latin instruction (Hunt 1980, 179). For further discussion, see Dahan, Rosier, and Valente 1995.

8. To the western, Christian mind, Latin was seen as distinct from both the speaker's mother tongue and all other languages (Dahan, Rosier, and Valente 1995, 265). Thus, as Jan Ziolkowski remarks (1985, 90), Latin grammar was "essential in a society which paid homage to a father language—to a language that many people learned to speak, write, and think but that no one knew from the cradle."

9. The arts in question here must include grammar, as the sophism posits attending to the sophism sentence "as much as you can [to find out] whether it is true or false" (*S* 9.8, 15th sophism: 987). Ever conscious of the needs of his students, Buridan's examples in the *Sophismata* show sensitivity to the fact of vernacular languages, e.g.: "let us assume that someone [who cannot read] has Latin as his mother tongue [*idioma latinum a matre*], just as we have French . . . he will know very well the signification of the spoken expression, '*Homo currit* [A man runs]'" (*S* 9.1, 1st conclusion: 831).

10. For beginning students in the schools, the most popular text was the *Ars Minor* of Donatus, a fourth-century grammarian who was Isidore of Seville's main source for the discussion of grammar in the first section of the *Etymologiae*. Again, the universities favored Priscian's *Institutiones Grammaticae*, together with the ever-expanding literature of abridgements, commentaries, glosses, lectures, and disputations on it. Especially influential in the latter connection was the *Summa super Priscianum* of Peter Helias, compiled in the 1140s. Jan Pinborg ("Speculative Grammar," *CHLMP*, 254) described Helias's *Summa* as the result of the "combined efforts" of earlier glossators, efforts "directed towards explaining the authoritative texts, towards systematizing the descriptional apparatus used by the authors [i.e., Donatus

and Priscian], and towards harmonizing the apparent or real contradictions which arose in a comparison of the grammatical and logical traditions." For further discussion, see Kneepkens 1995.

11. This picture of the place of Latin grammar in the university arts curriculum remains somewhat idealized, of course, as the influence of grammar gradually waned over the course of the thirteenth century. Much of the teaching of grammar appears to have moved from the university to the colleges and other smaller schools that grew up in its environs (Buridan, for example, must have studied grammar while a student at the Collège Lemoine). Grammar continued as a university subject, though in a more specialized form. According to C. H. Kneepkens (1995, 252–53), "grammar instruction at the universities became a sort of training in general linguistics and was dissociated from the exposition of authors and the teaching of Latin. To some extent this was a natural consequence of the rise of the universities. After all, the university as an institution was explicitly intended for higher, tertiary education. A student was expected to be well trained in Latin already on arrival at the university."

12. Pinborg, "Medieval Philosophical Literature," *CHLMP*, 16–17.

13. Chase 1926, 13.

14. Pinborg, "Medieval Philosophical Literature," *CHLMP*, 29.

15. The fact that many of Buridan's lectures have come down to us in more than one form because he lectured on certain texts (e.g., Aristotle's *Physics* and *De Anima*) more than once might seem an insurmountable obstacle to the proper editing of his work and to any study, such as the present one, which tries to advance a synoptic perspective on his thought. In my view, however, the editing problem is only apparent, and resolves itself immediately once it is realized that it is impossible to arrive at an authoritative text. The next best thing is to identify the various redactions of Buridan's lectures and to edit on that basis, giving some priority to final redactions on the grounds that they represent his thought at its most mature (though one should not regard them as completely authoritative, since the questions Buridan asks each time he delivered his lectures were partly determined by his current interests and the philosophical issues of the day). And as for the problem of saying what Buridan's philosophy is in the wake of a fluid textual tradition, I would reject this for the reason sketched at the beginning of this chapter. That is, it would be a mistake to try to determine Buridan's 'final form' teaching on the basis of the texts that we have, given that Buridan did not conceive of what he was doing in this way (which is why, e.g., those searching for Buridan's definitive defense of nominalism will search in vain). Rather than forcing the texts into some contemporary hermeneutical category, it seems better to identify the general trends and lines of argument that emerge from his writings, respecting the tentativeness with which he himself usually puts his conclusions.

16. The remark makes good on Buridan's promise in the Preface of this work "to say and write things [in the text which is the subject of the commentary] which differ from what [Peter of Spain] has said and written, whenever it appears to me suitable to do so" (*S* Preface: 4). He also makes contemporaneous observations aimed at the edification of his students, e.g., "concerning non-substantivated adjectives there is much disagreement among the professors [*inter doctores*]" (*S* 4.2.6: 237).

17. The structure of the question commentary was inherited from another oral genre, the *disputatio* or disputed question, a classroom exercise that attempted to follow

the dialectical procedure set out by Aristotle in *Nicomachean Ethics* VII.1.1145b2–7. See Anthony Kenny, "Medieval Philosophical Literature," *CHLMP*, 25.

18. *QM* VI.2: 33vb:

> Notandum quod artes quaedam sunt mechanicae vel manufactivae, et de illis est scientia practica, et illas faciunt laici quemadmodum sunt artes sutoriae et cupriae. Aliae sunt artes liberales, qui vocantur liberales ex eo impedite quod liberant intellectus introductos a curis secularibus et mundialibus. Et tales sunt septem scilicet grammatica, logica, rhetorica, musica, astrologia, geometria, et arithmetica. Et illarum primae tres sunt practicae scientiae. Vocantur autem practicae pro tanto quod sic instituunt hominem ad sermocinandum et orationem congruam proferendam et ad orationes ornandas et ad syllogismos proferendos et ad materiam inveniendam. Docent enim unde possit sermo Latinatus inveniri et significata vocabulorum dictionum et orationum et propositionum. Aliae autem quattuor sunt speculativae artes vel de illis traditur scientia speculativa pro tanto quia speculantur causas altissimas rerum ordines essentias rerum vel quasi omnia.

Weijers notes that one first finds the mechanical arts mentioned in this sense in the early twelfth-century school of St. Victor (1987 [1989], 51).

19. In a text that would have been familiar to most educated people in the Middle Ages, Cicero observes that "no workshop can have anything liberal about it [*nec enim quicquam ingenuum habere potest officina*" (*De officiis* I.150: 153). Echoes of this conception of manual labor as utterly servile can also be found in Paul at 1 Cor. 4:12 and 1 Thess. 2:9. Interestingly enough, Cicero goes on remark that among those occupations concerned with material gain, "none is more becoming to a free man [*nihil homine libero dignius*]" than agriculture. But this would have been understood by medieval readers as referring to the business or supervisory end of agriculture, which is proper to the lord, not to the subordinate activities of ploughing, seeding, sheep shearing, etc., which are proper to the tenants or vassals. And in any case, it is difficult to imagine Cicero doing any actual farming.

20. "We shall divide this book into nine treatises, the first of which is going to deal with propositions and their parts and attributes [*passionibus*]" (*S* 1.1.1: 4). Cf. Priscian's definition of expression: "An expression is a correct ordering of words, exhibiting a complete thought [*oratio est ordinatio dictionum congrua, sententiam perfectam demonstrans*]" (*Institutiones Grammaticae* ii, 15; Hertz 1855–59, vol. 1, 53). Later, Priscian speaks of the ordination of single utterances to words, and of words to "the construction of the perfect expression [*ad constructionem orationis perfectae*]," concerning which "we must most diligently inquire for the exposition of authors [*ad auctorum expositionem*]" (*Institutiones Grammaticae* xvii, 2; Hertz 1855–59, vol. 2, 108).

21. This is not to claim that the logical notion of supposition was developed from the grammatical notion. The origins of the *suppositio* terminology in the twelfth century are rather murky, and appear to involve several different traditions and strands of influence, not all of which are confined to the *trivium*. For further discussion, see Ebbesen 1987a, Kneepkens 1987, and Valente 1995.

22. Buridan often contrasts grammatical and logical practice: "an adjectival name, taken adjectivally, is such that just as it does not provide a suppositum for the verb [*non reddit suppositum verbo*] according to the grammarians, so also it does not

supposit, strictly speaking, according to the logicians. But if it is substantivated in the neuter gender, then it can provide a suppositum for the verb according to the grammarian, and it can also supposit according to the logician" (*S* 8.2.4: 648).

23. Chase 1926, 33.

24. For the classical definition of conversion, see Aristotle, *Prior Analytics* I.2–3, though the author(s) of the *Ars Montana* would have almost certainly been familiar with conversion via the old logic (*logica vetus*)—i.e., the Boethian tradition of propositional logic—where it appeared as a rule of syllogistic inference. For discussion, see Ebbesen, "Ancient Scholastic Logic as the Source of Medieval Scholastic Logic," *CHLMP*, 101–127, and Stump 1989, 31–66, 111–34.

25. Anonymous, *Abbreviatio Montana* [8d. "Conversions"], translated in Kretzmann and Stump 1988, 48. For the identification and dating (before 1140) of this text, see de Rijk 1966, 8, 22. For other early treatises exhibiting the question-and-answer format, see the two Oxford texts, *Logica 'Cum sit nostra'*, which was widely used in the schools and was apparently still in circulation in the fourteenth century, and the *Logica 'Ut dicit'*, which influenced it (de Rijk 1967, Part I, 416–47; Part II, 379–451).

26. Reilly 1993 documents a struggle over teaching methods in mid-century Paris which seems to have led a number of scholars, including Peter Helias, to leave the city. In their extant writings, Thierry of Chartres, Gilbert of Poitiers, William of Conches, and John of Salisbury all "lament what they regard as the commercialization of the teaching process [at Paris]. Instead of the master working for years with a small number of students who were gradually replaced with new ones, the teachers were faced with a flood of students which they could not control" (12).

27. Peter of Spain, *Summulae Logicales* I, 15; de Rijk 1972, 8, ll. 5–9. The lemma of this passage in Buridan's *Summulae* is virtually identical (*S* 1.6.2: 50).

28. For example, in the universal affirmative proposition 'Every man is an animal', the predicate is not distributed over the subject because there are some animals, such as Tawny the lion, which are not human. Cf. *QAnPr* I.8: "[significative] terms are said to be convertible with each other, and this is when, for whatever things the one supposits, the other supposits for those same things, and vice versa: e.g., the terms 'man' and 'risible' [*termini dicuntur ad invicem convertibiles, et hoc est quando pro quibuscumque unus supponit pro eisdem alter supponit, et e converso, ut isti termini 'homo' et 'risibile'*]."

29. *In Categorias Aristotelis libri quattuor*, PL 64.161D.

30. De Rijk (1967, Part 1, 116) describes the development as follows: "This shifting of interest of the grammarians away from the primordial invention and imposition of individual words to their syntactical function seems to have found its counterpart in—and, no doubt, to have stimulated—the parallel development on the side of the dialecticians, when the latter in their theories of signification transferred their main interest from the original imposition of words to the actual meaning of this word in this proposition as a result of its actual function in that proposition." These developments might in turn have been stimulated by a change in the study of theology. Margaret Gibson notes that by the last quarter of the eleventh century, the interest of theologians began to shift from speculative cosmology to "the analytical study and interrelation of specific points of Christian doctrine," a project which demanded "a certain preliminary facility in the *artes*," thereby bringing into play, as the old tradition of biblical commentary did not, "the analytical skills of the *Trivium*" (1969,

126). In any case, the nuances of relations between the grammarians and the dialecticians were many. For the development of grammar as a *scientia*, see Kneepkens 1995.

31. Abelard, *Logica 'ingredientibus'*, tr. Spade 1994, 38–39.

32. As de Rijk puts it (1967, Part 1, 189), "Abailard's whole logic of terms is overshadowed by the problem of *universalia*." I should make clear that by 'context', I mean something much broader than de Rijk when he points to the distinctively "contextual approach" taken by early twelfth-century logicians and grammarians (an approach which led to the rise of, among other things, terminist logic): "No longer were words studied as separate units quite apart from their linguistic context; rather . . . the statement (*propositio*), not isolated words, was taken to be the fundamental unit of meaning. The meaning of a word in its actual use in a propositional context was considered so important, indeed, as to lead to the introduction of a special terminology, centered around terms (i.e., words as parts of actual propositions) and their properties" (de Rijk, "The Origins of the Theory of the Properties of Terms," *CHLMP*, 161; cf. de Rijk 1967, Part 1, 113–17, 123–25). By 'context' I mean the larger set of discourse conditions and possibilities which govern the appropriate use of both terms and propositions, i.e., their 'complete setting', as it were, in the lives of those who use them. This would include such non-linguistic (or at least not obviously linguistic) factors as textual authority, genre, and authorial intention.

33. Margaret Gibson characterizes this specialization of the art of grammar in terms of its separation from the other liberal arts and especially from the *quadrivium*: "What Peter Helias had brought to commentary on Priscian was not so much new thinking as new realism. The modern student had neither the time, nor always the skill, to range easily throughout every field of learning. You chose your subject, and you mastered the required texts" (1992, 32).

34. Reilly 1993, 26–28.

35. Peter Helias, "*Liber Constructionum*" in *Summa super Priscianum*, ed. Reilly 1993, 832, ll. 5–15. Peter uses the same adjective, '*congrua*', for both grammatical and semantic agreement. Further illustrations of this conception can be found in Ebbesen 1981. See also John of Salisbury, *Metalogicon* I.15 (McGarry 1955). The first book of the *Metalogicon* is a wealth of information on twelfth-century conceptions of the relation between grammar and logic.

36. By teaching the logical notion of supposition through differentiation, Buridan sees himself as recapitulating its historical development: "this is how logicians have become accustomed to use these names [i.e. 'personal' vs. 'material' supposition], and this they were allowed to do, for names are significative by convention [*ad placitum*]" (*S* 4.3.2: 253). De Rijk notes that "material supposition in propositions of this type: '*homo est bissillabum* ['*homo*' is bisyllabic]' . . . was sometimes called the supposition of the grammarians by 12th-century logicians" (1962, 20).

37. Latin, of course, lacks definite and indefinite articles, so they must be supplied in English to make Buridan's point clear.

38. See also Buridan's resolution of the fallacies leading to redundancy (*nugatio*) and solecism (*solecismus*) in the seventh treatise: "those who do not know the rules of grammar and their exceptions are often deceived" (*S* 7.5.5: 600).

39. In contrast to the Abelardian picture, Buridan rejects as "superficial" any strategy that sets nonsense-sentences to one side because they are not "proper locutions." Thus, as long as a sentence satisfies the rules of congruence, it demands our full

logical consideration: "although a chimera cannot be seen, nor can a lunar eclipse be killed, yet the following are grammatical sentences according to the grammarian: 'A chimera is seen by you' or 'A lunar eclipse is killed by you', hence either of them has to be true or false in the form propounded" (*S* 9.4, 15th sophism: 912–13). One cannot help but be reminded here of Peter Helias's looser, more holistic understanding of the meaning of an expression as consisting not merely of its grammatical congruence, but also of its "agreement in meaning [*congrua sensu*]," i.e., the quasi-affective phenomenon whereby "the hearer understands something intelligibly through it."

40. Quoted in n. 20 above.

41. See Ria van der Lecq and H. A. G. Braakhuis, 1994, "Introduction" to *QE:* xxx–xxxv.

42. See Trentman 1970.

43. Panaccio 1999a, 53. See William of Ockham, *Summa logicae* I.1–3; *Opera Philosophica* I: 7–14.

44. Oddly enough, the features of this universal and naturally significative mental language must still be expressed in spoken and written terms because they are more accessible to us. This point is brought out by Marilyn McCord Adams: "Ockham would have admitted the notion of a basic scientific language ideally suited for describing the way things are, and would have identified it with the mental language. But while he regards the mental language as semantically primary, in that spoken and written words acquire significance by being conventionally related to concepts, he finds spoken and written language epistemically more accessible. And he sets out to describe the structure of mental language by considering which features of spoken and written language should be mapped onto it" (Adams 1987a, 289).

45. *QC* 1: 4, ll. 45–46 (cf. *S* 7.3.4: 522; *S* 9.1, 2nd conclusion: 832): "*voces non imponuntur ad significandum res nisi mediantibus conceptibus, quibus concipiuntur.*"

46. William of Ockham, *Summa logicae* I.1; *Opera Philosophica* I: 7–9.

47. On appellation, for example, see Scott 1966, 42, n. 76, and Biard 1989, 185–86. Part II, chapter 2 of Biard's book offers a more detailed comparison of the logic of Ockham and Buridan.

48. Peter King captures Buridan's style nicely here: "When is a term in personal supposition or material supposition? Unlike Ockham, Buridan does not try to give precise rules, but rather trusts to good sense and good logic (*S* 4.3.2: 252–58), usually taking context to decide" (King 1985, 40; I have altered the reference to fit Klima's translation).

49. Of course, the question of whether the *complexe significabile* is the adequate significate of the proposition was imported from what was originally a dispute between English Franciscans, i.e., Ockham, Walter Chatton, and Adam Wodeham. See Zupko 1994–97.

50. If we attend only to doctrine, the differences between Ockham and Buridan can appear insignificant. Claude Panaccio, for example, comments that their disagreement on what spoken words signify "can seem spectacular enough at first sight, although from a strictly theoretical point of view, in this particular case, it is a simple matter of terminology" (Panaccio 1999b, 298). As should be clear already, this book is anti-reductionist in its method in that it regards formal considerations (including matters of terminology) as crucially important for understanding what Buridan is trying to do as a philosopher.

51. See *S* 9.8: 952–97 and chapter 9 below. Ockham avoids paradoxes of self-reference by holding that a term cannot refer to itself (*Summa logicae* III.3; *Opera Philosophica:* 46), or at least that "self-reference is to be allowed except where it would lead to paradox—in short, it is licit except where it is illicit" (Spade 1974, 299).

52. Biard 1989, 196.

53. Not surprisingly, Buridan appeals to *Nicomachean Ethics* II.2.1104a3 for support here: "the accounts we demand must be in accordance with their subject matter."

54. A denominative term must be "concrete, deriving in its formation from its abstract form, as 'white' from 'whiteness'" (*S* 3.1.3: 146; cf. *S* 2.5.2: 127).

55. See the Prologue to Buridan's *Questions on the Nicomachean Ethics,* where he speaks of the need for a "moral logic" having "two parts, rhetoric and poetry, which differ as follows: rhetoric seeks a clear meaning and uses words retaining their proper signification; poetry, however, playfully attempts to obscure meaning through the metaphorical use of words, or in some other way [*huius autem moralis logicae duae sunt partes, scilicet rhetorica et poetria, quae sic differunt: quia rhetorica claram sententiam desiderat et verbis utitur in sua propria significatione retentis; poetria vero sententiam delectabiliter obscurare nititur per verborum transumptionem vel alio modo*]" (*QNE* I, Proemium: 2rb). For further discussion, see chapters 4 and 15 below.

56. *QIP* 5: 143, ll. 739–53:

> Sed mihi videtur, quod isti omnino non bene dicunt, quia sermo non habet in enuntiatione virtutem ex se, sed ex nobis ad placitum. Ideo si utamur sermone sicut ipso consueverunt uti philosophi et alii [*alli/alii*], nos nihil agimus contra virtutem sermonis, immo certe talem virtutem et potentiam habet vox, saltem litterata, quod ipsa est in potentia ad hoc, quod imponamus eam ad significandum quod volumus et quod ea imposita ad significandum utamus sicut volumus, scilicet vel significative vel materialiter; nec in hoc agendo agimus contra virtutem sermonis. Immo quod plus vox imposita ad significandum certam significationem sic est imposita, quod licite possumus uti ea secundum significationem sibi primo et principaliter institutam, vel secundum significationem similitudinariam vel metaphoricam, immo etiam secundum significationem contrariam significationi eius primariae, ut quando volumus loqui ironice. Immo tales usus conveniunt voci in virtute primariae significationis secundum attributionem ad eam, et ideo tales usus nequaquam sunt contra virtutem sermonis.

We can appreciate the rhetorical force of Buridan's objection to the literalists in the fact that he uses the strong adversative particle 'immo [on the contrary; indeed]' no fewer that four times in this one paragraph. A related discussion in the *Summulae* indicates that by ironical speech, Buridan intends to include sarcasm: "a father says ironically to his son: 'Oh, you are a very good boy', and by this he intends that the predicate 'good boy' should supposit not for a good boy but a bad one" (*S* 4.3.1: 252).

57. *QIP* 5: 142, ll. 700–701: "*sed nos possumus scire quomodo et ad quid imponebatur ad significandum nisi per usum auctorum.*" This remark is made in an argument at the beginning of the question, but it is the same position Buridan defends in the *resolutio*. For an example of Buridan practicing what he preaches, see the *Summulae*'s discussion of the topic from the whole-in-time and its part, which concludes, "on these grounds, I do not believe that Boethius's intention [i.e., in *De topicis differentiis*, 1188D27–28; Stump 1978, 52] to posit these *loci*—namely, the *loci* from the whole-in-

quantity, from the whole-in-mode, from the whole-in-place, and from the whole-in-time—as distinct from the *locus* from the superior to the inferior" (*S* 6.4.8: 439).

58. The reference to '*vetulae*' (lit. 'old women') is a commonplace in Buridan's writings, mentioned whenever he wants to appeal to the intuitions of experienced yet uneducated (and hence illiterate) folk as regards a philosophical claim. It should be pointed out that none of these references is pejorative in the sense that its purpose is to make fun of the elderly or ignorant. It is just that Buridan sincerely wonders from time to time what uneducated people think about the ideas he is discussing, such as whether it follows from God's omnipotence that God could make a contradiction come true (for discussion, see chapter 12 below). Cf. Aristotle, *Nicomachean Ethics* VI.11.1143b11–14: "Therefore we ought to attend to the undemonstrated sayings and opinions of experienced and older people or of people of practical wisdom not less than to demonstrations; for because experience has given them an eye they see aright."

vetule

59. *QIP* 5: 144–45, ll. 800–817:

> Ego statim respondeo, quod numquam ad hoc virtus sermonis nos obligavit, immo aliquando debemus sermones recipere secundum proprios sensus eorum et aliquando secundum sensus improprios, ut parabolicos vel ironicos, vel alios etiam valde remotos a sensibus propriis. Verbi gratia, si legimus libros doctorum, ut Aristotelis vel Porphyrii, debemus recipere sermones eorum secundum illos sensus, licet improprios, secundum quos illi doctores imposuerunt eos, et sic simpliciter debemus illos sermones concedere tamquam veros, quia recepti secundum illos sensus sunt veri. Sed tamen debemus dicere, quod secundum tales sensus positi, et quod si essent positi secundum suos sensus proprios, ipsi essent falsi. Et si legentes libros doctorum aliter reciperent sermones quam credant eos esse positos a doctoribus, ipsi essent protervi et dyscoli et non digni studere vel legere libros philosophorum. Similiter omnes sermones Bibliae vel Evangeliorum debemus simpliciter dicere esse veros et debemus eos recipere secundum illos sensus secundum quos positi sunt et secundum quos sunt veri; et aliter facientes essent erronei et blasphemi, vel forte haeretici. Sed tamen de multis illorum sermonum, licet nobis bene dicere quod essent falsi, si essent positi et recepti ad proprios sensus.

60. As Buridan observes in the seventh treatise of the *Summulae,* 'On Fallacies': "For someone who denies the authority of the wise and most reliable authors [*auctoritatem sapientium et probatissimorum*] or who speaks against them incurs the *meta* [i.e., the sophist's tactical goal] of implausibility, as was said earlier. Still, it is well known that not only poets but even the Bible, and all theologians, preachers, and philosophers often use figurative and parabolic expressions, not only according to their proper signification but even by attribution [i.e., with reference to their literal or primary signification]" (*S* 7.3.4: 520).

61. Courtenay 1984, 49.

62. *CUP* II, pp. 505–507, n. 1042 (the Latin text is excerpted in Courtenay 1984, n. 37):

> nulli magistri, baccalarii, vel scolares in artium facultate legentes Parisius audeant aliquam propositionem famosam illius actoris cujus librum legunt, dicere simpliciter esse falsam, vel esse falsam de virtute sermonis, si crediderint quod

actor ponendo illam habuerit verum intellectum; sed vel concedant eam, vel sensum verum dividant a sensu falso, quia pari ratione propositiones Bibliae absoluto sermone essent negande, quod est periculosum . . . nullus dicat simpliciter vel de virtute sermonis omnem propositionem esse falsam, que esset falsa secundum suppositionem personalem terminorum, eo quod iste error ducit ad priorem errorem, actores enim sepe utuntur aliis suppositionibus . . . nullus dicit propositionem nullam esse concedendam, si non sit vera in ejus sensu proprio, quia hoc dicere ducit ad predictos errores, quia Biblia et actores non semper sermonibus utuntur secundum proprios sensus eorum. Magis igitur oportet in affirmando vel negando sermones ad materiam subjectam attendere, quam ad proprietatem sermonis, disputatio namque ad proprietatem sermonis attendens nullam recipiens propositionem, preterque in sensu proprio, non est nisi sophistica disputatio. Disputationes dyalectice et doctrinales, que ad inquisitionem veritatis intendunt, modicam habent de nominibus sollicitudinem.

63. *QIP* 5: 145, ll. 818–36:

Nunc igitur propter modum loquendi consuetum ego dico, quod licet nobis uti sermonibus ad placitum, dum tamen non recipiamus eos secundum sensus falsos, ideo ad placitum et non proprie consuevimus per virtutem sermonis intelligere sensum eius proprium. Et sic cum dicimus propositionem esse veram de virtute sermonis, nos debemus intelligere per hoc, quod ipsa esset vera recipienti eam secundum sensum eius proprium; et cum dicimus propositionem esse falsam de virtute sermonis, debemus per hoc intelligere quod esset falsa recipienti eam secundum sensum proprium, licet simpliciter sit vera, quia recipimus eam secundum alium sensum, secundum quem est vera. Et si per talia verba nostra aliter intelligamus, male intelligimus. // Unde notandum est, quod eadem propositio vocalis potest esse mihi vera et tibi falsa, quoniam vocalis non est vera nisi designat mentalem veram. Unde ista propositio 'homo est species' posita a Porphyrio est mihi vera, quia recipio eam secundum suppositionem materialem et sic designat mihi mentalem et non falsam, sed veram in mente mea; sed forte est tibi falsa, quia non vis eam recipere nisi secundum sensum proprium, secundum quem designat tibi mentalem falsam.

I drop line 833 of Tatarzyński's edition, which repeats the previous line. Elsewhere Buridan makes the same point as regards different natural languages: "if it is written on the wall that a man is a donkey, then it is false for me, having this language, and it is true for you, assuming that you have some other language in which the term 'donkey' signifies precisely the same as what the term 'animal' signifies to us" (*S* 9.6, 5th conclusion: 932).

64. Otherwise, our language would consist of sophism sentences, which would undercut the possibility of language by, among other things, making communication impossible. Determinacy is prior to ambiguity.

65. Buridan's refusal to embark upon any systematic reform of ordinary language for logical purposes (though he sometimes advocates piecemeal reform, as we will see in the next section) is expressed early and often, e.g.:

But in the end we should note—since we can use names by convention [*ad placitum*], and many people commonly use this way of putting the matter—that with respect to every true proposition we say: 'It is so', and with respect to every false one we say: 'It is not so', and I do not intend to eliminate this way of speaking. But for the sake of brevity I may use it often intending by it not what it signifies on account of its primary imposition, but the diverse causes of truth and falsity assigned above for diverse propositions, as has been said. (*S* 9.2, 14th conclusion: 859)

Where two or more conventions are equally well established, Buridan usually indicates which one he prefers on pragmatic grounds. Thus, after presenting three descriptions of the fallacy of equivocation, he comments: "You may ask: 'Which one of these would you propose?' To this I reply that names name by convention; therefore, I do not reprove any of these ways of expressing the matter, but at the same time the third one seems to me to be most to the point" (*S* 7.3.2: 516).

66. The barrel hoop example was standard in discussions of the conventionality of spoken and written language. See William of Ockham, *Summa logicae* I.1; *Opera Philosophica* I: 9.

67. The *liber* example makes it easy to see why, in n. 6 above, Jacques de Vitry should have been so concerned with correct pronunciation. For the fallacy of accent in the Greek commentary tradition on Aristotle's *Sophistical Refutations,* see Ebbesen 1981a, 187–89.

68. The *loci classici* are Aristotle, *De Interpretatione* 1.16a3–8; Augustine, *De Trinitate* XV.10–11, *PL* 42, and *De Doctrina Christiana* II, 56–131; and Boethius, *Commentarii in librum Aristotelis 'Peri Hermeneias'* (both versions), Meiser 1877 and 1880. For further references and discussion, see Paul Vincent Spade, "The Semantics of Terms," *CHLMP,* 188–90. By the fourteenth-century, this acknowledgment had become the conventional—in fact, the unreflectively conventional—opening for discussions of signification in logic treatises.

69. Pinborg 1976, 76. The sentiment is echoed by Sten Ebbesen (1976, 146): whereas "his predecessors had paid lip-service to the often-repeated dictum '*voces sunt ad placitum*'," Buridan "takes it seriously." Ebbesen continues, noting that "Buridan's insistence that vocal language is arbitrary and that consequently investigation of it has no cognitive value takes him near to destroying traditional logic," and that Buridan "has burnt, or at any rate severely damaged, the bridges to grammar. Like many a modern logician he looks upon the linguists with a mixture of sympathy and disdain. Certainly, you may on occasion use an item or two from a theory that they have developed. But much of their talk is not particularly clever. And anyhow it is not logic." On my reading, this is true as regards any systematic connection between grammatical and logical doctrine—Buridan does not think that grammar is on a par with logic in this sense. However, as we saw above, he also treats grammar as the foundational discipline for logic in the sense that it is a practice whose rules make logic possible. From the perspective of the learning imparted from master to student in the arts curriculum, grammar and logic are continuous disciplines.

70. Among Buridan's predecessors, the thirteenth-century grammarian Pseudo-Kilwardby and the philosophers Roger Bacon and Robert Kilwardby were interested in the division of signs into the conventional and natural. Especially interesting are their analyses of interjection, a part of speech that appears to signify both naturally and conventionally at the same time. For discussion, see Rosier 1994, 85–94, and Ashworth 1999, 221–34.

71. *QDI* I.3: 16, ll. 4–23:

Dicendum est breviter quod cum sint propositiones orationes et termini mentales vocales vel scripti, Aristotiles in hoc libro solum fecit considerationem de
vocalibus propter hoc quod oportet disputationes in loyca uti. Et quia etiam determinare de natura et consideratione conceptuum pertinet ad librum De anima
vel ad librum Metaphysice, tunc restat loyco applicare voces conceptibus correspondentes ad arguendum debite et loquendum congrue. Ideo omne nomen de
quo hic agitur est vox. // Sed tu queres quomodo ille voces que sunt nomina et
verba, significant ad placitum: utrum ad placitum meum vel tuum. Dico quod
aliqua sunt nomina et verba significativa eorumdem et eodem modo uni toti
magne communitati, ut voces latine omnibus latinis et voces gallice omnibus
gallicis. Et non est in potestate mea vel tua auferre vel mutare huiusmodi significationem communem. Sed hoc fuit in potestate primi imponentis illud ydioma
vel primorum imponentium, qui ad placitum suum talibus vocibus tales significationes dederunt. Sed etiam adhuc multi inter se concordes possent fabricare
ad placitum unum ydioma quo inter se uterentur, sicud patet de illis qui loquuntur
inter se garganicum. Ymmo etiam ego tecum disputans vel te docens inpono voces
ad significandum ad placitum meum, dicendo: maior extremitas vocetur 'a' et
minor 'b' et conclusio 'c'. Possum enim aliter dicere, si michi placet.

72. Commenting on this same passage, Joël Biard observes, "the freedom which
the speaker has at his disposal in the case [of imposing signification at will] is opposed to the constraint represented by the linguistic community." The reason is clear:
"total arbitrariness is inconceivable where the function of language is essentially
communicative" (Biard 1989, 176, 178).

73. Klima, introduction to *S:* xlix. This is nicely illustrated by Buridan's *Summulae* discussion of local propositions, where, after presenting his own "general reason or
rule for the truth or falsity of temporal, local, and other propositions," he comments,
"Now this is a simple method. The other method, given by the author [i.e., Peter of
Spain], is complicated, for it requires a special account in each case" (*S* 1.7.8: 66).

74. See *S* 1.1.3: 8–9; *S* 9.2, 14th conclusion: 858–59.

75. See *S* 9.8, 2nd sophism: 956–58.

76. Buridan often points out that whereas the proximate object of scientific
knowledge is the conclusion of a demonstration, the remote object is the thing(s)
signified by the term(s) in that conclusion. See, e.g., *QIP* 1: 127, ll. 206–209; *TDUI:* 158,
ll. 14–34.

77. For Buridan, the categories represent divisions of language, not reality.
Thus, he argues that Porphyry did not introduce Aristotle's *Categories* as a piece of
prescriptive or speculative metaphysics, "but only to describe and distinguish [the cate-
gories] according to the different modes of predicating and to set forth their agreements and differences [*sed solum ea describere et distinguere secundum diversos modos
praedicandi et assignare inter ea convenientias et differentias*]" (*QIP* 14: 187, ll. 2356–57).
The actual number of the categories is contingent, relative to the circumstances of
inquiry (*QIP* 14: 183, ll. 2210–11).

78. See Aristotle, *Metaphysics* II.1: 993b30 and Buridan, *QDA₃* III.12: 132. Buridan
adds the parenthetical remark: "It is usually said that this is one difference between
divine and human knowledge, since divine knowledge is the cause of all other things,

whereas human knowledge is caused by other things. And it is like this for divine and human willing as well [*Solet dici quod haec est una differentia inter scientiam divinam et scientiam humanam, quia scientia divina est causa aliarum rerum omnium, et scientia humana est causata ab aliis rebus. Et ita etiam est de velle dei et hominis*]."

79. *QM* II.1: 8vb: "*nihil aliud est comprehensio veritatis quam comprehensio propositionis verae.*" The same point is made very clearly in the eighth treatise of the *Summulae*: "every definition is given for the sake of making the definitum known, and not for the sake of making it known to God, angels, or inanimate natures but to us, and it would not make it known unless it were itself better known to us" (*S* 8.2.6: 660).

80. "In another way, the comprehension of truth is taken for the adhesion or assent by which we assent or adhere to a true proposition [*Alio modo comprehensio veritatis accipitur pro adhaesione vel assensum quo assentimus vel adhaeremus propositioni verae*]" (*QM* II.1: 8vb)—which adhesion or assent is a function of the will, not the intellect. Elsewhere, Buridan says that he fixes on propositions as our means of grasping truth because only propositions, not mere concepts or terms, can solicit our assent or dissent (*QDA₃* III.12: 137). For Buridan's account of propositional attitudes in the face of "weak judgment [*iudicium debilis*]," see section 2 of chapter 15 below. For Buridan on the psychology of assent, see my "On Certitude" in Thijssen and Zupko 2001, 165–82.

81. What if Buridanian naturalism yields a philosophy no more empirically well founded than Isidorean etymology? I find such worries premature. The judgment that Isidore's system is unreliable was arrived at empirically and over the long haul, despite the fact that some of his derivations are correct, and independently of questions about the soundness of his naturalistic intuitions. Likewise, it would be wrong to judge the success of Buridan's philosophical program—its capacity to "speak the truth (*veriloquium*)," as he would put it—on anything but an a posteriori basis.

82. In this way, Buridan's sense of the natural is different from the grammarians' traditional distinction between natural and conventional signs. A sign is natural not because it comes to be without the intellect or will, but because it results from a process naturally suited or ordained to produce it, including (in the case of human beings) the deliberate activity of the intellect and will. In this sense, the contrast concept would not be 'conventional', but 'miraculous'.

83. *QE* 8, 3.1: 34, ll. 55–57: "*Termini mentales sunt significativi naturaliter. Alii vero termini sunt significativi ad placitum ex impositione voluntaria primi instituentis.*"

84. I speak here of personal supposition, i.e., where the term in question stands for what it signifies, rather than material supposition, where its reference is mediated by other concepts, as in the case of figurative discourse. For discussion, see chapter 4 below.

85. Therefore, "similar intentions do not thus produce similar or dissimilar suppositions or appellations by convention, except when it comes to material supposition" (*S* 7.3.10: 547). For discussion, see chapter 4.

86. *QDI* II.11: 100, ll. 30–33 (cf. *QDA₃* I.6: 129vb; *QDA₃* III.8: 73): "*Sed iste sunt mentales quia passiones idest conceptus anime sunt naturales similitudines harum rerum. Et voces non sunt significative earum, nisi secundum impositionem voluntariam ad placitum et mediantibus intentionibus anime.*" For discussion, see section 3 of chapter 13 below.

87. Though the converse is true, of course, in the process by which concepts are first formed.

88. For discussion, see chapters 12–13 below.

89. Again, the problem is that as empirical creatures, we cannot discern the formal identity (or difference) of two substances as such, but must always infer it "by means of accidental concepts" (*S* 8.2.4: 652). 'Substance' should be understood as referring to terms in the category of substance, not to things, since "there are no substances if by 'substances' we mean things subsisting per se, outside the activity of the soul, in the way horses or donkeys exist [*non sunt substantiae capiendo 'substantias' pro rebus per se subsistentibus praeter opus animae, sicut sunt equi vel asini*]" (*QM* VII.18: 53rb). Accordingly, "we should not understand by 'what it is' a quidditative or a causal definition . . . but by 'what it is' we should understand what it is that is meant [*dicitur*] by the name" (*S* 8.3.5: 677). It is the causal definition that the philosopher seeks, beyond the merely nominal definition assumed by the grammarian and by the logician, and the causal definition concerns the intrinsic causes of a thing, in the way that a whole is its parts (*QM* VII.21: 54vb–55ra; see also chapter 10 below). For discussion of the role of definitions in the science of psychology, see chapter 13 below and Gyula Klima, "Buridan's Theory of Definitions in His Scientific Practice" in Thijssen and Zupko 2001, 29–47.

90. *QM* VII.8: 46rb: "*accipiendo similitudinem large vel improprie non pro eadem qualitate, immo solum pro quadam appropriata convenientia agentis ad effectum.*" Buridan explicitly recognizes this as a departure from Aristotle: "I propose a different conclusion than the one Aristotle intends [*aliam conclusionem pono quam Aristotles intendit*]." In a related passage in his psychology, he asserts that no generic or specific similarity between cause and effect suffices to explain sense perception. His argument consists of the observation that in the case of vision, "the species of colors in the eye and the representation of color in the imagination or intellect do not seem to be of the same or of a similar nature, or belong to the same kind and species [*species colorum in oculo et representatio coloris in fantasia vel intellectu non videntur esse eiusdem vel consimilis nature, nec eiusdem rationis et speciei*]" (*QDA₃* II.18: 261; cf. *QDA₃* II.6: 77; for discussion, see chapter 12 below).

91. On this point, see Klima, introduction to *S:* xxxvi–vii and Klima 1988, 12–17.

NOTES TO CHAPTER 2

1. *QIP* 1: 126–27, ll. 176–80: "*Logica docens vocatur ex eo, quod docet quomodo et ex quibus constituendae sunt argumentationes tam demonstrativae quam dialecticae vel aliae. Logica vero utens vocatur, quia utitur argumentationibus ad probandum apparenter vel non apparenter aliquam conclusionem, in quacumque materia hoc fuerit.*"

2. *QIP* 2: 132–33, ll. 372–78: "*scientia speculativa non docet nos agere ea, de quibus ipsa considerat vel speculatur, nec docet nos speculationem tali modo. . . . Sed scientia practica proponit hoc esse faciendum vel ipsum esse taliter a nobis faciendum.*" Buridan thus locates himself (along with Albert the Great and William of Ockham) on one side of the medieval debate about the nature of logic as a *scientia*, or body of knowledge, against thinkers such as Radulphus Brito, who calls logic "speculative

(though not primarily speculative)" because it is aimed at the knowledge of "logical entities [*entia logicalia*]," rather than at pursuing the good, or some other extramental activity. For discussion, see Ebbesen 1991. See also n. 25 below.

3. Aristotle, *Nicomachean Ethics* VI.1.1139a11–16.

4. *QIP* 2: 130, ll. 292–302:

Dico igitur quod 'praxis' Graece idem est quod 'operatio' Latine, non tamen quaecumque operatio, sed operatio quae fit per intellectum et voluntatem libere. Unde si in nobis per nervos fiat nutritio, augmentatio, motus cordis vel pulmonis somnus vel vigilia, tales operationes non vocantur 'praxes' quia fiunt in nobis modo naturali, non voluntarie, nec de illis ut sic est scientia practica, sed speculative. Sed cum operabilia a nobis fuerint in potestate nostrae liberae voluntatis, scilicet quod faciamus ea vel non faciamus et quod sic vel aliter faciamus ea, tunc habitus docens nos quando et ubi debemus illa facere vel dimittere, et quomodo melius debeamus illa facere, et sic de aliis circumstantiis; talis habitus est practicus.

5. Buridan here follows a long tradition, going back to Boethius's division of the sciences in *De Trinitate,* of separating logic and grammar from the speculative sciences of metaphysics, mathematics, and physics. See also *QIP* 1: 126 and *QM* VI.2.

6. *QIP* 2: 132, ll. 345–50: "*Et ita logicus quantum esset ex parte logicae non curaret aliud nisi quod argumentum esset bonum ad conclusionem probandam, sive hoc esset pro iustitia servanda, sive hoc esset ad iniustificandum et destruendum bonum hominem vel ad auferendum sibi bona sua, sicut saepe arguunt advocati et conciliarii divitum hominum contra homines bonos et paupers.*"

7. "For thus it is said in *Nicomachean Ethics* VI that the end of prudence is to live well. For the prudent person intends the good in all human actions, and considers circumstances in order to do things in such a way that it benefits you and others as regards the welfare of the soul and the happy life [*Sic enim dicitur sexto Ethicorum, quod finis prudentiae est bene vivere. Bonum enim in omnibus actibus humanis prudens intendit et considerat circumstantias ut taliter agat, quod hoc prosit tibi et aliis ad salutem animarum et ad felicem vitam*]" (*QIP* 2: 131, ll. 335–38; cf. *Nicomachean Ethics* VI.5.1140a24–b4). In the passage referred to by Buridan, Aristotle points out that prudence is "not an art because action and making are different kinds of thing."

8. Thus, Buridan takes Isidore of Seville's traditional definition of logic as "the art of distinguishing truth from falsehood" a step further, claiming that "the aim of logic is not only the truth, or knowing the truth, but also constructing, or knowing how to construct, the patterns of argumentation which it considers [*finis logicae non solum est veritas vel scire veritatem, immo est facere vel scire facere argumentationes, de quibus ipsa considerat*]" (*QIP* 2: 132, ll. 364–66; cf. Isidore, *Etymologiae* 2.22.1). Buridan was probably influenced here by Albert the Great, who advanced the view that *argumentatio* was the principal subject of logic (see Marmo 1990, 161–63). Albert pointed out that unlike other sciences, logic has for its subject things which cannot exist without human activity, "for it aims at the production by its human possessors of pieces of reasoning (*argumentationes*)" (Ebbesen 1991, 269). I translate the Latin term '*argumentatio*' as 'patterns of argumentation' or 'argumentation', though Buridan understands it to include all of the integral and formal aspects of arguments: "an *argumentation* [as opposed to an argument] is not only that middle term [that proves the

conclusion], but rather a whole expression composed of the middle term and the extremities, which are contained in the premises and the conclusion" (*S* 6.1.2: 392).

9. Boethius, *De topicis differentiis* 1174D (Stump 1978, 30): "argumentation . . . is the unfolding of the argument by means of discourse [*oratio*]." Commenting on this passage, Sten Ebbesen remarks: "Wherever Boethius learned this distinction, I have little doubt that it is based on the Stoic distinction between incorporeals with a -μα name and corporeal entities with -σις name," e.g., the incorporeal '*pragma*' vs. the corporeal '*praxis*' ("Where Were the Stoics in the Late Middle Ages?" in Strange and Zupko, forthcoming).

10. *QIP* 1: 126, ll. 166–67: "*in quolibet libro Logicae demonstrantur multae conclusiones per sua principia propria et necessaria*"; *QM* IV.4: 15va: "*dialectica est communis et considerat de omnibus et sic universaliter est de ente.*"

11. Buridan includes "normative grammar [*grammatica regularis*]" among the arts or sciences that cannot be satisfactorily acquired without logic, but he is careful to distinguish this from "positive grammar [*grammatica positiva*]," which has to be learned first because it enables the master "to communicate with the disciple" (*S* 1.1.1: 6; see section 1 of chapter 1 above). Again, reasoning is seen as the perfection or completion of speaking.

12. "By reason of this generality, which it shares with metaphysics, [logic] has access to disputations that concern not only the conclusions but even the principles of all sciences" (*S* 1.1.1: 6). The idea that "the verbal universality of logic mirrors the real universality of metaphysics" goes back to Albert the Great, for whom, see Jordan 1992, 486.

13. *QM* IV.4: 15va: "*Et si quaeratur ubi traditur illa scientia dialectica, dicitur quod in libro Metaphysicae quantum ad conclusiones metaphysicales, et in libro Posteriorum quantum ad conclusiones posterioristicas, in libro Physicorum quantum ad conclusiones physicales, et sic de aliis. Unde in illis libris solent poni saepe et adduci rationes probabiles et disputative antequam demonstrative terminetur propositum.*"

14. Buridan says that *logica utens* "certainly is a science insofar as it uses demonstrative argumentation, whatever the subject matter" (*QIP* 1: 127, ll. 199–200).

15. McKeon notes that "Varro [116–27 B.C.E.] enumerated nine such arts which became, with the elimination of architecture and medicine, the seven medieval arts," and further, that "Isidore of Seville's *Origins* or *Etymologies* treats the seven liberal arts in the first three of twenty books before going on to the etymologies and natures of other things, including an alphabetically ordered dictionary in Book X" ("The Organization of Sciences and the Relations of Cultures in the Twelfth and Thirteenth Centuries," in Murdoch and Sylla 1975, 153).

16. Aristotle, *Metaphysics* VI.1.1026a6–19; XI.7.1064b1–3; *Physics* II.2.193b22–36. The division of speculative philosophy into mathematics, natural philosophy, and theology is also found in Boethius (*De Trinitate* II: *PL* 64, 1250A–B) and Avicenna (*Liber de philosophia prima*). The classification of *theologia* or *divina scientia* as a theoretical science traces its origins to Boethius, Cassiodorus, and Isidore of Seville (Weijers 1987 [1989], 49). It is worth noting that the Aristotelian origin of these distinctions was not evident to everyone, since some authors, e.g., attributed the distinction between speculative and practical knowledge to Avicenna.

17. Cf. also Albert the Great, whose influential position on the hierarchy of the sciences is discussed in Jordan 1992.

18. Charles Lohr details a thirteenth-century student's guide that does just this in "The Medieval Interpretation of Aristotle" in *CHLMP*, 84–86. Costantino Marmo notes that this same position, defended by Thomas Aquinas (*Expositio super librum Boethii De Trinitate*, q. 5, a. 1), "appears rather traditional: the subordination of the *quadrivium* to *mathematica*, conceived as part of theoretical philosophy along with *theologia* and *physica*, was merely a commonplace in the thirteenth century as well as in the twelfth century" (1990, 147). See also Weijers 1987 [1989], 47.

19. This is because it is only in his *Commentary on Aristotle's Physics* that Thomas says that the intermediate sciences have more in common with physics than with mathematics—an interpretation that seems to have been occasioned by a mistranslation of Aristotle at *Physics* II.2.194a7–8. Thomas's own view is actually the same as Averroes's, viz., that the middle sciences are closer to mathematics than to physics. See Thomas Aquinas, *Expositio super librum Boethii De Trinitate*, q. 5, a. 3, ad 6; *Summa Theologiae* IIaIIae, q. 9, a. 2, ad 3; *In II Physicorum*, lect. 3, n. 8. For discussion, see Maurer 1986, 43, n. 22.

20. Cf. Averroes, *In II Physicorum* 2, c. 71.

21. See n. 11 above.

22. QR I.1: "*nihil prohibet eam esse scientiam quantum ad multas conclusiones ipsius prout scientia proprie agitur primo Posteriorum, quia est habitus conclusionis necessarie demonstratae per sua principia.*" I am grateful to Bernadette Preben-Hansen for permission to consult her working edition of this text.

23. Buridan expresses here what had become the standard late medieval view of rhetoric. According to Costantino Marmo, "in the 1270s the classification of logic underwent a subtle modification which made rhetoric shift from its traditional place beside logic and grammar in the *trivium* to a position subordinate to logic, viz., as a part of Aristotle's *Organon*, or, in some cases, as a part of dialectic together with poetics" (1990, 146).

24. Biard 1998, 142. Weijers notes that in earlier authors, the term '*adminiculativa*' was usually opposed to '*principalis*' to indicate the basic distinction between primary and auxiliary sciences (1987 [1989], 43–44). See also McKeon 1942, 29–30. Cf. Buridan: "rhetorical argumentation is comprised within dialectical, whence rhetoric and poetic are parts of dialectic, as Aristotle says" (*S* 7.1.4: 499).

25. QNE Proemium: 2rb: "*Cum igitur non nisi secundum moralia sit innatus appetitus alienare iudicium rationis.*" There are interesting similarities between Buridan's views on the hierarchy of the sciences (and the place of rhetoric in it) and those of the earlier Parisian arts master, Radulphus Brito (c. 1270–1320), for whom, see Marmo 1990, 185–87.

26. Of course, in reconstructing Buridan's views on the place of logic in the division of the sciences here I do not mean to suggest that his remarks are without precedent. Far from it—Buridan was joining a discussion that was already at least half a century old, following the eclipse of the *trivium* in the thirteenth century. For the thirteenth-century debate, see Lafleur 1988 and Marmo 1990.

27. Subordination, of course, yields greater specialization. Thus, Buridan notes in his commentary on Aristotle's *De motibus animalium* that in this book, "we descend to the different species of motion in particular, e.g., to the fact that some animals fly, others swim, and so on [*in libro autem De animalibus descenditur specialiter*

ad diversitates species [species/speciales] motuum, ut quod quedam animalia volant, alia natant, et cetera]" (DMA I: 535).

28. *QDI* I.1: 6, ll. 10–15 (cf. *S* 4.3.2: 255–58): "*Subiectum enim proprium in hac scientia assignandum est 'enuntiatio', ita quod 'enuntiatio' non capiatur personaliter sed materialiter, quia hic determinatur principaliter de ea et de suis partibus, tam subiectivis quam integralibus et de suis passionibus, ut de oppositionibus et de equipollentis. Et omnino ibi consideratur de illo quod per se habet attributionem ad enuntiationem.*"

29. *QDI* I.3: 16, ll. 4–7: "*cum sint propositiones orationes et termini mentales vocales vel scripti, Aristotiles in hoc libro solum fecit considerationem de vocalibus propter hoc quod oportet disputationes in loyca uti.*" To the objection that we can form many propositions in our minds without giving them vocal expression, Buridan replies, "we speak here only of names that can occur in spoken propositions [*non loquitur hic nisi de nominibus que possent poni in propositionibus vocalibus*]." If there were a science of mental propositions, he says, it would be proper to psychology or metaphysics, not logic.

30. There is never any question of the conventionality of logical discourse in Buridan: "Note also that supposition is not called 'personal' because it is for persons, nor is it called 'material' because it is for matter. Therefore these names are being used here rather improperly. . . . But this is how logicians have become accustomed to use these names, and this they were allowed to do, for names are significative by convention [*ad placitum*]" (*S* 4.3.2: 253; cf. Ockham, *Summa logicae* I.64; *Opera Philosophica* I: 197). See also *QAnPr* I.1: "when I ask whether there is a science of the syllogism *simpliciter*, or whether in the *Prior Analytics* there is a determination about the syllogism *simpliciter*, you must not understand it such that the word, '*simpliciter*', is the determination of a syllogism, but rather, it must be understood such that it is a determination designating our way of speaking [*quando dico 'utrum de syllogismo simpliciter sit scientia', vel quando dico 'in libro Priorum determinatur de syllogismo simpliciter', vos non debetis intelligere quod haec dictio 'simpliciter' sit determinatio syllogismi; immo debet intelligi quod sit determinatio designans modum nostrum loquendi*]."

31. Because of exigencies of the question at hand, Buridan sometimes does not fully expand the range of objects of knowledge. There is always, at a minimum, both the proposition as the primary object and the things signified by the terms in that proposition as secondary objects (as in *QM* IV.3: 34va). But sometimes he mentions only the triad of propositions, terms, and things (*QIP* 1: 127–28; *QAnPr* I.1; *QAnPo* I.1; *QGC* I.1: 96va).

32. *QAnPo* I.1: "*et ita dicimus nos habere scientiam de animalibus et lapidibus, de deo et intelligentiis, et sic de aliis.*" Well aware that demonstrations meeting the formal requirements of Aristotle's *Posterior Analytics* will be few and far between—at least in our present epistemic circumstances—Buridan uses the second way of speaking about objects of knowledge to admit a wider range of knowable objects: "only in the first way is there knowledge of propositions, and not of all propositions, but only of those which are true and necessary, or at least those which are true for the most part. . . . In the second way, there is certainly knowledge of all things in the world . . . but not knowledge like that of a demonstrable conclusion [*primo modo solum est scientia de propositionibus et non de omnibus, sed solum de veris et necessaries vel saltem de illis quae ut in pluribus sunt verae. . . . Secundo modo est bene scientia de omnibus rebus mundi . . . sed non est sic de illis scientia tanquam de conclusionibus demonstrabilibus*]" (*QM* VI.3:

34va–vb). For discussion, see chapters 12–13 below and Eileen Serene, "Demonstrative Science" in *CHLMP*, 515–17.

33. See *QP* I.1: 2va: "it is obvious that we seek to have knowledge in the first three ways only to have knowledge in the fourth, for the artificer does not care to have knowledge of propositions and terms unless because he believes that on account of this, he will have knowledge of the things about which he intends to act and procure what is useful for himself [*Immo manifestum est quod non quaerimus habere scientiam de tribus priis modis nisi propter habere scientiam isto quarto modo, non enim curaret artifex de propositionibus et terminis nisi propter hoc crederet habere scientiam de rebus circa quas intendit agere et sibi utilia procurare*]."

34. *QAnPr* I.1: "*Et tunc dicendum est quod etiam isto modo habemus scientiam de syllogismis in isto libro Priorum: quia saepe termini ex quibus conclusiones hujus libri componuntur significant syllogismos et supponunt pro syllogismis.*"

35. *QAnPo* I.1:

Quia isti termini 'ens', 'unum', 'idem', 'diversum', 'causa', 'causatum', 'corruptibile', 'incorruptibile', et sic de multis aliis, significant omnes res mundi, et tamen ex istis terminis possunt componi multae conclusiones demonstrabiles, tam in physica quam in metaphysica. Igitur de omnibus rebus habetur scientia tam per physicam quam per metaphysicam, et, per consequens, de demonstrationibus. . . . Ultima conclusio est, descendens ad scientiam libri Posteriorum, quod de isto termino 'demonstratio' habetur scientia tertio modo, scilicet tamquam de termino ex quo conclusio demonstrata componitur. Et haec scientia habetur et traditur in isto libro Posteriorum, et non in Physica nec in Metaphysica. Multae enim conclusiones demonstrantur in isto libro quae componuntur ex isto termino 'demonstratio' tamquam ex subjecto propositionis; verbi gratia, quod demonstratio est ex veris vel quod demonstratio est ex necessariis.

36. Buridan's view of logic as a science of discourse reprises that of his Parisian predecessor Peter Abelard, who defends his own sermocinalism in characteristic fashion by viciously attacking the opposing view of logic as a *scientia rationalis*: "When we say, 'If it is a man, it is an animal,' if we refer to the sequence of our conceptions of the [atomic] propositions [included therein], as we would if we were concerned with the concepts themselves, then there is no truth to the consequence, since the one conception might subsist [in our minds] entirely without the other" (de Rijk 1970, 154; for discussion, see Kretzmann 1967, 370–71). However, despite (or perhaps because of) Abelard's criticisms, the Avicennian idea that logic is a *scientia rationalis*, concerned with second intentions, or concepts of concepts (in the way that 'species' signifies the concept of 'man'), became the majority view in the later Middle Ages and was variously defended by Thomas Aquinas, Henry of Ghent, Duns Scotus, Peter Aureol, William of Ockham, and Walter Chatton. The only thinkers who seem to have regarded logic as a *scientia realis* (though in quite different ways) were the *modistae* and Buridan's older contemporary, Walter Burley, who held that logical intentions are features of extramental reality. For an overview of the debate, see Knudsen, "Intentions and Impositions" in *CHLMP*, 479–95, and Ashworth, "Logic, Medieval" in the *Routledge Encyclopedia of Philosophy*, vol. 5, 750–51. For the history and evolution of the terminology—e.g., 'sermocinalis', which was unknown in antiquity—see Weijers 1987 [1989].

37. See Pinborg 1976, 76 and Ebbesen 1976, 146. For the details, see n. 69 of chapter 1 above.

38. Spade 1998, 407.

39. Perhaps that is why in the vast majority of cases Buridan prefers to speak of concepts as "conceiving" rather than as "signifying," though, as Paul Vincent Spade points out ("The Semantics of Terms" in *CHLMP*, 190, n. 9; cf. Biard 1989, 172), there are exceptions. Joël Biard contends that such anomalies should not make us lose sight of the fact that Buridan's logic, unlike Ockham's, focuses on spoken discourse: "To be sure, John Buridan sometimes speaks as if the domain of concepts were structured like a language. In fact, he speaks of mental propositions (signified by spoken propositions), and considers the agreement between concept and thing by means of supposition; in the same way, he recognizes that a concept is universal insofar as it signifies a multiplicity of singular things. But in the sophisms, when he considers the relations between word, concept, and thing, or distinguishes the different kinds of supposition, he understands language as in the first instance a collection of spoken propositions, [thereby] standing the Ockhamist hierarchy on its head (at the very least)... John Buridan's domain of study is fundamentally spoken language [*Le domaine d'étude de Jean Buridan est fondamentalement le langage parlé*]" (Biard 1989, 199). See also section 3 of chapter 1 above.

40. Buridan does not even consider Burley's suggestion that logic is a *scientia realis* concerned with the logical attributes of real things. No reason for this is apparent. It might be that he was concerned only to defend his own minority position against the conceptualists. Alternatively, he might not have known of Burley's work, or that the realist position was actually defended by someone other than the *modistae*.

41. See Kretzmann 1967, 374: "For one thing, as it had been presented by Priscian and Donatus, grammar was simply a set of observations about correct constructions without any attempt at explanation of the correctness, but only knowledge 'by causes' qualified as scientific. For another, even Peter Helias ... had maintained that there were as many grammars as there were languages; but a unified subject matter was a prerequisite of a science."

42. Siger puts it this way: "grammar is the *scientia sermocinalis*, which considers discourse and its properties [*passiones*] in general for the purpose of expressing principally concepts of the mind by means of interconnected discourse." The key claim, however, is that the "modes of being, or properties of things ... precede a mode of understanding as a cause precedes an effect," and that the same relation holds between concepts and significant utterances, and thus, by transitivity of causality, between modes of being and modes of signifying (*Summa Modorum Significandi*, ed. G. Wallerand, 93–94; tr. in Kretzmann 1967, 374–75). In what follows, I do not intend to go beyond Buridan's own remarks about the *modistae*, whose doctrines and writings are now much better understood by scholars. For discussion, see Rosier 1983, Rosier-Catach 1999, Marmo 1994, 1995, and 1999.

43. Spade 1988b, 187; 1998, 403. Although the influence of the Parisian *modistae* had waned by the 1320s, there continued to be pockets of resistance elsewhere. The heart of the movement was Erfurt, and the doctrine was still alive and well enough there to occasion "a ferocious attack on the existence of the *modi significandi*" by John Aurifaber in a public disputation around 1330 (Pinborg 1975, 287). Pinborg also sug-

gests that Buridan was the first to use Peter of Spain's *Summulae Logicales* as a logic text at the University of Paris, perhaps because it included a short treatise on the doctrine of supposition, one of the most useful devices in terminist logic (1976, 72). Be that as it may, Buridan evidently found Peter's treatment inadequate in numerous places, as we shall see.

44. I am indebted for this observation to Gyula Klima. See *S* 8.3.5: 675, n. 112.

45. The terminology was standard: "'doctrine' and 'discipline' are truly said to be relational terms because their corresponding concrete terms, viz., 'teacher' and 'student', are truly said to be relative to each other. For this reason, 'doctrine' and 'discipline' have a connotation beyond the name 'knowledge', viz., their being 'from the teacher' and 'in the student' [*doctrina et disciplina vere dicuntur ad aliquid, quia concretum eorum, scilicet doctor et discipulus, vere dicuntur relative ad invicem; unde doctrina et disciplina addunt connotationem super hoc nomen 'scientia', scilicet esse a doctore et esse in discipulo*]" (*QC* 14: 104, ll. 119–23; cf. *S* 3.5.10: 192).

46. *QIP* 1: 127, ll. 195–97: "*Et sic manifestum est quod logica docens, quam tradit Aristoteles in libris suis logicalibus, est vere scientia de argumentationibus tam dialecticis, sophisticis quam demonstrativis.*"

47. *QDI* I.1: 6, l. 19–7, l. 3:

In scientia autem libri Predicamentorum subiectum proprium assignari potest iste terminus vel ista oratio. . . . Deinde in libro Priorum subiectum proprium ponendum est iste terminus 'argumentatio'. Non tamen nisi secundum rationem restrictam, scilicet ea ratione solum qua dicitur illative, et non secundum rationem communem ad argumentationem dyalecticam et demonstrativam. // In totali autem loyca subiectum ponitur iste terminus 'argumentatio' sive tali vel alia restrictione. In libro Posteriorum argumentatio demonstrativa vel demonstratio, quod idem est. In libro Topicorum argumentatio dyalectica. In libro Elencorum argumentatio sophistica. In libro Retorice argumentatio rethorica. In libro Poetice argumentatio poetica. Que de eo dicitur 'poetica' quia fit ex quibusdam allicientibus animam ad audiendum et credendum, non ex natura vel circumstantiis factorum vel faciendorum inferendorum, sed ex admiratione verborum non communiter consuetorum vel ex occultatione sententiarum sub parabolis vel ex extraneis similitudinibus, aliquando etiam fictis non possibilibus. Admiratio enim allicit valde quia est delectabilis, sicut habetur primo Rethorice.

48. De Rijk 1962, 14–15; Kretzmann 1967, 371.

49. For discussion, see Black 1990.

50. Several versions survive of Buridan's *expositiones* and *quaestiones* on Porphyry's *Isagoge* and Aristotle's *Categories, De Interpretatione,* and *Prior* and *Posterior Analytics.* Buridan apparently wrote only a set of *quaestiones* on the *Topics* and *Sophistical Refutations.* See Michael 1985, 455–99.

51. Here we must remember that the arts curricula of the day prescribed the logical works of Aristotle as fulfilling the dialectical mandate of the *trivium.* That is, Aristotle's *Categories* (including the *Isagoge*), *De Interpretatione, Prior* and *Posterior Analytics, Topics,* and *Sophistical Refutations* were the books every arts master was supposed to teach in his lectures, usually in that order. See Pinborg, "Medieval Philosophical

Literature" in *CHLMP,* 17–19. For discussion of how Buridan's commentaries were actually produced, see Flüeler 1999.

52. This is not to say that Buridan intended to keep the practical and theoretical aspects of logic separate, so that never the twain shall meet. He helps himself to the library of logical *scientia* on a number of occasions in the *Summulae.* For example, in his fourth-treatise discussion of the rule that "no oblique name can in itself be a subject or predicate," he notes that many people would reject this rule. He then gives a defense of the rule set out in *quaestio* format, with his opponents' arguments given first, followed by his own view and arguments for it, and finally, his responses to the opponents' arguments. The rationale for using the *quaestio* format in a practical textbook becomes clear as he begins his defense of the rule: "I sufficiently proved [the rule] in q. 6 of bk. 1 of [my question-commentary on] *De Interpretatione.* I now shall repeat here some of the arguments I presented there" (*S* 4.2.6: 241; cf. *QDI* I.6: 24–31).

53. King 1985, xi.

54. Leaving aside Buridan's lengthy commentary and the numerous minor enhancements he makes to Peter's text *passim,* the major changes are as follows: (1) replacing the chapter on modal propositions in the first treatise with a newer and much expanded version, thereby increasing the entire length of the treatise by a third; (2) in the second treatise on predicables, providing a "more suitable" text for the seventh chapter on the comparative features of predicables (Peter's text mistakenly includes a discussion of univocal and equivocal predication at this point, material that strictly speaking belongs to, and is essentially repeated at the beginning of, the third treatise on categories—see de Rijk 1972, xciii); (3) replacing the fourth treatise on supposition with a brand new treatise on the same subject; (4) adding sections on modal syllogisms and the powers of syllogisms to the fifth treatise on syllogisms (Peter's fourth treatise), thereby tripling its length; and (5) adding two new treatises, an eighth on demonstrations and a ninth on sophisms. See Pinborg 1976, 74 and Boehner 1952, 83–84.

55. Scott 1966, 1–2; Pinborg 1976, 71. Peter's original *Summulae* continued to be successful, however, even in the wake of Buridan's commentary. For this, and for the question of the true identity of its author, see d'Ors 1997 and 2001.

56. Some manuscripts of the *Summulae* leave out the ninth treatise on sophisms, and there is evidence that Buridan himself thought of it as a quasi-independent treatise because he sometimes omitted it from his lectures. The English translation of the *Summulae* does include it (correctly, in my view), although the critical edition is based on manuscripts which omit it: "the ninth [treatise] will concern sophistic exercises [*practica sophismatum*]—but in this lecture-series I do not include the reading of this latter treatise along with the reading of the other eight treatises" (*S* 1.1.1: 5). The point is that even in the manuscripts of omission, Buridan counts the work on sophisms as the ninth treatise of the *Summulae.*

57. Part of the problem here is that because Buridan worked in a tradition governed by authoritative texts, many of his most original contributions are developed in response to specific problems raised by those texts. The result is that innovation occurs by means of supplementation, with the traditional account gradually transformed by attrition. For example, Buridan discusses modal syllogistic in four different works: *S, QDI, QAnPr,* and *TC* (see Knuuttila 1991, 484). He does not author an independent treatise on modal syllogisms, since to do so would be tantamount to asserting that Aristotle's account is mistaken rather than merely incomplete or imperfect. Where we

do have examples of independent treatises (e.g., *TC, TDUI*), they concern topics merely introduced by Aristotle, rather than given any authoritative treatment.

58. See chapter 1 above concerning the change in teaching styles necessitated by increasing enrollments at the University of Paris. By the first half of the fourteenth century, the numbers of matriculating students had reached an all-time high, and was diminished only by the Black Death at mid-century.

59. As we shall see, the *Summulae* is unique in the Buridanian corpus in this regard. Buridan's voluminous commentaries all inherit the general structure of the particular works to which they are addressed, so that there are, e.g., eight books of Buridan's question commentary on the *Physics* corresponding to the eight books of Aristotle's *Physics* (if a book from the source text was not "read," or commented upon—e.g., Books III and XI of Aristotle's *Metaphysics*—this fact is noted in the text of the commentary). But beneath that, Buridan's commentaries are organized much more loosely around pertinent lemmata in the case of *expositiones* and various problems inspired by the lemmata in the case of *quaestiones*. His independent, 'polemical' treatises are all short works aimed at articulating and refuting the views of certain opponents. For a comparison of the structures of Thomas Aquinas's and Buridan's *Quaestiones* on Aristotle's *Physics*, see Lang 1992, 164–71.

60. I here depart from Klima's translation, which leaves '*loci*' as an untranslated term.

61. The information in this table is derived from de Rijk 1972, lxxxviii–xcv.

62. See Kretzmann 1967, 372: "By the middle of the fourteenth century only signification and supposition were regularly recognized as properties of terms, and throughout the history of the *logica moderna* it was the supposition (*suppositio*) of terms on which the inquiry centered." See also Scott 1966, 29: "The theory of supposition is the core of terminist logic."

63. See de Rijk 1972, lxxxviii–xcv. The variety of orderings found in manuscripts not reflecting the Avignon order is further evidence that Peter's text was written when the various aspects of the *logica moderna* had not yet been fully developed.

64. Buridan understands his placing of the treatises based on the *logica vetus* or *ars vetus* before those based on the *logica nova* or *ars nova* to exemplify the natural order in which one should study logic. Accordingly, the terminology is explained in terms of logical, rather than historical, priority: "But why is one logic called the '*ars vetus*' and the other the '*ars nova*'? It can be reasonably replied that the matter of a thing is temporally prior to the thing [itself], which is made from it. And that which is prior in time is called 'older'. Now the terms and propositions which are the concern of the *Categories* and *De Interpretatione* are the material parts from which argumentations are constructed. Therefore, they can be called 'old' with respect to the whole of argumentation, and for this reason, the part of logic which treats of them is called the '*logica vetus*' [*Quare autem haec dicitur Vetus Ars et illa Nova? Potest dici rationabiliter, quod materia rei praecedit tempore rem quae fit ex ea, et illud quod praecedit tempore dicitur antiquius. Modo termini et enuntiationes, de quibus agitur in libris Praedicamentorum et Peri Hermeneias, sunt partes materiales ex quibus fiunt argumentationes. Ideo possunt dici Veteres in respectu totalis argumentationis et ob hoc pars logicae tractans de eis vocata est Logica Vetus*]" (*QIP* Proemium: 123, ll. 69–75).

65. De Rijk 1972, lv–lxi. De Rijk's dating is based on the traditional attribution of Peter's *Summulae* to Pope John XXI (d. 1277). It could have been written even

earlier if, as seems likely, Peter and John were not the same person. See d'Ors 1997 and 2001.

66. See de Rijk and Spruyt 1992, 9. Perhaps because so much attention is given to it in the twelfth treatise of the *Summulae*, the syncategorematic word 'every [*omnis*]' is mentioned only briefly and tangentially in Peter's *Syncategoreumata*, in a section of the second chapter devoted to the different kinds of negation (see de Rijk and Spruyt 1992, 87).

67. Norman Kretzmann, "Syncategoremata, Exponibilia, Sophismata," in *CHLMP*, 215.

68. *TDI* 18 (which gives a modern edition of *QP* III.18: 61ra–63vb) distinguishes between the categorematic and syncategorematic senses of 'infinite'; *QP* VI.4 between the categorematic and syncategorematic senses of 'whole'. For discussion of the former, see Thijssen 1991a, xiv–xvi; of the latter, see Zupko 1993, 180–81.

69. It is of course possible to treat the cause by redefining logical terms so as to eliminate the ambiguities, redundancies, and other 'ragged edges' of natural languages. The result would be something like the ideal pursued by logicians in the early part of the twentieth century, i.e., purely formal systems of axioms and well-formed formulae whose calculus is as well behaved as mathematics. But for medieval logicians, who still used the Aristotelian currency of natural language, this was not an option.

NOTES TO CHAPTER 3

1. Buridan treats the words 'proposition [*propositio*]' and 'enunciation [*enuntiatio*]' as synonymous (*S* 1.3.1: 22).

2. Buridan goes on to say that Peter of Spain correctly states that a spoken proposition signifies something true or false, "for it signifies a mental proposition, which is either true or false. But a mental proposition need not thus signify something true or false" (*S* 1.3.1: 22). Rather, a mental proposition simply is true or false. For Buridan, the transitivity of signification ends with concepts. As we saw in chapters 1 and 2, he prefers to say that concepts are the means by which we conceive of things, rejecting the idea of a naturally significant mental language. This has the important consequence of preserving signification as a three-place relation among (1) written terms, which conventionally signify (2) spoken terms, which conventionally signify (3) concepts. Likewise, Buridan follows Aristotle's lead in *De Interpretatione* 1.16a3–9, holding that although it is a matter of convention which written terms signify which spoken terms, and which spoken terms signify which concepts, what concepts are the likenesses of—i.e., what we conceive of by means of any given concept—is natural and the same for all, and hence not a matter of convention. The relation between concepts and things is accordingly proper to psychology, not to logic.

3. Buridan's text contains references to figures illustrating assertoric (*S* 1.5.1: 43) and modal (*S* 1.8.7: 82) oppositions, but not all manuscripts include the diagrams, even though the text explicitly invites the reader to compare the two figures. In his translation, Gyula Klima represents assertoric oppositions in terms of an 'Octagon of Oppositions'—which, he suggests, is more perspicuous in two dimensions than a flattened cube—and modal oppositions in terms of another cube, this time flattened out

to two dimensions (indeed, one can almost see where to cut the figure so as to make it into a cube), from an incunabular edition of the *Summulae* (Buridan 1499). For the diagrams themselves, I direct the reader to Klima's translation (*S* 1.5.1: 44–45; *S* 1.8.7: 83).

4. Modal (*de modo*) propositions are a species of categorical propositions which contain a 'mode' or determination of the copula verb affecting the way in which the predicate is said to belong to the subject, as in 'A man is necessarily an animal', 'A man can be running', or 'Socrates happens to be white' (*S* 1.8.2: 67–69). Assertoric (*de inesse*) propositions simply assert that some predicate belongs to a subject, as in 'A man is an animal', 'A man is running', or 'Socrates is white'. Buridan misleadingly borrows Peter of Spain's terminology when he speaks of assertoric categoricals as involving "the simple inherence [*de inesse*] of the predicate in the subject" (*S* 1.3.4: 29), despite the fact that, unlike Peter, his semantics attaches no metaphysical significance to this claim, i.e., as indicating the actual inherence of the form signified by the predicate in the thing(s) signified by the subject. Gyula Klima argues (correctly, in my view) that this use of '*de inesse*' is yet another example of Buridan's "habit of using old terminology and filling it with new content"—the "new content" in this case being his nominalist reinterpretation of the old inherence theory of predication in terms of the newer doctrine of supposition. For discussion, see *S* 1.3.4: n. 62 and the introduction to Klima's translation of the *Summulae*, liii–lxii.

5. These cubes of oppositions are clearly related to the traditional square of opposition, which is also discussed in Buridan's text (*S* 1.4.2: 37–39). The difference is that the square of opposition "constitutes an exhaustive division of non-equivalent propositions sharing both their terms in the same order," so that the propositions related therein are said to stand in opposition under one of four modes. The cubes of opposition, however, exemplify inference relations among more complex assertoric and modal propositions—hence the need for a third dimension to represent such propositions.

6. *TC* I.1: 17, ll. 9–10: "*reductae in primas causas per quas dicuntur tenere.*" I have always liked Peter King's analogy for the relationship between these two works: "the *Treatise on Consequences* [is] an advanced independent investigation in logic. If the [*Summulae*] was the textbook for Buridan's introductory course in logic, the *Treatise on Consequences* is a handbook to the logic graduate seminar" (King 1985, 6).

7. Hubert Hubien, Introduction to *TC*, 14.

8. Buridan's treatment of modes is significant in the history of logic in two respects, which can only be briefly mentioned here. First, as Simo Knuuttila has shown, Buridan reduces to twenty-eight the number of acceptable Aristotelian moods and makes no attempt "to reconstruct Aristotle's modal syllogistic as a uniform system" (Knuuttila 1991, 487). Like Ockham, Buridan realized that "there is no uniform reading which would make all Aristotelian moods valid," and that Aristotle's fragmentary insights would have to be supplemented with a newer, more systematic, modal semantics—a realization which led to some of the greatest innovations of fourteenth-century logic (Knuuttila 1996, 130–31). Second, Gyula Klima notes that in suggesting that "we treat modes analogously with signs, namely, so that 'necessary' is treated like 'every', 'impossible' like 'no', 'possible' like 'some', and 'possible ... not' like 'some ... not'" (*S* 1.8.7: 82), Buridan has effectively stated "the gist of the idea of modern possible-worlds semantics, which treats the intensional modal notions analogously to

the extensional notions of the quantifiers, in fact treating them as quantifiers over possible worlds or situations" (*S* 1.8.7: n. 123).

9. Buridan considers some of the metaphysical aspects of the problem of universals in *QM* VII.15, which again, asks about the signification of universal terms. For discussion, see chapter 10 below and de Libera 1996, 374–80.

10. Spade 1994, 1. Medieval philosophers widely regarded this as a glaring omission. Thus, Abelard writes in his *Historia calamitatum:* "This has always been the dialectician's chief problem concerning universals, so much so that even Porphyry did not venture to settle it when he deals with universals in his *Isagoge,* but only mentioned it as a 'very serious difficulty' " (Radice 1974, 60).

11. *QIP* 14: 187, ll. 2354–57: "*Sed Porphyrius non intendebat docere probare illa praedicabilia de subiectis suis, sed solum ea describere et distinguere secundum diversos modos praedicandi et assignare inter se convenientias et differentias.*" The language Buridan uses here, i.e., "to prove those predicables of their subjects," would have sounded old-fashioned to Parisian readers of the *Summulae,* since it harks back to the realist approach of the *logica antiqua.* William of Champeaux (c. 1070–1120), for example, held that a topical maxim "could prove inferences only if it were about the things those inferences concerned" (Martin Tweedale, "William of Champeaux" in the *Routledge Encyclopedia of Philosophy,* vol. 9, 729).

12. *QIP* 3: 135, ll. 459–65: "*ego dico cum aliis expositoribus, quod hoc genus 'universale' sive iste terminus 'universale' est subiectum vel obiectum primum et proprium in scientia libri Porphyrii, quia de eo et de suis speciebus, scilicet de 'genere' et 'specie' etc. determinatur principaliter in isto libro et de nullis aliis nisi secundum attributionem, quam habent ad ipsum 'universale' et ad species eius, et ab eius unitate haec totalis scientia dicitur una.*"

13. Thomas Aquinas makes substantially the same point (though without putting it in terms of the doctrine of supposition) in *Summa theologiae* Ia, q. 13, a. 9.

14. De Rijk 1972, xcii. The author of the *Logica* or *Summa Lamberti* is now believed to be Lambert of Lagny, not Lambert of Auxerre. See Gauthier, introduction to Thomas Aquinas, *Expositio libri Peryermenias* (Roma: Commissio Leonina) 1*.1, p. 53, and cf. de Libera 1982.

15. I include here, of course, Porphyry's *Isagoge,* or *Introduction* to Aristotle's *Categories,* which was always canonical in the *logica vetus.* The practical accompaniment to the *Isagoge* is Buridan's second treatise on predicables. As we saw above, the sciences of rhetoric and poetry, with their proper subjects of 'rhetorical' and 'poetic' argumentation, respectively, are not adjoined to the speculative sciences of physics, mathematics, and metaphysics, but belong to the practical sciences of ethics, politics, and economics, where they provide the "special logic" governing the persuasive and aesthetic argumentation of those disciplines.

16. *QDI* I.1: 6, ll. 19–20: "*In scientia autem libri Praedicamentorum subiectum proprium assignari potest iste terminus vel ista oratio. . . .*" The *QC* is the only one of Buridan's logic commentaries that does not contain any reflections on the status of logic as a science. Even his *Quaestiones in octo libros Topicorum Aristotelis,* which I was unable to examine for this book, asks in the very first question of Book I "whether dialectical argumentation is the subject in [the science of] dialectics" (Michael 1985, 495).

17. Peter of Spain in De Rijk 1972, 28; cf. Aristotle, *Categories* 2.1a20–22.

18. The ambiguity was perceived by most medieval readers of the text, although at least one modern interpreter regards it as "perfectly clear that Aristotle's fourfold classification is a classification of things and not names, and that what is 'said of' something as a subject is itself a thing (a species or genus) and not a name" (Ackrill 1963, 75). Still, the linguistic interpretation strikes me as eminently defensible, though I shall not take up the matter here. For discussion, see Garver 1974.

19. Abelard likewise insists upon such a "purely verbal reading" of the categories (Marenbon 1997, 109; see also Spade 1994, 29).

20. "We should also note that we do not posit separate universals as did Plato. For secondary substances signify the same substances as primary ones, but differently, for primary substances signify one substance in a singular manner, whereas secondary substances signify many commonly, and indifferently" (S 3.2.6: 160).

21. QC 3: 17–18, ll. 89–121:

non potest sumi horum praedicamentorum distinctio ex parte rerum, pro quibus termini praedicabiles supponunt, quia sicut prius arguebatur, eadem caliditas est actio et passio et quantitas et qualitas et ad aliquid; et idem Sortes est homo et albus et tricubitus et pater et agens etc. Nec potest eorum distinctio sumi simpliciter ex parte vocum, quia non oportet propter diversa idiomata mutare numerum, quem communiter ponunt philosophi. Et voces etiam imponuntur ad significandum ad placitum. Ideo plurificarentur praedicamenta ad placitum nostrum, quod est inconveniens. Sed sumuntur ex diversis intentionibus, secundum quas termini sunt diversimode connotative vel etiam non connotative. Ex quibus diversis connotationibus proveniunt diversi modi praedicandi terminorum de primis substantiis; et ita directe et immediate distinguuntur penes diversos modos praedicandi de primis substantiis. Si enim praedicentur in quid sive essentialiter de ipsis, tunc tales termini sunt de praedicamento substantiae; si vero praedicantur denominative in quale, tunc sunt de praedicamento qualitatis; et si in quantum, sunt de praedicamento quantitatis. . . . Cum enim quaerimus, quid est Sortes aut brunellus, aut quid est hoc, demonstrato lapide vel lingo aliquo, supponimus quod ipsum est aliquid, et quaerimus specificationem per terminus substantiae subiectos. Et etiam cum quaerimus, quantus vel qualis est Sortes, supponimus quod est aliquantus vel aliqualis, et quaerimus specificationem per terminus substantiae subiectos istis terminis 'quantum' vel 'quale' et sic de aliis. . . . Et quia, sicut dictum est, non habemus de omnibus quaesitiva communia toti generi, ideo etiam praedicamenta possumus distinguere secundum diversos modos generales significandi circa primam substantiam . . .

22. Buridan's remark here is almost a paraphrase of Abelard's position in his commentaries on the *Categories* and Porphyry's *Isagoge*, for which, see Marenbon 1997, 115.

23. Aristotle, *Categories* 8.8b25–10a26.

24. QC 3: 19, ll. 138–46:

Credo ergo, quod non possit aliter assignari vel probari sufficientia numeri praedicamentorum, nisi quia tot modos praedicandi diversos invenimus non reducibiles in aliquem modum praedicandi communiorem acceptum secundum aliquam unam communem rationem, ideo oportet tot esse. Sed etiam quia non invenimus praedicabilia communia, quae sub istis modis non contineantur vel ad eos reducantur, ideo non ponimus plura praedicamenta. Unde si aliqua praedicabilia communia inveniamus habentia alios modos praedicandi praeter dictos decem, apparet mihi omnino, quod non esset negandum, quin essent plura praedicamenta.

Cf. Abelard's remark that the division of the categories is based "rather on the meaning of words than the natures of things. Had Aristotle considered the natures of things, there is no reason why he should not have discerned more, or fewer, categories" (*super Praedicamentis*, 116, l. 35–117, l. 2 and ff.; *super Porphyrii* 54, 32–34; quoted in Marenbon 1997, 115).

25. *QC* 3: 20, ll. 153–59: "*Sed tamen mihi apparet pro certo, quod ista decem, si sint aliqua alia, sunt magis manifesta et continentia sub se maiorem pluralitatem praedicabilium. Ideo rationabiliter ista magis enumerari debuerunt, nec oportebat alia enumerare, dato etiam quod essent alia, quia ex consideratione et determinatione istorum decem erat facile de aliis, cum occurrerent, considerare et determinare secundum similitudinem vel proportionem ad ea, quae de istis determinata sunt.*"

26. *QC* 3: 25, ll. 283–87: "*Et diligenter inquisitores de illis circumstantiis et connotationibus diversis considerent, et secundum earum exigentiam reducant ad ista decem praedicamenta vel ad unum illorum vel ad congregationem multorum; quod si non sit possibile, concedantur alia praedicamenta.*" The similarity between the views of Buridan and Peter Abelard on the significance of the categories is quite striking. For Abelard's position, which John Marenbon sees as emerging from his method of *in voce exegesis,* see Marenbon 1997, 111–16.

27. See *S* 9.4, 3rd remark: 880: "we should note that the diverse modes of predication arise from the diverse positive modes of how the things appellated pertain to the things for which the terms supposit, as in response to the question 'What is it like?' [*in quale*] or in response to the question 'How much is it?' [*in quantum*], 'Where is it?' [*in ubi*], 'How is this related to that? [*in quomodo se habet hoc ad illud*], etc. And it is from these diverse modes of predication that the diverse categories are derived, as should be seen in the commentary on the *Categories* [*QC* 3: 14–29]."

28. *QC* 3: 29, ll. 374–76: "*Sed haec sic dixi exemplariter, ut per praedicta diligentes inquisitores haberent occasionem dicendi perfectius et de praedictis nominibus et de aliis.*" Following the reading of two manuscripts, I drop the words '*et modum*' following '*occasionem*' in the critical edition of this text.

29. Buridan seems almost impatient with those who keep raising the question of the number of the categories, as if the tendency to regard it as important suggests a lack of logical knowledge: "This question and other questions asking about the number of the predicates or predicables, or categories, or natural principles, or elements, etc., are exceedingly difficult and tedious especially for younger students, for whom it is necessary to explain logical and sophistical quibbles which are no longer of any concern to advanced students. And so, for the sake of the beginners, I propose some easy and truistic conclusions [*Ista quaestio et aliae quaestiones quaerentes de numero vel praedicatorum vel praedicabilium, praedicamentorum vel principiorum naturalium, vel elementorum, etc., sunt valdes difficiles et taediosae specialiter iuvenibus, quibus oportet explicare cavillationes logicas et sophisticas, de quibus provecti non amplius curant. Ideo propter beanos ego pono aliquas conclusiones faciles et trufaticas*]" (*QIP* 14: 183, ll. 2204–209).

Elsewhere, Buridan says that the term '*beanus*' is used of someone who "has been at Paris for only a year [*Beanus dicitur, quia solo anno fuit Parisius*]" (*QC* 3: 27, ll. 325–26).

NOTES TO CHAPTER 4

1. As T. K. Scott, Jr., puts it (1966, 29): "The theory of supposition is the core of terminist logic."

2. A sampler: Lambert of Lagny (fl. 1250, Paris), *Summa Lamberti;* Nicholas of Paris (fl. 1250, Paris), *Summe Metenses;* William of Sherwood (c. 1200–1272, Oxford), *Introductiones in logicam.*

3. That is because, as we are later told, the grammarian is offended by "ungrammaticality [*incongruitas*]," whereas the logician is offended by "falsity [*falsitas*]"— a concept which assumes that the proposition under consideration has already passed the test of grammaticality (*S* 4.2.6: 241). Cf. Buridan's discussion of whether non-substantivated adjectives can be subjects or predicates in a proposition: "And on this question we should have recourse to grammar, if the truth cannot be determined in logic" (*S* 4.2.6: 247). See section 2 of chapter 1 above.

4. The latter claim is not uncontroversial, as some terminist logicians argued otherwise. For example, Vincent Ferrer (1350–1419) held that only subject terms can supposit (Spade, "The Semantics of Terms," in *CHLMP*, 195).

5. See Scott 1966, 29–42; Spade, "The Semantics of Terms," in *CHLMP*, 192–96; King 1985, 35–36. Again, these issues are not without controversy, and so such generalizations are made at one's peril. Part of the problem is just the perennial one of how to express what medieval philosophers thought they were doing in a way that makes sense *to us*. But this characterization will suffice for our purposes, since it covers the way in which most terminist logicians, including Buridan, actually used the doctrine of supposition.

6. Lest anyone doubt how literally he wishes us to understand this act of pointing, Buridan notes that "one might indeed wonder because, although the term 'God' can supposit, nevertheless, whatever is pointed out by the pronoun 'this', [the term] is not verified of this pronoun, for this would require pointing out God, whom we cannot point out" (*S* 4.1.2: 223). Two solutions are offered: (1) we can 'point' to God with our intellects; and (2) God can be pointed to in principle, although not in fact, i.e., in our present condition as wayfarers.

7. See Reina 1957. A close second would be the ninth treatise, the *Sophismata,* which was translated into English (1966) and edited (1977) by T. K. Scott, Jr. The eighth chapter of this treatise on insoluble propositions was later re-edited and re-translated by G. E. Hughes (1982).

8. G. E. Hughes (1982, 13–17) is particularly helpful on this point.

9. Thus, "the term 'white' taken *simpliciter* supposits for the wall, milk, wine, etc." (*S* 7.4.2: 559). It should be noted, however, that the term 'white' is also connotative (or appellative, in the context of a proposition): "for it is clear that 'white' [*album*] supposits for a substance and appellates the whiteness as inherent in that substance" (*S* 4.1.4: 228). We might think of connotation as "a kind of indirect or an oblique form or signification" (King 1985, 20), one function of which is to signify a certain relation between an abstract concept and the thing that exhibits its concrete counterpart. The

doctrine plays an important role in Buridan's ontology, since it covers the evident fact that the same thing can be conceived of in a variety of ways, and so helps to explain some of the more complex modes of human discourse without reifying them. Thus, a term is said to be appellative if it signifies something for which it does not stand (e.g., 'white' is an appellative term in the proposition, 'Socrates is white', because it signifies whiteness, even though there is no whiteness as such for which it can stand). For discussion, see Scott 1966, 42–49; Pinborg 1972, 139–44; de Rijk 1976, 91–100; Maierù 1976, 101–114; King 1985, 17–22; Nuchelmans 1988; and Klima's introduction to his translation of the *Summulae*. The use of 'appellation' to refer to the connotation of a term in a proposition was standard among nominalists after Buridan, in contrast to thirteenth-century logicians like Peter of Spain, who used appellation rather than supposition to denote an actually existing object. See Ashworth 1974, 92–93.

10. To the modern reader, then, a medieval author's account of supposition has the potential to reveal that author's 'ontological commitments'.

11. See Ovid, *Tristia* 5.4.48; Juvenal, *Saturae* VII, l. 49. For the medieval history of the 'smiling meadow' metaphor, see Rosier-Catach 1997.

12. Recall Buridan's acknowledgment of rhetoric as the source of the 'special logic' of moral persuasion. Buridan associates figurative or 'transumptive' discourse with dialectic in the *Summulae*'s sixth treatise on topics: "The second section [of Peter of Spain's text] says that the first kind of transumption does not belong to the dialectician. And I believe that this is false. For rhetoric and poetry are parts of dialectic, but this kind of transumption, which is a parabolic way of speaking, maximally belongs to poetry, for it is in this way that we call God a lion in the Holy Scripture, not sophistically but poetically, for just as the lion rules over all other animals, so does God rule over anything; and this is how we refer [in the Apocalypse of John] to 'the animals covered with eyes in front and back'. And such ways of speaking yield dialectical and persuasive arguments" (*S* 6.5.9: 479; cf. *S* 7.1.4: 499).

13. Thus, Peter of Spain: "Simple supposition is the taking [*acceptio*] of a common term for the universal thing signified by it [*pro re universali significata per ipsum*]" (de Rijk 1972, 81). Early terminist logicians, it should be said, did not always agree about the divisions of supposition. Material supposition is not mentioned by Peter, though William of Sherwood includes it in his *Introductiones in logicam* 5.2 (Kretzmann 1966, 107).

14. William of Ockham, *Summa logicae* I.67; *Opera Philosophica* I: 201.

15. Thus, Peter of Spain remarks that in the proposition, "'Man is a species [*homo est species*]' . . . the term 'man' supposits for man in general [*homo in communi*], and not for any of its inferiors" (de Rijk 1972, 81). Likewise, for Ockham, rather than suppositing for extramental particulars, "a mental term suppositing simply supposits sometimes for itself, as in 'Man is a species' . . ." (Ockham, *Summa logicae* I.67; *Opera Philosophica* I: 207). For discussion, see Boehner 1952, 40; Berger 1991, 31–37.

16. Pinborg 1972, 143.

17. A similar point is made by Scott 1966, 31, n. 57.

18. The joke is repeated at *S* 8.7.9: 750. The point is from Aristotle, *Sophistical Refutations* (1.165a6–8): "It is impossible in a discussion to bring in the actual things discussed: we use their names as symbols instead of them; and we suppose that what follows in the names, follows in the things as well."

19. See *S* 7.3.4: 520 (quoted in n. 60 of chapter 1).

20. Notice also that this severs the traditional connection between personal and material supposition as varieties of proper supposition. For Buridan, the only proper supposition is personal supposition; all of the others are strictly speaking improper. Stephen Read has linked Buridan's position on material supposition as improper with the breakthrough doctrine—first fully realized in the work of Buridan's student, Marsilius of Inghen—that material supposition is possible only if materially suppositing terms are significative, or stand for what they signify. See Read 1999, 18 and S 7.3.4: 522, where Buridan considers 'Homo est species' as an instance of the fallacy of equivocation.

21. The qualification, 'at least in the first instance', is intended to cover the conventionality of signification beyond these primary acts of imposition, which in Buridan's view are naturally determined. He conveys this idea by saying that such concepts are acquired 'immediately [statim]', i.e., without deliberation: "from the singular visual cognition there immediately arises the universal intellectual cognition, and so when we see this man, we immediately think of [a] man" (S 4.5.3: 296). Nevertheless, it is clear that even the signification commonly and principally given to the term 'man' could be changed after the fact if everyone agreed to use that term in a different way. The case is somewhat more complicated with mental language, since it does not seem open to any individual language-user to change the significance of his/her concepts at will. But, as I have already argued, concepts can be changed indirectly as a result of the dialectical relationship Buridan takes to exist between concepts and spoken or written languages. Thus, someone who learns from a book that kangaroos are marsupials does not acquire a new concept, but augments or modifies the concept he already has. See section 4 of chapter 1 above.

22. Not surprisingly, terms in the propositions of logic are said to occur in material supposition, since logic concerns the conventional classification of significant utterances and patterns of reasoning and persuasion. Its objects are the immediate, rather than the ultimate, significates of terms. See S 4.3.2: 25–58.

23. For discussion, see the articles by Eleonore Stump, "Obligations: From the Beginning to the Early Fourteenth Century," and Paul V. Spade, "Obligations: Developments in the Fourteenth Century," in CHLMP, 315–41.

24. This suggests the accuracy of John Trentman's early assessment: "The dispute about suppositio simplex, its nature and use . . . was primarily a dispute about the significatio of general terms and secondarily and indirectly about ontology" (1969, 953).

25. Strictly speaking, concepts are not artifacts because they owe their ultimate signification to nature rather than to convention. Convention enters the picture when a concept is imposed to signify something other than its ultimate significate, as in the case of material supposition.

26. Indeed Buridan almost stands alone in his re-deployment of natural supposition, for as Scott 1965 observes, the concept "does not occur in many later logicians, such as Ockham, Walter Burley, Albert of Saxony, and Marsilius of Inghen" (670)—the latter two of whom were either students or followers of Buridan. However, Smithka 1991 has shown that natural supposition is used by Albert of Saxony, though it plays a much more limited role in his logic than in Buridan's. The other exception is the realist Vincent Ferrer, who discusses natural supposition "in what seems to be routine fashion" in his treatise De suppositionibus, written in 1372 (Scott 1965, 670).

27. I here adopt the variant reading 'praedicari' for 'participari [= to be a participant (in it)]' in the critical edition (de Rijk 1972, 81), thereby glossing over a point

of some controversy. Roughly, the debate concerns whether natural supposition was originally conceived as a property possessed by certain terms that is dependent (Boehner 1952, 33–34) or independent (de Rijk 1971–73) of their propositional context. Peter of Spain is ambiguous on the question, remarking only that a common term "taken as such [*per se sumptus*]" has natural supposition. On the side of the independence thesis, there does appear to be some connection between the tendency of early terminists to view predication as expressing the inherence of an attribute in a subject, so that a naturally suppositing term might plausibly be thought of as possessing this capacity independently of any proposition which actually expresses it. But against this, the dependence thesis argues that: (1) supposition is always assumed to be a property terms possess in the context of a proposition, and no early terminist, including both Peter of Spain and Lambert of Lagny, explicitly states otherwise; (2) the independence thesis appears to collapse the distinction between signification and supposition as semantic properties of terms (Smithka 1991, 137–40); and (3) the semantic independence of naturally suppositing terms can be understood intra- rather than extra-propositionally. More recently, Alain de Libera (1993, 389–91) has argued that both interpretations can be found among thirteenth-century logicians, and that Buridan's position has some affinities with that of the Parisian dialectician John Le Page (fl. after 1235). In any case, Buridan clearly ascribes natural supposition only to terms occurring in propositions, which is reflected in his classification of natural supposition as a division of common personal supposition (*S* 4.3.4: 259; see also *QAnPr* I.25).

28. See de Rijk, "The Semantics of Propositions," in *CHLMP*, 197–98. The latter, of course, expresses our modern, post-Fregean understanding of 'proposition'.

29. As Scott 1965 puts it, "Every proposition was token-reflexive, in the sense that it contained an implicit reference to the time of its occurrence" (658).

30. Buridan uses the technical term '*status* [= state]' to denote the range of reference of a term that has been neither ampliated nor restricted (*S* 4.6.1: 298, n. 95). Although the concept is fairly straightforward, rules for ampliation and restriction could be very complicated considering the referential nuances of the discourse they were intended to capture. Scott (1966, 33–34) provides a summary of Buridan's rules of ampliation, but even that is by no means complete. An example of restriction would be when, "in 'Socrates' donkey runs', 'donkey' is not taken for all donkeys, but only for those that are Socrates'" (*S* 4.6.3: 300).

31. "[Die Philosophie] lässt alles wie es ist," Ludwig Wittgenstein, *Typescript* 213 (the so-called 'Big Typescript' assembled in 1933), §89, s. 418; Klagge and Nordmann 1993, 176–77. The remark was later incorporated into the text of *Philosophical Investigations*, §124.

32. William of Ockham, *Summa logicae* III.2, 5; *Opera Philosophica* I: 513–14. Cf. Aristotle, *Posterior Analytics* I.8. For discussion, see Pinborg 1972, 158–68, and Adams 1987a, 451–56, who also offers some interesting suggestions about how Ockham might have dealt with the difficulties raised by his solution.

33. Again, for ways in which Ockham might have developed his position (none of which seems entirely satisfactory), see Adams 1987a, 451–56. It should perhaps be mentioned that the otherwise engaging discussion in Scott 1965 is not sensitive to these exegetical difficulties because it omits a crucial part of the text (cf. Scott 1965, 659, n. 27 and Ockham, *Summa logicae* III.2, 5; *Opera Philosophica* I: 513, ll. 46–49).

34. *QNE* VI.6 contains the most perspicuous account of Buridan's response to Ockham, along with his criticisms of four other opinions on the proper object of scientific knowledge. For discussion, see Scott 1965, 662–69. Natural supposition is also treated in *QAnPo* I.16–19 and *QM* IV.9.

35. *QNE* VI.6: 122vb: "*videtur enim mihi quod nomina quae significant res nullum consignificando tempus determinatum significant indifferenter res praesentes, praeteritas et futuras, nec mirum quia possum intelligere rem nullum cointelligendo tempus determinatum. Unde possum apud intellectum componere inter conceptum rei et conceptum temporis ita praeteriti vel futuri sicut praesentis, ut dicendo 'Caesar fuit', 'Caesar erit', et ita non est inconveniens aliquando terminum supponere pro praeteritis et futuris sicut pro praesentibus.*"

36. It is significant that in natural philosophy, Buridan does not expand the range of a naturally suppositing term's reference to include *possibilia*. As Simo Knuuttila has shown, this is a result of his statistical understanding of the necessity of scientific propositions, according to which genuine possibilities cannot remain unrealized (hence, there are no *possibilia* which do not occur in either the past, present, or future). But that said, there remains for Buridan, as for Scotus and Ockham, an equally important sense in which all nomic natural necessities are logically contingent (Knuuttila 1989, 175–76).

37. *QNE* VI.6: 123ra: "*Sed statim diceret aliquis, 'Domine, vos coinciditis cum opinione praecedente, quoniam dictae propositioni scibili vos assignatis sensum hypotheticam, et alii concedebant de talibus propositiones hypotheticas necessarias et scibiles.' Respondeo quod forte haec opinio et illa eandem intendebant sententiam, sed differunt secundum logicam in modo loquendi. Primi enim non concedunt in praedictis rebus propositionem categoricam in sensu categorico. Ego autem concedo eam esse veram secundum suppositionem naturalem.*"

38. The point of such exercises is a matter of some controversy, and one that is seriously underdetermined by the textbook evidence. Paul Vincent Spade has suggested that by Buridan's time, the modes of personal supposition had become an idle wheel: "By the early fourteenth century, the doctrine of modes as a theory of reference had been pretty much defeated. But once this had happened, the theory of modes of supposition was left with *no question to answer*. It was no longer a theory of reference; it was not . . . a theory of truth conditions or analysis. The theory was left with no task to perform. No wonder it has proved so hard for scholars to agree about what it was trying to accomplish. By the early fourteenth century, it was not trying to accomplish anything at all!" (1988b, 212).

NOTES TO CHAPTER 5

1. Cf. Aristotle, *Prior Analytics* I.1.24a21–b16. The goals of attaining knowledge and presenting opinions are covered in the *Summulae*'s sixth (on topics) and eighth (on demonstrations) treatises, respectively. The seventh treatise on fallacies complements the treatise on topics (a.k.a. 'dialectical *loci*') insofar as it addresses sophistical as opposed to genuine syllogistic arguments—"Therefore it is necessary that every *elenchus* properly so-called should be a syllogism" (*S* 7.1.1: 495). Buridan is here using standard terminology. As Sten Ebbesen notes (1987b, 119), "The term '*locus sophisticus*'

was used as a synonym of '*fallacia*' throughout the Middle Ages." In the same way, Ockham divides syllogisms into demonstrative, topical, and those which are neither demonstrative nor topical, the last division more or less coinciding with sophistical syllogisms (see Eleonore Stump, "Topics: Their Development into Consequences," in *CHLMP*, 294; and William of Ockham, *Summa logicae* III.1; *Opera Philosophica* I: 360).

2. Buridan begins his commentary on the *Prior Analytics* by noting that it promises "an account of demonstration, though not in all of its particulars, but [only] insofar as demonstrations are syllogisms—which is nothing other than to offer a general account of the syllogism itself [*in isto libro Priorum determinatur de demonstratione, non tamen appropriate, sed in quantum ipsa est syllogismus, quod nihil aliud est quam determinare communiter de ipso syllogismo*]" (*QAnPr* I, Proemium). What the science of the *Prior Analytics* is particularly concerned with is "the necessary entailment of the conclusion from the premises [*ad illationem necessariam conclusionis ex praemissis*]" in a syllogistic demonstration. This, in turn, is the logical foundation of the companion science of "demonstration with respect to the proof of the conclusion from necessary and evident premises [*demonstratio quantum ad probationem ex praemissis necessariis et evidentibus*]," which is developed in the *Posterior Analytics*.

3. I.e., whatever is said of all As may be said of any A (*dici de omni*); whatever is denied of all As may be denied of any A (*dici de nullo*). See Aristotle, *Prior Analytics* I.4 and Lagerlund 2000, 152–53. The first four modes of the first figure of the syllogism are said to be perfect because "they are evident consequences by virtue of *dici de omni et nullo*" (*S* 5.2.4: 322).

4. Ebbesen 1984, 98.

5. As we shall see below, this is very much in keeping with Aristotle's understanding of the syllogism.

6. Indeed, Green-Pedersen (1984, 275) believes that Buridan developed some of his basic ideas about consequences in his *QAnPr* II.5–6 discussion of Aristotle's claim that the false cannot follow from the true in a valid argument, although the true can follow from the false (see *Posterior Analytics* II.2–4). It has been thought for some time that Buridan also wrote an independent treatise on syllogisms that is preserved in a single Munich codex (Bayerische Staatsbibliothek, Clm 7708, ff. 68r–95r; for the identification, see Faral 1946, 6; Faral 1950, 46; Markowski 1976, 14; and Michael 1985, 536). However, having examined a copy of this manuscript, I can confirm that it is simply a copy of the fifth treatise of the *Summulae*, which appears to have circulated independently of the rest of the work.

7. Actually, Henrik Lagerlund (2000, 143) reminds us that it is controversial whether Aristotle's syllogisms should be interpreted as conditionals or rules of inference, and that "it cannot be said that Buridan takes any stand in this debate, since the logicians of the fourteenth century, including Buridan, treat both under the heading of consequences." See also King 1985, 59–60.

8. Contrast Buridan's *QAnPr*, which, although it does address modal syllogisms (I.30–40), makes no attempt to systematize the discussion of the fifth treatise of the *Summulae*. Rather, what we find there is a parallel effort to explain the same kinds of modal syllogism along quasi-Aristotelian lines. I would argue that the reason for this, following a suggestion by Simo Knuuttila, is that Buridan realized that no unified account of Aristotelian syllogistic, including both assertoric and modal syllogisms, was possible. According to Knuuttila, "Buridan probably thought that Aristotle's modal

syllogistic is a partial theory of valid modal deductions without a classification of the different types of fine structures made use of in dealing with modal premises. As the main lines of modal syllogistic in Buridan, Ockham, and Pseudo-Scotus are very similar in this respect, late medieval approaches to Aristotle can be characterized [as] deconstructive in the sense that there is no attempt to present it as a uniform whole" (1991, 487). I would agree, but add that Buridan's approach is deconstructive only when viewed from the Aristotelian perspective, and that there are numerous indications in the *Treatise on Consequences* that he has deliberately left it behind.

9. *TC* IV.3: 131, ll. 68–70: "*ad quascumque praemissas sequitur conclusio de necessario de modo affirmato ad easdem sequitur conclusio de contingenti de modo negato.*"

10. This is not to say that the rules given in the *Summulae* and *Treatise on Consequences* have different results. Although the overlap is not complete (*TC* adds some modes, but omits others discussed in *S*; and the accounts appear contradictory in two places), it testifies to Buridan's virtuosity as a logician that he was able to arrive at roughly the same list of valid modal syllogisms using both approaches. For a definitive comparison of the two works in this regard, see the table in the third appendix to Hughes 1989, 110–11.

11. William of Ockham, *Summa logicae* III.3: 38; *Opera Philosophica* I: 727–31. For discussion, see Boehner 1952, 54–70 and Adams 1987a, 437–45.

12. The "sifting-out" term is Boehner's (1952, 54), and is exactly what Boehner proceeds to do over the next fifteen pages. In the end, one can sense that he feels a certain frustration at the traditionalism of Ockham's account: "Other than purely logical, that is, formal, considerations have induced the 'Venerable Inceptor' to retain the two tracts on terms [i.e., the first two treatises of the *Summa logicae* on terms and propositions], despite the fact that he was at least vaguely aware that they were foreign to logic. In this point he simply followed tradition" (1952, 82).

13. See Kretzmann and Stump 1988, 281–311.

14. Ivan Boh, "Consequences," in *CHLMP*, 311. In response, it should be pointed out that the notion that any pre-Fregean logician (including Buridan) understood the priority of propositional logic has been very effectively criticized by Franz Schupp (1988).

15. Buridan's rules "are arranged in a different order: assertoric sentences, modal sentences, syllogisms of assertoric sentences, syllogisms of modal sentences. The most significant difference is found in the feature that Buridan's treatise has a long introductory section where the truth and falsity of sentences, and the definition and division of consequence are explained . . . in Buridan we find the kind of systematic treatment [of consequences] which will be typical for the rest of the Middle Ages, not in Ockham or Burley" (Green-Pedersen 1981, 289; see also Green-Pedersen 1984, 265–99; Bos 1976, 62; and Lagerlund 2000, 158).

16. *TC* I.1: 17, ll. 7–10: "*In hoc libro vellem tractare de consequentiis, tradendo sicut possem causas earum, de quibus multae sufficienter probatae sunt per alios a posteriori; sed forte non sunt reductae in primas causas per quas dicuntur tenere.*"

17. *TC* III.4: 92–93, ll. 263–73:

Et videtur mihi quod Aristotiles reputavit syllogismum non esse compositum ex praemissis et conclusione sed compositum ex praemissis tantum potentibus inferre conclusionem; ideo posuit unam potestatem syllogismi quod idem syllogismus possit concludere plura. Ideo Aristotiles in prima figura praeter quattuor modos directe concludentes et secundum modum loquendi consuetum posuit solum alios duos modos qui, etiam secundum modum loquendi consuetum, concludunt indirecte, scilicet Fapesmo et Frisesomorum, et illos qui solum concludunt secundum modum loquendi inconsuetum dimisit. Et non enumeravit Baralipton, Celantes, et Dabitis contra Barbara, Celarent et Darii, quia secundum dicta non differunt ab eis.

18. Hughes 1989, 102.

19. No one has done more to draw attention to Buridan's contributions in the field of modal logic than Hubert Hubien: "the medieval masters had constructed a logic of propositions, or propositional functors, for which one would look in Aristotle in vain. Without a doubt, we know today that the Stoics had already constructed one such theory, but what one finds in the writings of John Buridan and his school goes far beyond the fragments of the work of Chrysippus and his successors, which Boethius had transmitted to them. This logic is a modal logic, and it is not difficult to collect, in treatises *de consequentiis*, theses sufficient to constitute an axiomatic [deduction] system for Lewis's S3" (Hubien 1977, 224). Still, the precise nature of Buridan's accomplishment has proved difficult to characterize in modern terms. See Lagerlund 2000, 163–64.

20. Supposition is put to other uses in the fifth treatise, which I do not discuss here. These include appellation (*S* 5.6.8: 347–48), and an application of the modes of personal supposition to illustrate the rule of 'upward monotonicity' (*S* 5.8.2: 366–67; for discussion, see Klima's n. 57 on p. 366; see also Lagerlund 2000, 136–64).

21. Hughes 1989, 97.

22. See Knuuttila 1991, 487. See also Knuuttila, "Modal Logic," in *CHLMP*, 355–57 and Lagerlund 2000, 162–64.

NOTES TO CHAPTER 6

1. Cf. Boethius, *De topicis differentiis* I, 1173C–D: "It seems to me . . . that we ought to convey two divisions [of Topics], one dug out from the Greek books, the other taken from Cicero's *Topica*. To complete the investigation, we must explain in which ways each division differs from the other, in which ways each matches the other, and in what way each can contain the other" (Stump 1978, 29).

2. De Rijk 1972, xciii.

3. See Green-Pedersen 1984; Stump 1989; and Ebbesen 1993.

4. Ebbesen 1993, 38.

5. See Jan Pinborg, "Medieval Philosophical Literature," in *CHLMP*, 28–29: "The arguments adduced in a disputation have an almost fortuitous character and are certainly not always demonstrative. Their aim is principally to persuade the opponent, and because of that aim it is not necessary to start every argument from first principles. One can instead begin with commonly accepted propositions, either quotations from authorities or well-known maxims. One can also formally agree on some accepted propositions. The arguments are developed in the form of syllogisms, categorical or hypothetical, consequences, or dilemmas. Overt formal errors are exceed-

ingly rare, since such 'sophistical' moves could be detected immediately and thus defeat their author." As for what actually happened in the lecture halls, we have little
'hard' evidence (whatever that means, in the context of medieval life and literary
genres). But the general point is nicely captured by Sten Ebbesen (1993, 17): "I tend to
think that there is a continuous pedagogical tradition linking ancient disputation
with early medieval disputation. Be that as it may, however, what is certain is that medieval scholasticism represents the apogee of Aristotelian dialectic. The scholastic cul-
tivation of *quaestiones* and other forms of disputation is in its forms the sort of thing
Aristotle describes, and in its aims the sort of thing he envisages: a disputation carried
on just to train the members of a school in the art of argumentation; they can exercise
the art in debates with outsiders and thank their training for enabling them to deal
with people who do not share the school's beliefs; finally, the disputation is a fine instrument for serious philosophical analysis."

    6. Boethius, *De topicis differentiis* I, 1173C; Stump 1978, 29.

    7. Green-Pedersen 1984, 302.

    8. For discussion of Buridan on relations, see Schönberger 1994, 371−447.

    9. As Ebbesen (1993, 37) has shown, the temptation to interpret topical rela-
tionships Platonically was very real, since it "is actually what Boethius' explanations of
the nature and function of *loci* seems to require."

    10. Green-Pedersen 1984, 302: "Descriptions of the *locus* similar to or even iden-
tical with Buridan's are found in all the works from the 14th century which discuss the
nature of the *locus* at any length."

    11. *TC* I.3: 22, ll. 48−51: "*illa propositio est antecedens ad aliam quae sic se habet
ad illam quod impossibile est qualitercumque ipsa significant sic esse quin qualitercumque illa alia significant sic sit ipsis simul propositis.*" A textual nicety which needn't
detain us here: although adequate for his purposes, Buridan says that this definition
is strictly speaking false because the criterion of truth expressed in it, 'howsoever
[the proposition] signifies, it is so [*qualitercumque ipsa significat, sic esse*]' fails to
cover past tense propositions with terms whose significates no longer exist (*TC* I.1:
17, ll. 14−27).

    12. *TC* I.4: 23, ll. 16−19: "*Reducitur autem ad formalem per additionem alicuius
propositionis necessariae vel aliquarum propositionum necessarium quarum appositio
ad antecedens assumptum reddit consequentiam formalem.*"

    13. Buridan is careful to distinguish between merely assertoric (*de inesse*) propo-
sitions which are described in modal terms, such as 'Man is an animal [*homo est animal*]', and genuinely modal propositions such as 'Man is necessarily running [*homo
de necessitate currit*]', in which the modal notion is incorporated into the very *dictum*
of the proposition (*TC* II.1: 56, ll. 13−22). Modal consequences are addressed to
propositions of the latter sort.

    14. I am indebted for this insight to Green-Pedersen (1984, 290). As Green-
Pedersen notes, the association became explicit less than a generation after Buridan in
the work of his student, Albert of Saxony, for whom *loci* "must be material consequences" (1984, 317).

    15. Green-Pedersen 1984, 319.

    16. The passage is quoted from Peter of Spain, *Summulae* V, 2, "*argumentum est
ratio faciens fidem*" (de Rijk 1972, 55), who in turn quotes it from Boethius, *De topicis*

differentiis I, "*argumentum est ratio rei dubiae faciens fidem*" (*PL* 64: 1174C). What is interesting here is that the belief in question is a '*fides*' rather than an '*opinio*', the latter being the noun commonly used for objective descriptions of the contents of one's mind. In contrast, '*fides*', like its English derivative 'faith', would have connoted for a Latin speaker the affective side of a belief, i.e., its trustworthiness, reliability, authority, and in general the idea that the object of the belief is not just believed but *worthy* of being believed. Buridan would almost certainly have realized that Peter and Boethius were talking about subjective conviction, a relation between believers and beliefs more proper to psychology than logic. For discussion, see my "On Certitude," in Thijssen and Zupko 2001, 165–82.

17. Boethius, *De topicis differentiis* I, 1174D: "So the argument is the strength (*virtus*), mental content (*mens*), and sense of argumentation; argumentation, on the other hand, is the unfolding of the argument by means of discourse (*oratio*)" (Stump 1978, 30). Buridan actually quotes this passage in support of his interpretation (*S* 6.1.2: 392).

18. According to the *Oxford Latin Dictionary*, the neuter noun '*argumentum*' is derived from the conjunction of the third declension verb '*arguere*' (= show; prove; assert) with the noun suffix '-*mentum*', whose origins are not known. In assimilating '-*mentum*' to '*mens*', Boethius and Buridan were probably following some standard ancient etymology.

19. Aristotle, *Prior Analytics* II.23.68b14: "For every belief comes either through deduction or from induction." Cf. *Posterior Analytics* I.1; *Topics* I.1; *Rhetoric* I.2; Boethius, *De topicis differentiis* I, 1206D.

20. See Stump, "Topics: Their Development and Absorption into Consequences," in *CHLMP*, 283.

21. The distinction corresponds to the ways in which material and formal consequences are said to hold. According to Green-Pedersen, "as the medievals read Aristotle['s *Topics*], he claims that the *loci* occur in syllogisms. Now, the medievals uphold their traditional distinction between the syllogisms and the arguments confirmed by the *loci* insofar as they—or the overwhelming majority of them at least—think that the dialectical syllogism as such is not valid in virtue of a *locus*, but by its form, i.e., its figures and moods. This means that the dialectical syllogism presupposes the syllogism as such. It is not, however, just a syllogism, but it adds something to it, viz. that its premisses are plausible and that they are different things or sentences from the conclusion. In the syllogism as such, on the other hand, it does not matter if we infer something from itself, and both the premisses and the conclusion may be false" (1984, 341).

22. *QT* I.16: 371: "*solus syllogismus demonstrativus est argumentatio simpliciter perfecta quantum ad probationem conclusionis, quia in tali requiritur quod antecedens sit simpliciter evidens et notum sine formidine; tunc enim fit perfecta probatio.*"

23. Plato, *Timaeus* 52b. Although Buridan would probably have known of this remark (it is from the half of the *Timaeus* which survived in the Middle Ages in the Latin translation of Chalcidius), I am not aware of him ever referring to it.

24. Aristotle, *Rhetoric* I.1.1355a14–15.

25. The references are to Aristotle, *Posterior Analytics* II.19.100a7–9, and *Metaphysics* I.1.981a3–4.

26. Induction presents by far the most interesting species of dialectical argumentation, of course. And, in any case, Buridan is inclined to treat enthymemes as in-

complete syllogisms and examples as incomplete inductions. The latter, he says, can be reduced to an induction "by adding to the antecedent as many singular premises as would be sufficient for generating belief in the universal conclusion" (*S* 6.1.5: 400).

27. E.g., a locus should be named from the antecedent because it has the power to "generate a belief" about the consequent (*S* 6.3.1: 409); with regard to the *locus* from the subjective part to its whole, "every accident has a substance subjected to it, unless the opposite happens by a miracle. But the natural scientist [*naturalis*] would say that if the effect of the material cause exists, then its matter must also exist" (*S* 6.4.3: 426); and with regard to the locus from cause and effect, "we should not understand by 'follows' the consequence of the conclusion from the premise or premises, but that the cause is naturally prior to its effect or that the effect should occur by means of the cause or for the sake of it" (*S* 6.4.9: 440).

Notes to Chapter 7

1. The synonymy of '*locus sophisticus*' and '*fallacia*' throughout the Middle Ages has been pointed out by Sten Ebbesen, who also notes that "in twelfth-century works the fallacies or sophistical *loci* are paralleled to the dialectical ones, but there is no attempt to formulate sophistical maxims before the second half of the thirteenth century" (Ebbesen 1987b, 119).

2. Aristotle, *De Sophisticis Elenchis* 1.164a20.

3. De Rijk 1962, 12–13, et passim.

4. Aristotle, *De Sophisticis Elenchis* 1.165a10–11.

5. Contrast Buridan's attention to context with the approach of the *modistae* or speculative grammarians. As Costantino Marmo notes, "logicians who adhered to the modistic paradigm refused to acknowledge any relevance of the linguistic context for solving fallacies" (Marmo 1995, 170).

6. Aristotle, *De Sophisticis Elenchis* 2.165b1–11.

7. I here diverge from Klima's text, which translates '*causa apparentiae*' as 'cause of illusion' throughout. I prefer 'cause of appearance' because it preserves the connection with the epistemic term '*apparentia*', i.e., an impression that invites our assent. For discussion, see chapter 12 below.

8. Ebbesen 1987b, 115.

9. Sten Ebbesen, "Ancient Scholastic Logic as the Source of Medieval Scholastic Logic," in *CHLMP*, 124 and Ebbesen 1987b, 116–17.

10. Thus, "a fallacy is nothing other than a deception [*fallacia nichil aliud est quam deceptionem*]" (*QE* 5, 5.3.1.1: 21). Buridan holds adamantly to the 'No deception, no fallacy' principle, noting, e.g., that the fallacy of begging the question cannot involve an "identical claim that is assumed for the purpose of proving itself (since this would be ridiculous and would not deceive the respondent)" (*S* 7.4.4: 571).

11. The common element here seems to be the elimination of falsity: "every sophistic argumentation is to be solved by the abolition and manifestation of some falsity [*per interemptionem et manifestationem alicuius falsitatis*]. But there are falsities other than just the falsity of the premises, for sometimes we have a false consequence, sometimes a false proof, and sometimes a false contradiction. For, as is clear from bk. 5 of the

Metaphysics [V.29.1024b22–24], entities are said to be false in a sense because they are apt to appear to be such as they are not, or to be what they are not" (*S* 7.6.1: 602–603).

12. See also Ebbesen 1984, 103.

13. Aristotle, *De Sophisticis Elenchis* 4. The six fallacies *in dictione* are: equivocation, amphiboly, composition, division, accent, and figure of words. The seven fallacies *extra dictionem* are: *secundum quid et simpliciter,* accident, *ignoratio elenchi,* consequent, *petitio principii,* non-cause as cause, and treating many questions as one (*S* 7.2.4–5: 511–15).

14. Aristotle characterizes fallacies *extra dictionem* only negatively, as being "independent of language" (*De Sophisticis Elenchis* 4.165b24). The positive claim that cause of the appearance in such fallacies comes from things—e.g., in Peter of Spain: "a fallacy is called *extra dictionem* whose cause of appearance and cause of non existence is in the thing [*in re*]" (*Summulae* VII; de Rijk 1967, 145)—is a Stoic accretion, though it is doubtful whether medieval logicians would have recognized this, and in any case it is not known precisely how the Stoics understood the distinction. See Ebbesen, "Ancient Scholastic Logic as the Source of Medieval Scholastic Logic," in *CHLMP,* 124 and Ebbesen 1987b, 120–21.

15. In keeping with his focus on ordinary discourse, the language of "those who speak in a practical manner" (*S* 7.4.2: 561), Buridan's preferred view (he mentions two other views which he finds unacceptable, but does not wish to "reprove") is that the term 'equivocation' supposits for "the use of the equivocal term in its several significations." Thus, in the fallacy of equivocation, "the cause of appearance is the identity of that incomplex utterance in both matter and form, and the cause of defectiveness is the use of that word in its diverse significations" (*S* 7.3.2: 516). The 'matter' here refers to "the sounds and syllables that make up an incomplex word," whereas the 'form' covers "the various modes of uttering, accenting, separating, or connecting the various words that occur in the utterance of an expression" (*S* 7.2.3: 510–11).

16. As we saw in chapter 6 above, Buridan, following Boethius and Peter of Spain, defines argumentation as "an explication of an argument by means of an expression" (*S* 6.1.2: 392).

17. Likewise, "the appearance of syllogism, by which this fallacy [of accident] comes about, should not arise from the utterance but rather from the intentions and the things signified [*ex parte intentionum et rerum significatarum*], and it would occur in a like manner even if utterances were not taken into account, as was said earlier; were this not so, it would not be called a fallacy apart from words" (*S* 7.4.1: 549).

18. Buridan does not take the further step of suggesting that all *in dictione* fallacies are reducible to *extra dictionem* fallacies, presumably because there are no *in dictione* fallacies at the mental level, which is free of ambiguity.

19. See Ebbesen 1987b, 120–21.

20. See Aristotle, *De Interpretatione* 16a3–8; Boethius, *Commentarii in librum Aristotelis 'Peri Hermeneias',* ed. 2a, I, cap. *De signis; PL* 64: 407B); and section 4 of chapter 1 above. Peter King points out that for Buridan, "the relationship of one language to another is not holistic, but piecemeal. A particular inscription will be related to a particular utterance, a particular utterance to a particular concept" (1985, 7). This is correct, except—as we shall see in a moment—for the suggestion

that there is a language of concepts hierarchically aligned with conventional spoken languages.

21. The term 'mental language [*lingua mentalis*]' is, as far as I know, unattested in the medieval Latin tradition (in his important book on the subject, Claude Panaccio lists twenty-six different Greek and Latin cognates for "le discours intérieur" along with the authors in which they occur, but not this one; see Panaccio 1999b, 306–307). I would argue that this is for good reason: although '*lingua*', '*oratio*', and '*sermo*' were all used in an extended sense to mean 'language', '*lingua*' was primarily understood to mean the tongue, '*oratio*' the action of speaking, and '*sermo*' a conversation between two or more speakers. '*Lingua mentalis*' would have made sense to a Latin speaker only as a kind of metaphor, like 'mental muscle'. The key authority here was Augustine. In a remark often cited together with Aristotle and/or Boethius on the threefold division of terms, Augustine declares that the inner word "belongs to neither Greek, nor Latin, nor to any other language [*nec graecum est, nec latinum, nec linguae alicuius alterius*]" (*De Trinitate* XV.10, n. 19; *PL* 42: 1071). This inner word, "which is prior to every sound and to every thought of sound," is the inarticulate *logos* whose vision constitutes the wisdom of eternal things; it is "that word which belongs to no language, the true word of the true thing, having no nature particular to it, but deriving entirely from that knowledge from which it is born [*quod est verbum linguae nullius, verbum verum de re vera, nihil de suo habens, sed totum de illa scientia de qua nascitur*]" (*De Trinitate* XV.12, n. 21; *PL* 42: 1075). Buridan's older contemporary, William of Ockham, cites the first Augustine passage at the beginning of his *Summa logicae,* and, like Buridan, speaks of mental terms and mental propositions, but never mental language (*Summa logicae* I: 1; *Opera Philosophica* I: 7).

22. In support of the idea that the purpose of spoken language is to communicate our thoughts to others, Buridan quotes from Aristotle, *De Anima* II.8.420b29–33: "Not every sound, as we said, made by an animal is voice . . . what produces the impact [of air against the windpipe] must have soul in it, and must be accomplished by an act of imagination, for voice is a sound with meaning." Commenting on this passage, he remarks that "since an utterance cannot be uttered without some concept, every utterance signifies that the animal uttering it conceived something . . . 'significative utterance' [therefore refers] to something that notifies the man or animal hearing it what thing (or things) is (or are) conceived, and in what manner by the utterer (and I mean notifies, either by nature or by voluntary stipulation [*institutio*])" (*S* 1.1.4: 9–10). See also *QM* IX.5: 58va, where Buridan worries that the practice of refusing to distinguish the different senses of a proposition might cause "disputation and human communication to perish [*periret saepe disputatio et collocutio hominum ad invicem*]."

23. I here concur with the judgment of Paul Vincent Spade, "The Semantics of Terms," in *CHLMP,* 190. It is important to note that Buridan does not explicitly reject the idea of a naturally significant mental language. It is just that he makes almost no use of it. And although he sometimes attributes quasi-linguistic properties such as signification to concepts, he does so in a much more attenuated fashion than Ockham, preferring to speak about them (appropriately enough) in psychological terms. In my view, it is possible to read Buridan as an advocate of mental language only if we attach no significance to his choice of terminology here.

24. Thus, for example, Buridan notes in the eighth treatise of the *Summulae* that "a thoroughgoing investigation" of the question of whether adjectival nouns have nominal or real definitions "pertains to the *Metaphysics,* or, in a certain respect, to *On the Soul.*" There follows a discussion of whether "a sense apprehends only in a singular manner," referring the reader to Book II of his commentary on Aristotle's *De Anima* (*S* 8.2.4: 651).

25. *QE* 5, 5.3.1.3: 21–22: "*Fallacie autem extra dictionem dicuntur deceptiones provenientes a processibus ratiocinativis qui possent fieri si non essent signa ad placitum instituta. Hoc tamen non obstante etiam possunt fieri in signis ad placitum institutis.*"

26. Duns Scotus, *Ordinatio* I, d. 42, q. unica.; *Opera Omnia* VI: 348: "*quia sicut intellectus 'inclusus in naturalibus' tradidit omnem artem de syllogismo apparente, informi et defectuoso, sic posset solvi per illam artem ad dissolvendum omnem talem syllogismum, apponendo talem artem ad talem paralogismum.*"

27. *QE* 7, 3.3.4: 31: "*Dico ergo aliter quod ad paralogismos fallacie equivocationis respondendum est simpliciter concedendo vel simpliciter negando aliquam premissarum. Et ex hoc ostenderetur discursum non valere. Nichilominus ex superhabundantia et ad docendum alios et propter attendentes ne credant respondentem sibi contradicere et male respondere, respondens potest distinguere aliquam praemissarum et ostendere ignorantibus diversos eius sensus, quorum unus est verus et reliquus est falsus, licet hoc non oportet fieri de virtute sermonis.*"

28. There are interesting similarities between Buridan's connection of meaning with use and the discussion of the fallacy of equivocation in the *Ars Meliduna,* an anonymous logic text dating from the mid-twelfth century. See de Rijk 1967, 298.

29. Ria van der Lecq and H. A. G. Braakhuis 1994, "Introduction" to *QE*: xxx.

30. At issue is something like the following version of the principle of non-contradiction: "the same thing cannot at one and the same time both be and not be, or admit of any other similar pair of opposites" (Aristotle, *Metaphysics* XI.5.1062a1).

31. This is connected to Buridan's idea, developed in his *Sophismata* discussion of alethic paradoxes, that, taken literally, every proposition asserts itself to be true. For the details, see chapter 9 below.

32. Buridan here applies what we would recognize as standard truth-functional analyses for the logical connectives 'and' and 'or', i.e., where 'A and B' is true just in case A is true and B is true, but otherwise false, and 'A or B' is false just in case A is false and B is false, but otherwise true (*QE* 7, 3.3.3: 31). In her review of *QE*, E. J. Ashworth points out that in the *Summulae,* Buridan actually denies the doctrine that no proposition is to be distinguished with respect to propositions containing equivocal terms, and suggests this as evidence that the *Summulae* was composed before the 1340 statute (Ashworth in *Speculum* 72 [1997]: 1151–53; cf. *S* 7.3.4, 518–19).

33. The difference between the two forms of inquiry is never far from Buridan's mind. In his eighth treatise discussion of quidditative definitions, he says: "I believe we should reply that an adjectival name, taken adjectivally, is such that just as it does not provide a suppositum for the verb [*non reddit suppositum verbo*] according to the grammarians, so also it does not supposit, strictly speaking, according to the logicians" (*S* 8.2.4: 648).

34. Thus, "the illusion of syllogism, by which this fallacy [of accident] comes about, should not arise from the utterance but rather from the intentions and the things signified" (*S* 7.4.1: 549). Likewise, "context [*materia*]" and "style of speaking

[*modum loquendi*]" play a large role in many of the sophistical arguments discussed by Aristotle: "it is well known that those who speak in a theoretical manner [*loquentes pure speculative*] do not distinguish between particular and indefinite propositions where truth and falsity are concerned, but those who speak in a practical manner, about human actions, or morals, as do lawyers, jurists, and common people [*vulgares*], strongly distinguish between them" (S 7.4.2: 561). Later, Buridan specifies that his definition of 'antecedent' and 'consequent' is given "in the logicians' usage [*apud logicum*]" (S 7.4.5: 573).

Notes to Chapter 8

1. Boethius, *De divisione,* preface; Magee 1998, 4–5. It is worth noting that Boethius uses the Latin term '*peritia*' here, meaning skill, or knowledge acquired by experience.

2. In a remark showing that he was familiar with Boethius's text, Buridan notes that Boethius "calls attributes 'accidents' [*vocans passiones 'accidentia'*]" (S 8.1.6: 621).

3. The predicability test is met in all three cases, though the situation is more complicated in the case of denominative predicables since, as Buridan notes, Boethius "posits three kinds of division of wholes that are predicable denominatively of their parts, namely, [the division] of a subject into its accidents, that of an accident into its subjects, and that of an accident into accidents" (S 8.1.6: 621). The 'Of horses . . .' example illustrates the second kind.

4. Cf. *QM* VII.21: 54vb: "As for the concept of a definable term, its signification is in some way confused and explicable by some other terms, and so a definable term must be definitively resolvable into several terms [*de ratione termini diffinibilis est quod eius significatio sit aliquo modo confusa et explicabilis per aliquos alios terminus, et ita terminus diffinibilis debet esse diffinitive resolubilis in plures terminos*]."

5. Gyula Klima correctly points out that it is the entire phrase '*diffinitio explicans quid nominis*' that is properly rendered by 'nominal definition', since the Latin term '*quid nominis*' was understood to be just 'the meaning of the name'—which of course even utterances signifying simple concepts have ("Buridan's Theory of Definitions in His Scientific Practice," in Thijssen and Zupko 2001, 31, n. 5). Nevertheless, simplicity and subsequent usage make the translation of '*quid nominis*' by 'nominal definition' more appropriate.

6. As we have seen, it is precisely the lack of such skills of interpretation, or reading, that is exhibited in the activities of the "literalist" students and teachers targeted in the arts faculty statute of December 29, 1340.

7. Cf. *QM* VII.21: 54vb (cf. *QP* I.4: 5ra): "because there is no infinite regress in definitions or quidditative predications, it must be that at some point one reaches indefinable terms, viz., terms in quidditative and other predications which are not further resolvable using definitions into prior or more simple terms [*sed quia non proceditur in infinitum in diffinitionibus nec in praedicatis quidditativis, oportet aliquando venire ad terminos indiffinibiles, scilicet qui nec in praedicatis quidditativis nec in aliis amplius sunt diffinitive resolubiles in terminos priores vel simpliciores*]."

8. Buridan explicitly ties this point to its Aristotelian source: "in every reasoning, be it dialectical or demonstrative, it is necessary to know beforehand the nominal

definition of each term used in that reasoning, as Aristotle rightly states in bk. 1 of the *Posterior Analytics* [I.1.71a12–28]" (*S* 8.2.4: 642; cf. *QP* III.7: 50rb).

9. We should not try to discern the semantic complexity of a term from its syntax alone. Buridan notes that we could all conventionally agree to use the term 'D' to signify the concept signified by the proposition, 'A man runs', which would make 'A man runs' the correct interpretation or nominal definition of the term 'D'. Likewise, citing a traditional example, he points out that "a barrel hoop hanging in front of a tavern is a sign imposed conventionally to signify, and its interpretation is: 'Wine is sold in this house'" (*S* 8.2.3: 637; cf. *S* 9.6, 3rd sophism: 935, n. 142).

10. The idea that a quidditative, or real, definition "signifies more than the *definitum*" derives from the fact that the genus and difference terms of the *definitum* (e.g., 'animal' and 'rational' for 'man') signify more than the *definitum*, although, as Buridan emphasizes, they do not stand for more things, since "the genus is restricted by the difference added to it so as to supposit only for the items for which the *definitum* supposits" (*S* 8.2.4: 646).

11. This is nicely expressed by Gyula Klima: "a connotative term is what in modern parlance we would call a non-rigid designator of its supposita: it can cease to supposit for its supposita without their destruction, as a result of removing its connotata," in the way that 'wealthy man' will cease to supposit for someone who has squandered his fortune, although the man himself will continue to exist ("Buridan's Theory of Definitions in His Scientific Practice," in Thijssen and Zupko 2001, 38).

12. Buridan holds that complete demonstrative knowledge is beyond the reach of our cognitive powers. See *QP* I.5: 7rb: "And so I believe that no man has ever known anything perfectly, unless he is God, or a saint in heaven (and I am not going to say anything about this at present). . . . And it is certain that knowing stone or straw, sleep or wakefulness, perfectly in this way is exceedingly difficult or impossible for us. As far as we are concerned, it is a great thing if we can attain special knowledge of the several and principal causes of effects by knowing that they are effects of this cause, and how they are effects of this cause [*Et sic ego credo quod nunquam homo nisi fuerit deus vel beatus in patria, de quibus nihil dico modo, scivit aliquam rem perfecte. . . . Et certum est quod sic scire perfecte lapidem vel festucam, somnum vel vigiliam, est nobis valde difficile vel impossibile, et est nobis magna res si ad specialem notitiam plurium et principalium causarum effectuum possumus pervenire sciendo quod illae sunt huius effectuum causae et quomodo*]."

13. *QM* IV.9: 19vb: "*ideo videtur difficile a quo originaliter conceptus quo concipimus rem esse proveniat. Et videtur mihi esse dicendum quod res percipiuntur et iudicantur esse secundum quod percipiuntur tanquam in prospectu cognoscentis.*"

14. *QM* IV.9: 20ra: "*quoniam autem per intellectum absolvimus conceptum rei a conceptu talis praesentiae et etiam a conceptu habitudinis rei ad talem praesentiam, tunc imponimus res ad significandum per illa nomina 'essentia', 'homo', 'lapis'.*"

15. Aristotle, *Metaphysics* VII.12.1037b30–1038a35.

16. *QP* I.4: 5rb:

Item cum non sit processus in infinitum in diffinitionibus, sed necesse sit devenire ad terminos indefinibiles, et diffinitiones proprie non sint nisi terminorum substantialium, ut declaratum est vii Metaphysicae, et termini substantiales non diffiniuntur per terminos accidentales, ut ibidem dicitur, sequitur quod est devenire ad terminos substantiales indiffinibiles. Sed talibus terminis, scilicet substantialibus et indiffinibilibus, corresponderent conceptus substantiales simplices. Si enim corresponderent eis conceptus complexi et compositi ex simplicibus ipsi essent diffinibiles et diffinitive resolubiles per terminos et in terminos correspondentes illis conceptibus simplicibus ex quibus illi complexi sunt compositi. Item si conceptus substantialis hominis sit complexus, ponamus quod hoc sit ex tribus simplicibus, scilicet A, B, et C, tunc si nullus conceptus substantiae est simplex, A non esset nisi conceptus accidentis, et similiter nec B nec C. Igitur totum complexum ex eis non esset conceptus nisi accidentium et non substantiae, cum totum nihil sit praeter partes, sed hoc est absurdum, scilicet quod conceptus substantialis hominis non sit nisi conceptus accidentium.

17. It should perhaps be noted here that the medieval understanding of the subject/object distinction was precisely the opposite of our modern conception, where 'subjective' implies dependence on the perspective of the cognizing agent or subject, and 'objective' independence of this perspective. Subjects were understood by medieval thinkers in the Aristotelian sense as mind-independent subjects of attributes, whereas objects had intentional status, i.e., as objects of thought or sensation.

18. Clearly, the sort of consequence Buridan envisions here is entirely natural, as opposed to the deliberate and conventional process by which we characterize one proposition as a consequence of another.

19. *QP* I.4: 5va: "*intellectus naturaliter habet virtutem dividendi illam confusionem et intelligendi substantiam abstractive ab accidente et accidentes abstractive substantia et potest utriusque formare simplicem conceptum.*"

20. *QP* I.4: 5va: "*oportet quod illud tertium concurrens sit conceptus simplex, cum nec sit A, nec sit B, nec sit A et B simul, sed est aliud distinctum quod est formale propositionis mentalis cuius distinctione est affirmativa et negativa mentales de eodem subiecto et de eodem praedicato distinguntur.*" One might expect here the noun form of 'form', i.e., '*forma*'. But the nominalized neuter adjective '*formale*'—attested in both the 1509 Paris edition and the early fifteenth-century manuscript I used to check its readings (Vat. Lat. 2164: 4ra)—was a technical term in later medieval logic, referring to what we would now call the content of a proposition, as opposed to its particular mode of expression.

21. Thus, as Gyula Klima points out, Buridan concedes the existence of simple, connotative concepts which are not mere composites of simple non-connotative concepts plus syncategoremata—which happens to be Ockham's account of connotative concepts—but which "simply signify absolute things, connoting others as adjacent or non-adjacent to what they signify." One advantage of Buridan's approach, he argues, is that "we would not have to delay our semantics until we had provided nominal definitions of all connotative terms" (1993a, 48–49).

22. *QP* I.3: 4ra: "*Unde si naturalis considerat de homine, de planta, de aqua, hoc non est secundum conceptum simpliciter quidditativum sed respective ad suos motus et operationes.*" Thus, "the natural philosopher [*physicus*] does not have to know what a man is substantially, but by which movements and operations, and how and through which members and powers he is naturally suited to move and be moved, to act and be acted upon [*Physicus non habet scire quid homo est substantialiter sed quibus motibus et operationibus et quomodo et per quae membra et per quales virtutes ipse sit innatus movere et moveri, agere et pati*]" (*QP* I.3: 4ra). The terms I have translated as 'natural scientist [*naturalis*]' and 'natural philosopher [*physicus*]' were regarded by

Buridan as synonymous: "[the terms] 'by natural generation' and 'by nature' signify the same in Latin, as do 'physical' and 'natural' [*Idem autem significant 'physis generante' et 'natura' Latine, et similiter 'physicum' et 'naturale'*]" (*QDA₃* II.3: 38).

23. Again, "the natural scientist does not consider man or stone or whiteness absolutely, [i.e.] what each one of them is, for this pertains only to the metaphysician [*naturalis non considerat hominem lapidem vel albedinem simpliciter quid est unumquodque illorum, hoc enim pertinet ad solum metaphysicum*]" (*QP* II.6: 34rb; cf. *QM* VI.1: 33rb; *QDA₃* II.3: 34).

24. *QP* I.3: 4ra: "*primus et communissimus terminus substantialis sive non connotativus ponitur subiectum proprium in metaphysica, ut iste terminus 'ens' vel 'res' vel 'aliquid'.*"

25. *QM* VII.21: 54vb: "*Logicus enim ponit quod quid est est de aliquo termino diffinibili, et quaeritur eius diffinitionem . . . sicut Porphyrius ponit speciem componi ex genere et differentia.*"

26. See the passage quoted in n. 8 above. For the same reason, Buridan elsewhere refers to nominal definition as "the principle of instruction [*principium doctrinae*]" (*QP* III.7: 50rb).

27. *QM* VII.21: 54vb: "*diffinitio per genus et differentia solet logice vocari diffinitio formalis eo quod genus et differentia solent vocari formae. Et de ista diffinitione formali dicit Aristoteles in proemio De Anima quod tales diffinitiones sunt dialectice omnes et vane ad demonstrandum quia non manifestat causas rei et suorum accidentium sed solet dici quid nominis. Modo philosophus non vult sistere in tali declaratione nominis sed talia supponit vel a grammatico vel a logico et tunc vult inquirere quae res sit illa quam per talem terminum significatur.*"

28. *QM* VII.21: 54vb–55ra:

> Unde philosophus intendens non ad quid nominis sed ad quid rei quaerit non solum diffinitionem simpliciter quiddativam quae est per genus et differentiam, quia illa non est nisi declarans quid nominis. Unde si ego scio quid est animal rationale mortale, propter hoc nescio ego distincte quae res est illud animal rationale mortale, scilicet utrum sit una res simplex an composita, et si est composita ex quibus et quos partibus sit composita. Ideo philosophus ultra quaeritur diffinitionem causalem maxime quantum ad causas intrinsecas eo quod res de qua quaerimus est illae causae intrinsecae cum totum sit suae partes.

29. Cf. *S* 8.8.2: 760: "For example, if I formally know *propter quid* that there is a lunar eclipse, I do not only know that the earth is interposed and that there is a lunar eclipse, but I also know that there is a lunar eclipse because of that interposition, and to know this is to know that that interposition is the cause of the eclipse."

30. Aristotle, *De Anima* I.1.402b23–25.

31. *QM* VII.17: 52vb: "*termini substantiales de praedicamento substantiae non sunt omnino absoluti a connotatione accidentium saltem in impondendo oportet considerare accidentia . . . quamvis per illam ducamur ad notitiam substantia.*"

32. The point is not straightforward because the term 'vacuum', strictly speaking, signifies nothing. Accordingly, Buridan argues that it must correspond to a complex concept, which we expound by means of the nominal definition, 'place not filled with body [*locus non repletus corpore*]'. But he accepts the possibility that God could, by virtue of God's absolute power, annihilate the entire world inside the vault of

heaven, while preserving the heavens themselves—we might think of a glass sphere with all of the air inside removed—in the following terms: "if the lower world were annihilated and the vault of heaven remained, it would not be true to say that beneath the vault of heaven, there would be a vacuum, because beneath the vault of heaven, there would be nothing; but the vault of heaven itself, which was the place containing that inferior world, would be a vacuum, for the concave [i.e., inner] surface of the vault of heaven would first be a place filled with a body or bodies, and then a place not filled with body; therefore, that [inner] surface would be a vacuum [*si iste mundus inferior esset annihilatus, caelo remanente, non esset verum dicere quod infra caelum esset vacuum, quia infra caelum nihil esset; sed ipsum caelum quod erat locus continens ista inferiora, esset vacuum, nam superficies concava caeli est nunc locus repletus corpore vel corporibus, et tunc esset locus non repletus corpore; ideo illa superficies esset vacua*]" (*QDC* I.20: 95; cf. *QP* III.14: 57ra–rb).

33. For Buridan, doubt always presupposes knowledge: "for you would not raise a query about a knife if you had no concept of it whatsoever" (*S* 8.3.3: 671). Cf. *QAnPo* II.3: "the intellect would never ask about anything concerning which it has no precognition, such that it has no concept of the thing itself [*nunquam intellectus quaereret de quo non esset praecognitio, ita quod de se ipso nullam haberet notitiam*]."

34. The metaphor of syllogistic inference as a kind of movement (cf. Aristotle, *Posterior Analytics* II.13.97b31) is used by Buridan in his description of how we search for the middle premise: "And [the process] is similar to local motion, because every man who walks toward some place [*terminus*] also walks toward the middle, through which he must go. And if there were nothing in between him and that place, he would not be able to go through the middle, nor would he seek to go through it; on the contrary, he would already be there [*Et est simile sicut de motu locali, quia omnis (homo) vadens ad aliquem terminum vadit etiam ad medium per quod oportet transire, et si non esset medium inter ipsum et terminum, ipse non posset ire, nec quaereret (ire) ad illum terminum, immo jam haberet ipsum*]" (*QAnPo* II.3).

35. On Buridan's view, doubt always precedes the question: "in every question, properly so-called, something is known . . . and something is doubted and is asked. And neither the question nor the doubt comes to a close until what is sought has been found and manifested; however, when it is found and manifested, the doubt comes to an end, but not before" (*S* 8.12.1: 808–809).

36. For discussion, see Barnes 1969, 123–52, and Ackrill 1981, 94–106.

37. Aristotle, *Posterior Analytics* II.2.89b36–90a34. The ability immediately to hit upon the middle term in a demonstration is, of course, Aristotle's definition of quick-wittedness (ibid. I.34.89b10).

38. Barnes 1969, 124.

39. Buridan even suggests that Aristotle enumerates his list of four questions in *Posterior Analytics* II.1 "according to this kind of distinction [*secundum istum modum distinctionis*]," i.e., between the second- and third-adjacent senses of 'is' (*QAnPo* II.2).

40. The dog syllogism is from Barnes 1969, 124.

41. *QAnPo* II.4:

. . . nec conclusio demonstrationis scitur propria demonstratione nec terminus diffinitus ipsa diffinitione, immo demonstrative scitur res se habere ita sicut per conclusionem significatur se habere et per diffinitiones scitur quae res sit illa quae per terminum diffinitum significatur. Et si sic dicatur, tunc ponenda sunt duae conclusiones, correspondentes duabus primis. Prima est quod eadem res scitur diffinitive et demonstrative. // Secunda conclusio est quod licet eadem res demonstrative vel diffinitive sciatur, tamen hoc non est secundum ejus eandem appropriationem. Immo scitur demonstrative secundum appropriationem ejus complexam, affirmativam vel negativam unius termini de altero, et hoc intendimus cum dicimus conclusionem esse demonstrative scitam. Sed res scitur diffinitive secundum appropriationem ejus incomplexam, et hoc vocamus cum (dicimus) diffinibilem sciri diffinitive.

42. The innovation is tied to Buridan's doubts about whether purely quidditative definitions are available to the natural scientist. Previous thinkers (e.g., Thomas Aquinas, in *Summa Theologiae* 1a, q. 1, a. 1, ad 2) tended to be more sanguine about the possibility of scientific knowledge, and thus did not see any problem with extending the demonstrative paradigm to the natural sciences. For discussion, see chapter 13 below.

43. *QM* I.3: 4vb (cf. *QM* VI.1: 33rb; *QP* I.1: 2vb): "*Nulla enim scientia praeter metaphysicam habet considerare de quidditate rei simpliciter. . . . Similiter physicus non habet scire simpliciter quid est homo vel quid est asinus, licet possit talia describere per aliquos motus vel per aliquos operationes.*"

44. Metaphysical demonstrations "are said to be the most certain with respect to the method of demonstration, for their demonstrations proceed for the most part in the first mode of the first figure and with convertible terms. But they are not more certain than others [i.e., demonstrations in mathematics and the natural sciences] with respect to the certainty [*evidentia*] of their principles" (*S* 8.11.4: 801).

45. Of course, this means that it is possible to treat of the same subject under different sciences—a conclusion Buridan is happy to endorse: "But then you will ask: 'Who knows, then, the reason why [*propter quid*] circular wounds heal more slowly?' And I say that it is the interdisciplinary professional [*medius artifex*], who knows the external sciences [*scientias extrinsecas*]. For he knows by geometry that the edges of a circular figure are maximally distant on all sides, and he knows by medicine that for the healing of a wound its edges should come together, and the intermediate science, assuming this, provides the rest, applying the one to the other" (*S* 8.9.2: 777).

46. Klima, "Buridan's Theory of Definitions in His Scientific Practice," in Thijssen and Zupko 2001, 39–47.

47. Cf. *S* 8.2.4: 646–47 (quoted above).

48. Actually, the argument traps the demonstrator in a dilemma. As Gyula Klima puts it: "if the demonstration is valid, then its conclusion cannot essentially predicate the quidditative definition of the term 'soul', taking this term in the subject according to the concept expressed by its purely nominal definition. On the other hand, if the conclusion is interpreted as essentially predicating a quidditative definition of its *definitum*, then the demonstration is not valid" ("Buridan's Theory of Definitions in His Scientific Practice," in Thijssen and Zupko 2001, 42).

49. *QDA*₃ II.3: 35: "*quaedam est diffinitio dicens quid nominis, alia pure quidditativa, alia causalis, explicans non solum quid res est sed etiam propter quid est.*"

50. Klima, "Buridan's Theory of Definitions in His Scientific Practice," in Thijssen and Zupko 2001, 43.

51. Klima, "Buridan's Theory of Definitions in His Scientific Practice," in Thijssen and Zupko 2001, 45.

52. Because he generally subscribes to the "older interpretation," i.e., the inherence theory of predication, Thomas does not assume that the term 'soul' and its nominal definition must correspond to the same concept; thus, his definition of 'soul' can be a true '*quid nominis*', i.e., any old phrase giving the meaning of the name. But Buridan advocates the newer, identity theory of predication, and, unlike Ockham, also admits the existence of real connotative concepts, which "simply signify absolute things, connoting others as adjacent or non-adjacent to what they signify" (Klima 1993a, 47–48). For discussion of whether Thomas also accepted the identity theory, see Malcolm 1979 and Michon 1996.

53. See Ebbesen 1984, 103.

54. Gyula Klima offers the following explanatory note (*S* 8.5.2: 716, n. 199): "Buridan talks about the species of numbers, since for him numbers are concrete collections of concrete units. So, e.g., any group of three units, such as these three stones and these three people, are individuals of the species 'number three [*numerus ternarius*]'."

55. I say 'innumerable' here because Buridan does not actually claim that the principles of nature are infinitely many. Perhaps this is a consequence of the standard medieval assumption that creation is finite. In any case, he does seem to think that the empirical process by which such principles are generated is sufficiently open-ended to guarantee that "as far as we are concerned [*quoad nos*]," the number of truths encoded in nature will always outstrip our capacity to acquire and re-ordain them as "teachings [*doctrina*]." See *QAnPo* I.5.

56. Another example—which comes up in the third treatise, before the elements of demonstrative proof have been presented and discussed—is the principle, 'Every natural change requires an agent', in connection with which Buridan simply remarks that it can be stated "baldly, and without proof" (*S* 3.6.1: 194). There are also some borderline cases. In the ninth treatise, Buridan speculates on the epistemic status of a proposition expressing the truth conditions for affirmative categorical propositions, i.e., "for the truth of an affirmative categorical proposition it is required that the terms, namely, the subject and the predicate, supposit for the same thing or things; therefore, it suffices for its falsity that they do not supposit for the same thing. And perhaps this is not a conclusion but rather an indemonstrable principle, or, if it is a conclusion, it comes close to an indemonstrable principle" (*S* 9.2, 10th conclusion: 855).

57. Buridan's failure to 'talk the talk' as regards demonstrations in the natural sciences apparently led Eileen Serene to conclude that "Buridan considers demonstrative science only a small subset of science," and that he "seems willing in practice to relegate demonstrative science to a peripheral status" ("Demonstrative Science" in *CHLMP*, 516–17). But this does not explain why Buridan goes to such lengths in the *Summulae* to push demonstration beyond the paradigm of the A-form syllogism. To put the point in a Buridanian fashion, we may think of Serene's conclusion as true of demonstrations understood in the strict sense, but not of demonstrative argumentation considered more generally, which includes a vast number of indemonstrable principles that are certain and evident, but whose evidentness is not as absolute as that of the principle of non-contradiction. Thus, "absolute necessity or absolute perseity pertains to demonstrations properly speaking, but not necessity or perseity with qualification

[*necessitas simpliciter et perseitas simpliciter pertinent ad demonstrationes proprie dictas, et non necessitas vel perseitas secundum quid*]" (*S* 8.6.3: 734; cf. *S* 8.10.5: 787–88).

58. Aristotle, *De Anima* III.4.429a13 ff.; Averroes, *Commentarium Magnum in Aristotelis De anima* III.4: 386; III.5: 407.

59. The notions of appearance and assent are almost certainly Stoic in origin. As Cicero puts it, "Zeno used to clinch the wise man's sole possession of scientific knowledge with a gesture. He would spread out the fingers of one hand and display its open palm, saying 'An impression [*visum*] is like this'. Next he clenched his fingers a little and said, 'Assent [*adsensus*] is like this'. Then, pressing his fingers quite together, he made a fist, and said that this was cognition [*comprehensio*] (and from this illustration he gave that mental state the name of *katalepsis,* which it had not before). Then he brought his left hand against his right fist and gripped it tightly and forcefully, and said that scientific knowledge [*scientia*] was like this and possessed by none except the wise man" (*Academica* II.145; tr. Long and Sedley 1987, 253–54).

60. *QDA₃* III.2: 17: "*Nec apparet mihi quod auctoritates pro secunda parte sint bene fulcitae demonstrationibus, licet possent fulciri probabilis argumentis, de quibus etiam dicetur post.*"

61. Sten Ebbesen brings out this epistemic side of demonstration rather nicely: "Knowledge is an attitude to a true proposition. This attitude arises instinctively as soon as we have the same attitude to the premises and to the logical principle governing the syllogism. Our having this attitude to the premises may itself be the result of a proof, but a finite number of steps will take us back to indemonstrable propositions to which we have the attitude of knowledge without having any proof of them" (1984, 101; cf. *QAnPo* II.11).

62. The distinction is often drawn in terms of the relative firmness and evidentness of a principle: "although all first and indemonstrable principles, possessed by us in their appropriate manner, are firm and evident, yet there is one [i.e., the principle of noncontradiction] which Aristotle declares, in bk. 4 of the *Metaphysics,* to be the firmest and most evident and to be firmer and more evident than all or most others" (*S* 8.9.5: 782).

63. Also, with secondhand knowledge, there is the fear, noted in chapter 7 above, that "teachers are capable of saying what is false and even textbooks may contain falsehoods [*doctores possunt falsa dicere et in libris etiam falsa scribi possunt*]" (*QM* I.8: 7va; see also Ebbesen 1984, 103). Part of the concern here is that our assent is not grounded in the relevant particulars, since "the words of teachers and of books do not produce in students singular concepts, but common ones" (*S* 8.7.9: 750). At the level of principles, however, the grounding is the reverse, with principles of the subordinate sciences deriving their certainty and evidentness from the higher science: "the evidentness of specific terms and principles depends on the evidentness and assumption of general terms, principles, and conclusions" (*S* 8.11.5: 804).

64. Buridan is always sensitive to the pedagogical import of his work, in both its spoken and written forms: "we call the knowledge of the conclusion in the strict sense a cognition that is steadfast and enduring [*mansiva*] and one that enables someone to teach [*doctrinalis*] with certainty and evidentness" (*S* 8.7: 738); "doctrinal [demonstrations] are those by which we can teach students who know the customary significations of utterances without the presence of the things signified, and by writing down these demonstrations in books we can also teach their successors [the same conclusions]" (*S* 8.7.9: 749).

NOTES TO CHAPTER 9

1. The construction of the *casus* often took some ingenuity, as in Buridan's discussion of the sophism 'You will be a donkey': "The first [conclusion] is that an utterance like 'A man is a donkey' can be true, by positing that, by a deluge or by divine power, the whole of the Latin language is lost, because all those who knew Latin are destroyed, and then a new generation following them impose by convention the utterance 'man' to signify the same as that utterance signifies to us now, and the utterance 'donkey' to signify the same as the utterance 'animal' signifies to us now. This case is possible" (*S* 9.6, 1st conclusion: 930–31).

2. De Rijk 1962, 595.

3. For the historical background, see the articles by Eleonore Stump, "Obligations: From the Beginning to the Early Fourteenth Century" and Paul Vincent Spade, "Obligations: Developments in the Fourteenth Century" in *CHLMP*, 315–34 and 335–41.

4. For discussion, see Anthony Kenny, "Medieval Philosophical Literature" in *CHLMP*, 21–29 (the article is co-authored by Anthony Kenny and Jan Pinborg, but a note at its head indicates that Kenny is responsible for the sections on disputation).

5. Twentieth-century logicians made unicorns their non-existent creature of choice. But unicorns never played this role in medieval logic, presumably because they were thought to exist.

6. There is no satisfactory English translation of the term '*complexe significabile*' or its synonym, '*enuntiabile*', which means 'that which is capable of being expressed by a proposition [*enuntiatio*]'. I shall therefore keep the Latin in what follows.

7. Peter Abelard discusses virtually the same position in his *Logica ingredientibus*, 'Gloss on *De interpretatione*', although he does not use the phrase '*complexe significabile*' for the significate of a proposition. Instead, he refers to "their *dicta*, which are like things for propositions, although they are not essences at all [*dicta eorum, quae sunt quasi res propositionum, cum tamen nullae penitus essentiae sint*]" (Abelard, *Logica ingredientibus; Geyer 1919, 367, ll. 12–13*).

8. This discovery was made by the late Gedeon Gál, O. F. M., for which see Gál 1977.

9. Wood and Gál 1990, 181. For discussion, see Zupko 1994–97, 213–17.

10. Wood and Gál 1990, 192. See also Nuchelmans 1980b.

11. Wood and Gál 1990, 193.

12. Zupko 1994–97, 216–17. See also my review of Wood and Gál 1990 in *Speculum* 68, no. 1 (January 1993): 95–97.

13. Wood and Gál 1990, 195. The convention of indicating a *complexe significabile* with a noun-phrase, specifically a Latin accusative + infinitive construction, was almost universal among those who discussed the doctrine, including Buridan: "But others say that 'man drinking wine' is a certain complex signifiable, corresponding, on the part of the thing, to the corruptible proposition, 'A man drinks wine' [*Alii autem dicunt quod hominem bibere vinum est quoddam significabile complexum, correspondens a parte rei huic corruptibili propositioni 'homo bibit vinum'*]" (*QAnPr* I.5).

14. Wood and Gál 1990, 195.

15. For the chain of transmission, see Tachau 1988, especially "Epilogue: Adam Wodeham's First Parisian Readers": 353–83; Biard 1989, 181–85; Nuchelmans 1973, 227–42; and Nuchelmans, "The Semantics of Propositions" in *CHLMP*, 203–207.

16. Gál 1977, 70.

17. Trapp and Marcolino 1981, 8–9.

18. De Rijk 1994, 160. I here translate from the official record of Autrecourt's trial. Another text, with some differences in the order and wording of the articles of condemnation, derives from the published list of theses Nicholas was forced to recant in public. For the critical edition of both texts, see de Rijk 1994, 139–207. In an effort to link Autrecourt's views with Gregory of Rimini, Élie (1936, 37–40) contended that Autrecourt had once been a student of Rimini's, but this proposal has been discredited by Nuchelmans (1973, 237–38). For an excellent overview of Autrecourt's epistemological views, see the introductory essay by Christophe Grellard in Grellard 2001, 7–72.

19. Thijssen 1991, 171. Cf. Nuchelmans 1973: "As long as we do not know in what kind of context Nicholas of Autrecourt made his statements, the question of whether he was an adherent of the *complexe significabile* theory or not cannot be satisfactorily answered" (237–38).

20. I borrow the useful term "*aliquid-nihil* dilemma" from Thijssen 1991b, 167.

21. See Zupko 1994–97, 217–23.

22. Buridan offers no reason why *complexe significabilia* cannot be substances, but we may surmise that it is for the same reason that they cannot be creatures, i.e., "if they were creatures, then they would be some kind of eternal creature, which is against the faith [*si esset creatura, tunc esset aliqua creatura aeterna, quod esset contra fidem*]" (*QM* VI.8: 38vb).

23. As Gyula Klima notes, "in this way, Buridan manages to assign some credible semantic function to such sentential nominalizations without having to subscribe to a dubious ontology of eternal or quasi-eternal *enuntiabilia*, or *complexe significabilia*, distinct from ordinary substances and accidents" (*S* 9.1: 844, n. 28).

24. Indeed, the term '*complexe*' probably derives from the use of '*complexum*' as a synonym for '*propositio*'.

25. *QM* V.7: 31rb (cf. *S* 9.1, to the 5th sophism: 843–44): "*deus enim qui est simplicissimus non solum est incomplexe significabilis, immo etiam complexe, quoniam complexe significatur per illas propositiones 'deus est prima causa', 'deus est primus actus', et sic de aliis, et sic omnes res de mundo est complexe significabilis.*"

26. *QM* V.7: 31ra (cf. *S* 9.1, to the 5th sophism: 843–44): "*Alia conclusio videtur mihi ponenda contra hoc quod alii opinantur quod deum esse causam Sortis non est significabile complexe quod nec sit deus, nec Sortes, nec ambo, nec etiam aliqua dispositio inhaerens deo aut Sorti, quia ex quo tale nulli inhaeret ipsum per se magis subsisteret vel saltem aeque per se sicut homo vel lapis, et sic magis videtur esse substantia.*"

27. See Trapp and Marcolino 1981, 8–9.

28. *QM* V.7: 31ra: "*si possumus omnia salvare per pauciora, nos non debemus in naturalibus ponere plura, quia frustra fit per plura quod potest fieri per pauciora. Modo omnia possunt salvari faciliter non ponendo talia complexe significabilia quae nec sint substantiae, nec accidentia, nec per se subsistant, nec aliis inhaerant. Ideo talia non sunt ponenda.*"

29. Compounding the difficulty is the fact that we do not possess any works from both authors in a relevant genre, such as a *Sentences* commentary or a question commentary on Aristotle's *Metaphysics*. As a career arts master, Buridan did not lecture or write on theology, whereas nearly all of Wodeham's surviving writings are theological, the exception being his independent *Treatise on Indivisibles* (ed. Wood 1988). The views of Buridan and Wodeham on indivisibles are compared in Zupko 1993.

30. The qualification that the proposition must be "formulated" means that it must actually exist as an inscription or utterance, or else conceptually, i.e., "in my mind" (*S* 9.2, 3rd conclusion: 851). Like most medieval logicians, Buridan regards sentence-tokens, rather than types, as the proper subject matter of logic. As Hughes 1982 notes, "one important corollary of regarding propositions as sentence-tokens is that they are things that come into being and go out of existence, and that it is always a contingent matter whether a certain proposition (or indeed any equiform one) exists at a given time or not. Moreover, if a certain proposition does not exist at a certain time, then according to Buridan it cannot be either true or false at that time" (6; cf. *S* 9.1, to the 2nd sophism: 841; *S* 9.8, 1st sophism: 953).

31. *QM* VI.8: 39ra (cf. *QDA*₃ III.12: 134; *S* 9.2, 11th conclusion: 856):

ad falsitatem affirmativae nulla est causa quia nihil requiritur in re significata vel in rebus significatis, quia sufficit quod sit formata et non vera, si enim sit formata et non vera, sequitur quod est falsa. Modo ad hoc quod non sit vera non oportet aliquid esse a parte re significatae, sed sufficit non esse causam propter quam esset vera si esset vera . . . quia si nunquam fuisset vel etiam nunquam foret equus vel asinus, adhuc illa esset falsa 'equus est asinus' et ista vera 'equus non est asinus'. Et tamen huiusmodi falsitas non est in rebus significatis aliqua causa, nihil vero est in eis ex quo nihil sunt.

32. *QM* VI.8: 39ra (cf. *QDA*₃ III.12: 134): "*quaecumque causae requiruntur ad veritatem alicuius propositionis, eaedem requiruntur ad falsitatem suae contradictoriae.*"

33. Hourani 1972–73, 84.

34. Cf. Aristotle, *Metaphysics* VI.4.1027b25–27: "for falsity and truth are not in things—it is not as if the good were true and the bad were in itself false—but in thought; while with regard to simple things and essences truth and falsity do not even exist in thought."

35. In other writings, Buridan sometimes expresses these truth conditions in terms of a more traditional formula derived from a gloss on Aristotle: "Many people commonly say the opposite [viz., when they hold that every true proposition is true because howsoever it signifies, it is so in the thing or things signified], and take Aristotle in the *Categories* [5.4b9–10] to be authoritative when he says that an expression [*oratio*] is true or false because the thing exists or does not exist, for an expression is said to be true because the thing exists, i.e., because it is so in reality, and false because the thing does not exist, i.e., because it is not so in reality [*Oppositum dicunt multi communiter et accipiunt auctoritatem ab Aristotele in Praedicamentis dicente quod ab eo quod res est vel non est, dicitur oratio vera vel falsa, ab eo enim quod res est, id est, quod ita est in re, dicitur oratio vera, et ab eo quod res non est, id est, quod non est ita in re, dicitur oratio falsa]*" (*QM* VI.8: 38vb; cf. *QDA*₃ III.12: 133–38). But he makes it clear in the *Sophismata* that this is not his preferred way of speaking: "But in the end we should note—since we can use names by convention [*ad placitum*], and many people commonly use this way of putting the matter—that with respect to every true proposition we say: 'It is so [*ita est*]', and with respect to every false one we say: 'It is not so [*non est ita*]', and I do not intend to eliminate this way of speaking. But for the sake of brevity I may use it often intending by it not what it signifies on account of its primary imposition but the diverse causes of truth and falsity assigned above for diverse propositions, as has been said" (*S* 9.2, 14th conclusion: 859; cf. *QDA*₃ III.12: 134,

where he calls the traditional formula "a way of speaking of which I neither approve nor disapprove at present—but see my more complete account of this elsewhere [i.e., in the *Sophismata*] [*quam locutionem ad praesens nec probo nec reprobo, sed de hoc videatur alibi perfectior declaratio*]").

36. We might think of this along the following lines: "[the term] 'false' does not assert [of something] what [it is], but how [it is]" (*S* 7.3.10: 546).

37. *QDA₃* III.11: 123 (cf. *QP* II.3: 31ra–rb): "*nam res uno modo potest aliter et aliter se habere prius et posterius ad aliquod extrinsecum, sine aliqua sui mutatione, per mutationem illius extrinseci, sic enim columna prius mihi dextra sit posterius mihi sinistra.*" For the other two modes of accidental change, see chapter 11 below. The column example was traditional. Most everyone assumed it was from Boethius's *De Trinitate*, although the example there has one man approaching another stationary man, not a man approaching a column.

38. Cf. Aristotle, *Categories* 5.4a35–b2: "Statements and beliefs, on the other hand, themselves remain completely unchangeable in every way; it is because the actual thing changes that the contrary comes to belong to them. For the statement that someone is sitting remains the same; it is because of a change in the actual thing that it comes to be true at one time and false at another. Similarly with beliefs."

39. Cf. Aristotle, *Physics* II.3.195a13–14; *Metaphysics* V.2.1013b13–15. Likewise, Buridan suggests that absent causes are causes only in a metaphorical or 'attributive [*secundum attributivam locutionem*]' sense (*QDA₃* III.12: 138).

40. A sampler: Burge 1978; Hughes 1982; van der Lecq 1993a; Pironet 1993; Prior 1962; Roberts 1953; Scott 1966; Sirridge 1978; Spade 1975 and 1978.

41. A typical list of positions can be found, e.g., in the *Insolubilia* of Thomas Bradwardine, which was written in the 1320s. See Paul Vincent Spade, "Insolubles," in the *Stanford Encyclopedia of Philosophy*.

42. Another solution, which concedes that Socrates's proposition "is true and false at the same time," is rejected as sacrificing too much. The problem with this theory is that it makes it impossible to give the contradictory of Socrates's proposition, which means that it has no proper coordinates in Aristotelian logical space.

43. This is effectively Thomas Bradwardine's solution to the Liar (see Paul Vincent Spade, "Insolubles," in the *Stanford Encyclopedia of Philosophy*). But it was not without precedent. Among the others who defended Buridan's solution would have been Bonaventure, who, in the course of discussing one of Augustine's arguments for the existence of God (*Soliloquies* I.15)—i.e., that if no truth exists, then some truth exists; and if some truth exists, a First Truth exists—records the objection that the first inference fails because no proposition can entail its own contradictory. Bonaventure agrees, but adds the following qualification: "one must understand that an affirmative proposition makes a two-fold assertion, one which asserts the predicate of the subject, and the other which asserts that the proposition is true. . . . Contradiction is concerned with the first type of assertion, not the second. So when it is said that no truth exists [*nulla veritas est*], this proposition, insofar as it denies the predicate of the subject, does not imply its opposite, which is that some truth exists. But insofar as it asserts itself to be true, it implies that some truth exists [*infert aliquam veritatem esse*]" (*Quaestiones disputatae de mysterio Trinitatis*, q. 1, a. 1, ad 5; Latin text excerpted in Spade 1975, 53). For other advocates of this solution, see Paul Vincent Spade, "*Insolubilia*" in *CHLMP*, 249.

44. Cf. Buridan's earlier claim that contradiction requires not only the logical form of contradiction, but the speaker's intention (*S* 9.7, 2nd sophism: 943).

45. Pironet 1993, 294–95. Cf. Hughes 1982, 167–69.

46. Buridan's presentation of this alternative is somewhat complicated by the doctrinal claim that the 'nothing' signified by 'A man is a donkey' is not any kind of proposition, but rather 'that a man is a donkey [*hominem esse asinum*]', which is the *dictum* or sentential nominalization of that proposition (expressed in Latin by the accusative + infinitive construction). In Buridanian semantics, such a construction supposits for whatever both the subject and predicate terms of its corresponding proposition supposit for, provided the proposition is true; otherwise it supposits for nothing. Gyula Klima remarks that this is how "Buridan manages to assign some credible semantic function to such sentential nominalizations without having to subscribe to a dubious ontology of eternal or quasi-eternal *enuntiabilia*, or *complexe significabilia*, distinct from ordinary substances and accidents" (*S* 9.1, 844, n. 28). Buridan's sensitivity to the ontological dimensions of the problem emerges when he says that "'that a man is a donkey' is nothing, because a man cannot be a donkey [*hominem esse asinum nihil est, eo quod homo non potest esse asinus*]"—which also suffices for its falsity.

47. Paul Vincent Spade has drawn a further problem here to my attention: "if every proposition signifies *se esse veram*, and we're construing the infinitival expression personally, we've got a problem. For if the proposition is *false*, the infinitival expression has nothing it can signify, so that the proposition really *doesn't* have any additional signification at all, contrary to the whole point of the theory." If Buridan was aware of this as an additional problem for the first solution, he does not mention it.

48. As Hughes 1982 has suggested, the force of 'virtually' in 'virtually implies' is that the second proposition would be implied by the first only if the first is actually formulated (169). This emerges in a closing comment on the sophism in which Buridan remarks, "perfecting this solution, we have to say that every proposition, adding *that it exists*, implies that it is true" (*S* 9.8, 7th sophism: 970).

49. Of course, this holds only for affirmative propositions. Negative propositions are true if their subject and predicate terms *do not* stand for the same thing or things.

50. *TC* I.5: 26, ll. 41–44: "*Tamen credo quod omnis affirmativa esset vera cuius termini supponerent pro eodem modo proportionali suae formae, dum tamen nec formaliter, sive explicite, nec consecutive, vel implicite, asserit se esse falsam.*"

51. Paul Vincent Spade, "Insolubilia" in *CHLMP*, 253.

52. Cf. Anaximenes of Lampsacus, *Ars rhetorica quae vulgo fertur Aristotelis ad Alexandrum;* Fuhrmann 1966. For the Latin text Buridan probably used, see Grabmann 1931–32. Cf. also Aristotle, *Rhetoric to Alexander,* preface, 1420a5–b27. The commander metaphor is also used by Buridan of metaphysics: see *QM* VI.2: 34ra, quoted in n. 14 of the Introduction above.

Notes to Chapter 10

1. This is reminiscent of a passage in the "First Discussion, About the Natural Sciences," of the *Tahafut al-Tahafut* (= *The Incoherence of the Incoherence*), Averroes's reply to al-Ghazali's *The Incoherence of the Philosophers:* "we do not find that any of the ancient philosophers discusses miracles, although they were known and had appeared

all over the world, for they are the principles on which religion is based and religion is the principle of the virtues; nor did they discuss any of the things which are said to happen after death" (Van Den Burgh 1954, 322). It is unlikely that Buridan knew this discussion directly, however, and there is nothing similar in Averroes's *Commentarium Magnum in Aristotelis De anima',* which Buridan knew well.

2. Thijssen 1998. Thijssen's book is the best comprehensive study to date, though Courtenay and Tachau 1982, Courtenay 1989 and 1995, and Miethke 1991 are also very helpful.

3. Thijssen 1998, xii. The embedded quotation is from Bury, *History of Freedom of Thought* (London, 1913), 52.

4. That Buridan understood himself to be primarily in the business of teaching the authoritative texts of Aristotle should be clear in the following remark from the very first question of his commentary on the *Metaphysics:* "I say that of all of the intellectual virtues, metaphysics, or wisdom, is the best and most noble. Nevertheless, I exempt here intellectual dispositions supernaturally infused in us by God because Aristotle omits to mention them, and because it does not pertain to this faculty [i.e., of arts] to dispute about them [*dico quod Metaphysica sive sapientia est omnium virtutem intellectualium optima et nobilissima. Tamen excipio habitus intellectualis nobis a deo supernaturaliter infusos quia de hiis non intromisit se Aristoteles, nec pertinet de illis disputare ad istam facultatem*]" (*QM* I.1: 3rb).

5. In the notorious conclusion to his second letter to Bernard of Arezzo, Nicholas remarks that on his interpretation, "it follows . . . that in the whole of his natural and speculative philosophy, Aristotle had such certitude of scarcely two conclusions, and perhaps not even of one" (de Rijk 1994, 79). The certitude in question is that of reducibility to the principle of non-contradiction, which Nicholas defends as the only properly Aristotelian criterion for human knowledge. For the details, see section 1 of chapter 12 below.

6. Buridan never accuses a theologian of having exceeded his curricular mandate in so many words, since pronouncements of this sort would have been proper to bishops, juridical bodies of the Church and University, and other institutional authorities. He is more likely instead to point to the hubris in the offending teacher's remarks, as in his reference to the 1347 condemnation of the theologian John of Mirecourt: "I adhere to this conclusion [viz., that understanding and knowledge are dispositions distinct from the intellect and yet inhering in it] on the authority of the school of Paris and the Bishop who once summoned [the faculty] together because of the danger of many false opinions of Parisian teachers, and condemned these opinions. And the Bishop checked the arrogance of the University with the penalty of excommunication, so that they would no longer be held by anyone. And this was one of the condemned opinions: that our intellect is [the same as its] knowledge or understanding [*huic conclusioni adhaereo per auctoritatem studii Parisiensis et episcopi, qui quondam congregati propter periculum multarum falsarum opinionum Parisius seminatarum, condemnaverunt eas. Et adrogatum universitatis inhibuit episcopus sub poena excommunicationis ut non amplius ab aliquo tenerentur. Et haec fuit una de illis: scilicet quod intellectus noster esset scientia vel intellectio*" (*QDA*₃ III.11: 121; cf. *CUP* II, 1147, art. 28; for discussion, see Maier 1958, 331–39).

7. Aristotle, *Metaphysics* VI.1.1026a18; XI.7.1064b1.

8. Precedents for reading 'theology' as 'metaphysics' in this context—somewhat obscured by the fact that the incunabular edition erroneously gives '*metaphysica totalis*' for '*mathematica totalis*' and '*metaphysicus*' for '*mathematicus*' in lines 23 and 25 of folio 34ra—can be found in Robert Kilwardby, *De Ortu Scientiarum* LXVI.655 (Judy 1976, 22) and Thomas Aquinas, *In De trinitate* V, a. 4, as well as in Albert the Great, whose account is perceptively discussed in Jordan 1992.

9. *QM* I.2: 4ra–rb:

Notandum est quod hic non comparamus metaphysicam ad theologiam, quae procedit ex ignotis creditis quamvis non per se notis nec evidentissimus, quia sine dubio illam theologiam tenemus principaliorem et maxime proprie dictam sapientiam. Sed non in proposito non quaerimus nisi de habitibus intellectualis ex humana ratione et processu ratiocinativo inventis et ex nobis evidentibus deductis. Sic enim Aristoteles metaphysicam vocat 'theologiam' et 'scientiam divinam'. Unde in hoc differt metaphysica a theologia, quod cum utraque consideret de deo et de divinis, metaphysica non consideret de deo et de divinis nisi ea quae possunt probari et ratione demonstrativa concludi seu induci. Theologia vero habet pro principiis articulos creditos absque evidentia et considerat ultra quamcumque ex huiusmodi articulis possunt deduci.

10. As Thijssen (1998, 2) notes: "In many official documents and other texts, philosophers and theologians were exhorted not to cross the boundaries of their own fields—a reference to Proverbs 22:28—and not to become theologizing philosophers and philosophizing theologians."

11. *QM* I.2: 4rb (cf. *QAnPo* I.23): "*Similiter metaphysica est quaesita gratia sui ipsius, quia non ordinatur ad aliquod opus extrinsecum ipsa sit maxime speculative nec ipsa ordinatur ad alias scientias speculativas immo potius e converso cum ipsa sit principalissima et ordinatrix omnium aliarum scientiarum. Quod etiam ipsa sit principalissima apparet per hoc quod ipsa considerat prima et universalissima principia doctrinae per quae omnia alia principia aliarum scientiarum roborantur et declarantur, si indigeant declaratione.*"

12. A typical remark: "it is the task of metaphysics to show the various senses of mathematical principles in the way they should be presupposed and taken in mathematics" (*S* 8.11.4: 801–802).

13. As we shall see in chapter 12, Buridan sees the arguments of Nicholas of Autrecourt on the criteria for knowledge as posing a threat primarily to metaphysics and only secondarily or derivatively to the natural sciences.

14. Buridan argues that the distinction between the speculative sciences of metaphysics, physics, and mathematics originates from those incomplex principles, or terms, which are their proper subjects: being [*ens*] in the case of metaphysics, moveable being [*ens mobile*] in the case of physics, and what is measurable [*quantum*] in the case of mathematics. Of the ten Aristotelian categories or modes of inquiry, substance is said to belong to metaphysics; quantity, relation, and position to mathematics (though, as noted above, this is sometimes erroneously printed in the incunabular edition as 'metaphysics'); and quality, action, passion, time, and place to physics. The category of state, which Buridan interprets in the sense of someone having possessions such as a field or house, is relegated "to the practical sciences [*ad scientias practicas*]" (*QM* VI.2: 33vb–34rb). There are, of course, derivative senses in

which categories can be said to pertain to other speculative sciences, such as in connection with the four species of quality.

15. As we have seen, Buridan usually cites the case of the "old women [*vetulae*]" in this connection.

16. *QM* I.2: 4rb:

fundatum

... quando arguitur quod ipsa non est principalissima dico quod verum est si comparatur ad theologia fundamentam super articulos fidei. Sed illa circumscripta, ipsa est omnium aliarum scientiarum principalissima. Tota enim scientia legum et decretorum subiicitur morali scientiae sive morali philosophiae et ei subalternatur, nisi pro quanto decreta et decretales accipiunt aliquid ex theologia. Medicina autem ex toto subalternatur naturali philosophiae. Ideo illae non merentur dici scientiae principales. Quare autem nostra facultas sit infima? Potest dici quod hoc est propter divitias eorum qui alias profitent et quia etiam nostra facultas est valde communis. Continet enim grammaticam, logicam, rhetoricam, et ratione harum ipsa non meretur dici 'principalis'. Sed cum illis artibus ipsa etiam continet naturalem philosophiam secundum quam est principalis medicinae et moralem philosophiam secundum quam sit principalis legum et metaphysicam secundum quam est principalis simpliciter.

divitias

17. Peter of Spain, *Summulae Logicales* I.1; de Rijk 1972, 1.

18. The passage is also ambiguous about whether the riches in question are the material or the final cause of a scholar's teaching in one of the higher faculties, i.e., about whether one is inclined towards theology or law or medicine by the actual possession, or merely the desire to come into the possession, of greater lucre (or wisdom). I am grateful to my Classics colleague Garth Tissol for helping me to appreciate the nuances of this remark.

19. Buridan's general approach on questions of faith vs. physics is discussed by Edith Sylla in "*Ideo quasi mendicare oportet intellectum humanum:* The Role of Theology in John Buridan's Natural Philosophy," in Thijssen and Zupko 2001, 221–45. For the distinction between philosophy and theology in Thomas, see Sweeney 1990 and Kretzmann 1997, 23–53. Cf. also Thomas's Parisian contemporary Boethius of Dacia, who tries to solve the problem of the apparent contradiction between certain revealed truths and philosophical truths "by arguing that, not only is each discipline based on its principles, but its conclusions must be qualified by these principles" (Marenbon 1990, 267).

20. For discussion of these texts, see Paul Bakker, "Aristotelian Metaphysics and Eucharistic Theology: John Buridan and Marsilius of Inghen on the Ontological Status of Accidental Being," in Thijssen and Zupko 2001, 247–64.

21. The discussion of divine omnipotence in *QNE* X.5 is particularly interesting because it shows that Buridan is well aware that he could be seen as practicing theology without a license. After conceding that it is a consequence of God's absolute power that God could give someone the vision of beatitude while annihilating the love that would otherwise naturally accompany it, he says:

Nevertheless I neither approve nor disapprove of these statements, because they do not concern the science which Aristotle has given to us, and because they exceed [the mandate] of our Arts Faculty. In keeping with this mandate, and going no further, it was my intention to treat of moral questions in this book. And if I have sometimes crossed over [into the domain of the theologians], I believe that this has occurred incidentally. For it is certainly true that our Faculty aims to consider what further conclusions we can draw from certain assumptions, whether those assumptions are possible or impossible. And this holds for natural and moral terms alike.

[Haec tamen dicta nec approbo nec reprobo, quia sunt de scientia quam dedit nobis Aristoteles, et excedunt nostram artium facultatem, secundum quam tamen (et non supra), fuit intentio mea tractare de moralibus in hoc libro, et si aliquando ego transgredior, ego hoc reputo esse incidentaliter. Verum est tamen bene ad dictam nostram facultatem spectat considerare quid ex aliquibus positis possumus ultra concludere, sive illa posita sint possibilia sive impossibilia, et hoc tam in terminis moralibus quam naturalibus.] (*QNE* X.5: 213rb; revised text of Kilcullen 1996)

22. His remarks are quite explicit: "in this question [about whether relations are things distinct from the things they relate], I do not intend to say or to have said anything about the Holy Trinity of persons in divinity, but only about creaturely relations [*in hac quaestione nihil intendo dicere vel dixisse de ista sancta Trinitate personarum in divinis, sed solum de relationibus creaturis*]" (*QC* 10: 74, ll. 149–50).

23. Perhaps we should say, '*de jure* off-limits', as Buridan is not above occasionally teasing out the philosophical consequences of an article of faith: "As for the last [counter-argument] concerning divine foreknowledge, it is exceedingly difficult and pertains to the theologians. Nevertheless, I think that it should be resolved in keeping with what has already been said. For it was said that God knew from eternity that Peter's soul would not be annihilated. And yet it is possible that God never knew this, but that God knew from eternity the opposite, since it is possible for it to be annihilated, in view of the fact that God could annihilate it. And yet if it were annihilated, God knew from eternity that it would be annihilated [because] there is no change in divine knowledge [*Ad ultimam de praescientia divina, est valde difficile et pertinet ad theologos. Magis puto tamen quod sit solvendum secundum prius dicta. Dictum enim fuit quod deus ab aeterno scivit quod anima Petri non annihilaretur. Et tamen possibile est quod hoc nunquam scivit, immo quod ab aeterno scivit oppositum, quia possibile est quod annihilaretur, deus enim posset eam annihilare. Et tamen si annihilaretur, deus ab aeterno scivit quod annihilaretur, et non est mutatio in scientia divina*]." Buridan goes on to remark that this question is difficult "because our knowledge differs from God's knowledge, for our knowledge depends upon things, but God's knowledge is the cause of things [*quia differt nostra scientia a scientia dei, scientia enim nostra dependet a rebus, sed scientia dei est causa rerum*]" (*QM* VI.5: 37ra–rb).

24. Thomas puts this same distinction in terms of the *ratio* or concept under which the subject is considered: "although philosophy considers all existing things according to concepts [*rationes*] taken from creatures, there must be another science, which considers existing things according to concepts [*rationes*] taken from the inspiration of the divine light" (*In I Sent.*, Prol., q. 1, a. 1, ad 1; cf. *In De trinitate*, q. 5, a.1–4).

25. For this reason as well, Buridan never tries to compare the methods of philosophy and theology, let alone to suggest how the former might be subsumed by the latter. He is aware of the possibility of *rapprochement* between the two sides, if only by its absence from the Parisian scene: "it seems to me that this question [about whether it is possible for demonstration to cross disciplinary lines] is difficult first because

there has been exceedingly little discussion between the philosophers and the doctors [of theology], and second because it touches on the means of distinguishing the sciences, and it is even more difficult to assign whence, and in what way, the sciences originally received their distinction [*ista quaestio, ut mihi videtur, est difficilis, primo quia valde modicum discussa est inter philosophos et doctores, secundo quia tangit ad modum distinctionis scientiarum, et est multum difficile assignare unde et quo modo scientiae accipiant originaliter suam distinctionem*]" (*QAnPo* I.23). But his general view seems similar to Augustine's explanation of why he will not concern himself with persuading unbelievers that God exists: "I am not even sure that we ought to enter into discussion with them at all. To do so, in any event, would necessitate starting out all over again with a different approach, a different method, and different arguments" (*The Way of Life of the Catholic Church*, 6.10; Gallagher and Gallagher 1966, 11).

26. On the ontological side of the question of universals, Buridan's recognition of irreducible entities in the category of quantity distinguishes his nominalism from the even more reductionist approach of William of Ockham, who recognized only individual substances and qualities. For discussion, see Normore 1985.

27. Thus, Sten Ebbesen ("Where Were the Stoics in the Late Middle Ages?" in Strange and Zupko, forthcoming) observes that the whole Autrecourt debate depends upon "the conceptual apparatus of consequences with antecedents and consequents.... [Autrecourt] undermined the belief in substances by arguing that you cannot infer the existence of a substance from the existence of an accident unless you have built the notion of substance into that of accident, so that the consequent, 'there is a substance', is included in the antecedent, 'there is an accident'."

28. Hence his reference to such individuals as "wicked men," bent upon destroying the natural and moral sciences (*QM* II.1: 9ra).

29. See also Gyula Klima's article, "The Medieval Problem of Universals," in the *Stanford Encyclopedia of Philosophy,* especially sections 8–10.

30. Buridan's allusions to Plato on universals are fairly typical: see, e.g., *QM* VII.15: 50va–vb, and de Rijk 1992. On other topics, however, he is sometimes suspicious about whether a position handed down as Plato's is in fact Plato's. For example, after disposing of an argument introduced "on the authority of Plato [*auctoritate Platonis*]" for the role of separate substances in the generation of living things, he concludes, "and so in this way Plato's opinion is destroyed—if he in fact had an opinion of the sort we have ascribed to him [*ita igitur interimitur opinio Platonis, si habebat talem opinionem qualem ipsi imponimus*]" (*QM* VII.9: 47ra). For discussion of Buridan and Plato, see Schönberger 1994, 292–95.

31. For the meaning of twelfth-century nominalism, see the special issue of *Vivarium* (30, no. 1, May 1992) devoted to this topic.

32. See Peter King, "John Buridan's Solution to the Problem of Universals" in Thijssen and Zupko 2001, 1–27. In King's view Buridan's nominalism has three interrelated aspects: (1) the ontological thesis that there are no non-individual entities in the world; (2) the psychological thesis that some concepts, though metaphysically particular, can represent more than one individual thing; and (3) the semantic thesis that such concepts also function as common names in Mental Language.

33. Cf. *QIP* 4: 138, ll. 565–66. Buridan's treatment of transcendental terms is similar: "the subject of metaphysics is being, that is, the term 'being' [*subiectum . . . [est] ens, id est iste terminus 'ens' in metaphysica*]" (*QIP* 3: 135, ll. 449–50).

34. Buridan even regards it as conventional that we treat universals as second-intentional names (*TDUI:* 145–46). Universals are substances in the second mode of substance only, i.e., "they are terms in the category of substance [*sunt termini de praedicamento substantiae*]" (*QIP* 4: 140, ll. 635–36); likewise, "'universal' is a transcendent name [*universale est nomen transcendens*]," and such names occur on one level only (*TDUI:* 147); and as a form, a universal is a second intention (*TDUI:* 148).

35. Note also that the differences in universal names do not correspond to any real diversity in the things signified by those names, "but in the medium through which we arrive at the concepts by which those names are imposed [*sed in mediis per quae devenimus in conceptus a quibus illa nomina imponuntur*]" (*QIP* 11: 173, ll. 1853–54). The "medium" is the more common or general concept, e.g., of sensing, from which the common concept of everything sensitive is formed, and names such as 'animal' are imposed (*QIP* 11: 173, ll. 1847–50).

36. That the object of knowledge is a *complexum*, or proposition, rather than an *incomplexum*, or a term, follows from the fact that we can believe or know only what can be true or false, and only propositions can be true or false.

37. For discussion, see Normore 1985.

38. *QP* I.8: 11vb: "*non frustra ponitur huiusmodi magnitudo quia fuerunt rationes cogentes eam ponere per quas etiam apparet tanta vel maior utilitas illius magnitudinis in natura sicut albedinis vel nigredinis.*" For discussion, see Maier 1955, 214–15 and Adams 1987a, 184–85.

39. Note that this is assuming horses exist. Buridan argues that we can at least conceive of subjects without their *propria* or inseparable accidents—e.g., non-neighing horses or non-risible men—but that no such concept can supposit for anything. Thus, the inseparability of 'able to neigh' and 'horse' is expressed not by any purely conceptual or a priori conception, but rather in the claim that as long as there are horses, it can always be truly affirmed that horses are able to neigh. See *S* 2.6.5: 133–34.

40. De Rijk 1992. See also de Rijk 1980.

41. Abelard was by no means the first medieval philosopher to advocate a semantic approach to the problem of universals, although he did explore some of its related, psychological dimensions. The semantic approach itself goes back to Aristotle. According to Norman Kretzmann (1982, 492, n. 19), "a good part of the difficulty in the problem of universals is represented in, not merely historically started by, Aristotle's ambivalence in *Categories* and *De Interpretatione* regarding the distinction between linguistic and extralinguistic entities."

42. Spade 1994, 37.

43. Geyer 1919, 16.

44. See, e.g., Martin Tweedale, "Abelard and the Culmination of the Old Logic" in *CHLMP:* "What most associate Abelard with nominalists of the later Middle Ages such as Ockham, and even of our own time, such as N. Goodman and W. V. O. Quine, are his incessant efforts to show that dialectic and the *artes sermocinales* in general can be developed without their requiring us to believe in the existence of things other than those more or less ordinary ones described by *physica*" (154). Elsewhere, Tweedale argues that Abelard's main contention in answering "the question of what it is in things that permits us correctly to call them men or whatever" was "to deny explicitly that talking about 'being a man' or any such type commits us to some universal thing over and above the concrete individuals that share

such a type. In [Abelard's] view there is no way to proceed from these trivial semantic truths to the realist theory of universals. Logic is not a genuine path to realist metaphysics, no matter how much language may give the illusion that it is" (1976, 154).

45. Contrast Ockham, who insists that no part/whole relationship exists between universals and particulars (*Ordinatio* I, d. 2, q. 4 [*Opera Theologica* II: 118]; d. 2, q. 5 [*Opera Theologica* II: 158–59]; *Expositio Perihermenias*, c. 8 [*Opera Philosophica* II: 165]; for discussion, see Adams 1990, 6). For an overview of methodological differences between Oxford and Paris, see Alain de Libera, "The Oxford and Paris Traditions in Logic" in *CHLMP*, 174–87.

46. Spade 1994, 41.

47. Spade 1994, 48.

48. Of course, more needs to be said if this is to lead to a solution to the problem of universals. And it is far from clear that Abelard says all of the right things. Addressing the question of what makes common terms such as 'man' apply to individual men, he claims that the "common cause" of this imposition is the fact that discrete men all "agree in *being a man*," adding that the *status* of being a man does not count as a real universal because it is not a thing (Spade [tr.] 1994, 41–42). As Martin Tweedale notes, "Abelard helps himself generously to a host of non-things as well [as substances and forms, both of which are things]: *status, dicta,* natures, properties, states, and events, among others," leading Tweedale to conclude that "Abelard's theology is deeply committed to this way of having your ontological cake and throwing it away at the same time" (1988, 220–21).

49. Spade 1994, 50.

50. Spade 1994, 50. De Rijk describes this process of understanding universals, which Abelard says "must always come about by abstraction," as follows: "if one singles out certain 'things' (features) belonging to an object one does not deny or ignore other 'things', but only zooms in on some special aspects of the object" (1992, 59).

51. *QM* I.7: 6vb–7ra (the Latin text of this passage, based on two manuscripts and the 1518 edition, can also be found in de Rijk 1992, which I follow in correcting the incunabular edition's reading of '*ignorantia*' for '*incorruptibilia*' in the third sentence of this passage):

> Alia ponuntur esse universalia in significando vel representando, quia non significant determinate hoc vel illud, sed indifferenter omnia similis generis vel speciei; ut iste terminus 'homo' omnes homines, iste terminus 'color' omnes colores. Et sic universalia sunt termini significativi sive in voce sive in mente sive in scriptura. Et isti termini ita singulariter existunt vel in mente vel in voce, sicut iste color in pariete, quamvis dicantur universales in significando. Et isto modo concedendum est quod universalia sunt ita bene generabilia et corruptibilia in mente vel in voce sicut color in pariete.

52. *QM* VII.15: 50va: "[*aliquid*] *dicitur universale secundum praedicationem vel significationem quia de multis est praedicabile et indifferenter significat multa et supponit pro multis. Et tunc significatum ipsum oppositum est terminus singularis seu discretus qui una impositione significativum vel repraesentativum est unius tantum, ut Sortes, Plato. Et sic universale et singulare sunt termini mentales vocales aut scripti.*"

53. *QM* VII.15: 51ra: "*omne quod est in te ita singulariter existit sicut tu, et tamen hoc non obstante potest multa indifferenter significare; ideo universale secundum significationem bene existit in te.*"

54. On the influence of Boethius's *De divisione*, see Sten Ebbesen, "Ancient Scholastic Logic as the Source of Medieval Scholastic Logic" in *CHLMP*, 105–107, and John Magee, "Prolegomena" in Magee 1998, xxxiv: "in addition to the commentaries of Peter Abelard, Albert the Great, and Antonias Andreae, there is a wealth of glossed MSS, florilegia, and indirect evidence to suggest that *De divisione* proved of enduring interest to medieval students from the later tenth century on. This would have pleased Boethius, who in the proem evinces particular concern for the *utilitas* of the treatise in the context of the Latin-speaking world." Boethius also discusses part/whole relations in his two treatises on the topics, *De topicis differentiis* and *In Ciceronis topica*. These treatises gave rise to another mereological tradition based on the study of part/whole inferences, parallel to that found in medieval commentaries on *De divisione* and related treatises, which tended to focus on terms and propositions. For the texts, see Stump 1978 and 1988.

55. See Aristotle, *Metaphysics* V.25–26.1023b12–1024a10. Boethius found ample precedent for discussing mereological questions in the tradition surrounding the *Categories*. Porphyry, for example, uses the language of parts and wholes in the *Isagoge* to model relations between genus, species, and individual: "The individual then is included under the species and the species under the genus. For the genus is a kind of whole and the individual a part, while the species is both a whole and a part, although a part of one thing and the whole not *of* another thing but rather *in* other things. For the whole is in the part" (Spade [tr.] 1994, 7); "Genus and species, as has been said, have in common being predicated of several things. . . . It is also common to them to be prior to what they are predicated of, and for each of them to be a certain 'whole'" (Spade [tr.] 1994, 13). See also Magee 1998, xxxiv–lvii.

56. As opposed to division carried out with respect to accidents, of which there are likewise three kinds: of a subject into its accidents, of an accident into its subjects, and of an accident into accidents (Magee [tr.] 1998, 10–11).

57. I.e.: (1) a whole is divided with respect to quantity, whereas a genus is divided with respect to quality; (2) a whole is naturally posterior to its proper parts (since the whole perishes if any one of its parts is destroyed), whereas "every genus is by nature prior to its proper species"; (3) the "matter [*materia*]" of a whole is said to be the plurality of its parts, whereas the genus is the matter of its species; and finally, (4) a part is not always the same as its whole ("for a hand is not the same as a man, nor a wall the same as a house"), whereas "a species is always the same as its genus" (Magee [tr.] 1998, 14–15).

58. Magee 1998, 38–39.

59. Elsewhere in the treatise, Boethius suggests that such universals are called wholes because they "compose [*conjungere*]" the individuals which are said to be their parts: "A whole is divided into parts whenever we resolve [*resolvimus*] one or another thing into those elements of which it is composed, e.g. when I say that of things belonging to a house one is the roof, another the walls, another the foundation, or that a man is composed of soul and body [*hominem conjungi anima et corpore*], or when we say that the parts of man are Cato, Vergil, Cicero, and the single men who,

although being *particulars*, nevertheless combine to make up the sum total of man [*vim tamen totius hominis jungunt atque componunt*]. For man is not a genus and single men are not species; they are rather the parts out of which the whole of man is composed" (Magee [tr.] 1998, 8–9). That is to say, man, unlike animal, cannot be treated under genus into species division because it is composed not of species, but of individual human beings. Boethius treats species division as analogous to the division of a quantitative whole.

60. Magee [tr.] 1998, 40–41. See Magee's commentary on this and surrounding passages (144–53).

61. Dal Pra 1954, 157. Abelard also emphasizes the semantic approach in his *Dialectica:* "In the first and strict sense, division is said to be 'an expression [*oratio*] in which something is shown to be divided by something else'" (de Rijk 1970, 535).

62. That is, part/whole inferences are not what Abelard would call "perfect inferences," which are syllogisms or hypothetical consequences whose truth follows from the form of the sentences in which they are expressed (e.g., 'If every man is an animal and every animal is alive then every man is alive') (de Rijk 1970, 254).

63. Magee 1998, 38–39. Abelard also agrees with Boethius that 'whole' is generally said of what is continuous, or universal, or consisting of certain powers (Dal Pra 1954, 193).

64. Dal Pra 1954, 194. For discussion, see Henry 1991, 44.

65. Boethius does mention predication in his discussion of wholes consisting of powers: "For in that each and every part of [the soul] entails the predicate 'soul' it is brought into connection with the division of a genus" (Magee 1998, 40–41).

66. "Since the universal is a whole with respect to its individuals, that is why we call each single man a *particular*, i.e., receiving the predication of its whole . . ." (Dal Pra 1954, 193).

67. Dal Pra 1954, 160. I have not adopted Dal Pra's emendation of '*dicatur*' to '*dicantur*'. For Abelard, the universal whole is distinct from the genus: "The whole according to substance is rightly said of these, since the whole of them is the substance itself; but the genus of a species is not like this since, apart from the genus, the differentia of the species is also in the substance, but besides the species, there is nothing that enters into the substance of the individual. That is why 'whole' is rightly said of those individuals whose whole is a substance; that is also why Porphyry says that the individual parts of a species are not called species" (de Rijk 1970, 546).

68. De Rijk 1970, 546–47. De Rijk suggests that Abelard's reference to Porphyry here is actually to Boethius, *In Isag.* 212.15–16 and 215.18–216.2. This passage is also discussed in Henry 1991, 65–67.

69. As Porphyry says, "genera differ from species because species, even though they are predicated of several, are not yet predicated of what differ in species but only in number" (Spade 1994, 2). Abelard's restriction of the use of the term 'part' to the parts of a species or universal whole suggests that they share with quantitative parts the feature of individuality.

70. Spade 1994, 37; cf. Aristotle, *De Interpretatione* 7.17a39–40. It is hardly accidental, of course, that Abelard uses the same adverb (*singillatim*) in *De divisionibus* to describe the way in which the parts of a universal whole receive the predication of their whole.

71. Spade 1994, 40.

72. Cf. also Abelard's comment on Boethius's advice about how universal wholes should be divided (*De divisione* 888C), where he says that such divisions should be thought of as producing not the parts themselves, but names or terms which are "taken for" such parts: "In the same way also, those wholes which are universals [must be divided]; of men, for example, some are in Europe, etc. Since he [i.e., Boethius] must give an example of the division of a universal whole, he produces an example of the division of a subject into accidents. But because he could not enumerate every individual belonging to man, he posits those particular names for the individuals belonging to *man*. And this division must not be called the division of a universal whole into parts, but into what is taken for the parts [*sed in sumpta pro partibus*]" (Dal Pra 1954, 196).

73. De Rijk 1970, 574; cf. Henry 1991, 72–73.

74. Dal Pra 1954, 193–94; cf. Henry 1991, 44. Socrates's right arm is not Socrates, nor is one soldier or one cavalry division the entire army.

75. De Rijk 1970, 547; cf. Henry 1991, 47.

76. De Rijk 1970, 548. Abelard's suggestion that integral wholes are predicable of their parts only in the genitive also preserves the Boethian notion that unlike universal wholes, integral wholes are naturally posterior to their proper parts.

77. De Rijk 1970, 28–29; cf. Henry 1991, 80–81. Since each man belongs to the set of men, '... part of man' is predicable of each, with the name of the whole in the genitive case as is appropriate for integral wholes.

78. De Rijk 1970, 431; cf. Henry 1991, 80–81. Elsewhere, Abelard appears to base the distinction between mere plurality and aggregation on our use of what he calls "collective or comprehensive names [*nomina collectiva vel comprehensiva*]" such as 'populace [*populus*]' or 'rose-garden [*rosetus*]': "for a plurality of men is not said to be 'men [*homines*]' in the same way as it is said to be a 'populace [*populus*]', but only those gathered in one place are said to be a 'populace'. That is why the name 'populace' seems to be taken from a collection of men" (Geyer 1919, 171; cf. Henry 1991, 82–83).

79. Geyer 1919, 171; cf. Henry 1991, 83–84. Unlike multiple or aggregate wholes, such wholes do not retain their properties once divided (de Rijk 1970, 431). Again, this might be one of the reasons why Boethius says that discontinuous and universal wholes are divided "in the same way," although Abelard ignores this in his comment on the passage in question (de Rijk 1970, 196). The relation between the parts and the whole is in each case quite different.

80. Geyer 1919, 163; cf. Henry 1991, 50–51.

81. Henry 1991, 46–180.

82. De Rijk 1970, 555; cf. Henry 1991, 89–90.

83. This struggle has been well documented by D. P. Henry, who notes that "Abelard is immensely conscious of this lack of vocabulary for theorising about whole and parts" (1991, 49).

84. Geyer 1919, 194. Abelard does not comment on the fact that this (superior) definition of the human soul is also applicable to non-human souls.

85. Or, at least, the soul is predicable of its powers only taken as a whole. Conversely, Abelard remarks that when 'soul' is understood via its superior definition, the parts "do not need to be joined together with it in order to receive the predication of the whole, for the whole is predicated of the singular parts" (Geyer 1919, 197).

86. Rather, 'soul' in this sense shares with integral wholes the property of being predicable of its parts in the genitive: "the division of this kind of whole is made in this way: 'Of the soul, one part pertains to growth, another to sensation, and another to reason'" (de Rijk 1970, 555).

87. De Rijk 1970, 558.

88. In contrast, the universal whole man is (as Boethius suggests) formed from discrete individuals such as Cato, Virgil, and Cicero.

89. On this point, see Freddoso 1978. Furthermore, not only is a soul composed of parts of a certain kind, but "each and every one [of these parts] of the soul consists in its proper parts." In plants, for example, the vegetative power is said to consist of the powers of "sprouting, growing, producing flowers, and bearing fruit" (Geyer 1919, 197).

90. Unlike Abelard, Buridan wrote no commentary on Boethius's *De divisione,* although his discussion suggests that he was familiar with it, or at least with the general principles expressed therein. See, e.g., *QP* I.9: 13ra–rb.

91. For discussion, see E. J. Ashworth, "Logic, Medieval" in *The Routledge Encyclopedia of Philosophy,* vol. 5, 746–59.

92. See Martin Tweedale, "Abelard and the Culmination of the Old Logic" in *CHLMP:* "Of all the scholastic logicians writing while the old logic (*logica vetus*) was still virtually the whole of the logical curriculum in the schools, Abelard is generally conceded to have been the most profound and original" (143).

93. This fact may partly account for its eclipse. As Martin Tweedale writes, "[Abelard's] work should have formed the basis of a highly original development of the *artes sermocinales* and of philosophy in general in Western Europe. But this was not to be. Partly because of Abelard's poor reputation with church authorities, but mostly because of the influx of hitherto unavailable works by Aristotle and his Islamic commentators, Abelard's work was largely to be ignored in favor of the more comprehensive and systematic philosophy these new texts provided" ("Abelard and the Culmination of the Old Logic" in *CHLMP,* 157).

94. Buridan also remarks that Boethius and Aristotle both dismiss the sense of 'whole' in which it signifies the same as 'complete', but there is no evidence that Aristotle does so in the passage he cites, or that Boethius even recognizes such a sense in *De topicis differentiis.*

95. Avicenna accordingly regarded second intentions as the proper subject of logic. For discussion, see Christian Knudsen, "Intentions and Impositions," in *CHLMP,* 479–95. As terms of second intention, 'universal whole' and 'subjective part' are similar in function to the terms 'genus' and 'species', so that, Buridan says, "we call a common term taken absolutely a 'whole' with respect to itself taken with determination, just as we call the term 'animal' a universal whole with respect to the terms 'rational animal' and 'irrational animal', and consequently also with respect to the species man and brute animal [*terminum communem simpliciter acceptum, vocemus 'totum' respectu sui ipsius accepti cum determinatione, sicut istum terminum 'animal' vocamus totum universale ad istos terminos 'animal rationale' et 'animal irrationale', et per consequens etiam ad istas species homo et brutum]*" (*QDA₃* II.7: 87). Buridan is actually interpreting here what he takes to be Aristotle's view in *De Anima* II.2 on how the parts of the soul can be distinguished in definition. Elsewhere, he notes that specific universal wholes are composed of proper names, not individuals. Thus, if we impose the proper name 'A' on

water, and 'B' on half of it, "the name 'water' would be a universal whole with respect to the names 'A' and 'B', as is a species to its individuals" (*S* 6.4.4: 434).

96. *QIP* 3: 136, ll. 505–507: "*licet terminus 'universale' in anima tua vel in mea non habeat partes integrales, tamen habet partes subiectivas, scilicet quinque praedicabilia.*"

97. *QIP* 4: 140, ll. 657–59: "*non sicut totum integrale in partes ex quibus integratur, sed sicut terminus communis in terminos sibi subiectos.*"

98. He writes, "it is obvious that we are not concerned [here] with the other senses of 'whole', e.g., with 'whole' in the sense of 'universal whole', because the question [at hand] does not ask about these" (*QP* I.9: 12va). *QP* I.9 is occasioned by Aristotle's aside in *Physics* I.2 that "there is, indeed, a difficulty about part and whole, perhaps not relevant to the present argument [i.e., about the sense in which things are said to be one], yet deserving consideration on its own account" (185b10–12). Buridan's resolution of the question applies his teaching on the different senses of 'whole' in the *Summulae* (*S* 4.3.7.1: 267–68).

99. Buridan follows Peter of Spain in defining categorematic terms in two ways, viz., as (1) capable of standing in the subject or predicate position of a proposition (definition by predication); or (2) signifying something outside the mind *per se*, or ultimately (*S* 4.2.3: 232–33).

100. *QP* I.9: 12va: "*verbi gratia, divisim dicimus quod isti lapides pedales sunt pedales si uterque est pedalis, sed coniunctum dicimus quod isti lapides occupant spatium duorum pedum et congregatum ex eis.*"

101. See E. J. Ashworth, "Logic, Medieval" in *The Routledge Encyclopedia of Philosophy*, vol. 5, 752–53. Buridan uses the distinction often and without comment in his logical and philosophical writings, though a primer of sorts can be found in the *Summulae*: "if we want to convey the composite sense, then we utter the proposition continuously, and if we want to convey the divided sense, then we should put a sign of division immediately after the first categorical, as in the following example: 'A man is a donkey, and a horse is a goat or God exists'. But if the sign of division were not placed immediately after the first categorical, but after the second, in this way: 'A man is a donkey and a horse is a goat, or God exists', then the proposition would still be composite, just as it would be without a sign of division" (*S* 7.3.7: 531).

102. These are propositions in which the whole is said to be denominated from its parts, such as when we say that a man is curly because he has curly hair (*QP* I.9: 12rb), a function derived from the Aristotelian notion of paronymy, for which, see *Categories* 1a13–15.

103. Buridan also follows Peter of Spain in defining syncategorematic terms in two ways, viz., as (1) not capable of standing in the subject or predicate position of a proposition (definition by predication); or (2) not signifying something outside the mind *per se*, but only with another such significative term (*S* 4.2.3: 232–33; cf. *S* 9.4: 883).

104. *QP* I.9: 12va: "*implicat in se signum universale distribuens hoc nomen 'pars' ita quod idem valet dicere 'totus homo' et 'hominis quaelibet pars', vel 'totus Sortes' et 'Sortes quaelibet pars'.*"

105. *QP* I.9: 12va: "*unum est cuius quaelibet pars est divisibilis, ut equus, lapis, aqua; aliud est cuius aliqua pars est indivisibilis, in quibus autem quaelibet pars est divisibilis.*"

106. *QP* I.9: 12vb: "*Ego dico quod totum est suae partes, verbi gratia, 'totus equus est suae partes', ut patet per exponentes, 'equi quaelibet pars est suae partes', quilibet enim pars habet duas medietates et istae duae medietates secundum dicta prius. Sed in quibus aliqua pars est indivisibilis, negandum est quod totum sit suae partes, verbi gratia, 'non totus homo est suae partes', instantia enim est de anima intellectivae quae non est suae partes cum sit indivisibilis.*"

107. Unlike his categorematic exposition of 'whole' in his *Questions on Aristotle's Physics,* Buridan does not specify here that the parts in question must be integral, although this is clearly understood from their nature.

108. *QDA₃* II.7: 103: "*Et aliquis quaereret quomodo de proprietate sermonis haec locutio 'tota anima' debet exponi. Et videtur mihi quod differt dicere 'tota animae' et 'anima tota'. Dicatur ergo 'tota anima', id est 'quaelibet pars animae', et 'anima tota', id est 'animae quaelibet pars'.*"

109. Counterexample: If Socrates is in the house and Plato outside, then Plato's left ear is a human part not in the house, although of Socrates, each part is indeed in the house. I have modified Klima's translation so that it is consistent with my rendering of 'quaelibet' as 'each' in the passages quoted above (rather than as 'any', in Klima's text).

110. Still, even if an indivisible human soul lacks integral parts, why could it not be said to have formal, i.e., metaphysically constitutive, parts? The answer to this question lies in a piece of doctrine. Buridan says that "the human soul is simple and not substantially composite [*anima humana est simplex et non composita substantialiter*]" (*QDA₃* III.10: 108). By 'not substantially composite', he means that the intellective soul is neither a matter/form composite like material substances, nor, as might be suggested by *De Anima* III.5, a composite of distinct capacities in the form of the agent and possible intellects. The problem with assuming that the intellective soul is metaphysically composite is that such entities would be subject to corruption should their metaphysically distinct constituent parts in any way become separated from each other.

111. Scott 1966, 13. That Buridan both read and used Ockham's *Summa Logicae* has been demonstrated by Ria van der Lecq and Henk Braakhuis in their edition of Buridan's *QE*, xxx–xxxv.

Notes to Chapter 11

1. Thus, according to Thomas Aquinas, *Summa contra gentiles* III.46, "what [the soul's powers and habits] really are we discover from the qualitative character of their acts [*quid vere sint, ex ipsorum actuum qualitate invenimus*]." This is so because "the intellect must reach substance through the cognition of sensible accidents [*per sensibilium accidentium cognitionem oportet ad substantiae intellectum pervenire*]" (III.56).

2. The last of these features distinguishes Buridan's view from that of Averroes, who argues that the immaterial and everlasting part of the human soul (which he calls the 'possible intellect') is a singular being existing apart from individual human beings, but in such a way that it is simultaneously present to each one of them. Much of Buridan's own account of psychological inherence is developed in counterpoint to Averroes's *Commentarium Magnum in Aristotelis De Anima,* a work with which he was intimately familiar. See Zupko 1989, 457–505.

3. Aristotle, *De Anima* II.2.413b16–24.

4. *QDA*₃ II.7: 89: "*Prima est quod anima vegetativa et anima sensitiva* [*et ceterae* add. mss.] *in equo non sunt distincte secundum diversas partes corporis, sed per totum corpus animalis extensa est vegetativa et sensitiva et appetitiva.*"

5. *QNE* VI.3: 118vb: "*anima licet possit aliquas suarum operationum immediate exercere, immo non potest omnem. Verbi gratia, si ponamus in homine unam solam formam substantialem, scilicet animam intellectivam, quodlibet corpus humanum informetur qua, tamen sic est abstracta quod non est educta de potentia subiectivi nec extensa eius extensione propter quod etiam non indiget uti organo corporeo ad eius operationes principales, puta velle et intelligere. Tamen ipsa ad alias operationes exercendas indiget organo corporeo et certis dispositionibus qualitativis organi indiget, enim oculo ad videndum, aure ad audiendum, etc.*"

6. Buridan later allows that the intellective soul uses corporeal organs "ministratively [*ministrative*]" in carrying out its principal operations (*QNE* VI.3: 119ra). This is based on his view that the intellect of the wayfarer cannot (1) think without phantasms or images provided by the faculty of sense, specifically by the imagination, a cognitive power realized in physical organs, viz., (following Aristotle) in the heart (*QDA*₃ II.24: 401–402; III.15: 383; cf. Aristotle, *De Anima* III.7.431a16–17); or (2) exercise its power of volition without objects presented to it "under a good or bad aspect [*sub ratione boni vel mali*]," appearances that are ultimately derived from sensory images (*QNE* III.1–5: 36rb–40ra; *QDA*₃ III.15: 167–68; III.18: 199–205; see also chapter 15 below). The dependence of thinking and willing on corporeal organs is not expressed more strongly because of the conceivability of the intellective soul operating without them. In such a disembodied state, it is said to understand "by God's power and arrangement [*ex dei potentia et ordinatione*]" (*QDA*₃ III.6: 54). For discussion of Buridan on the sensory part of the soul, see Peter Sobol, "Sensations, Intentions, Memories, and Dreams," in Thijssen and Zupko 2001, 183–98.

7. *QDA*₃ II.5: 66–67:

> Sed tu rationabiliter queris utrum anima in pede equi sit visiva. Et ego dico quod sic, loquendo de potentia principali et remota, quia secundum se innata est videre, et videret in pede si Deus et natura formarent sibi oculum in pede. Tamen ipsa non est in pede potentia propinqua ad videndum, quia per potentiam propinquam debemus intelligere vel dispositiones requisitas cum principali agente vel ipsamet principalem potentiam habentem suas dispositiones requisitas ad operandum. Et cum est sine illis vocatur potentia remota. Nec est ista potentia frustra in pede, quia ibi exercet alias operationes.

Likewise, in his literal commentary on Aristotle's *De motu animalium*, Buridan argues that since it is the form of the body, the soul of an animal exists throughout its whole body, "but only in the heart insofar as it is the first mover of the body" (*DMA* VI: 551).

8. *QNE* VI.3: 119ra: "*unde si oculus esset talis in pede qualis est in capite quantum ad qualitativas dispositiones, utique nos oculo pedis videremus sicut oculo capitis. Ubique enim per totum corpus est animae substantia quae innata omnem suam operationem exercere ubi fuerit organicae dispositiones ad hoc requisitae.*"

9. Of course, the comparative term 'nobler [*nobilius*]' is being used here in the archaic sense of 'more impassible', in the way inert elements such as helium are sometimes referred to as 'noble gases'. The nobility of agency is also appealed to in a similar

argument on the negative side of QDA_3 III.1, which asks whether the human intellect is a passive power as regards what is intelligible. Thus, if the intellect were completely passive, it would follow "that the vegetative power would be more noble than the intellect, which is false. The consequence is obvious, because (1) it is active in relation to its object; (2) acting is nobler than being acted upon; and (3) that action must be judged nobler whose act is nobler [*sequitur quod potentia vegetativa esset nobilior intellectu, quod est falsum. Et consequentia patet, quia ipsa est activa in suum obiectum; et agere est nobilius quam pati; et illa actio debet iudicari nobilior cuius actus est nobilior*]" (QDA_3 III.1: 1). Cf. Siger of Brabant, who in his *Metaphysics* commentary connects nobility with (1) whatever is simpler in any genus, and (2) a cause vis-à-vis its effect (Maurer 1983, 226).

10. See Aristotle, *De Anima* II.3.414b24–415a14; cf. *De Anima* III.12–13; *De Caelo* I.2.286b26 ff.

11. QDA_3 II.4: 56:

dicitur quod Brunellus, per eandem eius essentiam et naturam, est Brunellus et equus et animal et vivens et corpus [*secundum se ipsum // corpus* mss.]. Et cum dicitur quod Brunello inest esse sensitivum secundum quod animal et non secundum quod vivens, nos per hoc intelligimus quod haec est vera per se et primo, 'animal est sensitivum' et non hoc, 'vivens est sensitivum'. Ita quod per 'inesse secundum quod ipsum' intelligitur praedicatio essentialis [*convertibilis // essentialis* mss.] terminorum vel prima in metaphysica [*immediate // in metaphysica* mss.] aut huiusmodi.... Ita quod ista locutio non erat de reali inhaerentia.

12. Aristotle, *De Anima* II.2.413b29.

13. QDA_3 II.7: 91: "*Secunda conclusio Aristotelis est quod ista nomina 'sensitivum' et 'vegetativum' attributa equo non sunt synonima, sed differunt secundum rationem, quia alia est ratio secundum quam intelligimus animam esse principium sensationis et secundum quam dicitur sensitiva, et alia est secundum quam intelligimus animam esse principium nutritionis et secundum quam dicitur nutritive, et sic de aliis.*"

14. Buridan does not, however, wish to say that the mediating qualitative dispositions or instrumental potentialities through which the soul exercises its operations (discussed in connection with the mutual extensionality principle) are really distinct from each other. The reason is that dispositions of this sort inhere in physical organs, from which it follows, e.g., that the eyes of an animal must be really and not merely conceptually distinct from its ears or nose (QDA_3 II.5: 64–67; QNE VI.3: 118vb).

15. A parallel concept, 'denomination by the much more principal part [*denominatio a parte valde principaliori*]', applies to terms denoting substances. Thus, although Socrates's bodily parts change over time, Socrates remains the same in the sense that his principal part, i.e., his soul, persists without substantial change throughout his life (QP I.10: 13vb; cf. QDA_3 II.7: 100–101; cf. QDA_3 III.11: 125; QDA_3 III.20: 217). The underlying logical principle is presented in the *Summulae:* "a predication is called 'non-essential', or 'denominative', if one term of it adds some extrinsic connotation over the signification of the other, as for example 'white' supposits for a man and appellates whiteness as pertaining to him. Therefore the predication 'A man is an animal' is essential, while the predications 'A man is white' or 'A man is risible' are denominative, for 'risible' appellates the act of laughing, although with the modality of aptitude (because 'risible' means the same as 'can laugh')" (S 2.5.2: 127). Thus, Buridan notes that we say that a term "denominates the whole on account of a principal part,

or on account of the unity resulting from the continuity of several parts succeeding each other in something, as in a river, or in some such manner . . . as, e.g., the term 'Seine' is a singular term, although it is not the same water that is now the Seine and that was the Seine last year" (*S* 2.1.1: 104). Cf. Cicero, *De finibus* V.30.92: "It is a universal rule that any whole takes its name [*appellatur*] from its most predominant and preponderant part."

16. *QM* IV.1: 13ra–rb: "*Dico quod eadem res valde diversis conceptibus concipitur, aut propter diversas proprietates in ea inventas aut propter diversa connotata extrinseca sive sibi inhaerentia, propter hoc enim eadem res significatur bene nominibus decem praedicamentorum, et sic apparet quod adhuc conceptus habent distinctionem originalem ex parte rerum significatarum, non tamen semper ex parte rerum quas significant sive pro quibus supponunt, immo saepius ex parte connotatorum.*"

17. Cf. Ockham, for whom connotative terms primarily signify what they are truly predicable of, and secondarily signify, or connote, other things, such as the abstract concept contained in its nominal definition (*Summa logicae* I.10; *Opera Philosophica* I: 35–38).

18. De Rijk 1976, 98–99.

19. *QDA₃* II.7: 94: "*Si dicamus quod animal sit praecise constitutum substantialiter ex materia prima et una forma substantiali quae non sit partium substantialiter dissimilium et diversarum rationum, tunc iste terminus 'animal', si sit terminus vere substantialis, non significant nec connotat huiusmodi organizationes.*"

20. Cf. Buridan's solution to the sophism, 'Today you ate raw meat' (*S* 9.4, 2nd sophism: 877).

21. Cf. *S* 7.3.10: 535–48 and section 3b of chapter 10 above.

22. Normore 1985, 198–99.

23. *QM* V.9: 32va:

. . . aliquando contingit quod terminus relativus concretus significat vel connotat non solum rem pro qua supponit et rem ad quam est comparatio, immo etiam connotat rem aliam vel inhaerentem alicui illarum vel forte aliquando extrinsecam: verbi gratia, si ego dico 'Sortes est similis Platoni', ille terminus 'similis' non solum significat et connotat Sortem et Platonem, immo etiam connotat qualitatem secundum quam ille est similis illi. Et ita si ego dico 'Sortes est aequalis Platoni', ille terminus 'aequalis' ultra Sortem et Platonem connotat magnitudines eorum. Et si dico 'albedo inhaeret lapidi' vel 'forma inhaeret materiae', tunc illa dictio 'inhaeret' connotat dispositionem additivam praeter formam et materiam, scilicet inseparabilitatem, ut dicebatur in alia quaestione. Similiter si ego dico 'Sortes distat a Platone', ille terminus 'distat' connotat rem aliam praeter Sortem et Platonem etiam extrinsecam Sorti et Platoni, scilicet dimensionem intermediam per quam Sortes distat a Platone.

24. The proposition, 'B is now an animal', obviously fits into the latter category, since the predicate, 'is now an animal', is first denied and later affirmed of B, a subject that is itself unchanging.

25. *QP* II.3: 31ra–rb:

Primus modus est si illud praedicatum sit connotativum alicuius extrinsici, tunc enim propter existentiam vel non existentiam aut propter aliam mutationem illius extrinseci possibile est illud contingere, ut homo est pater si est eius filius et illo non existente non est pater, et homo est dives si sunt divitiae sibi applicatae et est pauper si pereant vel alteri applicentur, et corpus A est propinquum corpori B si non sit aliud corpus intermedium vel vacuum et est remotum vel remotius si est intermedium corpus minus aut maius. Et propter aliud sic aliter se habere non requiritur aliqua eius mutatio aut suarum partium.

Neither of the other two ways Buridan mentions could apply to the case of 'B is now a horse'. The second way is intended to cover predicates connoting "the situation of the parts of a thing in relation to each other [*situm partium illius rei ad invicem*]," and specifically to the differing dispositions which result from the internal local motion of its parts, such that "there is nothing else afterwards which was not there before, and also nothing before which was not there afterwards [*nihil aliud est posterius quod non esset prius et nihil etiam erat prius quod non sit posterius*]." But none of the examples Buridan gives—Socrates first sitting and then standing; a spherical object becoming cubical—involves any gain or loss of integral parts. Likewise, the third way applies to predicates connoting qualities that are actually generated or corrupted at different times in a thing, such as whiteness in Socrates. For further discussion, see Normore 1985 and chapter 13 below.

26. QDA_3 II.7: 98: "*nec tamen est aliud quam ante erat, sed aliter se habet . . . esse enim 'totale' vel 'partiale' non solum significat esse aliquid sed etiam aliqualiter se habere vel non habere ad aliud.*"

27. QDA_3 III.17: 192: "*imaginor quod sicut deus assistit toti mundo et cuilibet parti eius principaliter et sine distantia, sicut quodammodo anima humana assistit toti corpori humano sine distantia. Differet tamen, quia deus non est forma inhaerens mundo, anima autem informat corpus humanum et inhaeret.*" Buridan repeats in this passage what he earlier reported as the opinion of Averroes (QDA_3 III.3: 22). He is generally on the same page as the Commentator where the nature of the human soul is concerned. In fact, Buridan sometimes writes as if the only difference between them is that he asserts, whereas Averroes denies, the actual inherence of the human soul in the human body.

28. The distinction is more common among theologians and was used, e.g., by both Duns Scotus and Ockham to explain the doctrine of transubstantiation. For discussion, see Adams 1987a, 186–201.

29. For Buridan, this follows from the assumption that indivisible animate forms such as the intellective soul are definitively rather than circumscriptively present in the bodies in which they inhere. As we saw above, the sensitive and vegetative souls are also predicable of each part of their material subjects, although this is for a different reason: the homogeneity principle guarantees the equal attribution of divisible animate forms to each part of the bodies in which they inhere, so that the integral parts of material things also "receive the predications of the whole to the extent that they are quidditative predicates [*recipiunt praedicationes totius quantum ad praedicata quidditativa*]" (QDA_3 II.7: 93; cf. QDA_3 III.17: 192–93).

30. Buridan actually begins by offering four "naturalistic" *reductio* arguments against Averroes, but these tend to gainsay rather than directly refute the Commentator's position. Briefly, he argues that a transcendent intellect would exist extrinsically to the substance it supposedly informs, and could not be numerically many—contrary to the evidence of experience. Hence, he argues that it must be unique—which is also contrary to experience—and finally that it would exist before

you do, even though it is in a sense your transcendent intellect (*QDA₃* III.4: 32–34, ll. 85–130; for discussion, see Zupko 1989, 470–73).

31. *QDA₃* III.4: 35: "*quando dicitur quod moveretur motibus contrariis, potest dici sicut de corpore Christi in hostia consacrata cum unus presbiter fert corpus Christi ad dextram et alter ad sinistram. Non enim corpus Christi per se movetur, nec motu sibi inhaerente, sicut nec magnitudo hostiae sibi inhaeret.*"

32. *QDA₃* III.4: 36:

Ad secundam instantiam, dicitur quod non distat a se, quia non est in manu et in pede commensurabiliter, cum non sit extensa extensione manus vel pedis. Et non est inconveniens idem esse non commensurabiliter in diversis locis ab invicem distantibus et secundum se totum, licet hoc sit modo supernaturali, ut corpus Christi simul est in paradiso et super altari (non enim corpus Christi in hostia super altari commensuratur magnitudine hostiae, sed est in qualibet parte hostiae, licet partes distent ab invicem, et non ob hoc distat a se). Et ideo consimiliter quodammodo intellectus est in manu et in pede, et in neutro commensurative, cum non sit extensus in aliquo illorum membrorum.

33. See *QDA₃* II.7 and chapter 10 above.

34. *QDA₃* III.4: 36: "*nihil secundum famosam et communem locutionem dicitur homo vel animal nisi substantia totalis, scilicet sic quod non sit pars alterius substantiae.*"

35. *QDA₃* III.4: 37: "*dicetur quod non est naturalis sed supernaturalis modus quo intellectus inhaeret corpori humano. Et certum est quod supernaturaliter, deus posset non solum formare non eductam de potentia materiae, immo etiam eductam separare a sua materia, et separatim conservare, et ponere in aliam materiam. Quare igitur hoc non esset possibile de intellectu humano.*"

36. Buridan also appeals to supernatural causes to explain the numerical diversity of human intellects (*QDA₃* III.5: 44).

37. *QDA₃* III.3: 22–23: "*Tertia opinio est veritas fidei nostrae, quae firmiter debemus credere: scilicet quod intellectus humanus est forma substantialis corporis inhaerens corpori humano, sed non educta de potentia materiae nec extensa de eius extensione, et ideo non naturaliter genita nec corruptibilis. Sed tamen non simpliciter perpetua, quia de novo creata. Et tamen sempiterna a parte post sic quod nunquam corrumpetur vel annihilibitur, quamvis deus de potestate eius absoluta eam potest annihilare.*"

38. Even so, Buridan's expressions of deference to theologians more often than not accompany, rather than replace, his own discussions of so-called matters of faith. See *QM* VI.5: 37ra (on divine foreknowledge); *QDC* I.20: 93 (on the existence of a body beyond the heavens); *QP* IV.8: 73vb–74ra (on the possibility of a vacuum); *QP* VIII.12: 121ra (on the thesis that God sets each of the celestial bodies in motion directly, with an impressed force or impetus): "I state this not as an assertion, but in order to seek from practitioners of divine theology what they would teach me in these matters about how they can occur [*sed hoc non dico assertive sed ut a divinis theologiis petam quod in illis doceant me quomodo possunt haec fieri*]."

39. For discussion of the theological controversy in connection with Ockham, see Adams 1987a, 186–201.

40. *QDA₃* III.3: 25–26: "*quamvis illa conclusio sit simpliciter vera, et firmiter fide tenenda, et quod rationes ad eam adductae sint probabiles, tamen non apparet mihi quod sint demonstrativae, ex principiis (fide circumscripta) evidentiam habentibus, nisi*"

*deus de gratia speciali et ultra communem cursum naturae nobis faceret illam eviden-
tiam, sicut ipse posset alicui facere evidentem articulum trinitatis vel incarnationis."*

41. Buridan elsewhere allows that there are theological arguments concerning the
nature of the soul—e.g., that Christ "assumed a complete and entire humanity [*as-
sumpsit sibi totam humanitatem et integram*]," including a sensitive soul—but says that
these produce a "great faith [*magnam fidem*]" in him, not knowledge (*QDA₃* III.17: 192).

42. *QDA₃* II.9: 138:

> Verum est quod certe magna est dubitatio si ponamus in homine solam ani-
> mam. Oportet enim istam esse intellectivam et indivisibilem, non extensam aliquo
> modo extensione materiae vel subiecti. Et tunc ista anima inextensa est anima
> sensitiva et vegetativa. Quomodo igitur, cum sensatio ponitur extensa exten-
> sione organi et materiae, poterit ipsa esse in subiecto indivisibili inhaerente et
> tamquam educta de potentia istius? Hoc videtur mirabile, cum forma non habeat
> extensionem nisi extensionem sui subiecti. Et quomodo divisibile et extensum
> poterit inhaerere indivisibili et inextenso? Hoc videtur mirabile. Et certe ego re-
> spondeo quod hoc est mirabile, quia mirabili et supernaturali modo anima hu-
> mana inhaeret corpori humano non extensa nec educta de potentia subiecti cui
> inhaeret, et tamen etiam toti corpori inhaereat et cuilibet parti eius. Hoc vere est
> mirabile et supernaturale.

43. Cf. Buridan's comment elsewhere concerning the possible relationship between the number of celestial motions and the number of intelligences: "one might
assume that there are many more separate substances than there are celestial spheres
and celestial motions, viz., great legions of angels, but this cannot be proved by demonstrative arguments originating from sense perception [*ista probari non possunt rationibus demonstrativis habentibus ortum ex sensatis*]" (*QM* XII.9: 73ra). Sometimes
Buridan confronts theological issues with what can only be described as intellectual
playfulness. Edith Sylla nicely characterizes his approach here: "Buridan does not exclude theology from physics, along the lines of Boethius of Dacia, nor does he over-
whelm physics with theology, along the lines of today's Creationists. Rather, in a mod-
erate way, Buridan introduces theological truths into the body of Aristotelian physics
and then shows, plausibly, that to draw inferences from physics plus theology, it is
necessary to add other hypotheses [e.g., to assume a reference frame for extra-cosmic
motion, or a 'time' to measure duration before creation]—to beg the human intellect" (*"Ideo quasi mendicare oportet intellectum humanum:* The Role of Theology in
John Buridan's Natural Philosophy," in Thijssen and Zupko 2001, 244–45).

44. See Hume, *An Enquiry Concerning Human Understanding*, X.1, and Augustine, *City of God*, XXI.8. For an overview of medieval approaches to explaining
mirabilia, see Hansen 1985, 50–73. For the epistemological consequences of Buridan's
conception of the miraculous, see chapter 12 below.

NOTES TO CHAPTER 12

1. See, e.g., Moody 1947 (rpr. in Moody 1975, 127–60); Weinberg 1948; Scott
1965; Scott 1971; Ebbesen 1984; King 1987; and Thijssen 1987.

2. See Scott 1971, 35–36 and Thijssen 1987, 255.

3. Scott 1971, 33–34.

4. For further discussion of Nicholas, see Lappe 1908; Moody 1947; Weinberg 1948; Scott 1971; Thijssen 1987; Adams 1987a, 607–25; de Rijk 1994, 1–37; and Grellard 2001, 7–72. See also n. 43 below for remarks on the proper translation of '*evidentia*'.

5. De Rijk 1994, 60–62. I have made occasional minor modifications in de Rijk's translation of the passages from Nicholas quoted in this chapter.

6. Nicholas presents his criterion as a necessary condition for certitude without actually stating that it is also a sufficient condition. Even so, as Marilyn Adams remarks, "he does not here mention any other necessary condition" (1987a, 611).

7. De Rijk 1994, 46–52.

8. Nicholas makes some of the same points in a letter (also extant) replying to a certain Aegidius (de Rijk 1994, 100–110).

9. By "formal experiences" Nicholas is referring to our ability to form a concept of substance, even though cognitions of this sort are without epistemic warrant.

10. De Rijk 1994, 64–74.

11. De Rijk 1994, 74.

12. De Rijk 1994, 72–74.

13. For example, Nicholas argues against Bernard that if, as Bernard assumes, your intellect has no intuitive knowledge of your own acts, then you cannot be certain about the existence of those acts (de Rijk 1994, 52). Nicholas himself appears to reject this assumption.

14. See especially Adams 1987a, 607–610.

15. De Rijk 1994, 48–54; 60.

16. These examples are drawn from *QM* II.1: 8ra–rb, *QDC* II.22: 227, and *QDA₃* II.11: 165–67.

17. *QM* II.1: 9rb (cf. *QNE* VI.11: 126vb; *QAnPo* I.2; *QDA₃* II.5: 67; *QDA₃* II.11: 172): "*si sensus naturaliter illudantus, intellectus habent inquirere quando homo sit et quando non, et habent corrigere iudicia illusoria.*"

18. See *QM* II.1: 9ra–rb; *QDA₃* II.11: 169–76.

19. *QM* II.1: 8rb–va (cf. *QAnPo* I.2):

> ... sensus possit illudi, ut communiter dicitur, et certum est quod species sensibilium possunt conservari in absentia sensibilium et organis sensuum, ut habetur De somno et vigilia, et tunc iudicamus de eo quod non est ac si esset, ideo erramus per sensum. Et difficultas augmentatur multum per ea quae credimus ex fide quia deus potest in sensibus nostris formare species sensibilium sine ipsis sensibilibus et longo tempore potest eas conservare, et tunc iudicamus ac si essent sensibilia praesentia. Modo ultra, tu nescis, cum deus hoc possit et maiora facere, utrum deus facere hoc vult, ideo tu non habes certitudinem et evidentiam utrum ante te sunt homines dum vigilas vel dormis, quia in tua dormitione posset deus facere species sensibiles ita clara, immo in centuplo clariores quam obiecta sensibilia possent facere. Ideo ita formaliter iudicares quod essent res sensibiles ante te sicut nunc iudicas. Ideo cum nihil scias de voluntate dei, tu non potes esse certus de aliquo.

20. *QM* II.1: 8va (cf. *QP* I.4: 4vb–5ra; *S* 6.4.13: 448): "*nec conclusio nec effectus potest cognosci per causam nec per causa per effectum, quia causa non continetur in effectu nec essentialiter nec virtualiter nec effectus per causam, quia causae sunt nobis*

minus notae . . . videtur quod nunquam possumus evidentiam habere de uno per aliud, quia non est evidentia nisi secundum reductionem ad primum principium quod fundatur in contradictione, sed nunquam de duobus diversis possumus contradicere."

21. In the text of the *Questions on Aristotle's Metaphysics,* this argument is presented before the argument just mentioned concerning the possibility of causal knowledge. For the record, the arguments inspired by Nicholas are numbers 11, 14, and 17 in the series of eighteen arguments given at the beginning of *QM* II.1. No great significance, of course, should be attached to the particular order in which opposing arguments are presented.

22. O'Donnell 1939, 237. For the significance of the term, 'habitus conjecturativus', see Weinberg 1948, 70, n. 32.

23. O'Donnell 1939, 237. The Latin text is worth quoting in full: "*cum probatur quod certitudo per propositionem quiescentem in anima quae est illud quod producitur ut in pluribus a causa non libera est effectus eius naturalis; quaero quid appellas causam naturalem; vel illam quae produxit praeteritum ut in pluribus et adhuc producet in futurum si duret et applicetur? Et tunc minor non est scita, etsi [esto // etsi mss.] quod aliquid sit productum ut in pluribus; non est tamen certum an sic debeat esse in futurum.*" Nicholas could have been reading Duns Scotus, who not only subscribes to the principle that what occurs in most cases by means of an unfree cause is its natural effect, but also expresses it in similar words: "*tamen expertus infallibiliter novit quia ita est et semper et in omnibus—et hoc per istam propositionem qui est quiescentem in anima: 'quidquid evenit ut in pluribus ab aliqua causa non libera, est effectus naturalis illius causae'*" (*Ordinatio* I, d. 3, p. 1, q. 4, n. 235; *Opera Omnia* III: 141–42).

24. *QM* II.1: 8va (cf. *QNE* VI.11: 127ra; *QP* I.15: 18vb–19ra; *QAnPo* II.11): "*experientiae ad concludendum universale principium non habent vim nisi per modum inductionis in multis et nunquam ex inductione sequitur universalis propositio nisi sit inductum in omnibus singularibus illius universalis, quod est impossibile.*"

25. Actually, in the *Summulae* Buridan points out that 'and so on for the [other] singulars' fails to be a proposition, and so a fortiori cannot be the premise which turns an inductive inference into a valid syllogism. Why couldn't 'and so on for the singulars' stand for a (very long) proposition? Buridan does not think this solves the problem: "I would reply that in saying 'Socrates runs and Plato runs . . . and so on for the singulars; therefore every man runs', if the clause 'and so on for the singulars' is taken in place of a proposition, then that proposition should be more clearly explicated, and one would have to scrutinize what that would be, but this is not easy to state" (*S* 6.1.4: 395). And the reason it would not be easy to state, of course, is that most of the singulars it covers are neither known nor certain.

26. As we shall see, this last sentence is crucial for understanding Buridan's reply to the corresponding skeptical argument.

27. *QP* I.4: 4vb–5ra: "*si A et B sunt alia ad invicem, nunquam esset contradictio A esse et B non esse.*" The principle, and its skeptical consequences, would have been known to anyone familiar with the *Summulae*'s eighth treatise on demonstration. See, e.g., *S* 8.5.2: 716–17, where we hear about "some people lecturing nowadays who say that no evident proof is possible in terms of which we conclude from the existence of one thing to the existence of another." Buridan accuses them of "ignorance of logic"!

28. The confusion over what Nicholas's views actually were is discussed in Courtenay 1972, 224–34. The main problem is that we do not have enough of Nicholas's lit-

erary corpus to support confident judgments about the nature of his teachings, the most crucial piece of missing evidence being his *Sentences* commentary. For more recent discussions of Nicholas and the official opposition to his teachings, see Tachau 1988, 335–52 and Thijssen 1998, 73–89.

29. *QM* II.1: 9rb–va (cf. *QAnPo* I.2):

dico quod effectus sciuntur per causam propter quid, quia causa est notiora etiam nobis quam propter quid effectus est. Similiter causa scitur per effectum quantum ad quia est, quia effectus gerit quandam similitudinem causae, ideo potest causam representare una cum naturali inclinatione intellectus ad veritatem. Quando etiam dicitur quod aliud per aliud non potest sciri conclusive nego et dico quod quasi sunt infinita principia per se nota aut per sensum aut per experientiam aut per inclusionem terminorum absque hoc quod indigeant demonstrari per principium primum.

30. Thus, when Buridan elsewhere remarks that the heart "is necessarily constitutive of a man himself, since he cannot exist without a heart [*cor est de necessaria constitutione ipsius hominis, quia non posset esse sine corde*]" (*QM* VII.11: 48ra), he is talking about natural and not logical necessity. The latter cannot be at issue, since it follows from Buridan's conception of divine omnipotence that there would be nothing contradictory in God's choosing to operate outside the common course of nature to preserve the life of a man whose heart had been removed. As he notes in his reply to skeptical doubts about the veridicality of the senses, "if God operates simply miraculously, it must be concluded that he can [*si vero deus simpliciter miraculose operetur, concludendum est quod potest*]" (*QM* II.1: 9rb).

31. As Scotus remarks, "I say that even though one does not experience all singulars, but many, nor experience them at all times, but often, nevertheless one infallibly knows that it is so always and in all cases. This is by means of the proposition reposing in the mind, 'Whatever happens in many instances [*ut in pluribus*] by means of a non-free cause is a natural effect of that cause', which is known to the intellect even though its terms have been taken from an erring sense" (*Ordinatio* I, d. 3, p. 1, q. 4, n. 235; *Opera Omnia* III: 141–42). Recall above that it is Scotus's version of the uniformity principle to which Nicholas apparently objects in the *Exigit*.

32. Buridan appears to have changed his mind about whether the intellect necessarily assents to propositions expressing first-mode principles. On at least one occasion, he states that such acts of assent are necessary (*QNE* VI.11: 127rb; cf. *QM* VII.6–7: 142va–144vb), but he elsewhere makes the weaker claim that when the intellect apprehends a first-mode principle, a man is "compelled without necessity" to assent to it "in such a way that he cannot dissent" from it (*QM* II.1: 8rb; cf. *QAnPo* I.2). The latter description, of course, allows for the possibility of deferring judgment by neither assenting nor dissenting. For Buridan on the act of deferment, see chapter 15 below. Even Nicholas concedes, "someone could, on the basis of custom or for some other reason, stop short [*resilire*], so that he doesn't assent indubitably to it, i.e., to the truth of the first principle" (O'Donnell 1939, 237).

33. *QM* II.2: 9vb (cf. *QAnPo* II.11). Other examples of first-mode propositions mentioned by Buridan: 'Nothing dead is alive'; 'The same thing cannot at the same time both be and not be'; 'It is necessary for each and every thing to be or not be'; 'There is something'; 'Every horse is an animal'; 'Iron is a metal'; and 'No hot thing is cold'.

34. *QM* II.2: 9vb (cf. *QNE* VI.11: 127ra):

... etiam sunt aliqua principia universalia quae propter experimenta in multis singularis consimilibus concedunt ab intellectu propter naturalem inclinationem intellectus ad veritatem, sicut quod omnis ignis est calidus, quod sol est calefactius, quod omne rheubarbarum est purgativum cholerae, quod omne quid fit fit ex aliquo praesupposito, quod omne mixtum est corporale, et sic de multis principiis naturalibus. Et ista principia non statim a principio cognoscuntur, immo possemus de eis diu dubitare. Sed ideo dicuntur principia quia sunt indemonstrativa et omnino non possunt demonstrari nec etiam probari per rationem formaliter concludendum. Immo solum conceduntur quia sicut vidimus in pluribus singularibus et in nullis potuimus invenire instantiam.

35. For Buridan on induction, see also *QP* I.15: 18vb–19ra; *QNE* VI.10: 127ra; *QAnPo* II.11; and *S* 8.5.4: 720–24.

36. Moreover, Buridan does not think Scotus's interpretation of the uniformity of nature principle, which he understands as claiming that the actions of causes and effects are to be explained in terms of their specific or generic similarity (a view he associates with Plato), is universally applicable. For in his view, "it is not necessary that the thing made be similar to the maker in either species or nearest genus [*non oportet factum esse simile agenti neque secundum speciem neque secundum genus propinquum*]," since animals are produced from non-animals by putrefaction, fire is produced by light and by striking a stone together with iron, and the first motion is produced by the prime mover (*QM* VII.8: 46rb). The most he is willing to concede is that it is necessary for there to be a certain likeness between any given cause and its effect, where the term 'likeness' is construed "broadly and figuratively [*large vel improprie*]" to refer "not to some quality, but only to a certain agreement belonging properly to the agent as regards the effect [*non pro eadem qualitate, immo solum pro quadam appropriata convenientia agentis ad effectum*]." But Buridan sees this agreement as applying only to particular causal events, i.e., to "the concurrence of singular passive dispositions and agents," not to causation in general. Furthermore, he does not regard it as a priori principle on the basis of which one can arrive at evident knowledge of causes and effects. The likeness which explains a causal event, be it specific, generic, or a matter of "a certain agreement," is still knowable only by experience. This interpretation of the uniformity of nature principle can also be found in Buridan's psychology, where he argues that no generic or specific similarity between cause and effect suffices to explain sense perception. As we have already seen, in the case of vision he notes that "the species of colors in the eye and the representation of color in the imagination or intellect do not seem to be of the same or of a similar nature, nor of the same kind and species" (*QDA*$_3$ II.18: 261—Latin text quoted in chapter 1, n. 90 above).

37. Thus, following Buridan's model of first-mode principles, one might argue that the existence of a cause is implied by and contained in the very idea of an effect, a view famously attacked by Hume (see *Treatise* I.iii. III). Buridan might look to be headed in this direction as far as the demonstration of effects from causes is concerned, since he states at least once that the existence of an 'actual' cause is sufficient for the existence of its effect, so that the effects of such causes may be posited of necessity. But he adds that causes are only called 'actual' when they are "taken together with some other causes or circumstances [*causae ... ut sumuntur cum aliquibus cau-*

sis aliis vel circumstantiis dicuntur actuales]." Thus, fire is the actual cause of burning only if it is sufficiently close to a combustible object that lacks the capacity to resist being burned (*QAnPo* II.9; cf. *QM* V.6: 30va; *QM* VI.5: 35vb; cf. also Aristotle, *Physics* II.3.195b16–17). But these sufficiency conditions also suffice to block any attempt to demonstrate the existence of effects from causes a priori, since their satisfaction is evident only a posteriori, or as Buridan would say, through the evidence of sense, memory, and experience (we can only tell whether or not a piece of wood is dry enough to burn by examining it, of course). So it is not surprising that this argument does not form part of Buridan's reply to skepticism about causal knowledge.

38. *QM* II.1: 9rb (cf. *S* 8.5.3: 717–19):

> dico quod non est illatio gratia formae, sed intellectus per naturalem inclinationem suam ad verum praedispositus per experientias assentit universali principio. Et potest concedi quod huiusmodi experientiae non valent ad evidentiam simpliciter, sed valent ad evidentiam quae sufficit ad scientiam naturalem. Et cum hoc etiam alia sunt principia ex inclusionibus vel repugnantiis terminorum vel propositionum quae non indigent experientiis, sicut est de primo principio. Immo haec est evidenter vera quod chimera est vel non est, hircocerus est vel non est, et quod homo est animal, si nota significatio terminorum.

39. *QAnPo* I.2 (cf. *QM* II.1: 8vb–9ra; *QAnPo* I.2; *QP* I.15: 18vb–19ra; *QNE* VI.11: 126ra–127vb; and *S* 8.5.1–4: 711–24): "*est notandum quod ad scientiam requiritur certitudo et evidentia; et adhuc duo requiruntur, scilicet certitudo veritatis et certitudo assensus. Dico primo 'certitudo veritatis', quia si firmissime et sine aliqua formidine assentiremus propositioni falsae, sicut faciunt haeretici, qui aliquando magis volunt mori quam negare illud cui ipsi assenserunt, tamen non est scientia propter talem assensum, quia deficit veritas et certitudo et firmitas veritatis.*"

40. For further discussion of belief, see: *QAnPo* I.32; *QM* II.1: 8vb–9ra; *QNE* VI.6: 122ra. Knowledge and belief (*opinio*) are compared in *S* 8.4.3: 703–706. For discussion of the psychology (as opposed to the epistemology) of assent, see my "On Certitude," in Thijssen and Zupko 2001, 165–82.

41. For Buridan, "the comprehension of truth is nothing other than the comprehension of a true proposition [*nihil aliud est comprehensio veritatis quam comprehensio propositionis verae*]." Besides the act of assenting to a true proposition, this can also be understood as "the formation or existence of a proposition in the mind [*formatio vel existentia propositionis apud animam*]," "the understanding of a true proposition in an objective mode [*intellectio propositionis verae per modum obiecti*]," or "the adherence or assent by which we assent or adhere to a true proposition [*adhaesio vel assensus quo assentimus vel adhaeremus propositioni verae*]" (*QM* II.1: 8vb).

42. *QAnPo* I.2: "*quia de propositione firmissimae et certissimae veritatis possumus dubitare, et sic non firmiter ei assentire, et tunc sic de ea non habemus scientiam.*" Our disposition to assent is manifested in a sequence of distinct cognitive acts: the act of apprehending a certain appearance or state of affairs, followed by the act of judging it to be so (*QM* II.1: 8vb–9ra; *QNE* VI.6: 122ra). Although the term 'appearance' (*apparentia*) has sensory connotations, Buridan says that it is used broadly to refer to any occurrent cognition; only in the strict sense does it refer to the actual object of the intellect's assent or dissent. 'Appearance' also has epistemic import, since it is applied to cognitions that 'look good', or have 'the ring of truth'. Thus, the 'readily believable

arguments' (probabiles rationes) on behalf of a certain position are said to produce an 'appearance' on behalf of the truth of that position (QDA₃ III.8: 200–203). Buridan argues further that propositions are distinct from appearances, since it is possible to form propositions which may or may not be true, e.g., 'The stars are even in number', for which there are "no arguments on one side or the other naturally suited to cause the appearance of one side rather than the other" (QDA₃ III.18: 202–203). The vast majority of propositions, however, will produce appearances that are either 'evident', 'sophistic', or 'plausible', making it possible for them to be connected with demonstrative, sophistic, or dialectical topics, respectively (S 6.5.6: 474).

43. Some commentators persist in translating 'evidentia' as 'evidence' despite the fact that Buridan understands 'evidentia' more narrowly as a way of being appeared to, i.e., as the quality or condition appearances have of being evident, rather than more broadly as the ground or reason used to justify beliefs. Indeed, if evidentia were not a quality of this sort, it could not be a proper object of the assenting or dissenting judgmental dispositions Buridan takes to be definitive of belief. In Buridanian terms, we would express the distinction by saying that the evidentness of an appearance is evidence that our assent to it is justified. It is apparently Cicero who introduces the Latin term 'evidentia' (along with 'perspicuitas') in philosophical contexts to translate the Greek term 'enargeia' (Academica 2, 6, 17), 'testimonia' being the preferred term for proof or grounds. Current usage of the English word 'evidence' blurs the distinction, of course, though it is interesting to note that 'evidence' did not come to mean the condition of being evident until the seventeenth century. Hume, for example, is obviously thinking of evidentness when he remarks, "Though there never were a circle or triangle in nature, the truths demonstrated by Euclid would for ever retain their certainty and evidence" (Enquiry Concerning Human Understanding, IV.1). One might wonder how construing 'evidentia' as a quality of appearances is compatible with the claim that Buridan's anti-skeptical remarks approximate an externalist theory like reliabilism, but this would pose a problem only if Buridan holds that evidentness of an appearance is the only circumstance relevant to the justification of its corresponding belief/judgment, which he does not. As we shall see, not all evident judgments are justified: e.g., my evident judgment while dreaming that Socrates is standing before me.

44. Aristotle's threefold division of problems and propositions into those concerned with ethics, natural philosophy, and logic, in Topics I.14.105b19–26.

45. There is also a third, weaker kind of evidentness, which suffices for acting morally well, "even though the judgment [on which our action is based] is false, due to invincible ignorance of some circumstance [licet iudicium sit falsum propter invincibilem ignorantiam alicuius circumstantiae]" (QM II.1: 9ra). But evidentness of this sort concerns standards of rationality in practical judgment rather than standards of knowledge in scientific judgment. Buridan says, e.g., that it is possible for a judge to act well and meritoriously in hanging an innocent man, provided witnesses and other evidence make it sufficiently apparent to him that the man is a murderer (for cases of non-culpable ignorance, see section 2b of chapter 15). It is partly in the hope of providing criteria for such judgments that Buridan elsewhere speaks of the need for a "moral logic" to govern reasoning in the practical sciences (QNE Proemium: 2rb; cf. S 8.7.5: 745). Peter King has argued that in practice, the same evidentness considerations that apply to moral judgments will also apply to scientific judgments, which are supposed by

evidentno

Buridan to exhibit the stronger variety of relative or *secundum quid* evidentness; thus, Buridan "gives up the question of truth for physical principles, offering instead a theory of warranted assertibility" (1987, 125–28). As will become clear below, I disagree with King's interpretation, since, quite apart from the question of divine intervention in the natural order, Buridan does think that external conditions pertain to the justification of scientific judgments, whereas the criteria for acting "well and meritoriously" are fully internal, based on evidence one is consciously aware of when the judgment is made. Thus, Buridan's judge may be praised from a prudential point of view for hanging an innocent man, even though he is not in what we would now describe as a strong epistemic position. The judge may nonculpably believe that the legal traditions of his community are authoritative as regards the guilt of the condemned man, even though that may be a very poor reason for believing that he is guilty.

46. *QM* II.1: 8vb (cf. *QAnPo* I.2; *S* 8.5.3: 717–19): "*homo cogitur sine necessitate ad assentiendum propositioni ita quod non potest dissentire.*" Buridan, however, may have changed his mind on this point. See n. 32 above.

47. *QM* II.1: 8vb–9ra: "*evidentia secundum quid sive ex suppositione . . . observaretur in entibus communis cursus naturae, et sic esset nobis evidentia quod omnis ignis est calidus et quod caelum movetur, licet contrarium sit possible per potentiam dei.*" I have avoided translating '*evidentia ex suppositione*' as 'conditional evidentness' or 'hypothetical evidentness', since, unlike Ockham, Buridan does not make the corresponding claim that scientific judgments are only conditionally or hypothetically necessary. Instead, he appeals to the older terminist notion of natural supposition to give the truth conditions for propositions expressing scientific judgments (*S* 4.3.4: 260–62; cf. *QNE* VI.6: 122vb; *QAnPo* I.16). See also, for discussion (of the history of the doctrine) de Rijk 1971–73; de Rijk, "The Origins of the Theory of the Properties of Terms," in *CHLMP*, 168–70; (of the doctrine as used by Buridan) Scott 1965, 669–73; and King 1987, 119–21.

48. Although God's miraculous action is the only source of *secundum quid* judgmental error mentioned in *QM* II.1, Buridan elsewhere shows much interest in the question of how scientific judgments go wrong in practice. For one thing, he says, although we naturally assent to 'Every fire is hot' and 'The sun is a warming agent', "this must be understood [in every demonstration in which those principles appear]: 'if no impediment occurs'." Impediments are part of the natural order, occurring whenever natural phenomena are prevented from turning out as nature intended because of deficiencies in matter or interference by other agents. Thus, plants are sometimes destroyed by heat, cold, or wind before they bear fruit; the fetus of an organism can die in utero; and some creatures are born with eyes that will never see or feet that will never walk. The extent to which nature can be impeded is discussed in *QDA*$_3$ III.19: 211–12 (from which these examples are taken), and *QP* II.12: 38vb.

49. See *QNE* IV.11: 126ra–vb; *QAnPo* II.11; *QM* I.8: 7va; *QP* I.15: 18vb–19ra. Again, it is not possible to experience every singular covered by an inductive generalization. In the case of 'Every fire is hot', no one can bring all singular fires into account, since no one can touch all of them, and, more significantly, *know* that those are all of them.

50. *QAnPo* II.11 (cf. *QAnPo* I.2; I.12; *QM* I.5: 6ra; I.8: 7va; *QP* I.15: 18vb–19ra; *QNE* VI.10: 127ra; cf. also Aristotle, *Posterior Analytics* II.99b20 ff.): "*dicendum est quod nobis est innata virtus quaedam inclinata naturaliter et determinata ad assentiendum veritati principiorum si sibi fuerint debite applicata, sicut ignis est naturaliter inclinatus ad comburendum cum sibi fuerit combustibile appositum, et illa virtus nobis*

innata est intellectus humanus." The *Summulae* adds that the intellect is naturally disposed to assent to truth in the way that "the swallow is disposed to make such and such a nest when it is time to lay eggs, even if without the use of senses it would not be able to do this" (*S* 8.5.4: 721).

51. *QM* I.8: 7va: "*sed tandem intellectus percipit in pluribus singularibus ita fuisse et non in aliquo fuisse instantiam, percipit ipse ergo per suam inclinationem naturalem ad veritatem consurgit ad consentiendum universali propositioni, ut quod omnis ignis est calidus.*" Cf. *QP* I.15: 19ra: "*intellectus, non videns instantiam nec rationem instandi, cogitur ex eius naturali inclinatione ad veritatem concedere universalem.*"

52. *QAnPo* II.11: "*licet intellectus indigeat inductione, tamen illa non est sufficiens ad determinandum intellectum nisi intellectus per suam naturam esset ad hoc inclinatus et determinatus.*"

53. *QAnPo* II.11 (cf. *QM* I.8: 7va; *QP* I.15: 18vb–19ra; *QNE* VI.11: 126vb–127ra): "*indigent primo judicio sensus, et memoria et experientia: verbi gratia, quod omnis ignis est calidus et quod omne rheubarbarum faciat choleram non statim concedit intellectus; unde posito quod numquam vidisses ignem vel, si vidisses, tamen non tetigisses, non esset intellectui tuo notum utrum omnis ignis sit calidus. Igitur ad hujus modi principia firmiter concedenda ab intellectu praeexigitur sensus, memoria et experientia, tali modo quod primo a sensu tu cognoscis istum ignem esse calidum et statim intellectus consequenter judicat ignem esse calidum.*"

54. *QNE* VI.11: 126vb: "*sensus seu sensualis inductio seu experientia non constituunt causaliter intellectivam cognitionem neque eius certitudinem.*"

55. The *lumen naturale*, of course, had a very respectable medieval pedigree. See Augustine, *Enchiridion* 17: "error in the soul is hideous and repulsive just in proportion as it appears fair and plausible when we utter it, or assent to it, saying, 'Yea, yea; Nay, nay'. . . . Yet so much does a rational soul shrink from what is false, and so earnestly does it struggle against error, that even those who love to deceive are unwilling to be deceived" (tr. Bourke 1974, 41–42). Cf. Buridan: "man as regards his intellect naturally desires to know, since each and every natural being desires and is inclined towards its perfection [*homo secundum intellectum appetit naturaliter scire, quia unumquodque ens naturale appetit et inclinatur ad suam perfectionem*]" (*QM* I.5: 5vb). Now according to one view, Buridan remarks elsewhere, the capacity to assent to truth is not acquired by the intellect, but "naturally implanted" in it: some call this capacity the agent intellect, whereas others, such as Averroes, refer to it as "the intelligible light," created by the divine intellect in the human soul at the same time as the soul. On another view, this capacity is an acquired habit identified with actual or habitual knowledge. Buridan opts for the first view, but sees no need to posit an intellectual light infused from above distinct from the agent intellect which, according to Aristotle in *De Anima* III.5 (430a15–16), is like a light with respect to the objects of our act of understanding (*QNE* VI.11: 127rb–va).

56. Buridan emphasizes, however, that the immediacy of assent should not be confused with immunity from doubt, especially where uneducated persons are concerned. He relates on several different occasions an anecdote in which he asks some old women whether "they can be sitting and not sitting at the same time" (*QM* II.2: 9vb)—or "running and not running" (*QM* IV.12: 21va); "eating and not eating" (*QNE* VI.11: 127vb) (he appears to have tried this several times)—to which they all immediately reply in the negative. But when Buridan mentions God's omnipotence and

ability to annihilate the entire world, asking them rhetorically, "Surely you believe that God could do this [i.e., cause you to be sitting and not sitting]?" their reply is "We do not know; God can do everything, and one must believe that God can do the impossible [*Et tunc petivi ab eis, 'Nonne creditis quod deus posset hoc facere?', statim respondebant, 'Nescimus. Deus potest omnia facere, et quod impossibilia deum posse facere credendum est'*]."

57. Of course, Buridan recognizes that people often assent to propositions, such as those expressing articles of faith, which are evident to them neither absolutely nor assuming the common course of nature (*QM* II.1: 8vb; *QAnPo* I.2).

58. The direct acquaintance of the knower with the known is an important principle in Buridan's theory of knowledge. He denies that scholars who have only heard or read that rhubarb cures or purges bile have certain knowledge (*certa scientia*) of that principle, since "teachers are capable of saying what is false, and even textbooks can contain falsehoods [*doctores possunt falsa dicere et in libris etiam falsa scribi possunt*]" (*QM* I.8: 7va; see also Ebbesen 1984, 103). Buridan here follows Augustine, who concedes in *De magistro* xi.37 that he "must believe rather than know" about the men who "vanquished King Nebuchadnezzar and his fiery furnace by their faithfulness and religion," since his acquaintance with that event is through scripture rather than his own experience.

59. Cf. Aristotle, *Nicomachean Ethics*, VII.3.1146b25.

60. *QNE* VI.11: 127rb: "*quantum ad secundum modum principiorum, non videtur esse dubium quin ad prompte, faciliter et firmiter dicendum verum indigeamus habitu acquisito superaddito intellectivae potentiae, quia potentia circa ea circa quae innata est dirigere et errare non est seipsa sine habitu superaddito determinata sufficienter ad firmiter et prompte et faciliter dirigere et nunquam errare.*"

61. Thus, the intellect assents to induction "when it sees no reason why it should not be so in all of the others [*nullam videns rationem propter quam non ita debeat esse in aliis*]" (*QNE* VI.11: 127ra; cf. *QM* II.2: 9vb; *QAnPo* I.2; I.12; II.11). Likewise, principles of natural science are not demonstrably or absolutely evident, but are rather made evident by induction, "through which the intellect, which, not seeing a counter-instance [*instantia*], or any reason for deferring judgment [*ratio instandi*], is compelled by its natural inclination to the truth to concede the universal proposition" (*QP* I.15: 19ra).

62. This is important for Buridan to establish, since he argues that the senses are good for us in two ways: "first, for the care [*procuratio*] of what is necessary and also useful in this life; second, for cognition and knowledge, since none of our intellective concepts can be produced in us without the aid of the senses [*sine ministerio sensuum*]" (*QM* I.6: 6ra).

63. Buridan indicates that he agrees with the reliability conditions for sense perception proposed by Themistius, but he rejects the idea that it is ever possible to judge infallibly, or "with perfect certitude [*cum perfecta certitudine*]," about proper sensibles, since that would require that the sense organ, the intervening medium, and the object of sensation all be perfectly disposed—something which almost never happens in practice, or if it does, only, as Buridan nicely puts it, "*in tali momento.*" He prefers to say that although not infallible, judgments about proper sensibles such as black or white, sweet or bitter, and so on, under the proper (not perfect) circumstances, are "certain and without any defect [*certe et sine aliquo defectu*]." Accordingly, he interprets Aristotle's remark in *De Anima* II.5 (418a12) about the impossibility of

error with respect to the proper sensibles as a claim about the degree to which they produce error relative to accidental sensibles: we are never completely mistaken about proper sensibles; about accidental sensibles, however, it is possible to be mistaken "not only in a few [degrees] or in part, but completely [*contingit non solum in pauco vel in parte sed in toto errare*]." This would be the difference between being mistaken about a shade of color and mistaking bile for honey, or copper for gold. See *QDA₃* II.11: 170–72, *S* 8.2.6: 662, and Sobol 1996, 505–13. For Themistius's reliability conditions, see Verbeke 1957, 132–33.

64. For these examples, see *QDA₃* II.11: 169; *QM* I.7: 7ra; *QDA₃* II.11: 174. Buridan treats the existence of something in the prospect of the perceiver as the paradigm case of perceptual reliability, claiming that the existence of an entity manifestly appearing before us "could not be proven more evidently than by the fact that it appears in the prospect of sense [*non posset evidentius probari quam quia apparet in prospectu sensus*]" (*QAnPo* I.4). Likewise, he argues that we know the existence of motion, colors, and the stars more evidently by sense than by reason (*QM* IV.12: 21vb).

65. *QM* II.1: 9ra (cf. *S* 8.4.4: 709): "*si vero deus simpliciter miraculose operetur, concludendum est quod potest, ideo non est evidentia sed solum ex suppositione sicut antedictum fuit quae est sufficiens ad scientiam naturalem.*"

66. For Scotus, see *Quaestiones Quodlibetales*, q. 6, a. 1; q. 7, a. 2; q. 13, a. 2; Alluntis and Wolter 1975, 135–37 (6.18–19); 162–72 (7.9–38); and 290–96 (13.27–47). For Ockham, see *Ordinatio* I, Prologue, q. 1, a. 1; *Opera Theologica* I: 31; 69. Scotus indicates that our knowledge of what is existent as such may be either sensory or intellectual. Likewise, Ockham says that it is possible for us to intuitively cognize both sensible particulars and particular mental acts, such as the acts of belief and love elicited from the dispositions of faith and charity, respectively. How did Scotus and Ockham view skepticism? Scotus was concerned to reply to Academic skepticism, but only insofar as he took the views of Henry of Ghent to have those same consequences. But even so, his dialectical strategy is to reject the skeptics' criterion of certainty, rather than reply to their arguments on a point-by-point basis (*Ordinatio* I, d. 3, p. 1, q. 4, nn. 229–45; *Opera Omnia* III: 138–48). And as for Ockham, there is simply no evidence that he was interested in refuting skepticism, or even aware of some of the skeptical consequences of some of his own views. For discussion of Scotus and Ockham on this issue, see Adams 1987a, 572–601, and John Boler, "Intuitive and Abstractive Cognition," in *CHLMP*, 469–75.

67. According to Ockham, experience certifies our capacity to cognize intuitively (*Ordinatio* I, Prologue, q. 1, a. 1; *Opera Theologica* I: 23), though the epistemic picture is complicated by his admission that God could cause us to have an intuitive cognition of a non-existent object. See Boler, "Intuitive and Abstractive Cognition," in *CHLMP*, 467–70.

68. *QM* VII.20: 54va (cf. *QP* I.7: 9ra; *QDA₃* III.8: 75–79): "*saepe illi conceptus sunt ficti, quia non habent in re extra convenientem correspondentiam, non est enim inconveniens quod sint conceptus singulares ficti, sicut etiam communes.*"

69. *QDA₃* III.8: 76: "*Quamvis ergo sensus exterior cognoscat Sortem vel albedinem vel album, tamen hoc non est nisi secundum speciem confuse repraesentatem cum substantia et albedine et magnitudine et situ secundum quem apparet in prospectu cognoscentis. Et ille sensus non potest distinguere illam confusionem, scilicet non potest abstrahere species substantiae et albedinis et magnitudinis et situs ab invicem. Ideo non*

potest percipere albedinem vel substantiam [*vel album* om. mss.] *nisi per modum existentis in prospectu eius. Ideo non potest cognoscere praedicta nisi singulariter"*; *QDA₃* III.8: 79 (*QP* I.7: 8vb; *QM* VII.17: 52va): "*dico quod cum intellectus a phantasmata recipit speciem vel intellectionem Sortis cum tali confusione magnitudinis et situs, facientem apparere rem per modum existentis in prospectu cognoscentis, intellectus intelligit illum modo singulari.*" Cf. *Summulae* 8.2.1: 633: "things cannot be cognized as singulars unless they are cognized as something in the prospect of the cognizer." For discussion of Buridan on singular cognition, see Miller 1985 and van der Lecq 1993b.

70. Descartes, *Fourth Meditation:* "I can see the impossibility of God's ever deceiving me. Any fraud or deception involves imperfection; the ability to deceive may to some degree argue skill or power, but the will to deceive is a sign of malice or weakness, and so cannot occur in God" (Anscombe and Geach 1971, 92–93).

71. For Buridan, the inscrutability of God's will is a consequence of his belief that "the will of God is infinitely more free and powerful than our will [*in infinitum voluntas dei sit liberior et potentior voluntate nostra*]" (*QP* VIII.2: 110va; cf. *QM* IV.12: 21vb).

72. *QM* IV.12: 21vb (cf. *S* 8.4.4: 708): "*deus in hoc non male ageret, etiam si annihilaret omnes homines et totum mundum, eo quod totum est simpliciter suum. Ideo si non male faceret annihilando hominem etiam iustum, videtur quod non male faceret si in aliquo crearet opinionem falsam, quoniam illa opinio falsa non esset iam mala.*"

73. See *QM* IV.12: 21va (cf. *QM* II.2: 9vb): "In another way, to err mentally concerning a first principle is to dissent from it or assent to its opposite. And concerning this, I say with Aristotle that it is impossible to be in error in this way about a first principle, at least naturally [*Aliomodo errare mente circa primum principium est ipsi dissentire vel eius opposito assentire. Et de hoc dico cum Aristotele quod impossibile est sic circa primum principium errare saltem naturaliter*]" (Aristotle argues in *Metaphysics* IV.3.1005b23 that it is impossible for anyone to believe the same thing to be and not to be, though, unlike Buridan, he does not restrict this claim to the natural order). The example that follows asks whether God could make us assent to a contradiction. Buridan concedes that he could, but denies that his doing so would violate his essential goodness because of the absolute dependency of all creatures on God, an assumption which blocks any appeal to ordinary (i.e., human) moral constraints on divine action. Buridan is noncommittal on the related question of whether God could produce contrary qualities in the same subject at the same time: "if this is possible by divine power, then one must say that contraries are not absolutely incompatible in being in the same thing at the same time, but incompatible in being [in the same thing] at the same time through a natural power [*si hoc est possibile per potentiam divinam, tunc oportet dicere quod contraria non repugnant simpliciter in essendo simul in eodem, sed repugnant in essendo simul per potentiam naturalem*]" (*QP* III.3: 43vb).

74. Although, as we saw in chapters 10–11, supernatural considerations do enter into Buridan's treatment of other topics, so that he considers the consequences of God's absolute power with respect to the possible existence of void space, the kind of motion exhibited by bodies in a vacuum, and the possible existence of other worlds distinct from our own, although he does not believe that any of these circumstances *in fact* obtains.

75. *Quaestiones de libris Meteorologicorum Aristotelis* I.8; Faral 1950, 95.

76. *QDA₃* II.10: 154: "*Notandum est enim quod, licet agens universale* [*universale* add. mss.] *quod est Deus possit unumquodque agere determinate sine alio agente* [*agente*

add. mss.] *determinato, tamen illa non diceretur actio naturalis sed miraculosa. In actionibus autem naturalibus, oportet, praeter universale agens, concurre particularis agentia determinata ad hoc quod potius fiat hoc quam illud, ut ignis agens determinat ad hoc quod fiat ignis, seu producatur, et non aqua, et semen equi ad hoc ut producatur equus, et non capra.*"

77. This same point is eloquently expressed by Buridan's student and disciple, Nicole Oresme: "to have recourse to the heavens is to destroy the knowledge of natural and moral philosophy, indeed, of all philosophy, since if I ask [*queram/queratur*] why Socrates is big, or healthy, or strong, or why this kind of grass grows in that meadow, or why the ass does not breed in Scotland, and so on, and you respond, 'Because such was the constellation in the heavens,' so would I be able to respond even more briefly, 'Since God wants it so'" (*Quaestio contra divinatores horoscopios;* Caroti 1976, 310).

78. Notice as well that Buridan's reply to Ultricurian skepticism avoids Locke's genetic fallacy of supposing that an account of the origins of various knowledge-claims has justificatory force. Buridan's view is rather that our own a posteriori standards of certainty, including our beliefs about how various perceptual and cognitive processes actually do operate, are sufficient for empirical knowledge. This explains why he is generally disposed to ignore skeptical worries rather than reply to them directly. In that respect, his view has much in common with contemporary reliabilism.

79. Needless to say, some aspects of contemporary reliabilist theory do not correspond easily or obviously to anything in Buridan. For example, Buridan would presumably want to reject deductive closure in the case of divine deception, since on his view, I can know that there is a stone in front of me without knowing what this implies, viz., that we inhabit a "normal" world (for other cases pertaining to deductive closure in Buridan, however, see Willing 1985). Likewise, I have found no indications that Buridan would follow contemporary reliabilists in rejecting the 'KK Principle' (i.e., 'if you know that P, then you know that you know that P'), since my knowing P is for him partly dependent upon both (1) my assenting to P, and (2) the fact that P is evident to me. Likewise, with respect to demonstrative knowledge, he remarks, "it is true that some people say that knowledge of the consequence is not required for knowing the conclusion, but [only] for knowing oneself to know the conclusion. But it still seems to me that this is required for knowledge of the conclusion" (*S* 8.4.2: 700). But again, my thesis is that Buridan's epistemology is most closely approximated and most charitably interpreted by reliabilism, not that Buridan is himself a reliabilist. The latter claim would quite rightly invite the charge of anachronism.

80. For discussion of this point, see Zupko 1999.

NOTES TO CHAPTER 13

1. According to Moody, "empiricism is a theory of method in the acquisition and evaluation of knowledge" (1958, 150–51; 1975, 292), a definition which he clarifies as follows: "in the narrower sense, empiricism is the doctrine that human knowledge is grounded on the kind of experience, mostly achieved through the five senses, whose objects are particular events occurring at particular times and in particular places. In this sense empiricism rules out direct intuition of suprasensory realities

such as Platonic ideas or immaterial substances, and it usually rejects a priori knowledge of necessary synthetic truths." That this definition should be treated only as a first approximation as far as the differences between thirteenth- and fourteenth-century philosophy are concerned, however, is suggested by Moody's awareness that both Aristotle and Thomas would satisfy it: "Thomas Aquinas himself took a major step along this road [i.e., of "philosophical empiricism"] when he rejected all a priori and suprasensory sources of human knowledge, holding with Aristotle that all human knowledge arises from sense experience" (1958, 155; 1975, 296–97). The differences Moody had in mind we may accordingly take to be a matter of degree, not of kind.

2. Moody 1958, 158; 1975, 299.

3. Indeed, historians of philosophy might be unusual in this regard because scholars in other disciplines, such as the history of science, have continued to use 'empiricism' as a descriptive term in their accounts of later medieval philosophy. See, e.g., Edward Grant's observation that "Jean Buridan was perhaps the quintessential empiricist of the Middle Ages" (1993, 86). Still, it is not my aim here to reconstruct what 'empiricism' means outside of philosophy, although my reading of that term as occasioned by Moody's thesis will of course have some bearing on the question. It is worth pointing out, however, that the strongest opposition to Moody on this point has in fact come from another historian of science, John Murdoch. In Murdoch's estimation, Moody "places too much emphasis on the role of empiricism in 14th-century philosophy," an error which "leads him to conclude that the orientation of philosophy was then 'toward positive science'" (1982, 174). Murdoch objects, "true, empiricist epistemology was dominant in the 14th century. But this did not mean that natural philosophy then proceeded by a dramatic increase in attention being paid to experience and observation (let alone anything like experiment) or was suddenly overwrought with concern about testing or matching its results with nature; in a very important way natural philosophy was not even about nature." In my view, Murdoch reads too much into Moody's ambiguous remarks about the implications of his thesis for "the positive sciences" in the later Middle Ages (see Moody 1958, 159; 1975, 300). Furthermore, his interpretation of the import of Moody's thesis seems guided by the assumption that if Moody is right, we should expect to find late medieval thinkers embracing something like logical empiricism—which of course they didn't (even Locke and Hume would fail to be empiricists on this criterion). In contrast, my working assumption is that Moody's thesis can be properly evaluated only by returning to its epistemological setting, regardless of any other implications he might have correctly or incorrectly drawn from it. And there is no doubt that Moody does sometimes overstate its significance. See n. 87 below.

4. By 'induction' I simply mean any species of non-demonstrative argument that reasons from some individuals of a certain class or type to others (typically, all others) of the same type. For most medieval logicians, both prior to the twelfth-century recovery of Aristotle and afterwards, inductive reasoning was thought to lack the necessity of the syllogism. See Martin Tweedale's discussion of Garland the Computist (whose *Dialectica* was composed c. 1100–1120/30) in this connection (1988, 199; for the dating of Garland's work, see Iwakuma 1992). More will be said below about the particular inductivist strategies employed by fourteenth-century philosophers.

5. What if late medieval philosophers did not understand what they were doing in terms of some definitive doctrine, but as a kind of method instead? An approach

that expects empiricism to conform to a certain doctrinal paradigm will fail to be sensitive to such changes.

6. These philosophers have two things in common which make them appropriate subjects for a comparison of this sort: (1) a philosophical reputation beyond their respective centuries (which is something of an understatement in the case of Thomas, of course); and (2) a contribution to the medieval genre of commentary on Aristotle's *De Anima*. The latter criterion rules out Ockham, of course, who wrote no commentary on *De Anima*.

7. See Aristotle, *De Anima* I.1.403a26–32.

8. Aristotle, *De Anima* I.1.402a6–8. Aristotle does, to be sure, begin by sketching a series of problems to which he hopes to find the solutions later on, which suggests that he views the nature of the soul as matter for further investigation, not as something that can be determined entirely a priori.

9. Thomas Aquinas, *Sentencia De Anima*, I.1: 7, ll. 206–11; *Opera Omnia* XLV, 1; tr. Pasnau 1999, 10. Cf. Aristotle, *De Anima* I.1.402b5–9.

10. Thomas Aquinas, *Sentencia De Anima*, I.1: 7, ll. 211–13; *Opera Omnia* XLV, 1; tr. Pasnau 1999, 10.

11. Thomas Aquinas, *Sentencia De Anima*, I.2: 9, ll. 2–4; *Opera Omnia* XLV, 1; tr. Pasnau 1999, 13.

12. Thomas Aquinas, *Sentencia De Anima*, I.2: 9, ll. 46–47; *Opera Omnia* XLV, 1; tr. Pasnau 1999, 15. Cf. Aristotle, *De Anima* I.1.403a10–11; III.4.429a18–28; III.7.431a14–16.

13. Thomas Aquinas, *Sentencia De Anima*, I.2: 10–11: ll. 69–81; *Opera Omnia* XLV, 1; tr. Pasnau 1999, 15.

14. Thomas Aquinas, *Sentencia De Anima*, I.2: 12: ll. 256–63; *Opera Omnia* XLV, 1; tr. Pasnau 1999, 20. Cf. Aristotle, *De Anima* I.1.403b17–18.

15. Thomas Aquinas, *Sentencia libri De sensu et sensato*, Proemium: 5, ll. 68–79; *Opera Omnia* XLV, 2. The Latin editors of Thomas's commentary on *De sensu* view his suggestion that a book on the intellect and intelligibles would be a book on metaphysics, not natural philosophy, as a possible departure from his teacher, Albert the Great, who not only composed a work with the title, *De intellectu et intelligibili,* but placed it together with his other works on natural science (Proemium: 5, notes on ll. 74–79). It is worth noting further that the subject's degree of abstraction from (or, conversely, contraction to) matter is also Thomas's criterion for separating the more specialized sub-disciplines of psychology from each other: "in the first place, Aristotle examined the soul in itself as a certain abstraction; second, he makes a study of the things which are souls, in keeping with a certain contraction or application to the body, but in general; third, he makes a study by applying all of this to particular species of animals and plants, by determining what is proper to each species. The first study, then, is contained in *De Anima;* the third study is contained in the books he has written about animals and plants [i.e., *Historia animalium, De partibus animalium, De plantis,* etc.]; but the middle study is contained in the books he has written about certain things which pertain in common either to all animals, or to several kinds of animals, or even to all living things. My present aim is to comment upon the latter books [i.e., *De sensu* and *De memoria*]" (Proemium: 4–5, ll. 40–54).

16. Thomas states that the subject of physics or natural philosophy is "mobile being conceived absolutely [*ens mobile simpliciter*]" (*Commentaria in octo libros Physicorum Aristotelis* I, c. 1, n. 4: 4, col. 2; *Opera Omnia* II). He then gives an inventory of

the more specialized works by Aristotle falling under this heading, noting that *De Anima* is properly concerned "with living things [*de animatis*]." Mark Jordan has this exactly right when he says that for Thomas, "the extension of physics into the study of the soul marks a new step in the hierarchy of the sciences," and that psychology in particular represents "the extension of physics 'upwards' towards ethics and metaphysics" (1986, 116–17).

17. *QDA*₃ I.1: 123ra–rb: "*in hac scientia quid nominis praesupponitur de anima, nec forte hic investigatur definitio animae nisi per habitum superiorem, scilicet meta-physicam. Ille enim definitiones entis* [f. 123ra–rb] *cuiuslibet per actum et potentiam quae in secundo libro permittuntur ad investigandum definitionem animae sunt de metaphysica cuius est stabilire aliarum scientiarum principia.*" Cf. *QM* VI.1: 33rb: "no special science [e.g., psychology] considers the quiddities of things according to their absolutely quidditative natures—unless, perhaps, by reference to a superior science. For the natural philosopher only considers things insofar as they are changeable, or in relation to change, e.g., how they move or are moved, how they are generated or corrupted, and how from these causes, or on account of them, they move or are moved in a certain way, [or] are made and corrupted in a certain way. And these [causes] are not quidditative natures [*nulla specialis scientia considerat quidditates rerum secundum rationes simpliciter quidditativas, nisi forte hoc sit supponendo a superiori scientia. Physicus enim non considerat de rebus nisi secundum quod sunt transmutabiles vel in ordine ad transmutationes, ut quomodo movent vel moventur, quomodo generantur vel corrumpuntur, et ex quibus causis vel propter quas sic movent vel moventur, fiunt aut corrumpuntur, et illae non sunt rationes quidditativae*]." Cf. also *QP* I.1: 2vb: "It is customary to treat some metaphysical questions in the special sciences because those special sciences have taken the determinations of such questions from metaphysics [*consuetum est aliquas quaestiones metaphysicales tractare in scientiis specialibus propter hoc quod illae scientiae speciales habent a metaphysica praesupponere determinationes illarum quaestionum*]." Buridan also contends that these nominal and therefore non-quidditative definitions do not pertain to demonstrative science. See *QAnPo* I.5: "But nominal definitions cannot be proved, because their terms signify conventionally [*diffinitiones dicentes quid nominis non possunt probari, quia significationes nominum sunt ad placitum*]." See also section 2 of chapter 8 above.

18. *QDA*₃ I.1: 122ra. This observation is made in an opposing argument at the beginning of the question, but Buridan does not disagree with it in his reply. In fact, as we saw in chapter 10, he makes a similar claim himself in *QDA*₃ III.15. Cf. Oresme, who remarks that since "the intellect has a recollective power [*virtus reservativa*], . . . theologians correctly state that one part of the rational soul exists with the assistance of a power of memory. Thus, we remember after death, although not as we do now [*non taliter ut nunc*]" (*QDA* III.11; Patar 1995, 396, ll. 16–19). Buridan also thinks that it is not the business of psychology to ask such 'theological' questions as, "whether Christ was a human being during the three days when his body was in the sepulchre without a soul, and his soul was among the dead without a body [*utrum Christus in triduo erat homo, scilicet quando corpus sine anima erat in sepulchro, et eius anima sine corpore in infero*]" (*QDA*₃ III.6: 53). Thomas, of course, addresses the very issue Buridan and Oresme regard as off-limits for natural philosophy in q. 15 of his *Questions on the Soul*, which asks whether a soul would be able to understand once it has been separated from its body.

19. *QDA₃* I.1: 122vb:

Et similiter modo intelligit Aristoteles quod quamvis anima esse inseparabilis a corpore, nec posset operationes suas existere sine corpore, tamen possibile est considerare de anima secundum seipsam considerando passiones et praedicata sibi [*sibi/sine*] convenientia secundum se et non [*non/nota*] toti corpori. Multa enim sunt talia, ut quod anima est actus corporis (hoc enim non est conveniens corpori, nec composito ex anima et corpore); et sic quod anima sit principium corporis secundum agens, secundum formam, et secundum finem; item anima dividitur in plures potentias secundum diversas operationes vitales; et sic de aliis.

20. That Buridan sees the primary aim of psychology as being the study of the dispositions and attributes proper to the soul in itself follows from his conception of animate qualities as predicates attributed to a subject in a proposition. Thus, he argues, "it is not the soul itself, but the term 'soul' that is the proper and adequate subject of this science [of psychology], because it properly supposits for animals. And if it is asked where that term is, I say that it is in my mind as far as my knowledge is concerned, and in your mind as far as your knowledge is concerned [*non anima sed ille terminus 'anima' est subiectum proprium adaequatum isti scientia, quia appropriate supponit pro animalibus. Et si quaeratur ubi est ille terminus, dico quod est in mente mea quantum ad scientiam meam, et in mente tua quantum ad scientiam tuam*]" (*QDA₃* I.1: 123rb).

21. *QDA₃* II.3: 34: "*Nota quod naturalis non considerat substantiae secundum rationes earum simpliciter quidditativas, sed solus metaphysicus. Physicus enim solum considerat substantias in ordine ad motum et operationes ipsarum. Et quia formae naturales, ad operationes suas, requirunt certam materiam et appropriatam per dispositiones qualitativas et quantitativas, ideo oportet quod naturales diffiniant formas per suas proprias materias. Ideo bene oportet animam diffiniri per corpus physicum organicum diffinitione naturali.*" So that the point is not lost on his audience, Buridan mentions it again in the replies to opposing arguments at the end of the question: "To the first counterargument, I say that souls and other substantial forms are not defined by the natural scientist according to quidditative and absolute concepts, but in relation to their matter and motion and natural operations [*Ad primam dico quod animae et aliae formae substantiales non diffiniuntur a naturali secundum conceptus quidditativos et absolutos, sed respective ad materiam et ad motus et operationes naturales*]" (*QDA₃* II.3: 39).

22. *QDA₃* I.1: 123ra: "*dico quod sufficit ad hoc quod illa scientia sit naturalis quod consideret de aliqua parte integrali vel essentiali [integrali vel essentiali/totali] entis mobilis in ordine ad operationes vitales.*"

23. Although Oresme opts for the second view, he feels no logically compelling reason for doing so. In fact, he describes both views as "certainly questionable [*bene dubia*]" (*QDA* I.1; Patar 1995, 98, ll. 13–16).

24. Oresme, *QDA* I.1; Patar 1995, 98, ll. 6–12.

25. Oresme, *QDA* I.1; Patar 1995, 99, ll. 37–46. Cf. Aristotle, *De Anima* I.4.408b13–15.

26. Oresme, *QDA* I.1; Patar 1995, 100, ll. 55–57.

27. Aristotle, *De Anima* I.1.402a10.

28. Thomas Aquinas, *Sentencia De Anima*, I.1: 6: ll. 145–47; *Opera Omnia* XLV, 1; tr. Pasnau 1999, 8. Cf. Aristotle, *De Anima* I.1.402a10 ff.

29. Thomas Aquinas, *Sentencia De Anima*, I.1: 6: ll. 161–63; *Opera Omnia* XLV, 1; tr. Pasnau 1999, 9.

30. Thomas Aquinas, *Sentencia De Anima*, I.2: 12: ll. 246–47; *Opera Omnia* XLV, 1; tr. Pasnau 1999, 19.

31. Thomas Aquinas, *Sentencia De Anima*, II.3: 78, ll. 21–25; *Opera Omnia* XLV, 1; tr. Pasnau 1999, 134. Thomas then contrasts the a posteriori method of demonstration in the natural sciences with the a priori method used in geometry where, he says, many definitions are treated "like conclusions [*sicut conclusiones*]" (78, ll. 46–48; tr. Pasnau 1999, 135; cf. Aristotle, *De Anima* II.3.413a13–20). After a digression proving that four-sided figures possess certain properties, he remarks that these examples are only partly relevant to the study of the soul, i.e., "with respect to [Aristotle's] demonstrating soul's definition. But there is no similarity with respect to his doing so through a demonstration stating the explanation [*demonstratione dicente propter quid*]" (79, ll. 104–105; tr. Pasnau 1999, 138). For additional evidence that Thomas views psychology as a demonstrative science, see *Summa contra gentiles* II.61: "But if, as he says [i.e., Averroes, in Book II, chapter 21 of his *Commentarium Magnum in Aristotelis De anima*], 'soul [*anima*]' is taken equivocally with regard to the intellect and other things, Aristotle would have first revealed the equivocation, and then defined it, as was his custom. Otherwise, he would have proceeded from equivocation—which is not [the method of] demonstrative science [*quod non est in scientiis demonstrativis*]" (*SCG* II.61: 428, col. 2, ll. 6–11; *Opera Omnia* XIII).

32. Thomas Aquinas, *Sentencia De Anima*, I.1: 6: ll. 168–71; *Opera Omnia* XLV, 1: tr. Pasnau 1999, 9.

33. Thomas Aquinas, *Sentencia De Anima*, I.1: 7: ll. 250–67; *Opera Omnia* XLV, 1: tr. Pasnau 1999, 11.

34. Aristotle, *De Anima* I.1.402a2.

35. *QDA₃* I.4: 126ra: "*Prima est quod scientia de anima est nobis valde difficilima et per consequens incertissima quantum est ex parte cognoscentis et inter cetera naturalium, scilicet circumscriptis deo et intelligentiis, quia intellectus noster est insensibilis. Et tamen ex parte nostramet ex debilitate nostri intellectus est, quod non possumus comprehendere nisi sensibilia vel per deductionem ex sensibili, ut dictum est. // Secunda conclusio est quod ex parte rei intelligendae, scientia de anima est certissima et facilima, quia inter cetera naturalia anima est altioris entitatis et maioris cognitionis.*"

36. *QDA₃* I.4: 126rb–va: "*Sed ipsa est difficilior et incertior simpliciter [simpliciter/ specialiter] quantum ad animam intellectivam quomodo illa se habeat ad corpus et ad materiam propter hoc* [f. 126rb–va] *quia non est extensa et non educta de potentia materiae, sed modo supernaturali adveniens est inhaerens corpori.*"

37. *QDA₃* I.4: 126va: "*ex parte maioris multitudinis [multitudinis/intellectionis] quaestionum dubitabilium, propter hoc quod ultra alias formas anima requirit in corpore diversas organizationes et habet valde multiplicatas organizationes et diversas potentias et operationes.*"

38. Oresme, *QDA* I.3; Patar 1995, 112, ll. 32–37. Bert Hansen suggests that Oresme was probably not acquainted with the *Phaedo* directly but through intermediate sources such as Cicero (1985, 276–77, n. 15). Or (we might add) through Cicero, via Buridan, who quotes this same passage in the *Summulae* in defense of an argument to the effect that it is necessary for a knower first to cognize all of the premises of a demonstration before he can be said to know its conclusion (*S* 8.3.7: 688).

39. Oresme, *QDA* I.3; Patar 1995, 112, l. 49 (cf. Aristotle, *Posterior Analytics* I.2.71b20–23; I.4.73a24–25): "The difficulty in psychology is because of two things,

viz., either on account of the remoteness being too great [*propter nimiam remo-tionem*], because one must produce many conclusions which are difficult to appre-hend (as is obvious in geometry, even though each conclusion is evident); [or] sec-ond, on account of the lack of evidentness of the consequence [*propter inevidentiam consequentiae*], because sometimes there is a non-formal consequence, and so it is difficult to see if it holds and why it holds." What does Oresme mean by 'non-formal consequence'? Buridan, whose teachings influenced Oresme, distinguishes between material consequences that hold absolutely and those that hold only as regards what is actually the case. Of the latter, he remarks that "a consequence is called 'actual' when, with things standing as they now stand, it is not possible for the antecedent to be true without the consequent—although this is possible absolutely speaking [*con-sequentia 'ut nunc' vocatur quando rebus stantibus ut nunc stant non est possibile an-tecedens esse verum sine consequente, licet simpliciter hoc sit possibile*];" thus, "a conse-quence as regards what is actual is valid if it can be reduced to a formal [consequence] by the addition of a true proposition, even if [that proposition is] contingent [*conse-quentia ut nunc est bona si possit reduci ad formalem per additionem propositionis verae, licet contingentis*]" (*QAnPr* II.19; cf. *TC* I.4). See also chapters 5 and 6 above. For the medieval history of formal consequence, see Schupp 1988, 44–75.

40. Aristotle, *De Anima* I.1.402b22.

41. I take this to be the general point of Aristotle's *Physics* I.1, which is for Buri-dan and Oresme the paradigm of reasoning in the natural sciences. Buridan in fact doubts whether most natural sciences would count as absolutely [*simpliciter*] demon-strative, since it is not necessary for the practitioners of a natural science to be directly acquainted with the essences of things, and hence with the origins of their causal principles. Thus, the phenomenon of eclipses could not be the subject of a Buri-danian demonstrative science. See *QP* I.1: 3vb; VI.3: 34ra–rb; for discussion, see n. 57 of chapter 8 above.

42. The title of QDA₃ I.6 is taken from a lemma of Aristotle's *De Anima* (I.1.402b22), translated into Latin by William of Moerbeke as, "*accidentia conferunt magnam partem ad cognoscendum quod quid est.*"

43. QDA₃ I.6: 128va: "*per accidens non cognoscitur substantia directa representa-tione, quia accidens et substantia valde sunt diversa, nec per discursum patet, quia non potest esse evidens consequentia de esse unius ad esse alterius, quia non potest reduci ad primum principium, quod fundatur in contradictione. Nunquam enim potest esse con-tradictio hoc esse et illud non esse, cum contradictio debet esse affirmatio et negatio eius-dem de eodem.*"

44. Rejecting an idea he associates with certain unnamed thinkers ("*aliqui*") who were apparently inspired by Averroes (*Commentarium Magnum in Aristotelis De anima* II.63: 225, ll. 39–42) to hold that sensation and imagination can apprehend "only accidents" and not the essences or "quiddities" of things, Buridan replies by ap-pealing to experience and common sense:

> I believe that sense perceives white and sweet rather than whiteness and sweetness. That is why a dog perceives someone who is calling him using his sense of hearing, and perceives the same person visually, for he judges that the one calling him is the one he sees. Thus, using his sense of sight, he runs up to the one calling him. And the dog does not judge that sound is color, but that the one calling him is the one colored. Nor does he run up to the sound, but, once the sound has ceased, he

runs up to the one who called him. And I believe that since accident and substance are one, it is easier to cognize substance and accident together confusedly than it is to cognize accident distinctly from substance, or conversely, for it is always more difficult to apprehend something distinctly than confusedly. For this reason, I do not believe that a dog makes judgments about whiteness in abstraction from substance, but about whiteness. Whiteness, however, is a substance that is white.

[Immo ego credo quod sensus percipit album et dulce potius quam albedinem et dulcedinem. Unde canis percipit vocantem se per auditum et eundem percipit per visum, iudicat enim vocantem esse quem videt, ideo per visum vadit ad vocentem. Et non iudicat canis quod vox est color, sed quod ille vocans est ille coloratus; nec vadit ad vocem, sed etiam voce cessante vadit ad ipsum qui vocavit. Et credo quod cum accidens et subiectum sint unica, facilius est confuse simul cognoscere subiectum et accidens quam accidens distincte a subiecto vel econverso, semper enim difficilius est distincte quam confuse apprehendere [*confuse apprehendere/conmiscere sive conmixtum comprehendere*]. Unde non credo canem iudicare de albedine abstracte a substantia, sed de albedino; albedinis autem est substantia, quae est alba.] (*QDA₃* I.6: 129ra)

This reflects Buridan's view that animate powers such as sense and imagination apprehend substance as the subject of accidents. Thus, although the dog is unable to apprehend the substance of his master per se, the fact that he naturally attributes representations of his master under different sensory modalities to the same subject shows that he is capable of apprehending substance per accidens.

45. *QDA₃* I.6: 128vb–129ra: "*ut ovis ex colore et figura et motu lupi sensibiliter elicit intentionem inimicitiae et fugit* [ff. 128vb–129ra] *ab eo, et ita intellectus cum sit virtus superior potest iterum ex intentionibus imaginatis elicere intentionem non imaginatam Ideo sic ex intentionibus accidentium sub imaginatione cadentium potest intellectus intentionem elicere substantiae.*" The wolf and sheep example was usually attributed to Avicenna. It occurs in the report of an opposing view here, but Buridan's response indicates that he has a similar interpretation.

46. *QDA₃* I.6: 129rb: "*Intellectus autem habet naturam et potentiam abstrahendi ab illa confusione conceptus proprios et distinctos quorum uno concipit substantiam sine accidente et alio accidens sine substantia.*"

47. It is important to notice that Buridan sees the uniformity of nature principle as having an affective dimension as well. Thus, in commenting on Aristotle's *De motibus animalium*, he says, "the limbs are exceedingly well suited to be acted upon by sensations and images, and are sufficiently close to them. Therefore, it is reasonable that if the senses or intellect judge that walking should occur, then immediately, i.e., we walk. And Aristotle says 'immediately', i.e., not absolutely right away, but very quickly, so that there does not appear to be any lapse of time [*membra sunt valde nata pati a sensibus et fantasiis et sunt sufficienter approximata. Ideo rationabile est, si sensus vel intellectus iudicant esse ambulandum, quod simul, ut est dicere, ambulamus. Et dicit Aristoteles simul, ut est dicere, quod non simpliciter simul, sed valde cito, ita quod non appareat tempus intermedium]*" (*DMA* V: 547–48).

48. *QDA₃* I.6: 129rb: "*sicut materia prima non potest recipere formas substantiales nisi praedisposita et praeparata per accidentia, ita nec intellectus notitias substantiarum quae sunt principaliores nisi praedispositus per notitias accidentium.*"

49. *QDA₃* I.6: 129vb: "*magna est convenientia accidentium ad substantias, caliditas enim est multum conveniens et naturalis igni* [*igni/substantiae*]. *Quando autem dicitur quod substantia et accidens sunt primo diversa, hoc conceditur quantum ad modos praedicandi secundum quos distinguuntur praedicamenta. Et etiam si multum distant secundum gradus entium et perfectionem, tamen diversa accidentia bene generant similitudines et repraesentationes* [*et perfectiones* add.] *diversarum substantiarum inquantum sunt naturales dispositiones earum.*"

50. Thus, the principle invoked in the third way above, viz., that effects resemble their causes, is treated by Buridan in other texts as evident only a posteriori. Anything stronger, of course, would simply beg the question against Autrecourt, whose argument is directed against the possibility of specifying such natural relationships a priori. Although Buridan's projectability judgments in the science of the soul tend to be made on the basis of predicates supplied by Aristotelian psychology, it is important to see, without being too anachronistic about it, that he is not thereby endorsing any kind of hypothetico-deductive solution to Autrecourt's objection, whereby the principles of Aristotelian psychology are seen as demonstrative on the assumption that accidents of the soul happen to resemble their subjects, or that God does not happen to be a deceiver, etc. That is because there is no evidence to suggest that he views the principles of Aristotelian natural philosophy as hypotheses awaiting confirmation by natural phenomena. Rather, our assent to such principles is the product of a twofold process arising from both the evidentness of particular judgments and the mind's natural inclination to assent to truth. Recall in chapter 12 the crucial role that judgments of sense, memory, and experience play in inductively causing our assent to empirical generalizations. Nor, in addition, does the corpus of Aristotelian natural philosophy represent any more than a source of working hypotheses for Buridan. As Moody observes, "Buridan not infrequently entertains alternative assumptions as being not only logically possible but also possibly preferable in accounting for the observed phenomena" (1970, 605). Indeed, Buridan sometimes criticizes the Aristotelian account on these very grounds, perhaps most famously in the case of antiperistasis, which he rejects in favor of the theory of *impetus* as an explanation of projectile motion. In psychology, the natural philosopher faces the slightly different problem of filling in the details where Aristotle's remarks are either sketchy or non-existent. The problem of intellectual memory, discussed in section 4 below, is a case in point.

51. *QDA₃* I.6: 129va:

> potest dici quod directa repraesentatione substantia cum accidentibus confuse repraesentat se sensui, et sensu mediante, intellectui, qui iam potest abstrahere modo dicto, etc. Dico etiam quod discursive possumus scire unum ex alio. Et ratio illa supponit falsum, scilicet quod nihil sit evidens nisi declaretur vel probetur per primum principium. Immo sunt tot principia indemonstrabilia [*propria* add.] quot sunt conclusiones demonstrabiles, prout debet videri primo Posteriorum. Quod etiam dicitur de syllogismo affirmativo etiam supponit falsum, scilicet quod non sit procedendum nisi per demonstrationes ex praemissis categoricis [*praemissis categoricis/principiis*].

52. Oresme, *QDA* I.4; Patar 1995, 115, ll. 10–13.

53. Oresme, *QDA* I.4; Patar 1995, 118, ll. 8–12.

54. Oresme, *QDA* I.4; Patar 1995, 119, ll. 38–48.

55. Oresme, *QDA* I.4; Patar 1995, 119, ll. 49–53; 56–59.

56. See Augustine, *City of God* XXI.8. For discussion, see Hansen 1985, 50–73 and chapter 12 above.

57. Oresme, *QDA* I.4; Patar 1995, 120, ll. 70–72.

58. Oresme's views on the reliability of natural knowledge are more complicated than I have suggested here. Edward Grant argues that unlike Buridan, Oresme appears to have a "double agenda" in natural philosophy, viz., "to replace superstitious explanations of phenomena with explanations based on natural causation, while at the same time depicting natural causation and natural knowledge as no more intelligible than the articles of faith" (1993, 105). Grant also sees each aspect of this agenda in evidence in different places: the former in Oresme's natural philosophy, the latter in his theology. Grant's findings merit further investigation, of course, but besides the fact that his thesis makes Oresme's position look divided against itself, the textual evidence mentioned in his article strikes me as compatible with a much less far-reaching sort of skepticism, viz., one concerning the ultimately knowability of the natural world as quantified by mathematics, rather than concerning natural knowledge in general. See n. 79 below.

59. Aristotle, *De Anima* III.4.429b8. The reason, adds Buridan in a comment on this passage, is that "if nothing remained in the intellect of the knower while asleep, he could not, while awake, deduce the conclusions that need to be deduced from many inferences any more than someone who was beginning to learn for the first time—which is false [*si in dormiente nihil remaneat in intellectu sapientis, tunc ipse evigilatus non posset magis conclusiones ex multis processibus deducendas deducere quam unus qui de novo inciperet addiscere, quod est falsum*]" (*QDA₃* III.15: 161–62).

60. Thomas Aquinas, *Sentencia De Anima*, III.8: 208, ll. 20–22; *Opera Omnia* XLV, 1: tr. Pasnau 1999, 352.

61. Thomas Aquinas, *Sentencia De Anima*, III.8: 209, ll. 43–50; *Opera Omnia* XLV, 1: tr. Pasnau 1999, 352–53.

62. On these modes, see Thomas Aquinas, *Summa Theologiae* I, q. 79, a. 6, ad 3: 271, col. 2; *Opera Omnia* IV.

63. Thomas Aquinas, *Summa contra gentiles* II.74: 470, col. 1, ll. 24–42; *Opera Omnia* XIII. The firmness argument is also found in the lighter treatment of intellectual memory in *Summa Theologiae* I, q. 79, a. 6: 270–71; *Opera Omnia* IV.

64. Thomas Aquinas, *Summa contra gentiles* II.74: 470, col. 2, ll. 37–45; *Opera Omnia* XIII. Cf. Aquinas, *Summa Theologiae* I, q. 79, a. 7: 272–73; *Opera Omnia* IV.

65. See Buridan, *QDA₃* III.11, which asks whether the intellectual act or disposition is the same as the intellective soul, or something added to it.

66. See Maier 1958, 331–39. Mirecourt's defense suggests that he might not have actually held some of the condemned views, but only mentioned them along with several other possible views as "readily believable [*probabile*]," letting "students choose whichever they wish." Buridan's citation of these articles from the 1347 condemnation of Mirecourt gives us a possible *terminus a quo* for dating the third and final version of his *Questions on Aristotle's De Anima*.

67. *QDA₃* III.11: 115 (see also Maier 1958, 332): "just as we suppose that this magnitude is the same as this figure, and that because it is differently disposed, it is sometimes a sphere and sometimes a cube or a pyramid . . . so also, many suppose that because this moveable thing is differently disposed, it is sometimes motion and

sometimes rest, sometimes upwards motion and sometimes downwards motion . . . therefore, as before, such a multitude [of moveable things and motions] would be posited pointlessly [*sicut nos ponimus quod haec magnitudo est idem quod haec figura et est aliquando sphaera et aliquando cubus vel pyramis . . . sicut etiam multi ponunt quod hoc mobile ex eo quod aliter et aliter se habet, est aliquando motus* [*et*] *aliquando quies, aliquando motus deorsum* [*et*] *aliquando motus sursum . . . ideo, ut prius, frustra poneretur talis multitudo*]."

68. *QDA*₃ III.11: 118–19:

> Iam ergo quidam quorumdam antiquorum resumpserunt opinionem, quam credo tempore moderno sufficienter improbatam, ita quod nullus amplius curaret de ea disputare: scilicet quod in nobis intellectus et scientia non different, sed sunt idem intellectus et intellectio et scientia, et omnis intellectio tua et omnes habitus intellectuales quibus tu intelligis vel consideras vel potes considerare sunt idem quod intellectus tuus. Et rationes difficiliores quas ad hoc adducunt sunt illae quas in principio quaestionis posuimus. Et maxime fundant se super hoc quod omnia possumus salvare per idem aliter et aliter se habere, sicut dicebatur de motu et figura. . . . Ideo propter tales rationes, aliqui antiquissimi posuerunt accidentia non esse entia distincta a substantiis suis, sed deberet dici 'modos substantiarum'. . . . Et hanc opinionem tenuerunt et tenent, ut puto, non quia credant eam esse veram, sed quia est difficile eos redarguere demonstrative.

Indeed, as Maier observes, Mirecourt himself concedes that on the question of whether thoughts [*cogitationes*] are distinct from the soul itself, "many think that here, they have at least a posteriori demonstrations. But I, on the contrary, don't know whether the arguments we have here can be said to be demonstrations" (1958, n. 104).

69. The first argument: "I adhere to the [opposite] opinion on the authority of the school of Paris and the bishop who once, having summoned the congregation together because of the danger of many false opinions of Parisian authors, condemned them. And the bishop checked the arrogance of the University with the penalty of excommunication, so that these opinions would no longer be maintained by anyone. And this was one of them, viz., that our intellect is the knowledge or intellection [*huic conclusioni adhaereo per auctoritatem studii Parisiensis et episcopi, qui quondam congregati propter periculum multarum falsarum opinionum Parisius seminatarum, condemnaverunt eas. Et adrogatum universitatis inhibuit episcopus sub poena excommunicationis ut non amplius ab aliquo tenerentur. Et haec fuit una de illis: scilicet quod intellectus noster esset scientia vel intellectio*]" (*QDA*₃ III.11: 121). The condemned proposition reads: "That it can probably be maintained [*probabiliter potest sustineri*] that a cognition or volition is not distinct from the soul—indeed, that it is the soul itself [*ipsa anima*]. And so those who hold this view are not compelled to deny a proposition known per se, or to deny anything, in admitting an authority" (*CUP* I, n. 1147, art. 28: 611). Rega Wood has suggested to me that Mirecourt's view here might owe something to Richard Drayton, regent master of the Franciscan school at Oxford c. 1324, whose works are mostly lost, but whom Adam Wodeham reports as holding that the act of fruition is not really distinct from the soul but is rather the same as the soul itself, like the wayfarer's act of love. Likewise, Wodeham's view of Drayton's position resembles Buridan's attitude towards Mirecourt's: "The conclusion of those arguments [i.e. Drayton's], if permissible, would be philosophically probable [*si esset*

licita, esset philosophice probabilis]." But even so, Wodeham counters that "love is a quality no less distinct from the soul than cognition," citing on his behalf article 85 of the Condemnation of 1277, viz., "that the knowledge of what is understanding does not differ from the substance of what is understanding [*"quod 'scientia intelligentiae non differt a substantia intelligentiae'"* (*Lectura secunda*, d. 1, q. 4, sect. 2; Wood and Gál 1990, 252–53; cf. *CUP* I, n. 473, art. 85: 548). Buridan's second argument is that "[Mirecourt's view that accidents are reducible to mere modes of substances] is contrary to what we hold concerning the sacrament of the altar, for there the accidents remain without a subject. Therefore, the substance of the bread, which was white and which had a certain size and shape, was not the whiteness, magnitude, and shape that remain in the sacrament because these remain and the substance of the bread does not remain. That is why this is a valid syllogism: 'The substance of the bread will not remain, and the whiteness will remain; therefore, the whiteness is not the substance of the bread' [*hoc est iam contra ea quae tenemus de sacramento altaris, ibi enim accidentia manent sine subiecto. Ergo substantia panis, quae erat alba, magna, et figurata, non erat albedo, magnitudo, et figura quae manent in sacramento, quia haec manent et substantia panis non manet. Unde bonus est syllogismus: 'Haec substantia panis non manebit, et haec albedo manebit; ergo haec albedo non est haec substantia panis'*]" (*QDA₃* III.11: 121–22). The condemned proposition reads: "That in the natural light of reason [*in lumine naturali*], there are no accidents, but everything is substance, and that if it were not for the faith, this must be assumed, and probably can be assumed [*potest probabiliter poni*]" (*CUP* I, n. 1147, art. 29: 611).

70. Buridan also gives a third argument, i.e., that the view that everything is substance seems to reduce to the absurdity that everything is ultimately the same:

> ... they could speak in the same way, using similar arguments, about the relation of substantial forms to matter: viz., that matter disposed in one way is fire; disposed in another way, it is water, air, or stone. And this was the opinion of Democritus and Melissus, who say that everything is one substantially. For it is said that they were not such as to believe that this man is the same in number as that one, but [they did believe this] of things that appear to be generated one from another, as if from earth A comes water B, and from water B comes grass C, and from grass C, horse D, and so on for every species of generable and corruptible thing. Then horse D is the same as what was water, air, and earth, for the same matter which they said is the entire substance of the thing was first earth, and then water, grass, and horse, differently disposed. But these remarks are extremely obscure and dangerous, for in this way, a donkey was once a stone, and a stone has always existed, and no horse or human being has ever been generated, although it has been made into a human being or horse. And these opinions have been sufficiently condemned by Aristotle [i.e., in *Metaphysics* I.4.985b5–20; VIII.2.1042b9–14; *De generatione et corruptione* I.1–2], and by others. In no way would I want to assent to them.

> [... similibus rationibus ipsi possent dicere de formis substantialibus ad materiam: scilicet quod materia uno modo se habens est ignis; alio modo se habens est aqua, aer, vel lapis. Et haec fuit opinio Democriti et Melissi et dicentium omnia esse unum substantialiter. Non enim erant ita fatui quod crederent illum hominem esse idem in numero cum illo, sed de hiis quae apparent ex se invicem generari: ut si ex terra A fiat aqua B, et ex aqua B herba C, et ex herba C equus D,

et sic de omnibus speciebus generabilium et corruptibilium, tunc equus D est idem quod fuit herba et aqua et terra, eadem enim materia quam dicebant esse totam substantiam rei fuit prius terra, et post aqua et herba et equus, aliter et aliter se habens. Haec autem dicta sunt valde obscura et periculosa, sic enim asinus fuit lapis, et lapis semper fuit, et nunquam equus vel homo fuit genitus, licet materia facta fuit homo vel equus. Et haec satis sunt reprobata per Aristotelem et per alios, et nullo modo vellem eis assentire.] (*QDA₃* III.11: 122)

71. *QDA₃* III.11: 122–23:

. . . 'aliter et aliter se habere' significat idem quod 'alio et alio modo se habere'. Si ergo intellectus noster nunc est una opinio, et cras erit opinio contraria, alio et alio modo se habens, iste modus non erit iste modus; ex quo modi ponuntur alii. Si ergo modi sunt plures et alii ab invicem, et intellectus non est nec erit alius, sed semper idem, necesse est intellectum esse alium ab illis modis et ab unoquoque illorum. Et tunc omnes difficultates quae erant de alietate vel identitate illarum opinionum, et maiores, revertuntur de illis modis. Ideo melius est statim stare in alietate illarum opinionum. Verum est quod intellectus sit contrarie opinans, alio et alio modo se habens, etsi illi modi sunt illi opiniones: sic etiam Sortes, prius albus et post niger, alio et alio modo se habet (et illi modi sunt albedo et nigredo). Accidentia enim sunt modi et dispositiones substantiarum secundum quorum variationem subiecta aliter et aliter se habet. Et omnino, aliter et aliter se habere requirit aliquam alietatem, et oportet quod illa detur in proposito, et non potest bene dari nisi illorum habituum ad invicem vel ad intellectum.

72. This is the distinction between three ways in which "something, while remaining the same, can be differently disposed, such that contradictory predicates are true of it—i.e., of the term suppositing for it—at different times [*aliqua res manens eadem tripliciter potest se habere aliter et aliter quod de ipsa, id est de termino supponente pro ipsa, verificentur praedicata contradictoria prius et posterius*]" (*QP* II.3: 31ra). The first two ways cover relational changes of material substances, i.e., (1) between a subject and what is external to it, and (2) between the integral (physical) parts of the same subject—neither of which apply to the intellect and its dispositions because the latter are conceived as qualities that are neither external to the intellect, nor among its integral parts (as an immaterial substance, the intellect strictly speaking has no integral parts). As an example of the first way, Buridan mentions a person moving such that a column is first on his right and then on his left; as an example of the second, a magnitude changing its shape from cubical to spherical (*QDA₃* III.11: 123; cf. *QP* II.3: 31ra–rb; for discussion, see Normore 1985 and chapter 11 above). The third way looks the most promising as a model for explaining psychological change: "if the [contradictory] predicate neither connotes something extrinsic nor the relation of the parts of that thing to each other, then no cause appears natural to me unless it is because something has been added, generated, or corrupted with respect to that thing. For in this way, a man is white and non-white, or first white and later black. And thus the distinction of forms and accidents from their substances can be known and defended [*si illud praedicatum nec connotat aliquid extrinsecum nec connotat habitudinem partium illius rei ad invicem, et tunc nulla causa apparet mihi naturalis nisi quia illi rei est aliqua res addita generata vel corrupta. Sic enim est homo albus et non albus, vel albus*

et niger prius et posterius. et sic potest sciri et argui distinctio formarum et accidentium a 〔2020〕
substantiis suis]" (QP II.3: 31rb).

73. *QDA₃* III.11: 124:

Si res tertio modo dicatur aliter et aliter se habere prius et posterius (scilicet circumscriptis exterioribus et quod eius partes non mutent situm ad invicem), tunc
alietas designata per 'aliter et aliter se habere' non potest salvari, nisi per generationem vel corruptionem alicuius dispositionis sibi inharentis et distinctae ab ea.   〔2020〕
Sic enim est de aqua, si prius est calida et post frigida; et de materia, si prius est
sub forma aquae et post sub forma ignis; et de intellectu, si prius fuit sic opinans
et post contrarie: nam homine dormiente, et omni repraesentatione sibi per sensum circumscripta, adhuc aliter haberet se posterius quam haberet se prius,
quod non potest salvari nisi per alietatem illarum opinionum ab invicem et ab   〔?〕
intellectu. Aliter non posset ostendi quin omnia essent unum modo quo opina-
bantur Parmenides et Melissus, sicut dixi prius.

74. See Maier 1958: "Each state and each change, each disposition [*modus se*
habendi] and each case of being differently disposed [*aliter et aliter se habere*], thus
signifies for Buridan a form-like accident or a form-like disposition in the subject in
question. This account also holds good for local motion, which is not mentioned here   〔20〕
[i.e., in *QDA₃* III.11], for Buridan certainly sees in it an 'absolute', [i.e.,] the inhering
accidents of a moving body, for which this account is largely true" (338). To this Maier
adds, "for Buridan . . . [local motion] is something internal which has a formal character and which virtually stands for an inhering quality of the mobile." For discussion
of the Buridanian theory of *impetus,* see Clagett 1959, 505–64.

75. Buridan's application of *impetus* theory to explain analogous phenomena
outside the context of projectile motion is not without precedent in the history of
philosophy. Avicenna, apparently influenced by Philoponus, introduces a related,
though less sophisticated, concept of impressed force, "*mayl* [inclination]," to explain
the continued motion of a body no longer in contact with its mover. Even more
interesting, he also distinguishes between three kinds of *mayl,* each of which is thought
to cause a different kind of motive effect: (1) psychic *mayl* (bodily motion due to will
and intention); (2) natural *mayl* (the gravitational acceleration of falling bodies); and
(3) unnatural or violent *mayl* (projectile motion). For discussion of the Islamic doc-   〔20〕
trine and its (as yet undemonstrated) influence on the Latin West, see Clagett 1959,
510–14; 547–48; Maier 1968, 127–41; and Grant 1977, 48–49. With respect to psychological *impetus,* Buridan's view also has some affinity with the Stoic notion of "*hormé*
[impulse]" as a motion of the soul: "In genus impulse is a movement of the soul towards something. In species it is seen to include both the impulse which occurs in rational animals and the one found in the non-rational . . . one would correctly define
rational impulse by saying that it is a movement of thought towards something in the
sphere of action" (John Stobaeus, quoted Long and Sedley 1987, 317). In their commentary, Long and Sedley describe Stoic impulses as "that activity of the soul's
commanding-faculty which converts its judgements of what it should pursue or avoid
into purposive bodily movements" (420). But again, there is no evidence that Buridan
knew about Stoic *hormé,* or that such a notion might have indirectly influenced his
own theory of *impetus.* One must be careful about taking the sense in which impetus is a doctrine too literally, however. For if Buridan instead conceives of it as an

explanatory mode, we should expect to find him unselfconsciously using it in a variety of contexts, none of which speaks to its necessary and sufficient conditions.

76. *QDA₃* III.15: 163: "*Secunda conclusio est quod ille habitus non est de natura vel specie intellectionis, sed differens ab eo solum secundum intensum et remissum, ut aliqui dicunt, ita quod cum est intensum est intellectio et cum est remissum non amplius dicitur intellectio sed habitus. Ista conclusio probatur, quia non existente actu intelligendi, est habitus remissus in eo qui parum studuit, ideo cito annihilatur nisi perseveret in studio. In eo autem qui longo tempore studuit, est iam habitus intensus, et difficiliter mobilis seu annihilabilis, licet non sit actualis intellectio.*"

77. Apparently, Buridan himself once subscribed to this view. In the first version of his *Questions on Aristotle's De Anima*, he says:

the intellectual habit is that same likeness which is called the species, connoting a greater firmness, and also the fact that it inclines the intellect. // To sum up, then, it is obvious that it is the same quality which, when it has been acquired and the intellect is not [actually] cognizing or understanding by means of it, is called an intelligible species; but when it has been firmly enough established in the intellect and is [actually] inclining the intellect, it is called a habit. It is obvious, then, in reply to the question that the intelligible species, that the act of understanding, and the intellectual habit are not distinct things, but the terms, 'intelligible species', 'act of understanding', and 'intellectual habit' signify the same thing being disposed in different ways.

[habitus intellectualis est illa eadem similitudo quae vocatur species, connotando maiorem firmitatem, et etiam quod inclinat intellectum. // Patet igitur recapitulando quod eadem qualitas quae, dum acquiritur, vocatur actus intelligendi, et quando acquisita est et intellectus non cognoscit nec intelligit per eam, vocatur species intelligibilis; sed quando est bene firmata in intellectu et est inclinativa intellectus, vocatur habitus. Patet igitur ad quaestionem quod species intelligibilis, actus intelligendi, habitus intellectualis non sunt res distinctae, sed isti termini 'species intelligibilis', 'actus intelligendi', 'habitus intellectualis' significant eandem rem, alio tamen et alio modo se habentem.] (*QDA₁* III.10: 459, ll. 23–34)

Buridan goes on to explain the causal connections between species, act, and habit: "I say that this [i.e., the phrase, 'a habit is generated from acts'] must be understood as follows: when any species produces an act of understanding on many occasions, that species is intensified and so firmly established in the intellect that it will in addition be named a 'habit' [*dico quod hoc debet intelligi quod, cum aliqua species multoties fit actus intelligendi, ipsa intenditur et ita firmatur in intellectu quod amplius nominabitur 'habitus'*]" (*QDA₁* III.10: 460, ll. 49–52).

78. *QDA₃* III.15: 163–64:

Item ponamus secundum adversarium quod intellectio sit forma intensa decem graduum eiusdem rationis, et habitus derelictus sit forma remissa quinque graduum, semper eiusdem rationis cum illis gradibus qui erant formae intensae. Cum ergo cessante actuali intellectione, corrumpuntur quinque graduum illi formae intensae, et constat quod cito et faciliter et quasi instanter cessat huiusmodi intellectio. Ideo cito et faciliter corrumpuntur illi quinque gradus, et tamen alii quinque remanentes habitus non corrumpuntur cito, sed sunt longe permanentiae et de difficili mobiles. Huius autem diversitatis inter quinque remanentes et quinque corruptos, nullus posset assignare causam ex qua ponuntur ad invicem eiusdem rationis, et quod intellectus nullus sibi determinat. Ideo ficticia et falsa erat positio adversarii.

79. Since Buridan does not identify his younger self as among those who subscribed to the view he is attacking in *QDA₃* III.15, it is difficult to say why he abandoned it. But his objection suggests that he might have thought that his early view did not fully consider the consequences of treating thoughts and dispositions as differing intensive magnitudes of the same quality. The question raised by this approach would appear to be whether mathematizing the distinction gives us a model of intellectual memory that fits the phenomena. If the aim of medieval philosophers who appealed to the intension and remission of forms in this way was, as Norman Kretzmann has suggested, to consider "abstract problems of mensuration in terms of arbitrarily assigned degrees ranging over intensive and extensive qualities alike," so that latitudes of forms were treated "as continua analogous to line segments and temporal intervals, degrees being the analogues for points and instants" (1977, 5), then one can ask whether the difference between thoughts and dispositions is purely a matter of degree. Buridan's objection sets out to embarrass his opponents by not allowing them to speak vaguely of the intensification and diminution, but insisting that actual (hypothetical) measures be assigned to the different psychological states mentioned. The result raises questions about the mechanism of such changes, i.e., why the form in question is not subject to the same speed of intensification/diminution between degrees 0–5 (*qua* disposition) as it is between degrees 5–10 (*qua* occurrent thought). In the absence of such an explanation, the speed distinction begins to look completely *ad hoc*. Buridan's criticism of this application of the doctrine of the latitude of forms has a certain resonance with the (limited, in my view) skepticism expressed by his younger colleague, Nicole Oresme, as regards the possibility of knowledge in natural philosophy. See n. 58 above. For discussion of medieval theories of the intensification and remission of forms, see Sylla 1973 and "The Oxford Calculators" in *CHLMP*, 540–63.

80. *QDA₃* III.15: 165: "*Cum autem intellectus actuatus fuerit per primas intellectiones, ipse est potens actu considerare de omnibus quae ex illis primis intellectionibus vel ex similibus aliis deductis fuerunt, et quorum habitus in eo remanserunt.*"

81. Buridan's view appears vulnerable to another kind of objection that he does not address here: viz., how one kind of psychological quality can be caused by another qualitatively (and not just quantitatively, as in the intension/remission view) distinct from it. For if the disposition is not the same kind of thing (*res*) as the thought, how can one figure in the generation of the other? Buridan might conceivably reply here that the generation of occurrent thoughts from intellectual dispositions is no more mysterious than the process by which the intellect is said to abstract "species or intentions [*species vel intentiones*]" of intelligible things from particular images generated by the sensory powers of the soul, or even the process by which the latter powers receive sensible species from things outside the soul. Notice that Buridan's argument for qualitatively distinct dispositions concerns the subject or medium of such objects, not the objects themselves. Thus, an actual thought and the disposition to have such a thought can both be about the same thing, even though they exist in distinct

modes as psychological qualities: "from the demonstration of some conclusion, e.g., that every triangle has three angles, a certain disposition is generated in the intellect, which is naturally suited to remain over time. And it remains in the intellect after the act of understanding has ceased and in the absence of the object [*ex demonstratione alicuius conclusionis, ut quod omnis triangulus habet tres angulos, generatur in intellectu quidam habitus, qui per tempus innatus est manere. Et manet in intellectu cessante actu intelligendi et in absentia obiecti*]" (*QDA₃* II.18: 289). The disposition and occurrent thought must be distinct on his view because the disposition has the natural capacity, once generated, to remain or endure (*manere*) in the intellect—a power that the occurrent thought does not have. Buridan also looks to causal or operational diversity as a means of distinguishing between the modes of being of species or intentions received in different faculties of the sensory part of the soul. Observing that, unlike species impressed upon the eye, species received in the imagination and common sense "do not require the presence of a bright or colored body, or even of a diaphanous medium, for their generation or retention," he concludes, as we have seen in chapters 1 and 12 above, that "the species of color in the eye and the representation of color in the imagination or intellect do not seem to be of the same or of a similar nature, nor of the same kind or type [(*species*) *in fantasia vel in sensu communi non indigent ad generationem sui vel permanentiam presentiam lucidi vel colorati vel etiam dyafani. Ideo species colorum in oculo et representatio coloris in fantasia vel intellectu non videntur esse eiusdem vel consimilis naturae, nec eiusdem rationis et speciei*]" (*QDA₃* II.18: 261). Again, Buridan's idea is that if the imagination can be affected by color in the absence of light, then its species must differ from that which activates the power of vision. For operational diversity as an indicator of specific difference, see chapter 11 above.

82. Oresme, *QDA* III.9: 380–81, ll. 18–51. For Mirecourt, see n. 66 above.

83. Oresme, *QDA* III.9: 382, ll. 74–75.

84. Oresme, *QDA* III.10: 387, ll. 91–97. Oresme does add a proviso here, viz., "except that the [latter] inclination [i.e., the gravity] is natural, and the inclination that is in the intellect is free," which looks to be a reference to the Scotistic distinction between the natural and voluntary orders. This distinction does not appear to play any role in Oresme's account, however, which is wholly concerned with the natural order.

85. Oresme, *QDA* III.10: 389–90, ll. 48–55.

86. Oresme, *QDA* III.10: 390, ll. 56–66.

87. Even conceding, as in n. 3 above, that Moody does sometimes overstate his case. In this category, I would place such remarks as, "the theologians of the later Middle Ages became philosophical empiricists, bequeathing to the modern world a critique of knowledge that might have pleased David Hume if he had known it in its fourteenth-century purity" (1958, 147; 1975, 289), as well as the related claim that "in epistemology Ockham's position was very nearly that of Hume" (1958, 156; 1975, 298). For a convincing refutation of this and other efforts to depict Ockham as the medieval Hume, see Adams 1987a: 551–629.

88. It is noteworthy here that Thomas's conception of physics is likewise closer to metaphysics than to any kind of natural science, whereas Buridan tends to group physics together with psychology and biology as natural sciences concerned with matter. For discussion of the gradual attenuation of teleological methods in natural philosophy between Thomas and Buridan, see Lang 1989.

Notes to Chapter 14

1. *QNE* Proemium: 2ra: "[philosophia moralis] *non contemplationis gratia, non enim inquit ut sciamus quid est virtus scrutamur, sed ut boni efficiamur qua nullum fuerit* [*fuerit/esset*] *utique proficuum eius.*" Cf. Aristotle, *Nicomachean Ethics* II.2.1103b26–28. Buridan quotes this passage directly from the Latin translation of Aristotle's text.

2. Aristotle, *Nicomachean Ethics* I.7.1098a16–17; X.7.1177a12–13. Buridan also cites Books I and X in this connection.

3. *QNE* Proemium: 2ra: "*animae nostrae virtutes et utiliter habitus et dispositiones et operationes in morali scientia pertractantur necesse est, ut ista scientia proponatur aliis etiam nobilitate speculationis.*"

4. Aristotle, *Nicomachean Ethics* II.6.1107a1–3; Buridan, *QNE* I.1: 2va; I.22: 21vb; II.14: 33ra.

5. *QNE* I.1: 2vb: "*Etiam licet actus humani sint contingentes in ordine ad hominem absolute sumptum, sunt tamen determinati in ordine ad suas causas, semper enim vel in pluribus actus virtuosi a virtute procedunt, et vitiosi ad vitio.*"

6. Let me make clear at the outset, however, that the remarks which follow are in no way intended to re-cultivate ground that has already been covered by James J. Walsh in a series of informative articles on the role of the virtues in Buridan's moral philosophy (see Walsh 1964; 1966a; 1966b; 1975; 1980; and 1986). Rather, the two projects are complementary. That is because, whereas Professor Walsh's work has mostly been concerned with how the virtues are related to each other, and with their role in Buridan's moral teleology, my concern in this chapter is with the question of how they got there in the first place, i.e., how virtues are generated and conserved as psychological attributes. This suggests that it is possible to approach the question of virtue in Buridan's ethics from two, quite different, directions: on the one hand, we can consider the virtues as component parts of a person's moral character, and ask how those parts fit together so as to produce actions consistent with either the immediate or ultimate goals of the agent (call this 'the practical approach'); and, on the other, we can examine the origin and metaphysical status of the virtues themselves in order to determine the relation between moral and natural agency (call this 'the speculative approach'). This chapter tells the speculative story.

7. Cf. *QNE* I.22: 21vb; II.14: 33ra; and Aristotle, *Nicomachean Ethics* II.6.1107a1–3.

8. *QNE* II.14: 33ra: "*Concedendum est quod virtus potest esse sine electione actuale praesente, sed non absque electione praevia, quia generatur ex operationibus elicitis seu ex electionibus praecedentibus.*"

9. *QNE* III.1: 37va: "*agens voluntarium potest se libere ad utrumque oppositorum determinare, ceteris omnibus eodemmodo se habentibus.*" Buridan describes this ability—which he calls '*libertas oppositionis*'—as the *differentia* between voluntary and non-voluntary agents, adding that free self-determination is "a natural property of a voluntary agent, just as the ability to laugh belongs to man [*proprietas naturalis agentis voluntarii, sicut posse ridere hominis*]" (*QNE* III.1: 37va). For choice as an act of the will, see *QNE* II.14: 33ra.

10. Cf. Aristotle, *Categories* 8.8b25–10a26.

11. Aristotle, *Categories* 8.8b27. Buridan knows the Aristotelian account well: "in the first species of quality, habit and disposition evidently do not differ in species, but only accidentally, e.g., with respect to being moveable easily or with difficulty [*in*

*prima specie qualitatis non videntur specie differre habitus et dispositio sed solum acci-
dentaliter, puta secundum facile et difficile mobile]" (QNE* II.7: 27va).

12. *QNE* II.8: 27vb: "*omnis forma generabilis et corruptibilis cuius esse non consistit in divisibili sit augmentabilis et diminuibilis.*"

13. Cf. Aristotle, *Categories* 8.8b35–9a3.

14. *QNE* II.8: 28ra: "*Sicut enim sanitas se habet ad corpus, ita virtus moralis ad
animam. Corpus autem dicitur sanum sub omni dispositione sub qua corpus, et secundum se totum et secundum suas partes, est innatum omnem operationem sibi debitam
prompte et delectabiliter exercere. Proportio autem humorum et qualitatum sub qua hoc
potest non est indivisibile, immo quotidie diversificatur ipso corpore non impedito a sibi
debitis operationibus. Ergo similiter erit de virtute morali.*"

15. As we shall see below, Buridan does allow for the existence in some individuals of perfect virtue, the most intense form of virtue, which does not admit of degrees.

16. *QNE* II.14: 33va: "*virtus autem moralis est principium quoddam actuum hu-
manorum secundum partem appetitativam, ut omnes concedunt.*"

17. Buridan takes himself to be following Aristotle here (his remarks are prefaced by "Aristotle also says that . . ."), but what Aristotle actually says is that a habitual disposition is possessed by that which is disposed "either in itself or with reference to something else" (*Metaphysics* V.20.1022b10–11). Unlike Buridan, he does not
specifically define habits in relation to passions. It should also be noted that Buridan's
use of the phrase '*habere passiones* [= (lit.) having passions]' is intended to cover both
the primary, receptive sense in which passions are felt by a cognizing subject, as well
as the secondary, active sense in which such feelings give rise to certain 'passionate'
behaviors, which the subject naturally exhibits as long as there are no impediments.
In the case of beings who have the capacity to deliberate, impediments can be internal
(e.g., determination by a contrary volition) or external (e.g., paralysis), but only external in the case of non-human animals. Cf. the distinction below between the will's
elicited and commanded acts, as well as that between the first and second acts of the
will discussed in chapter 15.

18. *QNE* II.14: 33rb: "*potentia proprie est principium activum vel passivum operationis. Virtus autem non proprie loquendo et principaliter, sed est determinatio quaedam
principii activi vel passivi ad taliter agendum vel patiendum. Unde non est proprie principium operationis sed qualitatis eius.*"

19. For Buridan's realism about modes applied to problems concerning the description of certain relational changes, see chapter 11 above.

20. *QNE* I.16: 14vb: "*virtutis usus, hoc est operatio secundum virtutem, distinguen-
dum erit de virtutibus.*"

21. *QNE* I.22: 20[xix]vb (the roman numerals in brackets in the folio reference
indicate a pagination error in the 1513 edition; the correct folio number is given first,
in arabic numerals): "*In ista quaestione doctores ad invicem adversantur valde nituntur
enim plures probare quod virtutes morales sint in appetitu sensitivo, alii autem quod in
voluntate.*" James J. Walsh (1986, 467) identifies the former view with Thomas Aquinas
(*Summa Theologiae* IaIIae, q. 56, a. 4) and the latter with Franciscans such as Gerard
of Odo (*Expositio in Aristotelis Ethicam* I, q. 56), who greatly influenced Buridan's
views on ethics. For the latter connection, see Walsh 1975.

22. *QNE* I.22: 21ra–rb: "*Et istae rationes demonstrant insolubiliter apud me quod
in appetitu sensitivo oportet aliquem habitum generari inclinantem ipsum versus iudi-*

cium rationis, vel versus ipsam voluntatem innitentem iudicio rationis ad hoc quod homo efficiatur virtuosus. . . . Et istae rationes, sicut dixi de appetitu sensitivo, cum aliis rationibus quae postea ponerentur demonstrant insolubiliter apud me quod in voluntate oportet aliquem habitum generari inclinantem ipsam versus iudicium rationis ad hoc quod homo efficiatur virtuosus." In his discussion of this passage (1986, 467), James J. Walsh describes Buridan's first conclusion as follows: "it is irrefutably demonstrated that such a habit is needed for a man to become virtuous. Such a habit is virtue, but he [i.e., Buridan] reserves the decision as to whether it is a moral virtue." But the "irrefutably [*insolubiliter*]" is applied in both cases not to moral virtue, but to its opposite, viz., to the habits generated in the sensitive appetite and will, respectively, which are inclined against the judgment of reason, and which virtue is supposed to overcome. Buridan does not designate the positive cases of the *doctores* opposed in this debate as "irrefutable," since, unlike them, he does not regard the conclusions (1) that moral virtue is in the will and (2) that moral virtue is in the sensitive appetite, as mutually exclusive. This makes it easier to see why Buridan should want to ask whether the habit inclining sensitive appetite against the judgment of reason "is formally [the same as] moral virtue or not," for if their inclining activity is the same, perhaps they can only be distinguished externally, in terms of their relation to the agent? As we shall see below, Buridan answers this question in the negative.

23. *QNE* I.22: 21rb: "*secundum ultimam in quid potentia potest, hoc est dictu, secundum opus perfectissimum in quid potentia potest.*"

24. *QNE* I.22: 21ra: "*in voluntate indigemus habitu quodam inclinante eam ad iudicium rationis ad hoc quod prompte et delectabiliter et sine strepitu consentiant rationi recte. Et formetur ratio sicut formabatur de appetitu sensitivo, et ille habitus nihil aliud esse videtur quam virtus moralis.*"

25. *QNE* I.22: 21rb: "*ad obediendum imperio perfecte voluntatis et iudicio rectae rationis . . . virtus voluntatis primo et principaliter diceretur virtus hominis secundum quod homo, non autem virtus appetitus, nisi ex consequenti et in ordine ad aliud.*"

26. Aristotle, *Nicomachean Ethics* I.13.1102a5. Buridan elsewhere distinguishes between that ultimate happiness which accompanies the beatific vision, and happiness attainable in this life, noting that his own inquiry concerns the latter: "we will say nothing here, however, about that true happiness which the saints enjoy in God's presence, but only about that happiness which pertains to this life, of which the philosophers speak using human reason [*sed tamen nihil hic de illa vera beatitudine dicemus, qua in patria sancti fruuntur, sed de illa sola huius vitae de qua philosophi humana ratione locuti sunt*]" (*QNE* I.10: 10rb). Buridan does return to the former topic, though, in *QNE* X. For discussion, see Walsh 1966a, 10–12, and Walsh 1980.

27. "Primarily" because the will is the ultimate source of action (though not, of course, of one's reason for acting): "the will moves the appetite in the first place, and, through its mediation, corporeal limbs and things outside the body. Therefore, no deed will be done well unless it has been done well voluntarily [*voluntas primo movet appetitum et eo mediante membra corporalia et res extra. Ideo non erit opus bene operatum nisi fuerit elective bene* (bene/bona) *operatum*]" (*QNE* II.4: 25va).

28. Elsewhere, in connection with "the interior activity which is willing or desiring [*velle vel appetere*]," Buridan remarks "that an activity of this sort is called an immanent action . . . not because it is immanent in the patient (for it would be said that every action is immanent in that way), but because it remains in the agent [*de interiori*

operatione quae est velle et appetere, quia talis operatio dicitur actio immanens, quid non est quia passo immaneat, sic enim diceretur omnis actio immanens, sed quia manet in agente]" (*QNE* II.3: 23vb).

29. *QNE* I.10: 10rb: "*Distinguenda autem sunt opera virtutum. Quaedam enim sunt ab ipsa virtute sive a potentia in qua virtus existit elicita et ei immanentia, ut ratiocinari, iudicari, eligere, et omnino velle et appetere. Alia sunt imperata et in membra corporea vel in res exteriores transeuntia, sicut dare pauperibus, bellare contra inimicos, unicuique quod suum est tribuere, vel etiam privative loquendo, a delectationibus abstinere, nemini iniuriam in inferre, etc.*"

30. *QNE* II.4: 25rb:

operationes virtutum moralium possunt assignari quadruplices. Primae quidem immanentes ipsi voluntati. Aliae vero immanentes appetitivi sensitive. Tertiae in existentes membris nostris corporalibus quibus organice utimur ad opera exterius exercenda. Quartae vero sunt extra nos ad exterius transeuntes. Verbi gratia, in operatione liberalitatis postquam ratio prudentialis iudicavit dandum esse tali tale donum, voluntas primo hoc eligit facere, ideo imperat inferioribus potentiis ad hoc faciendum. Secundo appetitus sensitivus conveniens imperio voluntatis appetit illud idem facere, ideo movet corporalia membra ad hoc faciendum. Tertio igitur membra corporalia motum illum ab appetitu recipiunt. Quarto vero possibile est in tali executione ut a membris motis motus in exteriores res recipiatur.

For the physics of locomotion, see Buridan's commentary on Aristotle's *De motu animalium,* in which he explains that an animal moves its limbs by spirit, which is a material substance with weight and lightness; the prime mover in locomotion, however, is the soul, which he places in the heart (*DMA* VI: 550). For discussion, see Peter Sobol, "Sensations, Intentions, Memories, and Dreams," in Thijssen and Zupko 2001, 183–98.

31. *QNE* II.3: 24vb: "*dicendum esse quod eodem modo sicut potentia cuius est virtus.*" He claims further that virtue can in general "be reduced to the same genus of cause as that power of which it is the virtue [*ad idem genus causae reduci cum ipsa potentia cuius est virtus]*" (*QNE* II.3: 24vb).

32. The "in themselves" qualification is important here because, as we shall see, Buridan denies that the virtues are necessarily of the same moral kind as their activities in relation to the agent, since it is possible for an agent to choose an action contrary to what virtue inclines him to do, or to perform an otherwise virtuous activity for the wrong reasons (*QNE* I.10: 10va–vb; cf. Ps.-Buridan [= Nicholas of Vaudemont], *QPol* VII.12: 106vb).

33. Since it is Buridan's view that the different powers of the soul—intellective, sensitive, vegetative, or appetitive—all belong to the same identical subject (i.e., a particular living thing such as Socrates or Plato), he argues that they are distinct from each other in reason or definition alone (*QDA*₃ II.7: 91; *QDA*₃ II.5: 63–64). Thus, the different names used to signify such powers—'intellective soul'; 'sensitive soul'; etc.— must be understood not as signifying distinct things, but the same thing "according to different natures [*secundum diversas rationes]*." For discussion, see chapter 11 above.

34. *QNE* II.4: 25vb: "*non est mirandum quod aliqui valde mirantur, videlicet quod in voluntate et in appetitu sensitivo diversae ponantur virtutes morales, id est ex assuefactione acquisitae, immo addendum est quod etiam ponendae sunt in potentia vegetativa et in similibus potentiis motivis seu quocumque modo operativis omnium membrorum.*"

35. Hence, Buridan's assertion that "a habit in the will itself is generated per se from activities of the will itself, i.e., from choices [*habitus in ipsa voluntate generatur per se ex operationibus ipsius voluntatis, hoc est ex electionibus*]" (*QNE* II.4: 25va).

36. *QNE* I.16: 16rb: "*virtus habet duplicem operationem: unam scilicet interiorem quae est vere finis virtutis, et illa operatio una cum virtute est quae perficit hominem et reddit hominem vere bonum. Alia vero habet operationem exteriorem secundum quam virtus suam bonitatem largitur aliis.*"

37. *QNE* I.16: 16rb: "*Pone enim quod rex francorum et unus pauper homo habeant in se virtutem fortitudinis aut liberalitatis secundum quas ipsi semper habeant voluntatem bonam et perfectam operandi fortiter et liberaliter quaecumque oportuerit. Vult Seneca quod istae virtutes et earum operationes non reddunt regem in se meliorem quam pauperem, sed reddunt regem toti patriae meliorem quam pauperem.*"

38. *QNE* I.10: 10vb: "*licet exteriores operationes hominum nobis appareant, interiores tamen de quibus hic loquimur quae vere reddunt hominem aut bonum aut malum nobis occultae sunt. Si quis enim oret deum, nescio utrum ficte vel devote, immo si quae saepe scimus male agere, dato aliquando optimam egerit operationem et optime, tamen putaremus eum fingere et non bene agere.*"

39. *QNE* I.10: 10vb: "*Igitur ex una operatione etiam optima non iudicamus hominem esse bonum, quamvis ea sit simpliciter melior quam ipse esset ex habitu sine operatione, habitus enim nobis sunt evidentiores et eligibiliores saltem arguitive cum signo, quoniam multotiens agere bonas operationes exteriores quae nobis sunt evidentes est signum boni habitus.*"

40. *QNE* I.1: 2va: "*virtus habet causas determinatas, scilicet rationem distinguentem inter bonum et malum, et voluntatem eligentem bonum et refutantem malum, et assuefactionem in operibus bonis secundam praedictam electionem voluntatis et iudicium rationis.*" Just before this, Buridan describes the characteristic activities of these three causes, respectively, as "knowing, willing, and persevering in the face of difficulty [*scire, velle, et perseverare in difficilibus*]."

41. There is a parallel passage in Ps.-Buridan (= Nicholas of Vaudemont), *Questions on Aristotle's Politics,* where Nicholas remarks that "moral virtue exists in us originally by nature [*virtus moralis inest nobis a natura initiative*] . . . excitatively and provocatively by nature [*a natura excitative et provocative*] . . . [and] perfectively by custom [*ex consuetudine completive*]" (Ps.-Buridan, *QPol* VII.12: 106ra). The claim that moral virtue exists in the second way "by nature" is an error or misprint, however, since the proof that follows indicates that the excitation or provocation occurs when "we are instructed by teaching and scientific knowledge [*per doctrinam seu notitiam scientificam docemur*]." Nicholas's account in *QPol* VII.12 is thus identical with Buridan's in *QNE* II.1: 22ra.

42. Cf. Ps.-Buridan (= Nicholas of Vaudemont), who defines habituation as "the generation, from frequent and multiple similar acts, of a habit inclined to producing and eliciting similar acts" (*QPol* VII.12: 106va). Actually, Nicholas offers two, almost identical, definitions of habituation in this passage, without indicating which he prefers: "habituation [*assuefactio*] can be described as follows: it is the generation, from frequent and multiple similar acts, of a habit inclined to producing and eliciting similar acts. Others define it in this way: habituation is the generation, from frequent and multiple acts, of a habit inclined to similar acts or activities [*actus seu operationes*]" (*QPol* VII.12: 106va).

43. As Buridan says, "virtue is generated from actions, where the 'from' refers to the habit of action or motion through which virtue is acquired [*virtus fit ex operationibus, prout 'ex' dicit habitudinem actionis vel motus per quem virtus acquiritur*]" (*QNE* II.3: 23vb); cf. "virtuous acts generate virtue [*actus virtuosi generent virtutem*]" (*QNE* II.8: 28va). Although he argues that virtue can only be generated from good and right actions, Buridan denies the converse, viz., that good and right actions can only be generated from virtue (*QNE* I.10: 10va). That is because human beings have the freedom to act virtuously (or viciously) at any time, and so to override their established habits of choice, "although this is difficult and exceedingly rare [*licet hoc sit difficile et rarum valde*]."

44. *QNE* II.5: 26ra: "*virtus in voluntate generatur per se ex electionibus ipsius voluntatis consonis rectae rationi, et constat quod similes electiones eliciuntur secundum generatam virtutem. Cum igitur electiones voluntatis sint bonae vel malae in genere moris ex eo quod sunt consonae vel dissonae rectae rationi, apparet quod huiusmodi electiones praecedentes virtutem et ex quibus per se generatur virtus et electiones sequentes virtutem sunt eiusdem rationis in genere moris.*" Again, "a habit is generated per se in the will itself from the activities of the will itself, that is, from choices [*habitus in ipsa voluntate generatur per se ex operationibus ipsius voluntatis*]" (*QNE* II.4: 25va).

45. Cf. *QDA₃* III.18: 203–205. Buridan thinks that the will's primary act of agreement/disagreement is a causally necessary, but not sufficient, condition of its secondary act of acceptance, rejection, or deferment, the modes of which are incompossible. See chapter 15 below.

46. *QNE* II.2: 23ra: "*Unomodo quod sit ad unum actum sic determinate quod non indigeat recipere ab alio impressionem aliquam ad exercendum [exercendum/exequendum] illum actum, sed impedimento non existente, ipsa est sufficiens exercere [exercere/exequi] ipsum, sicut est de gravitate ad locum deorsum.*"

47. Aristotle, *Nicomachean Ethics* II.1.1103a21–22. For discussion of Thomas Aquinas's use of this passage in the same context, see Inagaki 1987.

48. *QNE* II.2: 23ra: "*Aliomodo quod sit indifferens ad diversos actus, ita quod ad determinate prosequendum aliquem actum indigeat aliquam prius recipere impressionem determinantem ipsam ad illum actum, sicut ferrum potentiam habet movendi ad magnetem.*" Oddly enough, Buridan here puts the moving power in the piece of iron rather than in the magnet, although he says that the iron "is moved towards the magnet" a little further on (see next note).

49. *QNE* II.2: 23rb: "*per unum solum motum vel unam actionem solam potest sufficienter determinari ad actum, verbi gratia ferrum ut moveatur ad magnetem . . . assuefactio proprie sit ex multiplicatis operationibus consimilibus.*"

50. *QNE* II.2: 23rb: "*intellectus ita determinatus est ad assentiendum veritati primorum principiorum, scilicet omnino primorum et per se notorum capiendum, quod non potest assuefieri ad negandum. Sed de aliquibus principiis non omnino primis et per se notis potest bene assuefieri ad negandum, quia non est omnino determinatus ad veritates ipsorum secundum se.*" Cf. *QAnPo* II.11; I.2; I.12; *QM* I.5: 6ra; I.8: 7va; *QP* I.15: 18vb–19ra; *QNE* VI.1: 116va; VI.10: 127ra; cf. also Aristotle, *Posterior Analytics* II.99b20 ff. For discussion of this natural inclination, see chapter 11 above.

51. The point can also be expressed negatively: *evidentia* in favor of a given proposition also makes it more difficult for the intellect to dissent from it, although

this is always in principle possible in the case of empirical, a posteriori, propositions, since they are never perfectly evident. For discussion, see chapter 13 above.

52. *QNE* II.1: 22va: "*Et ideo videtur esse dicendum de virtutibus in nobis sicut de aliis formis naturalibus perficientibus suam materiam. quod in materia sua talem habent a natura inchoationem solum quod suum proprium susceptivum et perfectibile per eas. Et per consequens habens inclinationes naturaliter ad eas suscipiendas, sicut materia inclinatur ad formam. Et perfectibile ad suam perfectionem recipiendam praeexistit a natura in nobis, hoc enim susceptivum est potentia animae appetiva sive intellectualis sive sensualis.*"

53. *QNE* II.1: 22va: "*dicendum est quod illa temperantia vel fortitudo quae a nobis a nativitate inest non est virtus moralis neque principalis neque secundum quam homo dicatur simpliciter bonus, sed est habilitas quaedam et inclinatio ad faciliter talem virtutem suscipiendum.*"

54. The role of virtue in disposing the will to rightness is even more important from a practical point of view than that of experience in disposing the intellect to assent to true propositions. That is because in this life, there is no moral equivalent of first principles in the intellect—no actions, that is, whose moral rightness is self-evident and in the recognition of which we are compelled to act. Since all actions are particular, no action can manifest absolute goodness. Hence, the rightness of an action is always a matter of degree, so that it will often remain an open question which particular course of action is best from a moral point of view. Buridan wisely reserves the ascription of absolute goodness to divine actions, since only those have the requisite universality. Thus, even the saints or those who are on his view possessed of "perfected virtue [*perfecta virtus*]," can do wrong because of inexperience, although they do so non-culpably (*QNE* II.8: 28vb).

55. *QNE* II.6: 26vb: "*ex huiusmodi ergo volitionibus frequentatis fiet habitus inclinans et firmans voluntatem ad semper hoc volendum.*"

56. *QNE* II.8: 29ra: "*Possibile enim est quod bonum esset dare huic pauperi denarium unum, et adhuc esset melius dare sibi duos, et optimum esset dari sibi tres.*"

57. *QNE* II.2: 23ra: "*Et possumus etiam de hac distinctione dare exemplum in moralibus, potentia nam [nam/naturam] appetitiva est indifferens ad virtutem vel vicium vel etiam ad agendum studiose vel prave. Ideo ut determinetur operationibus determinantibus ad virtutem vel vicium, indiget etiam virtute morali sibi impressa determinante ipsam ad agere studiose, vel vicio determinante ad agere prave.*"

58. *QNE* I.21: 20[xix]va: "*oportuit propter vitae necessitates ante usum rationis quod natura fecisset appetitum sensitivum in suum obiectum tendentem ad sensus apprehensionem sine regimine rationis, et per consequens quod posset in aliud ab eo quod recta ratio dictat.*" Buridan describes as "irrational [*irrationalis*]" the will that tends to follow this natural ordination (*QNE* I.21: 20[xix]rb). Later on, he outlines five distinct stages in the acquisition of moral virtue (*QNE* II.10: 30rb).

59. *QNE* II.9: 29rb: "*sensus non potest sufficienter conferre inter obiectum sibi praesentatum et ea quae concomitantur ipsum vel consequuntur, aut etiam inter praesens et futurum.*"

60. *QNE* II.9: 29va: "*Ex hiis igitur videri potest quod virtus moralis triplicem habet effectum super appetitum sensitivum, unum scilicet quia refrenat ipsum ne nimis properanter sequatur iudicium sensus sed expectet iudicium rationis. Secundum vero quia determinat ipsum ad obediendum iudicio rationis quamvis iudicio [iudicio/indicio] sensus*

repugnet. Tertium autem sic temperat et ordinat delectationes et tristitias sensuales ut earum impetus nunquam trahere possit appetitum praeter vel contra iudicium rationis."

61. Walsh 1966a, 5.

62. *QNE* II.1: 22va; Latin text quoted at n. 52 above.

63. *QNE* II.14: 33va: "*Sciendum est tamen quod si inclinatio debeat verificari de omni passione, oportet quod non solum capiatur pro tendentia ad bonum habendum vel malum fugiendum, sed etiam pro fixione in bono adepto, sicut si diceremus quod grave non solum habet inclinationem ad locum deorsum quando est sursum, sed etiam quando est deorsum habet inclinationem ad ibi sistendum.*"

64. *QNE* II.7: 27va (cf. *QNE* II.8: 28rb–va): "*Sed dicamus solum quod de generatione virtutis potest proportionabiliter intelligi sicut de generatione luminis in aere. Una enim candela aliquid facit in aere et altera aliquid et idem lumen efficitur maius in aere, et sic de tertia candela et quarta. Ita etiam una operatio aliquid generat virtutis et secunda etiam aliquid et tertia et quarta, et fit illa forma quae cum perfecta fuerit dicitur virtus. Et sicut unum magnum corpus luminosum facit maius lumen in aere quam decem parva, ita una magna et excellens operatio plus generat de virtute quam decem remissae.*"

65. For discussion, see Clagett 1959, 505–540 and Grant 1977, 50–55.

Notes to Chapter 15

1. Exceptions here would be late thirteenth-century Latin Averroists such as Boethius of Dacia and Siger of Brabant, whose understanding of the philosophical enterprise was thoroughly, or "radically," Aristotelian, and who regarded philosophy and theology as irreconcilable fields of inquiry.

2. Thomas Aquinas, *Summa contra gentiles* IV.22.5 (emphasis added).

3. Thomas Aquinas, *Summa contra gentiles* III.88.1–5.

4. Thomas remarks that the gift of the Spirit "removes both that servitude in which the slave of passion infected by sin acts against the order of the will, and that servitude in which, against the movement of his will, a man acts according to law; its slave, so to say, not its friend" (*Summa contra gentiles* IV.22.6).

5. Thus, Thomas argues that we come to see God's essence not by any natural power, no matter how perfect: "the increase through intensification of a natural power does not suffice, since this vision is not of the same essential type as the vision proper to a natural created intellect" (*Summa contra gentiles* III.53.5). Later, he adds, "because of the feebleness of its intellectual light, man's soul is not able to acquire a perfect knowledge of the things that are important to man unless it be helped by higher spirits" (*Summa contra gentiles* III.81.1).

6. I should perhaps make clear that I am not counseling despair or fatalism with respect to our ability as historians of philosophy to reconstruct medieval accounts of the will's freedom, or even of mining them for insights that might shed light on modern concerns. The point is rather that such inquiries will yield fruits only by paying careful attention to context. It is not up to us to finish what a particular medieval thinker started by reworking his ideas into a coherent, fully rational system able to take on all comers, because that is not what medieval philosophers took themselves to be doing. As Mark Jordan has shown, Thomas did not even regard philosophy as an activity proper to the pursuit of Christian wisdom (1990, 6–7). Therefore, we

ought to be cautious. Even if the order we see in medieval accounts of the will looks enticing, it might not be the order intended by the author, and the intended order might not give the modern, secular philosopher any comfort.

7. Duns Scotus, *Quaestiones in Metaphysicam* IX, q. 15, n. 2; tr. Wolter 1986, 153; cf. *Lectura* I, d. 39, qq. 1–5, n. 54; *Ordinatio* IV, d. 49, n. 10. Scotus does not further specify the "elsewhere [*alibi*]" mentioned in the last line of the first passage. See also Etienne Gilson's discussion of another relevant passage from the *Ordinatio* (I, d. 39, q. 1, a. 3, n. 13) in Gilson 1952, 588–89.

8. Ockham, *Quodlibeta septem* I.16; tr. Freddoso and Kelley 1991, 75–76.

9. Duns Scotus, *Quaestiones in Metaphysicam* IX, q. 15, n. 3; tr. Wolter 1986, 159.

10. Augustine, *On Free Choice of the Will* I.12; tr. Williams 1993, 80–88. Augustine's primary aim in this work is to refute the Manichean views that (1) freedom of choice (*liberum arbitrium*) does not exist; and (2) moral good/evil results from the primordial struggle between forces of good and evil inherent in all moral agents.

11. Augustine, *On Free Choice of the Will* III.12; tr. Williams 1993, 72.

12. See Augustine, *Confessions* VI.iv (6). Augustine had himself embraced skepticism after rejecting Manicheism: "after the manner of the Academics, as popularly understood, I doubted everything, and in the fluctuating state of total suspense of judgement I decided I must leave the Manichees, thinking at that period of my scepticism that I should not remain a member of a sect to which I was now preferring certain philosophers" (*Confessions* V.xiv [25]; tr. Chadwick 1992, 89).

13. Augustine, *Confessions* VII.iii (5); tr. Chadwick 1992, 113–14.

14. Augustine, *Confessions* VII.xix (25); tr. Chadwick 1992, 129.

15. Augustine even mentions one of the standard tropes or modes of skeptical argumentation in the section immediately above the second quoted passage: "I learnt by experience that it is no cause for surprise when bread which is pleasant to a healthy palate is misery to an unhealthy one; and to sick eyes light which is desirable to the healthy is hateful" (*Confessions* VII.xvi [22]; tr. Chadwick 1992, 126; cf. Sextus Empiricus, *Outlines of Pyrrhonism*). Other hints of Augustine's weaker criteria for the rationality of belief can be found in *Confessions* V.xiv (25), where he remarks in connection with the Manichean view of the physical world and natural order that "consideration and comparison more and more convinced me that numerous philosophers held opinions more probable than theirs" (tr. Chadwick 1992, 89). Cf. also *Confessions* XI.xvii (35): "As I recite the words ['*Deus Creator Omnium*'], I also observe that this is so [viz., that the line consists of eight syllables], for it is evident to sense perception" (tr. Chadwick 1992, 241).

16. On the question of influence, it should be pointed out that Buridan prefers to discuss Augustinian ideas that have filtered through, and in the process been refocused by, other natural philosophers and theologians of the period, including both Duns Scotus and Ockham. He hardly ever quotes from Augustine directly, and when he does, it is to cite commonplaces with which most of his undergraduate students would have been familiar. Direct discussion of Augustine's views would have in most cases exceeded Buridan's mandate as an arts master, of course, since the study of Augustine as an authority was proper to the faculty of theology, where his work was read and discussed via the *Sentences* of Peter Lombard.

17. Nicholas of Autrecourt, *Exigit ordo executionis*; O'Donnell 1939, 237. For the significance of the term '*habitus conjecturativus*', see Weinberg 1948, 70, n. 32.

18. *QNE* III.1: 37rb (cf. *QNE* X.2: 206rb): "*dicunt quod experientia videtur esse talis quod immutationes voluntatis ab obiectis suis quibus ipsa necessitatur ad velle aut nolle non sunt nobis manifeste. Sed si essent nobis manifeste, nos experiremur quod ipsa voluntas in omni actu suo determinatur ab alio.*" Although this particular argument does not appear in Autrecourt's surviving works, he does defend a deterministic view of the will's causal power in the *Exigit ordo executionis:* "When, therefore, it is said that the will is related to opposites, this must not be understood of the individual as if any particular will were related to opposites. Rather, each is determined to a single thing, as has been said. But [the statement] must be understood [of the will] as a species. For one will is related to one object, another to its opposite" (O'Donnell 1939, 261–62; tr. Kennedy, Arnold, and Millward 1971, 157). Autrecourt's determinism seems based on the idea that "any cause, whether natural or free . . . has the capacity for only one effect of which it is the sufficient cause," to which he adds: "And so it is true to say of any cause in the world that, if it should not produce its effect, it is because it is obstructed, and not because it is free, as our opponents imagine" (O'Donnell 1939, 260, ll. 33–40; tr. Kennedy, Arnold, and Millward 1971, 155). Autrecourt does not name his opponents here, but he seems to be addressing any view that understands the will in Scotistic fashion as positively indeterminate. Autrecourt was specifically condemned, however, for claiming in the ninth letter of his correspondence with Bernard of Arezzo that the following consequences are "not evident: 'An act of understanding exists; therefore the intellect exists'; 'An act of willing exists; therefore, the will exists'" (de Rijk 1994, 149).

19. Later in the same question, Buridan mentions an inductivist objection to his conclusion that "a voluntary agent can freely determine itself to opposites with everything else remaining the same, for that is the natural property of a voluntary agent, just as the ability to laugh belongs to a man [*agens voluntarium potest se libere ad utrumque oppositorum determinare ceteris omnibus eodemmodo habentibus, ista enim proprietas naturalis agentis voluntarii, sicut posse ridere hominis*]," which ends on an interesting and decidedly skeptical note: "Some individuals, wishing to destroy this truth, argue maliciously by induction from other agents, saying that a solution which gives a single example contrary to induction in the proposed case is not consistent. For if this were true, it could be demonstrated that man is not risible by induction from all other animals [*aliqui male arguunt, volentes hanc veritatem interimere, per inductionem in aliis agentibus, et dicentes quod solutio non est conveniens quae contra inductionem dat instantiam in proposito solum. Nam si hoc esset verum, posset probari quod homo non esset risibilis per inductionem in aliis animalibus omnibus*]" (*QNE* III.1: 37va). Buridan replies that we are entitled to draw conclusions about some things by induction, from others only if they appear to have "the same nature [*eiusdem rationis*]" with respect to the predicate inductively ascribed to them. Presumably, the *differentia* of rationality would be sufficient to permit the ascription of rationality to human animals, but to block it with respect to other animals.

20. *QNE* III.1: 37va (cf. *QNE* III.3: 42va):

Et ideo simpliciter et firmiter credere volo fide una cum aliqua experientia et dictis [*et dictis/ex actibus*] sanctorum et philosophorum huic credulitate concordantibus et firmiter adhaerentibus quod voluntas ceteris omnibus eodemmodo habentibus, potest in actus oppositos, sicut dicebatur prius. Et nullus debet de via communi recedere propter rationes sibi insolubiles specialiter in hiis quae fidem tangere possunt aut mores, qui enim credit omnia scire et in nulla opinionum suarum decipi fatuus est. De festuca enim tibi sensibiliter praesentata formabuntur centum rationes vel quaestiones de quibus contrariae sapientissimi doctores opinabuntur, propter quod in qualibet harum deceptus erit alter ipsorum vel ambo. Ideo non miror si in hac altissima materia non possum per rationes et solutiones satisfacere mihi ipsi.

The first sentence adopts the emendation of Walsh 1964, correcting the reading of the incunabular editions against some of the manuscripts. There is also a remark just prior to this passage in which Buridan notes that "it seems in the first place obvious by experience [*videtur primo patere per experientiam*]" that the will "can freely determine itself to either of two alternatives, without anything else determining it, or even determine itself to neither alternative but remain suspended until it has rationally inquired which way is better or more expedient [*libere potest se determinare ad quodlibet illorum absque alio quocunque determinante ipsam, vel etiam potest ad neutrum illorum se determinare sed in suspenso manere, donec fuit inquisitum per rationem quae via fuerit expedientior vel melior*]" (*QNE* III.1: 36va).

21. As Carl Ginet puts it, "How can we be reproached for this belief if we cannot help having it?" (1990, 91).

22. Augustine, *City of God* XIX.10; tr. Bettenson 1984, 865. It is from Aristotle, of course, that Buridan acquires the aim of examining virtue as "the habit of choice [*habitus electivus*]," i.e., as a variable and quantifiable quality of the soul that determines how it both acts and is acted upon (*QNE* I.22: 21vb; cf. *QNE* II.14: 33ra; Aristotle, *Nicomachean Ethics* II.6 1107a1–3). See also chapter 14 above.

23. *QNE* Proemium: 2rb:

duplici logica seu dialectica indigemus: una quidem quae simpliciter docet modum inveniendi dubiam [et] veritatem (et illam vocamus logicam simpliciter vel dialecticam), et alia contracta quae docet modum quo simul et dubium et verum invenitur, et appetitus sic afficitur et disponitur ut determinet vel non impediat intellectum ad concedendum conclusum (et haec vocatur dialectica moralis, quae sub est dialecticae simpliciter sicut et subalternata, nam dialectica simpliciter respicit intellectum simpliciter). Rhetorica vero sive moralis dialectica respicit intellectum sub contracta ratione, scilicet secundum hoc quod trahibilis est per appetitum. Cum igitur non nisi secundum moralia sit innatus appetitus alienare iudicium rationis, hinc est quod in aliis artibus et scientiis sufficit nobis logica simpliciter, sed in moralibus indigemus logica speciali.

24. *QNE* Proemium: 2rb: for the Latin text, see chapter 1, n. 55 above.

25. Augustine, *De ordine*; Russell 1942, 313.

26. The voluntarist will is thus said to belong not to the natural order, but to the order of liberty. For Scotus, see *Quaestiones quodlibetales*, qq. 16–17; tr. Alluntis and Wolter 1975, 369–98; and *Quaestiones in Metaphysicam* IX, q. 15; tr. Wolter 1986, 144–73. For Ockham, see *Ordinatio* I, d. 2, q. 1; *Opera Theologica* I: 84–98; I, d. 3, q. 5: 450–51; *Reportatio* IV, q. 16; *Opera Theologica* V: 350–61; *Quodlibeta septem* I, q. 1; *Opera Theologica* IX: 7; qq. 16–17: 87–93. For a brief history and overview, see J. B. Korolec, "Free Will and Free Choice" in *CHLMP*, 629–41.

27. Thomas changed his views on the will during his lifetime in subtle but interesting ways that need not detain us here (cf. *In II Sententiarum* d. 24, q. 1, a. 2; *De veritate* q. 23, a. 1; q. 24, a. 6; *Summa Theologiae* IaIae, q. 82, aa.1–4; IaIae q. 83, aa.1–4;

IaIIae, q. 13, aa.1–5; *Summa contra gentiles* I.72; I.95; III.11; III.73; III.85). I follow most commentators in using the term 'intellectualism' to describe the position defended by Thomas on the will, although the term 'naturalism' is also used, and perhaps better describes the motivation of that position, as Marilyn Adams points out: "Usually, in the secondary literature, voluntarism is set against naturalism. Both the voluntarist and the naturalist among medieval philosophers believe in will and nature. But the former will tend to locate his baseline explanations of things in the will and its choices, whereas the latter will ground them in the natures of things" (1987b, 219). The 'nature' most relevant to the question of human freedom is, of course, the intellect.

28. This point has been nicely made in connection with Buridan's account of *akrasia* by Risto Saarinen (1986; 1993).

29. As we shall see below, Buridan exempts God here on the grounds that all human beings have God as their ultimate final end: "an agent is said to act freely by freedom of final ordering if it acts by chief purpose for its own sake and is said to act like a slave [*serviliter*] if it acts for the sake of another. Hence God alone acts simply and entirely freely [*solus deus agit simpliciter et omnino libere*]" (QNE X.2: 205rb–va; tr. McGrade, Kilcullen, and Kempshall 2001, 516—all further quotations from QNE X will be from this translation, cited by page number; all quotations from the Latin text of the 1513 edition have been corrected on the basis of Kilcullen 1996).

30. Cf. Thomas Aquinas, *Summa Theologiae* IaIae, q. 82, a. 2; IaIIae, q. 9, aa.1, 6; q. 13, a. 3.

31. For the Latin text, see n. 57 below. Cf. Thomas Aquinas, *Summa Theologiae* IaIae, q. 83, a. 4; IaIIae, q. 13, aa.1, 3.

32. Cf. Thomas Aquinas, *Summa contra gentiles* III.25–26, 37. Buridan offers several arguments on behalf of this assumption, the most significant of which is based on the imperfection of volition vis-à-vis cognition, as evidenced by the absolute dependency of the former on the latter. For example, to the objection that an old woman who loves God but with only a "dim conception [*modica noticia*]" of God would be more pleasing to God than an important cleric who does not really love God but nevertheless has a rich concept of the divine nature, he replies (with what he thinks would be Aristotle's position) that "the woman does not love God more than she judges that God is good and should be loved [*vetula non plus amat deum quam iudicet ipsum esse bonum et amandum*]" (QNE X.5: 214rb; 573). Accordingly, the woman's intellectual grasp of God, however flawed, is primary. For discussion, see Georg Wieland, "Happiness: The Perfection of Man" in *CHLMP*, 683–86.

33. Monahan 1954, 84. Although Monahan argues specifically that "Buridan's doctrine of human liberty of choice belongs to this intellectualist tradition," his reasons appear to conflate Buridan's account of free choice with his separate account of freedom of final ordination. The intellectualist character of freedom of final ordination should not by itself be a reason for likewise classifying freedom of choice, however.

34. Korolec 1974, 126 (cf. 138–41; 149–51; see also Korolec 1975, 71–72).

35. Saarinen 1986, 139. See also Saarinen 1993, 140–42.

36. Saarinen 1986, 139. These three views should be taken to range over modern readers who have specifically addressed themselves to Buridan's account of free choice (*libertas oppositionis*). For discussion of Buridan's general concept of human freedom, see Walsh 1964; 1966b (on Buridan's moral naturalism); and 1980 (on Buridan's "distinctive" moral teleology). Cf. also Krieger 1986, who, while mentioning the

voluntarist/intellectualist dispute in passing (153–54 and 183–84, n. 115), prefers to consider the question of freedom in Buridan's commentary from the standpoint of practical reason or prudence.

37. *QNE* III.2: 41rb: "*Et ita quantum ad actum volendi, dicam quod ipsa anima informata aliquo actu priori, puta vel iudicio de bonitate aut malitia volibilis vel quadam complacentia vel displicentia . . . potest se movere ad actum volendi. Sicut ergo eadem res, scilicet anima, dicitur voluntas passiva secundum quod potest actum volendi recipere, et dicitur voluntas activa secundum quod potest actum ipsum producere. Hoc autem est secundum quod informata est actu priori praedicto.*"

38. Buridan argues that it is their dependency upon prior intellectual and sensitive cognitions that separates both intellective appetite (properly called 'volition' or 'will') and sensitive appetite, respectively, from natural appetites such as the tendency unsupported heavy bodies have to fall (*QNE* III.5: 44va; cf. *QNE* I.4: 5rb). This dependency is expressed early and often in Buridan's writings in terms of the principle, "the will does not enter into intellectual cognition uncognized [*voluntas non fertur incognita in cognitione intellectuale*]" (*QM* XII.1: 65rb; cf. *QNE* III.9: 47rb). From this principle (Buridan's 'volitional transparency thesis'), it follows that as far as the operations of the will are concerned, nothing is hidden.

39. *QNE* III.3: 42[lxii]rb:

Ita iudicium, vel anima informata iudicio de bonitate vel malitia obiecti, primo generat in ipsa voluntate complacentiam quandam in obiecto vel displicentiam in obiecto, mediantibus quibus ipsa voluntas acceptare potest obiectum vel refutare, quae quidem acceptatio vel refutatio sunt iam actuales inclinationes voluntatis ad quas motus consequitur, si non fuerit impedimentum. . . . Modo ergo diceretur quod si obiectum fuerit voluntati praesentatum sub ratione boni, tunc statim causabitur necessario in ipsa voluntate dictus actus complacentiae. Et si fuerit sibi praesentatum sub ratione mali, causabitur actus displicentiae. Et si praesentetur simul sub ratione boni et mali, causabuntur in ea simul utrique actus, scilicet complacentia ex obiecto illo et displicentia.

Buridan evidently thinks this point important enough to refer to it again later, in his Book VII discussion of *akrasia:* "And the conclusion is proved just as it was proved in the third question of Book III that the will necessarily feels agreement in an apparent good [*Illa etiam conclusio probatur sicut in tertia quaestione tertii libri probatur quod in apparente bono voluntas necessario habeat complacentiam*]" (*QNE* VII.8: 145rb).

40. *QNE* III.3: 43ra: "*voluntas non sit libera sive domina sui primi actus . . . sed mihi videtur dicendum . . . quod actus simplicis complacentiae vel displicentiae non est actus volendi aut nolendi proprie.*" In fact, moral praise/blame is properly ascribed to an agent only when the agent overcomes/succumbs to temptations arising from the first act of the will: "Now it appears that in the aforementioned pleasure or displeasure, we neither merit anything nor do we sin, but only in the acceptance or rejection of the entire object. . . . For if it is asked of a continent man, 'Would you like to know such a woman [of ill-repute]?', he will not reply, 'You bet!', but he would say, 'I would, were it not disrespectful or sinful [*Modo videtur quod in complacentia vel displicentia praedictis, nec mereamur nec peccemus, sed in obiecti totius acceptatione aut refutatione. . . . Nam si petatur a continente viro, 'Vis tu cognoscere talem mulierem?', non respondebit, 'Volo', sed dicet, 'Vellem, si non esset inhonestum vel peccatum'*]'" (*QNE* III.3: 43ra). Although the

best literal translation of 'nolle' would be 'will against', I prefer 'nill' or 'nilling', which has the advantage of maintaining the parallelism between 'velle' and 'nolle'.

41. *QNE* III.3: 42[lxii]va: "*Sed quia acceptatio et refutatio sunt impetus ad actum prosequendum vel fugiendum, et isti motus, scilicet prosecutio vel fuga, propter contrarietatem sunt incompossibiles in eodem, ideo etiam non possunt simul in voluntate fieri huiusmodi acceptatio et refutatio. Sed voluntas libere potest acceptare opus illud sine refutatione, vel refutare sine acceptatione, vel etiam nec refutare nec acceptare sed differre, ut videtur mihi quod quasi quilibet homo experiri potest in seipso.*"

42. See Saarinen 1993, 140–42.

43. Buridan's identification of the acts of acceptance and willing [*velle*], and rejection and nilling [*nolle*], is made clear on a number of occasions: e.g., *QNE* III.3: 42va; III.2: 38ra; III.3: 43ra–rb; III.5: 44vb; III.7: 45vb; and VII.7: 144va.

44. For discussion, see Korolec 1974, 140–52.

45. Ockham, *Ordinatio* I, d. 1, q. 6; *Opera Theologica* I: 506. For evidence that Ockham's voluntarism is less undiluted than many commentators have thought, see Adams 1987b. Among modern philosophers, John Locke is perhaps the best-known defender of deferment as "the source of all liberty." See *An Essay Concerning Human Understanding* II.xxi.47–48.

46. *QNE* III.5: 44[lxiiii]vb (cf. *QNE* III.4: 44[lxiiii]ra): "*voluntas potest illud non velle quod per intellectum iudicatur esse bonum, aliter enim non esset domina sui actus.*"

47. *QNE* III.5: 44[lxiiii]vb (cf. *QNE* III.4: 44[lxiiii]ra; *QM* VI.5: 36vb): "*voluntas potest differre actum volendi ut antea fiat inquisitio si bonitati apparenti fuerit aliqua malitia consequens vel annexa. Potest etiam illud non velle propter annexam tristitiam vel laborem. Et eodemmodo, dicendum est quod voluntas potest non nolle quod intellectus iudicat esse malum.*" This passage might suggest that there are really five modes of activity proper to the Buridanian will: willing (*velle* or *acceptatio*), nilling (*nolle* or *refutatio*), deferring (*differre*), not willing (*non velle*), and not nilling (*non nolle*). But this assumption is not consistent with Buridan's insistence elsewhere that the will is active in the first three modes only (*QNE* III.3: 42va—quoted at n. 41 above). By mentioning not willing (*non velle*) and not nilling (*non nolle*) in this context, Buridan is specifying what kind of state the deferring will must be in relative to the other two modes, viz., that of not willing what appears good on account of some bad accompanying circumstance, or not nilling what appears bad on account of some good accompanying circumstance, since neither willing nor nilling is compossible with deferring. For discussion of Buridan's use of the concept of *non velle*, see Fabienne Pironet, "The Notion of '*non velle*' in Buridan's Ethics," in Thijssen and Zupko 2001, 199–220.

48. *QNE* III.5: 44[lxiiii]vb: "*voluntas non potest velle illud in quo intellectui nulla apparet bonitatis ratio, quoniam tale nullomodo esset praesentatum intellectui seu voluntati sub ratione volibilis. Et eodemmodo dicendum est quod voluntas non potest nolle, licet possit non velle, illud in quo nulla apparet intellectui ratio malitiae, quia tale nullomodo est praesentatum intellectui sub ratione fugibilis vel refutabilis.*"

49. *QNE* III.5: 44[lxiiii]vb: "voluntas potest velle illud quod aliquis modo iudicatum est esse bonum, sicut in adulterium apparuerit inhonestum et delectablile, voluntas non obstante inhonestate potest velle adulterium ratione delectationis vel potest non velle ratione inhonestatis. Et ita est de illo qui tempore tempestatis proicit merces in mare, et haec dicta satis ruerunt prius. Sic igitur patet quod voluntas potest velle contra partem iudicii, sed non contra totum vel praeter totum." Although Buri-

dan suggests only that the will can not will (*potest non velle*) the adultery on the basis of its being disrespectful, he elsewhere makes the stronger claim that the will can positively reject (*refutare*) the entire act for the same reason, and that the individual who does so is worthy of praise. Indeed, the ability to positively nill (*nolle*) the adultery despite its pleasurable appearance is the mark of the continent person (*QNE* III.3: 43ra—quoted at n. 40 above).

50. As Buridan remarks elsewhere: "because of its freedom, it cannot be that the *hans* will is able to will what is less good, since the will's freedom to choose has not been given to it—whether by God or by nature—because this is a bad thing, but because this is a good thing, since it is a condition pertaining to nobility or excellence, as everyone concedes [*ex sua libertate, non potest habere quod posset velle minus bonum, probatur quia illa libertas oppositionis quam habet voluntas non est sibi data, sive a deo sive a natura, propter suum malum, sed propter suum bonum, cum illa sit conditio pertinens ad nobilitatem et excellentiam, ut omnes concedunt*]" (*QNE* III.4: 43vb). Thus, "if the will is able to choose, it chooses the greater good by necessity [*si voluntas debeat eligere, ipsa necessario eliget maius bonum*]" (*QNE* III.4: 44[lxiiii]ra–rb).

51. *QNE* III.9: 47rb: "*quando quis, per omnem diligentiam quam potest vel quam tenetur apponere, non potest rem scire.*" Buridan adds, "we are not the cause or the masters of this ignorance, nor is it imputed to us [*istius ignorantiae nos non sumus causa neque domini, neque ista nobis imputatur*]." Cf. Ockham, *Quaestiones variae*, q. 8; *Opera Theologica* VIII: 428–29.

52. For the different, epistemic, considerations Buridan applies to moral and scientific judgments, see section 3b of chapter 12.

53. Buridan calls actions resulting from such deliberate ignorance "formally voluntary [*voluntaria formaliter*]." It is in this sense that he claims that it is "in the power of the will to command the intellect to desist from considerations of the greater good, and in that case, it could accept what is less good [*in potestate voluntatis imperare intellectui ut desistat a consideratione illius boni maioris, et tunc poterit acceptare minus*]" (*QNE* III.4: 44[lxiiii]ra).

54. *QNE* III.9: 47ra–rb (cf. *DMA* IV: 545): "*primo quidem quando volumus aliquod opus ad quod sequitur impedimentum usus rationis, ut ex nimia potatione sequitur ebrietas quae tollit usum rationis. Secundo modo quando volumus aliquam aliam operationem exercere qui, licet non tollat usum rationis, tamen impedit a consideratione eius quod debemus scire, ut si quis vult ludere dum debet audire praecepta domini. Tertio modo, ut si desides existentes, volumus esse otiosi et nihil laborare, ad quod ex negligentia sequitur non considerare circa illud ad quod tenemur et faciliter possumus scire.*" This form of ignorance is said to issue in actions that are "virtually voluntary [*voluntaria virtualiter*]." Cf. an act arising from invincible ignorance, which, Buridan says, "is not virtually voluntary, since it does not follow upon anything voluntary, nor is it formally voluntary [*non est voluntaria virtualiter, cum non sequatur ad aliquid voluntarium, nec formaliter*]" (*QNE* III.9: 47rb).

55. *QNE* I.21: 20[xix]rb: "*potest apparere quod tam voluntas quam appetitus sensitivus potest dici irrationalis, quia non habet in se rationem formaliter. Potest tamen dici utrumque rationale secundum quod utrumque natum est obedire et exaudire quod ratio dictat.*" *QNE* I.22: 21ra: "*Voluntas innata est principari appetitui sensitivi libere, sicut prius dictum fuit. Modo, sicut dicitur primo Politicae* [cf. Pol. I.6.1255b12], *expediens est amicitia servo et domino quod ad invicem hiis qui natura tales sunt. Ideo voluntas*

innata est habere quandam complacentiam appetitui sensitivi et comparati sibi, propter quod cum appetitus sensitivus fortiter inclinatus ad aliquid voluptuosum aut ad aliquid praeter iudicium rationis, voluntas trahitur ad idem, recedens a iudicio rectae rationis."

56. *QNE* VII.7: 144vb: "*voluntas prava sit innata pervertere iudicium intellectus.*" As we saw in chapter 14, Buridan concludes that virtue is an acquired habit which helps curb sensitive appetite by tempering and ordering sensual pleasures so that they appear less enticing to the rational agent.

57. *QNE* X.2: 207[ccxv]vb: "*intellectus et voluntas sic agunt libere libertate opposi-tionis, quae data est nobis finaliter ut tam secundum intellectum quam secundum volun-tatem agamus libere libertate finalis ordinationis, scilicet laudabiliter et bene ad nostram salutem et perfectionem.*" Cf. *QNE* I.10: 10vb, where Buridan argues that "virtue is for our ultimate benefit [*finaliter virtus prodest nobis*]" because it harmonizes our actions with right reason. E. J. Monahan (1954—see n. 33 above) evidently regards teleological considerations of this sort as decisive in his reading of Buridan as an intellectualist. Buridan also views freedom of choice as necessary for moral responsibility. To refute those who would deny free choice, he says, "we have little in the way of argument to dis-prove this sort of opinion except from our catholic faith, and because if it were true we would be necessarily predetermined in all our acts and consequently they would not be imputable to us for merit or demerit, which seems to conflict not only with our faith but also with the sciences and principles of morals [*parvas rationes habemus, nisi ex fide nostra catholica et quia si essemus in omnibus actibus nostris necessario praedeterminati, illi non essent nobis imputabiles ad meritum vel demeritum, quod non solum fidei nostrae sed etiam scientiis et principiis moralibus repugnant*]" (*QNE* X.2: 207[ccxv]ra; 527).

58. *QNE* X.5: 213rb; 567: "it remains only to see whether happiness consists in that perfect apprehension of God or in the consequent act of willing and loving. And I to assert, last, this fourth thesis: Human happiness consists in the apprehension or perfect understanding of God [*non restat nisi videre an felicitas consistit in illa perfecta dei ap-prehensione, vel in actu volendi et amandi consequente. Et melius placet mihi ponere quod in apprehensione sive intellectione perfecta ipsius dei consistit humana felicitas*]."

59. *QNE* III.3: 42[lxii]va: "*Ad cuius evidentiam est sciendum quod libertas secun-dum quam voluntas potest non acceptare quod sibi praesentatum fuerit sub ratione boni, vel non refutare quod praesentatum est sub ratione mali, prodest valde nobis ad vitae di-rectionem, pro tanto quia in multis in quibus prima facie sunt aliquae rationes bonitatis apparentes, latent saepe mille malitiae vel annexae vel consequentes. Propter quod ac-ceptare illud quod apparebat bonum esset nobis inconveniens et damnosum, et sic etiam, quod prima facie videtur esse malum habet aliquando bonitatem latentem, propter quam refutasse illud esset nobis malum.*"

60. Buridan is adamant, however, that the will has no role to play in the investiga-tive process itself beyond prompting it: "it is not for the will to discern if an object that appears good is really good or not [*voluntatis non est discernere si obiectum apparens bonum simpliciter sit bonum aut non bonum*]" (*QNE* III.3: 42[lxii]vb; cf. *QP* VIII.2: 110va–vb). Only the intellect can inquire into the status of an object as good or bad, i.e., as willable or not, and "as the intellect judges it to be good, so the will wills it [*sicut igitur hoc iudicat intellectus esse bonum, ita hoc vult voluntas*]" (*QNE* III.5: 44[lxiiii]va).

61. For the connection between epistemic and moral responsibility, see nn. 51–52 above. As Buridan notes, "if the judgment of the intellect was in error because of the in-vincible ignorance of some circumstance, then no sin will follow upon the judgment of

reason. But if it was in our power to correct such a judgment through diligent reasoning and investigation, there will be sin not only in our act of agreement [with that judgment], but also if we accept what has been so misjudged without further investigation [*si iudicium intellectus fuerit erroneum propter circumstantiae alicuius invincibilem ignorantiam, non erit peccatum sequi iudicium rationis. Sed si fuerit in nostra potestate tale iudicium corrigere per diligentem ratiocinationem et inquisitionem, peccatum erit non in sola complacentia, sed si quo ita disiudicatum est sine inquisitione ulteriori acceptemus*]" (*QNE* III.3: 43ra; cf. *QNE* III.9: 47rb; *QM* II.1: 9ra). Buridan sees deferment as playing a key role in our moral life, as a means whereby we can "avoid almost every depravity [*potest homo quasi omnem evitare pravitatem*]" (*QNE* III.4: 44[lxiiii]ra).

62. *QNE* X.5: 212va–vb: "*libertas non est nobis data finaliter ad malum sed ad directionem. Videamus igitur quod si iudicium de bonitate obiecti non sit perfectum? Tunc libertas de non acceptando iudicatum vel de minus acceptando expedit nobis vel statim ad non acceptandum malum vel ad tutelam seu ad cautelam ne forte acceptemus malum.*" "Accept less" here clearly means "accept what is *prima facie* less good," as we shall see below.

63. *QNE* VII.8: 145va (cf. *QNE*: III.3: 42[lxii]vb; III.4: 44[lxiiii]ra; III.5: 44 [lx–iii]vb):

> potestas enim non acceptandi bonum apparens vel non refutandi malum apparens non prodest nobis finaliter ut in huius modi non acceptatione vel non refutatione sistamus, sed ut ante obiecti acceptationem vel refutationem inquiramus de omni bonitate vel malitia quae illud obiectum consequitur vel ei annectitur, ut tandem quod est simpliciter melius acceptemus et quod est simpliciter peius refutemus. Ergo inquisitione facta plenarie, sic quod iudicium sit iudicium fit perfecte creditum omni sublata formidine, nihil ultra prodest potestas non acceptandi, sed obest quia per eam possumus frustrari bono nostro, etiam nobis manifeste ostenso.

For the same reason, the further inquiry which the will occasions in its act of deferment cannot be unending, since the goal of certainty is virtually unattainable for empirical creatures, at least in practical matters. Buridan seems to think that the will's capacity to act at any time upon the agreement it feels in some apparent good (or disagreement in some apparent evil) is enough to short-circuit any misguided attempt to reach certainty through deferment: "it would be totally useless if the will felt no agreement in what appears good or disagreement in what appears bad. For in the fact that it commands further investigation of this kind of object, it is obvious that our whole impulse to deliberate about what should be accepted or rejected would be removed—and that would very much be to our detriment [*Haec aliter utilitas auferetur tota, si voluntas in apparenti bono nullam haberet complacentiam vel in apparenti malo displicentiam. Ad quid enim ipsa imperaret de ampliori inquisitione circa tale obiectum, manifestum est quod totus noster impetus auferetur ad consiliandum acceptandis aut refutandis, quod esset nobis damnosum valde*] (*QNE* III.3: 42[lxii]vb). Accordingly, Buridan uses the term 'certain judgment' in practical contexts to signify firmness or stability of belief: "And by 'certain judgment' here, I do not understand the same as 'true or scientific judgment', but 'that which is firmly believed to the exclusion of all fear [of error]', for in this way true and even false opinion can be certain [*Et non intelligo hic per 'certum iudicium' idem quod 'iudicium verum vel scientificum', sed idem quod 'firmiter creditum omni exclusa formidine', sic enim contingit opinionem veram vel etiam falsam esse certam*]" (*QNE* VII.8: 145rb).

64. There is, accordingly, nothing in Buridan's discussion of deferment to suggest that it could act spontaneously, or contrary to the dictates of reason.

65. Indeed, Buridan sees this as the *differentia* or definitional difference between voluntary and non-voluntary agents (*QNE* III.1: 37va).

66. Buridan's argument for this is straightforwardly Aristotelian. See the entire passage from *QDA₃* III.20: 220, quoted in section 4 below.

67. Assuming, of course, that the will's choice is unaffected by either ignorance or impediment.

68. Indeed, it is from the incompossibility of these motions that Buridan infers the incompossibility of the elicited acts that give rise to them (*QNE* III.3: 42va; III.13: 50vb). Likewise, deferment tends to an act "by which it is able to command the intellect to inquire about that object [*per quam ipsa sit potens imperare intellectui de inquisitione circa illud obiectum*]" (*QNE* III.3: 41vb).

69. In these contexts, Buridan uses the verbs 'to deliberate [*consiliare*]', 'to consider [*considerare*]', and 'to inquire [*inquirere*]' almost interchangeably (we also find 'to investigate [*investigare*]' used in a preliminary argument in *QNE* III.4: 43rb). Although it might look as if deferment has a twofold commanded act, viz., moving the will to consider its object further, and suspending or blocking the act of either pursuing or avoiding it, the latter is merely the consequence of its incompossibility with either of the two alternative modes of action, not something the will actually does. That is, the will's non-acceptance or non-rejection of an object is an incidental effect of its deferment, since the deliberation it commands is in Buridan's view incompossible with actually pursuing or avoiding that object: "for the will can defer the act of willing, and so prevent its issuing in action [*potest enim voluntas differre actum volendi, et ita prohibere transitum ad opus*]" (*QNE* III.5: 45ra). The other point to notice is that Buridan often speaks of suspension as something that happens to the will passively, as a result of appearances external to it, rather than something in which it is actively engaged. Thus, he says that often, when readily believable considerations on each side of a question appear to him, "they hold me in suspense [*in suspenso tenebant me*]," until the matter can be further adjudicated by the intellect (*QNE* VII.6: 143rb).

70. *QNE* III.4: 43va: "*sicut voluntas nihil potest velle absolute nisi sit apprehensum, ita nihil potest prosequi vel fugere nisi quod iudicatum fuerit esse prosequendum vel fugiendum.*" This is actually part of an objection, but Buridan lets it stand in his reply, perhaps because he clearly assumes it elsewhere (see *QNE* VII.6: 143va; *QNE* VII.7: 144vb).

71. The logical possibility that the will could "stand firm" in its act of deferment, which is (quite rightly) never taken seriously by Buridan, is the most likely source of the example that has come down to us known as 'Buridan's Ass', in which a donkey starves to death because it has no reason to choose between two equidistant and equally tempting piles of hay. The example is nowhere to be found in Buridan's writings, although there are versions of it going back at least to Aristotle (see *De Caelo* 295b32). The best explanation of its association with Buridan is that it originated as a parody of his account of free choice by later critics, who found absurd the idea that the will's freedom could consist in inaction, i.e., in its ability to defer or 'send back' for further consideration any practical judgment that is not absolutely certain.

72. *QNE* III.5: 44[lxiiii]va: "*voluntas movet intellectum ad considerandum ut inveniat medium valens ad attingendum finem volitum. Hoc autem non posset esse*

nisi per intellectum sibi praesentatum sub ratione boni hoc quod est consiliari ad tale medium inveniendum."

73. *QNE* III.5: 44[lxiiii]vb (cf. *QNE* X.5: 213vb): "*dico quod voluntas nunquam movet intellectum ad consiliandum nisi intellectus praeiudicaverit quod considerare illud obiectum est bonum. Nec est inconveniens quod intellectus actus cognoscat aliquod obiectum sub una ratione, et dubitet de eo sub alia, et quod tunc iudicet bonum esse considerare ulterius circa ipsum.*"

74. That is, there is nothing in the texts to suggest that Buridan regards the normative status of deliberation as *sui generis,* such that it would be futile to try to evaluate it relative to other goods motivating the will. We could, of course, choose to defer in a situation of uncertainty if deferment seems no less reasonable than either willing or nilling (i.e., if deferment is tied with willing and/or nilling with respect to goodness), but then that would not go against the requirement that the will must choose the greater good. Ties are possible when fallible subjects are doing the evaluating.

75. This consequence of Buridan's account can be shown by means of the following argument, the premises of which are based on the passages referred to above:

P1 The will can accept only what appears to it under the aspect of goodness, and reject only what appears to it under the aspect of badness, or evil.

P2 Nevertheless, the will isn't compelled to choose optimally, since it can (i) choose some other object under the aspect of goodness, or (ii) choose to defer its act in order to consider its object further, even if the intellect has judged the object of that act to be prima facie good.

P3 If (i), then the will must be acting on the basis of only part of the corresponding intellectual judgment, since it can never will against the judgment as a whole, i.e., taking everything into account.

C1 But such less-than-optimal choices are attributable to ignorance (i.e., incomplete knowledge, where "something remains unknown, unconsidered, or unjudged"), or impediment (i.e., where the process of reasoning has somehow been obscured, e.g., by passion or sensitive appetite).

P4 If (ii), then the choice of the will is likewise consonant with intellectual judgment, since in order to have been chosen, the act of deliberation to which deferment gives rise must have appeared to the will under the aspect of goodness.

P5 But that deliberation must have appeared to the will as either (a) the optimal good; or (b) some less-than-optimal good. If (a), then the will was simply acting in accordance with intellectual judgment. If (b), then the will's choice must at some point be attributable to ignorance or impediment; otherwise, there would be an infinite regress (see P2 (i) above).

C2 Deferment is not a case of the will acting directly against the intellect. The idea that the ability to defer somehow purchases greater autonomy for the will is an illusion.

76. In fact, 'will' and 'intellectual appetite' are treated as synonyms by Buridan (*QNE* II.14: 33vb). Likewise, he does not see the intellect and will as distinct either from each other or from the substance of the soul; any differences we notice are due to their differing activities (*QNE* III.2: 41ra–42va). Recall his principle that "one does not argue to a diversity of substantial forms on the basis of any specific diversity in

operations at all [*non quaecumque diversitas specifica operationum arguit diversitatem formarum substantialium*]" (*QDA₃* II.4: 54), discussed in section 1b of chapter 11.

77. See Duns Scotus, *Ordinatio* III, d. 17 [Codex A: 160ra–rb]; tr. Wolter 1986, 182–83; *Ordinatio* IV, suppl. d. 49, qq. 9–10; tr. Wolter 1986, 186–87; *Quaestiones quodlibetales* 16.39, 16.43; tr. Alluntis and Wolter 1975, 382–85. For discussion, see John Boler's trilogy on Scotus on the will (Boler 1990, 1993, and 1994).

78. This becomes clear, e.g., when Buridan reports the opinions of some unidentified others:

> concerning the first argument there are contrary opinions . . . but there is a difference between a natural and a voluntary subject. A natural subject is necessitated by an agent, so that when the agent is present, it receives its act of necessity as long as there is no extrinsic impediment. But a voluntary subject is not necessitated by an agent, so that when the agent is present, it does not receive its act of necessity but has been predisposed to freely determine the subject to be acted upon by this object or that, or by the same object according to one reason or another. For otherwise, freedom would not be preserved.

> [Sed de prima videntur opiniones contrariae. . . . Sed est differentia inter passum naturale et voluntarium, quoniam passum naturale necessitatur ab agente ita quod agente praesentate, necessario recipit actus eius, si non fuerit impedimentum extrinsecum. Sed passum voluntarium non necessitatur ab agente ita quod agente praesentate, non necessario recipit actus eius, sed praeexigitur quod ipsum passivum determinet libere ad patiendum ab hoc obiecto vel ab illo, vel ab eodem obiecto secundum unam rationem vel aliam. Aliter enim libertas non salvaretur.] (*QNE* III.3: 41vb–42[lxii]ra; cf. *QNE* II.1: 22va; *QP* I.4: 6va)

Cf. also Buridan's discussion of common arguments raised in connection with article 151 of the Condemnation of 1277. To an argument concluding that a sufficiently disposed patient is bound to be acted upon by an agent proximate to it, he notes, "it is replied that the major is true of a natural agent, but not of a voluntary agent [*respondetur quod maior est vera de agente naturali, non de voluntario*]" (*QNE* III.1: 36vb).

79. *QNE* III.5: 44[lxiiii]va (cf. *QNE* I.4: 5rb):

> Nondum est quod appetitus sensitivus et appetitus intellectivus, qui dicitur voluntas, vocantur appetitus cognoscitivi non quia cognoscant secundum quod est communis ratio appetitus, sed quia actus ipsorum consequuntur necessario cognitionem praeviam obiectorum suorum. Appetitus enim sensitivus et appetitus intellectivus in hoc distinguntur contra appetitem naturalem: quia appetitus naturalis fertur in obiectum absque ipsius obiecti praevia cognitione. Qui igitur ponunt quod appetitus sensitivus aut voluntas ferri possit in incognitum negant propriam rationem ipsorum secundum quam distinguntur ab appetitu naturali.

As we saw in chapter 14, Buridan's account of the virtues likewise seeks to assimilate them to other natural forms that perfect their matter. In the case of the virtues, the subject is the will: "and so it appears that we must speak of the virtues in us just as we do of other natural forms perfecting their matter . . . and consequently, [of the will] as having inclinations naturally receptive to them, just as form is inclined to matter, and perfectible as regards receiving their perfection [*Et ideo videtur esse dicendum de virtutibus in nobis sicut de aliis formis naturalibus perficientibus suam materiam . . . et*

per consequens, habens inclinationes naturaliter ad eas suscipiendas, sicut materia incli-
natur ad formam, et perfectible ad suam perfectionem recipiendam]" (*QNE* II.1: 22va).

80. Buridan is willing to say that rational agents have a certain inclination to understand or will that is "in keeping with natural appetite [*secundum appetitum natu-*
ralem]," but no actual understanding or willing can occur without prior cognition
(*QNE* III.5: 44[lxiiii]va; cf. *QNE* III.4: 43vb–44[lxiiii]ra). Scotus, of course, would not
have classed the intellectual and sensitive appetites together as non-natural appetites,
since the actions of brute animals (which possess only sensitive appetite) simply follow upon their sensory cognitions, and are hence unfree (*Ordinatio* III, suppl. d. 26;
tr. Wolter 1986, 178–79; cf. *Ordinatio* II, d. 6, q. 2; tr. Wolter 1986, 466–71).

81. *QNE* III.1: 37va: passage quoted at n. 19 above. Although this remark is prefaced with the suggestion that it gives us the difference between voluntary and non-
voluntary agents, Buridan makes clear that he does not understand this in any Scotistic sense by adding, "for this is the natural property of a voluntary agent [*proprietas*
naturalis agentis voluntarii], just as the ability to laugh belongs to a man." It is also
worth noting here that as far as the powers of voluntary agents that are capable of exhibiting this property are concerned, Buridan does not regard freedom as proper to
the will. As we shall see in section 4 below, he also attributes it to the intellect: "from
two simple concepts the intellect can form a third simple concept by forming a
proposition. For in an intellect possessed of the simple concepts A and B, that intellect can freely form the proposition, 'A is B', or the proposition, 'A is not B' [*ex duobus*
conceptibus simplicibus potest intellectus formare tertium simplicem formando proposi-
tionem. Habitis enim in intellectu conceptibus A et B simplicibus, intellectus libere potest
formare istam propositionem, 'A est B', vel istam, 'A non est B']" (*QP* I.4: 5va).

82. Later, he appears to hedge on this slightly. See n. 50 above.

83. *QNE* II.2: 23ra: "*Sciendum est quod naturale aliquando distinguitur contra*
causale, aliquando contra violentum, aliquando contra accidentale, aliquando contra
supernaturale, aliquando contra disconveniens, aliquando contra animale seu volun-
tarium." The Latin passage ends, "sometimes [the natural] is contrary to the animal
or the voluntary." This is not a scribal error, nor is Buridan suggesting that we should
equate what is animal with what is voluntary. As he makes clear a little further on, if
we understand 'the natural' to signify what cannot be otherwise habituated, in the
way a heavy body is naturally determined in itself (*secundum se*) to fall, then many
animal movements will be opposed to nature because they stem from powers that are
indifferent to determinate motion and which can hence be otherwise habituated. In
this sense, we can never alter the natural disposition of a rock to fall, although we can
train a dog to fetch. Needless to say, as we saw in section 4 of chapter 1, this is not
Buridan's preferred understanding of 'natural (*naturale*)'.

84. This would appear to resolve the concerns raised by James J. Walsh that
Buridan's "distinction between voluntary and natural agents seems to imply that a
voluntary agent is a non-natural one," and that "Buridan does not explain in what
sense a non-natural agent can be said to have a natural property" (1964, 60–61).

85. For Buridan, the absolute dependency of the will on the intellect is further
reflected in the way its operations are patterned after the operations of the intellect:

> It can be said, then, that the soul itself is active and receptive of every intellection
> and every volition, but perhaps not entirely in the same way. Indeed, taken by it-
> self, a heavy substance is in potentiality to moving downward, and it can initiate

carnal

that motion insofar as it informs the act of heaviness. In this way, the soul, taken in itself, can receive an intellection and a volition, but cannot do [anything with] them except insofar as it has been informed by some prior act. . . . It seems to me, then, that once the soul has been informed by an intelligible object, it can form in itself an act of understanding, and once it has been informed by several simple acts of understanding, it can form in itself an act of compounding, and then an act of dividing (at least with respect to principles known in themselves), and later an act of discursive reasoning. And so consequently, I will say that as far as the act of willing is concerned, when the soul itself has been informed by some prior act, e.g., by either a judgment concerning the goodness or badness of something willable, or a certain agreement or disagreement, as will be discussed later, it can move itself to an act of willing.

[Potest ergo dici quod ipsa anima est activa et receptiva omnis intellectionis et omnis volitionis, sed forte quod hoc non est totaliter secundum idem. Immo substantia gravis secundum seipsam est in potentia ad movere deorsum, et potest agere illum motum secundum quem informat actum gravitatis. Ita anima secundum seipsam potest intellectionem et volitionem recipere, sed agere eam non potest nisi secundum quod aliquo priori actu informata. . . . Videtur ergo mihi quod anima informata ipsa intelligibili ab obiecto, potest in se formare actum intelligendi, et ipsa simplicibus intellectionibus informata, potest in se formare actum [com]ponendi, et postea actum dividendi, saltem quoad principia per se nota, et postea actum discurrendi, et sic consequenter. Et ita quantum ad actum volendi, dicam quod ipsa anima informata aliquo actu priori, puta vel iudicio de bonitate vel malitia volubilis, vel quadam complacentia vel displicentia, sicut dicetur post, potest se movere ad actu[m] volendi.] (QNE III.2: 41ra–rb)

86. Boler 1994, 42, n. 58.

87. QNE VII.7: 144vb: "*quia tamen plurimi doctores solemnissimi tenuerunt illas conclusiones, forte non oportet eas abjicere, quoniam etsi ratio superius adducta non demonstret, tamen cum eius probabilite videtur aliud etiam esse probabile.*" For a list of the articles, see Mandonnet 1908, 175–91. Article 166 condemns the view that right reason is sufficient for right volition, which the authors of the Condemnation associate with Pelagianism. Article 169, which is at least partly directed against Thomas Aquinas, condemns the view "that the will, as long as passion and actual, particular, knowledge remain in place, cannot act against [reason] [*Quod voluntas manente passione et scientia particulari in actu non potest agere contra eam*]." Buridan's wording of Article 169 differs slightly, and perhaps significantly, from the original (though one cannot rule out scribal error here): "That, as long as actual universal and particular knowledge are present, the will could not [will] the opposite—[this is an] error [*Quod stante scientia in universali et in particulare in actu quod voluntas non possit in oppositum—error*]" (QNE VII.7: 144vb).

88. QNE X.2: 205rb:

. . . solus deus agit simpliciter et omnino libere; omnia autem alia agentia in ordine ad ipsum deum agunt serviliter, quia omnia que sunt et agunt et sunt et agunt gratia ipsius dei; unde et nos debemus esse servi dei. Deus autem quicquid ad extra producit vel conservat ipse producit et conservat suiipsius gratia prima et principali intentione; omnia enim que sunt in ipsum deum finaliter ordinata sunt. Et tamen hoc non obstante agens particulare dicitur agere libere si agat suiipsius gratia magis principaliter quam gratia alicuius alterius finis particularis qui non contineat ipsum finaliter secundum naturalem finium connexionem et ordinem.

89. Aristotle, *Metaphysics* I.2.982b26–28.

90. *QNE* X.2: 205va: "*Et hunc modum libertatis ponit nobis Aristoteles, prohemio* Metaphysice, *dicens, 'Sed ut dicimus homo liber est qui suimet et non alterius causa est, sic et hec sola libera est scientiarum', id est metaphysica, 'inter humanas scientias; sola namque hec causa suimet est'. Et per metaphysicam intelligit theologiam a 'metha' quod est 'trans' et 'physis' quod est 'natura', et 'icos' quod est 'scientia', quasi 'scientia de transcendentalibus naturam'.*"

91. *QNE* X.5: 212vb: "*Utrum autem noticia sit perfecta quam secundum fidem habemus de trinitate in hac vita? Dico quod sic, quantum spectat ad statum viatoris—immo multo perfectior quam evidens et demonstrativa scientia quod triangulus habet tres, etc. Sed hoc non est contra corollarium, quia dicebatur 'de quibus innati sumus habere evidentiam'.*"

92. Duns Scotus, *Quaestiones in Metaphysicam* IX.15; tr. Wolter 1986, 155.

93. Wolter 1986, 10; 37.

94. *QNE* X.2: 207[ccxv]rb–va: "*manifestum est quod illi non ordinantur finaliter ad intellectum et voluntatem secundum naturalem finium ordinationem. Absurdum enim esset dicere quod illud quod mihi est disconveniens turpe et nocivum sit gratia mei, et in me finaliter ordinatum naturali ordinatione finium; immo manifestum est quod sic intellectus et voluntas non suiipsius gratia agunt principali intentione, sed gratia delectionum sensualium naturalibus suis perfectionibus contrariarum.*"

95. Maimonides, *The Guide of the Perplexed* I, chapter 60.

96. Aristotle, *De Anima* III.4.429b6–9.

97. Thomas Aquinas, *Sentencia libri 'De anima'* III.8.20–31; tr. Pasnau 1999, 352; cf. *Summa contra gentiles* II.73.41.

98. Aristotle, *Physics* VIII.4.255b1–4.

99. Thomas Aquinas, *Summa contra gentiles* II.73.41.

100. *QM* VI.2: 33vb: Latin text quoted at n. 18 of chapter 1 above.

101. *QDA₃* III.15: 167: "*potentia intellectiva est libera et non oportet quod potentia libera, omnibus requisitis ad causandum . . . sed potest, illis stantibus, producere oppositum, vel differre, et nec producere istum nec oppositum.*"

102. *QDA₃* III.15: 167–68: "*dico quod illa libertas non habet locum nisi in actibus voluntariis et in aliis consequentibus actuum voluntarium. . . . Sed in illis primis intellectionibus formandis nullus potest concurrere actus voluntarius, quia voluntas non fertur incognita in cognitione intellectuale, et nihil erat intellectum ante formationem primae intellectionis. Ideo non habet ibi voluntas locum, ea ratione qua dicitur 'voluntas'.*"

103. *QDA₃* III.15: 170–71: "*Et ut expeditum sit de illa materia, aliquis posset quaerere quomodo consequenter intellectus potest componere et dividere et discurrere. Ego dico quod intellectus, actuatus per primas et simplices apprehensiones plures, potest iam cum illis phantasmatibus manentibus complectere alios conceptus, aut affirmative aut negative. Quo facto, potest iterum plures illarum propositionum congregare et ordinare in syllogismo et inferre conclusiones alias sequentes. Et potest libere se transferre de una consideratione in aliam, et hanc dimittere et illam prosequi, in quibus fuerit praehabituatus.*"

104. Thus, acts of the will are 'options' in the true sense of the word, modes of free choice (*libertas oppositionis*) proper to the freedom by which we govern our practical lives.

105. Aristotle, *Metaphysics* I.2.982b25–28.

106. *QNE* X.3: 209ra: "*anima liberius se habet in producendo volitionem ea ratione qua dicitur intellectus quam ea ratione qua dicitur voluntas.*" Cf. Nicholas of Vaudemont: "when it is said that we are masters of our operations in the will [*secundum voluntatem sumus domini operationum nostrarum*], the reply is that we are not. Indeed, we are more principally masters of our operations in the intellect, because we will nothing unless it has been judged to be good by the intellect" (Ps.-Buridan, *QPol* VII.5: 98vb). Nicholas uses this same argument from metaphysical priority to reply to another objection, where he notes that the power to cause a man to be servile or free "is more principally and originally [*radicalius*] in the power of the intellect . . . because the will never moves in the direction of a good or bad act without being predisposed by the opinion of the intellect [*sententia intellectus praehabita*]" (Ps.-Buridan, *QPol* VII.5: 98vb–99ra).

107. Nevertheless, it would be premature to think of this as Buridan's final position, since it is not evenly reflected throughout his writings. He is constantly pulled by intellectualist and voluntarist concerns in his moral psychology. Some of the recalcitrant evidence on intellectual freedom is as follows: (1) in *QM* VI.5: 36vb, Buridan claims that the will can produce the elicited act of deferment all by itself, without any other determining agent, and that without such deferment, we would have no more freedom than a dog; (2) in *DMA* IV: 545, he says that sin occurs when a suitably inclined appetite does not "await the reasonings of the intellect [*non expectat ratiocinationes intellectus*]"; (3) in *Summulae* 8.4.2: 698, we are told that "free will may dispose a man to believe things that are far from evident"; and finally, (4) in *QP* I.4: 6vb, we get the argument that free will plays a role in moving premises around to construct demonstrative syllogisms, though it often leads to mistakes. Although none of these passages is so opposed to Buridan's understanding of intellectual freedom that the appearances cannot be saved (and certainly none constitutes evidence for Buridan being a voluntarist or even a hybrid voluntarist/intellectualist), it does look as if he was genuinely perplexed by the competing demands of authorities framing in the question.

108. Thomas Aquinas, *Summa contra gentiles* II.47.4.

109. Aristotle, *De Anima* III.10.433a17.

110. *QDA₃* III.20: 220 (cf. *QNE* VII.8: 145rb):

Deinde etiam, quando homo movetur secundum rationem et intellectum, Aristoteles ostendit quae ratio movet et quae non, dicens quod ratio speculativa non movet quia non concludit aliquid esse faciendum vel non faciendum, prosequendum vel fugiendum. Deinde etiam, ratio universalis practica non movet, ut si arguatur quod semper bene agendum est cum aptitudo affuerit; iuste autem agere est bene agere; ergo iuste est agendum. Ego per illam rationem non moveor. Sed ratio practica descendens ad singularia est quae movet, ut si arguo febricitas sitiens debet potare tisanam; sed ego sum febricitas sitiens, et hoc est tisana: statim movebor ad potandum, si non sit impedimentum.

111. Thomas Aquinas, *Summa contra gentiles* II.60.5; cf. Aristotle, *Rhetoric* I.2.1382a4.

112. Thomas Aquinas, *Summa contra gentiles* II.76.19.

113. Thomas Aquinas, *Summa contra gentiles* II.26.21.

114. Cf. the understatement with which Eleonore Stump begins an essay on the problem in Thomas: "It is difficult to develop a comprehensive and satisfactory account of Aquinas's views of the nature of human freedom" (1997, 576).

NOTE TO CHAPTER 16

1. Duns Scotus, *Quodlibetal Questions on God and Creatures*, Prologue; tr. Alluntis and Wolter 1975, 3.

· WORKS CITED ·

PRIMARY SOURCES

Ackrill, J. L., tr. 1963. *Aristotle's 'Categories' and 'De Interpretatione'.* Clarendon Aristotle Series. Oxford: Clarendon Press.

Alluntis, Felix, and Allan B. Wolter, trs. 1975. *John Duns Scotus, God and Creatures: The Quodlibetal Questions.* Princeton, N. J.–London: Princeton University Press.

Anscombe, Elizabeth, and Peter Geach, trs. 1971. *Descartes: Philosophical Writings.* Indianapolis: Bobbs-Merrill.

Aquinas, Thomas. 1882– . *Opera Omnia.* Roma: Commissio Leonina.

Averroes. 1562–74. *Aristotelis Opera cum Averrois Commentariis.* Venice. Photomechanically reprinted 1962. Frankfurt a. M.: Minerva.

Barnes, Jonathan, ed. 1984. *The Complete Works of Aristotle.* Revised Oxford Translation. Bollingen Series 71.2. Princeton, N. J.: Princeton University Press.

Bettenson, Henry, tr. 1984. *Augustine: City of God.* New York: Penguin.

✓Bos, E. P., ed. 1994. *Johannes Buridanus, Summulae: In Praedicamenta.* Artistarium, vol. 10, no. 3. Nijmegen: Ingenium.

Bourke, Vernon, ed. 1974. *The Essential Augustine.* 2d ed. Indianapolis: Hackett.

Buridan, John. 1499. *Perutile compendium totius logicae Ioannis Buridani cum praeclarissima solertissimi viri Ioannis Dorp expositione.* Venice. Photomechanically reprinted 1965. Frankfurt a. M.: Minerva.

———. 1509. *Subtilissimae Quaestiones super octo Physicorum libros Aristotelis.* Paris. Photomechanically reprinted 1964, as *Kommentar zur Aristotelischen Physik.* Frankfurt a. M.: Minerva.

———. 1513. *Quaestiones super decem libros Ethicorum Aristotelis ad Nicomachum.* Paris. Photomechanically reprinted 1968, as *Super decem libros Ethicorum.* Frankfurt a. M.: Minerva.

———. 1588 (actually 1518). *In Metaphysicen Aristotelis Questiones argutissimae.* Paris. Photomechanically reprinted 1964, as *Kommentar zur Aristotelischen Metaphysik.* Frankfurt a. M.: Minerva.

————. *Quaestiones in duos libros De Generatione et Corruptione Aristotelis.* Wissenschaftliche Allgemeinbibliothek, cod. Amplon. F. 357, ff. 96ra–129va, Erfurt. Unedited manuscript.

[Ps.-] Buridan, John [= Nicholas of Vaudemont]. 1513. *Quaestiones super octo libros politicorum Aristotelis.* Paris. Photomechanically reprinted 1969. Frankfurt a. M.: Minerva.

Caroti, Stefano, ed. 1976. "Nicole Oresme: *Quaestio contra divinatores horoscopios.*" *Archives d'histoire doctrinale et littéraire du moyen âge* 43: 216–310.

Chadwick, Henry, tr. 1992. *Augustine: Confessions.* Oxford–New York: Oxford University Press.

Chase, Wayland Johnson, tr. 1926. *The Ars Minor of Donatus.* University of Wisconsin Studies in the Social Sciences and History 11. Madison: University of Wisconsin Press.

Crawford, F. Stuart, ed. 1953. *Averrois Cordubensis: Commentarium Magnum in Aristotelis De Anima Libros.* Cambridge, Mass.: Medieval Academy of America.

Dal Pra, Mario, ed. 1954. *Pietro Abelardo Scritti Filosofici, Editio super Porphyrium, Glossae in Categorias, Editio super Aristotelem De Interpretatione, De Divisionibus, Super Topicae Glossae.* Roma-Milano: Fratelli Boca.

Denifle, Heinrich, O. P., and Emile Chatelain, eds. 1891–1894. *Chartularium Universitatis Parisiensis.* Vols. 1–4. Paris: Delalain.

Duns Scotus, John. 1950–. *Opera Omnia.* Edited by C. Balić et al. Roma: Commissio Scotistica.

Freddoso, Alfred J., and Francis E. Kelley, trs. 1991. *William of Ockham: The Quodlibetal Questions.* Vols. 1–2. Yale Library of Medieval Philosophy. New Haven, Conn.–London: Yale University Press.

Fuhrmann, Manfred, ed. 1966. *Ars rhetorica quae vulgo fertur Aristotelis ad Alexandrum.* Leipzig: Teubner.

Gallagher, D. A., and I. J. Gallagher, trs. 1966. *Saint Augustine: The Catholic and Manichaean Way of Life.* The Fathers of the Church 56. Washington, D. C.: The Catholic University of America Press.

Geyer, Bernhard, ed. 1919. *Peter Abelards Philosophische Schriften; I. Die Logica 'ingredientibus'; II. Die Glossen zu Porphyrius.* Münster: Aschendorff.

Grabmann, Martin, ed. 1931–32. "Eine lateinische Übersetzung der pseudoaristotelischen Rhetorica ad Alexandrum aus dem 13. Jahrhundert. Literarhistorische Untersuchung und Textausgabe." In *Sitzungberichte der Bayerischen Akademie der Wissenschaften. Philosophische-Historische Abteilung* 4. München: Die Akademie.

Green, R. P. H., ed. & tr. 1995. *Augustine, 'De Doctrina Christiana'.* Oxford: Clarendon Press.

Green-Pedersen, N. J. 1984. *The Tradition of the Topics in the Middle Ages: The Commentaries on Aristotle's and Boethius' 'Topics'.* München-Wien: Philosophia Verlag.

Grellard, Christophe, tr. 2001. *Nicolas d'Autrécourt: Correspondance, Articles Condamnés.* Paris: Vrin.

Hansen, Bert, ed. & tr. 1985. *Nicole Oresme and the Marvels of Nature.* Toronto: Pontifical Institute of Mediaeval Studies.

Hertz, Martin, ed. 1855–59. *"Priscianus: Institutiones Grammaticae."* In *Grammatici latini,* edited by Heinrich Keil. Vols. 2–3. Leipzig. Photomechanically reprinted 1961. Hildesheim: Georg Olms Verlagsbuchhandlung.

Hubien, Hubert, ed. 1976. *Iohannis Buridani Tractatus de consequentiis.* Philosophes Médiévaux XVI. Louvain: Publications universitaires.

———, ed. *Iohannis Buridani Quaestiones in duos libros Aristotelis Posteriorum Analyticorum.* Unpublished typescript.

———, ed. *Iohannis Buridani Quaestiones in duos libros Aristotelis Priorum Analyticorum.* Unpublished typescript.

Hughes, G. E., ed. & tr. 1982. *John Buridan on Self-Reference: Chapter Eight of Buridan's Sophismata.* An edition and translation with an introduction and philosophical commentary. Cambridge–London–New York: Cambridge University Press.

Hyman, Arthur, and James J. Walsh, eds. 1987. *Philosophy in the Middle Ages: The Christian, Islamic, and Jewish Traditions.* 2d ed. Indianapolis: Hackett.

Judy, Albert G., O. P., ed. 1976. *Robert Kilwardby OP, 'De ortu scientiarum'.* Auctores Britannici Medii Aevi 4. London-Toronto: The British Academy and the Pontifical Institute of Mediaeval Studies.

Kennedy, L. A., Richard E. Arnold, and Arthur E. Millward, trs. 1971. *The Universal Treatise of Nicholas of Autrecourt.* Medieval Texts in Translation 20. Milwaukee: Marquette University Press.

Kilcullen, R. J., ed. 1996. "Buridan, On Aristotle's *Ethics,* Book X." Online edition available from www.humanities.mq.edu.au/Ockham/wburlat.

King, Peter, tr. 1985. *John Buridan's Logic: The Treatise on Supposition; The Treatise on Consequences.* Dordrecht-Boston-Lancaster: Reidel.

Klima, Gyula, tr. 2001. *John Buridan: 'Summulae de Dialectica'.* Yale Library of Medieval Philosophy. New Haven, Conn.–London: Yale University Press.

Kretzmann, Norman, tr. 1966. *William of Sherwood's 'Introduction to Logic'.* Minneapolis: University of Minnesota Press.

Kretzmann, Norman, and Eleonore Stump, trs. 1988. *The Cambridge Translations of Medieval Philosophical Texts. Volume 1: Logic and the Philosophy of Language.* Cambridge–New York: Cambridge University Press.

Leach, Arthur Francis, ed. & tr. 1911. *Educational Charters and Documents.* Cambridge: Cambridge University Press.

van der Lecq, Ria, ed. 1983. *Johannes Buridanus, Questiones longe super librum Perihermeneias.* Artistarium, vol. 4. Nijmegen: Ingenium.

———, ed. 1998. *Johannes Buridanus, Summulae: De suppositionibus.* Artistarium, vol. 10, no. 4. Nijmegen: Ingenium.

van der Lecq, Ria, and H. A. G. Braakhuis, eds. 1994. *Johannes Buridanus, Questiones Elencorum*. Artistarium, vol. 9. Nijmegen: Ingenium.

Lindsay, W. M., ed. 1911. *Isidori Hispalensis episcopi Etymologiarum sive Originum libri XX. Scriptorum Classicorum Bibliotheca Oxoniensis*. Vols. 1–2. Oxford: Clarendon Press.

Long, A. A., and D. N. Sedley, eds. & trs. 1987. *The Hellenistic Philosophers*. Vols. 1–2. Cambridge–London–New York: Cambridge University Press.

Magee, John. 1998. *Anicii Manlii Severini Boethii 'De divisione liber': Critical Edition, Translation, Prolegomena, and Commentary*. Leiden-Boston-Köln: Brill.

Mandonnet, Pierre, ed. 1908. *Siger de Brabant et l'Averroïsme latin au XIIIme siècle, IIme partie: Textes inédits*. 2d ed. Les Philosophes Belges. Louvain: Institut Supérieur de Philosophie de l'Université de Louvain.

Maurer, Armand, ed. 1983. *Siger of Brabant, Quaestiones in Metaphysicam*. Louvain-la-Neuve: Editions de l'Institut Supérieur de Philosophie.

———, tr. 1986. *St. Thomas Aquinas, The Divisions and Methods of the Sciences. Questions V and VI of His Commentary on the 'De Trinitate' of Boethius*. 4th rev. ed. Toronto: Pontifical Institute of Mediaeval Studies.

McGarry, Daniel D., tr. 1955. *The Metalogicon of John of Salisbury: A Twelfth-Century Defense of the Verbal and Logical Arts of the Trivium*. Berkeley–Los Angeles: University of California Press.

McGrade, Arthur Stephen, John Kilcullen, and Matthew Kempshall, eds. 2001. *The Cambridge Translations of Medieval Philosophical Texts. Volume 2: Ethics and Political Philosophy*. Cambridge–New York: Cambridge University Press.

Meiser, Carolus, ed. 1877. *Boethius, Commentarii in librum Aristotelis Perihermeneias pars prior versionem continuam et primam editionem continens*. Leipzig: Teubner.

———, ed. 1880. *Boethius, Commentarii in librum Aristotelis Perihermeneias pars posterior secundam editionem et indices continens*. Leipzig: Teubner.

Migne, J.-P. 1800–1875. *Patrologiae cursus completus, sive biblioteca universalis, integra, uniformis, commoda, oeconomica, omnium SS. Patrum, doctorum scriptorumque ecclesiasticorum. Series Latina*. 221 volumes. Paris: Garnier Frères.

Miller, Walter, tr. 1913. *Cicero: De officiis*. Loeb Classical Library. Cambridge, Mass.: Harvard University Press.

Moody, E. A., ed. 1942. *Iohannis Buridani Quaestiones super libris quattuor De caelo et mundo*. Cambridge, Mass.: Medieval Academy of America.

O'Donnell, J. Reginald, ed. 1939. "Nicholas of Autrecourt " [contains Latin edition of Autrecourt's *Exigit ordo executionis*]. *Mediaeval Studies* 1: 179–280.

Pasnau, Robert, tr. 1999. *Thomas Aquinas, A Commentary on Aristotle's 'De anima.'* Yale Library of Medieval Philosophy. London–New Haven, Conn.: Yale University Press.

Patar, Benoît, ed. 1991. *Le Traité de l'âme de Jean Buridan [De prima lectura]*. Philosophes Médiévaux, vol. 29. Louvain: Éditions de l'Institut Supérieur de Philosophie, and Longueuil, Québec: Éditions du Préambule.

————, ed. 1995. *Nicolai Oresme: Expositio et Quaestiones in Aristotelis De Anima.* Louvain-la-Neuve–Louvain–Paris: Éditions de l'Institut Supérieur de Philosophie and Éditions Peeters.

————, ed. 1996. *Ioannis Buridani, Expositio et Quaestiones in Aristotelis 'De Caelo'.* Philosophes Médiévaux, vol. 33. Louvain-Paris: Éditions de l'Institut Supérieur de Philosophie-Éditions Peeters.

Pironet, Fabienne, ed. Forthcoming. *Iohanni Buridani Summularum Tractatus nonus: De practica sophismatum (Sophismata).* Critical Edition and Introduction. Artistarium, vol. 10, no. 9. Nijmegen: Ingenium.

Preben-Hansen, Bernadette, ed. *Iohannis Buridani Quaestiones in Rhetoricam Aristotelis.* Unpublished typescript.

Rackham, H., tr. 1971. *Cicero: De finibus bonorum et malorum.* Loeb Classical Library. Cambridge, Mass.: Harvard University Press.

Radice, Betty, tr. 1974. *The Letters of Abelard and Heloise.* Harmondsworth: Penguin Books.

Reilly, Leo, C. S. B., ed. 1993. *Petrus Helias: Summa super Priscianum.* Studies and Texts 113. Vols. 1–2. Toronto: Pontifical Institute of Mediaeval Studies.

Reina, Maria Elena, ed. 1957. "Giovanni Buridano: *Tractatus de suppositionibus.*" *Rivista critica di storia della filosofia* 12: 175–208, 323–52.

Rijk, L. M. de, ed. 1962. *Logica Modernorum: A Contribution to the History of Early Terminist Logic.* Vol. 1. Assen: Van Gorcum.

————, ed. 1967. *Logica Modernorum: A Contribution to the History of Early Terminist Logic.* Vol. 2, parts 1–2. Assen: Van Gorcum.

————, ed. 1970. *Petrus Abaelardus, Dialectica.* 2d rev. ed. Assen: Van Gorcum.

————, ed. 1972. *Peter of Spain: Tractatus (called afterwards 'Summulae Logicales').* Assen: Van Gorcum.

————, ed. & tr. 1994. *Nicholas of Autrecourt: His Correspondence with Master Giles and Bernard of Arezzo.* Leiden–New York–Köln: E. J. Brill.

————, ed. 1995. *Johannes Buridanus, Summulae: De Praedicabilibus.* Artistarium, vol. 10, no. 2. Nijmegen: Ingenium.

————, ed. 1999. *Johannes Buridanus, Summulae: De demonstrationibus.* Artistarium, vol. 10, no. 8. Nijmegen: Ingenium.

Rijk, L. M. de, ed., and Joke Spruyt, tr. 1992. *Peter of Spain (Petrus Hispanus Portugalensis), Syncategoreumata.* Leiden–New York–Köln: E. J. Brill.

Russell, Robert P. 1942. *Divine Providence and the Problem of Evil: A Translation of St. Augustine's 'De ordine'.* New York: Cosmopolitan Science & Art Service.

Schneider, Johannes, ed. 1983. *Iohannes Buridanus Quaestiones in Praedicamenta.* München: Beck.

Scott, Frederick, and Herman Shapiro, eds. 1967. "John Buridan's *De motibus animalium.*" *Isis* 58: 533–52.

Scott, T. K., Jr., tr. 1966. *John Buridan: Sophisms on Meaning and Truth.* New York: Appleton-Century-Crofts.

————, ed. 1977. *Johannes Buridanus: Sophismata*. Stuttgart–Bad Canstatt: Frommann-Holzboog.

Sobol, Peter Gordon, ed. 1984. "John Buridan on the Soul and Sensation: An Edition of Book II of His Commentary on Aristotle's Book of the Soul, with an Introduction and a Translation of Question 18 on Sensible Species." Doctoral dissertation, Indiana University.

Sobol, Peter, tr. 1996. "Jean Buridan on Sensation." In *Readings in Medieval Philosophy*, edited by Andrew B. Schoedinger, 493–513. Oxford–New York: Oxford University Press.

Spade, Paul Vincent, tr. 1994. *Five Texts on the Mediaeval Problem of Universals: Porphyry, Boethius, Abelard, Duns Scotus, Ockham*. Indianapolis: Hackett.

Stump, Eleonore, tr. 1978. *Boethius's 'De topicis differentiis'*. Ithaca, N.Y.: Cornell University Press.

————, tr. 1988. *Boethius's 'In Ciceronis Topica'*. Ithaca, N.Y.: Cornell University Press.

Szyller, Sławomir, ed. 1987. "Johannis Buridani, Tractatus de differentia universalis ad individuum." *Przeglad Tomistyczny* 3: 137–78.

Tatarzyński, Ryszard, ed. 1986. "Jan Buridan, Kommentarz do *Isagogi* Porfiriusza." *Przeglad Tomistyczny* 2: 111–95.

Thijssen, J.M.M.H., ed. 1991a. *John Buridan's 'Tractatus de Infinito'*. Artistarium Supplementa, vol. 6. Nijmegen: Ingenium.

Trapp, A. Damasus, O.S.A., and Venicio Marcolino, eds. 1981. *Gregorii Ariminensis OESA, Lectura super primum et secundum sententiarum*. Vol. 1. Berlin: Walter de Gruyter.

Van Den Burgh, Simon, tr. 1954. *Averroes' Tahafut al-Tahafut (The Incoherence of the Incoherence)*. Vols. 1–2. London: Luzac.

Van Riet, Simone, ed. 1977. *Avicenna Latinus: Liber de philosophia prima*. Louvain-Leiden: Peeters and Brill.

Verbeke, Gérard, ed. 1957. *Thémistius: Commentaire sur le traité de l'âme d'Aristote*. Louvain: Publications Universitaires.

Waszink, J.H., ed. 1962. *Timaeus a Calcidio translatus commentarioque instructus*. Vol. 4 of Plato Latinus, edited by Raymond Klibansky. London-Leiden: The Warburg Institute and E.J. Brill.

William of Ockham. 1967–85. *Opera Philosophica et Theologica*. 17 vols., edited by Gedeon Gál et al. St. Bonaventure, N.Y.: St. Bonaventure University Press and The Franciscan Institute.

Williams, Thomas, tr. 1993. *Augustine: On Free Choice of the Will*. Indianapolis: Hackett.

Wolter, Allan B., O.F.M., tr. 1986. *Duns Scotus on the Will and Morality*. Washington, D.C.: Catholic University of America Press.

Wood, Rega, ed. 1988. *Adam de Wodeham, Tractatus de indivisibilibus*. Boston: Kluwer.

Wood, Rega, and Gedeon Gál, O.F.M., eds. 1990. *Adam de Wodeham, Lectura secunda in librum primum sententiarum*. Vols. 1–3. St. Bonaventure, N.Y.: St. Bonaventure University Press.

Zoubov, Vassili, ed. 1961. "Jean Buridan et les concepts du point au quatorzième siècle." *Medieval and Renaissance Studies* 5: 63–95.

Zupko, John Alexander, ed. & tr. 1989. "John Buridan's Philosophy of Mind: An Edition and Translation of Book III of His 'Questions on Aristotle's *De anima*' (Third Redaction), with Commentary and Critical and Interpretative Essays." Doctoral dissertation, Cornell University.

Secondary Sources

Ackrill, J. L. 1981. *Aristotle the Philosopher.* Oxford: Oxford University Press.

Adams, Marilyn McCord. 1987a. *William Ockham.* Vols. 1–2. Notre Dame, Ind.: University of Notre Dame Press.

———. 1987b. "William Ockham: Voluntarist or Naturalist?" In *Studies in Medieval Philosophy,* edited by John F. Wippel, 219–47. Studies in Philosophy and the History of Philosophy 17. Washington, D. C.: The Catholic University of America Press.

———. 1990. "Ockham's Individualisms." In *Die Gegenwarts Ockhams,* edited by Wilhelm Vossenkuhl and Rolf Schönberger, 3–24. Weinheim: VCH/Acta humaniora.

Ashworth, E. J. 1974. *Language and Logic in the Post-Medieval Period.* Dordrecht-Boston: Reidel.

———. 1985. *Studies in Post-Medieval Semantics.* London: Varorium Reprints.

———. 1999. "Aquinas on Significant Utterance: Interjection, Blasphemy, Prayer." In *Aquinas's Moral Theory: Essays in Honor of Norman Kretzmann,* edited by Scott MacDonald and Eleonore Stump, 207–234. Ithaca-London: Cornell University Press.

Barnes, Jonathan. 1969. "Aristotle's Theory of Demonstration." *Phronesis* 14: 123–52.

Berger, Harald. 1991. "Simple Supposition in William of Ockham, John Buridan, and Albert of Saxony." In *Itinéraires d'Albert de Saxe: Paris-Vienne au XIVe siècle,* edited by Joël Biard, 31–43. Paris: Vrin.

Biard, Joël. 1989. *Logique et théorie du signe au XIVe siècle.* Paris: Vrin.

———. 1997. "Le système des causes dans la philosophie naturelle de Jean Buridan." In *Perspectives arabes et médiévales sur la tradition scientifique et philosophique grec,* edited by Ahmad Hasnawi et al., 491–504. Leuven-Paris: Peeters.

———. 1998. "Science et rhétorique dans les 'Questions sur la Rhétorique' de Jean Buridan." In *La Rhétorique d'Aristote: Traditions et commentaires de l'antiquité au XVIIe siècle,* edited by Gilbert Dahan and Irène Rosier-Catach, 135–52. Paris: Vrin.

Black, Deborah L. 1990. *Logic and Aristotle's 'Rhetoric' and 'Poetics' in Medieval Arabic Philosophy.* Leiden–New York–København–Köln: E. J. Brill.

Boehner, Philotheus, O. F. M. 1952. *Medieval Logic: An Outline of Its Development from 1250 to ca. 1400.* Chicago: University of Chicago Press.

Boh, Ivan. 1993. *Epistemic Logic in the Later Middle Ages.* London–New York: Routledge.

Boler, John. 1990. "The Moral Psychology of Duns Scotus: Some Preliminary Questions." *Franciscan Studies* 50: 31–56.

———. 1993. "Transcending the Natural: Duns Scotus on the Two Affections of the Will." *American Catholic Philosophical Quarterly* 67: 109–126.

———. 1994. "An Image for the Unity of the Will in Duns Scotus." *Journal of the History of Philosophy* 32: 23–44.

Bos, E. P. 1976. "John Buridan and Marsilius of Inghen on Consequences." In *The Logic of John Buridan*, edited by Jan Pinborg, 61–69. Copenhagen: Museum Tusculanum.

Braakhuis, Henk A. G. 1999. "Scientific Knowledge and Contingent Reality. Knowledge, Signification and (Natural) Supposition in Buridan's *Questions on 'De generatione et corruptione'*." In *The Commentary Tradition on Aristotle's 'De generatione et corruptione': Ancient, Medieval, and Early Modern*, edited by J. M. M. H. Thijssen and H. A. G. Braakhuis, 131–61. Studia Artistarium, vol. 7. Turnhout: Brepols.

Brower, Jeffrey. 2001. "Medieval Theories of Relations." In *The Stanford Encyclopedia of Philosophy* (Summer 2001), edited by Edward Zalta. URL = http://plato.stanford.edu/archives/sum2001/entries/relations-medieval/.

Burge, Tyler. 1978. "Buridan and Epistemic Paradox." *Philosophical Studies* 34: 21–35.

Bursill-Hall, G. L., Sten Ebbesen, and Konrad Koerner, eds. 1990. *De Ortu Grammaticae: Studies in Medieval Grammar and Linguistic Theory in Memory of Jan Pinborg*. Studies in the History of Language Sciences 43. Amsterdam-Philadelphia: John Benjamins.

The Cambridge History of Later Medieval Philosophy. 1982. Edited by Norman Kretzmann, Anthony Kenny, and Jan Pinborg. Cambridge–London–New York: Cambridge University Press.

Clagett, Marshall. 1959. *The Science of Mechanics in the Middle Ages*. Madison: University of Wisconsin Press.

Courtenay, William J. 1972. "John of Mirecourt and Gregory of Rimini on Whether God Can Undo the Past." *Recherches de théologie ancienne et médiévale* 39: 224–34.

———. 1984. "The Reception of Ockham's Thought at the University of Paris." In *Preuve et raisons à l'université de Paris: logique, ontologie et théologie au XIVe siècle*, edited by Zénon Kaluza and Paul Vignaux, 43–64. Paris: Vrin.

———. 1988. *Teaching Careers at the University of Paris in the Thirteenth and Fourteenth Centuries*. Texts and Studies in the History of Medieval Education 18. United States Subcommission for the History of Universities and University of Notre Dame Press, Notre Dame, Ind.

———. 1989. "Inquiry and Inquisition: Academic Freedom in Medieval Universities." *Church History* 58: 168–82.

———. 1995. "The Preservation and Dissemination of Academic Condemnations at the University of Paris in the Middle Ages." In *Moral and Political Philosophies in the Middle Ages: Proceedings of the Ninth International Congress of Medieval Philosophy*, edited by B. Carlos Bazán, Eduardo Andújar, and Léonard G. Sbrocchi, 1659–67. Vols. 1–3. New York–Ottawa–Toronto: Legas.

Courtenay, William J., and Katharine H. Tachau. 1982. "Ockham, Ockhamists, and the English-German Nation at Paris, 1339–1341." *History of Universities* 2: 53–96.

Dahan, Gilbert, Irène Rosier, and Luisa Valente. 1995. "L'arabe, le grec, l'hébreu et les vernaculaires." In *Sprachtheorien in Spätantike und Mittelalter*, edited by Sten Ebbesen, 265–321. Tübingen: Gunter Narr Verlag.

D'Ors, Angel. 1997. "*Petrus Hispanus, O.P., Auctor Summularum*." *Vivarium* 35: 21–71.

———. 2001. "*Petrus Hispanus, O.P., Auctor Summularum* (II): Further Documents and Problems." *Vivarium* 39: 209–254.

Ebbesen, Sten. 1976. "The *Summulae, Tractatus VII De fallaciis*." In *The Logic of John Buridan*, edited by Jan Pinborg, 139–60. Copenhagen: Museum Tusculanum.

———. 1981a. *Commentators and Commentaries on Aristotle's 'Sophistici Elenchi'*. Vol. 1: The Greek Tradition. Leiden: E. J. Brill.

———. 1981b. "The Present King of France Wears Hypothetical Shoes with Categorical Laces. Twelfth Century Writers on Well-Formedness." *Medioevo* 7: 91–113.

———. 1984. "Proof and Its Limits According to Buridan: *Summulae* 8." In *Preuve et raisons à l'université de Paris: logique, ontologie et théologie au XIVe siècle*, edited by Zénon Kaluza and Paul Vignaux, 97–110. Paris: Vrin.

———. 1987a. "The Semantics of the Trinity According to Stephen Langton and Andrew Sunesen." *Gilbert de Poitiers et ses contemporaines. Aux origines de la 'Logica Modernorum'*, edited by Jean Jolivet and Alain de Libera, 401–436. Napoli: Bibliopolis.

———. 1987b. "The Way Fallacies Were Treated in Scholastic Logic." *Cahiers de l'Institut du Moyen-Âge Grec et Latin* 55: 107–134.

———. 1991. "Is Logic Theoretical or Practical Knowledge?" In *Itinéraires d'Albert de Saxe: Paris-Vienne au XIVᵉ siècle*, edited by Joël Biard, 267–83: Paris: Vrin.

———. 1993. "The Theory of *Loci* in Antiquity and the Middle Ages." In *Argumentationstheorie. Scholastische Forschungen zu den logischen und semantischen Regeln korrekten Folgerns*, edited by Klaus Jacobi, 15–39. Leiden–New York–Köln: E. J. Brill.

———. 2000. "Radulphus Brito: The Last of the Great Arts Masters, or, Philosophy and Freedom." In *Miscellanea Mediaevalia 27: Geistesleben im 13. Jahrhundert*, edited by Jan A. Aertsen and Andreas Speer, 231–51. Berlin–New York: Walter de Gruyter.

Élie, Hubert. 1936. *Le complexe significabile*. Paris: Vrin.

Faral, Edmond. 1946. "Jean Buridan. Notes sur les manuscrits, les éditions et le contenu de ses ouvrages." *Archives d'histoire doctrinale et littéraire du moyen âge* 15: 1–53.

———. 1950. *Jean Buridan: Maître ès Arts de l'Université de Paris*. Extrait de l'Histoire littéraire de la France. Vol. 28, part 2. Paris: Imprimerie Nationale.

Flüeler, Christoph. 1992. *Rezeption und Interpretation der Aristotelischen 'Politica' im späten Mittelalter*. Vols. 1–2. Amsterdam-Philadelphia: B. R. Grüner.

———. 1999. "From Oral Lecture to Written Commentaries: John Buridan's Commentaries on Aristotle's *Metaphysics*." In *Medieval Analyses in Language and Cognition*, edited by Sten Ebbesen and Russell L. Friedman, 497–521. Copenhagen: Royal Danish Academy of Sciences and Letters and C. A. Reitzels Forlag.

Fredborg, Karin Margareta. 1976. "Buridan's *Quaestiones super Rhetoricam Aristotelis.*" In *The Logic of John Buridan,* edited by Jan Pinborg, 47–59. Copenhagen: Museum Tusculanum.

———. 1987. "The Scholastic Teaching of Rhetoric in the Middle Ages." *Cahiers de l'Institut du Moyen-Âge Grec et Latin* 55: 85–105.

Freddoso, Alfred J. 1978. "Abailard on Collective Realism." *The Journal of Philosophy* 40: 527–38.

Gál, Gedeon, O. F. M. 1977. "Adam Wodeham's Question on the *Complexe Significabile.*" *Franciscan Studies* 37: 66–102.

Garver, Newton. 1974. "Notes for a Linguistic Reading of the Categories." In *Ancient Logic and Its Modern Interpretations,* edited by John Corcoran, 27–32. Synthese Historical Library 9. Dordrecht-Boston: Reidel.

Geach, Peter T. 1972. *Logic Matters.* Oxford: Basil Blackwell.

Gelber, Hester. 2001. "Robert Holkot." In *The Stanford Encyclopedia of Philosophy* (Fall 2001), edited by Edward Zalta. URL = http://plato.stanford.edu/archives/fall2001/entries/holkot/.

Gibson, Margaret. 1969. "The *Artes* in the Eleventh Century." In *Arts libéraux et philosophie au moyen âge: Actes du IVᵉ congrès international de philosophie médiévale,* 121–26. Montréal-Paris: Publications de l'Institut d'Études Médiévales de Montréal and Librairie J. Vrin.

———. 1992. "Milestones in the Study of Priscian, circa 800–circa 1200." *Viator* 23: 17–33.

Gilson, Étienne. 1952. *Jean Duns Scot: Introduction à ses positions fondamentales.* Paris: J. Vrin.

Ginet, Carl. 1990. *On Action.* Cambridge–London–New York: Cambridge University Press.

Goddu, André. 1990. "Ockham's Empiricism and Constructive Empiricism." In *Die Gegenwart Ockhams,* edited by Wilhelm Vossenkuhl and Rolf Schönberger, 208–231. Weinheim: VCH/Acta Humaniora.

Grant, Edward. 1977. *Physical Science in the Middle Ages.* New York: Cambridge University Press.

———. 1979. "The Condemnation of 1277, God's Absolute Power, and Physical Thought in the Late Middle Ages." *Viator* 10: 211–44.

———. 1993. "Jean Buridan and Nicole Oresme on Natural Knowledge." *Vivarium* 31: 84–105.

Green-Pedersen, N. J. 1976. "The *Summulae* of John Buridan, *Tractatus VI De locis.*" In *The Logic of John Buridan,* edited by Jan Pinborg, 121–38. Copenhagen: Museum Tusculanum.

———. 1981. "Walter Burley, *De consequentiis* and the Origin of the Theory of Consequence." In *English Logic and Semantics: From the End of the Twelfth Century to the Time of Ockham and Burleigh,* edited by H. A. G. Braakhuis, C. H. Kneepkens, and L. M. de Rijk, 279–304. Nijmegen: Ingenium.

Henninger, Mark, S. J. 1989. *Relations: Medieval Theories, 1250–1325.* Oxford: Clarendon Press.

Henry, D. P. 1984. *That Most Subtle Question* (Quaestio Subtilissima)*: The Metaphysical Bearing of Medieval and Contemporary Linguistic Disciplines.* Manchester: Manchester University Press.

———. 1991. *Medieval Mereology.* Bochumer Studien zur Philosophie 16. Amsterdam-Philadelphia: B. R. Grüner.

Hourani, G. F. 1972–73. "Ibn Sina on Necessary and Possible Existence." *Philosophical Forum* 4: 74–86.

Hubien, Hubert. 1977. "Logiciens médiévaux et logique d'aujourd'hui." *Revue philosophique de Louvain* 75: 219–33.

———. 1981. "Buridan and Leśniewski on the Copula." In *English Logic and Semantics: From the End of the Twelfth Century to the Time of Ockham and Burleigh,* edited by H. A. G. Braakhuis, C. H. Kneepkens, and L. M. de Rijk, 415–25. Nijmegen: Ingenium.

Hughes, G. E. 1989. "The Modal Logic of John Buridan." In *Atti del Convegno internazionale di storia della logica: la teorie delle modalità,* edited by G. Corsi, C. Mangione, and M. Mugnani, 93–111. Bologna: CLUEB.

Hunt, R. W. 1980. *Collected Papers on the History of Grammar in the Middle Ages,* edited by G. L. Bursill-Hall. Amsterdam Studies in the Theory and History of Linguistic Science 3. Studies in the History of Linguistics 5. Amsterdam: John Benjamins.

Inagaki, Bernard Ryosuke. 1987. "*Habitus* and *Natura* in Aquinas." In *Studies in Medieval Philosophy,* edited by John F. Wippel, 159–75. Studies in Philosophy and the History of Philosophy 17. Washington, D. C.: The Catholic University of America Press.

Iwakuma, Yukio. 1992. "'*Vocales,*' or Early Nominalists." *Traditio* 47: 37–111.

Jordan, Mark D. 1986. *Ordering Wisdom: The Hierarchy of Philosophical Discourses in Aquinas.* Publications in Medieval Studies 24. Notre Dame, Ind.: University of Notre Dame Press.

———. 1990. *The Alleged Aristotelianism of Thomas Aquinas.* Etienne Gilson Series 15. Toronto: Pontifical Institute of Mediaeval Studies.

———. 1992. "Albert the Great and the Hierarchy of Sciences." *Faith and Philosophy* 9: 483–99.

Karger, Elizabeth. 1992. "Syllogistique Buridanienne." *Dialogue* 31: 455–58.

King, Peter. 1987. "Jean Buridan's Philosophy of Science." *Studies in the History and Philosophy of Science* 18: 109–132.

Klagge, James, and Alfred Nordmann, eds. 1993. *Ludwig Wittgenstein: Philosophical Occasions, 1912–1951.* Indianapolis-Cambridge: Hackett.

Klima, Gyula. 1988. *Ars Artium: Essays in Philosophical Semantics, Medieval and Modern.* Budapest: Institute of Philosophy of the Hungarian Academy.

———. 1991. "Latin as a Formal Language. Outlines of a Buridanian Semantics." *Cahiers de l'Institut du Moyen Âge Grec et Latin* 61: 78–106.

————. 1993a. "The Changing Role of *Entia Rationis* in Mediaeval Semantics and Ontology: A Comparative Study with a Reconstruction." *Synthese* 96: 25–58.

————. 1993b. "*Debeo tibi equuum:* A Reconstruction of the Theoretical Framework of Buridan's Treatment of the *Sophisma.*" In *Sophisms in Medieval Logic and Grammar,* edited by Stephen Read, 333–47. Dordrecht-Boston-London: Kluwer.

————. 1999. "Buridan's Logic and the Ontology of Modes." In *Medieval Analyses in Language and Cognition,* edited by Sten Ebbesen and Russell L. Friedman, 473–95. Copenhagen: Royal Danish Academy of Sciences and Letters and C. A. Reitzels Forlag.

————. 2000. "The Medieval Problem of Universals." In *The Stanford Encyclopedia of Philosophy* (Winter 2001), edited by Edward Zalta. URL = http://plato.stanford. edu/archives/win2001/entries/universals-medieval/.

Kneepkens, C. H. 1987. "*Suppositio* and *Supponere* in 12th-Century Grammar." In *Gilbert de Poitiers et ses sontemporaines. Aux origines de la 'Logica Modernorum',* edited by Jean Jolivet and Alain de Libera, 325–52. Napoli: Bibliopolis.

————. 1995. "The Priscianic Tradition." In *Sprachtheorien in Spätantike und Mittelalter,* edited by Sten Ebbesen, 239–64. Tübingen: Gunter Narr Verlag.

Knuuttila, Simo. 1989. "Natural Necessity in John Buridan." In *Studies in Medieval Natural Philosophy,* edited by Stefano Caroti, 155–76. Biblioteca di Nuncius, Studi e Testi I. Firenze: Olschki.

————. 1991. "Buridan and Aristotle's Modal Syllogistic." In *Historia Philosophiae Medii Aevi. Studien zur Geschichte der Philosophie des Mittelalters,* edited by Burkhard Mojsisch and Olaf Pluta. Vol. 1, 477–88. Amsterdam-Philadelphia: B. R. Grüner.

————. 1996. "Duns Scotus and the Foundations of Logical Modalities." In *John Duns Scotus: Metaphysics and Ethics,* edited by Ludger Honnefelder, Rega Wood, and Mechthild Dreyer, 127–43. Studien und Texte zur Geistesgeschichte des Mittelalters 53. Leiden–New York–Köln: E. J. Brill.

Korolec, J. B. 1974. "La Philosophie de la Liberté de Jean Buridan." *Studia Mediewistyczne* 15: 109–152.

————. 1975. "Les Principes de la Philosophie Morale de Jean Buridan." *Mediaevalia Philosophica Polonorum* 21: 53–72.

Kretzmann, Norman. 1967. "Semantics, History of." In *The Encyclopedia of Philosophy,* edited by Paul Edwards. Vol. 7, 358–406. New York–London: Collier–Macmillan–The Free Press.

————. 1977. "Socrates Is Whiter than Plato Begins to Be White." *Noûs* 11: 3–15.

————. 1982. "The Culmination of the Old Logic in Peter Abelard." In *Renaissance and Renewal in the Twelfth Century,* edited by Robert L. Benson and Giles Constable, 488–511. Cambridge, Mass.: Harvard University Press.

————. 1997. *The Metaphysics of Theism: Aquinas's Natural Theology in 'Summa contra gentiles' I.* Oxford: Clarendon Press.

Krieger, Gerhard. 1986. *Der Begriff der praktischen Vernunft nach Johannes Buridanus.* Münster: Aschendorff.

Lafleur, Claude. 1988. *Quatre introductions à la philosophie au XIIIe siècle. Textes critiques et étude historique*. Institut d'Etudes Médiévales. Montréal-Paris: Vrin.

Lagerlund, Henrik. 2000. *Modal Syllogistics in the Middle Ages*. Leiden-Boston-Köln: Brill.

Lang, Helen S. 1989. "Aristotelian Physics: Teleological Procedure in Aristotle, Thomas, and Buridan." *Review of Metaphysics* 42: 569–91.

———. 1992. *Aristotle's Physics and Its Medieval Varieties*. Albany, N.Y.: SUNY Press.

Lappe, Joseph. 1908. "Nikolaus von Autrecourt." In *Beiträge zur Geschichte der Philosophie des Mittelalters* 6. Münster: Aschendorff.

Leach, Arthur M. 1899. *A History of Winchester College*. New York: Charles Scribner's Sons.

van der Lecq, Ria. 1985. "John Buridan on Intentionality." In *Medieval Semantics and Metaphysics. Studies dedicated to L.M. de Rijk*, edited by E.P. Bos, 281–90. Artistarium Supplementa, vol. 2. Nijmegen: Ingenium.

———. 1993a. "The Role of Language-Levels in the Medieval Discussion on *Insolubilia*." In *Argumentationstheorie: Scholastische Forschungen zu den logischen und semantischen Regeln korrekten Folgerns*, edited by Klaus Jacobi, 277–92. Leiden–New York–Köln: E.J. Brill.

———. 1993b. "Confused Individuals and Moving Trees: John Buridan on the Knowledge of Particulars." In *John Buridan: A Master of Arts. Some Aspects of His Philosophy*, edited by E.P. Bos and H.A. Krop, 1–21. Nijmegen: Ingenium.

de Libera, Alain. 1982. "Le traité *De appellatione* de Lambert de Lagny (Lambert d'Auxerre)." *Archives d'histoire doctrinale et littéraire du moyen âge* 48: 227–85.

———. 1993. *La philosophie médiévale*. Paris: Presses Universitaires de France.

———. 1996. *La querelle des universaux: De Platon à la fin du Moyen Age*. Paris: Éditions du Seuil.

Madden, John, with Dave Anderson. 1985. *Hey, Wait a Minute, I Wrote a Book!* New York: Villard Books.

Maier, Anneliese. 1955. *Metaphysische Hintergründe der spätscholastischen Naturphilosophie*. Studien zur Naturphilosophie der Spätscholastik, vol. 4. Roma: Storia e Letteratura.

———. 1958. *Zwischen Philosophie und Mechanik*. Studien zur Naturphilosophie der Spätscholastik, vol. 5. Roma: Storia e Letteratura.

———. 1964–77. *Ausgehendes Mittelalter*. Gesammelte Aufsätze zur Geistesgeschichte des 14. Jahrhunderts, vols. 1–3. Roma: Storia e Letteratura.

———. 1968. *Zwei Grundprobleme der scholastischen Naturphilosophie*. Studien zur Naturphilosophie der Spätscholastik, vol. 2. 3d ed. Roma: Storia e Letteratura.

Maierù, Alfonso. 1976. "Significatio et connotatio chez Buridan." In *The Logic of John Buridan*, edited by Jan Pinborg, 101–114. Copenhagen: Museum Tusculanum.

Malcolm, John. 1979. "A Reconsideration of the Inherence and Identity Theories of the Copula." *Journal of the History of Philosophy* 17: 383–400.

Marenbon, John. 1990. "The Theoretical and Practical Autonomy of Philosophy as a Discipline in the Middle Ages: Latin Philosophy, 1250–1350." In *Knowledge and the Sciences in Medieval Philosophy*, edited by Monika Asztalos et al. Vol. I, 262–74. Helsinki: Yliopistopaino.

———. 1997. *The Philosophy of Peter Abelard*. Cambridge: Cambridge University Press.

Markowski, Mieczysław. 1976. "Johannes Buridans Kommentare zu Aristoteles' Organon in Mitteleuropas Bibliotheken." In *The Logic of John Buridan*, edited by Jan Pinborg, 9–20. Copenhagen: Museum Tusculanum.

———. 1984. "L'Influence de Jean Buridan sur les universités d'Europe Centrale." In *Preuve et raisons à l'université de Paris: logique, ontologie et théologie au XIVe siècle*, edited by Zénon Kaluza and Paul Vignaux, 149–63. Paris: Vrin.

Marmo, Costantino. 1990. "*Suspicio:* A Key Word to the Significance of Aristotle's *Rhetoric* in Thirteenth Century Scholasticism." *Cahiers de l'Institut du Moyen-Âge Grec et Latin* 60: 145–98.

———. 1994. *Semiotica e linguaggio nella scolastica: Parigi, Bologna, Erfurt, 1270–1330. La semiotica dei Modisti*. Roma: Istituto Storico Italiano per il Medioevo.

———. 1995. "A Pragmatic Approach to Language in Modism." In *Sprachtheorien in Spätantike und Mittelalter*, edited by Sten Ebbesen, 169–83. Tübingen: Gunter Narr Verlag.

———. 1999. "The Semantics of the Modistae." In *Medieval Analyses in Language and Cognition*, edited by Sten Ebbesen and Russell L. Friedman, 83–104. Copenhagen: Royal Danish Academy of Sciences and Letters and C. A. Reitzels Forlag.

Marshall, Peter C. 1983. "Parisian Psychology in the Mid-Fourteenth Century." *Archives d'histoire doctrinale et littéraire du moyen âge* 50: 101–193.

McKeon, Richard. 1942. "Rhetoric in the Middle Ages." *Speculum* 17: 1–32.

Michael, Bernd. 1985. *Johannes Buridan: Studien zu seinem Leben, seinen Werken und zu Rezeption seiner Theorien im Europa des späten Mittelalters*. Vols. 1–2. Doctoral dissertation, University of Berlin.

Michalski, Konstanty. 1969. *La Philosophie au XIV Siècle: Six Études*, edited by Kurt Flasch. Frankfurt a. M.: Minerva.

Michon, Cyrille. 1996. "Thomas d'Aquin et Guillaume d'Occam: précurseurs de Frege." *Les Études philosophiques* 3: 307–321.

Miethke, Jürgen. 1991. "Bildungsstand und Freiheitsforderung (12. Bis 14. Jahrhundert)." In *Die Abendländische Freiheit vom 10. Zum 14. Jahrhundert: Der Wirkungszusammenhang von Idee und Wirklichkeit im europäischen Vergleich*, edited by Johannes Fried, 221–47. Vorträge und Forschungen 39. Sigmaringen: Thorbecke.

Miller, Richard H. 1985. "Buridan on Singular Concepts." *Franciscan Studies* 45: 57–72.

Monahan, E. J. 1954. "Human Liberty and Free Will according to John Buridan." *Mediaeval Studies* 16: 72–86.

Moody, E. A. 1947. "Ockham, Buridan, and Nicholas of Autrecourt." *Franciscan Studies* 7: 113–46.

———. 1958. "Empiricism and Metaphysics in Medieval Philosophy." *The Philosophical Review* 67: 145–63.

———. 1970. "Buridan, Jean." In *Dictionary of Scientific Biography,* edited by Charles C. Gillespie. Vol. 2, 603–608. New York: Scribner's.

———. 1975. *Studies in Medieval Philosophy, Science, and Logic: Collected Papers, 1933–1969.* Berkeley: University of California Press.

Murdoch, John E. 1982. "The Analytic Character of Late Medieval Learning: Natural Philosophy without Nature." In *Approaches to Nature in the Middle Ages,* edited by Lawrence D. Roberts, 171–213. Binghamton, N.Y.: Center for Medieval and Early Renaissance Studies.

Murdoch, John E., and Edith D. Sylla, eds. 1975. *The Cultural Context of Medieval Learning.* Dordrecht-Boston-Lancaster: Reidel.

Normore, Calvin. 1985. "Buridan's Ontology." In *How Things Are: Studies in Predication and the History and Philosophy of Science,* edited by James Bogen and James E. McGuire, 189–203. Dordrecht-Boston-Lancaster: Reidel.

———. 1987. "The Tradition of Mediaeval Nominalism." In *Studies in Medieval Philosophy,* edited by John F. Wippel, 201–217. Studies in Philosophy and the History of Philosophy 17. Washington, D.C.: The Catholic University of America Press.

Nuchelmans, Gabriel. 1973. *Theories of the Proposition. Ancient and Medieval Conceptions of the Bearers of Truth and Falsity.* Amsterdam-London: North-Holland.

———. 1980a. *Late-Scholastic and Humanist Theories of the Proposition.* Amsterdam–Oxford–New York: North-Holland.

———. 1980b. "Adam Wodeham on the Meaning of Declarative Sentences." *Historiographia Linguistica* 7: 177–87.

———. 1988. "*Appellatio Rationis* in Buridan, *Sophismata,* IV, 9–15." In *Die Philosophie im 14. und 15. Jahrhundert. In memoriam Konstanty Michalski (1879–1947),* edited by Olaf Pluta, 67–84. Bochumer Studien zur Philosophie 10. Amsterdam: B. R. Grüner.

Paetow, Louis. 1910. *The Arts Course at Medieval Universities, with Special Reference to Grammar and Rhetoric.* Urbana-Champaign: University of Illinois Press.

Panaccio, Claude. 1999a. "Semantics and Mental Language." In *The Cambridge Companion to Ockham,* edited by Paul Vincent Spade. Cambridge: Cambridge University Press.

———. 1999b. *Le discours intérieur: de Platon à Guillaume d'Ockham.* Paris: Éditions du Seuil.

Pinborg, Jan. 1972. *Logik und Semantik im Mittelalter: Ein Überblick.* Problemata 10. Stuttgart–Bad Cannstatt: Frommann-Holzboog.

———. 1975. "A Note on Some Theoretical Concepts of Logic and Grammar." *Revue internationale de philosophie* 113: 286–96.

———. 1976. "The *Summulae: Tractatus I De introductionibus.*" In *The Logic of John Buridan,* edited by Jan Pinborg, 71–88. Copenhagen: Museum Tusculanum.

Pironet, Fabienne. 1993. "John Buridan on the Liar Paradox: Study of an Opinion and Chronology of the Texts." In *Argumentationstheorie: Scholastische Forschungen zu den logischen und semantischen Regeln korrekten Folgerns,* edited by Klaus Jacobi, 293–300. Leiden–New York–Köln: E. J. Brill.

————. 1998. "Bibliographie Spéciale sur Jean Buridan." URL = http://mapageweb. umontreal.ca/pironetf/download/JBBiblio.pdf.

Pluta, Olaf. 1986. *Kritiker der Unsterblichkeitsdoktrin im Mittelalter und Renaissance.* Amsterdam: B. R. Grüner.

Prior, A. N. 1962. "Some Problems of Self-Reference in John Buridan." *Proceedings of the British Academy* 48: 281–96.

————. 1969. "The Possibly-True and the Possible." *Mind* 78: 481–92.

Read, Stephen. 1999. "How Is Material Supposition Possible?" *Medieval Philosophy and Theology* 8: 1–20.

Reynolds, Suzanne. 1996. *Medieval Reading: Grammar, Rhetoric, and the Classical Text.* Cambridge–London–New York: Cambridge University Press.

Rijk, L. M. de. 1966. "Some New Evidence on Twelfth-Century Logic." *Vivarium* 4: 1–57.

————. 1971–73. "The Development of *Suppositio Naturalis* in Medieval Logic: Natural Supposition as Non-Contextual Supposition." *Vivarium* 9: 71–107, 11: 43–79.

————. 1976. "On Buridan's Doctrine of Connotation." In *The Logic of John Buridan,* edited by Jan Pinborg, 91–100. Copenhagen: Museum Tusculanum.

————. 1980. "The Semantical Impact of Abailard's Solution of the Problem of Universals." In *Petrus Abaelardus (1079–1142), Person, Werk und Wirkung,* edited by Rudolf Thomas, 139–51. Trier: Paulinus-Verlag.

————. 1992. "John Buridan on Universals." *Revue de Métaphysique et de Morale* 97: 35–59.

————. de. 1997. "Foi chrétienne et savoir humain: La lutte de Buridan contre les *theologizantes.*" In *Langages et philosophie: Hommage à Jean Jolivet,* edited by Alain de Libera et al., 393–409. Études de philosophie médiévale 74. Paris: Vrin.

Roberts, L. N. 1953. "Every Proposition Is False—A Medieval Paradox." *Tulane Studies in Philosophy* 2: 95–102.

Rosier, Irène. 1983. *La grammaire spéculative des Modistes.* Lille: Presses Universitaires de Lille.

————. 1994. *La parole comme acte. Sur la grammaire et la sémantique au XIIIᵉ siècle.* Paris: Vrin.

Rosier-Catach, Irène. 1997. "*Prata rident.*" In *Langages et philosophie: Hommage à Jean Jolivet,* edited by Alain de Libera et al., 155–76. Ètudes de philosophie médiévale 74. Paris: Vrin.

————. 1999. "Modisme, pré-modisme, proto-modisme: vers une définition modulaire." In *Medieval Analyses in Language and Cognition,* edited by Sten Ebbesen and Russell L. Friedman, 45–81. Copenhagen: Royal Danish Academy of Sciences and Letters and C. A. Reitzels Forlag.

Ross, David. 1949. *Aristotle.* 5th ed. London: Methuen.

The Routledge Encyclopedia of Philosophy. 1998. Edited by Edward Craig. Vols. 1–10. London: Routledge.

Saarinen, Risto. 1986. "Moral Weakness and Human Action in John Buridan's Ethics." In *Faith, Will, and Grammar,* edited by Heikki Kirjavainen, 109–139. Helsinki: Luther-Agricola Society.

———. 1993. "John Buridan and Donald Davidson on *Akrasia*." *Synthese* 96: 133–54.

———. 1994. *Weakness of the Will in Medieval Thought, From Augustine to Buridan*. Leiden–New York–Köln: E. J. Brill.

Schönberger, Rolf. 1994. *Relation als Vergleich: die Relationstheorie des Johannes Buridan im Kontext seines Denken und der Scholastik*. Leiden–New York–Köln: E. J. Brill.

Schupp, Franz. 1988. *Logical problems of the medieval theory of consequences, with the edition of the 'Liber consequentiarum'*. Napoli: Bibliopolis.

Scott, T. K., Jr. 1965. "John Buridan on the Objects of Demonstrative Science." *Speculum* 40: 654–73.

———. 1971. "Nicholas of Autrecourt, Buridan, and Ockhamism." *Journal of the History of Philosophy* 9: 15–41.

Sirridge, Mary. 1978. "Buridan: 'Every proposition is false' is false." *Notre Dame Journal of Formal Logic* 19: 397–404.

Smithka, Paula. 1991. "Ampliation and Natural Supposition in Albert of Saxony's *Quaestiones super logicam*." In *Itinéraires d'Albert de Saxe: Paris-Vienne au XIVᵉ siècle*, edited by Joël Biard, 137–48. Paris: Vrin.

Spade, Paul Vincent. 1974. "Ockham on Self-Reference." *Notre Dame Journal of Formal Logic* 15: 298–300.

———. 1975. *The Mediaeval Liar: A Catalogue of the 'Insolubilia'-Literature*. Toronto: Pontifical Institute of Mediaeval Studies.

———. 1978. "John Buridan on the Liar. A Study and Reconstruction." *Notre Dame Journal of Formal Logic* 19: 579–90.

———. 1988a. *Lies, Logic and Language in the Late Middle Ages*. London: Variorum Reprints.

———. 1988b. "The Logic of the Categorical: The Medieval Theory of Ascent and Descent." In *Meaning and Inference in Medieval Philosophy: Studies in Memory of Jan Pinborg*, edited by Norman Kretzmann, 187–224. Dordrecht-Boston-London: Kluwer.

———. 1998. "Late Medieval Logic." In *Medieval Philosophy*, edited by John Marenbon, 402–425. Routledge History of Philosophy 3. London–New York: Routledge.

———. 2001. "Insolubles." In *The Stanford Encyclopedia of Philosophy* (Fall 2001), edited by Edward Zalta. URL = http://plato.stanford.edu/archives/fall2001/entries/insolubles/.

Stock, Brian. 1983. *The Implications of Literacy. Written Language and Models of Interpretation in the Eleventh and Twelfth Centuries*. Princeton, N. J.: Princeton University Press.

Strange, Steven K., and Jack Zupko, eds. Forthcoming. *Stoicism: Traditions and Transformations*. Cambridge–New York: Cambridge University Press.

Stump, Eleonore. 1989. *Dialectic and Its Place in the Development of Medieval Logic*. Ithaca, N.Y.: Cornell University Press.

———. 1997. "Aquinas's Account of Freedom: Intellect and Will." *The Monist* 80: 576–97.

Sweeney, Eileen. 1990. "Metaphysics and Its Distinction from Sacred Doctrine in Aquinas." In *Knowledge and the Sciences in Medieval Philosophy*, edited by Monika Asztalos et al. Vol. III, 162–70. Helsinki: Yliopistopaino.

Sylla, Edith D. 1973. "Medieval Concepts of the Latitude of Forms: The Oxford Calculators." *Archives d'histoire doctrinale et littéraire du moyen âge* 40: 223–83.

———. 1993. "Aristotelian Commentaries and Scientific Change: The Parisian Nominalists on the Cause of the Natural Motion of Inanimate Bodies." *Vivarium* 32: 37–83.

Tachau, Katherine H. 1988. *Vision and Certitude in the Age of Ockham. Optics, Epistemology, and the Foundations of Semantics, 1250–1345*. Leiden–New York: E. J. Brill.

Taylor, Richard C. 1998. "Averroes on Psychology and the Principles of Metaphysics." *Journal of the History of Philosophy* 36: 507–523.

Thijssen, J. M. M. H. 1985. "Buridan on Mathematics." *Vivarium* 23: 55–78.

———. 1987. "John Buridan and Nicholas of Autrecourt on Causality and Induction." *Traditio* 43: 237–55.

———. 1991b. "The 'Semantic' Articles of Autrecourt's Condemnation. New Proposals for an Interpretation of Articles 1, 30, 31, 35, 57, and 58." *Archives d'histoire doctrinale et littéraire du moyen âge* 58: 155–75.

———. 1997a. "The Crisis over the Ockhamist Hermeneutic and Its Semantic Background: The Methodological Significance of the Censure of December 29, 1340." In *Vestigia, Imagines, Verba: Semiotics and Logic in Medieval Theological Texts (XIIth–XIVth Century)*, edited by Costantino Marmo, 371–92. Semiotic and Cognitive Studies 4. Turnhout: Brepols.

———. 1997b. "What Really Happened on 7 March 1277? Bishop Tempier's Condemnation and Its Institutional Context." In *Texts and Contexts in Ancient and Medieval Science*, edited by Edith Sylla and Michael McVaugh, 84–114. Leiden–New York–Köln: E. J. Brill.

———. 1998. *Censure and Heresy at the University of Paris, 1200–1400*. Philadelphia: University of Pennsylvania Press.

Thijssen, J. M. M. H., and Jack Zupko, eds. 2001. *The Metaphysics and Natural Philosophy of John Buridan*. Leiden-Boston-Köln: Brill.

Todorov, Tzvetan. 1995. *The Morals of History*. Translated by Alyson Waters. Minneapolis-London: University of Minnesota Press.

Trapp, A. Damasus, O. S. A. 1956. "Augustinian Theology of the 14th Century: Notes on Editions, Marginalia, Opinions and Book-Lore." *Augustiniana* 6: 146–274.

Trentman, John A. 1969. "Vincent Ferrer and His Fourteenth-Century Predecessors on a Problem of Intentionality." *Arts Libéraux et Philosophie au Moyen Âge*, Actes du Quatrième Congrès International de Philosophie Médiévale, 949–58. Montréal-Paris: Institut d'Études Médiévales and J. Vrin.

———. 1970. "Ockham on Mental." *Mind* n.s. 79: 586–90.

Tweedale, Martin. 1976. *Abailard on Universals*. Amsterdam: North-Holland.

———. 1988. "Logic: From the Late Eleventh Century to the Time of Abelard." In *A History of Twelfth-Century Western Philosophy*, edited by Peter Dronke, 196–226. New York: Cambridge University Press.

Valente, Luisa. 1995. "Langage et théologie pendant la seconde moitié du XIIᵉ siècle." In *Sprachtheorien in Spätantike und Mittelalter*, edited by Sten Ebbesen, 33–54. Tübingen: Gunter Narr Verlag.

Walsh, James J. 1964. "Is Buridan a Sceptic about Free Will?" *Vivarium* 2: 50–61.

———. 1966a. "Buridan and Seneca." *Journal of the History of Ideas* 27: 23–40.

———. 1966b. "Nominalism and the *Ethics*: Some Remarks about Buridan's Commentary." *Journal of the History of Philosophy* 4: 1–13.

———. 1975. "Some Relationships between Gerald Odo's and John Buridan's Commentaries on Aristotle's Ethics." *Franciscan Studies* 35: 237–75.

———. 1980. "Teleology in the Ethics of Buridan." *Journal of the History of Philosophy* 18: 265–86.

———. 1986. "Buridan on the Connection of the Virtues." *Journal of the History of Philosophy* 24: 453–82.

Weijers, Olga. 1987 [1989]. "L'appellation des disciplines dans les classifications des sciences aux XIIᵉ et XIIIᵉ siècles." *Bulletin du Cange* 46: 39–64.

Weinberg, Julius R. 1948. *Nicolaus of Autrecourt. A Study in Fourteenth-Century Thought*. Princeton, N. J.: Princeton University Press.

Willing, A. 1985. "Buridan and Ockham: The Logic of Knowing." *Franciscan Studies* 45: 47–56.

Ziolkowski, Jan. 1985. *Alan of Lille's Grammar of Sex: The Meaning of Grammar to a Twelfth-Century Intellectual*. Speculum Anniversary Monographs 10. Cambridge, Mass.: Medieval Academy of America.

Zupko, Jack. 1993. "Nominalism Meets Indivisibilism." *Medieval Philosophy and Theology* 3: 158–85.

———. 1994–1997. "How It Played in the *rue de Fouarre*: The Reception of Adam Wodeham's Theory of the *Complexe Significabile* in the Arts Faculty at Paris in the Mid-Fourteenth Century." *Franciscan Studies* 54: 211–25.

———. 1998. "Sacred Doctrine; Secular Practice: Theology and Philosophy in the Faculty of Arts at Paris, 1325–1400." In *Miscellanea Mediaevalia 26: What Is Philosophy in the Middle Ages?* edited by Jan A. Aertsen and Andreas Speer, 656–66. Berlin–New York: Walter de Gruyter.

———. 1999. "Substance and Soul: The Late Medieval Origins of Early Modern Psychology." In *Meeting of the Minds: The Relations between Medieval and Classical Modern European Philosophy*, edited by Stephen F. Brown, 121–39. Rencontres de Philosophie Médiévale 7. Turnhout: Brepols.

———. Forthcoming. "Self-Knowledge and Self-Representation in Later Medieval Psychology." In *Mind, Cognition, and Representation: The Commentary Tradition on Aristotle's 'De anima'*, edited by Paul Bakker and J. M. M. H. Thijssen. London: Ashgate.

Subtilissimae Quaestiones super octo Physicorum libros Aristotelis (QP)

Quaestiones in Rhetoricam Aristotelis (QR)

Quaestiones circa librum Topicorum Aristotelis (QT)

Summulae de Dialectica (S)

consequences (*cont.*)
  relation to syllogistic logic, 73–76
  relation to topical reasoning, 81–86

definitions
  causal, 111–12, 116–17, 294n89, 370n21
  and descriptions, 112–13
  logical doctrine of, 103–13
  nominal, 103–5, 170, 191, 195, 208, 369n17
  real (quidditative), 27, 104–9, 208, 324n10, 370n21
  role in demonstration, 115–17
demonstration. *See* knowledge, demonstrative
discourse
  conventional, 22–23, 26, 54, 67, 131, 159, 177, 270–72, 322n34, 324n9, 331n1. *See also* language, conventional vs. mental
  literal, 64–66, 97–99, 103
  mental, 25–26, 321n21, 321n23
  metaphorical, 17–22, 61–64, 97–99, 103
  relation to logic, 14–17, 30–31, 37–38, 94, 299n36, 322n34. *See also* logic, relation to conventional discourse
division
  logical doctrine of, 101–3
  metaphysical, 150–63
doubt
  basis for freedom of choice, 250–51
  and judgmental error, 186–87, 192–202, 256–57, 363n63, 399n63, 406n107
  as obstacle to assent, 121–22, 193, 362n56
  role in philosophical inquiry, 327n33, 327n35. *See also* knowledge and skeptical doubt

evidentness (*evidentia*), 88–89, 120, 179, 184–86, 193–94, 204, 237, 244–49, 261–62, 272, 330nn62–64, 360n43, 360n45, 363n61, 388n31, 406n107
experience
  immediate, 106, 121–22

freedom
  academic, 139–46
  of choice, 249–60, 267, 383n9, 392n20, 398n57, 402n78, 406n104
  divine, 261, 365n71, 394n29
  of final ordination, 250–51, 260–62, 267, 394n29
  of the intellect, 263–74, 382n84, 403n81, 406n107
  purpose of, 256–58, 260–62, 397n50
  and responsibility, 248, 269, 395n40, 398n57, 398n61, 402n78, 406n107
  of the will, 244–49, 259–60, 267, 402n78

grammar
  development of, 285n30, 286nn32–33
  divisions of, 34, 296n11
  and etymology, 6–7, 24–25
  and interpretation, 18–19, 21
  medieval art of, xvi, 3–10
  and pronunciation, 4, 21, 24–25, 282n6
  relation to logic, 7–8, 10–14, 24, 59–60, 98–99, 103–4
  status as a science, 34, 39
  teaching of, 5–6, 283n11
  and texuality, 5–7

happiness
  beatific vs. wayfarer, 250, 261–62, 385n26
  definition of, 227, 231, 270, 398n58
  relation to free choice, 227

ignorance
  culpable vs. non-culpable, 254–55, 397n51, 397nn53–54, 398n61
individuality
  semantic interpretation of, 53–54, 56
individuals
  cognition of, 121–22
inherence
  of dispositions in the intellect, 221–23
  mereological approach to, 171–75
  of souls in bodies, 164–82

Impetus 241–2
secundum motum

JACK ZUPKO is associate professor of philosophy at Emory University.